ENCYCLOPEDIA OF AMERICAN HISTORY

Contemporary United States
1969 to the Present

VOLUME X

ENCYCLOPEDIA OF AMERICAN HISTORY

ENCYCLOPEDIA OF AMERICAN HISTORY

Contemporary United States
1969 to the Present

VOLUME X

Donald T. Critchlow, Editor
Gary B. Nash, General Editor

Facts On File, Inc.

Encyclopedia of American History:
Contemporary United States (1969 to the Present)

Copyright © 2003 by Donald T. Critchlow
Maps Copyright © 2003 by Facts On File, Inc.

Editorial Director: Laurie E. Likoff
Editor in Chief: Owen Lancer
Chief Copy Editor: Michael G. Laraque
Associate Editor: Dorothy Cummings
Production Director: Olivia McKean
Production Manager: Rachel L. Berlin
Production Associate: Theresa Montoya
Art Director: Cathy Rincon
Interior Designer: Joan M. Toro
Desktop Designers: Erika K. Arroyo and David C. Strelecky
Maps and Illustrations: Dale E. Williams and Jeremy Eagle

Facts On File, Inc.
132 West 31st Street
New York NY 10001

Library of Congress Cataloging-in-Publication Data

Encyclopedia of American history / Gary B. Nash, general editor.
p. cm.
Includes bibliographical references and indexes.
Contents: v. 1. Three worlds meet — v. 2. Colonization and settlement —
v. 3. Revolution and new nation — v. 4. Expansion and reform — v. 5. Civil War
and Reconstruction — v. 6. The development of the industrial United States —
v. 7. The emergence of modern America — v. 8. The Great Depression and
World War II — v. 9. Postwar United States — v. 10. Contemporary
United States. — v. 11 Comprehensive index
ISBN 0-8160-4371-X (set)   ISBN 0-8160-4370-1 (v. 10)
1. United States—History—Encyclopedias. I. Nash, Gary B.
E174 .E53 2002
973′.03—dc21   2001051278

Contents

★ ——————————————————————————

List of Entries

About the Editors

General Editor: Gary B. Nash received a Ph.D from Princeton University. He is currently director of the National Center for History in the Schools at the University of California, Los Angeles, where he teaches American history of the colonial and Revolutionary era. He is a published author of college and precollegiate history texts. Among his best-selling works is *The American People: Creating a Nation and Society* (Addison Wesley, Longman), now in its fifth edition.

Nash is an elected member of the Society of American Historians, American Academy of Arts and Sciences, and the American Philosophical Society. He has served as past president of the Organization of American Historians, 1994–95, and was a founding member of the National Council for History Education, 1990.

Volume Editor: Donald T. Critchlow, St. Louis University, received a Ph.D from the University of California, Berkeley. He is the author of several books, including *Intended Consequences: Birth Control, Abortion and the Federal Government in Modern America* (Oxford University Press, 1999) and coauthor of the textbook *America: A Concise History* (Wadsworth, 1993).

Foreword

★ ——————————————————————————————————

The Encyclopedia of American History series is designed as a handy reference to the most important individuals, events, and topics in U.S. history. In 10 volumes, the encyclopedia covers the period from the 15th century, when European explorers first made their way across the Atlantic Ocean to the Americas, to the present day. The encyclopedia is written for precollegiate as well as college students, for parents of young learners in the schools, and for the general public. The volume editors are distinguished historians of American history. In writing individual entries, each editor has drawn upon the expertise of scores of specialists. This ensures the scholarly quality of the entire series. Articles contributed by the various volume editors are uncredited.

This 10-volume encyclopedia of "American history" is broadly conceived to include the historical experience of the various peoples of North America. Thus, in the first volume, many essays treat the history of a great range of indigenous people before contact with Europeans. In the same vein, readers will find essays in the first several volumes that sketch Spanish, Dutch, and French explorers and colonizers who opened up territories for European settlement that later would become part of the United States. The venues and cast of characters in the American historical drama are thus widened beyond traditional encyclopedias.

In creating the eras of American history that define the chronological limits of each volume, and in addressing major topics in each era, the encyclopedia follows the architecture of *The National Standards for United States History, Revised Edition* (Los Angeles: National Center for History in the Schools, 1996). Mandated by the U.S. Congress, the national standards for U.S. history have been widely used by states and school districts in organizing curricular frameworks and have been followed by many other curriculum-building efforts.

Entries are cross-referenced, when appropriate, with *See also* citations at the end of articles. At the end of most entries, a listing of articles and books allows readers to turn to specialized sources and historical accounts. In each volume, an array of maps provide geographical context, while numerous illustrations help vivify the material covered in the text. A time line is included to provide students with a chronological reference to major events occurring in the given era. The selection of historical documents in the back of each volume gives students experience with the raw documents that historians use when researching history. A comprehensive index to each volume also facilitates the reader's access to particular information.

In each volume, long entries are provided for major categories of American historical experience. These categories may include: African Americans, agriculture, art and architecture, business, economy, education, family life, foreign policy, immigration, labor, Native Americans, politics, population, religion, urbanization, and women. By following these essays from volume to volume, the reader can access what might be called a mini-history of each broad topic, for example, family life, immigration, or religion.

— Gary B. Nash
University of California, Los Angeles

Introduction

All periods in history can be said to undergo change, yet what made the last half of the 20th century in the United States significant was the rapid acceleration of technological and scientific advancement. These advances inevitably affected American society, culture, and politics as the nation confronted a new world. Advances in biomedicine, computers, electronics, materials engineering, energy resources, and other scientific fields promised to transform the way Americans lived, how long and how well they lived.

These new scientific and technological advances promised life's betterment. Yet this scientific and technological revolution that promised so much also enlarged the capacity for destruction. The application of new technology changed the conduct of war. Missiles could now be targeted to pinpoint locations; missiles with multiple nuclear warheads could be launched to wipe out entire cities; biological warfare created the means to spread disease throughout civilian populations.

The political and social consequences of this new age were not only fully apparent in the immediate aftermath of the terrorist attacks, but even before September 11. Socially the United States became a more diversified nation ethnically and culturally. While the native birthrate dropped, the population of America grew through immigration, both legal and illegal, from Mexico, Central and Latin America, Asia, and, to a lesser extent, Europe. These waves of immigration changed the United States culturally and politically. Americans now spoke more languages, while English was transformed as new words entered into the vocabulary. While Christianity continued to have the largest religious following, other religions, such as Islam and Buddhism, grew in membership. Even the kinds of foods Americans ate changed, as new cuisines from Mexico, Latin America, and Asia were introduced.

While the United States experienced cultural and political changes created by its increasingly diversified population, Americans extended their political and legal rights, in what became known as the "Rights Revolution." Eighteen-year-olds earned the right to vote through a new constitutional amendment. Legislation was passed in the 1960s that outlawed discrimination based on race, sex, national origins, and religion, and subsequent legislation and enforcement of the law ensured that equal opportunity, and at times, preferences, be given to ethnic minorities and women. As a consequence, African-American men and women found new opportunities economically and politically. More African Americans went to college; home ownership among African Americans increased; and more African Americans entered into the middle class. The number of African-American elected officials on the local, state, and national levels increased.

Similarly, women found new opportunities as well. By the 21st century, more women worked outside the home. The number of women in middle management and higher management increased. A woman running for public office no longer was a novelty. The Supreme Court ruled that women had a constitutional right to abortion. At the same time, other groups sought to extend their political and legal rights as well, including the physically challenged, gays, and First Nation people. Furthermore, new legal rights were extended to children, the aged, spouses, and other segments of the population. While some saw freedom and rights being extended and ethnic and cultural diversity being recognized, others feared that the national identity had been replaced by group identities.

While the United States had become the most powerful nation in the world militarily and enjoyed the affluence that came with having the largest economy in the world, problems of poverty among many segments of the population remained. The "inner city" of many of the nation's largest urban centers had experienced physical deterioration and remained places where poverty and crime prevailed. Other challenges confronted the nation as well. The traditional two-parent family structure had changed. Changes in industry and business brought about by new technologies meant that those without the educational skills could not find employment in this changing economy.

Internationally, the United States confronted problems created in part by the collapse of the Soviet Union, as ethnic and religious conflicts erupted. The threat of nuclear war with Russia had been lessened, but other nations had developed nuclear, as well as biological, warfare capabilities. The terrorist attacks on September 11, 2001, tragically revealed that Americans confronted a far different world than during the era of the cold war.

The entries in this volume, which cover the period from 1969 to the present, offer to the reader a knowledge of the momentous political, cultural, social, and technological changes that occurred in these years and, in doing so, provide an opportunity to engage the future.

—Donald T. Critchlow
Saint Louis University

ENTRIES
A TO Z

Aaron, Henry L. (Hank) (1934–)

Because of his tremendous accomplishments during his 23 seasons in major league baseball, many consider Henry Aaron the best baseball player in history. He hit more home runs, 755, than any player in major league history, surpassing Babe Ruth's mark of 714 on April 8, 1974, in a game against the Los Angeles Dodgers. He also holds the record for runs batted in with 2,297; he led the National League in home runs in 1957, 1963, 1966, and 1967; and he won the league batting title twice. He also won the Gold Glove for his defensive play in right field in 1958, 1959, and 1960, but it was the power of his bat that earned him the nickname "Hammerin' Hank."

Henry Louis Aaron was born the third of eight children on February 5, 1934, in Mobile, Alabama, to Estella and Herbert Aaron. His professional baseball career began in the Negro Leagues playing with the Pritchett Athletics, the Mobile Black Bears, and the Indianapolis Clowns. His experience in the major leagues began as a shortstop in the Milwaukee Braves farm system in 1952, and he made his major league debut in 1954 with the Milwaukee Braves (now the Atlanta Braves). At the end of the 1974 season, Aaron was traded to the Milwaukee Brewers of the American League and retired as a player after the 1976 season.

After retiring as a player, Aaron took the position of vice president for player development for the Atlanta Braves and was promoted to senior vice president in 1989. Currently Aaron is corporate vice president of community relations for Turner Broadcasting Systems and is a member of the Sterling Committee of Morehouse College. He was inducted into the National Baseball Hall of Fame in 1982, where he stands alongside Babe Ruth as the only other player to have an exclusive room dedicated to his singular contributions to the game of baseball.

See also AFRICAN AMERICANS; SPORTS.

—William L. Glankler

abortion

Abortion refers to the intentional interruption of a pregnancy before birth, resulting in or accompanying the removal of the fetus. Though the procedure has been allowed in all 50 states since 1973, abortion has remained a source of social, political, ethical, and religious debate. Abortion deals with fundamental issues of civil liberties, civil rights, and morality. Those who support abortion rights argue that the government must not interfere with a woman's right to choose whether or not to reproduce. Those who oppose abortion argue that it violates the rights of the unborn. Currently, case law and political mandates in the United States tend to favor the first interpretation. It is clear, however, that the debate over legalized abortion is far from resolved.

The first state laws explicitly forbidding the practice passed during the religious revivalism of the 1820s. By 1900 every state except one made abortion a serious crime. Changes in attitude arose from the post–World War II concern for overpopulation, as well as reproductive rights for women. In the immediate aftermath of World War II, WOMEN'S RIGHTS advocates joined forces with public policy research institutions like the Rockefeller Foundation and the Ford Foundation to control world overpopulation and extend reproductive rights for women through national and international family planning programs. Though the initial goals of family planning involved public education and inexpensive distribution of contraception, by the end of the 1960s the efforts had expanded to include legalized abortion. Concurrently, women's rights advocates campaigned for changes in the state statutes and succeeded in significantly loosening the abortion restrictions in 14 states before 1973. In 1973 the U.S. SUPREME COURT decision in *ROE V. WADE* and its companion case, *Doe v. Bolten,* found abortion to be protected by the constitutional right of privacy.

Roe declared unconstitutional any but the most lenient regulations on abortion during the earliest stages of

Pro-choice demonstrators in New York City, 1977 *(Hulton/Archive)*

pregnancy. States were allowed to restrict abortions during the last trimester, but only if they provided an exception for cases where the life of the mother was at risk. This landmark decision established two legal constructs. The first stipulated that women's right to privacy included their reproductive organs and processes, as well as those dependent human embryos formed therein. The second suggested that a threshold existed between utter dependency and human viability. According to the Court, "developing life" could expect greater protections under the law during the last trimester because it was more likely to sustain itself outside the mother's womb. The Court reasoned that the rights of the unborn superseded the mother's right to privacy upon viability. Both opponents and supporters remained unsatisfied by this decision; mothers were accorded more specific rights over their reproduction decisions, while at the same time, limited protections under the law were also extended to the unborn, according to their viability.

Both decisions produced immediate backlash in the mid-1970s. Only New York had laws on the books that met the stringent guidelines of the new decision. Alaska, Hawaii, and Washington possessed laws similar to New York's, and were able to meet the new standard set by *Bolton* by removing residency requirements. The laws of the remaining 46 states were invalidated. The attorneys general of Indiana and Montana claimed that the decision was inapplicable to their states, while legislators in Utah, Michigan, and Rhode Island attempted to pass laws setting the Court's ruling aside. The Court issued a directive prohibiting any deviations from the new *Roe* and *Bolton* standards. At the same time, it rejected the petitions of 15 states calling for a rehearing of the case. After this, states looked for less direct ways of restricting abortion. In 1977 the U.S. Congress passed the Hyde amendment ending federal funding of most abortions. By the end of the decade, 37 states followed suit by rescinding state funding for abortions, limiting advertising for abortion services, and requiring spousal consent for married women and parental permission for minors.

Throughout the 1970s and 1980s, the Supreme Court heard dozens of cases involving abortion regulations. In *Bigelow v. Virginia* (1975), the Court prohibited state restrictions on advertising. The following year, *Planned Parenthood of Central Missouri v. Danforth* (1976) prohibited laws requiring spousal consent, as well as those statutes requiring parental consent without providing the alternative of a judicial waiver. The Court reconsidered the question of parental consent several times, finally concluding that states could require parental notification by a physician as long as minors had access to judicial waivers. *Maher v. Roe* and *Beal v. Doe* upheld state restrictions of abortion funding, and *Harris v. McRae* upheld the Hyde amendment's prohibition of federally funded abortion services. Abortion rights advocates became increasingly concerned that the new decisions were chipping away at *Roe v. Wade*. In contrast, abortion opponents remained frustrated that none of them specifically questioned the basic assumptions of abortion rights.

Immediately following *Roe v. Wade,* the National Council of Catholic Bishops led the charge against the new interpretation through lobbying efforts, and initiated education programs emphasizing the innate value of all human life. Five years earlier in 1968 Pope Paul VI promulgated the encyclical *Humanae Vitae,* which officially proclaimed the church's opposition to contraception and abortion. Since legalized abortion was still a rarity at the time of the encyclical's release, most Catholics and non-Catholics were concerned principally about those sections regarding artificial contraception. While many leading American Catholics publicly disavowed the encyclical's prohibition of artificial BIRTH CONTROL, their disagreement did not extend to abortion. After 1973 most Roman Catholics supported their bishops in opposition to *Roe v. Wade*. At the same time, other religious leaders also voiced their opposition to legalized abortion. Many African-American leaders, such as Rev. JESSE L. JACKSON, feared that abortion represented a form of eugenics aimed at limiting the size and strength of the black community in America. (Jackson later changed his position on abortion and endorsed *Roe* during his run for the presidency in 1984.) Other conservative Protestant denominations, called "fundamentalists" because of their belief in a literal interpretation of the Bible, also came out strongly against abortion. By the end of the 1970s, 82 percent of regular attendees of Protestant and Roman Catholic services opposed abortion at any stage of pregnancy. Yet despite these initial efforts, the opposition to abortion took a long time to coalesce. Nearly a decade passed before a strong constituency arose to organize any consistent and coherent opposition to the already entrenched abortion policies.

During the same period, women's rights advocates successfully promoted abortion as a critical component of women's equality. They argued that limiting access to abortion services guarantees continued oppression of women by denying them basic rights of privacy. Organizations like the NATIONAL ORGANIZATION FOR WOMEN (NOW) and the National Abortion Rights Action League (NARAL) undertook large-scale advertising and lobbying campaigns to fight frequent state restrictions. These organizations were especially concerned with those regulations requiring waiting periods or spousal or parental consent. Many women's rights advocates, including RUTH BADER GINSBERG, looked to the EQUAL RIGHTS AMENDMENT (ERA) as a tool for guaranteeing abortion on demand.

Abortion did not become a major issue in national elections until the presidential race of 1984. Republican president RONALD W. REAGAN used his first term of office to promote constitutional protections for the unborn. In 1981 he supported the Human Life Bill introduced by Sen. JESSE A. HELMS (R-N.C.). The bill resulted in a series of Senate hearings to determine the point when human life begins. Though no conclusion was reached, the investigation sparked considerable public debate. It also served to divide Republicans and Democrats on the issue. In 1983 President Reagan published "Abortion and the Conscience of the Nation" in the *Human Life Review.* In it, he openly condemned *Roe v. Wade* as a flawed and unconstitutional decision similar to the 1857 decision *Dred Scott v. Sandford* (sic), which denied slaves any protection under the law, and the 1896 Court ruling *Plessy v. Ferguson,* which legalized racial segregation. Reagan called for a constitutional amendment that specifically included the unborn under federal protection. Within a year, Reagan also announced the Mexico City Policy, which ended all U.S. aid to international organizations that actively promoted or performed abortions as a form of birth control. Reagan successfully linked opposition to abortion to the base of Republican ideology. In 1984 the Republican Party platform adopted several specifically antiabortion planks against abortion, infanticide, and euthanasia. Abortion rights advocates relied on the Democratic Party to represent their issues. The 1984 Democratic platform contained planks that emphasized empowerment of women and minorities, including the commitment to public funding of and guaranteed access to abortion services without restrictions.

After Reagan's landslide victory, Democrats used their majority in the House to oppose the Republican administration's continued restrictions on abortion services. During his final year, Reagan issued the "Emancipation Proclamation of Preborn Children." The proclamation was largely symbolic, since he was not legally empowered to enforce his declaration that all fetuses deserve equal protection under the law. At the same time, the proclamation included a directive to the Department of Health and Human Services prohibiting abortion counseling at health facilities receiving federal funds. Opponents labeled this a "gag rule" and abortion rights advocates appeared at numerous presidential press conferences wearing white gags and carrying signs protesting the order, which remained in effect until 1993. After Republican GEORGE H. W. BUSH's election in 1988, Congress repeatedly passed bills requiring Medicare funding for abortion, which were vetoed on each occasion. Bush also vetoed legislation that would use fetal tissue from abortions for scientific research. Congress retaliated by overruling Bush's nominee for the Supreme Court, ROBERT BORK, who had explicitly criticized *Roe v. Wade* numerous times during his tenure as federal court judge. The presidents of NOW and NARAL supported Democratic Party efforts to oppose Republican policies and to promote abortion as a necessary right of all women. At the same time, the Republican policies had the support of Rev. Jerry Falwell's MORAL MAJORITY, the National Council of Catholic Bishops, and the majority of Protestant denominations, which believe that human rights begin at conception.

Three days after taking office, Democratic president WILLIAM J. CLINTON reversed the Reagan-Bush prohibitions on abortion counseling at federally funded clinics; lifted the ban on abortions at U.S. military bases; and overturned the Mexico City Policy. He also authorized the process for legalizing the controversial drug RU-486, which opened the way for self-administered abortions. The drug began clinical testing in 1995, and the FDA approved the pill in 2000 with President Clinton's endorsement. Clinton also signed the Freedom of Access to Clinic Entrances Act (FACE), which allowed large fines and jail terms against abortion opponents who interfered with access to abortion clinics. FACE provided specific federal penalties for what were otherwise misdemeanor charges. The Department of Justice, under Clinton's administration, also advised abortion providers to sue for civil damages under the RACKETEER INFLUENCED AND CORRUPT ORGANIZATIONS ACT, a 1970 racketeering statute originally designed to target organized criminals. As a result, protestors were forced to end many of their planned demonstrations for fear that they might be charged with felonies. In 1994 Clinton signed the National Institutes of Health Revitalization Act, which provided federal funds for fetal tissue research. In 1995 the Republican-led Congress passed a bill banning the use of "partial birth abortion," but Clinton vetoed the measure. One argument by opponents of the ban was that it did not contain an exception for cases when the life of the mother is endangered. Supporters of the ban countered with testimony by the American Medical Association indicating that partial birth abortion is never necessary to save the mother's life. Clinton vetoed a similar bill in 1997.

Abortion continues to be a heated issue in American politics, although polls show that the majority of Americans support *Roe,* while they accept the state regulations on abortion.

See also AKRON V. AKRON CENTER FOR REPRODUCTIVE HEALTH; FEMINISM; RELIGION; WEBSTER V. REPRODUCTIVE HEALTH SERVICES.

Further reading: Donald Critchlow, *Intended Consequences: Birth Control, Abortion, and the Federal Government in Modern America* (New York: Oxford University Press, 1999); Mark Graber, *Rethinking Abortion: Equal Choice, the Constitution, and Reproductive Politics* (Princeton, N.J.: Princeton University Press, 1996); Rickie Solinger, ed., *Abortion Wars: A Half Century of Struggle, 1950–2000* (Berkeley: University of California Press, 1998); Laurence Tribe, *Abortion: The Clash of Absolutes* (New York: W. W. Norton & Company, 1992).

—Aharon W. Zorea

Abscam

Abscam (a term derived from "Abdul Scam") arose in 1978 from a minor FBI investigation into stolen paintings. An informant involved with the case agreed to cooperate in exchange for a reduced sentence. He later introduced undercover agents to a circle of corrupt congressmen, which led to the formation of a special FBI Organized Crime Strike Force sting operation. This operation subsequently targeted 20 members of Congress and a host of minor officials. The operation included a fictitious Arab sheik, Kambir Abdul Rahman, and a front corporation, *Abdul Enterprises, Ltd.* Throughout 1979, undercover agents used fake business credentials to approach suspected congressmen and offer $25,000–$50,000 in exchange for aid in immigration matters, government contracts, hotel and casino permits, and other investments. FBI agents videotaped and recorded all encounters. A media leak by the FBI exposed the operation in February 1980. Within weeks, 19 people were indicted, including one senator and six House members (Sen. Harrison A. Williams, Jr. [R-N.J.]; Rep. John W. Jenrette, Jr. [D-S.C.]; Rep. Michael O. Myers [D-Pa.]; Rep. Raymond F. Lederer [D-Pa.]; Rep. Frank Thompson, Jr. [D-N.J.]; Rep. John M. Murphy [D-N.Y.]; Richard Kelly [R-Fla.]). The congressmen and their co-conspirators were eventually convicted of influence peddling, conflict of interest, bribery, and racketeering. They were sentenced to terms averaging two to three years, with fines ranging from $20,000 to $50,000. Toward the end of 1980, the enforcement bodies within the Senate and House each pursued their own independent investigations and began the process of expulsion. Five of the six congressmen faced reelection during the trial, and none were reelected. Before the onset of the next term, however, the House succeeded in expelling Myers, and was about to expel Jenrette, who chose to resign before the vote could be taken. Senator Williams also resigned moments before the Senate vote to expel him. Williams was only the third senator in history to be convicted of a felony and the first to face expulsion. Similarly, Myers became the first member of the House to be expelled since the Civil War.

Abscam raised a number of issues regarding freedom of the press, Department of Justice oversight, and impeachment procedure. Consumer advocate RALPH NADER and Attorney General Benjamin Civiletti, as well as civil libertarians, condemned the FBI leaks, which initially brought the scandal to public attention. Nader was particularly concerned that the leaks violated constitutional due process by convicting the suspect in the arena of public opinion even before the trial had taken place. The outcry inspired an internal Justice Department investigation, which eventually led to disciplinary action against two prosecutors and five agents, who received letters of censure (the lightest measure available). The U.S. SUPREME COURT heard the case, *Myers v. NBC* (1980), involving allegations that NBC improperly aired material evidence on television. The Court decided that the seriousness of the case warranted "public inspection" of the evidence and rejected Myers's argument. This ruling provided precedent for news organizations reporting on celebrated court cases, allowing them to broadcast limited discovery evidence as a matter of public interest. Additionally, the Senate and House debates over the expulsion of their members brought up serious questions concerning the discretion of the FBI. Most of the accused congressmen claimed they were victims of aggressive tactics, which placed them in situations of unavoidable entrapment. The appellate courts repeatedly rejected these claims, and a later Senate probe into the sting operation revealed no indiscretions. The ACLU called for clear definitions of entrapment and strict measures to limit FBI initiatives. Another question arose in the Senate regarding whether bribery, racketeering, and influence peddling warranted expulsion or whether it could be addressed by censure. Both Republicans and Democratic leaders argued that such mild treatment would undermine the integrity of the Senate. After five days of debate, expulsion became inevitable, and Senator Williams resigned before it came to a vote.

—Aharon W. Zorea

acquired immune deficiency syndrome (AIDS)

AIDS emerged in the late 20th century as a major epidemic affecting every nation in the world. The AIDS pandemic in America has led to major medical research findings on the nature of the disease. At the same time, the pandemic has caused an increase in the use of condoms among both heterosexuals and homosexuals. As a consequence, AIDS has effected major social changes in the United States in the ways Americans view and practice sexual relations.

AIDS is caused by the human immunodeficiency virus (HIV), of which there are two distinct types: HIV-1, responsible for the current worldwide epidemic; and HIV-2, a less virulent strain primarily located in West Africa. The HIV virus progressively impairs or kills the cells of the immune system, destroying the body's ability to fight certain cancers and infection.

The term AIDS refers to the most advanced stages of HIV infection. The United States' Centers for Disease Control (CDC) defines AIDS to include all HIV-infected persons having fewer than 200 CD4+ T cells (also called T4 cells, of which an average healthy adult has 1,000 or more). The center also includes in its definition 26 clinical conditions that affect people with advanced HIV. Most of these AIDS-defining conditions are opportunistic infections: life-threatening illnesses caused by microbes that ordinarily do not cause sickness in healthy people.

The most common method of HIV transmission is through sexual contact with an infected partner. During sex, the virus can enter the body through the lining of the vagina, vulva, penis, rectum, or mouth. Often HIV is spread through contact with infected blood, among intravenous drug users sharing syringes or needles contaminated with the virus. Prior to 1985, when heat-treating techniques were introduced to destroy HIV in blood products, and intense screening was begun to determine if the virus was present, the disease also was contracted through blood transfusion or contact with blood products. Pregnant women can transfer the virus to their fetuses during pregnancy or birth, although with proper drug therapy, the risk of infection is significantly reduced. HIV also is found in breast milk, and can be passed on to babies through an infected mother. Although minute traces of the virus can be found in saliva, no evidence exists that contact with saliva spreads the disease. Moreover, there is no proof that the disease is spread through tears, sweat, feces, or urine.

Although many do not develop any indications when first infected with HIV, some people experience flu-like symptoms within a month or two after exposure. These symptoms might include headache, fever, malaise, and enlarged lymph nodes, but they usually disappear within a normal period of time, and are easily mistaken for another viral infection. During this period, the person is highly contagious, with large quantities of HIV present in genital secretions. Although the disease's progress is highly variable, more severe symptoms may not surface for two years in children, and a decade or more for adults. This asymptomatic period, whether lasting a few months or more than 10 years, is marked by the pronounced multiplication of the virus in the body as it kills the immune system's cells. These cells are usually debilitated or destroyed with few or no symptoms for the infected person. As the immune system deteriorates, however, complications begin to arise. Usually the first indication of infection is lymph nodes that remain enlarged for several months. Other symptoms that may antedate the onset of AIDS by months or even years include weight loss, fatigue, recurrent sweats and fevers, frequent or persistent yeast infection (vaginal or oral), flaky skin or skin rashes, pelvic inflammatory disease that is unresponsive to treatment, or short-term memory loss.

Although the origin of the AIDS virus remains controversial, recent research supports the theory that HIV jumped from chimpanzees to humans, a process referred to as *zoonosis*. Whether this transfer of the virus from animal to human was due to the ingestion of the animals as a food source, the keeping of primates as pets, or from medical science itself through HIV-contaminated polio vaccines remains unproven. The implications of zoonotic transfer, if brought about because of human error, would give tremendous weight to the arguments against using animal organs to produce vaccines, or xenotransplantation (grafting of tissue from one species to an individual of another).

Regardless of the scientific debates surrounding the origin—important because determining the disease's origin is critical to finding the cure—the virus did not establish itself as an epidemic strain until the mid-20th century in Africa. The earliest and most authoritative evidence of HIV infection comes from a 1959 plasma sample from an adult male from the former Belgian Congo. Analysis of this sample suggests the ancestor of this strain may date to the 1940s or '50s, and was introduced to humans a decade or so earlier. The oldest suspected case of AIDS in the United States dates back to 1969, when an African-American teenager from Saint Louis died of AIDS-like symptoms. Tissue samples, frozen at the time of the young man's death, contained HIV or a closely related virus and indicated that the disease was present in the United States before 1970. The virus has also been found in tissue samples from a Norwegian sailor, his wife, and their daughter, all of whom died about 1976 of AIDS-like indications.

Since 1981, when the disease was first identified in the United States, more than 600,000 cases of AIDS have been reported, and as many as 900,000 Americans may be infected with HIV. The World Health Organization (WHO) estimated that at the end of 1999, 33.6 million people were living with HIV/AIDS worldwide. The WHO also estimated that 16.3 million adults and children have died since the beginning of the epidemic. Sub-Saharan Africa has the highest global prevalence of HIV/AIDS infection, with Asia the lowest. In the United States, the epidemic is growing most rapidly among minority populations and is a leading killer of African-American males. According to the CDC, the prevalence of the disease is six times higher in African Americans and three times higher among Hispanics than among whites.

See also BIRTH CONTROL; GAY RIGHTS MOVEMENT.

Further reading: Douglas Feldman and Julia Miller, eds., *The AIDS Crisis: A Documentary History* (Westport, Conn.: Greenwood Publishing Group, 1998); Randy Shilts, *And the Band Played On: Politics, People and the AIDS Epidemic* (New York: Viking Penguin, 1988); Gerald J. Stine, *Acquired Immune Deficiency Syndrome: Biological, Medical, Social and Legal Issues* (Englewood Cliffs, N.J.: Prentice Hall, 1993).

—Michele Rutledge

advertising

Since its inception, advertising has been an integral and influential part of the United States society and economy. With the explosion of new communication and media technology in the last half of the 20th century, it has become even more pervasive, demanded stricter regulation, and received much criticism. The advertising industry at the end of the 20th century is a complex triad of advertisers, the media, and the advertising agencies. All three have a vested interest in influencing consumer choice. Advertisers spent approximately $131 billion in 1992, a quarter of which was spent by the 100 top national advertisers. Although $29.5 billion was spent on TELEVISION advertising, more than half of the total advertising expenditures go to newspapers, magazines, and direct mailings. Direct mail advertising is the fastest growing segment of the industry, primarily because computerized mailing lists enable advertisers to pinpoint potential customers. Automobile manufacturers, retailers, the food industry, restaurants, and the entertainment industry advertise most heavily and accounted for almost 10 percent of the total advertising expenditures in 1992.

The advertising agency produces the advertisements for its clients and serves as a liaison between the advertisers and the media. The 1980s witnessed a number of agency mergers, resulting in the creation of huge mega-agencies that offered their clients integrated advertising, marketing, and public relations services.

Advertising media are a mixture of television, magazines, newspapers, direct mail, and radio, each with its own specific benefits. For example, television offers the most multifaceted delivery because of its visual and auditory components, but it cannot distribute coupons as the print media can. In 1992 newspapers earned the highest proportion of advertising expenditures, 23 percent of the total.

Pedestrians walk past large advertisements for sportswear in New York City. While advertising has always been part of the American landscape, in the last decade many parts of the country have seen a proliferation of billboards and advertising in public spaces. Some citizens and public advocate groups are beginning to protest the sexual nature of many ads. *(Spencer/Getty Images)*

Television earned 22 percent; direct mail, 19 percent; magazines, 5.3 percent; and radio, 6.6 percent.

Advertising functions in a legal and regulatory framework that includes government legislation, self-regulation by the industry, and media control. The U.S. SUPREME COURT interpreted the First Amendment to protect commercial speech in *Virginia State Board of Pharmacy v. Virginia Citizens Consumer Council* (1976), but to a lesser degree than it protects political expression. In *Posados de Puerto Rico v. Tourism Co.* (1986), the Court upheld a ban on casino advertising to Puerto Rican residents but did not restrict such advertising to foreign tourists. The Court deemed it in the government's interest to protect local residents from the evils of gambling and that the restriction was not excessive.

Beyond the courts, the Federal Trade Commission (FTC) is responsible for regulating advertising and restricting deceptive commercial speech. The criterion used is whether the consumer is harmed, not whether the ad is technically false. If an ad is determined to be harmful to the consumer, the advertiser is ordered to cease running the ad and is fined only if it fails to comply with that order. In rare cases, advertisers are ordered to run "corrective advertising," in which they are required to restate earlier claims accurately or to offer substantiation for their claims. In 1977 the FTC ordered Warner-Lambert to run a $10 million campaign telling consumers that Listerine did not "prevent sore throats and colds or lessen their severity," as its advertising had claimed. U.S. advertisers are also controlled by their own self-regulatory board, the National Advertising Review Board, that discourages misleading and deceptive practices. The media participate in advertising regulation through their power to refuse ads they consider unfit for their editorial or programming context. Advertisers also respond to organized public pressure.

The intense desire for and need for regulation indicate that advertising exerts a significant force on society and, because of this, advertising has experienced a good deal of criticism, especially since the regulatory pressures decreased in the early 1980s. Billboard advertising has been accused of marring the environment. Advertising, in general, has been charged with creating false demand among consumers through the use of negative emotions such as guilt, anxiety, or fears of inferiority. This criticism revolves around the belief that advertising presents false images of the average citizen as young, attractive, wealthy, and leisured. Strong criticism has also been leveled at the stereotypical images of women and minorities in many advertisements. These criticisms, and many others, have sparked a wide-ranging debate over the role of advertising in our culture by asking whether it is a shaper or a mirror of our society. Such debate has led to intense scrutiny and discussion of products advertised, the character and amount of advertising exposure, advertising content, and its influence on behavior.

An important impact of advertising arises from its financial support of the mass media. Advertising provides about two-thirds of print revenue and virtually all broadcast revenue. This has generated criticism that the media, therefore, do not see the public as their primary audience, but instead see them as bait for attracting potential advertising revenue. It is argued that media content, for the most part, is designed to attract those citizens whose spending power is greatest.

One of the most controversial aspects of advertising's social impact is in the realm of politics, where heavy media campaigns have been common since the 1952 presidential election. Criticism of political advertising centers on the issues of money and regulation. Since most of the money gathered for political campaigns is used for advertising, wealthier candidates have an unfair advantage and third-party candidates are not able to raise the funds that nominees of the two major parties do. The regulation issue stems from the fact that political claims are not subject to restriction as are product claims, and no law prohibits even the most blatant falsehoods, exaggerations, or distortions. The perceived context of unfairness and deception underpins the fervid criticism of political advertisement.

The U.S. advertising industry experienced a serious recession during the late 1980s but rebounded by the mid-1990s. Changes in communications technology, however, threaten the future of the industry. Although in the past technological developments have boosted the advertising industry, the upsurge of online media that combine entertainment with advertising, sales promotion, and interactive marketing is likely to fragment mass audiences, creating smaller but more sharply targeted markets, and will change the way advertising is created and sold.

See also AUTOMOBILE INDUSTRY; BABY BOOMERS; BUSINESS; CAMPAIGN FINANCE; CENSORSHIP; COMPUTERS; ECONOMY; INTERNET; MEDIA.

Further reading: Stuart Ewen and Elizabeth Ewen, *Channels of Desire: Mass Images and the Shaping of American Consciousness* (Minneapolis: University of Minnesota Press, 1992); C. Goodrum and H. Dalrymple, *Advertising in America: The First 200 Years* (New York: Harry N. Abrams, 1990).

—William L. Glankler

affirmative action

The term *affirmative action* refers to policies used to increase opportunities for minorities by favoring them in the awarding of government contracts, college admissions, and hiring and promotion. The intended purpose of such policies has been to help eliminate the effects of past discrimination, whether perpetrated by a specific entity or by society as a whole. Title VII of the 1964 Civil Rights Act, specifically banning employment discrimination, laid the groundwork for affirmative action, and the Equal Employment Opportunity Commission (EEOC) and the Office of Federal Contract Compliance served as the primary enforcement agencies.

President Lyndon B. Johnson first used the term *affirmative action* in an executive order when he declared that government contractors should "take affirmative action" to ensure that applicants and employees are not discriminated against with regard to race, religion, sex, or national origin. President RICHARD M. NIXON went beyond the concept of simply removing discriminatory barriers and became the first president to initiate federal policies to guarantee the hiring of minorities. In 1969 the Nixon administration implemented the Philadelphia Plan which required contractors on projects assisted by federal funding to set specific goals for hiring minorities. This plan was upheld in the federal courts in 1970 and 1971.

Beyond the Philadelphia Plan, affirmative action policies have been defined by a series of legislative initiatives and U.S. SUPREME COURT decisions. In *GRIGGS ET AL. V. DUKE POWER COMPANY* the Supreme Court held that Title VII bans discriminatory practices as well as overt discrimination. This prompted employers to actively recruit minorities in order to avoid discrimination lawsuits. Colleges and universities adopted affirmative action measures when the Equal Opportunity Act of 1972 extended the Title VII protections to educational institutions. Subsequent cases further defined and refined the meaning and scope of affirmative action. In *BAKKE* (1978) the Court upheld the use of factors such as race, gender, and ethnicity in evaluating applicants but declared unconstitutional the implementation of rigid quota systems. The Court ruled in *United Steelworkers v. Weber* (1979) that a temporary training program that gave preference to minorities was constitutional because it served to remedy past discriminatory practices.

The 1980s and 1990s saw the appointment of several conservative judges to the Court, resulting in the elimination of some affirmative action programs deemed unfair or too broad in their application. In *Wygant v. Jackson* (1986), the Court struck down a plan to protect minority teachers from layoffs at the expense of white teachers with greater seniority. The Court's ruling in *Ward's Cove Packing Company v. Antonio* (1989) revised the *Griggs* decision from 1971. *Ward's Cove* shifted some of the burden of proof to the employee filing the discrimination lawsuit by requiring the plaintiff to demonstrate that specific hiring practices created racial disparities in the workplace. Moreover, even if this could be shown, the Court ruled that such practices would be legal if they served "legitimate employment goals of the employer."

While these measures limited the scope of affirmative action policies, other developments buttressed them. In *Metro Broadcasting v. Federal Communications Commission* (1990), the Court upheld federal laws designed to increase the number of minority-owned television and radio stations. Also, in response to the Court's conservative rulings, Congress passed the CIVIL RIGHTS ACT of 1991 that strengthened antidiscrimination laws and essentially reversed the *Ward's Cove* decision.

During the 1990s, affirmative action programs were the center of controversy in local politics as well. In 1995 the regents of the University of California voted to stop all affirmative action in hiring and admissions for the entire state university system. The Fifth U.S. Circuit Court prohibited the University of Texas Law School from considering race or ethnicity in its admission process in 1996. Also in 1996 California voters approved Proposition 209, which ended all state-sponsored affirmative action programs. Many believed that this would result in similar rulings in other states, but efforts in Colorado, Florida, and Ohio failed to collect the requisite number of signatures for a similar ballot initiative.

Affirmative action has been highly controversial since its inception in the mid-1960s. Critics claim that such policies violate the principle that all individuals are equal under the law, and they argue that to discriminate against one group today to compensate for discrimination suffered by another group in the past is unjust and unconstitutional. They view affirmative action as legalized reverse discrimination that privileges women and racial minorities over men and whites. Advocates insist that because discrimination is unfair treatment of people who belong to a specific group, there ought to be effective programs that aid those groups who have been discriminated against. Moreover, they argue that affirmative action policies are the only feasible option to ensure an integrated society in which all people have an equal opportunity in employment, education, and other areas. They claim further that quotas for hiring, promotions, and college admissions will fully integrate institutions traditionally closed to minorities and women because of discrimination.

See also AFRICAN AMERICANS; AMERICANS WITH DISABILITIES ACT; EQUAL RIGHTS AMENDMENT; NATIONAL ASSOCIATION FOR THE ADVANCEMENT OF COLORED PEOPLE; NATIONAL ORGANIZATION FOR WOMEN; WOMEN'S RIGHTS AND STATUS.

Further reading: Herman Belz, *Equality Transformed: A Quarter-Century of Affirmative Action* (New Brunswick, N.J.: Transaction Publishers, 1991); Robert J. Weiss, *"We Want Jobs": A History of Affirmative Action* (New York: Garland Publishing, 1997).

—William L. Glankler

AFL-CIO   See labor

African Americans

After 1968, the year that many scholars assign as the end of the Civil Rights movement, African Americans made significant strides toward parity and integration with white Americans. Yet the importance of race in U.S. society and culture qualified and, in some ways, limited the degree of success experienced by African Americans. More militant attitudes among blacks, the reemergence of black separatism in the 1990s, ambiguous racial attitudes on the part of whites, a sporadic economy, and the passage of civil rights laws contributed to the shape of the African-American community in the late 20th century.

As of 1992 there were approximately 31 million African Americans, comprising about 12.5 percent of the U.S. population. Eighty-five percent live in urban metropolitan areas and 45 percent reside in the North and Midwest. The urbanization of African Americans resulted from migration to northern, midwestern, and western cities that began during the first two decades of the 20th century. Since the late 1970s the migratory trend has shifted toward the South and Southwest, a result of deteriorating economic opportunity in northern cities and of decreased discrimination and increased economic growth in the South and Southwest. Those moving, however, are those with the resources to do so. Those experiencing economic difficulty lacked the resources to move and the skills demanded by the growing economies in the South and Southwest.

One unfortunate characteristic of the African-American community is its disproportionate susceptibility to poor health, a situation that social science has shown is in large part a result of a group's relative wealth or poverty. African Americans, whose median incomes lag behind those of whites, experience higher mortality and higher rates of disease than do whites even though such statistics show marked improvement since the middle of the 20th century. Passage of the Civil Rights Act of 1964 and Medicare and Medicaid legislation in 1965 had a major impact on African-American health care. The targeting of maternal and child health care under Title V of the Social Security Act, the development of community health centers, and Head Start also had a positive impact on the health of African-American mothers and children. Such funding and policy initiatives helped reduce the racial gap for mortality and infant mortality, although the black infant mortality rate is more than twice the white rate.

Despite these improvements, African Americans face other health risks because of their relative poverty. The rising proportion of uninsured Americans has driven up Medicaid costs, a development that has led to a constriction of health services for the poor. For young urban African Americans, substance abuse, AIDS, and homicide are very serious risks. Homicide and AIDS are the first and second leading causes of death among young black males. Between 1960 and 1990 the proportion of deaths from homicide

among white men ages 15 to 24 rose from 3 percent to 12 percent, while for African Americans the figure jumped from 20 percent to 55 percent. High rates of teen pregnancy and childbirth persist among African Americans and represent a host of potential health risks ranging from the mother contracting AIDS or other sexually transmitted diseases to low-birth-weight babies. Cases of hypertension and tuberculosis also remain persistently high among African Americans.

African Americans also have made clear though incomplete gains in education. By 1990 there was only a two-year gap between black and white Americans in the average number of years of schooling. The racial gap in standardized test scores also narrowed appreciably. Between 1971 and 1990, test scores for African Americans showed significant improvement absolutely and in comparison with white students. Regardless of these significant improvements, black high school dropout rates, while overall at parity with whites, demonstrate a disturbing increase in inner-city schools, with some districts reporting dropout rates as high as 50 percent. The high dropout rate is one factor contributing to the decline in college entry among African Americans. In 1997, 48 percent of blacks entered college, a figure that approached

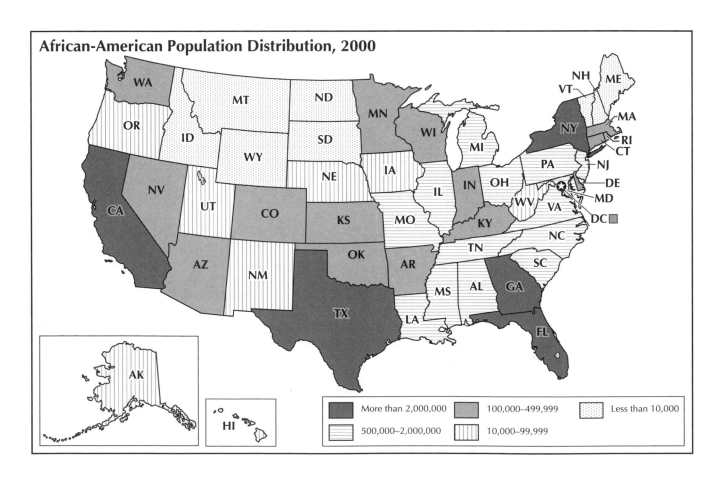

African-American Population Distribution, 2000

More than 2,000,000
500,000–2,000,000
100,000–499,999
10,000–99,999
Less than 10,000

parity with whites, but by 1993 only 32.8 percent of black high school graduates enrolled in college, compared with 41.4 percent of whites. There has been, however, a steady increase in college graduation among African Americans who attend college. Also, more black students receive degrees from "white" universities and colleges than from historically black colleges and universities, like Howard University in Washington, D.C.

Occupational status is another category in which African Americans have experienced unquestionable improvement since the middle of the 20th century. Measured by socioeconomic index scores that range from seven for domestic and day laborers to 74 for professionals, African Americans improved from an average of 15 in 1940 to 33 in 1990. Much of this improvement was the result of AFFIRMATIVE ACTION policies designed to increase both educational and employment opportunities for minorities. African Americans' improved occupational status is reflected in the continued growth of a class structure among them. While an African-American class structure has existed since the late 19th century, the latter half of the 20th century has witnessed a much sharper definition of that structure, based on occupational status and income. Between 1967 and 1992 the proportion of black households making less than $15,000 dropped only slightly, from 46 percent to 43 percent. The proportion of black households making more than $35,000, however, rose from 16 percent in 1967 to 25 percent in 1992. The proliferation of black-owned businesses contributed significantly to this social differentiation.

One impact of the black migration to northern and western industrial centers that began near the end of the 19th century was to place African Americans in proximity to better-paying jobs. Urbanized blacks had more access, though not unlimited access, to union jobs, low-level white-collar and civil service jobs. This greater access to better wages created a base of support for various black-owned businesses to emerge. By 1972 there were 187,600 black-owned businesses in the United States. By 1987 that figure more than doubled to 424,165, representing total receipts of more than $19 billion. According to *Black Enterprise*, the top 100 black-owned firms had total sales of $11.7 billion in 1995, a figure that represented only 1 percent of total U.S. receipts. Such a small proportion of the overall U.S. economy is a consequence of the relatively small size of black-owned businesses. In 1969, 94 percent were sole proprietorships and 84 percent had no paid employees. By 1977, although the number of black-owned firms had grown by 41 percent, 70 percent of them were still in personal services and retail. Even as late as 1987 the majority of these businesses were still concentrated in the food and service industries. Auto dealerships comprised the majority of the top 100 firms and produced more than 40 percent of the list's total sales in 1993 and 1994.

While these figures indicate economic progress, it is not an unalloyed progress. Forty-three percent of black households made less than $15,000 in 1992, placing nearly half of African Americans dangerously close to the poverty line. Moreover, although the black middle class is growing, the general position of blacks in relation to whites is inferior. Black males, especially, tend to be in lower-level jobs than whites in the same industries. For example, in 1990 the median earnings of black women approached parity with white women (about 98 percent), but median earnings for black males were 70 percent of white males. In sales, black males earned only slightly more than half what white males earned. Unfortunately, increased educational opportunities for African Americans do not seem to have eliminated this gap. It is true that younger, well-educated, two-earner black households have family incomes comparable to white families. For black males, however, even four or more years of college did not improve their income beyond 76 percent of white male income in 1991.

Although black family income is less than two-thirds that of whites, it has been responsible for sustaining a wide range of viable black institutions, including churches and schools, fraternal organizations, insurance firms, and various media enterprises. Along with black-owned businesses, black religious institutions are the most important among African Americans. African Americans are overwhelmingly Protestant Christians and, as black institutional organizations, the Baptist and Methodist churches are the largest and most significant. The National Baptist Convention, U.S.A., National Baptist Convention of America, and the Progressive Baptist Convention combine for a membership of more than 9 million. The largest black Methodist organization is the African Methodist Episcopal Church, which is also the oldest independent black church in the United States. African Americans have demonstrated a significant countertendency to the trend of Americans becoming less "churched," as participation by whites in mainstream Protestant churches declined significantly in the late 20th century. This countertendency has been most prominently manifested in the recent growth of Evangelicalism. The major exemplar of this intensely religious movement among African Americans is the Church of God in Christ, which finds its roots in Pentecostalism.

Throughout its history, the black church has served as more than merely a religious institution. It is a social institution that is central to the vitality of the African-American community and, as such, serves as social club, center for political activity, and as seedbed for community and political leadership. Black religious institutions have been a critical element in civil rights activism and have produced many of the most prominent leaders of the African-American community, such as JESSE L. JACKSON or the Reverend Al Sharpton, a Brooklyn, New York, activist and cleric who ran for the U.S. Senate in 1994. Reverend William Gray was a Democratic congressman from Philadelphia in 1979, was a vice chairman of the Congressional Black Caucus, served as chairman of the House Budget Committee in 1985, and was majority whip in 1989. Andrew Young, also a pastor, had a distinguished political career as a U.S. congressman (1971–77), as U.S. ambassador to the United Nations (1977–79), and as the mayor of Atlanta (1982–90).

Another prominent religious/activist institution is the NATION OF ISLAM. Under the leadership of LOUIS FARRAKHAN, the Nation of Islam has increased its ideological presence among younger, urban African Americans. It emphasizes racial pride, self-help, black business development, and a conservative family-oriented morality, and is the primary proponent of the late-20th-century form of separatist black nationalism. The Nation of Islam has enjoyed increased popularity among young African Americans primarily because of the positive feeling of "blackness" it has engendered, not because of any specific theological tenets. More secular institutions, such as the NATIONAL ASSOCIATION FOR THE ADVANCEMENT OF COLORED PEOPLE (NAACP) and the National Urban League, have been less influential in the 1980s and 1990s than they were in the first two-thirds of the 20th century. Both organizations failed to develop a national political strategy and have increasingly come under attack for their reliance on non-black sources of financial support.

That African Americans leveled such criticism at their own institutions was indicative of the ideological milieu within the black community. On one hand was a group of conservatives, including U.S. SUPREME COURT Justice Clarence Thomas, united by the claims that institutional and personal racism had declined sufficiently. On the other hand was a group of progressives or liberals, whose members included Jesse L. Jackson and Cornel West. This group insisted that racism was still prevalent in American society. Because of that, African Americans could not compete fairly without further public and private compensation for past discrimination and deprivation.

This neat division became blurred over the issue of integration versus nationalism, an issue that revolved around the ultimate goal for African Americans and the best strategy for attaining that goal. Some black intellectuals argued that racism was so fundamental to American society that integration as full-fledged members was both impossible and undesirable for blacks. Nationalists such as Louis Farrakhan argued that even if integration were preferred, white Americans would always "sell out" black Americans to preserve their own racial interests. Others, like Clarence Thomas and Jesse L. Jackson, insisted that integration into the dominant society was necessary in order to be able to fulfill one's dreams, or it was a goal in and of itself that would allow people to be judged regardless of skin color. The complexity of the issue allowed one to be a conservative nationalist (Louis Farrakhan), a liberal nationalist (Derrick Bell), a conservative integrationist (Clarence Thomas), or a liberal integrationist (Jesse L. Jackson).

The shape of African-American society at the end of the 20th century was indeed unique culturally, politically, demographically, and economically. Contending ideologies of separatism and integration among African Americans, coupled with larger economic, cultural, and political forces, created a community partially at peace with its uniqueness and with the larger American community, yet clearly restive about the forces, both external and internal, that continue to inhibit its progress.

See also AARON, HENRY; *BAKKE (REGENTS OF UNIVERSITY OF CALIFORNIA V. ALLAN BAKKE);* CIVIL RIGHTS ACT OF 1991; EVANGELICAL CHRISTIANS; FARMER, JAMES L.; *GRIGGS ET AL V. DUKE POWER COMPANY;* HILL, ANITA FAYE; JACKSON STATE UNIVERSITY; MOVIES; MUSIC; POPULAR CULTURE; POWELL, COLIN L.; RACE AND RACIAL CONFLICT; RELIGION; SPORTS; TELEVISION.

Further reading: Walter Allen and Reynolds Farley, *The Color Line and the Quality of Life in America* (New York: Russell Sage Foundation, 1987); Andrew Hacker, *Two Nations: Black and White, Separate, Hostile, Unequal* (New York: Scribner, 1991); Clifton Marsh, *From Black Muslims to Muslims: The Transition from Separatism to Islam, 1930–1980* (Metuchen, N.J.: Scarecrow Press, 1984).

—William L. Glankler

African nations (foreign policy)

United States foreign policy toward African nations during the COLD WAR was inconsistent and often at odds with the stated commitment of the United States to democracy and development. During the cold war, the United States often overlooked repression, injustice, corruption, and economic mismanagement in African countries such as Kenya, Somalia, Sudan, and Zaire. The United States and the Soviet Union both saw important reasons for acquiring allies in Africa, but Africa was never seen as a primary strategic region by either side during the cold war. Nevertheless, both the United States and the Soviet Union remained active in African affairs.

Until 1975 the United States and the Soviet Union limited their involvement in African nations. After 1975, though, the Soviet Union became directly involved in several African nations through the use of Cuban troops and East German and Soviet supporting staff. The United States response to this change in Soviet policy was initially confined to supplying limited amounts of arms and cash to anticommunist forces. By the late 1970s more than 40,000 troops from Cuba, East Germany, and the Soviet Union had been deployed across the African continent. The governments of Angola, Mozambique, Ethiopia, the People's Republic of the Congo, and Benin all claimed to be based on Marxist-Leninist principles, while Libya had a treaty of friendship with the Soviet Union.

The white regime in South Africa posed a particularly complex problem for U.S. policymakers throughout the 1970s and 1980s. President RICHARD M. NIXON relaxed pressure on the white minority regimes there because the National Security Council (NSC) assured him that the white leaders were there to stay and that change would only be possible by working through them. The NSC told the president in NSC Memorandum 39: "There is no hope for the blacks to gain the political rights they seek through violence, which will lead only to chaos and increased opportunities for the Communists."

By 1975 three factions in Angola fought for control of the country, with the United States covertly aiding one of the antimarxist factions. At the same time, the Soviet Union supplied Angolan marxists with large amounts of aid and supported the introduction of Cuban troops into the conflict. When the U.S. Congress learned of American covert involvement in the conflict, Congress acted to prevent any further intervention. Nevertheless, Secretary of State HENRY KISSINGER continued to work behind the scenes to maximize U.S. influence (and minimize Soviet influence) in African nations that were making the transition to majority rule.

South Africa remained a problem area for the United States. President GERALD FORD employed economic pressure to end apartheid (the strict segregation of and discrimination against black South Africans), but when President JAMES EARL CARTER, JR. came into office in 1977, the United States initiated a more aggressive policy toward South Africa to end minority rule. During Carter's presidency, South Africans agreed to hold elections, dismantle apartheid, and concede independence to Namibia.

President RONALD W. REAGAN's policies toward Africa reflected growing tensions with the Soviet Union. Reagan emphasized the importance of U.S. national security in American relations with Africa. Reagan's security program had five components: foreign military sales, economic support funds, grants of military assistance, international military education and training, and peacekeeping operations. Through these programs Reagan sought to diminish the dominance the Soviet Union had obtained in Africa during the 1970s.

Moreover, Reagan sought to display American military strength when confronted with hostile regimes in Africa. In August 1981 Reagan ordered the use of force against Libya, a nation considered a major source of world terrorism. U.S. Air Force jets shot down two Libyan planes after they fired upon the American planes.

The end of the cold war changed the way U.S. policymakers looked at Africa. With the end of the cold war, President GEORGE H. W. BUSH delegated responsibility for African policy to midlevel officials and placed U.S. relations with African countries on the back burner. President WILLIAM J. CLINTON continued a similar policy toward Africa, although his wife, HILLARY CLINTON, traveled to Africa on a goodwill tour. As a result African nations often received a high priority only when it became necessary for the United States, under United Nations auspices, to intervene in the name of human rights, as it did in Somalia.

In December 1992, shortly before leaving office, President Bush sent American troops to Somalia in a humanitarian effort to relieve famine and anarchy in northeast Africa. Once in office, President Clinton gave command of U.S. forces in Somalia to the United Nations, to undertake "nation-building" in the devastated country. On October 3, 1993, U.S. Army Rangers became involved in a disastrous raid on an enemy warlord's headquarters, leading to the deaths of 18 American soldiers, the wounding of 78 others, and the parading of American bodies through the streets. Clinton called for the withdrawal of American forces within six months and replaced Secretary of Defense Les Aspin, who had come under heavy criticism by the U.S. military. The withdrawal of American forces left Somalia in continued chaos and induced a reluctance within the Clinton administration to become militarily involved in Africa, even when it confronted genocide in other African nations.

Throughout the last three decades of the 20th century, U.S. interests have intersected with Africa at three points: in a drive for economic access to Africa's resources and investment opportunities; in cold war competition and internationalization of African conflicts; and in United Nations and other multilateral negotiations. As different U.S. presidents have entered the White House, the relationships with African nations have crossed the spectrum from ambivalence to covert military involvement. Now that the cold war has ended, the United States is developing new relations with African nations that focus on the economic relationship and internal African stability.

See also DEFENSE POLICY; FOREIGN POLICY.

Further reading: Gerald J. Bender, James S. Coleman and Richard L. Sklar, eds. *African Crisis Areas and U.S. Foreign Policy* (Berkeley: University of California Press, 1985); Michael Clough, *Free at Last? U.S. Policy toward Africa and the End of the Cold War* (New York: Council on Foreign Relations Press, 1992); Peter Duignan and L. H. Gann, *The United States and Africa: A History* (Cambridge, U.K.: Cambridge University Press, 1984); John

Lewis Gaddis, *Strategies of Containment: A Critical Appraisal of Postwar American National Security Policy* (New York: Oxford University Press, 1982); Jennifer Seymour Whitaker, ed., *Africa and the United States: Vital Interests* (New York: New York University Press, 1978).

—Leah Blakey

Age Discrimination Act of 1975

As an amendment to the Older Americans Act of 1965, this act protects people of all ages from discrimination based upon age. Specifically this law provides that "no person in the United States shall, on the basis of age, be excluded from participation in, be denied the benefits of, or be subjected to discrimination under any program or activity receiving Federal financial assistance" (42 U.S.C. Section 6102). The Office for Civil Rights (OCR) of the Department of Health and Human Services enforces the act in federally funded health and social service programs. The act allows particular exceptions to the broad stipulation against discrimination based on age. While it prohibits discrimination on the basis of age (maximum or minimum) at private institutions that receive federal assistance, it does not prohibit discrimination when the action "reasonably takes into account age as a factor necessary to the normal operation or the achievement of any statutory objective of such program or activity; or the differentiation made by such action is based upon reasonable factors other than age" (42 U.S.C. Section 6103). This law does not apply to any activity or program established under the authority of any law that provides benefits or assistance to people based upon their age, or upon established criteria for participation, in age-related terms, or that describes intended beneficiaries or target groups. Other exceptions include using factors other than age that have a direct and substantial relationship to the program, and as well as criteria for programs that offer special benefits to children or elderly persons.

—Michele Rutledge

Agnew, Spiro T. (1918–1996)

Relatively unknown in the Republican Party, Maryland governor Spiro Agnew was a surprise selection by Republican presidential nominee RICHARD M. NIXON for his vice presidential running mate in the 1968 campaign. Agnew's role in the campaign was reminiscent of Nixon's during the 1952 and 1956 presidential campaigns, attacking the Democrats while the presidential candidate avoided excessive controversy. Agnew became known for his quips, "When you've seen one slum, you've seen them all," and "Hubert Humphrey [the Democratic party nominee] is squishy-soft on communism."

Agnew's role in the Nixon administration remained limited. He was assigned to head the Office of Intergovernmental Affairs, created in 1969 to facilitate relations between state governors and the federal executive branch. Agnew also served as chair of the Space Advisory Committee. Nonetheless, governors from large states ignored Agnew and spoke directly with the White House. In addition, Agnew's support of a manned mission to Mars further estranged him from the White House. Furthermore, Agnew's views on foreign policy—supporting bombings in Cambodia and Laos publicly, opposing détente and the opening of China—resulted in his being left out of the decision-making process.

In 1973 the U.S. attorney in Baltimore investigated Agnew for accepting bribes from real estate developers in exchange for building contracts when Agnew held local and state offices in the 1960s. Already in the midst of WATERGATE, Agnew could not stop the investigation without attracting attention. After being denied an impeachment proceeding and receiving a court ruling that a sitting vice president could be indicted, Agnew pleaded "no contest" in federal court on October 10, 1973, and was fined $10,000, received a three-year suspended sentence, and was disbarred. After resigning the vice presidency, Agnew retreated into retirement and never returned to public life. He died September 18, 1996, of leukemia.

—John Korasick

agriculture

Although more than half of the world's population depends on agriculture for their source of livelihood, farmers account for only 2 percent of the American workforce. At the same time, however, American farms produce more than a quarter of the world's wheat and corn, and America ranks as the third leading exporter of rice. This inverse relationship between the number of farmers and their high yields reveals the degree to which agriculture continues to be influenced by modern technological innovations in transportation, communication, and the biological sciences.

After World War II, returning soldiers often left their rural homes and migrated to the cities to pursue urban professions; by 1960 the number of farmers had fallen by nearly 40 percent. Despite this massive loss of farm workers, the expanse of American farmland remained relatively stable, declining only 4 percent, and in 1960 the average size of each farm increased by almost a third to 303 acres. The trend continued for every decade after; the number of farm workers fell by a third, the total acreage of farmland declined by only 4 or 5 percent, and the average farm grew by 10–20 percent. By 1990 there were 4.5 million farmers (2.6 percent of the labor force) who worked 987 million acres (13 percent less than in 1960) with an average farm size of 461 acres. Increasingly, much of this farming took place on corporate-owned farms, leased to individual farmers. During this same period, the average yield per farmer increased nearly 300 percent: one farm worker in 1965 could produce enough food and fiber for 35 people; by 1993 a single worker provided for more than 100 people. Because of the importance of agriculture to the American economy, the United States government aided farming through farm subsidies, funding for agricultural research, purchase of surplus agricultural products distributed through the food stamp program, and foreign trade policies.

Since World War II, agriculture in the United States has experienced a silent revolution. The more obvious innovations in personal COMPUTERS often obscure the more mundane advances in agriculture and animal husbandry. The unpredictable nature of weather and ecology guarantees an element of risk in any farming endeavor. As early as the 1950s, agricultural scientists tried to limit the extent of that risk by experimenting with genetic engineering of crops to ensure higher yield, greater tolerance to heat and frost, and greater resistance to insects and disease. One way to increase yield is to shorten the maturation cycles of a given crop; for example, the shorter growing period of dwarf varieties of rice allow for an additional growing cycle per year. Another way to increase yield is to increase the size and amount of product, for example, more ears of corn per stalk, or more quarts of milk per cow. Other modifications of crop tolerances have allowed grain sorghum, which was originally a tropical plant, to be grown as far north as North Dakota. Moreover, the higher tolerance to temperature and moisture fluctuations compounded by the stronger resistance to insects and disease also help ensure consistently higher yields. The farming community generally recognized the significance of these scientific innovations, and by 1970 more than 850,000 students were enrolled in agricultural education courses outside of the farmstead.

During the 1960s and 1970s, scientists relied primarily on controlled mating systems; the desired traits that occur naturally in two or more species of plant are transferred to a more commonly cultivated species through cross-pollination to form new hybrids. Over successive generations, the desired traits are enhanced while the undesirable traits are extinguished. Beginning in the 1980s, developments in genetic engineering allowed scientists to manipulate traits directly at the chromosome level. This opened the way for hybrids between species that would otherwise be incompatible through the natural mating process. Given the enormous genetic variability that exists throughout the plants in the world, the number of possible combinations is virtually unlimited.

Other innovations in communication and transportation have directly influenced agriculture. The interstate

Participants at a protest organized by farm aid officials to raise awareness of the plight of family farms in America *(Smith/Getty Images)*

highway system helped liberate farmers from dependence on a fixed rail system and further expanded the range of available markets. An increase in all-cargo airplane routes during the 1970s was especially helpful for farmers dealing in fresh fruit or vegetables. By the 1980s agriculture was becoming specialized on a global scale. Developing nations no longer had to rely on diverse crop production, and could instead focus on the crops best adopted to their climate. Though the United States exports more than $50 billion a year in agricultural products, it still imports $37 billion a year in other specialty goods. The advances in transportation allow Israeli farmers to sell fresh tomatoes in Alaskan markets with no noticeable degradation of quality.

Similarly, innovations in personal computing technology during the 1990s enabled farmers to more precisely manage their planting, fertilizing, and harvesting schedules. Dedicated computing instruments are included in most farm implements, and can be easily taken to each farm site for direct analysis. These advances allow fewer farmers to manage larger operations; in 1965 it took corn farmers five labor-hours to produce 100 bushels of wheat, but by 1987 it took half that time. Larger farms are more economically efficient because they can arrange for volume discounts in purchasing grain, seed, or fertilizer. They can also arrange more stable markets by contracting directly with processors, thus avoiding the middle distributors. In addition, large farms typically require smaller investments in machinery per acre.

This push toward greater economies of scale has forced American farmers to adopt more sophisticated methods for procuring the necessary capital investment. Land remains the greatest single expense for farmers; the total worth of farm assets was $861.5 billion in 1992, with real estate accounting for $671 billion of that amount (78 percent). As a result, many modern farmers rent the land they manage, rather than own it directly. Another strategy avoids the costly investment in specialized farm equipment through outside contracts for specific services. A modern American farmer might rent his land; contract an airplane operator to seed, fertilize, and apply herbicide and pesticides; and contract a neighbor farm to harvest his crops. Ranchers employ similar contracts for sheep shearing, dehorning, or artificial insemination of their livestock.

Agriculture in America has experienced significant changes toward greater specialization and intensive development—not all of which have been welcomed by the American public. During the mid-1960s, César Chávez organized 60,000 migrant farm workers in California in an attempt to ensure higher wages and benefits. Through a series of strikes, boycotts, and marches, Chávez forced growers to sign union contracts with the labor supply. In 1970 he called on consumers to boycott grapes until the growers agreed to his demands, and an estimated 17 million Americans stopped buying grapes. In 1975 California governor Jerry Brown signed the Agriculture Labor Relations Act, which established collective bargaining for farm workers throughout California.

To the general public, Chávez helped create a public image of "corporate farmers" who exploit workers and small family operations to reap greater profit. During the 1980s, many farmers fell into heavy debt and were forced to sell their farms. Statistically, the decline in farm workers remained the same as had been experienced in each previous decade, but since most of those who left during the 1980s were forced out by debt rather than by choice, the farm "crisis" assumed greater proportions in the public eye. Country singer Willie Nelson organized three Farm Aid concerts to benefit indebted farmers from 1986–88. In

1990 Congress responded to the rise in farm bankruptcy by passing the Food, Agriculture, Conservation, and Trade Act and the Omnibus Budget Reconciliation Act to increase farmers' flexibility in planting while still allowing government support and subsidies.

Another area of public discontent stems from the new scientific methods of production. Starting as early as the 1960s, but becoming ever more vocal in the 1990s, several naturalist groups formed to protest modern farming techniques. Originally inspired by the use of toxic pesticides during the 1960s, modern natural food advocates often oppose the use of any artificial fertilizers, special growth hormones, or biogenetic engineering. They argue that modern farming techniques promote cancers and may produce other disease and deformities. Many animal rights advocates oppose all meat and dairy production as examples of cruelty to animals. Lobbying efforts by these activists, consumer advocates, and other interest groups led to more stringent Food and Drug Administration regulations for processing plants, and the passage of stricter truth-in-labeling laws. These changes encouraged meat and dairy associations to pursue more aggressive advertising campaigns. With the exception of a slight increase in the number of local farmer's markets, the public discontent has had little impact on the general trend in American agriculture.

Agriculture remains the basic element upon which every civilization must depend. Modern agriculture in the United States has evolved into a highly sophisticated and specialized industry requiring a decreasing percentage of total resources. Though science and technology may contradict the traditional images of a pastoral rural society, they remain an intricate part of farming today.

See also ECONOMY; IMMIGRATION.

Further reading: Randal S. Beeman and James A. Pritchard, *A Green and Permanent Land: Ecology and Agriculture in the Twentieth Century* (Lawrence: University Press of Kansas, 2001); M. C. Halberg, *Economic Trends in U.S. Agriculture and Food Systems since World War II* (Ames: Iowa State University Press, 2001).

—Aharon W. Zorea

Akron v. Akron Center for Reproductive Health

Since the 1973 decisions of ROE V. WADE and *Doe v. Bolton*, the U.S. SUPREME COURT heard cases that repeatedly sought clarification regarding the degree to which state statutes could require parental notifications for minors seeking ABORTION. *Akron v. Akron Center for Reproductive Health* (1983) represents the Court's fluctuating position on the question. The issue arose three years after *Roe*, in *Planned Parenthood Association of Central Missouri v.*

Danforth (1976), which overturned a Missouri statute requiring spousal consent, as well as parental consent for minor children. The *Danforth* decision was affirmed by *Bellotti v. Baird* (1979), which overturned a similar Massachusetts law specifically requiring parental consent for minors seeking abortion. The Court argued that states must provide alternative forms of authorization, including the ability of a local judge to determine whether the minor is sufficiently mature to make the decision on her own. The trend barring all minor consent requirements was undermined by *H. L. v. Matheson* (1981), which upheld a Utah statute requiring doctors to inform the parents of unemancipated minors, "if possible."

In the 1980s Akron, Ohio, passed a local ordinance which required: (1) in-hospital performance of all second trimester abortions; (2) physician-conducted pre-abortion counseling to ensure informed consent; (3) parental consent for unmarried minors; (4) proper disposal of fetal remains; and (5) a 24-hour waiting period between the time a woman signs a consent form and the time an abortion is performed. In *Akron v. Akron Center for Reproductive Health* (1983), the Court struck down each of the provisions, with a specific argument against each. With regard to parental consent, the Court reaffirmed *Bellotti v. Baird*, which required an alternative for parental consent.

Akron (1983) was seriously undermined seven years later by *Hodgson v. Minnesota* (1990), which, in a 5-4 decision, upheld a Minnesota statute requiring both a 48-hour waiting period for minors and a two-parent notification requirement, as long as judicial waivers allowing a judge to make exceptions and authorize an abortion without informing the parents when the court believed it to be in the girl's best interests. During that same summer, *Ohio v. Akron Center for Reproductive Health* upheld a state's right to require abortion providers to notify the parents of minors before performing an abortion on them; again, on the condition that minors had access to judicial waivers. *Akron* (1983) was fully reversed two years later by a pair of decisions handed down one day apart, *Planned Parenthood of Southeastern Pennsylvania v. Casey* (June 28, 1992), and *Casey v. Planned Parenthood* (June 29, 1992). The Court upheld Pennsylvania statutes requiring parental consent by abortion providers, as well as 24-hour waiting periods to ensure informed consent. The Court, however, maintained the 1976 *Danforth* decision and struck down a provision requiring spousal notification.

—Aharon W. Zorea

Alaska Native Claim Settlement Act (1971)

President RICHARD M. NIXON signed the Alaska Native Claim Settlement Act (ANSCA) into law in 1971. In exchange for dismissing future Alaska Native land rights claims, the federal government transferred title of 44 million acres, along with $462.5 million to be paid immediately from the federal Treasury and an additional $500 million from future oil-revenue sharing. Settlement benefits were dispersed through 12 separate regional tribal corporations and 200 local villages. Qualifying Alaskans had to possess at least one-fourth Indian, Aleut, or Eskimo ancestry. Approximately 80,000 Alaska Natives qualified, each receiving 100 shares of corporate stock. A 13th corporation was later added to account for those Alaska Natives living outside the state of Alaska. Alaska Natives were barred from transferring their shares to non-Natives for 20 years to prevent premature alienation. In 1991 the shares became transferable and were liable to state taxation.

The ANCSA represented a culmination of a long history of conflict over land rights between Alaska Natives and the European and American settlers who came to form the majority population of the state. The legacy of Alaska Native land claims dates back to when the United States first acquired Alaska in 1867, but they were not again specifically addressed until 1959, when Alaska applied for admission into the Union. Conflict arose when Congress authorized the newly formed state to select 130 million acres of land from the federal government holdings without accounting for Alaska Native land claims. The discovery of oil intensified the pressure for an immediate resolution, which came about within five years. The resulting ANSCA settlement amounted to nearly four times the cumulative settlements of all previous Alaska Native claims in the United States.

Critics claimed that the corporate structure of the settlement threatened to alienate unsuspecting Alaska Natives from their rightful shares. By the end of the 1970s, some corporations orchestrated lucrative lease agreements with oil companies, while others met with financial failures. Despite predictions to the contrary, however, the threat of corporate bankruptcy did not translate into Alaska Native alienation from their rightful claims. Federal recognition of Alaska Native corporations as a political unit arose as one of the undisputed benefits of the ANCSA. Moreover, it served as precedent for other Alaska Native claims, including a successful movement in Quebec, Canada, as well as new reparations movements posed by other minority groups in the United States.

—Aharon W. Zorea

Albert, Carl B. (1908–2000)

Albert was the 46th Speaker of the House of Representatives from 1971 to 1976, a period in which the major political issues of the VIETNAM WAR, the WATERGATE SCANDAL, and the ENERGY CRISIS placed unusual demands on Congress.

Carl Bert Albert was born on May 10, 1908, in Oklahoma. After graduating from Oxford University on a Rhodes scholarship in 1934, Albert worked for three years for the Federal Housing Administration, during which time he was admitted to the Oklahoma Bar. Albert spent six years practicing law and in 1941 entered the armed forces as a private in the Judge Advocate General's Corps.

Leaving the service as a lieutenant colonel in 1946, he was elected as a Democrat to the House of Representatives for the Third District of Oklahoma, a position he retained until his retirement in 1976. Albert was majority whip from 1955 to 1962; majority leader from 1962 to 1971, and in 1968 he chaired the turbulent Democratic Convention in Chicago.

As Speaker of the House, Albert was immediately drawn into the highly charged issue of the Vietnam War. Albert, who favored a peaceful ending of the war only on terms acceptable to the United States, faced opposition from within his own party by those who demanded immediate withdrawal. In 1973 Albert clashed with President RICHARD M. NIXON over the president's impoundment of congressional funds for domestic social programs, a move that Albert viewed as a challenge to the constitutional separation of powers. The Watergate scandal placed Albert in a unique position. After the resignation of Vice President SPIRO AGNEW, Albert, as Speaker, was next in line to the president. Albert resisted pressure to hasten impeachment and did not hinder the appointment of GERALD FORD as vice president, preferring to move cautiously in the impeachment proceedings.

Under Albert, the position of the Speaker gained more influence in policy matters, most notably in the right to nominate all majority party members of the Rules Committee. At the same time, the WAR POWERS ACT expanded the Speaker's role in foreign policy. Albert retired in 1976, although his term officially ended on January 3, 1977. He died in Oklahoma in 2000.

—Stephen Harding

Albright, Madeleine K. (1937–)

Madeleine Korbel Albright, a naturalized American citizen who was born in Czechoslovakia, has served in many U.S. government positions related to FOREIGN POLICY, culminating in her being appointed the first female secretary of state of the United States. She came to the United States as a child following the communist takeover of what is now the Czech Republic. She earned her doctorate in political science at Columbia University.

She began working in politics in 1975 when she served as a fund-raiser for then-senator Edmund S. Muskie while he was running for the Democratic presidential nomination. She later served as an adviser for foreign policy

during WALTER F. MONDALE's, MICHAEL S. DUKAKIS's, and WILLIAM J. CLINTON's presidential campaigns. In 1993 President Clinton repaid her hard work by appointing her ambassador to the United Nations. Then, in 1996 Clinton nominated Albright as the first female secretary of state for the United States.

Albright has been spoken of by many as a key strategist and policymaker for many years. Only one year after joining Senator Muskie's team, Albright was officially signed on as his chief legislative assistant. Due to Muskie's membership on the Senate Foreign Relations Committee, Albright immediately began focusing on foreign relations. In 1978 Albright moved to the National Security Council under Zbigniew Brzezinski, where she was a congressional liaison focusing on foreign policy legislation. In the 1984 presidential campaign she worked as Walter Mondale's foreign policy coordinator, and then in the 1988 campaign she served as a senior foreign policy adviser to Michael Dukakis. Her position papers on foreign policy during the 1992 election led to President Clinton's appointing her a delegate to the United Nations. The U.S. Senate unanimously confirmed her nomination, and she was sworn into office on January 28, 1993. At this time President Clinton named Albright to the National Security Council. On December 5, 1996, President Clinton nominated Albright as secretary of state to replace Warren Christopher. She was unanimously confirmed by the U.S. Senate and sworn in on January 23, 1997, as the first female secretary of state and the highest-ranking female in government. As secretary of state she pursued an aggressive foreign policy in protecting human rights and emerged as a leading advocate of American intervention, through United Nations auspices, in Serbia during Clinton's second term in office. She also became known as a proponent of "nation-building," and as such, urged American participation in the United Nations' efforts to build democratic regimes, especially in the former Yugoslavia.

—Leah Blakey

Amendments to the U.S. Constitution

The American people have demonstrated a distinct preference for seeking change within the system, rather than attempting changes to the system itself. After more than 200 years of existence, the U.S. Constitution has only been permanently altered 25 times. Remarkably, only six amendments proposed by Congress failed to win the necessary approval from two-thirds of the state legislatures to become ratified, which suggests that Congress does not advocate systemic change without some prior assurance of widespread popular support. Since 1968, this trend became less consistent; Congress approved three constitutional amendments between 1971 and 1978, and only one was ratified.

The TWENTY-SIXTH AMENDMENT (1971) established a uniform voting age of 18 years. Prior to that, state legislatures determined voting age independently. Only four states recognized a voting age below 21: Hawaii set the age at 20, Alaska at 19, and Georgia and Kentucky recognized 18-year-old voters. Efforts to lower the voting age began long before 1971, when soldiers during World War II complained that they were old enough to fight, yet were denied the right to vote. As president, former general Dwight D. Eisenhower publicly supported the idea of lowering the voting age, as did President Lyndon B. Johnson. Both men failed to initiate legislation that would effect national change. By the 1960s, however, the demographic pressures of the post–World War II BABY BOOM generation combined with a growing ANTIWAR protest movement to force a federal response. In 1970 Congress passed a Voting Rights Act, which officially lowered the voting age in all federal, state, and local elections. Despite widespread support for the new changes, some state legislatures opposed the manner in which they were achieved. The Oregon legislature immediately challenged the law, arguing that it violated Section One of Article 2 of the Constitution, which guaranteed the right of each state to determine the voting age requirements for its own elections. The U.S. SUPREME COURT upheld their challenge and repealed the law in *Oregon v. Mitchell* (1970). With unprecedented speed, Congress responded with a proposed constitutional amendment, which was ratified faster than any previous amendment in history, in just over three months.

In March 1971 Congress proposed the EQUAL RIGHTS AMENDMENT (ERA). It explicitly stipulated "equality of rights under the law shall not be denied or abridged by the United States or by any State on account of sex." The bill was initially proposed in 1923 by Alice Paul, a radical activist of the woman's suffrage movement who had helped win ratification of the Nineteenth Amendment just three years earlier. At the time, representatives of both sexes who feared it would invalidate special workplace protection for women, and might even make them subject to the military draft, rejected the ERA proposal. The Republican Party endorsed a version of the ERA in its party's platform in 1940, but failed to win support in Congress. The ERA was resubmitted as a tool for feminist empowerment in the early 1970s, and approved 84-8 by the Senate. Six states ratified the amendment in just two days, and a year later it was approved by 30 of the 38 states required for ratification. Proponents of the ERA maintained that it would ensure equal rights for women without having to have individual laws in a myriad of areas.

In 1973 PHYLLIS SCHLAFLY began the Stop ERA movement, which opposed the amendment for many of the same reasons opponents in the 1920s rejected it. She argued that some of the amendment's unintended consequences would deprive women of the existing rights and benefits of their sex, including child support, lower insurance rates, and immunity from the draft. Stop ERA gained widespread support from conservative women and evangelical Protestant women who feared the amendment might cause more harm than good. Though the original seven-year deadline for ratification was extended another three years, the pro-ERA supporters failed to rally the support necessary for ratification. The amendment died in 1982.

The ERA amendment was still being debated in the state legislatures when Congress proposed another amendment providing statehood for the District of Columbia (D.C.) in August 1978. The Twenty-third Amendment gave D.C. residents the right to vote for presidential tickets in 1961, and five years later, President Johnson appointed a mayor and a city council to handle administrative issues. In 1971 residents were allowed to elect a nonvoting delegate to the House, and 10 years after that, in 1981, they were allowed to elect the mayor and the city council members directly. Walter Fauntroy, a nonvoting delegate, lobbied extensively during the 1970s for statehood. Congress proposed the necessary amendment in 1978, which was quickly ratified by several states. Opponents arose equally fast, however, arguing that the amendment would create a separate category of "nominal" statehood. In addition, Republicans feared that D.C. would become a Democratic state. Opponents proposed that a better solution would be to dissolve the federal district and incorporate the land into the existing state of Maryland. The proposal failed to win further support, and no effort was launched to extend the 1985 deadline. During the 1990s, President WILLIAM J. CLINTON repeatedly touted support for D.C. statehood, but failed to initiate any significant efforts to achieve that goal.

Even though Congress has not proposed any new amendments since 1978, the Twenty-seventh Amendment was ratified in 1992, prohibiting congressional pay raises until after the subsequent election in the HOUSE OF REPRESENTATIVES. The purpose behind the amendment is to prevent legislators from voting themselves a raise without first giving the voters an opportunity to vote them out of office during the next election cycle. James Madison submitted the original proposal in 1789 as part of a legislative package of 12 amendments known as the Bill of Rights. Ten of the amendments were ratified in 1791, and the two remaining proposals were largely ignored; the reapportionment amendment was rejected as untenable, and the compensation amendment had passed only six states. Since the proposal did not include a statute of limitations, it remained on the books for 80 years until Ohio became the seventh state to ratify it in 1873—largely as a symbolic protest against a massive retroactive salary increase that the federal government had passed earlier. It remained undisturbed until the early 1980s, when an economics major from the University of Texas, Gregory D. Watson, unearthed the amendment during his research and launched a vigorous campaign for ratification. Colorado became the eighth state to ratify it in 1984; over the course of the next eight years, 31 states followed suit with Michigan and New Jersey bringing the necessary two-thirds majority in 1992. As the Twenty-seventh Amendment, James Madison's proposal endured the longest ratification process in American history.

Numerous groups have launched efforts to mobilize support for additional amendments, including explicit protection for the rights of unborn children, protection for prayer in school, a special prohibition against flag burning, and the legalization of marijuana. These measures, however, have not garnered congressional approval, and have not been debated except as tentative proposals.

See also ELECTIONS; FEMINISM; WOMEN'S RIGHTS AND STATUS.

Further reading: David E. Kyvig, *Explicit and Authentic Acts: Amending the U.S. Constitution, 1776–1995* (Lawrence: University Press of Kansas, 1996).

—Aharon W. Zorea

American Independent Party (AIP)

The American Independent Party (AIP) was established in 1968 primarily as a means for Alabama governor GEORGE C. WALLACE to launch a third-party presidential campaign. The AIP consisted of 50 separate state parties, of which only 12 used the American Independent label. Through the Wallace campaign's tight control of election activities and the high media profile that accompanied their candidate, the party qualified for inclusion on the ballot in all 50 states. Wallace selected former air force general Curtis LeMay as his vice presidential candidate. The campaign was based on Wallace's populist rhetoric in an attempt to appeal to disgruntled voters, especially his opposition to the Civil Rights movement and his hawkish stance on the VIETNAM WAR. Wallace attempted to limit the influence of the right wing on his campaign, especially the John Birch Society, and discouraged other candidates from running on the AIP platform, although 14 candidates ran for the House of Representatives in California. Wallace intended his campaign to deny an electoral college majority to either major party and to set the groundwork for a presidential bid in 1972. While he did not achieve his aim, Wallace received almost 10 million popular votes and 46 electoral votes—at that time the largest popular vote ever received by a third party.

After the election Wallace kept his distance from the American Independent Party. The party split in 1969 into the American Party, which supported Wallace, and the more conservative National Committee of Autonomous State Parties. Although Wallace ran in the 1972 Democratic presidential primaries, he was careful not to alienate either section. An assassination attempt on Wallace in May 1972, which left him paralyzed from the waist down, effectively ended his presidential ambitions. The two organizations then united under the American Party banner and nominated John G. Smith, a member of the John Birch Society, as presidential candidate and Thomas Anderson as his running mate. In the 1972 election they managed to receive only a little over 1 million votes, about 1.4 percent of the popular vote.

After the election the party split again, with Anderson gaining control of the American Party and William K. Shearer, the chair of the California section, forming a dissident group as a new American Independent Party. In the 1976 election the American Party nominated Anderson as presidential candidate. The American Independent Party nominated former Georgia governor Lester Maddox, thwarting an attempt by conservatives including Richard Viguerie, William Rusher, and Howard Phillips to take over the party. The combined vote of both parties in the 1976 election was 0.4 percent of the popular vote.

Since 1976 the American Independent Party has run in fewer states and supported its last presidential candidate, John C. Rarick, in 1980. The AIP still fields candidates in a few states, mainly California, and is a state affiliate party to the Constitution Party, supporting their presidential nominee, Howard Phillips, in 1996 and 2000.

See also ELECTIONS; POLITICAL PARTIES; WALLACE, GEORGE CORLEY.

—Steve Hardman

Americans with Disabilities Act (ADA)

The Americans with Disabilities Act, passed in 1990, was the culmination of decades of activism to make American society more accessible to people with disabilities. The disability rights movement emerged in the wake of the Civil Rights movement of the 1960s. Rejecting paternalistic treatment toward people with disabilities, the movement achieved numerous legislative victories in the years leading up to the ADA.

Beginning in 1968 with the Architectural Barriers Act, Congress passed a series of laws to provide access to some public facilities, public transportation, and public educational institutions. The Rehabilitation Act of 1973 prohib-

Disabled demonstrators rally in Los Angeles, California, to protest the State of California's challenge to the Americans with Disabilities Act of 1990 in the Supreme Court
(McNew/Newsmakers)

ited job discrimination by the government and by recipients of federal assistance.

In 1986 the National Council on Disability, an independent federal agency, declared the piecemeal efforts of Congress inadequate and raised the call for comprehensive civil rights legislation for the disabled. First introduced in 1989 in the House of Representatives by Anthony Coelho (D-Calif.), and in the Senate by Tom Harkin (D-Iowa), the ADA mandates workplace accommodation and access to public transportation and public accommodations such as restaurants and retail stores. In addition, telephone companies are mandated to provide relay services to individuals using telecommunication devices for the deaf. Finally, the act prohibits coercion, threats, or retaliation against the disabled or those aiding the disabled in asserting their rights.

The House passed the final version in July 1990 by a 377-28 margin and the Senate passed the bill by a 91-6 margin. The Americans with Disabilities Act, public law 101-336, was signed by President GEORGE H. W. BUSH on July 26, 1990, and went into effect in 1992.

—John Korasick

Anderson, John B. (1922–)

John Bayard Anderson gained national attention when he challenged Ronald W. Reagan for the Republic Party nomination in 1980. When he lost the nomination to Reagan, Anderson launched an independent campaign for the presidency under the auspices of the National Unity Party. Prior to his presidential bid, Anderson had served in the U.S. House of Representatives from the state of Illinois. He was born February 15, 1922, in Rockford, Illinois, to E. Albin and Mabel Edna (Ring) Anderson. He attended Rockford public schools, and the University of Illinois at Urbana, graduating in 1946. He later earned a law degree from Harvard University Law School, in 1949. During World War II Anderson enlisted in the United States Army and served from 1943–45 in the Field Artillery where he received four battle stars. He served as adviser on the staff of the U.S. High Commissioner for Germany from 1952–55. Anderson married Keke Machakos on January 4, 1953; they had five children. In 1960 he was elected as a Republican to the 87th Congress and to the nine succeeding Congresses (January 3, 1961–January 3, 1981).

Anderson broke with the Republicans in 1980 after his unsuccessful bid for the party's nomination and ran as the National Unity Party candidate for the presidency against incumbent Democrat JAMES EARL CARTER, JR., and Republican nominee RONALD W. REAGAN. In the three-way race, Anderson received about 7 percent of the total popular votes. In 1984 Anderson attempted a second run for the presidency, but quickly withdrew to make a bid for a congressional seat under the banner of the National Unity Party of Kentucky, which proved unsuccessful.

Following the 1980 campaign, Anderson accepted a series of visiting professorships at Stanford University (1981), University of Illinois College of Law (1981), Brandeis University (1985), Bryn Mawr College (1985), Oregon State University (1986), University of Massachusetts (1986), and Nova University (1987). His writings include *We Propose: A Modern Congress and Republican Papers* (contributor, 1968); *Between Two Worlds: A Congressman's Choice* (1970); *Congress and Conscience* (ed., 1970); *Vision and Betrayal in America* (1975); *The American Economy We Need* (1984).

See also ELECTIONS; POLITICAL PARTIES.

—Michele Rutledge

Anti-Ballistic Missile Treaty (ABM Treaty under SALT I) (1972)

President RICHARD M. NIXON and Soviet premier Leonid Brezhnev signed the Anti-Ballistic Missile (ABM) Treaty on May 26, 1972. The agreement was one of two documents to come out of the first Strategic Arms Limitations Talks (SALT I), which had its origins in a U.S.-Soviet summit meeting five years earlier on June 23, 1967. The ABM Treaty limited the defense strategies of both sides in an attempt to guarantee deterrence through a strategy of Mutually Assured Destruction (MAD).

The origins of an antiballistic missile defense system date back to the early 1950s, when the Defense Department experimented with crude defensive strategies against nuclear attacks. They concentrated on developing missiles that could shoot down nuclear-armed enemy bombers, because, at the time, neither side had the ability to accurately guide intercontinental-range ballistic missiles. The project was shelved as priorities shifted to larger weapons with more conventional conveyance systems. After 1957, however, the Soviet launch of the world's first satellite (*Sputnik*) caused many observers to fear that the United States had fallen behind in missile technology (causing what was known as the "missile gap"), which resulted in a reexamination of a missile defense system. In 1958 the Nike Zeus project was conceived, which consisted of a large acquisition radar, smaller target tracking and missile radars, and an interceptor missile. In 1963, after five years of study and a recommendation from the Joint Chiefs of Staff, the secretary of defense, Robert McNamara, chose to end the program because he worried that it was unreliable and that it would undermine the larger strategy of deterrence.

Advocates of nuclear deterrence argued that global peace required both sides of the COLD WAR to maintain relative parity; the guarantee that a first strike would be answered with immediate nuclear retaliation served to deter nuclear war. This concept of Mutually Assured Destruction (MAD) dominated American DEFENSE POLICY throughout most of the cold war. A successful missile defense threatened to undermine the system by removing the guarantee of retaliatory destruction, which might encourage one side to launch a first strike. Moreover, a missile defense might lead to further arms buildup as the Soviets built more weapons in an effort to overwhelm American defenses. President John F. Kennedy and Defense Secretary McNamara wanted to limit or pull back this buildup and resisted the ABM defense. Republican critics of McNamara's decision to scrap the Nike Zeus project, including RONALD W. REAGAN and PHYLLIS SCHLAFLY, argued that any agreement on arms limitation would be unilateral, since the Soviets could not be trusted to keep their end of the treaty. Throughout the mid-1960s, Republicans pushed for both stronger offensive and defensive weapons.

The American Trident missile makes its maiden flight at Cape Kennedy. (*Hulton/Archive*)

In response to growing criticism, McNamara announced the Sentinel Defense System in 1967, also known as Nike X. It would rely on faster Phased Array Radars in conjunction with nuclear-tipped interceptors, called Sprint missiles. In addition, another interceptor, the Spartan missile, with longer ranges, would be used to defend against high-atmosphere attacks. The Sentinel Defense System was the first attempt at a layered defense and was the first true ballistic missile system. McNamara advertised the program as "light defense," useful against minor third-party nations, or accidental launches from the Soviet Union. Since it was designed as a point defense, rather than a general defense, it would not undermine the doctrine of mutually assured destruction. Though some labeled it the "anti-Republican missile system," the Republican criticism that McNamara was compromising national security continued unabated; they wanted a strong general defense that could protect all citizens.

In March 1969, shortly after President Richard M. Nixon entered office, he announced he would strengthen the Sentinel system by adding a modified phased-deployment concept, which he named the Safeguard program. It extended the perimeter of employment out to 1,000 miles, and in effect reconfigured the "light defense" into the stronger "general defense" that the Republicans had called for. The announcement carried diplomatic ramifications; the Soviets had brought up the issue of ABM limitations during the U.S.–Soviet summit that President Lyndon B. Johnson attended in New Jersey in 1967. McNamara's announcement of the Sentinel Defense prompted the Soviets to call for their reduction. They did not, however, call for an end to all ABM defenses—only a limitation. The Soviets had begun developing their own missile defense system in 1955, and had already deployed an untested anti-satellite system in 1965. Some American observers feared that the Soviet development was actually further advanced than their own, with possibly more successful results. They feared that the security of a strong missile defense might prompt some Soviet policymakers to consider first-strike options. These American analysts hoped that the Soviets might react to news of the more powerful Safeguard program by calling for an end to all ABM systems, which would in turn help restore the system of parity that MAD depended on.

Eight months after Nixon's announcement, the United States and the Soviet Union entered into the first SALT talks. As expected, the Soviets demanded a treaty to limit ABM development before they would agree to future limitation talks. U.S. negotiators called for a complete ban on all ABM systems, but the Soviets refused. After three years of negotiation the two sides agreed to limit the number of ABM systems to 200 launchers and interceptors equally divided into two widely separated deployment areas along the national borderlines (which would prohibit a nationwide defense network). The resulting ABM Treaty (1972) was modified two years later, cutting the number of deployment sites in half, from two to one. Though the ABM Treaty served as a necessary catalyst for later SALT talks, American policymakers did not consider it a significant concession because American nuclear defense strategies never depended on ABM systems. The United States built a deployment site in Grand Forks, North Dakota, during 1975–76, but it was quickly dismantled to free up resources for other priorities.

U.S. commitment to national missile defense changed in the late 1970s, as advances in computing technology made a viable defensive network more feasible, and after Republican president Ronald W. Reagan entered the White House. He had lobbied for a stronger national defense since the late 1960s and remained committed to it as president. On March 23, 1983, Reagan announced his STRATEGIC DEFENSE INITIATIVE (SDI), which included space-based laser technology as well as land-based missile systems. SDI drew immediate criticism from the NUCLEAR FREEZE MOVEMENT, which feared the start of another arms race and the destabilization of nuclear deterrence. In January 1984 Reagan reported evidence that the Soviets had violated the ABM Treaty by installing a centrally located defense system (the Krasnoyarsk radar system), and that SDI was necessary for homeland defense. Two years later, in October 1985, U.S. National Security Adviser Robert McFarlane further announced that SDI did not fall under ABM Treaty proscriptions because it was based on "other physical particles" (like lasers) and that it was limited to research facilities, which the treaty explicitly permitted. Nevertheless, Democratic lawmakers strongly criticized the program as expensive, ineffective, and possibly dangerous.

SDI remained a strong research priority throughout the 1980s and early 1990s during President GEORGE H. W. BUSH's administration. It was eventually ended in July 1993 when President WILLIAM J. CLINTON announced that his administration would adopt a "narrow" interpretation of the ABM Treaty, which excluded SDI-like research and development. Though Clinton made numerous commitments to exploring the possibility and necessity of a missile defense system, including the "3-plus-3" program of 1996, he never allocated resources toward its development. In March 1997 Clinton joined Russian president Boris Yeltsin in signing a joint statement affirming the principles of the 1972 ABM Treaty. These efforts were met with strong criticism from Republican lawmakers who called for a return to Reagan-Bush strategic defense proposals. Within six months of entering office, President GEORGE W. BUSH announced his full commitment to SDI research, which he believed would be necessary to defend the United States from rogue nations. Seven months later, on December 14, 2001, President Bush gave formal notice to Russia that the United States was pulling out of the 1972 ABM Treaty.

See also CATHOLIC BISHOPS' LETTER; CONSERVATIVE MOVEMENT; DEFENSE POLICY; DÉTENTE; STRATEGIC ARMS LIMITATION TREATIES.

Further reading: Lawrence Freedman, *The Evolution of Nuclear Strategy*, 2d ed. (New York: St. Martin's Press, 1989); K. Scott McMahon, *Pursuit of the Shield: The U.S. Quest for Limited Ballistic Missile Defense* (Lanham, Md.: University Press of America, 1997); Walther Stützle, Bhupendra Jasani, and Regina Cowen, *The ABM Treaty: To Defend or Not to Defend?* (New York: Oxford University Press, 1987); James J. Wirtz and Jeffrey A. Larsen, eds., *Rockets' Red Glare: Missile Defenses and the Future of World Politics* (Boulder, Colo.: Westview Press, 2001).

—Aharon W. Zorea

antiwar movement—Vietnam

Opposition to the VIETNAM WAR—composed of leftist college students, pacifist religious groups, peace activists, and citizens of all ages—clearly indicated the divisive effects of the war on American society. Beginning as early as April 1965 with a march on Washington that consisted of more than 25,000 people, the antiwar movement served as a common cause for the growing counterculture of the 1960s and 1970s and a major component of the social turbulence of the same period.

Various impulses including the fear of being drafted, a commitment to peace, and the loyalty of a small minority to Ho Chi Minh's revolutionary ideology transformed college campuses into staging grounds for antiwar rallies and "teach-ins"—lengthy series of speeches denouncing the war and the United States's involvement in it. In October 1965 the National Mobilization to End the War in Vietnam ("the Mobe") organized more than 80,000 people in demonstrations nationwide and disrupted the 1968 Democratic National Convention in Chicago. On November 15, 1969, nearly a quarter million people marched against the war in Washington, D.C. The most famous incident connected with the antiwar movement occurred in May 1970 on the campus of KENT STATE UNIVERSITY, where Ohio National Guardsmen fatally shot four students while dispersing an antiwar demonstration. In addition to protests, demonstrations, and teach-ins, young men protested the war by burning draft cards, failing to register, or fleeing to Canada or other countries. By 1972 more than 30,000 "draft dodgers" had fled to Canada and thousands more to Sweden or Mexico. During the war, more than half a million men committed draft violations.

Many clergymen, educators, and businessmen disapproved of the government's Vietnam policies beginning in the mid-1960s, and their numbers continued to grow throughout the conflict. This growth, fueled by the constant flow of war images into America's living rooms via television, reflected a trend in public opinion that, by mid-1971, was solidly in favor of U.S. withdrawal from the war even if such withdrawal meant the collapse of the South Vietnamese government.

There was also political opposition to the war. In 1966 Senator William Fulbright initiated public hearings to determine whether pursuing the war in Vietnam served the national interest. Disillusion with the war grew throughout President Lyndon B. Johnson's administration. Secretary of Defense Robert McNamara worked quietly to reduce U.S. military presence in Vietnam and resigned after failing to persuade Johnson to do so. More significant politically was the growing influence of the antiwar faction in Congress. In June 1973, Senators Frank Church of Idaho and Clifford Case of New Jersey wrote into the fiscal 1974 budget an amendment forbidding the use of any American forces "in or over" Indochina, thus removing the guarantee of American air support if South Vietnam was attacked again. Other fiscal reductions followed when Congress reduced military aid to South Vietnam from $2.1 billion in 1973 to $1.1 billion in 1974 and $700 million in 1975. On March 20, 1975, Senators Adlai Stevenson III and Charles Mathias introduced legislation requiring the termination of all aid to South Vietnam by June 30 of that year.

This increased congressional opposition to American aid and involvement in Indochina reflected a crack in the anticommunist consensus in FOREIGN POLICY. During the 1970s the leadership of the Democratic Party had concluded that ideological anticommunism had been detrimental to the country and had led to American involvement in Vietnam. Because of this, during President JAMES EARL CARTER, JR.'s administration, Democrats refused to react aggressively to the growing military power of the Soviet Union. Mozambique, Angola, and Ethiopia all came under pro-Soviet rule in 1975. Soviet encroachment occurred in other areas throughout the late 1970s but the Carter administration opted for a policy of conciliation, hoping to allay any Soviet fears. In 1977 Carter cancelled the B-1 bomber program, as well as the neutron bomb program, and asked for no Soviet concessions in return.

The influence of the protest activity and public opinion is still debated by scholars. It is clear that the antiwar movement in the United States boosted North Vietnamese morale by convincing Hanoi that America's spirit to fight would certainly wither. It is likely that the movement figured prominently in President Lyndon Johnson's decision not to run for reelection in 1968 and played possibly a larger role in RICHARD M. NIXON's victory over the Democrat Hubert Humphrey, who, as Johnson's vice president, was unable to dissociate himself from the president's war policies. Also, the dramatic nature of the protests and the power of public opinion may ultimately have set the parameters of the conflict and prevented an even wider war. Clearly the antiwar movement contributed to America's "neo-isolationist" sentiment that was manifested after the war by a strong public distaste for the assumption of responsibility for other nations' affairs.

See also ARMS RACE; CHICAGO EIGHT; COLD WAR; DEFENSE POLICY; LIBERALISM.

Further reading: Charles DeBenedetti, *An American Ordeal: The Antiwar Movement of the Vietnam Era* (New York: Syracuse University Press, 1990); Kenneth Heineman, *Campus Wars: The Peace Movement and American State Universities in the Vietnam Era* (New York: New York University Press, 1993).

—William L. Glankler

arms race

The Soviet-American arms race was well underway by 1968 because the interests of the two superpowers were impossible to reconcile. The United States felt it necessary to have a multitude of arms at its disposal to halt communist expansion throughout the world, while the Soviet Union saw the U.S. move to contain Soviet expansion as a ploy to disguise its capitalist desire to dominate the world's resources and then use the resources to destroy the international communist movement. Thus, the two nations prepared to deter a major attack or to win if war did erupt by building arsenals that by the conclusion of the COLD WAR were large enough to completely destroy both nations if they successfully struck all of their targets.

The United States maintained the lead in the arms race with the Soviet Union well into the 1970s, excluding the areas of intercontinental ballistic missiles (ICBMs) and antiballistic missile systems (ABMs). The Soviet Union focused its entire economy on catching up with the United States, and by the mid-1970s a number of experts claimed that the Soviets had succeeded in at least matching the United States arsenal, although other experts disputed this. This in turn led to the United States increasing its weapon development and deployment programs in the early 1980s. As the number of nuclear weapons increased, many believed that the chance they would be used increased as well. U.S. defense policy makers nevertheless continued to argue for additional weapons. They stated that since the Soviets had at least parity, if not an advantage, a Soviet first strike could leave the United States with too few remaining weapons to react effectively. This would leave U.S. cities open to retaliation from the Soviets' second and third strikes. Therefore, they argued the United States needed not only more nuclear weapons, but also more accurate targeting systems to ensure that U.S. retaliation would devastate the Soviet Union. U.S. defense planners hoped this ability to destroy vast areas of the Soviet Union with a second or third strike capability would deter the U.S.S.R. from launching a nuclear attack in the first place.

There were many efforts undertaken in the 1970s and 1980s to control the nuclear arms race. The efforts met with only limited success, because neither side was willing to trust the other to adhere to the agreement. The Strategic Arms Limitation Talks (SALT I), signed in 1972, placed limits on strategic launch vehicles but not the missiles they launched. The ANTI-BALLISTIC MISSILE TREATY, which was also signed in 1972, limited the development and deployment of defensive systems. The Nuclear Nonproliferation Treaty (NPT), which went into effect in 1970, attempted to curb the horizontal spread of nuclear weapons, but in reality it did little to truly stop a nation that was dedicated to developing a nuclear arsenal.

President RONALD W. REAGAN's defense advisers had a definite strategy for waging the cold war. It was outlined in a national security decision directive (NSDD-13), which was leaked to the public in 1982. It stated that the United States should have the capability to wage a protracted nuclear war, which would involve repeated, well-planned, limited nuclear strikes against targets in the Soviet Union. Further details called for the nuclear decapitation of Soviet military and political leadership, as well as destruction of Soviet lines of communication. To meet this objective, the Reagan administration planned to spend $180 billion in a five-year period. This money was to be spent in part on 100 MX intercontinental ballistic missiles, 100 B-1 bombers, 400 air-launched cruise missiles, 3,000 sea-launched cruise missiles, and 15 Trident submarines with 360 Trident I submarine-launched ballistic missiles. Development programs were also to begin on a Stealth bomber, the Trident II missile, space-based antisatellite weapons, and improvements in U.S. command, control, communications, and intelligence systems.

The Soviet Union responded with shock and anger to the plans of the Reagan administration. Many thought that the expense involved in maintaining pace with the United States would be too overwhelming for the Soviet economy. The Soviet Union launched several efforts to revive détente and negotiate arms control agreements that would curb the United States's dramatic increase in its nuclear stockpile. During Reagan's second term, serious work was started to slow or halt the arms race between the two superpowers.

The downward spiral in the arms race had already begun when President GEORGE H. W. BUSH entered the White House in 1988. The Soviet Union appeared to be taking the lead in reduction of deployed nuclear weapons, but chaos soon erupted in Eastern Europe as the Soviet sphere crumbled. One of the largest arms control agreements of the decade, the Strategic Arms Reduction Treaty (START), was stalemated on several occasions due to Soviet domestic unrest and the outbreak of the Persian Gulf crisis in August 1990. By the fall of 1991 the Soviet Union itself was crumbling into several independent nations, and its successor, Russia, had little money left to devote to arms to fight a strategic nuclear war with the United States. Thus, the end of the cold war marked the end of the dramatic superpower arms race that had lasted for over four decades.

See also DEFENSE POLICY; FOREIGN POLICY; STRATEGIC ARMS LIMITATION TREATIES; STRATEGIC DEFENSE INITIATIVE.

Further reading: Ronald E. Powaski, *Return to Armageddon: The United States and the Nuclear Arms Race, 1981–1999* (New York: Oxford University Press, 2000).

—Leah Blakey

ARPANET   See Internet

art and architecture

Art

Art, beginning in the 1970s, entered a new, postmodern stage. There was no dominant style or movement; artists could "do their own thing." While some, especially minority, artists used their art to make political statements, others felt that art was no longer a worthwhile means of expressing personal or political statements. Art became highly conceptual, referring to nothing but itself.

During the 1960s, three artistic movements had flourished and provided consistency in the art community—pop art, op art, and minimalism. While these movements lost much of their influence, they did not simply disappear. Pop art used images drawn from popular culture. Using common objects and images—soup cans, comic strips—pop artists transformed everyday objects and images into works of art. Pop art did not glorify the creative process; rather, it celebrated mechanical creation and the repetitiveness of mass media.

Leaders in pop art were Andy Warhol, Roy Lichtenstein, and George Segal. Warhol, a former commercial illustrator, used images of common objects and reproduced them in altered colors. By displaying them as art, Warhol gave them shock value. Lichtenstein painted enlarged frames of comic strips based on war or romantic entanglements. This created a parody of a serious event. Segal was a sculptor who made plaster casts of people, either standing or engaged in everyday activities. The figures would then be placed with real objects to create a surreal effect. Op art meant to create pulsating optical effects through the repetition of shapes. There is no sense of depth in these works, further removing the painting from any illusion of reality. Like the other movements, there is little effort to instill deeper meanings. The best-known American op artist is Richard Anuszkiewicz. Minimalism is the use of geometric shapes or other simple units in sculpture or painting. Minimalists' use of new media—metal, plastics, Plexiglas—was an exciting new development. A leader of this movement was Donald Judd.

This use of new media foreshadowed many developments in art in the 1970s and 1980s. Site sculpture, also known as earth art, the utilization of new media on a grand scale, appeared on the scene. These sculptures were temporary; recording the creation and destruction of the piece was part of the art. One of the best-known pieces is the *Spiral Jetty* created by Robert Smithson in Utah in 1970. By depositing 6,000 tons of earth in the Great Salt Lake, Smithson laid the foundation for a 1,500-foot-long spiral of black rock and salt crystals that extended into the lake. By altering the lake in this way, the artist was able to alter the viewer's perception of the lake. Other notable site sculptors included Richard Serra, whose sculpture *Tilted Arc*, consisting of three steel plates, was installed in New York City's Federal Plaza. One of his goals was to "dislocate" the beauty of the plaza. The piece prompted protests and petitions for its removal. Christo gained notoriety by wrapping synthetic material on natural and man-made objects. In 1971 he hung a huge orange curtain across a canyon in Colorado, entitling it *Valley Curtain.*

Nam June Paik and Bruce Nauman exemplify sculpture on a smaller scale. Paik created sculptures using multiple television sets on which messages flashed by, conveying the fleeting nature of information. Nauman incorporated flashing lights and images that bombard the viewer with disturbing and disagreeable words, thoughts, images, and sounds. What should be apparent from these examples is that art was not a commodity. People could not buy a Serra or a Nauman. Art was neither decorative nor meaningful; art was meant to shock.

In the late 1970s and the 1980s there was a return to image-based painting. Neoexpressionism, very influential in the 1980s, rejected the impersonal art of minimalists. Vigorous brushwork increased the expressiveness of the work. Leaders of the Neoexpressionists were David Salle and Eric Fischl. Another group, the photorealists, continued the detached attitude of the pop artists, creating detailed paintings that look like photographs. The work of Chuck Close and Audrey Flack exemplify photorealism.

The use of new media in art was not limited to industrial material or lights. Art in the 1970s and 1980s was often focused on the process as much as the end result. A natural extension of this was performance art. Performance art relied on its immediacy and its temporary nature. Much like the earth art, the process was as much a part of the art as the actual piece. An example of performance art is Laurie Anderson's *Duet on Ice*. In the piece, Anderson played violin while wearing skates embedded in blocks of ice. The piece ended when the ice melted.

Not all art was devoid of meaning. There was a certain amount of issue-oriented art. Minorities used art to express group pride and identity. Among feminist artists, photographer Cindy Sherman used photographs to comment on female stereotypes. African-American artist Melvin Edwards dealt with violence against African Americans. Robert Mapplethorpe celebrated homosexuality in his photographic exhibits.

The public was generally baffled by art trends during the last third of the 20th century. With the development of noncommercial forms such as earth art, performance art, and the complex multimedia productions, photography became the most respected and collectable art of the era. In the 1980s nostalgia for classical art created a demand for the works of Wyeth, Picasso, and Pollock. Classical art became a commodity and began selling for record prices. Corporate funding for the arts skyrocketed and many corporations exhibited modern art in their lobbies. While some artists bemoaned the new commercialism, others responded to the money. This development led some art critics to predict that art in the 21st century will become more decorative.

Architecture

American architecture since 1970 is marked by two design approaches. The first is international modernism, which rejects historic styles and ornament and emphasizes pure utilitarian functionalism. The massive skyscrapers built during the late 1960s and the early 1970s, buildings like the John Hancock Center and the Sears Tower in Chicago and the World Trade Center in New York (destroyed in a terrorist attack in 2001) exemplify international modernism.

The next, and more popular style is referred to as postmodernism. Postmodern architecture ranges widely, from designs resembling international modernism to those based on ancient or Renaissance models. In response to the sterility of international modernism, postmodern architecture embraces decoration, combining curves and lines to create visually interesting buildings. Some postmodern architects apply postmodern ideas to the international style. In contrast to those embracing the grand scale of skyscrapers and airline terminals are those architects who employ postmodern variations on historical forms and details. An example of this is Charles Moore's Piazza d'Italia in New Orleans. Moore employed classical forms but used modern materials, constructing the Ionic capitals of the columns out of stainless steel. This mix of material and design is referred to as ironic postmodernism. Other variations of postmodern architecture include latent classicism and archaeological classicism. In latent classicism the classical elements are present, but not obvious. In archaeological classicism, the building is drawn directly from classical models, sometimes as a copy. By the 1990s the dominant variant of postmodernism was creative postmodernism. This variant adapted traditional details into modern buildings without the bizarre additions of ironic postmodernism.

One of the results of postmodern architecture is an increased emphasis on comfort and decoration. The old modernism had concentrated on showcase buildings for the wealthy, and functional office towers, which were bland and sterile structures surrounded by concrete. Postmodern designs, based on aesthetics and community, offer a connected, "natural" environment for people.

The 1990s also saw other schools of architecture, in deconstructionism, most notably Frank Gehry's buildings,

The Sears Tower in Chicago *(Boyle/Getty Images)*

and new modernism with its nonlinear, curved building forms. By the turn of the century, postmodernism was on the wane, being replaced by new schools of architectural thought.

See also CENSORSHIP; MORALITY; MOVIES; MUSIC; POPULAR CULTURE; POSTMODERNISM.

Further reading: Michael Archer, *Art since 1960* (New York: Thames & Hudson, Inc., 1997); Leland M. Roth, *Understanding Architecture: Its Elements, History and Meaning* (New York: HarperCollins, 1993).

—John Korasick

Asian Americans

Asian Americans have been characterized as a "successful" minority. Their educational achievements and economic success compare favorably with, or exceed, the national averages. Yet while "Asian American" is a convenient label, it includes many groups from diverse national and cultural backgrounds, making broad generalizations misleading.

People of Asian heritage have been present in the United States in large numbers since the 19th century. This original group included people from China, Japan, Korea, and the Philippines. These original immigrants settled and established a support system for future immigrants from their individual homelands, laying the foundation for future success.

In the 1960s about 7 percent of all immigrants were from Asia, equivalent to about 20,000 people per year. By the mid-1980s, these figures increased to 44 percent and about 264,000 per year, with many of these new immigrants being refugees from Southeast Asia—Vietnam, Cambodia, and Laos. Much of this increase was due to change in immigration law, established by the Immigration Act of 1965.

The Immigration Act was the first real reform in immigration policy since the National Origins Act of 1921. The Immigration Act abolished quotas that favored immigrants from northwest Europe by allotting 20,000 slots annually for each nation. Family reunification and emphasis on occupational skills became the primary criteria for incoming persons. Spouses, immediate relatives, and minor children of U.S. citizens were exempted from the numerical limitations placed on each nation. The system was gradually phased in between 1966 and 1968. In 1969 immigrant visas were distributed, for the first time, without any national preference.

All Asian-American groups experienced tremendous growth following the adoption of the Immigration Act. As of the 1990 census the five leading Asian-American populations came from China, the Philippines, Japan, India, and Korea. All of these groups, except the Filipino Americans and Japanese Americans, witnessed their populations more than double between 1980 and 1990. The Indian-American and Korean-American populations each grew by 125 percent during the 1980s and the Chinese-American population increased by 104 percent. The fastest-growing Asian-American group was the Vietnamese, who increased their numbers by nearly 135 percent between 1980 and 1990.

Among those who benefited most under the liberalized immigration statutes were Southeast Asians, with most arriving in the United States since 1965, and especially since the fall of Saigon in 1975. These people arrived in two waves. First came educated individuals from Vietnam. The second wave consisted of Vietnamese, Cambodians, and Laotians, all of whom tended to be poorly educated. This influx of people from Southeast Asia was a direct result of the VIETNAM WAR. The flight of refugees from the region, following the American withdrawal, inspired the Indo-China Refugee Act of 1975, which allowed 200,000 Vietnamese and others from the region to enter the United States exempt from the normal procedures and limitations. In 1978 Congress acted to allow the entrance of 85,000 Vietnamese refugees. The Refugee Act of 1980 again reduced restrictions on Southeast Asians, allowing 95,000

people entrance in 1980, 86,000 in 1981, and an additional 66,000 between 1983 and 1991.

According to the Bureau of the Census, the Asian-American population grew from 1.5 million in 1970 to 8.8 million in 1994, accounting for about 3 percent of the total population. Growing at a rate of 4.5 percent a year, immigration accounts for 86 percent of the increase. In terms of geographic location, 60 percent of Asian Americans lived in the western United States. Sixty-six percent lived in the states of California, New York, Hawaii, Texas, and Illinois.

As of 1994 nine of 10 Asian-American men and eight of 10 Asian-American women had at least a high school diploma. Forty-six percent of men and 37 percent of women had a bachelor's degree, as compared with 28 percent of Caucasian men and 21 percent of Caucasian women.

The 1994 median income for college-educated Asian and Pacific Islander Americans age 25 and older was $41,220 for men and $31,780 for women as compared to $47,180 for Caucasian men and $32,920 for Caucasian women, a difference described as statistically insignificant. Dual-income families were about 60 percent for both Asians and Caucasians. The poverty rate, in 1993, was 14 percent for Asians compared with 8 percent for Caucasians, a result many attributed to the more recent arrivals of Asian immigrants, including the Hmong, Cambodians, and Laotians, who entered the country with less education and support on arrival.

In 1994 the average family size was 3.6 for Asian Americans and 3.1 for Caucasians. Seventy-three percent of Asian-American households had three or more people, compared with 55 percent of Caucasian households. Twenty-two percent of Asian-American households had five or more members, compared to 12 percent of Caucasian households.

The median age in 1990 for Asian Americans was 30 years, compared with a national average of 33 years of age. Only 6 percent of Asian Americans were aged 65 or older, as compared to 13 percent nationally.

In 1990, 67 percent of Asian Americans of working age were in the labor force as compared with 65 percent nationally. Sixty percent of Asian women were working as compared with 58 percent for the rest of the population. In fields of occupation 33.3 percent of Asians worked in technology, sales, or administrative jobs, compared with 33 percent for the rest of the country. Thirty-one percent worked in managerial or professional occupations as compared with 26 percent for the rest of the United States.

The 2000 census shows that of the total population of the United States—281.4 million—11.9 million, or 4.2 percent, reported themselves as Asian. This number included 10.2 million people, or 3.6 percent, who reported only Asian and 1.7 million people, or 0.6 percent, who reported Asian as well as one or more other races. The census used the term "Asia" to encompass people whose origins are from the Far East, Southeast Asia, or the Indian subcontinent, including Cambodia, China, India, Japan, Korea, Malaysia, Pakistan, the Philippine Islands, Thailand, and Vietnam.

Regionally 48.8 percent live in the West; 18.8 percent in the South; 11.7 percent in the Midwest; and 20.7 percent live in the Northeast. Of these, 51 percent live in three states: California (4.2 million), New York (1.2 million), and Hawaii (0.7 million). In California, the largest concentration of Asians is in the San Francisco Bay Area, and the second largest concentration is in Los Angeles.

Other statistics collected in the 2000 census are also revealing. Of the Asian-American population, the largest group is Chinese (non-Taiwanese) at 2.3 million, followed by Filipinos at 1.8 million, and east Indians at 1.6 million. Cen-

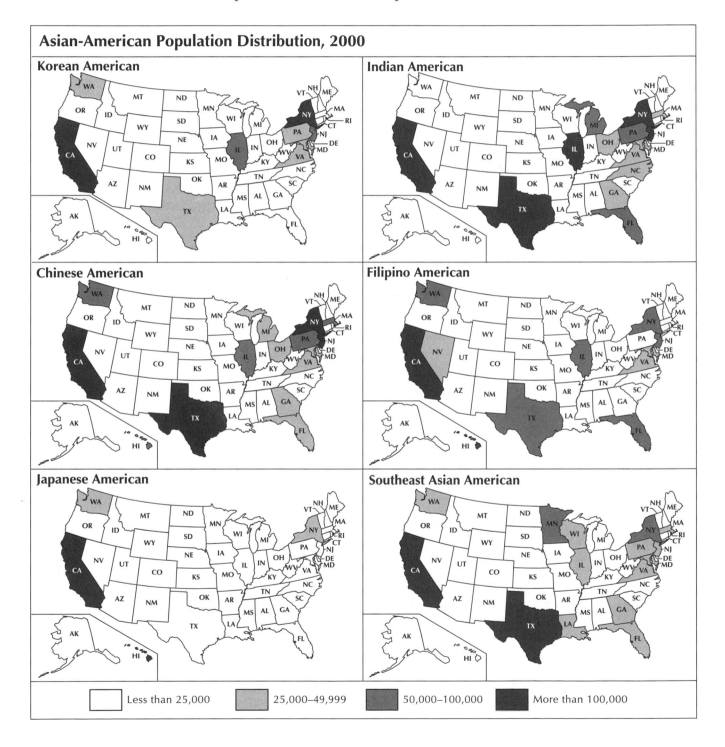

Asian-American Population Distribution, 2000

Korean American

Indian American

Chinese American

Filipino American

Japanese American

Southeast Asian American

Less than 25,000   25,000–49,999   50,000–100,000   More than 100,000

sus records also show that 39 percent of Asian Americans are employed in managerial positions, 86 percent have a high school education, and 53 percent own their own homes.

In addition, the March 2000 Current Population Survey (CPS), not to be confused with the Census 2000 results, revealed that 44 percent of Asians and Pacific Islanders age 25 and over had a bachelor's degree or higher. Asian and Pacific Islander families tend to be relatively large. For example, 23 percent of Asian and Pacific Islander married-couple families had five or more members. There were 2.5 million Asian and Pacific Islander families, of which 13 percent were maintained by women with no spouse present and 7 percent by men with no spouse present. In 1999 Asians and Pacific Islanders had a record-low poverty rate of 10.7 percent.

See also IMMIGRATION REFORM AND CONTROL ACT (1986).

Further reading: Juanita Tamayo Lott, *Asian Americans: From Racial Category to Multiple Identities* (Walnut Creek, Calif.: Alta Mira Press, 1998); Wendy L. Ng, ed., *Reviewing Asian America: Locating Diversity* (Pullman: Washington State University Press, 1995).

—John Korasick

assassinations

Political assassinations in the United States are rare. Yet during the 1960s, the nation experienced a rash of assassinations: Medgar Evers, 1963; President John F. Kennedy, 1963; and Malcolm X, 1965. Then, on April 4, 1968, Rev. Martin Luther King, Jr., was shot to death while standing on the balcony of the Lorraine Motel in Memphis, Tennessee. Authorities quickly apprehended James Earl Ray, who confessed to the murder, and sentenced him to 99 years. Many suspected that Ray acted as part of a larger conspiracy of southern racists, but no accomplices were ever identified. Ray later recanted his confession, but his appeal for a new trial was rejected. Just two months after King's murder, Senator Robert Kennedy

Surrounded by police officers and secret service agents, President Ronald W. Reagan waves to spectators outside the Hilton Hotel, Washington, D.C., seconds before an assassination attempt. *(Hulton/Archive)*

was fatally shot on the night of his victory in the California Democratic primary. The shooter, Sirhan Sirhan, was apprehended at the scene and later convicted of first-degree murder.

Later, Congress took up the question of assassination. At first, congressmen investigated whether the United States was involved in assassination attempts outside the American border. In 1975 a Senate committee led by Senator Frank Church published their discovery that American intelligence operatives under President Kennedy's administration were involved in plans to assassinate the Cuban dictator, Fidel Castro. The report caused some to question Castro's involvement in Kennedy's assassination. The following year, Congress reopened investigations into President Kennedy's and King's assassinations. After two years of study, the committee refuted reports of Cuban involvement in Kennedy's assassination but suggested a conspiracy of at least one other shooter involved with his death. The committee arrived at similar conclusions for the King assassination.

Two assassination attempts were made on Gerald Ford when he was president of the United States, but both failed. One attempt was made by a mentally ill woman and another by a cult member of the Charles Manson "family" (a counter-culture group that had committed a series of brutal murders in Southern California), but both attempts failed.

In 1980 Mark David Chapman killed the former leader of the Beatles music group, John Lennon, outside his New York apartment. A year later, evidently inspired by the Chapman killing and the movie *Taxi Driver* and one of its stars, Jodie Foster, John W. Hinckley shot President RONALD W. REAGAN in the chest on March 30, 1981. The president survived the assassination attempt, but a District of Columbia police officer, a Secret Service agent, and Reagan's press secretary, James S. Brady, were also wounded. Hinckley was later found not guilty by reason of insanity and committed to a mental hospital. In the 1990s, the entertainment industry capitalized on America's conspiracy fascination with sensational accounts, such as Oliver Stone's *JFK,* and the television series *The X-Files;* each alleged elaborate criminal conspiracies with possible government involvement. These claims had no factual support; nevertheless, they became a common theme in popular entertainment. The public atmosphere of the late 1990s became so sympathetic to allegations of government conspiracy that Coretta Scott King, Martin Luther King's widow, and other family members supported James Earl Ray's appeal efforts, based on their conviction that a much larger conspiracy was responsible for King's death. Ray died in prison with no successful appeals.

—Aharon W. Zorea

automobile industry

In the last four decades of the 20th century, the three major auto manufacturers in the United States have faced challenges to their domination of the market. Environmental and safety concerns, the instability of the world economy, and increased foreign competition forced the manufacturers to make radical structural changes while attempting to meet increasing demands from consumers in a competitive market.

In the late 1960s and early 1970s, U.S. auto manufacturers, in particular General Motors, were still reeling from Ralph Nader's exposé of the auto industry in his book *Unsafe at Any Speed* (1965; rev. ed. 1972), which exposed the design deficiencies of the Chevrolet Corvair. The manufacturers were accused of abusing their corporate power and knowingly producing defective cars. While the manufacturers responded by introducing safety features they were also faced with growing competition from abroad. Volkswagen, Toyota, and Nissan all began to increase sales in the United States during the 1970s. The Organization of Petroleum Exporting Countries (OPEC) embargoes on oil in 1973 and 1979, and the economic recessions of the 1970s led to the increased popularity of cheaper and more fuel-efficient imports. In 1970 the U.S. government introduced the National Air Quality Control Act (better known as the Clean Air Act), which required auto manufacturers to reduce auto pollutants; the government also set new standards for fuel economy, placing extra demands on the U.S. auto manufacturers. Japanese manufacturers were able to capitalize on the problems in the U.S. market and increase their market share, so that by the end of the 1970s, Japanese imports accounted for almost 25 percent of market sales.

Japanese manufacturers also benefited from a more efficient and modern manufacturing infrastructure. U.S. manufacturers responded by adopting many of these methods, known as "lean production," and began to introduce smaller cars. These changes, which included increased quality control, the development of automated production techniques, and the introduction of just-in-time ordering, helped the U.S. manufacturers slowly recover. However, the cost of reorganization resulted in extreme financial difficulties for the manufacturers; Chrysler in particular was on the verge of bankruptcy, and increased layoffs, employee reorganization, and the exportation of manufacturing work overseas in the 1970s brought the manufacturers into conflict with the United Auto Workers Union.

Increased global competition and emerging new markets since the 1980s had profound effects on the national character of auto manufacturers. Japanese and German manufacturers established plants in the United States, and

Computer technology has led to great changes in industrial design and manufacturing. Here, robots operate on an assembly line at a Ford Motor Company plant in Michigan. *(Hulton/Archive)*

in the 1990s U.S. manufacturers established joint ventures or invested in overseas companies. Chrysler and Daimler-Benz merged in 1998 while maintaining separate brands, and Ford bought Volvo in 1999. General Motors has arrangements with manufacturers in Japan and Fiat in Italy. By the late 1990s the national origin of any car became increasingly difficult to ascertain.

Since the 1970s, energy and environmental concerns have increased, and forced manufacturers to develop more fuel-efficient and environmentally friendly vehicles. In 1993 a joint initiative between the U.S. government and auto manufacturers established the Partnership for a New Generation of Vehicles (PNGV) which aims at producing more ecologically efficient vehicles using new forms of fuel technology such as electricity or natural gas.

Auto manufacturers have also had to respond to growing consumer demand for increased comfort and safety. Since the 1980s, a growing economy and increased global competition has seen the rise in the popularity of four-wheel drive (4WD) and luxury vehicles. The biggest demand has been for sport utility vehicles (SUVs) that combine the off-road and safety features of the Jeep with the passenger comforts of luxury cars. In 1996 sales of light trucks and vans (LTVs), which includes SUVs, represented 44 percent of new vehicle sales in the United States.

The difficulty for auto manufacturers of balancing consumer demand with environmental concerns became pronounced in 2000 when the president of Ford Motor Company, William Clay Ford, publicly acknowledged the inefficiency of Ford's SUVs and the threat they pose to the environment. In the same year, Ford was also forced to recall a large number of its fleet due to defective tires made by the Firestone Company in a blaze of publicity reminiscent of the Corvair controversy in the late 1960s. The need to balance environmental and safety concerns with the pressures of increasingly specific consumer demand in a globally competitive market is the major challenge faced by the U.S. auto manufacturers in the 21st century.

See also BUSINESS; CHRYSLER CORPORATION LOAN GUARANTEE ACT; CONSERVATION AND ENVIRONMENTAL MOVEMENTS; ECONOMY; ENERGY CRISIS; LABOR.

—Stephen Hardman

B

baby boomers

The baby boom generation, considered to be those Americans born between 1945 and 1965, has had considerable social, political, and economic impact during the last half of the 20th century. In 1995 people in this age group (aged 30–50) constituted approximately 33 percent of the United States population. Being such a large proportion of the population ensures their demographic importance well into the 21st century.

The sudden post–World War II population boom altered family and work patterns. In 1995, 77 percent of baby boom women were in the workforce and earned more than 70 percent of what baby boom men earned. Both of these rates are part of an upward trend that shows no signs of reversing. The increasing rate of women's participation in the workforce and their increasing salaries have created more wealth for families and individuals in the expanding middle-income group in the United States, a group largely responsible for stimulating the suburbanization of U.S. cities during the 1970s and 1980s. Approximately 25 percent of the 44.5-million baby boom householders in 1995 earned $70,000 or more. In 1997, 53 percent of people aged 30–34 owned homes while 74 percent of those aged 45–49 owned homes. Because of this increase in wealth and the concomitant stimulus to consumer activity, baby boomers played a significant role in generating the economic boom of the 1990s.

The baby boomers affected the economy in less positive ways as well. For example, according to a 1997 Maritz AmerPoll, middle-aged Americans are less likely to visit shopping malls than any other group and, when they do visit malls, they spend less time there. As a result mall sales growth per square foot did not keep even pace with inflation in the late 1990s. The baby boom generation also adversely affected the labor market. The graduation of large numbers of baby boomers from college in the 1970s and 1980s depressed entry-level wages for people with college degrees. Moreover, as the large influx of boomer work-

ers aged, the U.S. workforce grew older, with the proportion of workers under the age of 25 decreasing from 20.3 percent in 1980 to 14.3 in 1997. The women and boomers who flooded the job market during the 1970s had gained training and experience by the 1990s, however. As a result, the negative effect on entry-level jobs caused by the aging of the labor force reversed itself and college graduates' starting salaries rose rapidly.

Not only have baby boomers altered the national economic landscape by generating more wealth, contributing to an increasingly vigorous consumerism, and altering the labor market, they have had a political impact as well. BILL CLINTON's political success has been attributed to baby boom voters. To many boomers, Clinton was one of their own. He was highly educated, experimented with marijuana, avoided the VIETNAM WAR, married a working woman, had one child, grappled with marital problems, and was always willing to renegotiate his commitments. Identification with the most influential segment of the population helped Clinton win election in 1992 and reelection in 1996.

The baby boom also redefined the significance of children in society—in how they were cared for and educated, and in their place in the economy. Dr. Benjamin Spock revolutionized the notion of childcare by responding to the increased number of children in the population. His child-rearing manual, *The Common Sense Book of Baby and Child Care* (1946) advocated a more nurturing and less rigid approach to child rearing, a notion that seemed at odds with the shifting cultural attitudes toward FAMILY LIFE, women's role in the family, and the emphasis on self-fulfillment. Spock's book sold more than 50 million copies by 1998. The increase in the number of children contributed heavily to the development of educational psychology by increasing the demand for specialists to design and evaluate instructional materials, training programs, and tests. As the baby boomers aged during the 1960s and 1970s, college enrollment exploded and fueled the tremendous growth of colleges and universities. Not only did this make a college education more accessible, it also provided impetus and participants for college-centered social unrest during the 1960s and early 1970s. Finally, the simultaneous growth of the consumer economy and the increasing number of children, as well as the new significance of the child, made possible the founding and growth of retail establishments that specifically catered to the needs of children and infants, such as Toys "R" Us, founded in 1957.

Beyond the influence the boomers have had on American social, political, and economic development, they also represent significant challenges for the future. Similar to the way their numbers fueled the growth of universities in the 1960s and 1970s, their children (a second baby boom) are swelling the college and university student bodies in the late 20th and early 21st centuries. More important, as boomers age they will accentuate the overall aging of the U.S. population. Because of this, the political influence of this large middle-aged group has already brought to the political forefront issues surrounding health insurance, Social Security, Medicare, and retirement.

See also ANTIWAR MOVEMENT; RECREATION; SPORTS; WOMEN'S RIGHTS AND STATUS.

Further reading: Marc Freedman, *Prime Time: How Baby Boomers Will Revolutionize Retirement and Transform America* (New York: Public Affairs Press, 2000).

—William L. Glankler

Bakke (Regents of the University of California v. Allan Bakke) (1978)

This U.S. SUPREME COURT case, which limited racial preferences in admissions policies of state universities, represented the first major constitutional test of AFFIRMATIVE ACTION. The Court ruled that university admission policies could not use quotas to achieve racial balance, but could give special consideration to members of minority groups, with the goal of achieving ethnic variety in a student body.

Allan Bakke, a white engineer, applied to the University of California Medical School at Davis in 1972 as one of 2,664 applicants for 100 openings. Eighty-four openings were filled through the regular admissions process while 16 were filled through a special admissions program designed to address the school's paucity of African-American, Asian, Latino, and Native American students. This affirmative action program, established in 1970, had less stringent grade point average and standardized test score requirements than did the regular admissions program and the 16 positions could be filled only by members of the aforementioned minorities. After being rejected twice by the school and after discovering that his grades and test scores were higher than those of several applicants who had been admitted under the special program, Bakke sued the university under Title VI of the Civil Rights Act of 1964.

Believing that he had been rejected only because he was white, Bakke claimed that being denied admission violated the act's provision forbidding racial or ethnic privileges in programs supported by federal funds. Moreover, Bakke argued that the university's practice of establishing specific positions for minorities denied him his Fourteenth Amendment right to equal protection of the law.

The university argued that, although racial characteristics were irrelevant to state objectives, it was compelled to implement its special admissions program out of concern for the victims of past and continuing racial discrimination. The university also claimed that the program produced some very practical benefits. It enriched medical education by providing an ethnically and racially diverse student body, provided successful role models for minority youth, and provided for improved medical services in minority communities. Both the state trial court and the Supreme Court, however, ruled that the program's racially exclusionary nature constituted a quota system that, without evidence of any prior discrimination on the part of the university, denied equal protection.

The U.S. Supreme Court upheld the lower court's decision, ruling (5-4) that public universities could not establish fixed racial quotas as part of their admissions policies and ordered that Bakke be admitted. The Court, however, also ruled that public universities could consider racial factors, such as the overall racial composition of an incoming class, when making admissions decisions as long as such decisions did not include the use of racial quotas, but the justices were split on their reasons and filed six separate opinions. One group of justices addressed the statutory issue rather than the constitutional issue and argued that Title VI's prohibition against the exclusion of any individual on racial grounds from a federally funded program was sufficient grounds for their finding in Bakke's favor. Another group argued that race-conscious remedies were proper only if necessary to redress past racially motivated injuries and achieve an important state purpose. Justice LEWIS POWELL cast the deciding vote based on the exclusionary nature of the school's admissions program. Because Bakke had been completely excluded from competing for the school's 16 special positions, his right to equal protection under the Fourteenth Amendment had been denied. Powell found that there existed no past constitutional or legal violation for which racial quotas would be necessary. Powell did agree, however, that in a truly competitive process, racial considerations could be utilized as a means for creating diversity in the student body.

Despite predictions, *Bakke* ultimately had little practical effect on public universities' admissions programs. *Bakke* did not provide a definitive answer on affirmative action. Moreover, it complicated the matter, heightening the tension between an individual's claim to equal protection and treatment by the state, and that state's responsibility to promote some measure of equality among its citizens. It settled only the narrower issue of racial quotas in admissions policies of state-supported institutions and left the question of affirmative action's appropriateness in other realms to later cases. The case, however, prefigured the political and legal battles that would surround affirmative action and racial preference in the 1980s and 1990s.

See also AFRICAN AMERICANS; BRENNAN, WILLIAM; BURGER, WARREN; CIVIL RIGHTS ACT OF 1991; EDUCATION; GRIGGS ET AL. V. DUKE POWER COMPANY; REHNQUIST, WILLIAM.

Further reading: Timothy J. O'Neill, *Bakke and the Politics of Equality: Friends and Foes in the Classroom of Litigation* (Middletown, Conn.: Wesleyan University Press, 1985); Bernard Schwartz, *Behind Bakke: Affirmative Action and the Supreme Court* (New York: New York University Press, 1988).

—William Glankler

Bennett, William J. (1943–   )

William J. Bennett emerged in the 1980s as a major intellectual figure in the conservative movement, serving as head of the NATIONAL ENDOWMENT FOR THE HUMANITIES and secretary of education in RONALD W. REAGAN's administration, and then drug czar in the GEORGE H. W. BUSH administration.

He was born in Brooklyn, New York, in 1943. He earned an undergraduate degree in philosophy at Williams College in 1965, before completing a doctorate in political philosophy at the University of Texas in 1970. The following year, he earned a law degree from Harvard University. Bennett taught philosophy for 10 years at various universities and was recognized with 21 honorary degrees before he was 37.

In 1976 Bennett worked as director, president, and later as executive director of the National Humanities Center in North Carolina. A year after President Ronald W. Reagan took office, Bennett received an appointment to serve as chairman of the National Endowment for the Humanities. In 1985, at the start of Reagan's second term, Bennett was moved to the Department of Education, where he served as secretary for four years. During his tenure, Bennett emphasized strict standards, a core curriculum, and character education. He maintained direct contact with America's public schools by traveling around the country to personally teach in primary and secondary classrooms. Before he left the office, he had taught in 115 schools.

President George H. W. Bush declared war on illegal drugs shortly after taking office and named Bennett to be the nation's first drug czar, who directed the Office of National Drug Control Policy. Both Presidents Reagan and Bush emphasized a strong antidrug policy, and cocaine and other drug use declined by 70 percent between 1985 and 1991, although many critics saw this war on drugs as controversial and argued that more federal funding should go to drug rehabilitation programs. Bennett applied the same vigor he used as secretary of education to the war against drugs. He made more site visits, but this time to crack houses, hospitals, prisons, and therapeutic communities. Within a year, Bennett helped overthrow the heads of all four major international illegal drug trafficking organizations, including the Colombian Medellín and Cali cartels.

Bennett left government in 1990, but has remained a leader in conservative values and education. Following public office, he became a Distinguished Fellow at the Heritage Foundation and codirector of Empower America (with Rep. JACK F. KEMP [R-N.Y.], former U.S. Representative to the UN Jeane Kirkpatrick, Rep. Vin Weber [R-Minn.], and Gov. Lamar Alexander). After leaving office, Bennett became a best-selling author with such books as *The Death of Outrage: Bill Clinton and the Assault on American Ideals, The Book of Virtues,* and *Our Sacred Honor.*

—Aharon W. Zorea

Bilingual Education Act (1968)

Also referred to as Title VII, the Bilingual Education Act mandated that schools provide bilingual education programs. The act was aligned with Title VI of the Civil Rights Act of 1964 as part of President Lyndon Johnson's "war on poverty." Based on the idea that the increasing number of linguistically and culturally diverse children attending U.S. schools were not receiving an education equal to that of native English speakers, bilingual education was intended to provide the basis for future economic success, eliminating poverty among immigrants.

Initially, the act did not recommend any specific program of instruction. Financial assistance was provided to local agencies to use on a number of approved activities, including bilingual education, history and cultural studies of target populations, early childhood education, and adult education for parents.

The rationale behind the act was upheld by the SUPREME COURT in *Lau v. Nichols* in 1974. The court ruled that schools must provide language skills to students in addition to facilities, textbooks, teachers, and curricula. There could be no equality of treatment if the students could not understand the material. Also in 1974, Congress reauthorized the act. This time it defined bilingual education as instruction in English with the student's native language used only to the extent necessary to allow the student to progress through the system. Thus the native language was only to be used to facilitate the acquisition of English, not as a source of cultural enrichment for the child. In addition, Congress included Native Americans under the act. Grants were established for teacher and instructional material development as well. Finally, Congress established the Office of Bilingual and Minority Language Affairs, which later became part of President JAMES EARL CARTER, JR.'s Department of Education in 1980.

Reauthorization of the act occurred in 1978, 1984, 1988, and 1994. In 1978 the act was redefined to mean its purpose was to allow children to achieve competence in English. In 1984 the reauthorization mandated bilingual education as a transition to the use of English alone. In 1988 Congress enacted legislation that restricted a student's enrollment in a bilingual education program to a three-year limit. This regulation sought to ensure that bilingual students would be mainstreamed into English-speaking classes.

Bilingual education has become a major political issue. Proponents argue that students need to learn to read in their native language in order to successfully learn English. Opponents argue that students in bilingual programs master neither language and the result is poor performance and a high dropout rate. The core of the debate is whether the United States is the proverbial "melting pot" or a multicultural nation with not one but many equally valuable cultures. This debate has resulted in the passage of referendums in California and Arizona promoting "English-only" education. Other states with large immigrant populations such as New York and Texas have resisted similar efforts. While governor of Texas, GEORGE W. BUSH indicated that he favored the continuation of bilingual education as long as it proved effective in the transition to English proficiency.

See also IMMIGRATION; MULTICULTURALISM; POVERTY.

—John Korasick

birth control

Any method of avoiding or postponing pregnancy is called birth control. The debate over the morality of preventing conception has existed since the early 19th century, but the debate became especially heated and divisive during the 1960s when birth control became a public policy issue. At the end of the 20th century the issue of birth control was complicated dramatically by the multiplying methods of birth control available to women and men.

The desire to control pregnancy is as ancient as some methods of birth control. In traditional societies, women understood that prolonged breast-feeding inhibited ovula-

tion and, therefore, helped prevent conception. Withdrawal is also a traditional form of birth control in which the male withdraws from intercourse before ejaculation. Condoms, although not an ancient form of birth control, have been available to men for centuries. A female condom became available in the early 1990s. Natural family planning is based on the female monthly menstrual cycle and is often referred to as the rhythm method. The calendar method was developed in 1930; the ovulation method and the sympto-thermal method were developed later.

Mechanical, pharmaceutical, and surgical advances multiplied during the late 20th century and provided a wider array of birth control options. Mechanical devices include intrauterine devices (IUDs), the diaphragm, and the cervical cap, all used by women to prevent pregnancy in different ways. The most important pharmaceutical advance was the birth control pill, introduced in 1961. Others include injectable contraceptives (a synthetic hormone that is injected to suppress ovulation and create an environment in the uterus unfavorable to conception) and the drug RU-486, or "the morning-after pill" (a pill that may be taken soon after unprotected intercourse to prevent pregnancy). The Norplant device marries mechanical and pharmaceutical options. Introduced in 1990, it consists of several tiny rubber tubes implanted under the skin of a woman's arm where they slowly release the hormone progestin and prevent pregnancy for five years. Surgical options include sterilization and abortion. The male vasectomy and the female tubal ligation are virtually permanent forms of birth control that render the male sterile and the female infertile. ABORTION is the removal of a developing embryo or fetus from the uterus.

Along with the proliferation of birth control options, the latter half of the 20th century experienced a shift in attitudes toward birth control and an intensification of the debate over it. The 1960s witnessed a multitude of changes that impacted the nature of the birth control debate and made birth control and its various methods a central cultural and political issue. The SEXUAL REVOLUTION, driven by an increasingly pervasive ethic of pleasure, removed the connection between sexual activity and reproduction. Concerns about overpopulation and poverty, dating back to the 1950s and voiced by such persons as John D. Rockefeller III, raised serious questions about the efficacy of uncontrolled pregnancy. At the same time, groups such as Planned Parenthood of America voiced concerns about reproductive rights for women, a concern echoing women such as Margaret Sanger earlier in the century. The Civil Rights movement and the women's movement highlighted the rights aspect of the birth control issue. The introduction of the birth control pill in 1961—which, when used properly, is nearly 100 percent effective—made it quite simple for women to control pregnancy. Finally, the U.S.

SUPREME COURT removed the last legal barrier to the availability of contraceptive devices when it struck down Connecticut's law banning the distribution of contraceptives in *Griswold v. Connecticut* (1965).

Most important, during the 1960s the federal government began to take a more active role in the birth control movement. President Lyndon Johnson placed family planning second in importance only to the pursuit of peace in his 1967 State of the Union Address. That same year legislation was enacted that cemented family planning's place in public policy. The Foreign Assistance Act allowed $35 million for family-planning programs. With the Social Security amendments of 1967, 6 percent of the funds allotted for the Child Health Act were set aside for family-planning services. By 1968 the Office of Economic Opportunity funded over 120 family-planning clinics, and by 1969 the federal government had appropriated nearly $50 million for family planning and contraceptive services.

The federal government's involvement in family planning and birth control continued apace during the early 1970s and the administration of RICHARD M. NIXON. In 1970 Congress enacted the Family Planning Service and Population Research Act that established separate funds for birth control services. By 1973 Congress had authorized $382 million for family planning, research, and educational services.

The character of the debate over birth control changed in 1973 with the Supreme Court's decision in *ROE V. WADE*. In this decision, the Court recognized a woman's right to have an abortion in the first trimester of pregnancy and allowed for special circumstances, such as protecting women's health, during the second trimester. The Court rested its decision on a woman's right to privacy and, consequently, the case transformed what was essentially a legal and moral problem into an irreconcilable argument over rights—the right of women for abortion versus the right of the fetus for life. The acrimony over this issue extended to the grassroots level and polarized the American public, resulting in more than just legislative battles. PRO-LIFE AND PRO-CHOICE groups marched and rallied, family-planning centers were picketed and firebombed, physicians who performed abortions were harassed, and some were assassinated.

The controversy, however, was not only about abortion, but also about birth control in general and the federal government's funding of it. For example, the Black Panthers and other African-American nationalist groups declared that federally funded birth control and family-planning services were nothing more than government-run programs designed to slowly exterminate the black race. Roman Catholics also figured prominently in the debate. In 1968, Pope Paul VI issued the encyclical *Humanae Vitae*, which reaffirmed the church's opposition to artificial contraception, and advocated "responsible parenthood" in which married couples controlled pregnancy through the use of natural family planning, or the rhythm method. Although many American Catholics balked at this encyclical and the church became more liberal during the 1980s and 1990s, the Roman Catholic Church still officially promotes only natural family-planning methods. While American religious attitudes softened considerably toward the use of artificial contraception during the last three decades of the 20th century, the religious and moral foundation for the opponents of abortion remained solid.

The moral arguments rested on the belief that all human life is sacred and that a human fetus, from the moment of conception, was life and was a "person." These beliefs manifested themselves in 1981 in the Human Life Amendment, introduced by Senator Orrin Hatch (R-Utah) and another amendment supported by Senator Jesse Helms (R-N.C.). The amendment would have established that from the moment of fertilization, the fertilized egg is a "person" under the constitution and is entitled to all of the rights and privileges afforded each living individual. Moreover, it would have overruled *Roe v. Wade* and would have held doctors, husbands, social workers, and health professionals liable for violation of the amendment. A fallback bill was introduced by Senator Mark Hatfield (R-Oreg.) that proposed eliminating federal funding for abortion, and allowing the right to choose an abortion to vary from state to state. These proposed pieces of legislation reflected the divisive and highly partisan nature of the debate over abortion and, implicitly, over birth control in general that continue into the 21st century.

As the 20th century came to a close, the arguments for and against birth control remained essentially the same. Those opposed generally argued from the standpoint that contraception interfered with God's laws and infringed on the rights fundamentally inherent in human life. Those in favor of contraception offered more secular and less philosophical arguments. They argued that limiting family size, delaying family commitments, or not having children at all might be necessary for a better life. In addition, proponents of artificial contraception argue vigorously for the fundamental right of a woman to control her own body, and the constitutional right to privacy. Moreover, they argued that birth control is essential in addressing issues of maternal age and health, genetic disorders, and overpopulation. Although the fundamental arguments show little change, the position of birth control as a cultural issue has changed radically during the 20th century. Social, political, and technological changes during the latter half of the 20th century made birth control so prominent that the issue became the flash point of what sociologist James Hunter called a "culture war." Finally, the fact that birth control had become so firmly entrenched in the arena of public policy ensured that the culture war would continue well into the 21st century.

See also BIRTHRATES: CHRISTIANITY; FAMILY LIFE; FEMINISM; MARRIAGE; MORAL MAJORITY; NATIONAL ORGANIZATION FOR WOMEN; RELIGION; *WEBSTER V. REPRODUCTIVE HEALTH SERVICES;* WOMEN'S RIGHTS AND STATUS.

Further reading: Donald T. Critchlow, *Intended Consequences: Birth Control, Abortion, and the Federal Government in Modern America* (New York: Oxford University Press, 1999); James Reed, *From Private Vice to Public Virtue: The Birth Control Movement and American Society since 1830* (New York: Basic Books, 1978).

—William L. Glankler

birthrates

From a record low of 14.0 in 1975, the United States birthrate (measured in number of live births per 1,000 women between the ages of 15 and 44) showed a marked increase through 1990 when it reached a high of 16.7. Since 1990, however, the birthrate has experienced a significant decrease, falling to 15.2 in 1994 and to 14.4 in 1998. At the end of the 20th century, the U.S. birthrate accounted for only 64 percent of the country's population growth. Fluctuations in birthrates are generally attributed to the age cohort known as the BABY BOOMERS (those born between 1945 and 1964), the legalization of abortion, the wider acceptance of various forms of birth control, and the changing status of women in American society since the late 1960s.

The relative decline in the birthrate over the last three decades of the 20th century was largely a result of the aging of the baby boomers. By 1990 most "boomer" women had passed beyond their childbearing years. The spike in the birthrate between 1985 and 1990, when it increased from 15.7 to 16.7, likely reflected the wish of many "boomer" women to have children later in life in order to pursue careers. This, along with the desire to have fewer children, clearly affected the overall trend in the birthrate between 1970 and 1998 and reflected the changing status of women in American society. The existence of a greater emphasis on women's rights, along with a larger population of women produced by the baby boom, was largely responsible for the increase in the birthrate for unmarried women from 29.4 in 1980 to 44.0 in 1997. The impact of the baby boom generation on the declining birthrate is more fully understood when considering that 16 million legal immigrants have come to the United States since 1976 and that foreign-born women statistically, on average, have more children than native-born women.

The legalization of ABORTION in 1973 and the increased acceptance and introduction of new forms of BIRTH CONTROL have greatly influenced the drop in the birthrate for women between the ages of 15 and 19. Overall the teenage birthrate dropped from 62.1 in 1991 to 52.3 in 1997. Although the rates for AFRICAN AMERICANS (90.8) and HISPANIC AMERICANS (97.4) are nearly triple that for white women (36.0), they too showed significant decreases during the same time period.

Moreover, the death rate is also declining—a process that, coupled with the declining birthrate, is aging the U.S. population. At the end of the 20th century, demographic forces presented new political and social challenges for the nation.

See also AGE DISCRIMINATION ACT (1975); FAMILY LIFE; FEMINISM; IMMIGRATION; POPULATION TRENDS; PRO-LIFE AND PRO-CHOICE MOVEMENTS; SEXUAL REVOLUTION; WOMEN'S RIGHTS AND STATUS.

—William L. Glankler

Boland Amendment

Passed by Congress on October 11, 1983, the amendment prohibited the Defense Department, the Central Intelligence Agency (CIA), or any other government agency from providing funds or military aid to the CONTRAS for the purpose of overthrowing the Nicaraguan government. The amendment was sponsored by Democratic representative Edward Boland of Massachusetts, but strongly opposed by RONALD W. REAGAN's administration. Representative Boland wrote the amendment in reaction to the April 1983 news story that the CIA had aided in the planning and execution of contra attacks on oil sites in several Nicaraguan locations. Attached to the 1983 fiscal year Defense Appropriations Bill, the amendment was renewed each year through fiscal year 1986. President Reagan sought to circumvent the amendment by using the National Security Council (NSC) to supervise covert military aid to the contras. Overseen by National Security Advisors Robert McFarlane and John Poindexter and directed by U.S. Marine Lt. Col. OLIVER L. NORTH, the operation was successful in raising private and foreign funds for the fighting, but it did not remain secret because the details were made public through the IRAN-CONTRA AFFAIR hearings, a congressional investigation into this operation.

See also DEFENSE POLICY; FOREIGN POLICY.

—Leah Blakey

Bork, Robert (1927–)

Born in 1927, Robert Bork is the most famous nominee to the U.S. SUPREME COURT ever rejected by the U.S. Senate. His confirmation ordeal coined a new verb, *bork*—to attack (a candidate or public figure) systematically, especially in the media. He is also the leading judicial critic of judicial activism in the post–World War II era. Bork received his B.A. from the University of Chicago in 1948 and his law degree in 1953. His legal and academic career during the 1960s, 1970s, and 1980s includes various tenures on the Federal Appellate Court and the U.S. Court of Appeals, a partnership in a Chicago law firm, and a position on the faculty at Yale Law School. Since 1988 he has been a senior fellow at the American Enterprise Institute. He is the father of three and author of three books.

Bork's passion for intellectual controversy led him to give up a lucrative law practice to teach at Yale Law School. His provocative style made him a stimulating scholar and teacher. It also led him to develop a close friendship with fellow professor and constitutional scholar Alexander Bickel. By the time he met Bickel, Bork was a formidable scholar of antitrust law, espousing libertarian views.

Public life affected Bork's legal thinking after he was appointed solicitor general, the Justice Department's third-ranking position, in 1973. He became embroiled in President RICHARD M. NIXON's WATERGATE SCANDAL when Nixon ordered Attorney General Elliot Richardson to fire Special Prosecutor Archibald Cox. Richardson resigned rather than obey Nixon's order. Nixon then fired Richardson's deputy, William Ruckelshaus, when he likewise refused to fire Cox, so Bork became acting attorney general. Bork decided Nixon possessed the power to fire Cox, so Bork fired him.

At the end of his term as solicitor general, Bork returned to Yale, where he completed *The Antitrust Paradox* (1978), a treatise on federal antitrust law. Bork continued his criticism of undemocratic judicial activism in articles and speeches, even after appointment as a federal judge to the U.S. Court of Appeals for the D.C. Circuit in 1982. He postulated a position of "original intent" that argued judges could discern the purpose of the Constitution's authors if they were careful and humble enough to use its written text as their guide.

From his "original intent" stance, Bork denounced the Warren and Burger Courts for rewriting the Constitution and its amendments. He argued that the justices usurped the powers of democratic state legislatures by discovering an implied "right" to sexual privacy in the 1965 *Griswold v. Connecticut* and 1973 ROE V. WADE rulings. Bork also theorized that nonpolitical speech, such as PORNOGRAPHY and obscenity, was not protected by the First Amendment, thus allowing communities to legislate their own standards on such speech.

When Justice LEWIS POWELL announced his retirement in 1987, President RONALD W. REAGAN nominated Bork to fill the vacancy. Powell had been the fifth or "swing" vote on a closely divided court. Bork came under criticism from abortion rights, civil rights, and labor interest groups. Despite voiced support from sitting Justices White and Stevens, the Senate, 58-42, rejected Bork's nomination. In 1988, shortly after the rejection of his nomination, Bork resigned from the circuit court to write and speak his mind about public affairs, authoring two best-selling books.

See also SUPREME COURT.

Further reading: Robert Bork, *The Antitrust Paradox: A Policy at War with Itself* (New York: Free Press, 1978); *The Tempting of America: The Political Seduction of the Law* (New York: Free Press, 1989); *Slouching towards Gomorrah: Modern Liberalism and American Decline* (New York: Free Press, 1996); and Ethan Bronner, *Battle for Justice: How the Bork Nomination Shook America* (Boston: Anchor Press, 1990).

—Christopher M. Gray

Branch Davidians

The Branch Davidians are a religious sect with origins in the Seventh-Day Adventist Church. They are best known for their standoff with federal agents in Waco, Texas, in 1993 that resulted in the death of 86 of their members.

Formed in 1959 by Ben Roden, the Branch Davidian Seventh-Day Adventists believe that they are God's chosen people for the last days prior to the end of the world. Central to their theology is their belief in the coming of a messiah who will be able to explain the Seven Seals of Revelation, a series of prophecies contained in the Book of Revelation. Whoever can explain the Seven Seals will unlock the true meaning of the Bible. Many believed that David Koresh had that ability.

Ben Roden died in 1978 and left his wife, Lois, as president of the church. Vernon Howell joined the organization in 1981 and experienced his first vision from God in 1983, generating friction between himself and George Roden, Lois Roden's son. Howell eventually seized control of the group and, in 1990, changed his name to David Koresh: "David" for the biblical King David of the Israelites, and "Koresh," Hebrew for Cyrus, the Persian king who freed the Israelites from Babylon.

The Branch Davidians came under suspicion, based on reports by previous Branch Davidian members, in late 1990 and early 1991 from California, Michigan, and Texas law enforcement agencies for possible weapons violations. In February 1993 the Bureau of Alcohol, Tobacco, and Firearms (ATF) began its investigation of possible weapons violations as well as allegations of sexual and physical child abuse within the group's compound outside Waco, Texas. The ATF attempted to serve a warrant on David Koresh on February 28. A gun battle ensued in which six Branch Davidians and four ATF agents were killed. At this point the Federal Bureau of Investigation (FBI), under the auspices of U.S. Attorney General JANET RENO, assumed control of the matter and initiated a 51-day siege of the Branch

Davidian compound, during which several Branch Davidians left the compound.

At the outset, David Koresh agreed to surrender if the FBI broadcast one of his sermons live on March 2. The FBI complied, but Koresh reneged on his promise to surrender. Koresh offered another compromise on April 14, saying that he would exit the compound peacefully once he had completed his manuscript explaining the Seven Seals. Completing his explanation of the core of the Branch Davidian theology would have established him as the messiah in the eyes of his followers. Whether Koresh would have surrendered after completing this task will never be known.

On April 19 the FBI launched an assault on the compound. When the Branch Davidians resisted, the FBI used tear gas to subdue those inside the compound. Approximately six hours after the raid began, fires broke out inside the compound, and FBI agents reported hearing gunfire inside as well. The fire resulted in the death of 86 Branch Davidians, while nine escaped and were arrested. Of the nine, eight were convicted on charges ranging from voluntary manslaughter to weapons violations.

Following the tragic loss of life at Waco, criticism mounted against the FBI and the Justice Department, claiming that the agents involved, and Attorney General Janet Reno, were not justified in their use of force and that federal agents were responsible for the fire that destroyed the compound. In August 1999 a document surfaced indicating that the FBI had used incendiary tear gas in the assault, an allegation that the FBI had previously denied. In response to this new evidence, Janet Reno appointed former senator John C. Danforth to investigate the incident. On July 21, 2000, Danforth issued a report exonerating both the FBI and the Justice Department. The evidence in the report showed that the fires began inside the Waco compound and were likely started by the Branch Davidians. The Danforth report also concluded that federal agents did not initiate the conflict by firing their weapons at the complex, but only did so later, after those inside resisted, and that the actions undertaken by the FBI and approved by Janet Reno did not constitute an improper use of armed force.

Further reading: Robert Emmet Long, ed., *Religious Cults in America* (New York: H. W. Wilson, 1994); Stuart A. Wright, ed., *Armageddon in Waco: Critical Perspectives on the Branch Davidian Conflict* (Chicago: University of Chicago Press, 1995).

—William L. Glankler

Brennan, William J., Jr. (1906–1997)

William J. Brennan, Jr., served as an associate justice of the U.S. SUPREME COURT from 1956 to 1990 and is recognized as a leading practitioner of liberal judicial activism, as well as one of the most influential public officials of the post–World War II era. Brennan received his B.A. from the University of Pennsylvania in 1928 and an LL.B. from Harvard Law School in 1931. He served on the New Jersey Appellate Court, Superior Court, and Supreme Court between 1949 and 1956 and was the father of three children.

Brennan's outlook was shaped by two reformist mentors, including his father, William, Sr., a Democratic labor leader and municipal official in Newark, New Jersey; and New Jersey Supreme Court Justice Arthur Vanderbilt, a Republican and famed legal innovator. Brennan's father stressed to his son that justice must be secured for underprivileged people. Vanderbilt emphasized how important proper procedure and due process were to securing individual liberty. Brennan's legal thinking was influenced by Harvard University law professor Felix Frankfurter. Brennan applied the lessons he learned from these men in his efforts to ensure that the law satisfied the evolving "demands of human dignity."

When Justice Sherman Minton retired in 1956, a presidential election year, President Eisenhower sought a replacement who was both Roman Catholic and Democratic, to help him win votes with those two blocs. Attorney General Brownell, a friend of Arthur Vanderbilt, selected Vanderbilt's protégé, Brennan. Brennan joined the Court as a recess appointment, before receiving Senate confirmation in 1957.

Chief Justice Warren quickly made Brennan his closest friend and adviser on the Court. The two conferred weekly during Court terms to review cases and plot strategy to win majorities. Justice Brennan always asked his new law clerks what the most important principle of constitutional law was. He then gleefully answered his own question by holding up the five fingers of one hand and exclaiming: "You can't do anything around here without five votes." Only Chief Justice John Marshall equaled Brennan at persuading a Supreme Court majority to vote his way. Brennan was a genius of persuasion and knew exactly how to win a colleague's agreement. He was the only justice who read all certiorari petitions to the Court. Brennan also boasted an encyclopedic memory of Supreme Court case law. Using these skills, Brennan led the Earl Warren, WARREN BURGER, and early WILLIAM REHNQUIST Courts to revolutionize the American public order in favor of his "jurisprudence of dignity."

Brennan venerated the Bill of Rights. He believe it applied directly to the states (known as incorporation). The First Amendment's freedom of expression was of particular importance to him. In *Roth v. United States* (1957), the Court redefined obscenity in a way that loosened state and local regulation of material once regarded as pornographic.

Justice William J. Brennan, Jr. *(Robert Oakes, National Geographical Society, Collection of the Supreme Court of the United States)*

The Court also amended libel law in *New York Times v. Sullivan* (1964), making it nearly impossible for public figures to win suits against the news media. *New York Times v. U.S.* (1971), the Pentagon Papers case, freed the media to pursue government secrets even of national security importance. In *Texas v. Johnson* (1989) and *U.S. V. EICHMAN* (1990), the majority struck down state and federal statutes prohibiting burning of the American flag. Brennan also joined majorities in the Warren Court in decisions that banned public prayer in schools and mandated strict separation of church and state.

Earl Warren thought the most important case of his tenure was *Baker v. Carr* (1962), a Brennan opinion. This Tennessee case revolutionized American democracy by compelling state legislative reapportionment to eventually bring about an unprecedented "one person, one vote" distribution. When reapportioning, a state's rural interests had often favored themselves at urban districts' expense. Opinion polls showed popular support of the decision in favor of reapportionment, but some scholars thought this case usurped state self-government, and others noted that American republican self-government was historically hostile to proportional representation.

Brennan led another 5-4 vote in *Furman v. Georgia* (1972), striking down the death penalty for violating the

Eighth Amendment's prohibition of cruel and unusual punishment. Only Justice Marshall joined with Brennan's argument against the death penalty after the Court reversed itself four years later in *Gregg v. Georgia* (1976). The Court succeeded in incorporating the Bill of Rights into state criminal procedure, but rising crime rates rendered these reforms unpopular with law enforcement officials and the public at large. These decisions directly assisted the defeat of Justice ABE FORTAS's nomination to be chief justice in 1968, thus allowing President RICHARD M. NIXON to replace Earl Warren with Warren Burger in 1969.

Brennan also played an important role in changing racial and gender law. In *Cooper v. Aaron* (1958), he wrote a unanimous opinion justifying the Court's power to order state governments to racially integrate schools. His opinion in *Green v. New Kent County* (1968) became the basis for all federally mandated school-busing programs. Brennan joined the majority in justifying AFFIRMATIVE ACTION racial quotas in *Gaston v. U.S.* (1969), *GRIGGS ET AL. V. DUKE POWER* (1971), and the *BAKKE* (1978) case. *Cooper v. Boren* (1976), a 7-2 opinion written by Brennan, prepared the ground for gender quotas throughout American life by applying the equal protection clause to laws discriminating between the sexes. Brennan also openly endorsed the EQUAL RIGHTS AMENDMENT.

Brennan aided the feminist movement by ruling for sexual liberation cases. He supported the implicit "right to privacy" in *Griswold v. Connecticut* (1965) and relied on the "right to privacy" in *Eisenstadt v. Baird* (1972), a 6-1 opinion legalizing the distribution of contraceptives to unmarried people. This case set up *ROE V. WADE* (1973), which legalized ABORTION. *Roe* rewrote the abortion laws in all 50 states. Brennan found himself a target of especially bitter criticism, since he was the only Roman Catholic on the Court and yet had nullified abortion and contraceptive laws upholding central tenets of his church's teaching. To the nascent conservative movement, *Roe* became the symbol of an out-of-control, activist Supreme Court.

After President Ronald W. Reagan's appointment of Justice William Rehnquist as chief justice, Brennan found all but his revolutionary reapportionment decisions whittled away or even overruled. But Brennan stubbornly voted his conscience. He lent support to the emerging gay liberation movement in his *Bowers v. Hardwick* (1986) dissent. He continued to lobby Court members, especially his replacement, Justice DAVID SOUTER, after stepping down in 1990. He also continued to reap the adulation of law professors. Brennan remained a controversial figure even after death. His funeral mass in 1997 was marred by a large, loud protest of anti-abortion activists.

Further reading: Raoul Berger, *Government by Judiciary* (Cambridge, Mass.: Harvard University Press, 1977);

Alexander Bickel, *The Supreme Court and the Idea of Progress* (New York: HarperCollins, 1970); John Hart Ely, *Democracy and Distrust* (Cambridge, Mass.: Harvard University Press, 1980); John T. Noonan, Jr., *Private Choice: Abortion in America* (New York: Free Press, 1979); David Savage, *Turning Right: The Making of the Rehnquist Court* (New York: John Wiley & Sons, 1992).

—Christopher M. Gray

Breyer, Stephen (1938–)

Stephen Breyer began his tenure as an associate justice of the U.S. SUPREME COURT in 1994. Breyer received a B.A. from Oxford University in 1961 and an LL.B. from Harvard Law School in 1964. He is a professor at Harvard Law School and served as judge on the Senate Judiciary Committee as well as on the U.S. Court of Appeals before serving on the Supreme Court. He is married to the former Joanna Hare and has three children.

President BILL CLINTON appointed Breyer to fill the Court vacancy created by Justice Harry Blackmun's retirement. Since he was an exceptionally well-qualified nominee, with moderate to liberal views on law, the Democratic Senate confirmed him easily.

Breyer offered few surprises as a Supreme Court justice. He exhibited the same attributes there that he had on the First Circuit. His opinions on economic cases displayed a mastery of regulatory problems, especially on antitrust matters. On free speech and moral issues, he tended to rule in liberal fashion, though some critics complained he did not value the First Amendment enough.

Breyer applied this analytical approach even to controversial cases like the *Stenberg v. Carhart* (2000) "partial-birth" abortion decision and the *Bush v. Gore* (2000) presidential ballot ruling.

—Christopher M. Gray

Buchanan, Patrick J. (1938–)

Pat Buchanan has been a senior adviser to three U.S. presidents and has three times sought the Republican nomination for the presidency. In 2000 he sought election as the presidential candidate for the REFORM PARTY, and is perhaps best recognized for his outspoken brand of conservatism. Buchanan was born in Washington, D.C., attended Jesuit schools, and received his master's degree in journalism from Columbia University in 1962. At the age of 23 he accepted a position with the *St. Louis Globe Democrat* and became the youngest editorial writer on a major newspaper in America. Between 1966 and 1974 he was an assistant to RICHARD M. NIXON and was the White House director of communications for RONALD W. REAGAN from 1985 to 1987. During his years in the White House, Buchanan wrote FOREIGN POLICY speeches and attended four summit meetings, including Richard M. Nixon's historic trip to China in 1972.

After leaving the White House in 1974, Buchanan became a syndicated columnist and founding member of three TELEVISION talk shows: NBC's *The McLaughlin Group* and CNN's *Capital Gang* and *Crossfire*. Buchanan unsuccessfully challenged GEORGE H. W. BUSH for the Republican presidential nomination in 1992 and lost to Senator ROBERT DOLE in 1996. He left the Republican Party in 1999, running unsuccessfully as the Reform Party's candidate for president of the United States in 2000. Throughout his career, Buchanan's controversial comments on such contentious issues as IMMIGRATION and RACE AND RACIAL CONFLICT have led many to accuse him of being a white supremacist and an anti-Semite. He remains, however, a highly influential spokesperson for many conservatives in contemporary American society.

—William L. Glankler

Buckley, William F., Jr. (1925–)

As founder, owner, and editor of *National Review* magazine, William Buckley is recognized as the intellectual godfather of the post–World War II CONSERVATIVE MOVEMENT. Born in 1925, Buckley received his B.A. from Yale University in 1950, founded the *National Review* in 1955, hosted the television show *Firing Line* from 1966 to 1999, and has written over 40 books.

Buckley unified the quarreling factions of the American intellectual right into a coherent ideological movement by founding and editing *National Review* magazine. He also correctly identified RONALD W. REAGAN, a *National Review* subscriber, as the leader able to bring the conservative movement to political victory, 13 years before the 1980 elections.

Buckley's family background fused the various cultural strands of the modern American conservative coalition. Both his Texan father, William F. Buckley, Sr., and Louisiana-born mother, Aloise, were traditionalist southern Roman Catholics who venerated God, family, and country while loathing all forms of secular social engineering, especially communism. His father also indoctrinated his children with a distrust of Franklin Roosevelt's New Deal, at home and abroad. Albert Jay Nock, a libertarian writer and friend of the elder Buckley, inspired young Bill with his notion of "the Remnant," an elite of superior characters who would uphold moral and intellectual standards.

After army service, Buckley joined his brother James at Yale and began making "the Remnant" a reality. He befriended two dissenters from liberal orthodoxy: Yale political science professor Willmoore Kendall and classmate Brent Bozell. Bozell married Buckley's sister Priscilla.

Kendall recruited Buckley for the CIA. Both men later became founding senior editors of *National Review.*

While chairman of the Yale *Daily News* during his senior year, Buckley aroused the campus by proudly trumpeting his illiberal views. He also determined to write a book exposing how Yale indoctrinated its students with hostility to Christianity, the free market, and aggressive anticommunism. Buckley wrote the book just after graduation and while serving with the CIA in Mexico, under a then-obscure case officer, E. Howard Hunt. Buckley called his book *God and Man at Yale.* Published in 1951, it became a best-seller, making its 25-year-old author a national intellectual celebrity. Harvard dean of Arts and Sciences McGeorge Bundy, a precocious Yale alumnus, launched a vitriolic attack on the book in *The Atlantic Monthly.* Buckley shocked all liberal intellectuals by rebutting Bundy's attack in an even more vitriolic answer in the same magazine. For the first time since Henry Cabot Lodge, Sr.'s death, the American right had a dashing, patrician champion who could effortlessly debate liberal thinkers. And this champion emerged only a year after Lionel Trilling denied that there were any genuine conservative ideas.

Seeing Bundy bloodied enraged the liberal establishment. They vilified Buckley's "bigoted" Roman Catholic and southern background, thereby increasing book sales. Buckley enraged liberals even further by cowriting a scholarly defense of Senator Joseph McCarthy's anticommunist crusade, *McCarthy and His Enemies,* in 1954. A year later, Buckley joined with Bozell to found a conservative magazine with these distinguished ex-leftist intellectuals: Willmore Kendall, Max Eastman, James Burnham, John Chamberlain, Willi Schlamm, and John Dos Passos. The name of the new magazine was *National Review.* Later, Buckley added his sister Priscilla as managing editor and friend Whittaker Chambers as senior editor to the staff. Buckley was indispensable to the magazine because only he, with his charm, humor, patience, and money, could keep such a fractious staff working together.

National Review became the beacon of American conservatism. Its publisher, William Rusher, inspired the draft of Barry Goldwater for president in 1964. Brent Bozell ghostwrote *Conscience of a Conservative* for Goldwater. Buckley distanced himself from the John Birch Society in 1961 because they were not part of "the responsible right." He acquired a newspaper column while also publishing almost a book per year. Buckley ran for mayor of New York City in 1965 against liberal Republican John Lindsay. His television theatrics in the mayoral race brought him a syndicated television show in 1966, *Firing Line.*

Buckley recognized he was not a deep thinker, but he saw his duty to spur the movement on with columns, debates, speeches, and television appearances, and to identify new talent in ideas and politics. Buckley aided the careers of many young writers and editors. They include such famous names as Garry Wills, John Leonard, George Will, John McLaughlin, Hadley Arkes, Joseph Sobran, Peter Rodman, Lawrence Kudlow, Richard Brookhiser, and David Frum.

In 1967, Buckley touted California's new governor, Ronald W. Reagan, as the political future of American conservatism in a long magazine profile. While Reagan was the butt of jokes across the nation, Buckley foresaw that this B-movie actor could win the presidency and overthrow Democratic liberalism.

During the conservative disasters and disappointments of the 1960s and 1970s, Buckley maintained his faith in Reagan. Even when the two fiercely disagreed about both HENRY KISSINGER's foreign policy and the PANAMA CANAL treaty, Buckley continued to urge Reagan on to the White House, standing by him loyally in his 1976 challenge to Gerald Ford. In 1980, Buckley's judgment was triumphantly vindicated by Reagan's election and resulting presidency. Many Reagan aides were former *National Review* staffers. CIA director William Casey was an old-time NR hand who drew up the magazine's original articles of incorporation.

In 1991, Buckley stepped down as editor in chief of *National Review* to become editor at large. He retired from *Firing Line* in 1999 and from speechmaking in 2000.

Further reading: John P. Diggins, *Up from Communism* (New York: Columbia University Press, 1975); John Judis, *William F. Buckley Jr.: Patron Saint of the Conservatives* (New York: Simon & Schuster, 1987).

—Christopher M. Gray

Burger, Warren E. (1907–1995)

Warren Burger served as chief justice of the U.S. SUPREME COURT from 1969 to 1986. Burger was born into a humble Minnesota working-class family. He early displayed a talent for artistry in painting and sculpture, but decided to apply himself to night law school. In 1938 Burger befriended Harold Stassen, who was elected Minnesota's "Boy Governor" that year. Stassen's patronage proved invaluable to both Burger's personal practice and his role in Minnesota Republican Party politics between 1938 and 1952. Burger acted as floor manager for Stassen's presidential campaigns at both the 1948 and 1952 Republican Party National Conventions. In the close contest between Eisenhower and Robert Taft for the 1952 Republican presidential nomination, Burger played a crucial role. He switched the Minnesota delegation, pledged to its favorite son, Stassen, over to Eisenhower, thereby nominating the latter. Eisenhower's aide, Herbert Brownell, was favorably impressed by Burger's conduct at the 1952 convention.

When Brownell became Eisenhower's attorney general, he named Burger head of the Justice Department's Civil Division. In 1956 Brownell persuaded Eisenhower to appoint Burger to the most prestigious federal appellate court, the U.S. Court of Appeals for the D.C. Circuit. Burger became one of the few advocates of judicial restraint on a liberal circuit. During the 1960s, Burger strongly denounced the Warren Supreme Court's judicial activism, especially in criminal procedure cases. He became the foremost federal judicial critic of Warren rulings. Earl Warren tried to retire early in 1968 to forestall RICHARD M. NIXON from appointing Burger as his replacement after the elections. Warren's gambit failed; Burger became chief justice a year later.

Despite Nixon's hopes, Burger did not lead a conservative judicial counterrevolution as chief justice. Burger failed to lead or inspire the Court with either his intellect or his character. His court rolled back some Warren Court decisions on criminal issues such as the death penalty. However, the Burger Court, as its leading scholar Earl Maltz argues, proved far more liberal than the Warren Court on cases involving regulation of racial and gender discrimination, government secrecy, and sexual conduct. Associate Justice WILLIAM J. BRENNAN, JR., leader of the liberals on the Court, consistently outmaneuvered Burger to obtain majorities on important Supreme Court cases.

In 1971 Burger wrote the opinion for two unanimous 9-0 Court decisions, both involving North Carolina petitioners, aimed to remedy past and present racial discrimination. *Swann v. Charlotte-Mecklenburg County School Board* upheld judicially mandated and supervised school busing. *GRIGGS ET AL. V. DUKE POWER* held that an employer had to show "business necessity" for requiring a high school diploma or an IQ test of an employee; otherwise the employer was in violation of Title VII, specifically for discrimination against African Americans based on "disparate impact." Both these unanimous rulings represented the judicial activism railed against by critics of the Warren Court. Burger backed away from these opinions in future busing and affirmative action cases such as *BAKKE* (1978). From the mid-1970s on, Burger usually concurred with Rehnquist's conservative opinions on racial discrimination.

In *U.S. V. NIXON* (1974), Burger persuaded the Court to speak unanimously 8-0 (Rehnquist recused himself) in ordering President Nixon to hand over his recorded tapes of White House conversations to WATERGATE special prosecutor LEON JAWORSKI. Burger's opinion argued presidential executive privilege immunity was conditional to circumstances, and not absolute. This ruling of the Burger Court compelled President Nixon to resign from office in disgrace.

United States v. Nixon was not the most controversial Burger Court ruling. Perhaps the most far-reaching decision issued by the Burger Court was *ROE V. WADE* (1973), which legalized ABORTION. Inspired by Justice Brennan's leadership, it transformed abortion laws in most of the states and territories. Burger joined the majority in this case in order to limit the reach of the ruling by assigning the majority opinion.

After publication of Bob Woodward's and Scott Armstrong's best-selling book *The Brethren* (1979), Burger's reputation across the intellectual-political spectrum plummeted. This book claimed that Burger enjoyed little respect or trust among his colleagues on the Court and liberal Justice Brennan and conservative Justice Rehnquist actually dominated the Court's proceedings. Under RONALD W. REAGAN's administration, Attorney General EDWIN C. MEESE III and his aides persuaded Burger to step down in 1986 in a double switch, replacing him with Rehnquist and filling the open seat with Justice ANTONIN SCALIA.

—Christopher M. Gray

Bush, George H. W. (1924–)

George Herbert Walker Bush served as the 41st president of the United States during the historic transition at the end of the COLD WAR. For his role in organizing the unprecedented global alliance against Iraq during the PERSIAN GULF WAR of 1991, Bush received the highest approval rating (89 percent) ever measured for an American president to that date. Ironically, by mid-1992, Bush also received one of the lowest ratings (30 percent), due to poor economic conditions that accompanied the transition to the post–cold war world. He was defeated after one term by Arkansas governor WILLIAM J. CLINTON in 1992.

Bush was born in Milton, Massachusetts, on June 12, 1924. He was the second of five children born to Prescott and Dorothy Walker Bush. His father served in the U.S. Senate, representing Connecticut from 1952–83. George Bush served as a U.S. Navy pilot in the Pacific in World War II and received the Distinguished Flying Cross. In late 1944 he married Barbara Pierce. They had six children together, including George Walker, who was elected president of the United States in 2001. He graduated Phi Beta Kappa in economics from Yale University in 1948 and moved to Texas to work in the oil industry, starting three separate companies.

In 1964 Bush won the Republican Party's nomination for U.S. Senate. Bush lost the election, but received 43.5 percent of the vote, which was remarkable considering that Texas was traditionally a Democratic state, and that year's leading Texan candidate, Lyndon B. Johnson, carried the presidential election. In 1966 Bush became the first Republican to represent Houston in the House of Representatives. As a freshman congressman, Bush won an important seat on the House Ways and Means Committee. He supported extending the vote to 18-year-olds and voted to end the draft. He was reelected in 1968, but gave up his seat to run against former Democratic congressman Lloyd Bentsen for a seat in the Senate. He lost the election, but was named U.S. ambassador to the United Nations by President RICHARD M. NIXON. In 1973, Nixon named Bush chairman of the Republican National Committee after Nixon's landslide victory.

In 1974 President GERALD FORD named Bush as envoy to China. By December 1975, Ford asked him to serve as director of the Central Intelligence Agency (CIA). He resigned in January 1977, shortly after President JAMES EARL CARTER, JR. took office.

Bush made a long-shot bid for the presidency in 1979. He announced his candidacy in early May and came in a strong second out of the field of six Republican contenders during the primaries. Bush ran as a moderate, criticizing Reagan's campaign pledge to cut taxes, which, Reagan argued, would inspire economic growth and allow increases in military spending, while balancing the budget. Bush described it as "voodoo economics," which Democrats and the media remembered long after the election. By May 1980, however, he recognized former California governor RONALD W. REAGAN's overwhelming popularity and withdrew from the race. Bush was in agreement with Reagan on social policy, and thereby helped balance the ticket as a moderate conservative when he was nominated to run as vice president. The Reagan-Bush team defeated President Carter by a wide margin.

Bush was forced to rise to the occasion of leadership just three months after taking office. On March 30, 1981, John W. Hinckley, Jr., tried to assassinate President Reagan. While Reagan recovered, Bush assumed many public functions of the presidency. In 1984 the Reagan-Bush ticket won reelection with 525 electoral votes; the largest electoral landslide in history. When Reagan underwent intestinal surgery in July 1985, he formally transferred the power of his office to Bush, who then became the first designated acting president of the United States.

Toward the end of Reagan's administration, the Republicans were already planning on promoting Bush as the next president. With a $12 million campaign chest, Bush quickly outdistanced his other Republican rivals, Kansas senator BOB DOLE and Christian televangelist Pat Robertson. Bush campaigned on the promise of a "kinder and gentler America" which included social conservatism, environmental protection, and a solid pledge of no new taxes. After winning the nomination, Bush surprised many by selecting the relatively young Indiana senator, DAN QUAYLE, to be his running mate. In August, media-generated scandals related to the IRAN-CONTRA AFFAIR, and the so-called "wimp factor," arising from Bush's inevitable com-

George H. W. Bush and Dan Quayle *(George Bush Presidential Library)*

parison to the charismatic Reagan, placed the Bush-Quayle ticket consistently behind in the polls. The Democrats nominated Massachusetts governor MICHAEL DUKAKIS, who chose long-time Bush rival Senator Lloyd Bentsen of Texas as his running mate. By mid-autumn, Bush managed to reassert his independence from Reagan's shadow and gained the offensive by emphasizing Dukakis's record in Massachusetts. In the November election, the Bush-Quayle ticket achieved a solid 53 percent of the vote, winning 40 states and 426 electoral votes. At the same time, however, the Democrats increased their majority in the House.

The "wimp" image quickly disappeared as Bush asserted his foreign policy program. At the start of his term, Bush declared war on illegal drugs. In October 1989, U.S.-backed military forces launched a coup attempt against PANAMA dictator and drug-lord Manuel Noriega. After the first attempt failed, President Bush sent 12,000 more troops to join the 12,000 already stationed in the Canal Zone. Noriega finally surrendered from his refuge in the Vatican diplomatic mission on January 3, 1990. He was sent to Florida where he was convicted on charges related to drug trafficking and racketeering. Bush later pledged $1 billion to help rebuild Panama. The following month, Bush held a summit in Cartagena, Colombia, with the presidents of the three largest drug-producing nations: Peru, Bolivia, and Colombia. They reached an accord promising to limit both supply in South America and demand in the United States. At the same time, Bush pursued a diligent program to end the cold war to bring the USSR back into the "family of nations." Between the summer of 1989 and the autumn of 1990, Bush met with Soviet leader Mikhail Gorbachev three times to discuss arms and troop reduction, trade agreements, and even economic aid. Whether due to Reagan-Bush policies or increasing domestic pressure, the Soviet Union underwent significant change at this time, leading to the collapse of communism in the Soviet Union and Eastern bloc countries. On November 9, 1989, the Berlin Wall, a symbol of Soviet control in Eastern Europe, was taken down. Though the cold war was not entirely over, by the time Saddam Hussein's Iraqi army invaded Kuwait on August 2, 1990, a major thaw had taken place.

The invasion of Kuwait placed an estimated 10 percent of the world's petroleum reserves under Iraqi control. Hussein's army began concentrating along the Saudi Arabian border, thereby threatening another 25 percent. To prevent Iraq from positioning itself to control more than a third of the world's oil supplies, Bush organized a multinational political and military alliance with European, Asian, and Middle Eastern nations. The task involved forging relationships between nations that had long traditions of mutual suspicion and hostile relations, including Israel, Egypt, France, and the USSR. Bush wisely chose to facilitate the operation through the UN Security Council, which approved a resolution authorizing the use of force if Iraq did not remove its occupying forces from Kuwait by January 15, 1991. The United States deployed hundreds of thousands of troops to the gulf along with joint forces of nine other nations. On January 12 Congress approved military action in the gulf, and on January 16 "Operation Desert Storm" began with the multinational force initiating sustained air bombardment of Iraq. On February 24 the ground-based attack began, and continued for 100 hours until the Iraqi troops had been pushed out of Kuwait. Bush later endured criticism for ending the attack before reaching Baghdad, but he believed the UN mandate called only for the removal of Iraq and the security of Mideastern oil reserves. Shortly after the Persian Gulf War, Bush and Soviet leader Mikhail Gorbachev signed a final treaty reducing existing arsenals of ballistic missiles, and by the end of the year, the Soviet Union dissolved. By mid-1991 Bush's approval rating reached 89 percent.

On the home front, Bush shifted emphasis away from military preparedness and toward a domestic tranquility. Bush supported the Clean Air Act of 1989, the AMERICANS WITH DISABILITIES ACT of 1990, and the CIVIL RIGHTS ACT of 1991. The eight years of military buildup under Reagan's administration had contributed to a deficit of $141 billion before Bush took office, so Bush pledged to reduce the military. However, the cuts in funding had negative effects on those directly and indirectly dependent on military contracts. At the same time, Bush encountered a crisis in the savings and loan industry, which had resulted from deregulation of the industry under Reagan's administration. As a result of this crisis, the federal government provided $126 billion to bail out many of these institutions. Moreover, despite the military cuts, the annual deficit still increased to $220 billion, and the national debt reached $3.2 trillion. Because of these figures, Bush hoped to keep the 1990 budget under control in a way that was acceptable to both Democrats and Republicans. The resulting deal promised to reduce the deficit by $500 billion in five years. Conservative Republicans, however, became irate because Bush broke his "no new taxes" pledge during the presidential campaign. In six weeks, Bush's approval rating slipped 20 points.

In 1991 Bush believed it was necessary to ensure fiscal responsibility and a balanced budget. Later that year, he proposed the NORTH AMERICAN FREE TRADE AGREEMENT as another support for the new post–cold war economy. Many Americans, however, interpreted the treaty as further evidence that Bush placed foreign policy ahead of domestic problems, and that he was out of touch with working Americans. During the 1992 election, his Democratic rivals, BILL CLINTON and his running mate ALBERT GORE, JR., gave their promise of a better economy. They also used Bush's broken tax pledge repeatedly to criticize Bush. At the same time, Texas billionaire H. ROSS PEROT joined the race as a third-party candidate and drew many Republicans and independents who had become disillusioned by the double impression of Bush's broken tax pledge and the mild recession underway in 1990. Bush lost the election with 36 percent of the vote to Clinton-Gore's 43 percent, while Perot attracted 21 percent of the vote.

Bush returned to Texas with his wife, Barbara, and settled back into private life. He kept silent throughout the Clinton-Gore administration and its numerous scandals. In 1994 Bush's oldest son, GEORGE W. BUSH, became governor of Texas, and his second oldest, Jeb Bush, later became governor of Florida. In 2000 George W. Bush ran for president with Dick Cheney, his father's secretary of defense, as vice president. He became president after a Supreme Court decision in his favor granted him the requisite electoral college votes.

See also ELECTIONS; POLITICAL PARTIES.

Further reading: George Bush, *Man of Integrity* (Eugene, Oreg.: Harvest House, 1988); George Bush and Brent Scowcroft, *A World Transformed* (New York: Alfred

A. Knopf, 1998); John Robert Greene, *The Presidency of George Bush* (Lawrence: University Press of Kansas, 2000); Herbert S. Parmet, *George Bush: The Life of a Lone Star Yankee* (New York: Simon & Schuster, 1997).

—Aharon W. Zorea

Bush, George W. (1946–)

George Walker Bush began his service as the 43rd president of the United States on January 20, 2001. Entering the office amid controversy and much partisan division, Bush promised to unite the nation through compassionate conservatism and political civility. Eight months later, the nation was rocked by terrorist attacks on the twin towers of the World Trade Center in New York City, and on the Pentagon in Washington, D.C. These attacks left more than 3,000 dead and hundreds wounded. The event transformed the attitude of the nation and completely redirected President Bush's agenda.

George Walker Bush is the eldest son of former president GEORGE H. W. BUSH and Barbara Pierce Bush, and is sometime referred to by the press as "George W." to distinguish him from his father. He was born on July 6, 1946, in New Haven, Connecticut, while his father was finishing his degree at Yale University after World War II. The family moved to Midland, Texas, a few years later, and George was joined by five siblings: John (commonly known as "Jeb," who became governor of Florida in 1999), Neil, Marvin, Dorothy, and Robin, who died of leukemia in 1953 at the age of three. Like his father, Bush attended Philips Academy in Andover, Massachusetts, and graduated from Yale University with a degree in history in 1968. He served as a jet fighter pilot in the Texas Air National Guard. He left the service as a lieutenant in 1973 to go back to school, and earned a master's of business administration from Harvard Business School in 1975. He returned to Midland, Texas, and founded Arbusto, an independent oil and gas exploration company, named after the Spanish word for "bush." Two years later, he married former teacher and librarian Laura Welch; in 1981 she gave birth to their twin daughters, Jenna and Barbara.

The younger Bush entered politics in 1978, when he campaigned as a Republican in a large West Texas district for a seat in the U.S. House of Representatives. He proved to be a successful fund-raiser, but eventually lost by six points to Democratic state senator Kent Hance. Bush returned to the oil business, but kept a hand in politics throughout the 1980s; he provided early financial support for Phil Gramm's successful senatorial campaign in 1984, and later worked on his father's presidential campaign as an adviser and speechwriter in 1986 and 1987. During his father's campaign, Bush later reported that he reached a turning point in his life; shortly before his 40th birthday. He committed himself to his faith as a Christian, gave up alcohol entirely, and generally approached his professional duties with greater seriousness. Bush sold his interests in the oil business and served as his father's chief liaison to Christian conservatives during the 1988 campaign.

After the election, Bush used the money from his oil investments to become part owner of the Texas Rangers professional baseball team, serving as the team's managing partner. In 1994 he made his second entrance as a political candidate in a gubernatorial campaign against the very popular incumbent Democrat, Ann Richards. Bush campaigned on welfare reform and devolution to local government of control over schools; he won the election and became the 46th governor of the state of Texas. During his first term, Bush demonstrated a remarkable ability to unite opposing factions and succeeded in passing most of his campaign goals through a Democratic-controlled legislature, including tort reform, antidrug, and anti-CRIME measures. He also secured bipartisan support for a $1 billion tax cut, while still providing substantial increases in funding for public EDUCATION. In 1998, Bush became the first Texas governor to be elected to consecutive four-year terms, winning 68 percent of the vote.

The Texas governor announced his intention to run for president of the United States in June 1999. He

George W. Bush *(Getty Images)*

campaigned as a "compassionate conservative," stressing tax cuts, limited government, partial privatization of Social Security, and welfare reform, while also advocating increased funding for education, and school choice, known to its critics as school vouchers. He promised a new tone in politics by emphasizing respect and bipartisan cooperation with all members of Congress. Bush swept the Republican primaries, despite a strong challenge from Senator John McCain (R-Ariz.) By early March, he was able to concentrate on his campaign against his probable Democratic challenger, Vice President ALBERT GORE, JR. In July, Bush announced that his choice for running mate was Richard B. Cheney, a former representative from Wyoming who had also served as defense secretary for the elder Bush during the Persian Gulf War. Bush was behind in the polls before the first televised debate on October 3. The debates reinvigorated his campaign, however, and despite widespread criticism that the Texas governor was an incompetent public speaker, the press and the public opinion polls proclaimed Bush the victor in each of the three debates. The same polls suggested that Gore was too stiff and mechanical, while the Texas governor seemed the more honest and believable candidate. By the week before the election in November, the two candidates were virtually even.

On election night, the news networks announced results for Florida, giving its 25 electoral votes to Gore after most but not all the voting stations had closed. Their predictions were based on exit polls of voters, and statistical analysis showing that returns from outstanding districts could not change the outcome. Nonetheless, as more polling stations reported their returns, the news networks changed their figures and declared Bush the winner, at which point Gore called the Texas governor to concede the election. As the night wore on, however, and certain key districts reported a large number of discarded, spoiled, and otherwise disputed ballots, largely in Democratic districts, the news networks retracted their declaration of a Bush victory and ended their broadcasts by stating that the vote was too close to call. Meanwhile, Gore rescinded his concession and waited for official returns of the vote count in Florida. Officials in the Gore and Bush campaigns debated balloting procedures and the certification process in state and federal courts. Though the Florida State Supreme Court eventually ordered a statewide recount, the U.S. Supreme Court found that time had run out and ruled 5-4 to stop the recount, letting the original count stand. The decision gave Bush Florida's 25 electoral votes, providing him with a total of 271 votes for an electoral majority of one vote.

In his victory speech on December 13, Bush emphasized his bipartisan approach to politics and promised to serve as a leader of "one nation" and not "one party." After eight years of partisan conflict, most members of the national media and Congress dismissed the possibility of a "new tone" in Congress as unrealistic; the national media described Bush as a president without a public mandate, and Democrats insisted that Bush's presidency was illegitimate. For a short time, these predictions seemed to come true. Though the Republicans maintained a majority in both houses of Congress after the 2000 election, Vermont senator James Jeffords quit the Republican Party and declared himself an independent in May 2001, thereby giving control of the Senate to the Democratic Party. Nonetheless, Bush succeeded in passing an 11-year, $1.35 trillion tax cut bill that reduced the top income tax rate to 35 percent and resulted in the refunding of $300 to millions of middle-income taxpayers.

On September 11, 2001, 19 terrorists hijacked four separate commercial jets and aimed them at American landmarks; two struck the twin towers of the World Trade Center in New York City, a third struck the Pentagon, and a fourth was prevented from reaching its target, presumably in Washington, D.C., by a passenger uprising. The acts were the most destructive foreign attack ever launched on American soil; it resulted in the deaths of more than 3,000 people and a loss of billions of dollars to the American ECONOMY. The horror of the events united America unlike anything the recent generation had experienced.

Earlier partisan conflicts disappeared, and President Bush received unqualified support from the Congress, which passed a series of emergency response bills at the president's request. On September 20, George Bush gave a national address before a joint session of Congress and outlined the nation's retaliatory response against the terrorists who launched the attack and against global terrorism wherever it is found. More than three-quarters of the nation saw the address live, and another 14 percent saw rebroadcasts or excerpts later. Within two weeks, President Bush received a 90 percent approval rating, the highest of any president in modern history, barely edging out his father's peak rating of 89 percent during the Persian Gulf War and President Harry S. Truman's 87 percent rating at the close of World War II.

See also CONSERVATIVE MOVEMENT; ELECTIONS; POLITICAL PARTIES; REAGAN, RONALD W.; TERRORISM.

Further reading: William E. Leuchtenburg, *In the Shadow of FDR: From Harry Truman to George W. Bush* (Ithaca, N.Y.: Cornell University Press, 2001); Alice V. McGillivray, Richard M. Scammon, Rhodes Cook, eds., *America at the Polls, 1960–2000, John F. Kennedy to George W. Bush: A Handbook of American Presidential Election Statistics* (Washington, D.C.: CQ Press, 2001).

—Aharon W. Zorea

business

The revolution in COMPUTER technologies in the late 20th century produced mixed results for American businesses. Since the 1960s, innovations in communication and data processing encouraged greater consolidation of resources, resulting in giant conglomerates and multinational corporations. Later innovations in personal computing and the advent of the INTERNET helped to moderate this trend by the mid-1990s. The rate of major mergers declined, while the number of smaller, technology-focused startup companies increased. The market adjustment during the first quarter of 2001 and continuing well into 2002 threatened to undermine the effect of this new technology sector, but the long-term changes remain undetermined.

In 2000 most American businesses fell into one of three categories: individual proprietorship, partnership, and corporations. Seventy-five percent of American companies are small businesses, while less than 1 percent are large corporations holding assets of $250 million or more. Yet that 1 percent dominates production and exchange in the national economy, causing some observers to fear that they hold an unfair advantage over small businesses that cannot enjoy similar economies of scale. This fear is especially pronounced when large corporations buy out their smaller competitors. Though mergers between corporations began in earnest in the late 1950s and early 1960s, the number of unfriendly mergers increased significantly by 1970. In 1968 Congress passed the Williams Act, limiting hostile takeovers by requiring aggressor companies to publicly notify targeted companies of their intent. The goal of the legislation was to allow targeted companies sufficient time to gather extra resources and purchase outstanding stock before control shifted to the aggressor company. The act enjoyed minimal success, and within two years, Congress passed even more stringent notification requirements. These new regulations were undermined by innovations in telecommunication and information processing, which improved the efficiency of large centralized administrations and generally encouraged more corporate mergers, friendly or otherwise, throughout the 1970s. The difficulty in amassing the billions of dollars necessary to finance these mergers remained the last obstacle limiting their size.

Several factors coalesced in the early 1980s to remove the remaining limits on the size of corporate mergers. With the election of President RONALD W. REAGAN, the political environment became more conducive to large corporate takeovers; his business-friendly campaign created a sense that the Department of Justice would require a higher standard of evidence for antitrust suits than in previous administrations. Additionally, the Reagan administration deregulated a number of industries that had traditionally been heavily constrained by federal oversight agencies, including energy, broadcasting, airline and ground transportation, and finance. Deregulation of banking and securities industries encouraged novel forms of financing; American companies more actively sought foreign investment and experimented with nontraditional bond strategies, including leveraged financing and high-yield bonds. Financier Michael Milken dominated the investment banking industry with high-yield bonds; working on the assumption that traditional credit ratings were more conservative than actuality, Milken purchased bonds with poor credit ratings and then resold them to investors at a profit, based on the belief that most bonds would remain solvent long enough to yield high returns. His success earned Milken the often-pejorative title of "junk bond king." At the same time, many oil and gas firms enjoyed unprecedented cash reserves as a result of profits gained through oil and gas prices created by the ENERGY CRISIS in the 1970s, which not only encouraged expansion into other areas, but also made them targets for takeover. Excess cash reserves cause a company's value to exceed the stock-offering price, which attracts buyers who willingly go into debt to acquire the company knowing they can use the cash reserves to pay the financing. With innovative financing techniques, buyers with very little expendable cash were able to arrange takeovers of very large corporations on credit, and then use the targeted company's cash reserves or liquidate its holdings to pay for the purchase.

These changes in the political environment, deregulation, and excess cash reserves forced a restructuring of the business community in America toward even larger conglomerate corporations. Restructuring affected industries with the most rapid technological development as well as those with inefficient management, including oil and gas, tires, broadcasting, financial services and insurance agencies. Some of the most famous mergers in 1989 involving a billion dollars or more include the $4.2 billion merger of Time and Warner communications, and the $25 billion hostile takeover of Nabisco by R. J. Reynolds. In 2000 only eight nations had budgets as large as the transnational corporations General Motors, Daimler Chrysler, Ford, and Wal-Mart, each of which earned more than Canada, Spain, and Sweden combined.

Public reaction to the wave of megamergers during the 1980s was generally negative. Business journalists reported that financiers like Michael Milken made hundreds of millions of dollars in commissions, while other corporate raiders, like Ivan Boesky, made similar amounts for purchasing companies with the sole goal of liquidating their assets. Drawn by the public debate, the Department of Justice and the Securities and Exchange Commission began investigating improprieties in the industry as early as 1985. Other critics included longstanding Wall Street investment houses, which felt threatened by the innova-

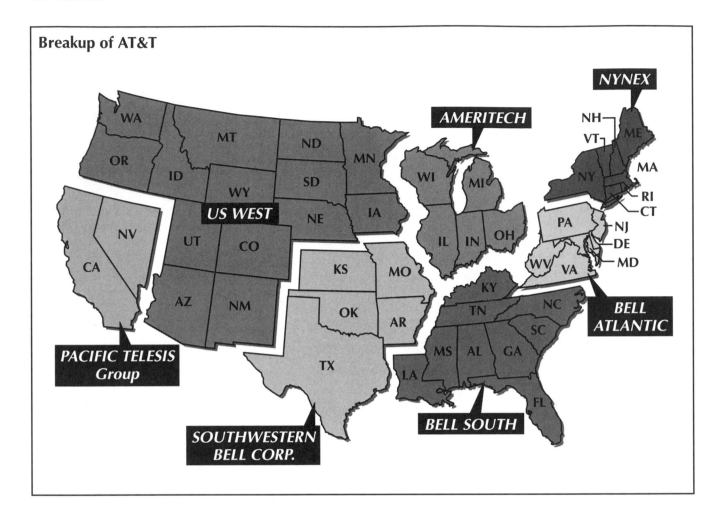

Breakup of AT&T

tions, as well as big businesses that feared that these new financing schemes made even the largest corporations vulnerable to hostile takeovers. To add fuel to the fire, the stock market suffered the largest one-day crash in history on October 19, 1987. Though the crash failed to produce an economic depression, it nevertheless inspired great political distress.

Shortly thereafter, the savings and loan industry suffered serious setbacks requiring a multibillion dollar bailout from Congress. Problems arose in the saving and loan industry when Congress deregulated it, allowing companies to become overextended in poor investments, often engineered by unscrupulous managers. Public sentiment remained antagonistic to the new corporate culture, and the federal agencies responded with a series of highly publicized indictments based on laws against insider trading and other stock manipulation practices. The punishments were made more severe under laws against racketeering. In 1987 Ivan Boesky was sentenced to three years in prison and fined $100 million. Three years later, in a separate case,

Michael Milken, who is still credited with revolutionizing modern capital markets, pleaded guilty to six felony counts of fraud, unrelated to racketeering or insider trading. He was banned for life from securities trading, sentenced to two years in prison, and fined $47 million.

Critics point to the 1980s corporate culture as a "decade of greed" characterized by corporate raiders, leveraged buyouts, insider trading, and sophisticated securities fraud. Business practices, such as securities fraud, undermined confidence in the integrity of financial markets, while leveraged buyouts often left companies with huge debts. Supporters of these mergers noted that the movement forced companies to adjust to modern economic conditions by trimming middle management positions, reducing redundancy, and investing more heavily in research and development to maintain their competitive advantages. Some analysts attribute the stock market's explosive growth in the 1990s to the added efficiency of large corporations, which they claim provided the venture capital to launch newer technology sectors of the economy.

Other analysts doubt the impact of the 1980s business retrenchment on the 1990s boom. Additional tangible results of the market restructuring included the widespread use of consumer credit, the decline of large retail stores, and the rise of discount stores and national retail chains that specialize in one type of product, such as hardware, books, music, toys, or groceries. Whether these innovations represent benefits or detriments to the welfare of society is a matter of opinion.

With the creation of the Internet and the World Wide Web in the early 1990s, the rate of megamergers began to decline, while the rate of small combinations increased. New technology companies rose from obscurity to claim millions of dollars in profits, to be later purchased by a larger corporation. The success of the new technology sector had its own dangers. The Department of Justice and the attorneys general of several states filed an antitrust suit against software manufacturer Microsoft. Microsoft lost its much-publicized case, but won an important appeal in late 2001, which resulted in a more favorable settlement offer. After a decade of adjustment to the new technology sectors, the trend toward large corporate mergers continued, as Daimler-Benz joined with Chrysler in a $75 billion merger in 1998, and the Internet service provider AOL joined with media giant Time-Warner in a $165 billion merger in 2000.

In 2001 the technology-heavy NASDAQ index fell 40 percent during the first quarter, pulling the Dow Jones Industrial Average down by 10 percent. Some analysts attributed the drop to a shift in demand from personal computers toward alternative wireless technologies as well as unexpected plateaus in returns from electronic commerce. Others described it as a natural market adjustment stemming from the uncritical investment in technology firms that had no real profit potential, but relied instead on inflated confidence in future success. Most analysts remained convinced that the full extent of this technology revolution was still unfolding.

See also CRIME; ECONOMY; RACKETEER INFLUENCED AND CORRUPT ORGANIZATIONS ACT; TECHNOLOGY.

Further reading: Daniel Fischel, *Payback: The Conspiracy to Destroy Michael Milken and His Financial Revolution* (New York: HarperCollins, 1995); Robert Sobel, *Dangerous Dreamers: The Financial Innovators from Charles Merrill to Michael Milken* (New York: Wiley, 1993).

—Aharon W. Zorea

Byrd, Robert (1917–)

Since his election to the U.S. Senate, Robert Byrd has played an important role as a leader in the Democratic Party. He is the second-longest serving senator in U.S. history and is considered by many one of the greatest parliamentarians in the history of the Senate.

Born in 1917 in North Wilkesboro, North Carolina, he was left a virtual orphan after his mother died when he was one year old. His aunt and uncle raised him in West Virginia, living in various communities in the bituminous coalfields. Unable to afford college, he worked as a gas station attendant, a produce salesman, a meat cutter, and a welder. During World War II, Byrd contributed to the war effort by becoming a welder in wartime shipyards in Baltimore, Maryland, and Tampa, Florida. Byrd then joined the Ku Klux Klan to help win election to the West Virginia House of Delegates in 1946. (He later apologized publicly for his membership in the KKK.)

After serving two terms in the West Virginia House, he was elected to the U.S. Senate in 1959. In 1967 he was selected as secretary of the Democratic conference, and in 1971 as Senate Democratic whip. In 1977 he became Senate Majority Leader, a position he held from 1977 to 1980 and from 1987 to 1988. He was Senate Minority Leader from 1981 to 1986. Because of his parliamentary effectiveness, he played a critical role in shaping major legislation during those years. Although Byrd voted against the Civil Rights Act of 1964, he later endorsed affirmative action and women's rights. Also, as a leading senior senator, he was able to direct federal funding to his home state of West Virginia for public buildings, state highways, relief for unemployed coal miners, and education.

In 1988 Byrd surrendered Majority Leader status to become chairman of the Appropriations Committee. In 1989 he was elected president pro tempore of the U.S. Senate. His four-volume history of the U.S. Senate received much praise from scholarly critics. As senator, he has been perceived by his colleagues on the Democratic side as a centrist and a statesman.

He is married to his former high school sweetheart, Erma Ora James. They have two daughters, who are now married with children.

Further reading: Robert Byrd, *The Senate, 1789–1989*, 4 vols. (Washington, D.C.: U. S. Government Printing Office, 1989–1994).

—Christopher M. Gray

C

campaign finance

Elected officials are expected to represent the interests of their constituency regardless of its members' economic status. Even the appearance that wealthy contributors might have greater influence and access to politicians could undermine the public's confidence in their representative government. Consequently, Congress has enacted numerous regulations limiting types and kinds of campaign contributions. In 1925 the Corrupt Practices Act became the first consolidated federal law to address the issue of election campaign finance ethics. It required campaign treasurers to report all contributions of $100 or more; placed limits on candidate expenditures; and prohibited solicitation of funds from employees of government and government-related industries. The act was rarely enforced, and could be easily sidestepped.

The Federal Election Campaign Act (FECA) of 1971 reconsidered the question of federal campaign finances, establishing strict parameters on election spending for primaries, runoffs, general elections, and even party conventions. All candidates were required to provide full and timely disclosure reports, and specific limits were established on media advertising, and personal and individual contributions. Corporations and unions were barred from direct contributions, but were permitted to solicit funds from members, employees, and stockholders. Such donations could be used to pay for the overhead costs of political action committees (PACs), which in turn pay campaign expenses. The FECA was further amended in 1974 to include an option of public matching funds for presidential primaries and nominating conventions; spending limits for all federal elections; individual contribution caps of $1,000 per candidate; and an aggregate cap of $25,000 per year. In addition, PACs were permitted to contribute $5,000 per candidate, per election, and all limits on media advertising were removed. Congress created the Federal Election Commission (FEC) to administer and oversee campaign law.

In 1976 the U.S. SUPREME COURT upheld the main provisions of the FECA in *Buckley v. Valeo*, including individual contribution limits, disclosure requirements, and matching public funds. The Court further held that limits on individual candidate expenditures from their personal funds amounted to violations of the First Amendment guarantee of free speech. In 1988, the Court concluded in *Communication Workers of America v. Beck* that unions could not contribute funds to political candidates over the objections of due-paying nonmember employees. The clash between free speech and campaign finance reform intensified in 1998, when the Court ruled in *Colorado Republican Federal Campaign Committee v. Federal Election Committee* that contributions to political parties were independent of individual candidates' expenditures, and thus were not covered by legislative spending caps; this ruling legitimized a dramatic increase in these indirect, "soft" money contributions between 1992 and 1996 (222 percent) and again between 1996 and 2000 (71 percent). Even relative to total contributions, soft money increased from 18 percent in 1992 to 28 percent in 1996, and 40 percent in 2000.

Though individual congressmen proposed campaign finance reform bills during every session since 1974, the issue gained prominence in the 1984 and 1998 elections and became a subject of Ronald W. Reagan's farewell address in 1988. Senator John McCain (R-Ariz.) and Senator Russell Feingold (D-Wisc.), working in conjunction with Representatives Christopher Shays (R-Conn.) and Marty Meehan (D-Mass.), proposed the Bipartisan Campaign Reform Act of 1997, which would have barred all soft money contributions. This time, reform forces got a boost from the media attention given to accusations of fund-raising improprieties leveled against President WILLIAM J. CLINTON, as well as the exorbitant costs of running political campaigns, which often favored incumbent officeholders who usually found it easier to raise money than their challengers did.

Specifically, the McCain-Feingold bill forbade national parties, federal officeholders, and candidates from soliciting, receiving, or spending any funds that were not directly subject to federal election laws. It reiterated the prohibition on the use of federal buildings for fund-raising. Additionally, it included federal election year campaign activities that had previously not been under FEC jurisdiction, including voter registration drives, and get-out-the-vote efforts. A filibuster by Senate Republicans barred the bill from coming to a vote. It was reintroduced in 1999 and managed to pass the HOUSE OF REPRESENTATIVES, but was again blocked by Senate Republicans.

Senator McCain concentrated heavily on the issue of campaign finance during his primary bid for the Republican presidential nomination in 2000. Many in the media saw his successes at the start of the campaign as a popular mandate for campaign finance reform. The issue received prominent attention through the rest of the election, even after McCain suffered a defeat to Texas governor GEORGE W. BUSH, who explicitly opposed the McCain-Feingold bill. Despite the attention paid by media and politicians alike, the average amount of money raised in the Senate, House, and presidential campaigns for 2000 broke all previous records, totaling more than $2.2 billion. The public response was mixed. Polls consistently indicate that three-quarters of respondents want some form of campaign finance reform. Yet, from a field of 28 important political issues, campaign finance consistently ranked 24th throughout the 2000 election year. Nevertheless, Senator McCain and Congressman Shays submitted the same Bipartisan Campaign Finance Reform bill to the 107th Congress in June 2001. Nine months later it passed by a vote of 240-189 in the Republican-controlled House and by 60-40 in the Democratic-controlled Senate. President Bush signed it into law on March 27, 2002. On the same day, the National Rifle Association and Senator Mitch McConnell (R-Ky.) filed separate suits challenging, as a violation of the First Amendment, the "soft money" provision that prohibited independent organizations from advertising their interests during a campaign.

See also ELECTIONS; POLITICAL PARTIES.

—Aharon W. Zorea

Camp David accords

The historic Camp David accords were forged in 1978 between Israel and Egypt at the U.S. presidential retreat at Camp David, Maryland. The official agreement was signed on March 26, 1979, by Israeli prime minister Menachem Begin and Egyptian president Anwar el-Sadat. Under the pact, Israel agreed to return the Sinai peninsula to Egypt, a transfer that was not completed until 1982. In a joint letter, the two nations also agreed to negotiate Palestinian autonomy measures in the Israeli-occupied West Bank and Gaza Strip, but little progress was made on this issue until the 1990s, due to the other Arab states' dislike of the agreement.

Since the declaration of Israeli statehood in 1948, armed conflict has been a staple of Arab-Israeli relations. This armed conflict exploded in the Six-Day War of June 1967, which pitted Israel against Egypt, Syria, and Jordan. The next full eruption of conflict was the October War of 1973. This episode placed Israeli troops against a barrage of soldiers from Egypt, Syria, Jordan, Kuwait, Iraq, and Saudi Arabia. Both of these conflicts ended in Israeli victory.

The Six-Day War and the October War combined to make the Arab-Israeli conflict one of the most intractable political problems in the world. After each war, Israel attempted to turn conquered land into settlement areas. These settlements were located in the West Bank, Gaza, and the Sinai, and threatened to further undermine efforts at peace, because their existence linked Israeli domestic politics with retaining this conquered territory. Israel virtually ignored United Nations resolutions designed to make taking land during war illegal. The Arab states, although defeated in both major outbursts of violence, had demonstrated a strong military capability coupled with the intent to damage and even destroy Israel. Powers outside the Middle East were extremely interested in these events because of their coordination with an oil embargo. The Arab nations also cooperated in their refusal to recognize Israel as a nation. As such, they refused to undertake diplomatic relations with the Jewish state. Thus, by the mid-1970s both Israel and the Arab nations had established antagonistic and perpetually conflicting positions.

The United States searched for a diplomatic answer to the stalemate in the Middle East for many years, trying several programs such as U.S. pressure on Israel coupled with Soviet pressure on Egypt. The election of JAMES EARL CARTER, JR., created a new opportunity for U.S. diplomacy in the situation. He entered the White House with an open mind regarding the Middle East, and his chief diplomatic advisers saw the situation in a different light than had previous administrations. President Carter's plan for the Middle East focused on restoration of the pre-1967 borders, full normalization of Arab-Israeli relations (coupled with subsequent recognition of Israel's inherent right to existence), a reconvened Geneva conference on a comprehensive settlement, the right of self-determination for Palestinians in a Palestinian homeland, the full participation of the Soviet Union in peace negotiations, and the full participation of the Palestine Liberation Organization (PLO). President Carter met with the nations' individual leaders in an attempt to sell his plan, but all Middle Eastern parties with the exception of President Sadat of Egypt were reluctant to pursue the new president's proposals.

U.S. president Jimmy Carter meets with Egyptian president Anwar el-Sadat at Camp David, Maryland, September 1978 (Hulton/Archive)

In September 1978 President and Mrs. Carter welcomed President Sadat and Prime Minister Begin to Camp David, where the three would meet for several days in an attempt to reach a peaceful understanding regarding the Middle East. Initially President Carter met individually with each of the leaders, assuring each that he understood their security concerns and that he would work toward solid guarantees for them. Both sides were resolute about their security needs and demonstrated no indication of flexibility. On the second day of the conference, President Sadat presented President Carter with a "Framework for the Comprehensive Peace," which examined in detail every major issue and presented a hard line toward Israel. President Sadat also gave President Carter a memo outlining concessions that Egypt would accept. President Sadat expressed to President Carter his trust that the American president would use the concessions at the appropriate time.

The following day Prime Minister Begin and President Sadat met face to face with President Carter. While these high-level meetings were occurring, Secretary of State Cyrus Vance was meeting with his counterparts in the Israeli delegation. In all of the meetings, Israel's overwhelming desire to retain land became apparent. On the fifth day of the conference President Carter developed a list of "Necessary Elements of Agreement" for the group developing the American peace proposal. At the conclusion of the first week of meetings, President Carter outlined his priorities: 1) sovereignty in the West Bank and Gaza would not be resolved at this time, 2) the settlement question would have to be added to any agreement, and 3) an Israeli agreement to withdraw from the Sinai would be concluded at these meetings.

Signing the Camp David accords began rather than concluded a path to peace. On September 27, 1978, the Israeli Knesset voted to approve the Camp David accords and to withdraw the Israeli settlements in the occupied Sinai. Three major problems still existed after the meeting at Camp David. These were: the timetable for Israeli withdrawal from the Sinai, the exchange of ambassadors, and the future of the West Bank/Gaza territories.

See also FOREIGN POLICY.

—Leah Blakey

capital punishment

Capital punishment is the most severe form of penalty that a state can impose on a criminal. Capital CRIMES are those that require a punishment of death, which in the United States is carried out by hanging, electrocution, gas, firing squad, and most commonly, lethal injection. The American criminal justice system has traditionally recognized capital punishment as appropriate for the protection of civil society. In 1967, in response to numerous lawsuits questioning its arbitrary implementation, the courts imposed a moratorium on all death sentences until they could determine whether or not the penalty violated constitutional due process and whether it amounted to cruel and unusual punishment. In 1972 the U.S. SUPREME COURT decided in *Furman v. Georgia* that the current justice system had no standards by which to distinguish capital offenses from noncapital crimes. In this light, the Court ruled that the implementation was arbitrary and constituted a violation of the Eighth Amendment's prohibition of cruel and unusual punishment. Throughout the country, death row prisoners had their sentences commuted to life in prison. Thirty-five states quickly enacted new statutes establishing standards for capital crimes, and in 1976 the Court accepted these modifications as constitutional in *Gregg v. Georgia.* The following year, in *Coker v. Georgia,* the Court ruled that the death penalty for rape was "grossly disproportionate and excessive," further concluding that capital crimes must cause death. Since then, with the exception of treason, murder is the only capital offense approved by the Court. During the 1980s, several states enacted legislation making nonlethal crimes, such as car-jacking and drug-dealing, capital offenses. As of 2002, however, the Supreme Court had not tested these cases.

Public opinion is mixed on whether the United States should continue to allow capital punishment. Supporters rely on five general arguments to justify the death penalty: for the defense of society, for justice, for deterrence, for retribution, and for revenge. Many conservative groups support the death penalty as necessary for the sake of justice, while stressing the need for deterrence and defense of society. Opponents argue that capital punishment violates human rights, is arbitrarily implemented, and inherently is cruel and unusual. Traditionally, opponents tended to be political and social liberals. During the 1990s, however, these stereotypes were challenged. President WILLIAM J. CLINTON and his vice president, ALBERT GORE, JR., vocally supported capital punishment. In contrast, the Roman Catholic Church, which traditionally tolerated the penalty, has become outspoken in its opposition. During his 1999 tour of the United States, the conservative Pope John Paul II directly linked capital punishment and abortion as elements of a modern "culture of death." The advent of DNA tracking in criminal investigations has also served to raise doubts about the reliability of the American judicial system to impose such a permanent penalty. One 1999 study examined appellate briefs over a 23-year period and discovered that prejudicial errors were discovered in 68 percent of the capital cases. Though not all of these errors led to a reversal, 7 percent of the defendants were later found to be innocent. In 1999 this trend prompted the Republican governor of Illinois, George H. Ryan, to declare an emergency moratorium on capital sentences until his state's 66 percent error rate could be more closely examined.

See also EVANGELICAL CHRISTIANS; JUDICIAL WATCH; LIBERALISM; MORALITY.

—Aharon W. Zorea

Carter, James Earl, Jr. (Jimmy) (1924–)

James Earl Carter, Jr., popularly known as "Jimmy," served as the 39th president of the United States. He was just the type of political outsider, representing integrity and reform, that the public eagerly wanted after the WATERGATE SCANDAL and America's loss in the VIETNAM WAR. In 1976, with the help of his running mate, Senator WALTER F. MONDALE of Minnesota, Carter narrowly defeated Republican incumbent GERALD R. FORD. Once in office, however, Carter's political inexperience hampered his efforts at lasting reform; his administration was frustrated by high inflation and unemployment rates, a debilitating energy crisis, and a weakened military and diplomatic presence overseas. Renominated by the Democratic Party in 1980, Carter was soundly defeated by Republican challenger RONALD W. REAGAN. In his later service as a private citizen, he earned international respect as an elder statesman, selfless humanitarian, and nonpartisan mediator.

Jimmy Carter was the first president elected from the Deep South since before the Civil War. He was born to James Earl Carter, Sr., and Lillian Gordy Carter on October 1, 1924, in the small farming town of Plains, which was little more than a railway stop located in southwestern Georgia. His father was a peanut farmer and a small store owner who later became involved in local politics and eventually won a seat in Georgia's House of Representatives, where he served until he died. His mother was a registered nurse and proved to be the stronger influence in Jimmy's life as a model of public service, including volunteering for two years' work for the Peace Corps in India at the age of 68.

While still in high school, Jimmy decided to attend the United States Naval Academy at Annapolis, Maryland. He received an appointment in 1942 and later graduated in the top 10 percent of his class. Shortly thereafter, he married his hometown sweetheart, Rosalynn Smith. During the six years that Carter served as a naval officer, they added three sons to the family: John William (born 1947), James Earl III (born 1950), and Donnel Jeffrey (born 1952). A daughter, Amy Lynn, was born much later in 1967. While in the navy, Carter worked as a training officer aboard the USS *Mississippi* and volunteered for submarine duty for two years aboard the USS *Pomfret.* In 1951 Carter was assigned to the first vessel built after World War II, and earned his qualifications for submarine commander. The next year, he joined the nuclear submarine program under Admiral Hyman Rickover. After attending graduate-level courses in nuclear physics at Union College in Schenectady, New York, Carter returned to the Naval Reactors Branch of the U.S. Atomic Energy Commission in Washington, D.C., where he assisted in the design and development of the power plant in the nation's first nuclear submarines, including the USS *Seawolf*. When his father died in 1953, Carter resigned his commission and returned to Georgia to take over the family business.

Racial segregation loomed as the most pressing issue facing southerners during the 1950s, and Jimmy Carter took a courageous stand against it. Carter suffered social and economic backlash when he became the only white man in Plains who refused to join the pro-segregation White Citizens' Council; his white neighbors organized a temporary boycott of his business. In 1962 Carter ran for a seat in the Georgia State Senate but lost the primary by a few votes. He appealed the results, arguing that election fraud, including stuffed ballot boxes, robbed him of his true victory. Carter won the appeal and eventually won the election. Along the way, he also made a name for himself as a reformer opposed to corruption and government waste. He advocated more efficient government planning and bureaucracy, and more critical consideration of the budgets.

After winning reelection in 1964, he immediately set his sights on higher posts. In 1966 Carter announced his plans to run for Georgia governor. The decision was ill timed, and Carter lost the gubernatorial nomination during the primaries, far behind the popular segregationist, Lester Maddox, who eventually became governor.

Carter later said that the 1966 defeat caused him to be disillusioned with politics and life in general. His sister Ruth, who was a Christian missionary, helped him get over the disappointment and further guided Jimmy toward a deeper religious experience. From that point on, Carter freely referred to his faith, "born-again Christian," as an integral part of his political decision making. He returned to the campaign trail in 1970 to run for governor, this time with much more caution. After a hard-fought campaign, Carter won the election by appealing to rural conservatives, but in so doing he alienated his black constituents and carried less than 10 percent of the state's black voters in the general election.

Once in office, however, Governor Carter quickly returned to his social liberalism and actively spoke against segregation, promoted civil rights by specifically appointing women and minorities to bureaucratic positions in the state government, and even displayed a portrait of the recently martyred civil rights leader, Martin Luther King, Jr., in the state capital. He also pushed for strict banking regulations and stronger consumer protection laws, state-sponsored health care, increased funding for education, and wide-reaching reforms of the state's prisons and mental health facilities. His most highly praised achievement, however, was the reorganization of the state's 300 agencies into 22 larger departments, which earned him an antiwaste reputation. He publicly announced his candidacy for the president for the 1976 election shortly thereafter.

The pool of Democratic presidential hopefuls included nine other candidates with considerably more national experience than Carter had. Yet Carter presented the fresh image of an honest, down-to-earth politician, a born-again Christian, and gentleman planter. This appealed to many Americans who had become weary of the Watergate scandal. Moreover, Carter's emphasis on domestic reform, economic security, and moral values provided welcome change for those discouraged by American involvement in Vietnam. Furthermore, many Democrats, anxious about the threat posed by George Wallace, sought a southern politician who could take away voters from the former governor of Alabama. Carter won the Iowa caucuses by organizing a grassroots campaign, which also mobilized evangelical voters. He then went on to win the primary in New Hampshire and finished first in 17 of the 30 primaries he entered, winning the Democratic nomination. He also chose Walter F. Mondale, senator from Minnesota, as his running mate.

James Earl Carter, Jr. *(James E. Carter Presidential Library)*

The combination resounded with the public, and Jimmy Carter enjoyed a 30-point lead immediately following the Democratic convention.

It did not last, however, and by the time President Gerald Ford accepted his party's nomination, Carter's lead had dwindled significantly. Carter promised to bring an outsider's perspective to the White House, as well as promising a more muscular defense and foreign policy. Carter also criticized Ford for failing to address the problems of an economic recession and high inflation.

Ford took advantage of Carter's tendency to rely on ambiguities in his campaign speeches by shifting the national debate away from the public image of integrity toward a more specific discussion of the issues. Ford argued Carter's platform was dangerous to the economy because it would produce higher inflation and require higher taxes. By November, Carter barely edged out Ford with 49.9 percent of the popular vote to Ford's 47.9 percent.

Carter took a decidedly populist agenda to the office, which he put into effect immediately; he stripped the White House of many of its traditional formalities, including suspending the playing of "Hail to the Chief" in his presence, and restricting the use of his portrait in government offices. He also sold the presidential yacht, limited White House limousine service, discontinued long-standing traditions of presidential balls and state dinners, and significantly reduced the White House staff. He also tried to streamline the federal agencies in much the same way he had redesigned Georgia's state agencies. The federal bureaucracy, however, held such a great constituent base that Congress was reluctant to act, and Carter was unable to force the changes. He fulfilled his campaign promise by creating a Department of Energy and a Department of Education. Congress, however, rejected his proposal for a new department for consumer protection.

Despite Democratic control of Congress, Carter suffered a strained relationship with both houses. Though Carter's status as a Washington outsider helped elect him to the White House, it served to undermine his presidency in the long run; he had little success in his political relations with Congress. These administrative handicaps were magnified by the especially severe winter in 1977, which prompted serious shortages of natural gas. Carter responded with a number of emergency measures, including asking Congress for temporary authority to regulate prices and oil supplies; enactment of special "windfall" taxes on oil companies to discourage allegations of price gouging; economic incentives for research into alternative energy sources; and a national conservation campaign. Despite the flurry of federal enactments, the energy crisis produced a dramatic rise in inflation. Carter also imposed additional credit restraints, which some critics blamed for causing declines in auto and housing sales. An unusual combination of high inflation and market recession, which became known as "stagflation," ensued, and the public sentiment turned strongly against Carter's administration. By July 1980, Carter received the lowest approval rating of any president to that date.

In FOREIGN POLICY, Carter found mixed success. Foreign policy under Carter was marked by two shifts. Initially Carter, through his secretary of state, Cyrus Vance, pursued a policy of making human rights and democratic principles the basis and measure of American foreign policy. As a consequence, anticommunism in foreign policy was downplayed. Escalating confrontation with the Soviet Union, especially after its invasion of Afghanistan in December 1979, led Carter to take a more aggressive stance toward the Soviet Union. Still, Carter enjoyed a number of foreign policy successes.

In 1977 Carter replaced the 1903 PANAMA CANAL Treaty with a new version that recognized Panama's complete sovereignty over the Canal Zone within 20 years. The treaty was controversial, since many Americans feared this forfeiture would leave the United States vulnerable. Pointing to this, as well as to Carter's earlier decision to pardon all Vietnam-era draft evaders and his refusal to approve development of the neutron bomb and a B-1 bomber plane, critics accused Carter of being soft on defense matters.

Carter's greatest success in foreign policy came when he brokered an unprecedented peace agreement between Egyptian president Anwar el-Sadat and Israeli prime minister Menachem Begin that later resulted in the signing of a peace treaty on March 26, 1979.

This was arguably the high point in Carter's foreign policy. In the summer of 1979 the Soviet Union invaded Afghanistan, and U.S.-Soviet relations deteriorated rapidly afterward. In response, he discontinued the second round of Strategic Arms Limitations Talks (SALT II) with the Soviet Union and accelerated the military arms buildup that he had begun earlier. He also boycotted the 1980 Olympics in Moscow (which led to the Soviet boycott of the Los Angeles Olympics in 1984). Carter tried to improve relations with China by formally recognizing their revolutionary Communist government and by severing ties with the traditionally American-supported Nationalist regime in Taiwan.

Carter's foreign policy came under further criticism when militant Islamic revolutionaries, led by fundamentalist Ayatollah Ruhollah Khomeini, overthrew the shah of Iran, Mohammad Reza Pahlavi, who had ruled for 37 years. After the shah fled to the United States, a group of Iranian supporters of the ayatollah stormed the U.S. embassy in Tehran in November 1979 and took 66 American hostages. Negotiations for the release of the hostages moved slowly and were aggravated by an abortive military rescue attempt in April 1980. The hostages remained captive throughout the remainder of Carter's administration and plagued his campaign for reelection.

Further damaging Carter, the president's brother, Billy, was discovered to have received $220,000 from Libya for unknown reasons. Even though a later congressional investigation found that American foreign relations were unaffected by the payment, the appearance of impropriety involving a Middle Eastern government hostile to the United States undermined Carter's credibility.

President Carter received his party's nomination for the 1980 presidential election, but only after a formidable challenge by Senator Ted Kennedy (D-Mass.) who had rallied the party's liberal wing to his side. The fight with Kennedy left the Democrats bitterly divided. After winning the nomination, Carter told aides that he believed he could easily defeat the Republican nominee, RONALD W. REAGAN. His underestimation of Reagan proved his undoing on election day. Reagan won in a landslide, winning 50 percent of the popular vote to Carter's 41 percent of the vote, and third-party candidate John Anderson's popular vote of 9 percent. The Republicans also gained control of the Senate for the first time in 26 years.

Carter's approach to social problems proved more effective after he left office than it had been while he was president. In 1982 he founded the Carter Center at Emory University in Atlanta, Georgia, where he also taught. The center dedicates itself to championing human rights and to peaceful resolution of conflicts around the globe. During the 1980s, Carter and his wife became known as spokespeople for numerous charitable causes, including Habitat for Humanity, which is a nonprofit organization that builds houses for the poor. By the 1990s, Carter had assumed the role of elder statesman; he was asked to monitor elections in South American countries in 1989–90 and in Haiti in 1994. He also served as mediator for the UNITED NATIONS after North Korea's violation of the 1968 Nuclear Nonproliferation Treaty in 1994. He was repeatedly called upon during the many armistices of the Balkan conflicts of the late 1990s. Carter was awarded the Nobel Peace Prize in 2002.

See also CAMP DAVID ACCORDS; ECONOMY; EVANGELICAL CHRISTIANS; FOREIGN CORRUPT PRACTICES ACT (1977); IRANIAN HOSTAGE CRISIS; TAIWAN.

Further reading: James Earl Carter Jr., *Keeping Faith: Memoirs of a President* (New York: Bantam Books, 1983); ———, *The Blood of Abraham: Insights into the Middle East* (Boston: Houghton Mifflin Company, 1985); ———, *Turning Point: A Candidate, a State, and a Nation Come of Age* (Boston: Houghton Mifflin Company, 1993); ———, *Talking Peace* (New York: Random House, 1993); Kenneth

E. Morris, *Jimmy Carter, American Moralist* (Athens: University of Georgia Press, 1996).

—Aharon W. Zorea

Catholic Bishops' Letter (The Challenge of Peace) (1983)

On May 3, 1983, the National Conference of Catholic Bishops promulgated a pastoral letter on war and peace, *The Challenge of Peace: God's Promise and Our Response.* Addressing Roman Catholics and non-Catholics alike, the American bishops restated the moral implications of war, nuclear stockpiling, and other policies of nuclear deterrence. The letter came during the last phase of the COLD WAR, which had culminated in a renewed ARMS RACE between the United States and the Soviet Union. Furthermore, the letter appeared in the midst of RONALD W. REAGAN's first term in office, when he had taken a tough stance against the Soviet Union, calling it an "evil empire." The letter, in effect, encouraged peace activists who were calling for a "nuclear freeze" in the arms race, while at the same time creating great controversy among anti-Soviet conservatives who supported the administration defense buildup.

From the start of his pontificate in 1978, Pope John Paul II sought to reduce the threat of nuclear war and promote the cause of global peace. In two addresses to the United Nations, the pope recognized that nuclear deterrence could temporarily prevent war, but warned that it was ultimately unsatisfactory because it relied on the threat of global destruction. He asked that any future efforts toward peace include a genuine commitment to disarmament and implored the assembled nations to devote as much energy to spiritual renewal as they did to technological innovation.

The National Conference of Catholic Bishops applied the pontiff's principles specifically to the policies of the United States. *The Challenge of Peace* recognized the nation's right and duty to protect itself from unjust aggression but condemned even the defensive use of nuclear weapons because they indiscriminately kill innocent civilians and noncombatants. The bishops urged the United States to pursue bilateral verifiable agreements that would halt the testing, production, and deployment of nuclear weapon technology; significantly reduce existing stockpiles; encourage global restrictions on the sales of conventional weapons; and establish a global authority with which to police the nonproliferation of all weapons of mass destruction.

The bishops' letter came under immediate attack by conservative groups who believed that the call for disarmament was naïve and counterproductive. NEOCONSERVATIVES such as Max Kampelman and Roman Catholic conservatives such as George Weigel criticized the bishops in a well-publicized campaign and countered that unilateral disarmament was dangerous and that the Soviet Union had failed to live up to arms reduction treaties in the past. Realistic arms control, these opponents maintained, could only be accomplished by tough-minded negotiations with the Soviet Union that allowed for on-site inspection and verified arms reductions.

See also ANTI-BALLISTIC MISSILE TREATY; DEFENSE POLICY; FOREIGN POLICY; IRANIAN HOSTAGE CRISIS; KISSINGER, HENRY; NUCLEAR FREEZE MOVEMENT.

—Aharon W. Zorea

censorship

In the United States, censorship refers to government restriction of public exposure to certain forms of expression. The First Amendment guarantees the individual rights of free speech and a free press, but it has never been interpreted to mean that all forms of expression are legal, or that the press is free from all obstruction. The courts have generally accepted laws barring citizens from engaging in activities that might harm the public good; for example, shouting "fire" in a crowded theater when there is no danger may cause a stampede; public obscenity may offend public sensibilities; publication of troop movements may compromise national security; and the publication of unsubstantiated rumors may inflict irreversible damage on another's reputation. These types of acts have always been liable to censorship. The question of censorship, therefore, involves a balance between an individual's right of expression through speech or the press, and the society's need for public order.

Freedom of the press has been most challenged when newspapers threaten public order or national security, yet even in these cases, the Court has tended to favor the press. In 1969 the Court ruled in *Brandenburg v. Ohio* that the First Amendment protects radical papers that call for violence and the use of force. Two years later, in *New York Times v. United States* (1971), better known as the Pentagon Papers case, the Court concluded that the government must assume the "heavy burden of showing justification" for censoring even classified information. Since 1971, the issue of censorship of the press has largely been settled, though the advent of cable TELEVISION and the INTERNET has brought new dimensions to the debate, particularly as it relates to legal process and obscenity. In 1995 the widely publicized murder trial of former football and television star O. J. Simpson prompted many observers to criticize the MEDIA for their exhaustive coverage, which may have unduly influenced the jury's verdict.

Critics charged the television networks with influencing the national presidential elections in 1980, 1988, 1996, and 2000, when they called the outcome before all the polls had closed; critics argued that many undecided voters changed their decision during the last hours in order to claim support for the "winning side."

Whether the framers of the First Amendment initially intended protection only for the content of political expression and not subjects that might violate public mores is a topic of heated debate among constitutional scholars. Those opposing restrictions on free speech, even involving the publication and dissemination of pornographic materials, argue that MORALITY cannot be legislated in a pluralistic society and therefore censorship on the basis of obscenity falsely imposes a narrow Judeo-Christian view of decency, and thus severely limits protected forms of artistic expression. Supporters replied that the claim of artistic expression was only a façade used by the sex industry to legalize pornography and desensitize society to the dangers of obscenity, which include child prostitution, sexual addiction, and the breakdown in family relationships.

In the 1957 decision *Roth v. United States*, the Supreme Court ruled that obscenity was not protected under the First Amendment, and that states could enact laws prohibiting the mailing of "lewd, lascivious, or filthy" materials. Seven years later, however, the Court loosened its standards of obscenity with *Jacobellis v. Ohio* (1964), which established the test for obscenity as "whether to the average person, applying contemporary community standards, the dominant theme of the material, taken as a whole, appeals to prurient interests." This definition opened the way for changing definitions of obscenity and, as a result of the "SEXUAL REVOLUTION" of the late 1960s and early 1970s, most courts have tended to find that "community standards" have relaxed, favoring the rights of individual expression over the needs for public censorship. Congress responded to increasing technological innovations, permitting easier distribution of PORNOGRAPHY in the home through cable and Internet connections, when it passed the Communications Decency Act (CDA) of 1996, which criminalized the "knowing" transmission of "obscene or indecent" messages to any recipient less than 18 years of age. The next year, in *Reno v. ACLU* (1997), the Court struck down the CDA because the language did not clearly define obscenity and therefore violated First Amendment protections.

In the 1990s American society embraced with unprecedented enthusiasm an increasing tolerance of moral diversity. Critics argued that, though the new atmosphere promotes tolerance of controversial subjects, it includes an unspoken censorship under more traditional Judeo-Christian values. Many Roman Catholics were offended by artworks that they felt mocked their faith, and by works that were explicit attacks on it. Critics in the field of academia feared that the resulting demand for POLITI-

CAL CORRECTNESS severely censored what they could teach. Free-speech advocates for the new atmosphere claimed that critics had exaggerated the offense, and that society benefited from controversy since it inspires constructive debate. The courts have not addressed the issue of de facto, or "reverse," censorship and have shown no indication they are likely to do so in the future.

See also SUPREME COURT.

—Aharon W. Zorea

"Chicago Eight"

The "Chicago Eight" were eight radical activists who were tried for conspiracy to instigate a riot at the Democratic National Convention in Chicago in August 1968. The alleged conspirators included Tom Hayden and Rennie Davis of Students for a Democratic Society (SDS); Abbie Hoffman and Jerry Rubin, cofounders of the Youth International (Yippie) Party; Dave Dellinger, a pacifist and leader of the fall 1969 mobilization demonstration in Washington, D.C.; John Froines, a radical activist professor; Lee Weiner, a street organizer and movement activist; and Black Panther Party leader Bobby Seale. After Seale was gagged and chained to his chair by the order of the judge, his case was separated from the other seven.

These men, part of the National Mobilization to End the War in Vietnam ("The Mobe"), organized more than 5,000 activists to participate in protest activities throughout the week of the Democratic Party convention in Chicago. Yippies Hoffman and Rubin planned street theater and demonstrations, including presenting a pig as their presidential nominee and threatening to pour LSD in the city water supply. Chicago mayor Richard Daley vowed to maintain order and reinforced his police force with armored vehicles and additional men. On the night of August 28, Chicago police confronted protesters jamming North Michigan Boulevard. Using clubs and tear gas, the police injured many activists, other bystanders, and more than 60 television cameramen and journalists. Images of bloodied protestors and rampaging police filled the evening news coverage that poured into American households. These images subsequently damaged the campaign of Democratic Party nominee Hubert Humphrey and helped win the election for Richard M. Nixon, the Republican Party nominee, who ran on a campaign calling for "Law and Order," as well as national reconciliation.

The Walker Commission, appointed to investigate the violent events, concluded that the Chicago police had provoked the crowd and had been encouraged by Mayor Daley. The commission's report found that they had engaged in a "police riot." Despite this finding, Chicago authorities arrested the "Chicago Eight" for conspiracy to commit a riot.

The trial itself was politicized from the beginning, because it highlighted President Nixon's campaign to reassure Americans who were disturbed by campus unrest, racial violence, and the apparent lack of patriotism of antiwar activists. The controversial behavior of both the defendants and Judge Julius Hoffman quickly turned the trial, held in Chicago from October 1969 to March 1970, into a media circus. Six of the eight defendants were convicted on various charges. All convictions were overturned on appeal because of Judge Hoffman's alleged bias and procedural errors.

See also ANTIWAR MOVEMENT; VIETNAM WAR.

—William L. Glankler

Christian Coalition

Founded in 1989 by Marion Gordon "Pat" Robertson, Christian Coalition (CC) is a grassroots political movement comprised of conservative EVANGELICAL CHRISTIANS. Robertson, a religious leader who first became a candidate for the 1988 Republican nomination, was defeated by Vice President GEORGE H. W. BUSH.

After the demise of Jerry Falwell's MORAL MAJORITY in 1989 and the apparent foundering of the Christian Right, Pat Robertson, along with his associate Ralph Reed, proposed the formation of an organization for Christian grassroots activism and an "American Congress of Christian Citizens" at an organizational meeting held in Atlanta on September 25, 1989. Under the name "Christian Coalition," the group decided to follow both proposals, but by March 1990, the Congress approach was dropped, and the group focused solely on grassroots action.

Christian Coalition's organizing mission was to represent evangelical and "pro-family" Roman Catholic Christians at the local, state, and federal levels, to speak publicly and issue media statements, to train leaders for political and social action, to provide political information to constituents, and to protest alleged anti-Christian bias and defend the legal rights of Christians. Specific goals include anti-ABORTION and anti-PORNOGRAPHY legislation, support for local control of EDUCATION, tax reform, and protecting religious freedom. Initial membership figures in 1990 claimed 25,000 Christian Coalition members. This figure climbed to 57,000 by the end of 1990, with 125 local chapters and an annual budget of $2.8 million. By December 1996 the organization reported receipt of $24.9 million in donations from supporters. In October 2000, the organization purported to represent over 2 million members and supporters, had an affiliate in every state, and over 2,000 local chapters.

Christian Coalition utilizes TELEVISION broadcasts and maintains its own INTERNET site. Here interested persons can participate on-line in citizen activism, be alerted to pending legislative information, and respond to the national organization, various members of Congress, the MEDIA, or their local chapter.

The CC regularly produces three publications. The *Congressional Scorecard* is published semiannually, and shows the voting records of senators and representatives on conservative issues chosen by the Christian Coalition. State affiliates produce similar materials regarding voting in the state legislatures. *Religious Rights Watch,* published monthly, is a single-page announcement that reports violations of the legal rights of Christians. *Christian American,* initiated in 1990 as a quarterly newsletter, is the principal vehicle of communication from the national organization. In 1991 the newsletter format was changed to a monthly tabloid newspaper featuring a section by Robertson, as well as syndicated columnist like PHYLLIS SCHLAFLY and Cal Thomas. The publication changed again in 1995 to a magazine format published six times a year with content similar to its predecessor, but less confrontational in its delivery.

The Christian Coalition opened a lobbying office in 1993 in Washington, D.C., to keep track of legislation, influence administration officials and Congress, work in association with other lobbying groups, and represent the CC before the national media. The CC reportedly spent $5.9 million on Washington lobbying activities in the first half of 1996. Through this office, information is disseminated to constituents through *Christian Coalition Live,* the Internet, e-mail, fax, and direct mail.

Most of the CC constituency identifies with the platform of the Republican Party. At the 1996 Republican National Convention, the Christian Coalition maintained a sophisticated communication system that connected floor whips to the CC members among the delegates. For the 2000 presidential election, the Coalition published a goal of recruiting 100,000 volunteers to serve as liaisons between their churches and local CC chapters, and to distribute 70 million voter guides to have information in every congressional district. These actions have not gone unnoticed by watchdog groups, and in 1996 the Federal Election Commission (FEC) filed a civil lawsuit against the Christian Coalition for illegally aiding the 1990, 1992, and 1994 Republican campaigns. After losing this lawsuit in 1999, the Christian Coalition reorganized.

See also POLITICAL ACTION COMMITTEE; POLITICAL PARTIES; RELIGION.

Further reading: Robert Boston, *The Most Dangerous Man in America? Pat Robertson and the Rise of the Christian Coalition* (Amherst, N.Y.: Prometheus Books, 1996); Justin Watson, *The Christian Coalition: Dreams of Restoration, Demands for Recognition* (New York: St. Martin's Press, 1997).

—Michele Rutledge

Christianity   See religion

Chrysler Corporation Loan Guarantee Act (1979)

In 1979 Chrysler Corporation was on the verge of bankruptcy, and the U.S. government agreed to provide the company with $1.5 billion in federal loan guarantees under the Chrysler Corporation Loan Guarantee Act of 1979. This bailout, which was passed by Congress in December 1979 and signed into law by President JAMES EARL CARTER, JR., on January 7, 1980, was the largest amount of direct federal assistance ever given to a private corporation.

Chrysler, along with Ford and General Motors, had deteriorated as costs of meeting federal regulations governing emission controls and fuel economy increased, while the economy suffered the recessions of the 1970s, and the cost of oil rose due to the OPEC embargoes. Chrysler argued that government regulations had affected Chrysler unfairly because it produced fewer cars than Ford and General Motors, making the extra cost per vehicle higher. Chrysler's new chairman, Lee Iacocca, who joined the company in 1978 from Ford, also admitted that Chrysler had a record of bad management. It had left the company unprepared to meet its commitments, as foreign automobile imports, especially from Japan, entered the country to meet consumer demand for fuel-efficient cars following the oil price increases. In the third quarter of 1979 Chrysler reported a net loss of $460.6 million and a projected loss for the year of $1.5 billion, more than any business had lost at that time.

Chrysler approached Congress for federal aid, sparking an intense debate on the role of the government in a free-market economy. The resulting act provided Chrysler with $1.5 billion in loan guarantees on condition that the company could raise another $2 billion. In granting assistance, proponents in Congress argued that the cost to taxpayers of a Chrysler bankruptcy, in the form of substantial unemployment, economic distress, worker compensation, and the loss of tax revenues, necessitated government intervention. Proponents further stressed the importance of maintaining a strong national auto industry in the face of increasing overseas competition.

Opponents of the act argued that the government should not be in the business of bailing out a private company, in effect, its wealthy stockholders. At this time a fierce public debate over the role of government in the marketplace arose, as business groups and conservative organizations called for further economic deregulation (started in the Carter administration), increased fiscal responsibility in Congress, and downsizing of government in general. At the same time, some economists, such as Robert Reich, were calling for increased government planning along the lines of the "Japanese" model, in which the government subsidized private corporations and industrial development.

Following the federal bailout, Chrysler used the $3.5 billion to drastically reduce operating costs, develop a new range of fuel-efficient vehicles, and mount an aggressive advertising campaign. In 1981 Chrysler showed a small profit and by 1984 announced record profits of more than $2.4 billion, having paid off the federal loan guarantees seven years early.

See also AUTOMOBILE INDUSTRY; BUSINESS; ECONOMY.

—Stephen Hardman

Civil Liberties Act (1988)

The Civil Liberties Act of 1988, signed into law by President RONALD W. REAGAN, authorized reparation payments to all Japanese Americans and Alaskan Aleuts who were interned, relocated, or evacuated from their homes during World War II. Representative THOMAS FOLEY (D-Wash.) introduced the measure to the House with 125 cosponsors on January 6, 1987. The bill officially recognized that the United States committed a "grave injustice" when it uprooted more than 120,000 citizens and permanent residents of Japanese ancestry, and Alaskan Aleuts living on certain islands during World War II and relocated them in internment camps. It further recognized that they were not responsible for any acts of espionage or sabotage, nor did they pose any security risk. The bill acknowledged that the actions were "motivated by racial prejudice, wartime hysteria, and a failure of political leadership." It apologized on behalf of the nation for the wrongs committed and requested the president to offer full pardons for any Japanese Americans convicted of violating the laws or executive orders related to the internment process. It further authorized the U.S. Treasury to offer reparation payments of $20,000 to each Japanese American, and $12,000 for affected Aleuts who suffered as a result of these wartime measures.

In August 1987 the bill passed the House by a vote of 243-141. By April of the following year, the Senate approved the bill by a vote of 69-27. It was signed into law August 10, and the Office of Redress Administration (ORA) was formed to advertise for, identify, and find all those who might be eligible for reparation payments. The law provided a window of 10 years for all eligible individuals to submit their claims. Before officially closing on February 5, 1999, the office paid out 82,219 claims, leaving 79 claims pending. An additional 133 cases involving Japanese Americans who had been removed from Latin America could not be processed under existing laws. Ten days before the ORA closed, the federal government set-

tled the claims of these Latin-American Japanese in *Mochizuki v. United States*, which allowed partial settlements of $5,000. On May 14, Congress authorized emergency funds with which to pay all outstanding claims.

See also ALASKA NATIVE CLAIM SETTLEMENT ACT; ASIAN AMERICANS; NATIVE AMERICANS; WAR POWERS ACT.

—Aharon W. Zorea

Civil Rights Act (1991)

Signed into law on November 21, 1991, by President GEORGE H. W. BUSH after months of public debate over civil rights issues, the Civil Rights Act was a compromise measure with bipartisan support that amended and clarified certain aspects of the Civil Rights Act of 1964. Its purpose was to strengthen federal civil rights laws, to provide for damages in employment discrimination cases, and to clarify provisions of the 1964 act relating to "disparate impact" actions. Essentially, this congressional action on civil rights was a response to decisions by the U.S. SUPREME COURT that limited the scope and weakened the protections of federal civil rights statutes.

The Civil Rights Act of 1991 achieved this goal by reversing a series of U.S. Supreme Court decisions. For example, it reversed the Court's decision in *Ward's Cove Packing Co. v. Antonio* (1989) in which the Court ruled that an employer could justify a discriminatory practice by proving that it was a "business necessity." The new act eliminated the claim of "business necessity" as a justification for intentional discrimination. Additionally, in reversing the Court's decision in *Patterson v. McLean Credit Union* (1989), the 1991 legislation broadened the language of the Civil Rights Act of 1964 to extend the law's protection to employees' claims of post-hiring racial harassment. Finally, the new legislation narrowed the opportunities for challenging affirmative action policies in the courts by reversing the Court's decision in *Martin v. Wilks* (1989).

The Civil Rights Act of 1991 had political repercussions, as well. Because it clarified and broadened the civil rights protections of previous legislation, especially by curtailing the ability to challenge affirmative action, President Bush had previously denounced the legislation as a "quota bill," thus voicing the opinion of his constituency. By signing the bill, Bush only furthered the alienation of conservatives and Reagan Democrats that had begun when, in 1990, he reneged on his campaign promise not to raise taxes.

—William L. Glankler

Clinton, Hillary Rodham (1947–)

Hillary Rodham Clinton, United States senator (D-N.Y.), attorney, author, and children's rights activist, was the first career woman to become First Lady and the first First Lady to become a United States senator. She was born Hillary Diane Rodham on October 26, 1947, in Chicago. Her family was staunchly Republican and in 1964 Hillary Rodham worked for the Goldwater presidential campaign. Shortly after arriving at Wellesley College in Massachusetts, she was elected president of the Young Republicans' Club. Over the four years at Wellesley, however, Hillary Clinton's political and ideological affiliations changed dramatically, and in 1968 she volunteered for the presidential campaign of antiwar Democrat Eugene McCarthy. After graduating with honors, she attended Yale Law School, where she became a protégée of children's advocate Marian Wright Edelman. In 1973, she served as a staff member for the Judiciary Committee of the U.S. HOUSE OF REPRESENTATIVES during President RICHARD M. NIXON's IMPEACHMENT inquiry. In 1974 she moved to Arkansas to marry law school classmate WILLIAM J. CLINTON. There she became a law professor at the University of Arkansas in Fayetteville and, after their marriage in 1975, joined the prominent Rose Law Firm. In 1978 Bill Clinton was elected governor of Arkansas.

As First Lady of Arkansas, Rodham came under criticism for keeping her maiden name. Nonetheless, she took an active public role and became involved in education issues, founding the Arkansas Advocates for Children and Families, and chairing the Arkansas Educational Standards Committee. She also served on the board of the Arkansas Children's Hospital. Her daughter, Chelsea, was born in 1980. Clinton was named Arkansas Woman of the Year and Young Mother of the Year in 1984.

In 1993 Hillary Rodham Clinton accompanied her husband to the White House after he defeated incumbent GEORGE H. W. BUSH with 43 percent of the popular vote. President Clinton immediately named her to chair the Task Force on National Health Care Reform, from which she promoted a program for universal health insurance. The plan was submitted to the Democratically controlled Congress in September 1993, but met with fierce Republican opposition. Since both Clintons touted their health care reform agenda as the primary goal of their first year in office, its failure counted as a major defeat for the administration. During the same year, Rodham Clinton was also criticized for her role in firing seven members of the White House travel office. She then became the target of media rumors concerning WHITEWATER, a failed real estate development the Clintons had invested in 15 years earlier.

In addition to these political setbacks, 1993 brought personal difficulties for Rodham Clinton. In April her father, Hugh Rodham, died of a stroke after lingering for weeks in a Little Rock, Arkansas, hospital. In July, Vince Foster, a close friend and former law partner who had come to Washington at her request to serve as White House counsel, committed suicide. Foster's death inspired yet another round of rumors of conspiracy that continued to plague Rodham Clinton and her husband, and in January 1994 Attorney General JANET RENO appointed Robert B. Fiske, Jr., as a special counsel with broad authority to investigate charges relating to the Whitewater development. In August Fiske was replaced by KENNETH STARR. Over the next two years, Rodham Clinton was the focus of Starr's inquiry; no charges were ever brought.

After the political failure of her health care initiative and the negative press coverage of Whitewater and the White House travel office, Rodham Clinton returned to child welfare advocacy and in 1996 wrote *It Takes a Village and Other Lessons Children Teach Us*, which discussed her view on raising children in contemporary society. The following year, she hosted two conferences at the White House on children's issues, where she advocated federal support for day care. As a goodwill ambassador, she became the most widely traveled First Lady in American history,

Hillary Rodham Clinton *(Getty Images)*

visiting countries in six continents to promote human rights, education, childhood immunization, socialized health care, and economic empowerment for women. This reentry into the limelight was again accompanied by political scandals. In 1998 her husband, Bill Clinton, lied about his involvement in a sexual scandal with a 22-year-old White House intern, Monica Lewinsky. The day after President Clinton forcefully denied the affair, Rodham Clinton again became a center of controversy when she described a segment of her husband's critics as a "vast right-wing conspiracy." Though this scandal led to her husband's impeachment, many critics contend that Hillary actually benefited with a boost in popularity from those who sympathized with her as a victim of the ordeal.

Though technically a resident of Arkansas, in 1999 Rodham Clinton began to explore the possibility of running for the New York seat in the U.S. Senate soon to be vacated by Democrat Patrick Moynihan. She did not officially declare her intention to run until February 6, 2000. On May 20, five and a half months before the election, New York City mayor Rudolph Giuliani dropped out of the race for health reasons, and Republicans chose congressman Rick Lazio to run for the seat. The New York race proved to be one of the most hotly contested elections in the nation with almost $60 million spent, most of which went to negative advertising on both sides. On November 7 Rodham Clinton decidedly beat Lazio with 55 percent to 43 percent to become the first woman senator from New York, and the only First Lady to win public office.

See also ELECTIONS; RENO, JANET; STARR, KENNETH.

—Aharon W. Zorea

Clinton, William J. (Bill) (1947–)

William Jefferson Clinton, 42nd president of the United States (1993–2001), served following the end of the cold war. The last president of the 20th century, Clinton presided over the longest economic boom, but revelations of an affair and his attempt to deceive the public about it generated great controversy and the first presidential IMPEACHMENT since 1869.

Clinton was born William Jefferson Blythe III on August 19, 1946, in Hope, Arkansas. His father, William Jefferson Blythe, Jr., was killed in an automobile accident before his birth. His mother, Virginia Blythe, to support her son, left the child with his grandparents while she moved to New Orleans to study nursing. In 1950 his mother earned her degree and reunited with her son. She married Roger Clinton in 1961, at which time William Blythe's name was changed to Clinton. Clinton was a good student and demonstrated strong leadership skills. In 1962 he was selected to participate in a youth leadership conference in Washington, D.C., and, inspired by President John F. Kennedy, decided on a career in politics. After graduating from high school, Clinton entered Georgetown University to study international affairs. While at Georgetown, Clinton worked as an intern for his home-state senator and political mentor, J. William Fulbright. After earning his degree in 1968, Clinton won a Rhodes scholarship to attend Oxford University. Clinton's activities during this time haunted his future presidential campaigns. Clinton opposed the VIETNAM WAR and attended antiwar rallies while at Oxford. When his one-year draft deferment expired, Clinton applied to the Reserve Officers Training Corps in an attempt to get an extension. Clinton later withdrew the application and returned to Oxford. Letters Clinton wrote in this period were later read as evidence of his draft evasion by critics and idealism by supporters. Revelations that he experimented with marijuana at this time likewise rekindled old controversies when Clinton ran for president.

When Clinton returned from Europe, he entered Yale University Law School, where he met his future wife, Hillary Rodham. Clinton began his political career in 1972 when he directed the presidential campaign of GEORGE MCGOVERN in Texas. In 1973 Clinton earned his law degree and returned to Arkansas to teach law at the University of Arkansas.

In 1974 Clinton mounted an unsuccessful bid to oust incumbent Republican congressman John Paul Hammerschmidt, garnering 48 percent of the vote. Ms. Rodham had come to Arkansas to aid in the campaign and began teaching at the University of Arkansas. The Clintons married in 1975. In 1976 Clinton, running unopposed, was elected state attorney general. That same year, he also managed the Arkansas campaign of Democratic presidential aspirant JAMES EARL CARTER, JR. In 1978 Clinton was elected governor of Arkansas in a landslide victory. At age 32, he became the youngest governor in the United States since 1938. During his first term, Clinton focused on improving the state education and highways systems and bringing women and minorities into senior job positions. Unpopular policies, Rodham's independence, and the federal decision to house thousands of Cuban refugees in Arkansas alienated many voters, and he was defeated in his reelection bid in 1980. Clinton returned to the office of governor two years later after moderating his liberal rhetoric and abandoning some of his more unpopular policies. He was reelected in 1984 and 1986.

While governor, Clinton's priorities were education, economic development, and welfare reform. During his administration, Arkansas increased teacher salaries, mandated teacher competency exams, and instituted standardized testing to track student progress. These reforms improved Arkansas's high school graduation rate to the highest of any southern state, and thereafter more

Arkansans entered college. Incomes in the state increased 61 percent, though they remained below the national average. Clinton pursued welfare reforms that required the able-bodied to get job training or education to receive benefits.

From 1986 to 1987 Clinton served as chairman of the National Governor's Association where he tried to spread his education and welfare reforms. In 1990 he cofounded the Democratic Leadership Council, which was devoted to shifting the party to the political center in an attempt to appeal to voters lost in the 1980s to RONALD W. REAGAN and GEORGE H. W. BUSH.

In 1991 Clinton announced he would seek the 1992 Democratic presidential nomination. Despite early controversy stemming from his activities at Oxford and allegations of extramarital affairs, Clinton outdistanced the other challengers and captured the Democratic nomination. Clinton benefited from more prominent Democrats' choosing not to challenge the Republican incumbent, George H. W. Bush, who had received historically high approval ratings following the Persian Gulf War. He also benefited from a recession that turned public opinion against Bush in the months leading up to the election. Clinton seized on the issue of the ECONOMY, famously reminding his staff, "It's the economy, stupid." He promised health care reform, welfare reform, tax cuts for the middle class, and tax increases for the wealthy. He also pledged to protect reproductive rights and called for deeper cuts in defense spending with the end of the COLD WAR. Clinton and his running mate, U.S. senator ALBERT GORE of Tennessee, took their message of change and economic renewal to the American people, traveling by bus and holding town meetings. Clinton extended his appeal beyond traditional voters by making use of new and unconventional media outlets such as MTV and late-night TELEVISION talk shows. Voters elected Clinton with 43 percent of the vote to George Bush's 38 percent, and H. ROSS PEROT's 19 percent on his new Reform Party ticket.

Amid high expectations for fundamental change, Clinton reversed a number of Republican policies from the previous years. He ended the ban on fetal tissue research, repealed the "gag rule" on abortion counseling at federally funded clinics, and appointed record numbers of women and minorities to senior positions in his administration. The early days of his term were not easy. Most notably, his proposal to end the ban on homosexuals in the military met with widespread and vehement opposition.

One centerpiece reform for Clinton's first term was to be health care. Under the direction of the First Lady, an administration plan was conceived to establish a national health care system. The administration enacted gun control legislation (the Brady law), passed a historic deficit-reduction package, and passed the Family and Medical Leave Act, which mandated employers to provide workers with paid leave for childbirth and family illness.

Clinton's FOREIGN POLICY program was as ambitious as his domestic agenda, and as with the domestic agenda, his administration would find it difficult to carry out its plans in a rapidly changing world. Called, "Assertive Multilateralism," Clinton's policy saw the collapse of the Soviet empire as clearing the way for a regime of collective security arrangements and international law that, with varying degrees of earnestness, had been the primary rhetorical goal of U.S. foreign policy since 1916. At the same time, Clinton believed the end of the cold war freed America's substantial military resources for other missions, such as the suppression of "rogue states," the bolstering of tottering governments, and peacekeeping in regions of civil strife. Finally, the policy elevated the "soft power" of economic and trade ties to the same status as military and diplomatic approaches, and called for closer international policy cooperation to fight transnational criminal and terrorist groups.

In September 1993 an attempt to destroy the World Trade Center office complex in New York City gave Clinton clear notice that the new multipolar world order was filled with danger and instability. In response, Clinton called for the expansion of the FBI and other U.S. law enforcement agencies into foreign operations. He also implemented efforts to prevent nuclear, chemical, and biological arsenals of the disintegrating Soviet empire from falling into terrorist hands.

In December 1992 President George H. W. Bush had sent 28,000 U.S. troops to the strife- and famine-plagued nation of Somalia as part of a United Nations effort to ensure that international relief supplies were delivered to their intended recipients. On October 3 of the following year, as this humanitarian mandate had been changed into a "state-building" mandate, U.S. troops attempting to arrest local warlord Muhammad Farah Aideed encountered severe resistance. In a pitched battle lasting through the next day, these American troops faced hostile forces on the streets of Mogadishu, the nation's capital. Later, the bodies of two American soldiers killed in the battle were dragged through the streets by cheering crowds in scenes broadcast around the world.

The disaster in Mogadishu had substantial policy and political fallout. Clinton, already politically vulnerable because of his controversial lack of military service, adopted constructive guidelines on future deployment of American forces. Secretary of Defense Les Aspin resigned, and the administration's ambitious effort to overhaul the military was shelved. U.S. forces were withdrawn from Somalia on March 31, 1994. Russian elections, held in December 1993, under a new constitution drafted by President Boris Yeltsin, yielded a stunning victory by nationalist candidates who had campaigned explicitly against American world leadership and Yeltsin's closeness to Washington. A month later, a chastened Yeltsin rejected Clinton's "Partnership for Peace" proposal to create a collective security regime for Europe. In response, Clinton began U.S. support for the expansion of NATO membership into the former Soviet satellite states of Eastern Europe.

Clinton did not fare any better in bringing an end to the genocidal "ethnic cleansing" and bitter civil war in Bosnia. Clinton had criticized his predecessor throughout the 1992 campaign for inaction in Bosnia and the related fighting that resulted from the collapse of Yugoslavia in December 1990. As president, however, Clinton found it impossible to convince NATO to agree to any intervention without the guarantee of significant numbers of American ground troops. Clinton refused to make such a commitment until a crisis erupted in the fall of 1994, when UN peacekeeper soldiers were taken hostage. Clinton was also sharply criticized for his slow response in Bosnia and for his inaction in the Rwandan genocide of April to June 1994.

Clinton had varied success with the three remaining problems inherited from Bush. Deteriorating relations with the hard-line communist regime in North Korea, spurred by that nation's support for international TERRORISM and attempts to develop its nuclear arsenals, led to a dangerous and swift military escalation in May and June of 1994 between North and South Korea that was averted when former U.S. president Jimmy Carter negotiated a settlement.

The former president was also to play a role in the effort to restore democracy to HAITI. A 1991 coup d'état by General Raoul Cédras had driven from power the democratically elected president, Jean-Bertrand Aristide, an avowed socialist and excommunicated Roman Catholic priest. In the aftermath, thousands of refugees from the impoverished island nation began migrating to the southern shore of the United States. Clinton's gubernatorial reelection had been undermined in part by a similar refugee crisis 12 years earlier, and he was acutely sensitive to the political impact of such a migration. The administration brought tremendous pressure on Cédras, culminating in the Governor's Island Accord, in which the general agreed to restore Aristide, in return for personal amnesty and a lifting of American sanctions. When Cédras appeared to be hedging on the agreement, Clinton issued an ultimatum to Cédras to abide by the agreement or face forcible expulsion. Eventually a team led by former president Jimmy Carter convinced Cédras to leave his country, paving the way for a peaceful transition. Clinton also dealt forcefully with Iraq, dispatching troops to Kuwait in 1994 and ordering air strikes in 1996 when it became clear that Iraq had violated the restrictions placed on it at the end of the PERSIAN GULF WAR.

William Jefferson Clinton *(Getty Images)*

International economics was given a high level of attention in Clinton's administration. Clinton believed that the GLOBALIZATION of markets was an inevitable historical process, fueled by technological progress. He further believed that the liberalization of trade agreements, the elimination of tariffs and other nationally based barriers, and the integration of the regulations and legal structures of national economies was in the ultimate interest of prosperity in general and American prosperity in particular. In his first term, Clinton's trade views led him into conflict with the organized LABOR and the ENVIRONMENTAL MOVEMENT, two key constituencies of his party's coalition. During the 1992 campaign, Clinton had criticized the early drafts of the NORTH AMERICAN FREE TRADE AGREEMENT (NAFTA) for lacking provisions regarding worker rights, workplace safety, pollution, and environmental impact. He promised to force the inclusion of safeguards on these issues into the final agreement, as well as any future trade agreements. As in Bosnia, however, Clinton found the United States's clout with its allies to be less than imagined, and he ultimately accepted the inclusion of a series of unenforceable protocols on these concerns. The cries of betrayal among many of Clinton's key supporters were loud, especially when the president secured Senate ratification on the pact through a high-profile personal lobbying effort. The GENERAL AGREEMENT ON TARIFFS AND

TRADE of that same year also lacked the promised provisions. Clinton also reversed his campaign opposition to increased trade preferences for the People's Republic of China, further alienating human rights and democracy activists.

In 1994 a series of press investigations and rumors surrounding a real estate development in which Clinton had invested in 1978 led to the appointment of an INDEPENDENT COUNSEL. The WHITEWATER development was first brought to national attention on March 8, 1992, by the *New York Times*. The story reported that Clinton and his wife had invested in a development company run by James McDougal, a former U.S. Senate aide and political ally. Five years later, after the development had become moribund (it later went bankrupt), McDougal purchased the Madison Guaranty, a small savings and loan institution. In the national savings and loan crisis that soon followed, the Madison Guaranty became insolvent, but not before retaining the Rose Law Firm, and its attorney, Hillary Clinton. The fact that Mrs. Clinton's firm had a client S & L that was overseen, in part, by a regulator appointed by Mr. Clinton, and that both of them were investors in another company owned by the S & L's owner, seemed pregnant with the possibility of impropriety.

The Clintons and their allies dismissed this press speculation as petty rumor-mongering of old enemies. In response the Clintons became mistrustful of the press and refused to release financial and personal files to journalists. Nonetheless, the suicide of White House counsel Vincent Foster, in July 1993, set up yet another round of speculation.

Yielding to public pressure and the media outcry, on January 20, 1994, Attorney General JANET RENO appointed Robert B. Fiske, Jr., as a special counsel with broad authority to investigate charges related to the Whitewater development. On August 5 KENNETH STARR replaced Fiske.

Further problems arose when an Arkansas state employee, Paula Corbin Jones, filed a civil lawsuit against Clinton, claiming that his propositioning of her while he was governor constituted sexual harassment. Clinton's allies claimed that Jones's lawsuit was financed and championed by Clinton's conservative political opponents. (Later, a settlement was reached between Clinton and Jones.)

By 1994, Republicans gained control of the SENATE and the HOUSE OF REPRESENTATIVES. The new Republican majorities called for fundamental reform of the federal government and the social contract to create "the opportunity society." Labeled the "Gingrich Revolution" after the charismatic new Speaker of the House, NEWTON GINGRICH, new legislation was enacted regarding federal trade regulations, as well as business and consumer regulations. Under political pressure from the right, Clinton moved to

the political center to undercut Republican popularity, much to the dismay of the liberal wing of his party.

Despite their political differences, Clinton and the new Republican congressional majority negotiated a compromise welfare reform act. Clinton also managed to push through a significant increase in the minimum wage. By 1996, a surging economy and a falling federal deficit were seen by the majority of voters to be a vindication of Clinton's economic program. In November Clinton was reelected with a little less than 50 percent of the vote, while his opponent, Senate Majority Leader ROBERT DOLE, the Republican nominee, received nearly 42 percent of the vote, and Reform Party candidate Perot garnered 8 percent of the vote.

During his second term, Clinton urged on the Congress a plan to balance the federal budget by 2002. Furthermore, Clinton was able to present a balanced budget proposal for the 1998 fiscal year. At the end of that year, he announced a surplus for the fiscal year, after two decades of deficits. Despite a booming economy, Clinton's second term was marred by further scandal. In 1997 charges were made by Republicans that the Clinton-Gore campaign had participated in illegal fund-raising activities in 1996. The controversy intensified in May 1998 when a former Democratic fund-raiser admitted that he had accepted illegal contributions from a Chinese military official.

On May 27, 1997, the U.S. SUPREME COURT unanimously rejected Clinton's request to delay the Paula Jones lawsuit until he left office. In the months that followed, the hostility between the White House and the independent counsel increased dramatically. On January 12 Linda Tripp, who had secretly recorded the confidences of former White House intern Monica Lewinsky, released tapes in which Lewinsky described a series of intimate relations with the president that had occurred in the White House. On January 16 Starr was given authority by a grand jury to investigate Tripp's charges that Clinton had encouraged Lewinsky to lie under oath in the Jones case. In his testimony the next day before the grand jury hearing, Clinton relied on narrow definitions and legal technicalities to deny that he had engaged in sexual relations with Lewinsky. On January 21 Clinton denied the affair to the media, a denial he repeated in more forceful terms five days later. Clinton issued similar denials to his cabinet, his staff, his family, and members of Congress. These denials before the grand jury and the media became part of the later impeachment in Congress.

As the existence and contents of the Tripp tapes and other incriminating evidence were revealed over the next few weeks, however, Clinton's statements were clearly shown to be false. On August 17, 1998, Clinton testified before a grand jury. In a nationally televised address that same evening, Clinton admitted that he had engaged in an inappropriate relationship with Lewinsky, but strongly denied that he had done anything illegal.

Starr delivered his report on the Lewinsky affair to the House of Representatives on September 9, 1998. The report concluded that Clinton's actions "may constitute grounds for impeachment," a conclusion that the president's allies disputed. Public opinion had soured on Clinton with the revelation of the affair and the lies he had initially told about it. Critics of the Starr report wondered how an investigation of a 1978 land development had turned into an inquiry into the president's recent intimate relationships. Others believed that impeachment was too severe a penalty for the offenses. The diverging views of Clinton's character, the merit of the charges, the manner of the investigation, Clinton's conduct during the investigation, and the appropriate penalties for Clinton's action led to a deep rift in public opinion and stirred further partisan acrimony.

In December a divided House approved two articles of impeachment charging the president with perjury and obstruction of justice. The impeachment trial was held in the Senate from January 7 to February 6, 1999, and resulted in an acquittal. Those supporting the president's removal argued that Clinton was guilty of the charges, that he had disgraced his office, and that the failure to punish him would apply a different standard to the president from that applied to average citizens. Clinton's defenders maintained that the crimes he was charged with were rarely prosecuted and that the alleged offenses did not meet the definition of impeachable crimes described in the Constitution.

Although Clinton was not removed from office, the impeachment crisis did have a profound effect on his second term by consuming the attention of the White House and Congress for over a year.

Although the Lewinsky inquiry paralyzed domestic politics, Clinton was continually challenged by international problems during his second term. An economic crisis in Asia, beginning in Thailand, then spread to Indonesia, South Korea, and the Philippines, and—as their economies sputtered—to Hong Kong, Malaysia, and Japan. As major corporations and banks were caught in the Asia recession, Brazil, the leading economy of South America, was plunged into recession, and the Russian economy, struggling with the transition to a free market, collapsed. Clinton's administration organized a successful international effort to avert world recession.

The Middle East also loomed large in Clinton's second term. Iraq's repeated refusal to comply with the international arms inspections required after the Persian Gulf War led to U.S. and British ultimatums to allow inspectors free access. Each time, Iraq backed down at the eleventh hour, only to resume its defiant stance once the threat had passed. In December 1998 Clinton ordered extensive bombing designed to cripple Iraq's military.

On August 7 an Islamic fundamentalist and terrorist organization, associated with bin Laden, bombed U.S. embassies in Kenya and Tanzania, killing 12 Americans. Clinton responded with air strikes on terrorist camps in Afghanistan and a factory in Sudan believed, at the time, to be manufacturing chemical weapons for bin Laden. These U.S. attacks proved ineffectual in countering an extensive worldwide terrorist network that had been developed by bin Laden and his associates.

Clinton's efforts to negotiate peace between the Israelis and Palestinians also failed. The Wye River Memorandum of October 1998 appeared to pave the way for Palestinian self-government, but Clinton's last-minute efforts to achieve a permanent settlement in the closing days of his administration proved unsuccessful.

More successful was the Good Friday Agreement in Ireland. Negotiated by Clinton's personal envoy, former Senate leader GEORGE MITCHELL, the treaty brought decades of armed conflict in Northern Ireland to a close.

The most notable foreign crisis of Clinton's second term was the KOSOVO conflict. In February 1998 Serbian president Slobodan Milosevic began a military crackdown on the ethnic Albanian population and other Islamic inhabitants in Kosovo. A small, armed separatist movement swelled into a full-fledged revolt in the face of this aggression. Clinton negotiated a cease-fire in November, but by January the fighting had resumed. In February peace talks collapsed, and Milosevic began a campaign of "ethnic cleansing," attempting to drive the Albanian and Islamic majority from the country through mass murder and terror. In March Clinton led a U.S.-NATO coalition in a campaign of aerial bombardment designed to destroy Serbian military capability. Clinton and NATO achieved victory using only air power. Milosevic was driven from power in October 2000 and brought to trial for genocide in 2001.

During the presidential election of 2000, Clinton remained largely marginalized because of Democratic candidate Al Gore, Jr.'s strategy of distancing himself from the controversy that had surrounded Clinton.

Because of his perjury before the grand jury, the Supreme Court ordered him to resign from the Supreme Court Bar, thus preventing him from arguing cases before the nation's highest court. In addition, the Arkansas State Bar Association suspended Clinton's license for five years. He currently divides his time between Little Rock, where he is constructing his presidential library; New York City; and Washington, D.C. He continues to work for many charitable causes.

See also BUSH, GEORGE H. W.; BUSH, GEORGE W.; CAMPAIGN FINANCE; CLINTON, HILLARY RODHAM.

Further reading: William C. Berman, *From the Center to the Edge: The Politics and Policies of the Clinton Presidency* (Lanham, Md.: Rowman & Littlefield, 2001); Charles O. Jones, *Clinton and Congress, 1993–1996: Risk, Restoration, and Reelection* (Norman: University of Oklahoma Press, 1999); Steven E. Schier, ed., *The Postmodern Presidency: Bill Clinton's Legacy in U.S. Politics* (Pittsburgh: University of Pittsburgh Press, 2000).

—John Korasick

cold war (end of)

When RICHARD M. NIXON was elected president in 1968, the cold war was beginning its third decade. The ideological conflict between the United States and the Soviet Union had stalemated. The avowed American goal of containing communism had met with mixed results. The governments of Eastern Europe, China, Cuba, North Korea, and North Vietnam had become communist. The United States had successfully blocked communist expansion in Greece and South Korea and was currently attempting to prevent South Vietnam from becoming communist. Within the next 25 years the nations of Eastern Europe would overthrow communism, the symbol of the cold war—the Berlin Wall—would fall, and the Soviet Union would collapse.

Nixon and his foreign policy adviser, HENRY KISSINGER, changed the philosophy of the nation's foreign policy. Rather than focusing on the ideological conflict, the new policy assumed that nation-states pursued certain strategic aims, regardless of their system of government. As a result, the new administration believed that U.S. and Soviet interests were not necessarily in conflict in every instance. This policy, known as DÉTENTE, improved U.S.-Soviet relations for a time. Negotiations between the two nations resulted in trade agreements, and the sale of U.S. wheat and technology to the Soviets in 1972. That same year Nixon and Soviet leader Leonid Brezhnev signed the first Strategic Arms Limitation Treaty (SALT I), which limited the development of antiballistic missile systems and froze the number of intercontinental ballistic missiles and submarine-based missiles for five years.

While the United States and the Soviet Union were negotiating on arms control and trade, a European-led initiative resulted in the lessening of tensions in Europe. Since the end of World War II, Berlin had been a divided city, with the Soviets in control of one sector of Berlin, and the Western Allies—France, Britain, and the United States—in control of the rest of the city. Berlin lay within the boundaries of East Germany and the issue of Western access to the city had resulted in numerous crises over the years. In 1961 a wall was constructed by the Soviets to prevent the emigration of East Germans to the West. In 1970 the West German chancellor, Willy Brandt, with the

approval of the United States, initiated talks that led to the recognition of the eastern border of East Germany by West Germany, the normalization of access to West Berlin and the establishment of relations between the two German states. These events demonstrated that the United States accepted the postwar division of Europe.

After lengthy negotiations, Nixon made a visit to the People's Republic of China in 1972. The primary purpose of this initiative was to establish a relationship with mainland China, which had been at odds with the Soviet Union since the death of Stalin in 1953. The Nixon-Kissinger policy was to play the two communist giants against one another, and thereby, create a balance of power between those nations.

Although the United States and the Soviet Union maintained détente for the next 20 years, international tensions in the Middle East, Central Asia, Africa, and Central America continued to test diplomatic accommodation between the two countries. One of the first tests came in 1973 with the Yom Kippur War in the Middle East. This war began when Egypt and Syria, using Soviet weapons, attacked Israel, an ally of the United States. The attack on Israel was halted with the support of the United States. When Brezhnev threatened to take unilateral military action to end the conflict, the United States responded by placing its military on alert. This show of American power prevented Soviet intervention into the crisis and enabled Kissinger to negotiate a cease-fire, preventing the Soviets from enhancing their power in the region. As a result, the United States became the most influential power there, a state of affairs the Soviets resented deeply.

Following the end of war in Vietnam in 1973, Nixon would claim that the United States had successfully defended South Vietnam from the communist North. Nonetheless, in 1975 North Vietnam defeated the government of South Vietnam and unified the country under a communist regime. In 1975 Cambodia and Laos fell to communist insurgents. As a result of these communist victories, Southeast Asia was seen as a "win" for the Soviets.

During this period a debate arose within U.S. foreign policy circles that resulted in an upward revision in official estimates of Soviet military capability, especially nuclear capability. Furthermore, some political analysts argued that the Soviet Union had embarked on an adventuristic foreign policy to exploit social and political problems in developing nations in Africa and Latin America.

Further difficulties emerged in Africa. Rhodesia (present-day Zimbabwe) and Angola became focal points of tensions between the United States and the Soviet Union. A key tenet of the détente strategy was to avoid direct confrontation. The rivalry was instead played out through U.S. and Soviet support of "client state" local powers in their battles with one another.

A particularly difficult situation emerged in the Portuguese colony of Angola. In 1975 liberation movements within Angola forced the Portuguese to grant the colony independence. Fearing Soviet intervention, the United States became involved in an internal civil war in post-colonial Angola as three factions vied for power—the Frente Nacional de Libertação de Angola (FNLA), the Popular Movement for the Liberation Front of Angola (MPLA), and the National Union for the Total Independence of Angola (UNITA). The Soviets supported the MPLA, which assumed power; the Chinese supported the FNLA; and the United States provided covert aid to both the FNLA and UNITA. The intervention of South Africa on behalf of UNITA caused most Angolans to accept Soviet support and Cuban military advisers, to prevent the spread of South Africa's system of racial separation and white domination known as apartheid.

U.S.-Soviet relations became increasingly acrimonious during the Carter years (1977–81). Carter wanted to focus on human rights in his foreign policy. Carter's administration aggressively supported dissident organizations such as Poland's "Solidarity" movement, in spite of the objections of the Soviet leadership. Carter also moved forward with an arms control agreement to replace SALT, which was due to expire in 1977. In June 1979 Carter and Brezhnev signed the SALT II treaty, but Carter pulled it from consideration by the U.S. Senate after the Soviet invasion of Afghanistan later that year.

Growing tensions between the superpowers became apparent in a crisis that erupted in the Horn of Africa, when war broke out between Ethiopia and Somalia. The United States had supported the Ethiopians since 1953. The Soviet Union had provided military and technical assistance to Somalia since 1963. When a marxist coup overthrew the government in Ethiopia in 1974, relations with the United States soured. In 1976 Ethiopia signed an arms agreement with the Soviets. In response, the United States began supporting Somalia against the Soviet-supported government of Ethiopia. When war broke out between Somalia and Ethiopia in 1977, however, the United States did not supply arms to the Somalis; meanwhile, the Soviets supplied arms to the Ethiopians, and Cuban troops arrived to defend the nation. The U.S. failure to aid its new ally tarnished its image in the region.

After the 1977 Soviet invasion of Afghanistan, the United States significantly hardened its position toward the Soviet Union. In addition to pulling SALT II from Senate consideration, Carter imposed an embargo on grain and technology sales to the Soviets and ordered an American boycott of the 1980 Olympic Games in Moscow. Carter stepped up defense spending increases and ordered the registration of all 18-year-old males for a potential military draft.

Presidents Gorbachev, Reagan, and Bush at the close of the cold war era, New York harbor *(Ronald W. Reagan Library)*

In 1980 RONALD W. REAGAN, a strong anticommunist, was elected president of the United States. Reagan's administration believed that official estimates had dramatically and dangerously underestimated Soviet conventional and nuclear military capabilities. Reagan persuaded Congress to support a peacetime military buildup and increase the budget for CIA covert operations against Soviet-backed liberation movements in Africa and Central America. Reagan rejected détente, regarding the Soviet Union as "the focus of evil in the modern world." He called for an end of the prevailing policy of "mutually assured destruction" in favor of the development of an extensive missile defense system commonly referred to as "Star Wars." At the same time, Reagan pursued an aggressive policy to defeat communist insurgencies in the Western Hemisphere. In 1983 Reagan sent a force of marines to overthrow a marxist government in Grenada. Reagan also stepped up military assistance to the government in El Salvador in its war against communist guerrillas, supported by a newly formed leftist regime in Nicaragua. Beginning in 1981 the Reagan administration also funneled money to anticommunist resistance fighters in Nicaragua—the CONTRAS. In 1982 Congress passed the BOLAND AMENDMENT, a resolution barring further aid to the contras, in response to their misappropriations and human rights abuses. Efforts by the administration to continue funding, in spite of the law, led to a congressional investigation into what became known as the IRAN-CONTRA AFFAIR.

In 1985 Mikhail Gorbachev acceded to the leadership of the Soviet Union and inaugurated a series of legal and economic reforms. In 1987 the United States and Soviet Union signed the INTERMEDIATE-RANGE AND SHORTER-RANGE NUCLEAR FORCES TREATY (INF), which called for the destruction of intermediate-range missiles. The two sides also agreed to resume the Strategic Arms Reduction Treaty (START) talks, which had become stalled earlier in Reagan's administration. Gorbachev ordered the withdrawal of Soviet troops from Afghanistan, ended the support of the Nicaraguan government, and urged Soviet-backed governments in Eastern Europe to undertake political and economic reforms.

Gorbachev's policies of perestroika (political restructuring) and GLASNOST (political openness) were a response to the failing Soviet economy. The new Soviet openness and refusal to support crackdowns in satellites states emboldened Eastern European dissidents. By 1989 communist governments in Eastern Europe were coming under intense pressure from their citizens. Beginning in Poland, then Czechoslovakia, Hungary, Bulgaria, and Romania, regime after regime fell. When the democratic changes began in Eastern Europe, the Soviets were in no condition to stop the collapse. On November 9, 1989, the Berlin Wall, the symbol of the permanence of the cold war, was torn down by euphoric East and West German crowds. An anti-Gorbachev coup failed in August 1991, and four months later the Soviet Union was officially abolished.

See also ANTI-BALLISTIC MISSILE TREATY; ANTIWAR MOVEMENT—VIETNAM; DEFENSE POLICY; FOREIGN POLICY; SPACE POLICY.

Further reading: Stephen E. Ambrose and Douglas G. Brinkley, *Rise to Globalism: American Foreign Policy since 1938* (New York: Viking Penguin, 1997); Ralph B. Levering, *The Cold War: A Post–Cold War History* (Arlington Heights, Ill.: Harlan Davidson, Inc., 1994).

—John Korasick

Committee on the Present Danger   See conservative movement

computers

The last quarter of the 20th century witnessed a revolution in computing technology that substantially changed the face of American society, especially those sectors involved in research, production, commerce, defense, communication, and entertainment. Though simple mechanical calculating devices have been around since the 17th century, the first electronic calculating machines did not appear until the 1930s. Throughout the decades immediately preceding World War II, computing technology developed slowly through a combination of private sector and academic experimentation. The Moore School of Electrical Engineering at the University of Pennsylvania built the first successful electronic digital computer called the Electronic Numerical Integrator and Computer (ENIAC) in 1946. It weighed 60,000 lbs., measured 18 feet high and 80 feet long, and required 500 miles of wiring to link nearly 18,000 vacuum tubes together. It used 180,000 watts of electrical power to produce a computing power of 100,000 operations per second. One of its practical applications was to compute the feasibility of the hydrogen bomb. The cost of these giant computers led to the development of a cooperative relationship between land grant universities, major corporations, and government research agencies. The first significant advance from these large machines occurred in 1948, when physicists John Bardeen, Walter H. Brattain, and William B. Shockley at Bell Telephone Laboratories invented the transistor, which replaced costly and fragile vacuum tubes that limited the capacity of computers. In 1957 Jack Kilby designed the first true integrated circuit, or "chip," which permitted the giant computers developed during and immediately after World War II to be scaled down by including transistors, resistors, and capacitors on the same germanium wafer. In 1971 American engineer Marcian E. Hoff successfully incorporated hundreds of components onto a smaller silicon chip, which he called a "microprocessor." The reduction in size and expense of complex computing power opened the way for the gradual shift of computing technology from the large mainframe computers of research agencies to personal computers for small businesses and homes.

In 1974 Micro Instrumentation Telemetry Systems introduced the Altair 8800, which became the first truly personal computer to come to the market, even though it was sold primarily to hobbyists. Three years later, the Tandy Corporation came out with a similar product that included a keyboard and cathode ray tube (CRT) screen. In 1976 Stephen Wozniak and entrepreneur Steven Jobs joined forces to start Apple Computers, which soon became the fastest-growing company in U.S. history. In 1981 IBM introduced a personal computer with a standard operating system written by Bill Gates at the Microsoft Corporation, which could be used by a variety of hardware manufacturers, making personal computers more accessible to small businesses and home use. The effect on the economy was dramatic: the bull market lasted for the remainder of the century, creating a mutually reinforcing cycle where each new level of computing power led to the means for developing the next level.

Personal computers shown in a shopping center *(Getty Images)*

During the 1980s, the scale of computer chip technology improved 100-fold, increasing from 125,000 to 10 million circuits on a single chip size of a fingernail. During the 1990s, the rate of advance continued, to the point where personal computing power rivaled the power of larger mainframe computers, thus bridging the gap in technology between large corporations and small businesses. By 2001, only the largest corporations, research universities, and certain government agencies still relied on supercomputers. In 2000, the U.S. Department of Defense ordered construction of the world's most powerful supercomputer, the Cray T3E-1200™, capable of 1.3 teraflops (trillion calculations per second), which can almost track each particle in a simulated nuclear explosion. Analysts expect to develop a 100-teraflop computer with full nuclear simulation capabilities by 2005.

Concurrently, software designers endeavored to make the increasingly sophisticated technology more accessible to nonspecialized computer users through similar generations of operating systems and business-application software. The trend in the software industry, however, led toward less competition and more conformity of standards.

The Microsoft Corporation became one of the largest corporations in the world, and its founder, Bill Gates, became the world's richest man. Their success, however, drew fire from competitors. Their Windows operating system became so inclusive and so dominant (with 90 percent market share) that many smaller companies complained that they were deprived of a fair opportunity to compete. In May 1998 Microsoft was indicted by 20 state attorneys general and the U.S. Department of Justice for antitrust violations. Microsoft was found to be a monopoly in 1999, and in June 2000 was ordered to be broken up. An appeals court overturned the breakup ruling the following year, but nevertheless confirmed the verdict that Microsoft was a monopoly and maintained that position through practices that inhibited a competitive marketplace. The corporation avoided a full breakup in a settlement deal in late 2001.

Advances in computer technology, whether in the personal computer market or at the supercomputer level, have changed the way many Americans live and work: engineers and designers use computer-aided design (CAD) software to test and develop new products without the need for scale models; computer-aided manufacturing (CAM) has transformed production and research facilities, permitting microscopic precision with near-perfect reproduction; and computer-aided instruction (CAI) has improved public safety with flight simulators, while also opening up a new sector of distance learning and on-line education. Yet, these advances are not without their social risks.

One question that is particularly troublesome for a constitutional system is the effect these technologies have on personal privacy. As early as the 1960s, concerned observers worried that the efficiencies of computerized record keeping could tempt public and private organizations to collect more personal information than their records required, and then exchange the surplus data with other organizations that could use it for their advantage. For example, law enforcement agencies might trade information with tax and licensing agencies, or medical, credit, or banking institutions might sell personal information to employers or government agencies. These real possibilities prompted Congress to enact a number of privacy acts intended to safeguard personal information. Privacy advo-

Microsoft chairman Bill Gates *(Getty Images)*

cates feared that existing laws were incapable of addressing the problems posed by vast information networks that cross international boundaries. Others feared that too much regulation might stifle the natural evolution of a budding industry, especially within the area of electronic commerce and telecommunication.

State and federal legislatures responded by imposing a number of Fair Information practices, typically requiring the full disclosure of the gathering process and uses of personal information by certain sectors—including credit, insurance, banking, and law enforcement. They also established rules of confidentiality and gave those whose data is recorded the right to inspect, correct, and challenge collected information. Privacy advocates maintain that the safeguards do not go far enough and condemn the new commercial database files and consumer profiles.

The advent of widespread access to the INTERNET in the early 1990s prompted a number of equally perplexing questions regarding copyright, intellectual PROPERTY RIGHTS, and PORNOGRAPHY. Advances in telecommunication software opened the way for inexpensive or free Internet service providers (ISPs), which enabled casual computer users to conveniently and anonymously swap documents, images, and audio pieces around the world with little or no loss of quality. In 1995 Congress attempted to modify the existing copyright laws to accommodate the new technology, but the rate of technological advancement increases so quickly that finding a definitive solution has been difficult. In 2000 Napster, an on-line site dedicated to free music trading, incited a flood of lawsuits from major record labels, distributors, and performers. Though the courts eventually barred Napster and other sites from the practice, the technology to record and distribute high-quality music had already promulgated beyond controllable limits.

On another front, public and private corporations have had to guard against increased security threats as both thrill-seekers and criminals use Internet connections to break into and steal or sabotage corporate records, including credit card numbers and trade secrets. Law enforcement groups are also concerned that websites that incorporate Instant Communication Relays (IRC), which allow people to send messages and files instantly, may provide dangerous forums for minors. Throughout the late 1990s, federal and state law enforcement agencies were forced to establish special squads to investigate child pornography rings as well as pedophiles who use the Internet to meet their targets, leading to physical child molestation. Even legal uses of the Internet have prompted concern for its effect on social health; many psychologists claim that the anonymous stimulation of chat rooms and easily accessible pornography can be alienating, leading to disruption in personal and family relations, broken marriages, loss of workplace productivity, and even loss of employment.

In 1965 Gordon Moore observed that each new wave of technology provided the necessary platforms for the next generation of smaller and faster developments. He postulated that the rate of advance for computing technology should double every two years—a prediction that analysts refer to as "Moore's Law." Since then the actual rate has been closer to 18 months, but has remained nonetheless consistent, though as of 2000 the width of current circuitry was measured in atoms. Since the 1990s, personal computers have become both more prominent, and somewhat archaic. The prevalence of multiprocessors with wireless communication components in cell phones, handheld personal digital assistants, automobile navigation systems, household appliances, and even clothing has served to deemphasize the importance of dedicated computing boxes. The future direction that such growth will take is still unpredictable. Scientists are working on optical processors, which utilize laser and gas technology to arrive at a completely new platform of computing technology, independent of the current integrated-circuit design.

Other scientists are developing Quantum computers, which combine biological processes with digital components. It is quite possible that the full impact of the computer revolution will not be seen for several more decades.

See also BUSINESS; CRIME; GLOBALIZATION; HUMAN GENOME PROJECT; MEDIA; MOVIES; POPULAR CULTURE; RECREATION; SCIENCE AND TECHNOLOGY; SPACE POLICY; TELEVISION.

Further reading: Thierry Bardini, *Bootstrapping: Douglas Engelbart, Coevolution, and the Origins of Personal Computing* (Palo Alto, Calif.: Stanford University Press, 2000); Les Freed, *The History of Computers* (New York: Ziff Davis Press, 1995); Paul Freiberger and Michael Swaine, *Fire in the Valley: The Making of the Personal Computer* (New York: Osborne/McGraw-Hill, 1984); M. Mitchell Waldrop, *The Dream Machine: J.C.R. Licklider and the Revolution that Made Computing Personal* (New York: Viking Press, 2001).

—Aharon W. Zorea

Congressional Budget and Impoundment Control Act (1974)

Article I of the United States Constitution gives Congress control of the "purse strings"—the power to tax and spend. Beginning in fiscal 1971, the deficit began a rapid rise with no warning. In October 1972 RICHARD M. NIXON proposed a plan that would set a mandatory ceiling of $250 billion for the fiscal year 1973 budget. The plan also called for giving the president unprecedented authority to reduce or elimi-

nate spending on specific programs, thereby shifting spending authority away from Congress.

Congress rejected Nixon's plan, and in response, Nixon began impounding congressional appropriations by refusing to spend them. Presidential impoundment was not unprecedented. President Thomas Jefferson had impounded funds in 1803 that were meant to build gunships to patrol the Mississippi River on the grounds that the Louisiana Purchase had moved the nation's border far west of the river. President Harry Truman had impounded funds for the air force on the grounds that they were excessive. Nixon cited these examples as evidence that impoundment was an established presidential prerogative. The greatest differences were that no previous president had impounded so much, around $8 billion, and none had attempted to scrap entire government programs.

Democratic senator Sam Ervin of North Carolina led the charge against Nixon's action. Charging that impoundment was contemptuous of Congress under Article I of the Constitution, Ervin introduced a bill to limit the president's power to impound. The Senate approved an anti-impoundment bill in May 1973. The HOUSE OF REPRESENTATIVES passed a similar measure in July 1973.

Democratic representative Richard Bolling of Missouri was the paramount figure in reconciling the two measures. First, the impoundment authority of the president was codified under two clauses: rescission—permanent cancellation of funding requiring congressional approval, and temporary deferral of expenditure, which could stand unless overturned by Congress. The act created budget committees in the House and Senate, established the Congressional Budget Office, and set a process of setting spending and revenue targets.

The final version of the act passed the House on June 18, 1974, and the Senate three days later. Embattled, President Nixon signed the legislation July 12, 1974. Its most striking achievement was the regularization of the budget process, although budget deficits continued to remain a serious financial problem for the federal government.

In retirement, Richard M. Nixon wrote that the budget and impoundment act was a clear usurpation of presidential power by the Congress.

See also ECONOMY.

—John Korasick

conscription, end of

United States policy during the COLD WAR was to maintain large enough armies to fight regional wars against communism as well as maintain a standing army deployed in areas that might erupt into larger, more dangerous wars. Authorities believed that the only way to acquire enough manpower to fulfill these imperatives was through conscription.

As a consequence, President Harry Truman reinstituted the draft during the Korean War. With the Vietnam War in the 1960s, however, criticisms of the draft grew, as some students burned their draft cards, demonstrated at draft board centers, and refused military service. Furthermore, critics of the draft argued that the conscription system allowed middle-class whites to receive college deferments, while African Americans and other ethnic minorities, as well as white working-class youth, were drafted in the military.

During the presidential campaign of 1968, RICHARD M. NIXON sought to exploit this resentment toward the draft by mentioning the possibility of ending conscription, even though he attacked student antiwar demonstrators. In the meanwhile, proposals for ending the draft were made in Congress. Polls showed that Americans generally supported the end of national conscription.

The end did not finally occur until January 27, 1973, when the Paris Accord was signed with the goal of ending the VIETNAM WAR. At this time, Secretary of Defense Melvin Laird stated, "I wish to inform you that the armed forces henceforth will depend exclusively on volunteer soldiers, sailors, airmen and marines. Use of the draft has ended." Accompanying this statement was the decision to rely solely on the national guard and reserve troops to fill support roles for regular U.S. military forces when crisis situations required increased manpower mobilization. Selective Service registration remained, as did the possibility that those registered might have a military obligation, but since 1973 the draft has not been reinstated.

See also DEFENSE POLICY.

Further reading: Thomas Reeves and Karl Hess, *The End of the Draft: A Proposal for Abolishing Conscription and for a Volunteer Army* (New York: Random House, 1970); Gordon C. Zahn, *War, Conscience, and Dissent* (New York: Hawthorn, 1967).

—Leah Blakey

conservation, environmentalism, and environmental policy

Although Rachel Carson's 1962 seminal study, *Silent Spring,* is credited with launching the modern environment-conscious movement in the United States, conservation issues have been part of the national landscape since the late 19th century. Carson's inquiry, which gave scientific evidence that supported findings of unhealthy levels of toxins in our bodies and in our environment, provided the stimulus for the environmental movement that coalesced in the late 1960s.

The modern environmental movement is distinguished from earlier activity by its foundation in rigorous science. The German biologist Ernst Haeckel coined the term "ecology" (a branch of science concerned with the interrelationship of organisms and their environments) in 1866; nearly a century later, the designation was still virtually unknown to those outside the field of biology. *Silent Spring,* in conjunction with the increasing viability of this unique field of study, helped foster a new approach to the role of scientific inquiry in the United States. Science had increasingly been regarded as a handmaiden to industrial capitalism; environmental science contradicted this view. Ecology identified the various ways that human interaction with nature and the environment had been both dangerous and disruptive and, by the 1970s, provided a scientific foundation for environmental advocacy.

Biologist Barry Commoner, author of *The Closing Circle: Nature, Man and Technology* (1971), conjoined scientific study with social justice issues, and called for ecology to bring environmental equity to Western society through radical economic, social, and political changes. Commoner's maxims "Nature Knows Best," "Everything Must Go Somewhere," "There Is No Such Thing as a Free Lunch," and "Everything Is Connected to Everything Else," rapidly entered public discourse.

Environmental concerns were widespread in America by the early 1970s. This awareness was brought sharply into focus by the celebration of the first Earth Day on March 21, 1970. Wisconsin senator Gaylord Nelson conceived the event and enlisted others, who linked the celebration to ANTIWAR and civil rights issues. American endorsement of Earth Day signified that the general population was conscious of their national and global environment, as well as showing concern about conserving natural resources. Earth Day proved to be a seminal event in the contemporary environmental movement.

In 1972 the Club of Rome, a private international group of scientists, issued *The Limits to Growth.* Although primitive in comparison to later computer models, this study analyzed the effect of long-term uncontrolled population growth, industrial output, and resource consumption, and how they affected pollution and food supplies. Their results predicted a neo-Malthusian global failure, and the collapse of humanity by the early 21st century.

Nature and conservation groups like the Sierra Club, the Wilderness Society, the National Wildlife Federation, and the Nature Conservancy have existed since 1892, but in the 1970s new organizations emerged to participate in the environmental movement, including the League of Conservation Voters, Natural Resources Defense Council, Friends of the Earth, and others. The focus of these and other new nongovernmental organizations (NGOs) encompassed a range of issues including protection of the environment, conservation of natural resources and wildlife, as well as such other issues as energy efficiency, nuclear winter, global warming, population growth, and pollution control. Also in the 1970s, new public interest research groups (PIRGs), concerned with a range of issues including some environmental issues, emerged to force public disclosure and government action against air pollution, toxic dumps, nuclear waste, and contaminated water supplies. Environmentalism was professionalized during the 1970s, but amateurs continued to play a dominant role in the movement. As with other movements during this era, environmentalism also found radical adherents, who came together in Greenpeace and the Earth First! Movement. The more extreme environmentalists utilized sit-ins, demonstrations, and occasionally espoused "eco-tage," the destruction of power lines, logging equipment, and the occasional ski lodge.

The federal government responded to public desire for greater conservation and environmental involvement, passing the Wilderness Act in 1964, which facilitated the creation of roadless, protected regions. A series of wildlife protection legislation was passed in 1968, 1971, and 1973: respectively, the Wild and Scenic Rivers Act, the Wild Free-Roaming Horse and Burro Act, and the Endangered

Species Act. The latter has proved to be a source of contention between those seeking to preserve animals like the snail darter fish and spotted owl, and fishing and logging interests.

The National Environmental Policy Act (NEPA) is the foundation for contemporary environmental policies. It was signed into law by President RICHARD M. NIXON on January 1, 1970, in response to polls that showed strong mainstream support for federal protection of the environment. NEPA's mandate required all federal agencies to protect the environment. To facilitate this, the Council on Environmental Quality (CEQ) was created. By the end of 1970, the CEQ proposed the formation of a separate agency, the Environmental Protection Agency (EPA), in order to evaluate solid waste, air, and water pollution as different types of the same problem. The EPA was created that year as an independent agency. In 2000, the agency had an operating budget of $6.7 billion and a workforce of 18,000.

During the course of the 1970s, important environmental legislation was enacted, including the Clean Air Act of 1970, the OCCUPATIONAL SAFETY AND HEALTH ACT (1970), the Water Pollution Control Act (1972), the Safe

Workers clean up part of a waste oil spill on the Rouge River, Michigan. *(Bill Pugliano/Getty Images)*

Drinking Water Act (1974), and the Comprehensive Environmental Response Compensation and Liability Act (1980). The result of these and other mandates was the addition of millions of acres to the federal wilderness system, the requirement of environmental impact assessments on major construction projects, and the cleaning up of American lakes and streams

One important legislative act dealing with land-based hazardous waste was the Resource Conservation and Recovery Act of 1976. Prior to this act, hazardous waste was stored in pits, ponds, or slag piles, or shipped to undisclosed sites. Following the discovery of toxic dumps in places like "Love Canal," in Niagara Falls, New York, public pressure encouraged federal regulation to control treatment, generation, transportation, and destruction of hazardous materials. The Superfund, initiated by Congress in 1980 in response to Love Canal, was mandated to identify and clean up hazardous wastes. Within a decade of its inception, the Superfund was sharply criticized as being incredibly slow and inefficient. Although some 1,250 sites around the country have been identified, only 180 had been cleaned up, at a cost of some $6.7 billion.

In 2002 Americans spend more than $124 billion per year to facilitate federal environmental statutes and regulations. In an effort to curb these expenditures, reformers offer three possibilities to revise current environmental policy. The first advocates direct government regulation of all activities affecting the environment. The second relies on federal guidance to shape environmental policy but market-based incentives to implement it. The third suggests that with a properly contrived plan of PROPERTY RIGHTS, augmented by contract and tort law, market forces could take care of the environment without the need for government interference.

Issues of how to best protect the environment while maintaining a healthy economy, although not necessarily incompatible goals, have given rise to political and policy debates at the local, state, and national levels, through third-party political organizations and major POLITICAL PARTIES. Many activists have turned to the GREEN PARTY as a means of focusing the nation's attention on environmental issues. The debate over drilling for oil resources in the arctic wilderness in Alaska, blocked in the Senate in 2002 over President GEORGE W. BUSH's wishes, illustrates that debate over the environment and maintaining the nation's energy supplies will continue into the future.

See also ECONOMY; ENERGY CRISIS; POPULATION TRENDS; SCIENCE AND TECHNOLOGY.

Further reading: Frances Cairncross, *Costing the Earth: The Challenge for Governments, Opportunities for Business* (Cambridge, Mass.: Harvard Business School Press, 1991); Mark Dowie, *Losing Ground* (Boston: MIT Press, 1995); Al Gore, *Earth in the Balance: Ecology and the Human Spirit* (New York: Dutton, 1992); Robert Gottlieb, *Forcing the Spring* (Washington, D.C.: Island Press, 1993).

—Michele Rutledge

conservative movement

The election of RONALD W. REAGAN to the presidency in 1980 represented the growth of a powerful conservative movement that emerged in America following World War II. Conservatism as a political force, however, was not a single movement per se, but a confluence of a variety of individuals, groups, and organizations with differing ideological, cultural, and political perspectives on the meaning of the word "conservative." What conservatives shared, however, was a general distrust of centralized government, New Deal liberalism, and marxism, and a faith in individual endeavor, property rights, and the rule of law.

Throughout the 1950s conservatives remained generally isolated and without great political influence. The primary focus of conservatives remained anticommunism directed toward the Soviet Union. In the 1950s conservatives generally fell into two camps: traditional conservatism and libertarianism. Traditional conservatives were represented by WILLIAM F. BUCKLEY, founder of the *National Review;* scholar Richard Weaver; political philosopher Leo Strauss; and historian Russell Kirk. These traditional conservatives expressed a belief in transcendent values and maintained that American culture had become increasingly relativistic. Russell Kirk's *The Conservative Mind,* published in 1953, argued for the importance of tradition, community, and organic society, as articulated by political philosopher Edmund Burke in the 18th century.

Libertarianism, although sharing many values of traditional conservatism, emphasized the importance of the free market and individualism. In this respect, libertarians attributed less importance to tradition and the transcendental values found in Judeo-Christianity. Libertarians were influenced by economists such as Friedrich von Hayek, author of *The Road to Serfdom* (1948), which warned of encroaching state socialism in the West and in the United States. Influenced by Hayek, Frank Chodorov founded the Intercollegiate Society of Individualists in 1952 to promote the libertarian cause and free-market economics. University of Chicago economist Milton Friedman promoted free-market economics through his writings, which led to his receiving a Nobel Prize in 1976. In addition, many libertarians were influenced by Ayn Rand, a Russian émigré author whose best-selling novels, *Atlas Shrugged* (1957) and *The Fountainhead* (1943) promoted the virtues of individualism and capitalism and savagely attacked Judeo-Christian values.

In the 1950s conservatives and libertarians united in their opposition to communism. Anticommunism emerged as a potent force during the 1950s and would be carried into the 1960s. In the early years of the COLD WAR, the grassroots anticommunist movement was composed of a number of separate organizations and leaders including Christian Anticommunist Crusade, headed by Australian physician Fred Schwarz; the Cardinal Mindszenty Foundation, founded by PHYLLIS SCHLAFLY and her husband, Fred Schlafly; and the opportunistic Christian Crusade founded by Billy Hargis. In 1958 candy manufacturer Robert Welch founded the John Birch Society, but many conservatives shied away from the organization when it was revealed that Robert Welch had accused President Eisenhower of being a conscious agent of the Soviet Union.

This anticommunist movement laid the foundation for the modern conservative movement, which came fully of age with the nomination of U.S. senator Barry Goldwater (R-Ariz.) on the Republican presidential ticket in 1964. Although Goldwater was easily defeated by incumbent president Lyndon Johnson, conservatives gained important organizing and fund-raising experience. Goldwater won 23 million votes. The political and social upheavals of the 1960s, especially the extension of the welfare state under President Johnson's Great Society, racial riots and the Black Power movement, the Vietnam War, and student protests fed the growth of political conservatism.

This political backlash against the Great Society enabled conservatives to win elections and gain national visibility. In 1968 RICHARD M. NIXON won the White House. The Nixon administration, however, disappointed conservatives with his support for DÉTENTE, the opening of relations with mainland China, arms control treaties with the Soviet Union, and the expansion of the federal government with economic and environmental legislation and civil rights. Conservatives sought to challenge Nixon in 1972 by backing Representative John Ashbrook (R-Ohio) in the primaries, but this campaign failed to get off the ground. Following the WATERGATE SCANDAL, which forced Nixon to resign from office, conservatives were demoralized and isolated.

Conservatism revived, however, as activists seized upon two critical issues: abortion and feminism. In 1972 Congress passed the EQUAL RIGHTS AMENDMENT (ERA). The STOP-ERA movement, led by Phyllis Schlafly, mobilized conservative women across the country to prevent state ratification of this amendment. In this campaign, EVANGELICAL CHRISTIAN women and Mormons became politically involved. The U.S. SUPREME COURT's decision, *ROE V. WADE* (1973), which found ABORTION to be a constitutional right, created a backlash among Roman Catholics and other religious groups and led to a grassroots pro-life movement. Finally, environmental protection legislation

enacted in the Nixon administration activated American business, as well as western ranchers and farmers. In 1973 the Heritage Foundation, a conservative think tank in Washington, D.C., was founded by Paul Weyrich, Edwin J. Feulner, and Joseph Coors.

The GERALD FORD administration further disappointed conservatives, and in Republican primaries in 1976, RONALD W. REAGAN challenged Ford, leaving the GOP sharply divided between its liberal and conservative wings. This division, along with a weak economy, Watergate, and Ford's gaffes during the campaign, helped JAMES EARL CARTER, JR., the Democratic nominee, win the presidency.

During the Carter administration, conservatives mobilized to take control of the Republican Party, bringing new constituencies into the party from evangelical Christian voters and white voters in the South, as well as making inroads among Catholic voters in the North. In doing so, conservatives sought to tie social issues such as abortion, prayer in schools, and the ERA to traditional Republican issues of free-market economics, limited government, fiscal responsibility, and strong military and national defense positions. In response to what was perceived as a weak and vacillating foreign policy toward the Soviet Union, including defense cutbacks and arms control treaties such as the STRATEGIC ARMS LIMITATION TREATIES, intellectuals like Jeane Kirkpatrick, Richard Perle, William Kristol, Norman Podhoretz, and Gertrude Himmelfarb attacked what they called the "culture of appeasement." New organizations were established such as the Committee for the Free World and the Committee on the Present Danger to promote a tougher stance toward the Soviet Union. This movement became known as NEOCONSERVATISM. Neoconservatism was characterized by its interest in FOREIGN POLICY and DEFENSE POLICY and, in general, showed less interest in social issues.

The mobilization of a New Christian Right, led by televangelists Jerry Falwell (the MORAL MAJORITY) and Pat Robertson (the CHRISTIAN COALITION, directed by Ralph Reed), imparted further momentum to the conservative movement. The Christian Right attacked secular humanism, moral relativism, and sexual permissiveness, which were perceived as leading to the breakdown of the traditional family. Concerns with the American family's breakdown led to the creation of a pro-family movement represented by Phyllis Schlafly's Eagle Forum and Gary Bauer's Family Research Council. These new organizations and groups were labeled by the press as the New Right.

Critics accused the New Right of introducing religion into politics and ignoring the constitutional separation between church and state. Furthermore, they charged that the New Right was exploiting racial anxieties of whites and fears about changing gender roles that had been brought about by the feminist movement. In doing so, critics argued, the New Right was creating a politics of "intolerance" that failed to recognize ethnic and religious diversity in a pluralistic society.

Reagan's election as president in 1980 brought conservatives to power, culminating a 40-year effort. Reagan pursued a conservative agenda of tax cuts, economic deregulation, and a defense buildup. In doing so, Reagan became a hero to the conservative movement. The Reagan administration, however, did not achieve everything that conservatives wanted, especially on the so-called social issues—abortion and prayer in schools. Nonetheless, the success of the conservative agenda on fiscal matters and economic deregulation pushed the Democratic Party in the 1990s to the right on these issues, even while the party moved generally to the left on many social issues, especially reproductive rights for women.

Discord arose among conservatives after Reagan left office in 1988. Many conservatives remained suspicious of GEORGE H. W. BUSH, whom Reagan designated as his heir apparent. This discord was reflected in journalist PATRICK BUCHANAN's unsuccessful primary challenges to George H. W. Bush in 1988 and 1992 on a program of economic protectionism, immigration restriction, and cultural issues. Bush's loss of the White House to WILLIAM J. CLINTON in 1992 suggested that the "Reagan revolution" had failed to produce a political realignment. Conservatives rejoiced, however, when Republicans, under NEWTON GINGRICH, (R-Ga.) swept the off-year election and captured control of Congress in 1994, but it was not until the election of GEORGE W. BUSH in 2000 that conservatives regained the White House, although some conservatives initially supported his primary rival, Senator John McCain (R-Ariz.) for the nomination.

During the 1990s, fissures within the conservative movement became evident. The different agendas among conservatives led to divisions among the neoconservatives (who were primarily Jewish), Roman Catholics and southern Protestants of the Old Right, and libertarians. In the 1990s, with the end of the cold war social issues became dominant for some conservatives. Cultural conservatives such as former Reagan official William Bennett and constitutional scholar ROBERT BORK denounced what they saw as the cultural and moral decay of basic American values. Allan Bloom's best-seller, *The Closing of the American Mind* (1987) argued that "POLITICAL CORRECTNESS" had distorted American education, subverting society's moral and spiritual traditions. As a student of Leo Strauss, Bloom attacked modernism for eroding traditional values. Former radical David Horowitz, in a series of books and articles, indicted radicals of the 1960s as a "destructive generation" that had fostered racial tensions and cultural disorder.

As the conservative movement entered the 21st century, conservatives often divided over a wide range of issues—American military intervention, abortion, gay rights, immigration, and free trade—but they agreed upon fundamental issues concerning the need to downsize the federal government, the need for a strong military and national defense, and policies that they believed would promote family values, individual responsibility, and economic opportunity. The conservative movement changed American politics, moved both parties to the right on fiscal issues, and stirred debate about cultural and moral order in society.

Further reading: David Brooks, ed., *Backward and Upward: The New Conservative Writing* (New York: Vintage Books, 1996); George H. Nash, *The Conservative Intellectual Movement in America since 1945* (New York: Basic Books, 1976).

—Donald T. Critchlow

contras

The contras were a group of counterrevolutionaries opposed to the ruling Sandinista government in Nicaragua during the 1980s. President RONALD W. REAGAN authorized the funding that enabled the formation of the contras.

In Nicaragua the Sandinista National Liberation Front had overthrown the dictatorship of Anastasio Somoza in 1979. Although the new Sandinista government expanded its ties with noncommunist nations, it also strengthened its relationship with Cuba and other nations of the socialist bloc. The Reagan administration viewed this as an indication of further communist expansion in the Western Hemisphere and, therefore, as a threat to U.S. national security. In 1981 the United States suspended economic aid to Nicaragua, and Reagan authorized nearly $20 million for the recruiting, training, and arming of Nicaraguan counterrevolutionaries who would engage in irregular military operations against the Sandinista government. These insurgents, who came to be called contras, operated out of bases on the border areas of Honduras and Costa Rica, and numbered approximately 15,000 by the mid-1980s. They never presented, however, a serious military threat to the Sandinistas, but they did cause millions of dollars in damage to the Nicaraguan economy by attacking local police and military units, farms and cooperatives, shipping, and other civilian targets. The Sandinistas eventually expanded their military and implemented counterinsurgency strategy and tactics, which enabled them to contain and demoralize the contras by the late 1980s.

U.S. involvement with the contras deepened during the mid-1980s. In response to evidence alleging human rights abuses by the contras, Congress passed in

1984 the BOLAND AMENDMENT that prohibited any direct or indirect U.S. military aid to them. In violation of this law, the Reagan administration in 1985 and 1986 undertook a covert campaign by which a portion of the funds raised through illegal arms sales to Iran were funneled to the contras in Nicaragua. This operation was uncovered in 1986 and the ensuing scandal came to be known as the IRAN-CONTRA AFFAIR. In 1987 Congress voted against supplying any further aid to the contras, and the same year saw the locus of the Nicaragua conflict move from the military to the political sector. The contras formally demobilized in June 1990 under the auspices of the peacefully elected government headed by the National Opposition Union coalition.

See also BUSH, GEORGE H.W.; GRENADA; LATIN AMERICA; NICARAGUA; NORTH, OLIVER L.

—William L. Glankler

Cox, Archibald, Jr. (1912–)

Archibald Cox Jr., a Harvard Law School professor, author, and attorney, is best known as the special prosecutor whose investigation of the WATERGATE scandal led to the resignation of President RICHARD MILHOUS NIXON in 1974.

Archibald Cox was born May 17, 1912, to Frances Perkins Cox and Archibald Cox, Sr., in Plainfield, New Jersey, and was the great-grandson of William Maxwell Evarts, the attorney who defended President Andrew Johnson at his impeachment trial in 1868. Cox was the oldest of seven children. He completed his bachelor's degree at Harvard University in 1934, and graduated magna cum laude in 1946 from Harvard Law School. In 1937 he married Phyllis Ames. Following four years in Washington during World War II, Cox accepted a faculty position at Harvard Law School, specializing in labor law. Under President Harry Truman, Cox served as chair of the Wage Stabilization Board. Under Presidents John F. Kennedy and Lyndon B. Johnson, he served as solicitor general, a position that would later cause President Nixon to question Cox's motives during the Watergate scandal.

Despite his lack of prosecutorial experience, Archibald Cox was appointed by Attorney General Elliott Richardson in 1973 to investigate the alleged Watergate cover-up and illegal activity in the 1972 presidential campaign. As special prosecutor, a newly created government position, Cox was given a broad mandate with unprecedented investigative independence and authority in this case. After learning of the existence of secretly taped conversations held in the White House, Cox demanded specific tapes be made available to him. Nixon, citing national security issues and claiming executive privilege, withheld the recordings. The U.S. Court of Appeals overrode Nixon and ordered him to surrender the tapes. Nixon offered to submit edited transcripts

of the recordings, but his proposal—using Senator John Stennis (D-Miss.) as mediator and limiting any future access to unsubpoenaed tapes and presidential materials—was unacceptable. Nixon then ordered Richardson to fire Cox. Rather than comply with the president's order, the attorney general, as well as the deputy attorney general, William Ruckelshaus, resigned from office. Solicitor General ROBERT BORK, as acting attorney general, proceeded to execute Nixon's mandate. The firing of Cox and the resignations of Ruckelshaus and Richardson became collectively known as the Saturday Night Massacre.

Cox returned to academic life, serving as a visiting professor at Cambridge University and teaching law at Boston and Harvard Universities. Cox also served from 1980–92 as the chair of Common Cause, a citizens' lobbying group founded in the 1970s that emphasizes campaign finance reform.

—Michele Rutledge

crime

Forty percent of all federal criminal laws enacted from 1850 to 2000 were passed between 1970 and 2000. During the same period, the United States has enjoyed a general reduction in the number of victims of crime. Though the number of victims of violent crime increased 5 percent from 1973 to 1981, and another 16 percent from 1989 to 1994, the intervals between witnessed even greater decreases; the number of victims fell 14 percent between 1981 and 1989, and 48 percent from 1994 to 2000. The mid to late 1990s also saw a 75 percent drop in the incidence of rape and 50 percent drops in the number of robberies and aggravated assaults. Similarly, the number of victims of property crimes, including burglary and theft, fell 75 percent from 1974 to 2000, with the most significant decreases occurring between 1979 and 1984, when the rate fell 25 percent. Auto theft was the only anomaly; after a gradual decline from 1975 to 1985, the rates increased 50 percent between 1985 and 1991. Yet even auto theft experienced a 50 percent decline over the whole period from 1974 to 2000.

Despite the overall decline in the number of victims involved in crimes, the number of incarcerated criminals has skyrocketed; America's prison and jail populations rose 383 percent between 1980 (just over half a million) and 2000 (just under 2 million). The difference between the numbers of victims and the numbers of incarcerated criminals reflects the growing number of drug-related crimes. Some advocates for drug legalization contend that drug use is a "victimless crime" because the user and the perpetrator are one and the same. Opponents of drug legalization maintain that there is no way to estimate the numbers of families and friends harmed by drug abuse, or whether the legalization of drugs would actually lead to lower crime rates.

This unique imbalance between victim and offenders reveals a general shift in the nature of crime in America. The overall rate of crime actually increased 25 percent since 1970, but prior to 1970, most crimes dealt with violence or property without involving drugs. By the early to mid-1970s, drug use and drug trafficking gradually assumed a central role. To some extent, this shift is also related to a gradual decline, in major urban centers, of organized crime, which has been replaced by smaller, less organized, youth street gangs. This phenomenon resulted in a decline of certain kinds of property crimes and violent crimes related to extortion and intimidation. Since the new youth gangs concentrated on drug trafficking, they used violence, not merely for intimidation, but to eliminate the competition. The result was a demographic shift in the murder rate. Prior to 1985 most murders were committed by 25- to 34-year-olds. After that date, the murder rate by perpetrators 14 to 24 years old rose dramatically, while the rate for those aged 25 years and above declined proportionately. While the rate of murder for young white males doubled, similar rates for young black males tripled. The mean age of murder victims experienced similar shifts; in some inner-city neighborhoods, the life expectancy of black males was 25 years. By 2000 law enforcement agencies estimated that one out of four black males would be incarcerated in state or federal prisons. Another effect of this shift is that Americans who are not involved in illicit drugs are less likely to become victims of street crime, while those who are involved are more likely to become either victims or prisoners.

The federal government can take some credit for the decline in organized crime. Following the 1967 *Report of the President's Commission on Law Enforcement and Administration of Justice,* Congress passed the Organized Crime Control Act (OCCA) of 1970. Included as Title IX was the RACKETEER INFLUENCED AND CORRUPT ORGANIZATIONS ACT (RICO), which allowed law enforcement agencies to increase the normal fines and penalties of certain crimes, usually at levels three times the norm, when they are committed by organizations. Though the Department of Justice waited almost 10 years before using it, the act has since become a prosecutor's favorite tool for combating organized crime. The 1980s witnessed a string of widely publicized mob trials, including the Pizza Connection, prosecuted by the office of U.S. Attorney for the Southern District of New York Rudolph Giuliani, involving 23 defendants in a $1.6 billion heroin-smuggling operation; and the murder trials of John Gotti, the late head of the Gambino crime family, who was acquitted in two successive RICO cases in 1986, earning him the nickname "the Teflon Don." FBI tapes later revealed that Gotti bribed jurors and witnesses to win the acquittals. He was finally convicted and sentenced to life imprisonment after a third trial in 1991, when his underboss, Salvatore "Sammy the Bull" Gravano, testified against him. For most of the 1960s to the 1980s, organized crime controlled trucking in New York's garment district, the Fulton Fish Market & Union, and shipping in JFK International Airport, and governed unions involved with the Javits Convention Center, waste hauling, and construction. The result was a hidden extortion tax that merchants passed on to consumers. During the 1980s, the FBI effectively broke mob control in each of these areas and in similar strongholds across the country. Though John Gotti gained more fame than other mob leaders, he reigned during a time when organized crime was already greatly weakened.

The federal government has experienced mixed success in its efforts against the new wave of drug crimes. Congress passed the Comprehensive Crime Control Act in 1984, which included forfeiture provisions for all drug offenses and increased funding for law enforcement agencies. While the law resulted in more arrests for cocaine trafficking, the numbers and violence of youth gangs seemed to increase as well. Two years later, in the 1986 Anti-Drug Abuse Act, Congress addressed the gang problem directly by adding additional penalties for juveniles who commit drug crimes.

In 1989 President GEORGE H. W. BUSH declared a "war on drugs" and created a drug czar, WILLIAM J. BENNETT, to lead this campaign against drugs by coordinating federal agencies involved with drug enforcement, promoting drug rehabilitation, and public awareness programs. At the same time Congress appropriated additional funds for drug enforcement and drug rehabilitation programs. In the years that immediately followed, drug use and its related crime rates fell, only to rise again five years later.

In 1993 Congress enacted, with the endorsement of WILLIAM J. CLINTON's administration, the Brady Handgun Prevention Act, named after President Ronald W. Reagan's press secretary, left disabled following an attempted assassination of the president with a recently purchased handgun. The act required handgun buyers to wait five days before the purchase of the weapon for authorities to undertake background checks. The following year, Congress enacted the Omnibus Crime Control and Safe Streets Act (1994), which substantially increased federal involvement in crime prevention. The act permitted 30.2 billion to be given over a six-year period in block grants to states for police recruitment, prison construction, and prevention programs. The act also banned 19 types of assault weapons, and allowed judges to waive minimum sentences for nonviolent, first-time drug offenses. The act expanded the number of federal capital crimes. It also provided additional penalties for "hate crimes" (federal crimes committed

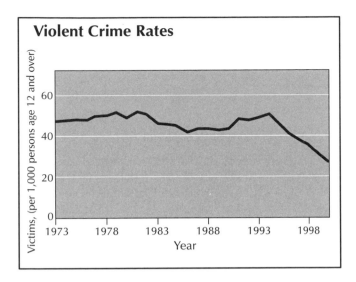

Violent Crime Rates

Victims, (per 1,000 persons age 12 and over)

Year

harsher penalties for repeat offenders. Other experts favor more preventive measures, including less incarceration time for nonviolent offenders, and more rehabilitation programs for drug offenders. This camp often sees drug use and drug-related crimes as a reflection of social problems in the inner city. The declining crime rates do not adequately prove the case for either side, because the American prison population continues to increase, topping 1 million in 1990, and 1.3 million in 2000. Similarly the population in jails, which hold inmates for terms less than one year, increased nearly 400 percent during the same period, reaching 621,149 in 2000. A debate continues between those who say increasing prosecution is responsible for lower crime rates, and others who think increases in federal criminal legislation have only produced more criminals to be incarcerated.

See also CAPITAL PUNISHMENT; NARCOTICS.

against victims selected for their race, religion, ethnicity, gender, disability, or sexual orientation. Finally the act imposed a "three strikes, you're out" policy, which mandated life imprisonment for criminals convicted of three violent felonies.

Experts remain divided in their approach to crime. One camp tends to promote stronger law enforcement measures, including more consistent enforcement of the laws, longer sentences, fewer opportunities for parole, and

Further reading: David Arthur Jones, *History of Criminology: A Philosophical Perspective* (Westport, Conn.: Greenwood Press, 1986); U.S. Department of Justice, *Challenge of Crime in a Free Society: Looking Back, Looking Forward* (Washington, D.C.: U.S. Government Printing Office, 1997); U.S. Department of Justice, *Compendium of Federal Justice Statistics* (Washington, D.C.: U.S. Government Printing Office, 1993–1999).

—Aharon W. Zorea

D

Dayton accords

In November 1995 peace negotiations were held in Dayton, Ohio, to work out the details of an agreement that provided for settlement of the war in Yugoslavia. This conflict began in April 1992 after nationalist Serb snipers fired on peaceful demonstrators in Sarajevo. Bosnia-Herzegovina, after seceding from the Yugoslav Federated Republic, was recognized by the West in May 1992 as an independent state. Bosnian Serbs, supported by Serbian leader Slobodan Milosevic, immediately began an armed war with the goal of dividing the republic along ethnic lines. Reports of "ethnic cleansing"—the mass murder and/or dispossession of non-Serbs—and other atrocities soon reached the international press. U.S. president WILLIAM J. CLINTON became a vocal advocate for a search for peace. The peace conference worked out the details of an accord that provided for an Implementation Force (IFOR) made up of NORTH ATLANTIC TREATY ORGANIZATION (NATO) peacekeeping troops, and national elections to be held in September 1996. The United States supplied 20,000 soldiers to the operation. Although imperfect—the concerns of Albanians in KOSOVO were not considered— the Dayton negotiations made progress toward ending the war and ethnic cleansing in the Balkans. The presidents of Bosnia, Serbia, and Croatia signed the agreement, which confirmed the division of Bosnia and Herzegovina.

See also FOREIGN POLICY.

—Michele Rutledge

defense policy

When President RICHARD M. NIXON entered office in 1969 he sought to pursue a policy of détente with the SOVIET UNION. This policy entailed establishing better relations with the USSR through trade and arms control; opening relations with mainland China; and ending the war in Vietnam. As part of this policy, the administration introduced the Nixon Doctrine, which stated that allies would do the fighting instead of U.S. troops. This doctrine was a response to the U.S. backlash to its involvement in the VIETNAM WAR, and an outgrowth of the détente strategy of avoiding direct confrontation between the superpowers. Under this doctrine, the United States continued to support its allies, including the South Vietnamese government, through military and foreign aid.

While seeking better relations with the Soviet Union, Nixon continued a nuclear strategy of "mutually assured destruction" (MAD), in which the United States would be able to retaliate to any nation's nuclear attack with nuclear weapons. At the same time, he sought to shift Soviet and U.S. nuclear weapons away from civilian targets. Nixon moved away from his predecessor's defense policy of "flexible response" and toward a new defense policy of "strategic sufficiency." This new policy replaced the goal of nuclear and military superiority, for which both superpowers had been striving for decades. "Strategic sufficiency" required the United States to have the nuclear capability to deter a nuclear attack launched by the Soviet Union. This was to be accomplished by convincing the Soviets that even after receiving a nuclear strike, the United States would still be able to retaliate with an unacceptable amount of nuclear force.

In 1972 the United States and the Soviet Union signed the first Strategic Arms Limitation Treaty (Salt I). It limited both nations to a maximum of 200 antiballistic missiles (ABM) and two ABM systems. A separate agreement froze for five years the number of intercontinental ballistic missiles (ICBMs) and submarine-launched ballistic missiles (SLBMs). These treaties formalized a strategy of mutual deterrence, the view adopted by both sides as the surest guarantee against nuclear attack.

In pursuing the SALT agreement, Nixon pressured reluctant liberals in Congress to support the development of new weapons systems. Nixon gave the go-ahead to a new kind of missile called a "multiple independently targeted reentry vehicle" (MIRV). Each of these missiles carried three to 10 separately targeted warheads, so fewer missiles could launch more bombs. The introduction of MIRV technology, in effect, accelerated the arms race.

Coming into office in 1974, President GERALD FORD continued Nixon's defense policy. In the aftermath of the Vietnam War, Ford, under pressure from Congress, agreed to cuts in defense. President Ford also dismissed James R. Schlesinger, who had served as secretary of defense in the Nixon administration, because he called for more money to be spent on defense. Schlesinger wanted the money to be allocated to conventional forces, which he believed were essential to American engagements in "limited" wars. Schlesinger also questioned the nature of the arms control policy being pursued by Secretary of State HENRY KISSINGER.

Meeting with Soviet leader Leonid Brezhnev in Vladivostok, Siberia, in late 1974, Ford made progress toward a new arms control treaty. The following year Ford and Brezhnev signed an accord in Helsinki, Finland, with 31 other nations, recognizing Europe's post-1945 political boundaries and agreeing to respect human rights. The Helsinki agreement drew criticism from "hawks" in both the Democratic and Republican Parties because it agreed to recognize the Soviet regimes in Eastern and Central Europe. Furthermore, critics accused the Soviet Union of continuing to violate human rights by suppressing dissidents and Russian Jews.

Defense policy in JAMES EARL CARTER, JR.'s administration is best described as equivalence and countervalence. President Carter worked toward the balancing of the United States and the Soviet Union in the nuclear arena. Initially Carter supported continued cuts in the defense budget with Congress. At the same time, Carter continued to rely on a nuclear capability based on a strategic triad of ICBMs, SLBMs, and bombers. Yet within these parameters, fierce debates during the next four years would be sustained within the administration and in Congress over a range of defense issues, including the development of a new B-1 bomber; the best platform for delivering a new mobile ICBM, the MX missile; the development of a neutron bomb; and the deployment of Pershing II missiles in Europe to counter the Soviet Union's deployment of mobile missiles in Eastern Europe.

In 1979 Carter negotiated a new arms control treaty, SALT II, with the Soviet Union, which called for further cuts in both nations' nuclear arsenals. The treaty acknowledged essential "parity" in the nuclear forces. Agreement called for each nation to stop construction of new fixed ICBMs, to leave the fixed sites in place, and not to convert light ICBMs into heavy ones. In addition, each nation would limit the number of its MIRVs and cruise missiles. The Soviet Union would dismantle 200 MIRV'd ICBMs, while the United States pledged not to test cruise missiles

with a range greater than 600 kilometers. The treaty was set to expire in 1985. A Joint Statement of Principles for SALT III called for further negotiations to set parity, while reducing overall levels of armaments.

When Carter submitted this treaty to Congress, however, he ran into strong opposition from members of his own party and Republicans who argued that the Soviets had not lived up to either the earlier Salt I agreement or the Helsinki Accords. Shortly before Carter signed the agreement, Senator Henry Jackson (D-Wash.) had declared that the treaty favored the Soviets and that to sign it would be "appeasement in its purest form." Although the Joint Chiefs of Staff endorsed the treaty, one of their representatives on the negotiating team resigned and testified against SALT. In addition, outside Congress, the treaty drew heavy criticism. The Committee on the Present Danger, a lobbying group organized in 1975 against détente, attacked the treaty as representative of a "culture of appeasement." Warning that it offered a means for the Soviet Union to achieve nuclear supremacy, through such loopholes as the absence of on-site inspections to verify that the agreement was being honored, Senate critics blocked the treaty from coming to a vote in 1979. Following the Soviet invasion of Afghanistan in December 1979, Carter withdrew the SALT II agreement in January 1980.

As tensions had mounted with the Soviet Union over its nuclear buildup and its involvement in Africa and Central America, Carter had urged increases in military expenditures. With the invasion of Afghanistan, Carter escalated defense spending, which had begun to increase shortly before the invasion. In June 1980 President Carter announced a countervailing strategy meant to convince the Soviet Union that the United States had the capability and the intent to launch a counterattack against the U.S.S.R. that would yield unacceptably great destruction of targets such as political and military control establishments, military forces, and the industrial areas of the Soviet Union. This shift toward selecting civilian targets reversed Nixon's declared policy of targeting only military sites. President Carter also continued to push European NORTH ATLANTIC TREATY ORGANIZATION (NATO) members to increase their defense spending and thus their share of responsibility.

When President RONALD W. REAGAN took office in 1981, he set out to enhance the ability of the United States not only to win a nuclear war but also to survive one. Throughout his first term, Reagan and his secretary of defense, Caspar Weinberger, continued to call for the largest peacetime military buildup since the outbreak of World War II in Europe. In his first year as president he announced his five-point plan for increasing U.S. capabilities: improvement of communications, command, and control systems (C3); modernization of the strategic bomber; new SLBM deployment; improvement of survivability and accuracy of new ICBMs; better strategic defense of the United States. Under this plan, he ordered production of 100 B-1 bombers and 100 MX-ICBMs, and called for the development of a stealth aircraft and the Trident II SLBM, as well as the enhancement of U.S. air-surveillance systems and anti-satellite systems (ASAT). President Reagan repeatedly fought Congress, which did not want to appropriate the money for funding these programs.

In March 1983 Reagan called for a Strategic Defense Initiative (SDI), derided by its critics as "Star Wars," a science-fiction fantasy movie. SDI called for a 20-year research and development project, with costs ranging from $100 billion to $1 trillion. While this proposal was being debated, the Reagan administration went ahead with plans made at the end of the Carter administration to deploy medium-range ballistic and cruise missiles in Europe. As a consequence, the Soviets withdrew from arms control talks.

Also during his first term, President Reagan aggressively employed U.S. troops in Third World countries to halt the spread of regimes that were unfriendly to the United States. He sent troops into GRENADA in 1983 and bombed Libya when the nation was found to be responsible for an international TERRORISM incident.

In his second term, Reagan appeared to reverse his defense policy toward the Soviet Union. In the next four years, Reagan had more meetings with the leader of the Soviet Union than any of his predecessors. He met with Mikhail Gorbachev, who had became party chairman in early 1985, at summits in Geneva in November 1985; in Reykjavik, Iceland, in October 1986; in Washington in December 1987; in Moscow in June 1988; and in New York that same year. As a result, détente was revived. More important, in December 1987 the two leaders signed the Intermediate Nuclear Forces treaty in which the two powers agreed to withdraw and destroy all intermediate-range missiles deployed in Europe. The following year, December 1988, in a speech before the UN General Assembly in New York Gorbachev announced that Russia would unilaterally reduce its military forces by 500,000 men and 10,000 tanks over the next two years.

President GEORGE H. W. BUSH came into office at the end of the COLD WAR. The significant changes in world affairs led the Bush administration to reformulate U.S. foreign and defense policy away from an ideological approach, as dictated by the cold war, toward a more pragmatic attitude. President Bush saw the beginning of a new era of defense planning when ethnic hostilities erupted across the world as the cold war ended. Conflicts became increasingly local, resulting in decreased justification for international defense. Beginning in fiscal year 1992 defense budgets began to diminish. This caused the subsequent closing of hundreds of military bases and a decrease in the number of U.S. servicemen stationed in Europe.

As the dominant military power now in the world, the United States under Bush assumed a greater role as an "international policeman"—working cooperatively with western European allies and the United Nations to preserve international stability. Often this meant military intervention into local areas. For example, in December 1989 Bush deployed U.S. troops to dethrone an unfriendly regime under dictator Manuel Noriega in PANAMA. In this intervention, 55 Panamanian National Guard troops and 23 U.S. soldiers lost their lives in 72 hours of fighting. The United States captured Noriega and placed him on trial in Miami, where he was convicted and sentenced for drug trafficking.

The Bush administration confronted a major international crisis on August 2, 1990, when Saddam Hussein, the dictator of Iraq, invaded his oil-rich neighbor, Kuwait. Bush organized an international coalition to oust Iraq from Kuwait. The United States led the United Nations to pass a series of resolutions demanding that Iraq withdraw, while at the same time the United States assembled a military force of 700,000 from 28 countries, stationed in Saudi Arabia. After the expiration of 12 UN resolutions calling for Iraq's withdrawal, Bush launched military action in what became known as the PERSIAN GULF WAR. After six weeks of bombing, UN forces launched a ground assault that liberated Kuwait, within 100 hours, on February 27, 1991. Although Hussein remained in power, he promised to allow arms inspectors into his country to ensure that all weapons of mass destruction, specifically nuclear, chemical, and biological weapons, had been destroyed and were not being developed. The UN continued an arms and economic embargo on Iraq, but Hussein soon was creating problems in the region by his refusal to cooperate with UN inspectors and his support of international terrorists.

When WILLIAM J. CLINTON won the presidency in 1992, he blended the use of military force and moral suasion in his defense and foreign policy. Confronted with the complexities of the post–cold war world, the Clinton administration was hesitant to deploy American forces unilaterally. During his eight years in office, Clinton continued to experience an uneasy relationship with the American military, in part because of his emphasis on multilateral military intervention, his downsizing of the military, and because of what critics said was his avoidance of military service during the Vietnam War. Furthermore, when he first assumed office, he ordered the military to include gay men and women in its ranks. The chairman of the Joint Chiefs of Staff, COLIN POWELL, was so upset with this policy that six months later, Secretary of Defense Les Aspin issued orders forbidding the military to inquire into the sexual orientation of service personnel. This "don't ask, don't tell" policy satisfied neither advocates nor opponents of including homosexuals in the military. Relations between the military and the administration did not get any better under Aspin, who failed to develop a rapport with the heads of the uniformed services. In late 1993 Aspin was fired, after 18 American marines lost their lives during a firefight in Somalia.

Aspin was replaced by William Perry, who served as the next secretary of defense between 1994 to 1997. He established a closer working relationship with the armed services and provided leadership as the military adopted a new generation of lighter weapons and more maneuverable ships, planes, and armored vehicles. In his second term, Clinton appointed Republican senator William Cohen to serve as secretary of defense.

During Clinton's tenure in office, the United States for the first time in its history had military forces in 100 nations around the globe. Under Clinton, American military troops were increasingly used to promote human rights abroad. These military interventions had mixed results. In the East African country of Somalia, the Clinton administration inherited a major U.S. military humanitarian operation. Shortly before leaving office, Bush had dispatched 28,000 U.S. ground troops to create what he called a "secure environment" for food distribution in this war- and famine-ravaged country. When Clinton came into office, however, he turned this relief effort over to a UN force, so that by July only 4,000 U.S. troops remained in Somalia as part of a "nation-building" force. On October 3, U.S. forces became engaged in a firefight with Somali warlord Muhammad Farah Aideed, leaving 18 marines killed. By the end of 1993, Clinton had withdrawn the remainder of the U.S. force. One major consequence of the failure of this mission was that the Clinton administration did not respond to a genocidal war by the Hutu-dominated government against the Tutsis in the East African country of Rwanda.

Clinton's efforts to restore the democratically elected government of Jean-Bertrand Aristide in Haiti with the threat of UN-backed American military action proved more successful in 1994, although subsequent Haitian governments proved less than democratic. In a rigged election, Aristide returned to power for a second term in June 2000.

The Clinton administration also became militarily engaged in the former Yugoslavia to promote human rights. In 1991 civil war had broken out in Bosnia, a province of Yugoslavia. The Bush administration avoided getting involved in conflict in the Balkans region, although it supported an embargo on exporting arms to the warring parties, which included Orthodox Christian Serbs, Catholic Croats, and Muslim Bosnians. The conflict intensified in the summer of 1995, precipitated by a Serb attack on the Muslim town of Srebrenica, which led to ethnic cleansing and the rape of thousands of Muslim women and girls. The Clinton administration joined NATO allies in launching air strikes against the Serbs, who were forced to withdraw to Yugoslavia. On November 1, representatives of Yugoslavia and the newly independent former Yugoslavian province of Croatia met at the U.S. Air Force base in Dayton, Ohio, where on November 21 the DAYTON ACCORDS were signed, lifting the siege of Sarajevo and creating the independent state of Bosnia. The United States agreed to lead an International Implementation Force (IFOR) of approximately 60,000 soldiers to maintain peace in Bosnia. The United States contributed 20,000 troops to this mission. Although Clinton pledged that these troops would be withdrawn by 1996, by 2000 the United States still had 8,000 troops in the area.

In March 1999 further troubles came in the region when Yugoslav president Slobodan Milosevic refused to withdraw his armed troops from the Yugoslav province of Kosovo. Because the United States feared that Milosevic would initiate an ethnic cleansing program against Albanian Muslims in this province, the United States and European members of NATO launched a bombing campaign against Milosevic's troops. Although Secretary of State MADELEINE ALBRIGHT and National Security Advisor Samuel R. "Sandy" Berger believed that the air campaign would force Milosevic to surrender in a matter of days, Milosevic sent the Yugoslav army on a rampage inside Kosovo. Moreover, the bombing of Yugoslavia appeared to unite the Serbs around Milosevic. Only on June 10, 1999—after seven weeks of intensive bombing—did Yugoslavia accept defeat. Over 60,000 troops from the United States and NATO entered Kosovo to supervise the return of refugees and to keep peace, but deep and historic hatreds remained between the Muslims and the Serbs. Few within the administration supported the end of the Kosovo war because it had lasted much longer than expected, and critics claimed that the war was "a perfect failure" that made conditions worse in Kosovo through military intervention. Few claimed it was absolutely successful, although Clinton defenders said that Kosovo was a much better place than it would have been absent NATO intervention.

The election of President GEORGE W. BUSH in 2000 brought a major refocus on American defense policy. During the campaign, Bush revived the proposal of creating a continental defense against nuclear missile attack, as well as a promise to "rebuild" the military and to increase pay for uniformed servicemen. Once in office, Bush pressed this agenda, but on September 11, 2001, the United States confronted its greatest attack since Pearl Harbor, when 19 terrorists hijacked four commercial airliners and slammed two of them into the twin towers of the World Trade Center in lower Manhattan and one into the Pentagon in northern Virginia, outside of Washington, D.C. A fourth airliner crashed before it reached its target. The terrorist attackers were identified as part of a worldwide terror network associated with a Saudi Islamic fundamentalist, Osama bin Laden. Bush declared a war on terrorism and then launched an international military assault against bin Laden's bases in Afghanistan, a country governed by a fundamentalist Islamic regime.

Thus from the initiation of the cold war at the end of World War II until today, the United States evolved from a nation preparing defensively for nuclear war in a bipolar world to one preparing defensively for terrorism, which could come in any form from any corner of the globe.

See also ANTI-BALLISTIC MISSILE TREATY; ARMS RACE; FOREIGN POLICY; TERRORISM.

Further reading: Patrick Glynn, *Closing Pandora's Box: Arms Races, Arms Control, and the History of the Cold War* (New York: Basic Books, 1992); John Lewis Gaddis, *Strategies of Containment: A Critical Appraisal of Postwar American National Security Policy* (New York: Oxford University Press, 1982).

—John Korasick and Leah Blakey

détente

Détente was the word President RICHARD M. NIXON used to describe his FOREIGN POLICY for the relaxing of tension in Soviet-American relations. The word has varied and interesting meanings. It is French and normally means "calm," "relaxation," or "easing," but it can also mean "the trigger of a gun." Détente policy was a U.S. invention that policymakers hoped the SOVIET UNION would understand and emulate. There is not a word in Russian that exactly means, "détente." The closest equivalent is *razriadka,* which can mean "lessening" or "reduction," but it can also mean "discharging" or "unloading." The diversity of the various meanings of the name of President Nixon's policy adequately fits the policy, which had an unexpected diversity of outcomes.

Richard M. Nixon's ascendancy to the presidency in 1969 brought about a marked change in U.S. policy regarding the Soviet Union—one that in many ways relaxed the tension between the two superpowers. As early as February 1969 on a trip to West Berlin, President Nixon called for an end to the tension surrounding that city. Since the end of the COLD WAR, Berlin had been a hot spot of contention, a city divided between the communist-controlled East and the allied-controlled West. Although Nixon's speech did not call for a reduction of U.S. forces stationed in West Germany, it indicated that his administration wanted to pursue a more concerted effort to bring Soviet and U.S. leaders together to discuss their differences and minimize direct military competition. Secretary of State HENRY KISSINGER stated in 1974 to the Senate Foreign Relations Committee: "Détente encourages an environment in which competitors can regulate and restrain their differences and ultimately move from competition to cooperation."

The difference between détente and the previous policy of "containment" became evident when President Nixon and Soviet premier Leonid Brezhnev signed a series of treaties allowing cultural and trade exchanges, and the selling of U.S. wheat to the Soviet Union. More important, the two leaders signed the first strategic Arms Limitation (SALT I) Treaty in May 1972. This policy became the cornerstone of détente.

SALT I comprised an Interim Agreement on Strategic Offensive Arms and an Anti-Ballistic Missile (ABM) Treaty. The Interim Agreement was set to expire five years after it was adopted. The ANTI-BALLISTIC MISSILE TREATY, which placed limits on ballistic missile defense deployment, development, and testing, was to last indefinitely, with reviews every five years. It limited the defense strategies of both sides in an attempt to guarantee deterrence through Mutually Assured Destruction (MAD).

Further evidence of Nixon's new approach to foreign affairs was seen when, in 1972, he visited the People's Republic of China in February and then the Soviet Union three months later. The following year, the Paris Accord was signed, calling for a cease-fire in the VIETNAM WAR, thus demonstrating once again the relaxation of tensions.

Détente continued into GERALD FORD's presidency as well. In his "State of the Union" message to Congress on April 12, 1975, President Ford stated: "[T]he United States and the Soviet Union share an interest in lessening tensions and building a more stable relationship. . . . But we cannot expect the Soviet Union to show restraint in the face of United States weakness or irresolution. As long as I am president, we will not permit détente to become a license to fish in troubled waters. Détente must be and I trust will be a two-way street." President Ford followed up on this idea of détente later the same year in Helsinki, when he joined 34 other world leaders in accepting the post–World War II boundaries in Europe and affirming the spirit of détente.

In the Carter administration (1977–81) détente came under serious criticism, as hawks within both the Republican and Democratic Parties alleged that the Soviet Union was violating human rights in its country by suppressing dissidents and not allowing its Jewish citizens to emigrate; by its arms build-up; by its unwillingness to relax its control in Eastern-bloc satellite nations; and its active support of revolutionary movements in Africa and Central America. These charges called for U.S. policy to take a harder stance toward the Soviet Union. One consequence of this stiffening became evident when the Senate refused to vote on a Carter-negotiated SALT II agreement, which would have further limited the arms race. Following the Soviet invasion of Afghanistan in 1979, relations between the Soviet Union and the United States became further strained.

These tensions followed into RONALD W. REAGAN's administration, which rejected a policy of détente with the Soviet Union. Indeed, when Reagan denounced the U.S.S.R. as an "evil empire," relations deteriorated so seriously that arms control talks between the two countries stalled. In his second term, however, Reagan swung back toward a policy of détente and was able to negotiate new arms treaties with the Soviets that radically reduced both nations' nuclear arsenals and withdrew medium-sized missiles from Europe. The final breakup of the Soviet Union led to the end of the cold war and called for new diplomatic initiatives in the post–cold war world.

See also ARMS RACE; STRATEGIC ARMS LIMITATION TREATIES.

Further reading: Paul Y. Hammond, *Cold War and Detente: The American Foreign Policy Process since 1945* (New York: Harcourt Brace, 1975); George Schwab and Henry Friedlander, eds., *Détente in Historical Perspective* (New York: Cyrco, 1975).

—Leah Blakey

Dole, Robert (1923–   )

Robert Dole was one of the most prominent Republican politicians during the latter half of the 20th century. Under the Republican banner, he ran as a vice presidential candidate with Gerald Ford in 1976, made a serious race for the presidential nomination in 1980 and 1988, and won the Republican presidential nomination in 1996, only to lose the general race to incumbent WILLIAM J. CLINTON that year. He served in the U.S. Senate from 1969 through 1996, emerging as a leader of the party. Although initially aligned with the conservative wing of the party, he proved to be a pragmatic politician. As the Republican Party moved to the right, Dole faced opposition from conservatives and would be challenged in the Republican primaries in 1986 by PATRICK BUCHANAN.

Born in Russell, Kansas, in 1923, Dole received a public education before entering the University of Kansas. In June 1943, after finishing his sophomore year, he enlisted in the U.S. Army to serve in the 10th Mountain Division in the liberation of northern Italy. He was wounded twice in battle, for which he received two commendations, including a Purple Heart. A German artillery shell left him disabled for life. He was discharged from military service in July 1948, after convalescing for three years for his wounds.

He returned to Russell, Kansas, to complete his B.A. degree at the University of Kansas, and an LL.B. from Washburn Municipal University. He married his first wife, Phyllis Holden, in 1948. A staunch Republican, Dole began his political career in 1951 as a member of the Kansas House of Representatives and served in this body until 1953. He was elected to four consecutive terms as Russell County attorney from 1952 to 1960. He entered the U.S. HOUSE OF REPRESENTATIVES in 1961, winning reelection in 1964 and 1966. In 1968 he won election to the U.S. SENATE and was reelected in 1974, 1980, 1986, and 1992. He left his seat in 1996 to become the Republican nominee for president.

As a U.S. senator, he established a distinguished record, serving on the standing committee on agriculture, and later as chairman of the Senate Finance Committee. In 1971 President RICHARD M. NIXON appointed Dole Republican National Committee chairman in 1971 for his service to the party. In 1972 he divorced his first wife and later met and married his second wife, Elizabeth Hanford. Following the Watergate scandal, Dole faced his toughest challenge for reelection to the Senate in 1974. Criticizing his opponent, Representative William R. Roy, for supporting abortion, Dole barely won the election, carrying only 50.8 percent of the popular vote.

In 1976 GERALD R. FORD picked Dole to be his vice presidential running mate as a means of holding the conservative wing of the party, which had rallied around a primary challenge by RONALD W. REAGAN. Dole acquired a reputation as a forceful speaker in this campaign, for his vigorous criticisms of the Democratic ticket of JAMES EARL CARTER, JR. and WALTER F. MONDALE. This reputation hurt him in his failed 1980 campaign for president; both Reagan and runner-up GEORGE H.W. BUSH defeated Dole easily in the party primaries.

Dole gave Republican conservatives a mixed performance during Reagan's presidency. Dole never concealed his skepticism about Reaganite conservatism, although he effectively served as chairman of the Senate Finance Committee to push through tax cuts in 1982. His wife, Elizabeth Dole, also served the Reagan administration in a number of high posts.

In 1988 Dole challenged George H. W. Bush in the Republican primaries. After Bush defeated Dole in the New Hampshire primary, he went on to easily win the general election. As president, Bush named Elizabeth Dole secretary of labor. In 1992, Dole campaigned for Bush, but Democrat WILLIAM J. CLINTON won the general election.

As Senate minority leader, Dole battled Clinton's legislative program. His tactics aided the Republicans in taking both the Senate and House in the 1994 elections. In 1996 Dole once again threw his hat into the presidential arena, and after a tough primary battle against Pat Buchanan, who won the New Hampshire primary, Dole went on to win the Republican presidential nomination. He resigned his Senate seat to free himself to campaign. But he never seriously threatened Clinton's polling lead, and lost the general election.

During his political life, Dole established a reputation for his acerbic wit, his loyalty to the Republican Party, and his public service. He served as adviser to the UN Food and Agricultural Organization in 1965, 1968, 1974–75, 1977, and 1979; and the National Commission for Social Security Reform in 1983. After leaving elected office, he continued public service as national chairman of the World War II War Memorial Campaign.

See also CONSERVATIVE MOVEMENT; ELECTIONS; POLITICAL PARTIES.

Further reading: Richard Ben Cramer, *What lt Takes: The Way to the White House* (New York, 1992); Bob and Elizabeth Dole et al., *Unlimited Partners* (New York: Simon & Schuster, 1996).

—Christopher M. Gray

Dukakis, Michael S. (1933–)

Born in suburban Brookline, Massachusetts, in 1933 to Greek immigrant parents, Michael Stanley Dukakis lived a classic American success story. Educated at Swarthmore College and Harvard Law School, with a tour in the U.S. Army in between, Dukakis became active in Massachusetts politics, first serving as a member of the Brookline Town Meeting. He became a member of the state legislature in 1962, winning reelection in 1964, 1966, and 1968. As a state legislator he sponsored the first no-fault auto insurance.

After a failed run for the office of lieutenant governor in 1970, Dukakis was elected governor in 1974. Inheriting a record deficit, Dukakis went back on a campaign pledge not to raise taxes, which cost him his bid for renomination. Dukakis taught at the Kennedy School of Government, a division of Harvard University, from 1979 to 1982. He returned to the governorship for a second term in 1982 and oversaw what came to be known as the "Massachusetts miracle," the revival of old industry and the introduction of new industry into the state. Dukakis was voted the "most effective governor" by the National Governor's Association in 1986 and won election that year to a third term. In 1987s Dukakis announced his intention to run for the 1988 Democratic presidential nomination. Outlasting rivals like Senator ALBERT GORE and U.S. Representative Richard Gephardt, Dukakis captured the nomination and picked Texas senator Lloyd Bentsen as his running mate. Stressing "competence" over "ideology," Dukakis ran an uninspiring campaign.

In an election characterized as one of the most negative in history, Republican nominees GEORGE H.W. BUSH and J. DANFORTH QUAYLE charged Dukakis with being soft on crime. The infamous WILLIE HORTON television ad was run by Bush supporters to highlight accusations that Dukakis was too liberal. The ad featured a convicted felon, Willie Horton, who had been released from prison by Dukakis only to commit a brutal rape. Furthermore, running on a pledge not to raise taxes, Bush attacked Dukakis for having raised taxes in his first term as governor of Massachusetts. In addition, Dukakis failed to respond to Bush's portrait of him as a "card-carrying" liberal. In the end, Bush easily won the election. Although Dukakis's race for the presidency marked another setback for Democrats in the Reagan-Bush years, his candidacy offered a transition as the party sought the political center. Dukakis promoted fiscal responsibility and called for greater efficiency in government. The next Democratic presidential nominee, WILLIAM J. CLINTON, followed Dukakis, this time successfully, in reaching middle-class voters. The 1988 presidential campaign was significant in another way: The negative campaign used on both sides—although the Horton ad was especially flagrant in this regard—left many with a sour taste after the election. As a result, in the next presidential election, Bush was constrained from appearing too negative in his attacks on his Democratic opponent, Clinton.

Following the election, Dukakis returned to Massachusetts to finish his term as governor. At this time, he faced a declining economy in Massachusetts as unemployment began to rise. He announced he would not seek reelection and left office in January 1991.

Since 1991 Dukakis has been a visiting professor of political science at Northeastern University, teaching courses in government and public policy. He has also taught at the University of Hawaii, the John F. Kennedy School of Government, Florida Atlantic University, and at the University of California, Los Angeles. Dukakis has authored numerous articles on public policy, particularly health-care reform. As a board member of Amtrak, he has called for the federal government to provide larger subsidies to support a national rail system.

See also ELECTIONS; POLITICAL PARTIES.

—John Korasick

E

Eagleton, Thomas F. (1929–   )

Thomas Francis Eagleton gained national attention during the presidential election of 1972 when he was forced to withdraw as the vice presidential nominee for the Democratic Party after it was revealed that he had undergone electric shock treatment for mental depression.

Born in 1929, Eagleton was a rising star in Democratic politics during the 1960s and became the youngest St. Louis prosecuting attorney (1956), Missouri attorney general (1960), and lieutenant governor (1964). In 1968 Eagleton challenged and defeated the incumbent Democratic senator, Edward V. Long, who was embattled after being linked with a scandal involving the Teamsters Union.

As a U.S. senator, Eagleton's liberal credentials in his first year were unimpeachable; he amassed a 90 percent favorable rating with the liberal Americans for Democratic Action. In 1969 he cosponsored a resolution making political reform in South Vietnam a precondition for continued American support during the VIETNAM WAR—believing that the United States was supporting an unpopular regime. By 1972 he supported immediate U.S. withdrawal from the war. He supported the draft, reasoning that an all-volunteer army would become a refuge for those unable to find other employment.

In 1972 Eagleton was selected by GEORGE S. MCGOVERN to be the Democratic vice presidential candidate. At the culmination of a convention marred by disorganization, McGovern and his aides met on the morning of July 14, 1972, nomination day, to decide on a running mate. Eagleton's name appeared on the final list, but the first choice was Boston mayor Kevin White. White was dropped because of opposition from the delegates. The next choice, Wisconsin senator Gaylord Nelson, refused the nomination but recommended Eagleton, largely known as a blue-collar labor liberal. Twenty minutes before the convention deadline, Eagleton was offered and accepted the nomination.

Shortly after Eagleton accepted, the *Detroit Free Press* ran a story and McGovern received a tip that Eagleton had undergone shock treatments in the 1960s. When confronted, Eagleton acknowledged that he had been hospitalized on three occasions and received shock therapy and counseling after pushing himself too hard during election campaigns. Eagleton had not been forthcoming because he considered the matter private and no longer relevant. McGovern scheduled a press conference during which he reaffirmed his choice. But there were serious concerns about having a man with a history of mental illness next in line for the presidency, especially with the specter of the assassination of John F. Kennedy still relatively fresh in the public mind. Eagleton resigned his spot on the ticket July 31, 1972. He received praise for his candor, and his continued support of McGovern and his own replacement, ROBERT SARGENT SHRIVER, JR. Although Richard M. Nixon won reelection, advocates for the disabled credited Eagleton's situation with lifting the stigma of mental illness.

Eagleton ran for and was reelected to the Senate in 1974. A solid Democrat, Eagleton earned a reputation as a champion of labor and civil rights, and an opponent of military spending. In 1980 Eagleton was again elected in an exceptionally close race. He did not seek reelection in 1986, retiring from the Senate in January 1987. Eagleton returned to St. Louis and accepted a partnership with the law firm of Thompson & Mitchell. Eagleton also became a professor of public affairs and political science at Washington University, teaching courses in public policy and legislative politics. He is also the author of two books: *Our Constitution and What It Means* (1987); and *War and Presidential Power* (1974).

—John Korasick

economy

The U.S. economy enjoyed spectacular growth in the first 20 years after World War II, with the gross national product doubling from 1945 to 1965. Inflation, or increase in prices, was low; unemployment was under control. However, from the late 1960s through the early 1980s, the economic picture changed to one of steep inflation, high unemployment, and regular recessions, or decreases in economic activity. The economy rebounded in the 1980s, fell into a slight recession in 1991–92, then boomed throughout the rest of the decade. In 2001 the economic picture changed again, this time for the worse. Behind the twists and turns of the U.S. economy since 1968 lay numerous factors, including wars, shifting oil prices, a high national debt, and the trend toward worldwide economic integration known as globalization.

In the late 1960s the federal government's finances began to stagger under the costs of the VIETNAM WAR and of new social programs associated with President Lyndon B. Johnson's Great Society, and Johnson's reluctance to raise taxes to offset rising inflation. The national debt, the amount of money owed by the federal government, climbed 70 percent in 10 years, from $313.8 billion in 1965 to $533.2 billion in 1975. (By comparison, the debt had risen only 15 percent from 1955 to 1965.) Furthermore, ballooning energy costs and rising labor costs created inflation. The rate of inflation climbed from 1.6 percent in 1965 to 9.1 percent in 1975. In 1971 the United States also faced, for the first time in decades, a deficit in its balance of payments, with the amount of money paid out to foreign countries exceeding the amount received.

American economic problems in the 1970s were linked to an international slowdown in growth and acceleration of inflation. Yet some countries, notably Japan and West Germany, fared better than others, raising talk of American decline relative to other nations. American manufacturers, particularly in the automobile, steel, and textile industries, lost ground to foreign competitors, resulting in massive layoffs. Unemployment was made worse in the post-1968 era by increasing automation, which reduced the need for employees, and the rise of a global labor marketplace, in which American businesses moved factories overseas to take advantage of cheap labor abroad. Workers could find jobs in the growing service sector—for example, in retail stores, restaurants, and health care—but these jobs were typically lower-paying than manufacturing jobs. The position of workers in the late 20th century was further weakened by the declining power of labor unions and the growing might of corporations that became ever bigger through mergers with smaller companies.

In August 1971, to combat the nation's economic troubles, President RICHARD M. NIXON announced the New Economic Policy, which began with a 90-day freeze on wages and prices; a temporary 10 percent surcharge on imports; and an end to redemption of dollars in gold. Other steps followed, including federal budget reductions; estab-

lishment of the Cost of Living Council, to plan and monitor increases in wages and prices; and tax measures to stimulate growth. Despite these policies, inflation again accelerated, and Nixon reimposed the wage and price freeze in 1973. Wage and price controls ended in 1974, but inflation remained a problem. The economy worsened in 1973–74 because of political events overseas and at home. In the winter of 1973–74, the Organization of Petroleum Exporting Countries (OPEC), composed predominantly of Arab oil-producing nations, imposed an embargo, or block, on oil shipments to the United States and other industrial nations in retaliation for their support of Israel in the Yom Kippur War (1973). In what was called the energy crisis, the embargo and a subsequent fourfold rise in oil prices drove inflation higher and caused worldwide recession and fuel shortages. In the midst of these difficulties, Nixon was distracted by the Watergate scandal at home, which forced his resignation in August 1974 and brought his vice president, GERALD R. FORD, to office.

By 1976, the unemployment rate was at 9 percent and inflation at 5.8 percent and rising. "Stagflation," a combination of recession and inflation, had become commonplace, with recessions occurring in 1970 and 1973–75. Ford's program of voluntary price controls, called Whip Inflation Now (WIN), failed, and Ford lost the 1976 election campaign to Democrat JAMES EARL CARTER, JR. Carter's economic policies also enjoyed little success; they included support for development of alternative energy sources, reduction of the federal bureaucracy, a windfall profits tax to cut profit gouging, and a plan to increase the dollar's value.

Once again, foreign political events had an impact on the American economy. In 1979, the shah of Iran, a leading oil-exporting nation, was overthrown and replaced with a theocratic Islamic government. This overthrow, known as the Iranian Revolution, led to a second energy crisis, with a new spiral of rising oil prices and shortages, marked in the United States by gasoline rationing and long lines at the gas pumps. Iranian revolutionaries took scores of Americans hostage in November 1979, and Carter was unable to secure their release. A new recession took hold, and Carter was charged with responsibility for the "misery index," the inflation rate added to the unemployment rate. In 1980 these figures were 13.5 percent and 7.1 percent, respectively, for a total of 20.6 percent. Independent of the president, the Federal Reserve Board, which had raised interest rates from the mid-1970s, kept these rates high, raising the cost of borrowing for both government and business. Toward the end of Carter's administration, Paul Volcker was appointed to serve as chairmen of the Board of Governors of the Federal Reserve System (the Fed).

In 1980 voters rejected Carter's reelection bid and instead elected Republican candidate Ronald W. Reagan, who promised a conservative approach known as supply-side economics or, more commonly, Reaganomics: lowering taxes and reducing regulation in the hope of stimulating investment and growth, while also cutting government spending and decreasing the size of the federal government. Under Reagan, Congress approved the largest tax cut in U.S. history, reducing personal and business income taxes by 25 percent from 1981 to 1983, while slashing government spending on social services. Simultaneously, out of commitment to the cold war against the Soviet Union, Reagan dramatically increased military spending, creating large budget deficits, or excesses in government spending over revenues received. The national debt doubled from $998 billion in 1981 to $2.1 trillion in 1986.

At first, Reagan's policies had little impact on the misery index. In the midst of a recession in 1982, unemployment rose, reaching 11 percent by 1983, its highest level since the Great Depression. Volcker, as head of the Fed, continued to maintain high interest rates as a means of controlling inflation, but this had the effect of reducing the money supply and slowing economic activity, bringing on recession and lowering tax revenues, making it harder still for the government to balance its budget.

Volcker attacked the problem of rising inflation rates by adopting a more restrictive monetary policy. Throughout the 1980s, he led a global crusade against inflation with some success. In the mid-1980s, however, a resurgence in unemployment and a stagnant economy forced Volcker to support some increases in monetary growth. Alan Greenspan, his successor appointed in 1987 by President Reagan, maintained similar vigilance against inflation. His method, however, differed in that he placed more stress on limiting federal involvement in the economy—rather than promoting economic growth through direct federal intervention, Greenspan preferred to maintain a tight control over inflation through subtle changes in interest rates. This policy proved successful in the 1990s, which earned him the respect of policymakers in both parties.

Aided by lower oil prices in the mid- and late 1980s, the economy at last revived. A bull market, a period in which stock prices rise, began in 1982. Inflation fell to about 3 percent by 1984, unemployment to 7.6 percent. The personal computer industry, born in the mid-1970s, became an engine of growth, with the software company Microsoft growing into an economic giant. Discount department stores such as Wal-Mart also did well in the 1980s, as did the health-care industry, due in large part to scientific advances and an aging population in greater need of medical treatment.

The economic boom continued through the 1980s. Still, there were signs of trouble: a stock market crash in 1987, an insolvent (financially unsound) savings and loan system, a growing gap between rich and poor, persistent

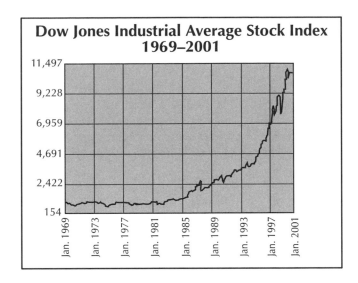

Dow Jones Industrial Average Stock Index 1969–2001

budget deficits and trade deficits (excesses of imports over exports), and the ever-rising national debt. Critics contended that Reagan's cuts in social spending lengthened the recession by suppressing demand. Proponents of the policies claimed that tax cuts helped end the recession and break the cycle of stagnation that had plagued the economy since the Vietnam War, observing that, under Reagan, the economy rebounded and personal wealth on a per-capita basis increased across socioeconomic and racial lines.

In mid-1990 the United States entered a new recession, for which Democrats blamed the Reagan-Bush economic policies. Having made an election promise of "no new taxes," Bush was criticized for raising taxes in a deficit-reduction package put forward by congressional Democrats. In the 1992 presidential campaign, Democrat WILLIAM J. CLINTON defeated Bush by making the economy the central issue. As his campaign staff put it, "It's the economy, stupid."

In March 1991 the economy began to grow again, and for 10 years the nation enjoyed the longest economic expansion on record. Unemployment, inflation, and interest rates were all low, and stock prices climbed. The boom was fed in part by technological innovation, particularly the rise of the Internet as a digital medium for communication and commerce. It was aided by Clinton policies, including deficit reduction and cutbacks in government spending. Clinton gave strong support to free trade, the lifting of economic barriers that discouraged exchange of goods and services between countries. Clinton convinced Congress to ratify the NORTH AMERICAN FREE TRADE AGREEMENT (NAFTA), which took effect in 1994, joining the United States, Mexico, and Canada in a free-trade zone. He also won adoption of the 1994 treaty, the GENERAL AGREEMENT ON TARIFFS AND TRADE (GATT), which advanced globalization by cutting tariffs, or trade barriers, around the globe and creating the WORLD TRADE ORGANIZATION (WTO) to administer trade laws.

In 1998 the federal budget was balanced for the first time since 1973, and the government enjoyed surpluses, not deficits, for the remainder of Clinton's tenure. Debate continues over the causes of the boom, with credit being variously attributed to the 1980s tax cuts, the 1990s deficit reduction, the 1980s decline in heavy manufacturing, the 1990s technology boom, and the ongoing processes of globalization and trade liberalization. Still, some Americans voiced concern about the continuing gap between the rich and the nonrich: According to one report, the average real income for the wealthiest one-fifth of Americans grew by 15 percent in the 1990s, while that of the middle class grew by less than 2 percent, and that of the lowest-income families did not grow at all. Concerns were also raised about the potential pitfalls of globalization, including the growing political power of multinational corporations unaccountable to electorates; the unequal position of Third World countries burdened by debt; and the lack of enforceable regulations protecting the environment and the rights of workers in a global marketplace. The stability of the U.S. economy was threatened in 1999 by ripples from an economic crisis in Asia that had begun in 1997.

In 2000 and 2001 economic growth began to slow and the stock market, which had soared in the 1990s, began to decline. Technology stocks were especially hard-hit: many Internet companies, known as dot-coms, failed not long after having been unveiled to great fanfare. Amid concerns that the long economic expansion might be ending, Republican GEORGE W. BUSH emerged victorious over Clinton's vice president, ALBERT GORE in the closely contested presidential election of 2000. Bush quickly won congressional approval of a $1.35 trillion program of tax cuts that he argued would promote economic growth, but that critics said would plunge the government back into deficit spending.

In March 2001 the 10-year expansion of the U.S. economy ended and a recession began. Unemployment rose, and production and sales fell. The already bad economic conditions were made worse by the terrorist attacks of September 11, 2001, in which the destruction of the World Trade Center killed thousands, devastated New York City's economy, and provoked the United States into war in Afghanistan. Fear of terrorism kept Americans at home, hurting the travel and tourism industries and their suppliers. Stocks plummeted; unemployment rose from 4.9 percent in September to 5.4 percent in October. In December, Enron Corp., once the world's largest energy trader, filed the largest corporate bankruptcy claim in U.S. history. Alan Greenspan again relied on interest-rate cuts to stimulate the economy, which, when combined with President Bush's taxes cuts, helped to stabilize the economy during the sec-

ond quarter of 2002. The terrorist attack nevertheless exacted a large price and the prospect of large budget surpluses in the near future appeared to be less certain.

See also AGRICULTURE; GLOBALIZATION; INFLATION; INTERNET; POVERTY RATES; TECHNOLOGY.

Further reading: Jack Beatty, ed., *Colossus: How the Corporation Changed America* (New York: Broadway Books, 2001).

—George Ochoa and Aharon W. Zorea

education, higher

Institutions of higher education provide instruction beyond the high school level. Colleges and universities provide requisite training for individuals wishing to enter professional careers. In addition, these institutions attempt to develop and enhance students' analytical skills, insight, and creativity.

The predominant types of higher education in the United States include community colleges, state or local universities, liberal arts colleges, professional schools, military academies, and proprietary institutions. Other types include agricultural colleges, technical colleges, teachers' colleges, and colleges affiliated with religious denominations. Community colleges typically offer the first two years of basic undergraduate course work. Most also offer technical training, vocational education, and adult educational programs. Often students complete the first two years of their college education in community colleges and then transfer the credits to a four-year college. Other community college students pursue technical, vocational, and other pre-professional programs. Typically, community colleges have lower tuition rates than four-year colleges and universities and therefore offer significant advantages, especially to "nontraditional" students. So-called "traditional" students are those who have graduated high school and are between the ages of 18 and 24. The nontraditional population may also include first-generation college attendees.

Universities usually are made up of colleges and professional schools that comprise the academic departments of the institution. For instance, a university may include a college of arts and sciences in addition to professional schools of engineering, medicine, law, and education. Universities offer higher education leading to a bachelor's degree, in addition to graduate and professional programs leading to master's and doctoral degrees. Colleges and universities in the United States may be public and supported by the government, or they may be private, independently run institutions. Most public colleges and universities in the United States are state institutions, although a few four-year colleges supported by either municipalities or the federal government also exist. State boards of higher education usually provide funds for these schools and administer their programs of instruction. Most state governments establish systems, like the University of California or the State University of New York systems, which encompass groups of interconnected college or university campuses.

Since 1969, increasing numbers of high school graduates continued their education at colleges and universities. From the mid-1970s through the later 1990s, enrollment has continued to rise in these institutions at a rate of 13 percent. Between 1987 and 1997, enrollment rose from 12.8 million to 14.3 million students. Although numbers dipped in the years 1992 to 1995, these figures were overshadowed by large increases in the late 1980s. Much of this growth came from women's enrollment. During the decade between 1987 and 1997, the number of men enrolled grew 7 percent, while the number of women rose by 17 percent. Part-time enrollment increased by 9 percent compared with 15 percent in full-time enrollment. In addition to the enrollment in accredited two-year colleges, four-year colleges, and universities, nearly 400,000 students were attending nondegree-granting, postsecondary institutions by the late 1990s.

Women have played a major role in the increase of enrollment between 1986 and 1999. The enrollment of women in college grew from 6.6 million in 1986 to 8.3 million in 1999, a 25 percent increase over the period. As a share of total college enrollment, 56 percent of all college students in 1999 were women, compared with just over half the college population in 1986.

More women than men earn associate, bachelor's, and master's degrees. In addition, the number of women receiving all types of degrees has increased more rapidly than for men. Between 1987–88 and 1997–98, the number of bachelor's degrees awarded to men increased by 9 percent, while those awarded to women rose by 28 percent.

Since the mid-1980s, the number of women in graduate schools has exceeded the number of men. During the late 1980s and the 1990s, the number of male full-time graduate students expanded by 22 percent, compared with 68 percent for full-time women. Among part-time graduate students, the number of men fell by 1 percent compared with a 15 percent increase for women.

Recent figures from the Department of Education show that of the 1,184,000 bachelor's degrees conferred in 1997–98, the largest numbers of degrees were in the fields of business (233,000), social sciences (125,000), and education (106,000). At the master's degree level, the largest fields were education (115,000) and business (102,000). The largest fields at the doctor's degree level were education (6,700), engineering (6,000), biological and life sciences (5,000), and physical sciences (4,600).

The pattern of bachelor's degrees by field of study has shifted significantly in recent years. Engineering and engineering technologies declined 12 percent between 1987–88 and 1992–93, and then posted a further 5 percent decline between 1992–93 and 1997–98. Computer and information sciences grew rapidly during the 1970s and mid-1980s, but dropped 22 percent between 1987–88 and 1997–98. Degrees in other technical fields have been driven upward in recent years, in part by increasing numbers of female graduates. For example, biological science degrees increased 28 percent between 1987–88 and 1992–93, and then rose 40 percent between 1992–93 and 1997–98. During the later period, the number of male graduates grew 30 percent, while the number of female graduates grew 50 percent. After declining by 5 percent between 1987–88 and 1992–93, the number of male graduates in the physical sciences rose 1 percent between 1992–93 and 1997–98. The number of female graduates in the physical sciences increased by 6 percent in the first period and rose a further 30 percent in the second half. Although the number of male graduates in agriculture and natural resources grew by 25 percent between 1992–93 and 1997–98, the number of female graduates grew by 66 percent.

Although the number of older students had been increasing more rapidly than the number of younger students, this trend is beginning to change. Between 1990 and 1997, the enrollment of students under age 25 increased by 2 percent. During the same period, enrollment of persons 25 and over grew by 6 percent.

Additionally, the proportion of American students in higher education who are minorities has been increasing. In the mid-1970s, 16 percent were minorities, compared with 27 percent 20 years later. Much of the difference can be attributed to rising numbers of Hispanic and Asian students. The proportion of Hispanic students rose from 4 percent to 9 percent, and the Asian and Pacific Islander proportion rose from 2 percent to 6 percent during that time period. The proportion of black students fluctuated during most of the early part of the period, before rising slightly to 11 percent in the later 1990s.

College enrollment increased from nearly 3 million in 1986 to 14.5 million in 1992. By 1999 this figure grew to 14.8 million. By the year 2011, college enrollment is projected to rise to between 17.7 and 18.2 million, with figures ranging from 16 to 23 percent since 1999. The projected number of women is expected to soar to nearly 60 percent by the first decade of the 21st century. Male enrollment had increased from 5.9 million during the mid-1980s to more than 6 million in the early 1990s, before decreasing slightly in 1995. Thereafter, it increased to 6.5 million in 1999.

More people are completing college. Between the later 1980s and the 1990s, the number of associate, bachelor's, master's, and doctor's degrees all grew. Associate degrees increased 28 percent; bachelor's degrees increased 19 percent; master's degrees, 44 percent; and doctor's degrees, 32 percent during this period.

Just over half of the students who enrolled in a four-year colleges in 1989–90 had finished their degrees by spring of 1994. About 7 percent of students had completed an associate degree or other certificate below the bachelor's degree, 15 percent of the students were still enrolled in a bachelor's degree program, and 24 percent were no longer working toward a bachelor's degree.

By the late 20th century, nearly 5,000 accredited institutions offered degrees at the associate degree level or above. These included more than 2,000 four-year colleges and universities, and nearly as many two-year colleges. Institutions awarding various degrees in 1997–98 numbered 2,465 for associate degrees, 1,910 for bachelor's degrees, 1,416 for master's degrees, and 517 for doctor's degrees. Despite the sizable numbers of small, degree-granting colleges, most students attend the larger colleges and universities. In fall 1997, 40 percent of institutions had fewer than 1,000 students, although enrollment at these campuses accounted for 4 percent of college students. While 10 percent of the campuses enrolled 10,000 or more students, they accounted for 50 percent of total college enrollment.

See also BABY BOOMERS; EDUCATION, HOME SCHOOLING; EDUCATION, PRIMARY AND SECONDARY; GENDER GAP; JACKSON STATE UNIVERSITY; KENT STATE UNIVERSITY.

Further reading: Diane Ravitch, *The Troubled Crusade: American Education, 1945–1980* (New York: Basic Books, 1983); Jeffrey A. Cantor, *Higher Education Outside of the Academy* (San Francisco: Wiley, 2000); Hugh Graham, *The Uncertain Triumph.* (Chapel Hill: University of North Carolina Press, 1984); Barry M. Franklin, *From "Backwardness" to "At Risk": Childhood Learning Difficulties and the Contradictions of Reform.* (Albany.: State University New York Press, 1994).

—Michele Rutledge

education, home schooling

Home schooling is a form of education that began to climb in popularity in the 1970s and continues to gain momentum in America, especially among EVANGELICAL CHRISTIANS and others dissatisfied with the curriculum and conditions of public schools. The term defines students being schooled at home instead of in a public or private school, those whose enrollment in private or public schools does not exceed 25 hours a week, and those who are not at home because of a temporary illness.

Research suggests that although home schooling initially expanded in the 1970s within a homogeneous sub-group of middle-class, white, Christian families, it seems to be an emerging trend among a wider range of American families. In 1994 the number of children ages 6 to 17 who were home-schooled was 345,000. By 1996 the number had nearly doubled to 636,000. According to the 1999 Parent Survey of the National Household Education Surveys Program, an estimated 850,000 students nationwide were being home-schooled, nearly 2 percent of all school-aged American students.

Of the total home school population, 82 percent are home-schooled only; the other 18 percent attend private or public schools part time.

Many factors influence the decision to teach children at home. These reasons include the expectation of being able to give a better education at home; moral or religious motivation; a desire for high educational achievement; dissatisfaction with public schools' curriculum; and anxiety about school environment, including peer pressure, safety, and drugs.

Often school districts or public schools offer support for home schoolers by providing parents with materials and books, places to come together, and the opportunity for home-schooled children to attend classes and engage in extracurricular activities at the school. Only a small percentage of home schoolers enroll in classes, however, or use either textbooks or libraries when they are made accessible by public schools. Many home schoolers express antipathy or even hostility toward utilizing public school resources.

Home schoolers typically share several common characteristics: high percentages are two-parent families, typically with only one parent participating in the labor force; large family size; and high parental scholastic accomplishment. The percentage of students who are home schooled is similar for both boys and girls and across elementary, middle, and high school grades.

See also EDUCATION, HIGHER; EDUCATION, PRIMARY AND SECONDARY; FAMILY LIFE; MORALITY; RELIGION.

—Michele Rutledge

education, primary and secondary

Public education in the United States consists of programs of instruction offered to children and adolescents through individual school districts administered by state and local governments. Ultimately, educational authority resides with the states, but the federal government has a history of facilitating specific educational programs considered to be in the national interest. This action in the field of education has further federalized, in effect, American schooling. Moreover, federal civil rights laws mandate that all schools conform to national standards of educational equality. In landmark statutes passed in 1958, 1965, and 1972, Congress for the first time broached problems related to improving instruction in primary subjects like science, mathematics, and foreign languages and enhancing educational opportunity for low-income children.

During the course of the 20th century, most states assumed a more active regulatory role than in the past, incorporating school districts into larger areas with common procedures. Prior to World War II, there were over 117,000 school districts in the United States; by 1990 the number had decreased to just over 15,000. State officials often supported efforts to equalize local school district expenses by using state funds and state laws to ensure more equitable per pupil expenditures, regardless of the wealth or poverty of individual districts. Local property taxes financed 68 percent of public school expenses in 1940, while the states contributed 30 percent. By 1990 states and local districts each contributed 47 percent to public school revenues. The federal government contributed the majority of the remaining funds.

Educational achievements of the 1960s and 1970s were impressive. The number of children attending public schools nearly doubled between 1945 and 1975. Almost 60 million students were attending schools in the United States by 1970, and more than $78 billion annually was spent on education. In 1970, three out of every four Americans were graduating from high school, two out of every five were going to college, and nearly a million people were earning a college or university degree every year. Substantial changes were made in teacher education programs, and significant modifications were introduced to the school curricula.

In spite of these gains, there were disturbing trends in the American education system. During the late 1960s and throughout the 1970s, cities began to reject bond issues designed to provide revenue for the schools. Concurrently, the achievement of many schools left much to be desired. In 1975 the College Entrance Examination Board disclosed that Scholastic Aptitude Test (SAT) scores had declined steadily since 1964. Reports over the next few years identified appalling deficiencies in the school system. A Carnegie Foundation report, *The Quest for Common Learning* (1981), decried general education in the United States and

Students at work on their laptops at the Discovery Charter School in Tracy, Colorado *(Sullivan/Getty Images)*

asserted that an inordinate amount of specialized courses and haphazard selection of topics and themes had resulted in curricular chaos. The report found that secondary students received good grades, although most students did not appear to work very hard in school, supporting widespread complaints about unqualified students being passed from grade to grade.

A series of investigations and recommendations for improvement followed the Carnegie report. Sponsored by President RONALD W. REAGAN's administration and appointed by the National Commission on Excellence in Education, an 18-member panel presented its findings in a report entitled *A Nation at Risk* (1983). The link between demanding schools and a sound ECONOMY was the thesis in this educational document of the late 20th century. The report blamed the public schools for a weak economy and demanded more academic requirements and higher standards and test scores, to overcome the low scholastic achievement of American students. Statistics in the document suggested students from other industrial societies outperformed their Americans counterparts on international academic tests.

By 1980, more than 2 million of the nation's instructors (75 percent of the total) were members of the American Federation of Teachers or the National Education Association. In the eyes of critics, the teachers' unions were more motivated by salary and job security issues than by new teaching techniques and student scholastic development. Several state legislatures passed antiunion measures restricting the rights of tenure, implementing merit pay procedures, and making it easier to dismiss teachers. The states, already involved in the financing of the schools, began to establish standards of performance and statewide testing programs for accountability of teachers and administrators. The pressure for accountability and reform increased in the early 1980s. Concurrently, the position of the federal government grew through the increasing amounts of educational appropriations by Congress and the creation of the Department of Education. This department was created by Congress in 1979 during the JAMES EARL CARTER, JR. administration and officially established in May 1980. A movement in the 1980s to institute national standards and to determine national priorities in education prompted opposition and controversy. The larger issue of federal involvement in education reflected partisan disputes.

A Nation at Risk continued to focus states' attention on raising education standards throughout the 1980s and 1990s. Many parents, teachers, administrators, and government officials held that only a concerted, centralized reform movement could surmount the manifest shortcomings of American education. Because the apparent crisis in student performance was based primarily on test-score results, most states had put into place reform tactics that emphasize more frequent and effective state testing and more state-legislated curriculum requirements. Some educators also suggested using test results to either allow or restrict a student's access to higher education or the job market. Although there is widespread support for such examinations, few states have mandated them.

Federal involvement in schools since the 1980s has been expressed less by legislation providing money for new programs than by government reports and proclamations that schools were performing insufficiently. *A Nation at Risk* and many subsequent federal reports and studies on the condition of schooling sparked a vigorous school reform effort at local and state levels.

Public school enrollment from kindergarten through grade eight rose from 29.9 million in the fall of 1990 to an estimated 33.5 million in the fall of 2000. Enrollment in the upper grades rose from 11.3 million in 1990 to 13.5 million in 2000. The increase from 1990 to 2000 was most rapid in the elementary grades, but this pattern is expected to change. The growing numbers of young pupils who have been filling the elementary schools will cause significant increases at the secondary school level during the next decade. Between the fall of 2000 and the fall of 2010, public elementary enrollment is expected to remain fairly stable, while public secondary school enrollment is expected to rise by 4 percent. Public school enrollment is projected to set new records every year until 2005.

Elementary enrollment has risen faster than the number of schools, with the average elementary school size increasing as a result. Regular elementary schools grew from an average of 433 students in 1988–89 to 478 in 1998–99. During the same time period, the average secondary school size rose from 689 to 707. The rising numbers of alternative schools, which tend to be small, have mitigated the increase in the average size of secondary schools. The average size of regular secondary schools, which exclude the alternative schools, special education, and vocational education schools, rose from 697 to 786 between 1989 and 1999. In 1994, 11 percent of American students in elementary and secondary schools attended private institutions. Most of these attended Catholic schools. Increasing numbers of American children are eschewing institutional education at both private and public schools, turning to home schools as their alternative.

Increasing numbers and proportions of children are being assisted in programs for the disabled. During the 1990–91 school year, 11 percent of students were served in these programs compared with 13 percent in 1998–99. Some of the increase since 1990–91 may be ascribed to the increasing percentage of children identified as learning-disabled, which rose from 5 percent of enrollment to 6 percent of enrollment in 1998–99.

The increase in American high school attendance was one of the most conspicuous developments in U.S. education during the 20th century. From 1900 to 1996 the percentage of teenagers who graduated from high school grew from approximately 6 percent to roughly 85 percent. During the course of the 20th century, most states passed legislation extending compulsory education laws to the age of 16. The 20th-century high school was a uniquely American invention. More so than either primary schools or colleges, high schools demonstrated the American ideal that education could successfully address a growing list of individual and social concerns.

At the beginning of the 21st century, educational thought and debate centered on how schools can promote individual mobility and the economy. Issues like governmental vouchers for financing private education, test scores and their administration, and the United States's ranks among other industrial nations continued to be the subject of intense deliberation.

See also EDUCATION, HIGHER; EDUCATION, HOME SCHOOLING.

Further reading: Amy Guttmann, *Democracy and Education* (Princeton: Princeton University Press, 1987); Hugh Graham, *The Uncertain Triumph: Federal Education Policy in the Kennedy and Johnson Years* (Chapel Hill: University of North Carolina Press, 1984); Edythe Margolin, *Young Children, Their Curriculum, and Learning Processes* (New York: MacMillan Publishing Company, 1976).
—Michele Rutledge

elections

Elections in the United States since 1968 have been anything but consistent. In 1984, President RONALD W. REAGAN carried the highest popular vote (over 54 million), the highest number of electoral votes (525 out of 538), and the most states (49, tied with President RICHARD M. NIXON in 1972, although Nixon won only 43.3 percent of the popular vote in 1968) of any president in history. Yet, just eight years later in 1992, President WILLIAM J. CLINTON entered the office with only 43 percent of the electorate as well. In the 2000 presidential election, however, it was nearly a dead heat between GEORGE W. BUSH and ALBERT GORE, JR. The participation rate of the voting-age population declined 10 points after 1968, and has remained relatively steady since. During the 1960s, turnout for presidential elections hovered between 60 and 64 percent, and the percentages for off-year (nonpresidential) elections stayed in the upper 40s. Beginning in 1972, turnout has fluctuated between 49 and 55 percent, with off-year elections following similar patterns in the upper 30s. These numbers might suggest declining voter participation. The number of eligible voters increased after 1968 as a result of immigration and civil rights initiatives, but the percentage of active voters—those voting—has remained relatively constant since World War II. Exactly why voting participation has declined—or if it has declined in any significant way—remains a point of discussion among scholars.

In general, the American electoral college system discourages third-party candidates. Each state is given a number of electoral votes equal to its combined number of senators and representatives in Congress. After a presidential election, the popular vote is tallied in each state and the party with the most votes takes all the electoral votes. The candidate with a majority of the 538 electoral votes wins the office. The framers of the Constitution developed this system to include a territorial representation among the popular vote; a strict popular voting system might provide large population centers with a greater political voice than rural centers. For example, three cities of 10 million residents would have more voice than 10 states with only 2 or 3 million people each. In the 18th century, this was of particular concern, since the more rural southern states shared interests that were at odds with the more populated northeastern states. Since candidates must secure majorities in multiple states to be able to have a chance of winning the presidency, American politics favors the candidate with the strongest party mechanism. Most voters prefer not to support a candidate from a nonestablished party, and as a result most third-party presidential candidates face overwhelming odds.

Since the Civil War, third parties received electoral votes only six times, the last occurring in 1968 when American Independence candidate GEORGE C. WALLACE managed to win 46 electoral votes. Only Robert LaFollette (1924) and H. ROSS PEROT (1992) managed to win even half the votes of the first runner-up. Despite these odds, third-party candidates can carry significant influence in national elections. With the exceptions of John F. Kennedy in 1960 and George W. Bush in 2000, every one of the 15 presidents elected with a minority plurality lost his majority to a strong third party. Most often, the third-party candidates splinter votes from a major party to give the election to a minority candidate; in 1912 President Woodrow Wilson won after Roosevelt stripped Taft of more than half his votes; in 1992 President Clinton won after Perot diverted votes away from GEORGE H. W. BUSH (although some observers said that Perot drew an equal number of voters away from Clinton); and in 2000, George W. Bush won after GREEN PARTY candidate RALPH NADER took votes from former vice president Gore.

A more dispersed constituency distinguishes the third-party campaigns of 1992, 1996, and 2000 from campaigns in 1972 and before. In prior elections, serious third-party candidates enjoyed clear demographic advantages in at

Gore and Bush supporters face off during a protest December 11, 2000, outside the U.S. Supreme Court in Washington, D.C. *(Wong/Newsmakers)*

least one or more states. In 1968 segregationist George Wallace received 46 electoral votes from just over 13 percent of the popular vote, because he held strongholds in five southern states and represented a strong local constituency. In contrast, Perot garnered nearly 20 million votes and 19 percent of the popular vote, and yet earned no electoral votes in the 1992 election; nor did he gain any after winning 8 percent and 8 million votes in 1996. This was because Perot's Independent Party and later REFORM PARTY had no central stronghold; he gained national recognition through media outlets, and not from a local constituency base. The Green Party's Ralph Nader received fewer than 3 million votes in 2000 (2.7 percent), but probably had an effect on the election. Democrat Gore edged Republican George W. Bush in the popular count by half a million votes, but Bush achieved a narrow victory with 271 electoral votes, one more than required, after a controversial dispute over Florida's election returns. Three previous presidents won elections despite losing the popular vote: John Quincy Adams in 1824, Rutherford B. Hayes in 1876, and Benjamin Harrison in 1888. In 2000, controversy again

erupted when Gore challenged the Florida election results. Voter exit-polling had indicated a Gore victory in the state, but a high level of disqualified ballots had left Bush with a lead of 327 votes out of some 6 million cast. Gore sought to have the ballots reexamined in four populous counties. A highly charged legal and political struggle ensued in which both candidates maneuvered to ensure their victory through the courts. On December 8, the Florida Supreme Court ordered a reexamination of the rejected ballots across the state, but the next day the U.S. SUPREME COURT stayed this decision. On December 12, the Court found 7-2 that Florida's law was flawed because it lacked uniform counting standards and further ruled, 5-4, that time had run out for recounts, effectively confirming a Bush victory.

Some opponents of the electoral college used the public anxiety over the 2000 election to push for electoral reform, specifically by ending the electoral college system altogether in favor of a strict popular vote. Supporters of the current system criticized these alternatives with many of the same arguments posed by the original framers of the Constitution, primarily that direct election of the president would provide advantage to urban centers. The 2000 election suggests that the interests remain divided; Gore's 1 percent popular advantage arose from a small number of large urban centers on the East and West Coasts, where he gained 71 percent of the vote. On a rural level, however, President Bush won a 78 percent majority of the voters; or 2,434 of the nation's 3,111 counties—leaving Gore with only 677.

See also ANDERSON, JOHN B.; BUCHANAN, PATRICK J.; CARTER, JAMES EARL, JR.; DOLE, ROBERT; DUKAKIS, MICHAEL S.; FERRARO, GERALDINE A.; FORD, GERALD R.; JACKSON, JESSE L.; MCGOVERN, GEORGE S.; MONDALE, WALTER F.; POLITICAL PARTIES; QUAYLE, J. DANFORTH.

Further reading: Robert L. Dudley and Alan R. Gitelson, *American Elections: The Rules Matter* (New York: Langman, 2001); Congressional Quarterly, *Congressional Elections, 1946–1996* (Washington, D.C.: Congressional Quarterly, Inc., 1997); Gary L. Gregg, II, *Securing Democracy: Why We Have an Electoral College* (Wilmington, Del.: Intercollegiate Studies Institute, 2001); Bill Sammon, *At Any Cost: How Al Gore Tried to Steal the Election* (Washington, D.C.: Regnery Publishing, Inc., 2001); Jeffrey Toobin, *Too Close to Call: The Thirty-Six Day Battle to Decide the 2000 Election* (New York: Random House, 2001).

—Aharon W. Zorea

Energy, U.S. Department of (creation of)

The U.S. Department of Energy originated from the federal Energy Policy Office created in June 1973. The extreme shortages the United States faced in the areas of electricity, gasoline, and heating oil forced the government to address the lack of policy in this area. This ENERGY CRISIS marked 1973 as the year of factory and school shutdowns, commercial-airline flight cancellations, electrical brownouts, major city blackouts, and long lines at gas stations. President RICHARD M. NIXON responded by formulating a national energy policy, which led to the creation of the federal Energy Policy Office. President Nixon named William Simon as its head. Simon's first actions were to order refineries to produce more heating oil rather than gasoline, to initiate year-round daylight savings time, to ask drivers not to exceed 50 miles per hour, and to require gas stations to limit individual sales as well as operating hours.

President JAMES EARL CARTER, JR., inherited many of the same problems that President Nixon had fought. President Carter, with the help of his Energy Secretary James Schlesinger, formulated an energy policy within the first 90 days of Carter's inauguration. The plan called for a myriad of programs, including the creation of the Department of Energy, which was activated on October 1, 1977. The

new department assumed the responsibilities of the Federal Energy Administration, the Energy Research and Development Administration, the Federal Power Commission, and parts of several other agencies. The department's task is to provide a comprehensive and balanced national energy plan, including research and development of energy technology, marketing of power, energy conservation, the nuclear weapons program, and an energy data collection and analysis program.

The primary focus of the department evolved over time. At the end of the 20th century, the department's primary objectives were to ensure the energy security of the United States, to maintain the safety and reliability of the nation's nuclear stockpile, and to develop innovations in SCIENCE AND TECHNOLOGY.

See also CONSERVATION; ENVIRONMENTALISM; ENVIRONMENTAL POLICY.

—Leah Blakey

energy crisis

The early 1970s witnessed a rapid change in the United States attitude toward energy consumption. Through the 1950s and 1960s Americans had become accustomed to expanding energy consumption with little concern about cost or availability. Beginning in 1971, however, the ORGANIZATION OF PETROLEUM EXPORTING COUNTRIES (OPEC) began to raise the price of oil, and then initiated an oil embargo on the United States in 1973. This embargo coincided with a weakening U.S. economy, and resulted in high inflation and fuel rationing, which brought into question the United States dominance, since 1945, of the world economy. The dependence on oil from the Middle East and the severity of the economic crisis brought into sharp relief the ability of the United States to determine its own domestic economic and political agendas. While the crisis was eventually overcome, it raised a number of questions, in particular the issues of national security tied to Middle East politics, the domestic economy's relationship to the world economy, and the viability of the reliance on oil.

At heart was the ability of the United States to maintain an independent, yet powerful, role in the global arena. A number of factors contributed to the energy crisis. On August 15, 1971, President RICHARD M. NIXON announced a new economic policy to respond to a faltering ECONOMY. As well as implementing a range of wage and price controls, Nixon imposed a 10 percent surcharge on all imports, as well as revoking the U.S. commitment to sell gold to other central banks at $35 an ounce, thereby taking the dollar off the gold standard. OPEC countries, concerned with the adverse effects on oil revenue, began to raise prices, especially as the dollar began to depreciate against the price of oil. The effect on the domestic price of fuel was compounded as American oil companies began to raise their own prices to protect their profits.

These difficulties were compounded when the United States supported Israel against Arab nations in the Yom Kippur War in 1973. OPEC responded by halting the supply of oil to the United States, Western Europe, and Japan. This embargo, which began on October 16, 1973, caused the price of oil to rise to unprecedented levels and aggravated an already weak U.S. economy. Long queues for gasoline, the introduction of rationing, and accelerated inflation brought home to many Americans the United States's precarious dependence on foreign oil. The decision by President Nixon in December 1973 not to switch on the lights on the national Christmas tree to conserve energy was a symbolic confirmation of a national crisis.

With the ending of the oil embargo on March 18, 1974, the crisis appeared to be over. Despite the continued high price of oil and the fragile nature of Middle East politics, consumption quickly returned to pre-1973 levels. A natural gas shortage during the winter of 1976–77, however, brought energy to the forefront of national politics once again, when President JAMES EARL CARTER, JR. declared a national emergency on February 2, 1977. During 1977 Carter announced a series of energy conservation measures and on August 4, 1977, Congress passed the Department of Energy Organization Act. The new U.S. DEPARTMENT OF ENERGY was opened on October 1, 1977, with former secretary of defense James R. Schlesinger as its first secretary. Events in the Middle East, however, once again took control of U.S. attempts to regulate energy consumption. The civil war in Iran in 1979, in which the shah, who had been a longtime ally of the United States, was ousted, caused severe problems between OPEC and the United States. The disruption to oil production and the complications of political allegiances resulted in OPEC's increasing the price of oil. OPEC announced an immediate price increase of 14.5 percent and, by June 1979, raised the average price of a barrel of oil by more than 50 percent. President Carter addressed the nation on July 15, outlining his proposals to deal with the new energy crisis. Central to Carter's plan was the need for energy conservation at home, the development of new sources of energy and a reduction in the reliance on imported oil, and deregulation of domestic oil prices. Although Congress deregulated oil in 1980, domestic oil companies raised their prices, causing another large increase in gasoline prices.

In the 1980s, as the United States increased its own domestic production of oil and attempted to improve end-user efficiency, prices returned to more moderate levels. Apart from a brief price increase during the Persian Gulf crisis in 1990–91, OPEC has managed to stabilize the price of oil, although in late 1999 OPEC cut production, thereby raising the price of gasoline in the United States. The issue of energy remains at the forefront of domestic policy. Problems with energy shortages in California and other states in 2001 revealed continued problems of supplying consumers with energy needs.

See also AUTOMOBILE INDUSTRY; ECONOMY; FOREIGN POLICY; INFLATION; IRANIAN HOSTAGE CRISIS.

—Stephen Hardman

environmental movement See conservation, environmentalism, and environmental policy

Equal Access Act (1984)

The Equal Access Act of 1984, formally known as Title VIII of the Education for Economic Security Act of 1984, requires public secondary schools to allow student religious groups the same access to school facilities that other student groups enjoy. The law was born out of the perception, widely held by public school administrators, that the establishment clause of the First Amendment required them to prohibit any religious activity by students at any time on school property. As a result, Congress held numerous hearings investigating whether administrators violated the rights of public school students to free speech, free association, and free exercise of religion. The U.S. SUPREME COURT had earlier ruled in *Widmar v. Vincent* that state-funded universities could not deny facility access to campus religious groups, and Congress concluded that younger, secondary-school-age students were being denied these same basic rights of expression. During the summer of 1984, with overwhelming bipartisan majorities in both houses, Congress passed the Equal Access Act to end discrimination against student groups based on religion.

Six years later, in *Board of Education of Westside Community Schools v. Mergens* (1990), the Supreme Court upheld the constitutionality of the Equal Access Act, concluding that secondary-school-age students are mature enough to distinguish between a school's tolerance and a school's endorsement of religious expression. They further ruled that even one "non-curriculum-related" group on campus can trigger the Equal Access Act; that the definition of "non-curriculum" must be broadly defined; and that religious groups must have the same access to school media, including school newspapers, bulletin boards, and public address systems, that any other student group enjoys. The Court specifically warned, however, that *Mergens* did not affect earlier decisions prohibiting state-initiated or state-led prayers at school functions and Bible reading in the public school classroom. In a famous quote, the Court recognized a "crucial difference between government speech endorsing religion, which the Establishment Clause forbids, and private speech endorsing religion, which the Free Speech and Free Exercise Clauses protect." As such, religious student groups were permitted access to public school facilities provided they did not receive specific school endorsement; that teachers or outsiders served only as nonparticipatory monitors, who are present only to ensure the safety of the students and school property; and that school officials retain the authority to prohibit groups that substantially interfere with the orderly conduct of the schools' educational activities. The Equal Access Act of 1984, and the subsequent Supreme Court decision that upheld it, not only brought up issues of free speech and the separation of church and state, but it also reaffirmed the constitutional rights of students.

See also EDUCATION; RELIGION.

—Aharon W. Zorea

Equal Rights Amendment (ERA)

The Equal Rights Amendment was a proposed amendment to the U.S. Constitution that failed to be ratified after passing Congress by a two-thirds majority in 1972. The struggle over ratification proved to have both symbolic and substantive importance regarding the role of women in American society, and the need to amend the Constitution to ensure female equality. No other amendment to the Constitution, with perhaps the exception of slavery abolition, national Prohibition, and women's suffrage, drew as much controversy and attracted such sizable numbers of activists to the debate over ratification.

The proposed amendment made its first formal appearance soon after the 1920 adoption of the Nineteenth Amendment that enfranchised women. In July 1923 the ERA was unanimously endorsed by the National Women's Party at a convention in Seneca Falls, New York. Shortly afterward, the ERA was first introduced in Congress in 1923 by Republican senator Charles Curtis through the efforts of Alice Paul, a militant feminist leader of the National Women's Party. Paul saw the amendment as a way to achieve full legal equality for women. This amendment drew opposition from other feminists who believed that women faced special circumstances and needed to be protected through special legislation that favored women, thereby distinguishing them from men. The proposed ERA, if added to the U.S. Constitution, would outlaw this special legislation requiring every federal and state law to treat men and women the same. Advocates of protections for women, such as National Consumers' League leader Florence Kelley, excoriated the ERA. In the Senate, Kelley was supported by pro-labor Democrats such as Thomas Walsh. The female-labor protectionist view dominated the one-day Senate hearings in 1929 and in 1931.

In the 1930s the ERA was revived when the National Federation of Business and Professional Women endorsed a version of the ERA in 1937. Further support over the next few years came from the General Federation of Women's Clubs, the National Association of Women Lawyers, and the National Education Association. Other women's organizations, however, continued to oppose the ERA, including the League of Women Voters. Congressional hearings in February 1938 reflected these divisions, but nonetheless the ERA reached the Senate floor in 1938 and the House floor the following year. In 1940 the Republican Party platform endorsed the ERA. The Democratic Party endorsed the ERA in its party platform four years later. In Congress, the ERA issue cut across party lines. Conservative New York Republican senator James W. Wadsworth, for example, opposed the ERA, while conservative Republican senator Robert Taft (Ohio) and liberal Democrat Helen Gahagan Douglas (Calif.) supported it. In 1950 a modified ERA amendment was approved in the Senate, 63 to 19. During debate over the ERA, Senator Carl Hayden (D-Ariz.) had attached a rider stating that "the provisions of this article shall not be construed to impair any rights, benefits, or exemptions conferred by law upon the persons of the female sex." ERA supporters opposed the Hayden rider, and as a result the bill failed to come before the House for a vote.

The emergence of a new women's movement in the late 1960s added momentum to the drive for the ERA. In October 1967 the newly formed NATIONAL ORGANIZATION FOR WOMEN (NOW) voted overwhelmingly to endorse the Equal Rights Amendment. In Congress, the chair of the House Judiciary Committee, Emanuel Celler, who supported women's protective labor legislation, held up the ERA in his committee. In the summer of 1970, Representative Martha Griffiths (D-Mich.) rallied a majority of her House colleagues to have the ERA discharged from the Judiciary Committee. On August 10, 1970, after only one hour of debate, the House approved the amendment in a vote of 352 to 15. Senate supporters, including Birch Bayh (D-Ind.) and majority leader Mike Mansfield (D-Mont.), brought the House-approved ERA directly to the floor. Senator Sam Ervin, Jr. (D-N.C.), attempted to attach a series of riders to the amendment, protecting women's interests concerning the military draft, alimony and child custody rights, and unfair labor practices. They failed to gain support in the Senate. Differences arose about time limits for state ratification, however, and as a result the 91st Senate adjourned without taking action.

The House again passed the ERA on October 12, 1971, after rejecting the Wiggins Amendment, which would have exempted women from compulsory military service and which also would have preserved other laws "which reasonably promote the health and safety of the

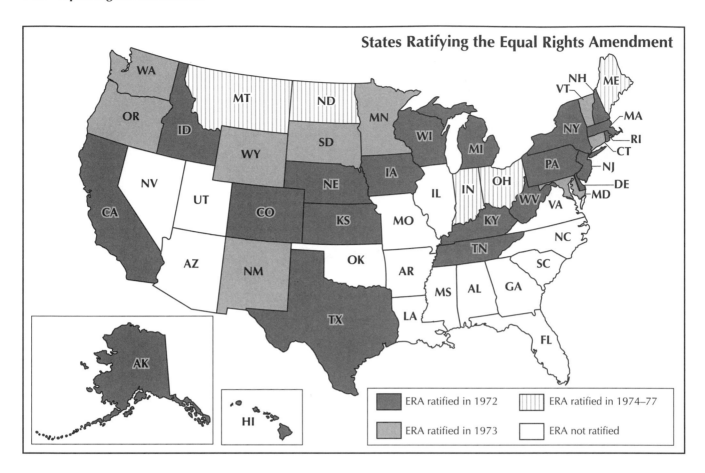

States Ratifying the Equal Rights Amendment

ERA ratified in 1972
ERA ratified in 1973
ERA ratified in 1974–77
ERA not ratified

people." An overwhelming majority of the House, 354 votes, supported the ERA, while only 23 members voted no, of whom one was the senior female member, Representative Leonor Sullivan (D-Mo.). In the Senate, Sam Ervin proposed nine separate ERA amendments to protect the traditional rights of women. Every one was defeated on a roll-call vote on March 21 and 22, 1972. As a result the ERA passed the Senate by 84 to 8. Congress granted seven years for the amendment to be ratified by three-fourths of the states. Meanwhile, in January 1973, the U.S. SUPREME COURT legalized ABORTION. This decision was to have profound implications in debates about women's rights in the 1970s and 1980s.

Within its first year after passage by Congress on March 22, 1972, 30 states ratified the ERA, requiring only eight more states to ratify it. At this point opposition to the ERA began to mobilize on the grassroots level. Leading the campaign against the ERA was PHYLLIS SCHLAFLY, a longtime conservative activist from Alton, Illinois. She brought to the campaign a keen political sense for organizing, argument, and lobbying. Within months of her entrance into the fight, STOP ERA groups had emerged across the country. Senator Sam Ervin supported her

efforts. Some women's groups joined in the opposition, starting with the National Council of Catholic Women. In addition, the AFL-CIO opposed ERA until 1975. As the STOP ERA movement gained momentum, Schlafly effectively drew support from EVANGELICAL CHRISTIANS, Mormons, Orthodox Jews, and Roman Catholic women across the country. Supporters of ERA organized around the National Organization for Women, led by Eleanor Smeal, and ERAmerica, an umbrella organization of labor, women, and liberal groups. At the same time pro-amendment groups organized on the state level. NOW's campaign focused on raising funds for local and state advertising, supporting local and state NOW chapters, and hiring professionals, supported by volunteer activists, to lobby state legislatures. The struggle over the ERA occurred in state capitals, where legislatures voted again and again on ERA.

As support for the ERA waned in key states and it appeared that the amendment would not receive the necessary state votes for ratification, Congress voted to extend the March 22, 1979, deadline to June 30, 1982. Following the extension, both sides concentrated their efforts on five critical states, Illinois, Florida, North Carolina, Missouri, and Oklahoma. No state ratified the ERA after the time extension. Five states that had ratified ERA earlier rescinded their ratifications. A federal court held the ERA time extension unconstitutional and rescissions constitutional, but the U.S. Supreme Court let the time run out, so that it was unnecessary to determine these issues with finality.

The five states (of the 35 states that initially approved ERA) that rescinded their previous ratification were Nebraska (March 15, 1973); Tennessee (April 23, 1974); Idaho (February 8,1977); Kentucky (March 16, 1978); and South Dakota (March 1, 1979). Fifteen states never ratified ERA including Alabama, Arizona, Arkansas, Florida, Georgia, Illinois, Louisiana, Mississippi, Missouri, Nevada, North Carolina, Oklahoma, South Carolina, Utah, and Virginia. The Illinois legislature voted on the ERA every year from 1972 through 1982; the Florida legislature considered it nearly every year, the North Carolina and Oklahoma legislatures every two years. The last state to ratify the ERA was Indiana in January 1977. The ERA was highly controversial and intensely debated, and the votes drew hundreds of spectators.

During the ratification period, the GERALD R. FORD and JAMES EARL CARTER, JR., administrations enthusiastically supported the ERA. Both the Republican and Democratic Parties endorsed the ERA, until 1980 when Republicans withdrew their endorsement in their party's platform.

The struggle over the ERA rallied thousands of American women to both sides of the debate. Supporters argued that an amendment was necessary to protect women from credit, employment, housing, and other forms of gender discrimination. Supporters claimed that the amendment would not affect personal relationships within marriage. Opponents, led by Schlafly, argued to the contrary, that the ERA would require women to be drafted and put in military combat equally with men, abolish the right of a wife to be supported by her husband, require funding of abortions with taxes, granting of marriage licenses to same-sex couples, and make unconstitutional all laws that gave one sex different rights from the other.

The success of the anti-ERA movement revealed the growing strength of the CONSERVATIVE MOVEMENT in the United States, which would eventually lead to RONALD W. REAGAN's election in 1980.

See also AMENDMENTS TO THE U.S. CONSTITUTION; FEMINISM; GENDER GAP; MORAL MAJORITY; RELIGION; WOMEN'S RIGHTS AND STATUS.

Further reading: David E. Kyvig, *Explicit and Authentic Acts: Amending the Constitution, 1776–1995* (Lawrence: University of Kansas Press, 1996).

—Donald T. Critchlow

evangelical Christians

An Evangelical is a person who subscribes to the theological position that individuals need a personal experience with God, asserts the religious authority of the Holy Bible, and feels under obligation to share his or her faith with others. Evangelicals, found in both conservative and mainstream Christian denominations, also share the common characteristics of a strong commitment to their faith. They believe that salvation comes through God's grace, not works, and in Christ's perfection, in the presence of Satan, and being "born again." The experience of conversion—being "born again"—is an act of repentance of sin and acceptance of Jesus Christ as savior.

In a doctrinal sense, many Evangelicals are drawn toward the view of dispensational premillenialism—the conviction that biblical prophecies related to Christ's return have yet to be fulfilled. In this belief system, according to his own time, God will turn away from an Israel that rejects the Messiah, and rescue the church immediately before the Great Tribulation (the "rapture"). The last days then would follow, in which the Antichrist would come, the battle of Armageddon would be fought, the Messiah would return for the Second Coming, and finally God's kingdom on Earth would appear. Although several prominent Evangelicals, including Billy Graham and Pat Robertson, advocate the doctrine of dispensationalism, it does not necessarily reflect the views of all Evangelicals. Conversely, many adhere to a general postmillennialism, the belief that Christ will return at an unknown date to establish his kingdom on Earth, or amillennialism, the belief that the millennium is a symbolic reference to the current era prefacing the Second Coming and the Last Judgment. The common point to all Evangelicals is the belief that Christ will return to Earth some day.

Evangelicalism encompasses a diverse number of Protestant denominations. The term originates from the Greek *euangelion* meaning "the good news," or "gospel." Modern usage comes from the series of 18th-century and 19th-century revivals that swept through North America. The transition from sect to denomination of both Baptists and Methodists took place during this era, and both grew to be the two largest Protestant groups in the United States. The large influx of non-Protestant immigrants in the late 19th and early 20th centuries diminished the strength of Evangelicals, but Evangelicalism still remains a strong element in American culture

Contemporary Evangelicalism remains a diverse movement. In the 21st century, Evangelicals retain historical doctrines of conversion through belief in and salvation by Christ; active expression of their faith; belief in the authority of scripture; and effort to convince others of their beliefs. But in the post–World War II period, religious leaders Harold John Ockenga and Billy Graham, in reaction against the perceived separatist, anti-intellectual fundamentalist movement of the 1920s and 1930s, shaped these convictions. The founding of the National Association of Evangelicals in 1942 helped bring together some 50 denominations into an organization whose goal is to represent evangelical interests on social, cultural, spiritual, and political issues.

As a group, evangelical Christians eschewed political involvement, focusing more on missions, evangelism, and caring for each other. But the 1976 Democratic presidential candidate JAMES EARL CARTER, JR., who confidently declared his born-again status, encouraged Evangelicals' involvement in politics—an area they had not been part of en masse since the early 20th-century temperance movement. Even more noticeable politically was the emergence and participation of groups like Concerned Women for America and the MORAL MAJORITY. In 1989 the CHRISTIAN COALITION was organized.

Evangelicals have many reasons for engagement in politics, including concerns over changing societal mores; a desire to effect change within society; and dissatisfaction with POPULAR CULTURE and mass MEDIA. Some cite their involvement in politics as a way to lessen the impact of the federal government, whose role has expanded into areas traditionally overseen by family, church, or local government. Yet, no Evangelical consensus exists in this group, which claims liberals and leftists as members as well. Prior to the 1970s, many Evangelicals were Democrats; in the late 1990s and early 2000s, the movement seems to have shifted toward a moderately conservative and predominantly Republican base.

See also FAMILY LIFE; MORALITY; RELIGION.

Further reading: Randall Balmer, *Mine Eyes Have Seen the Glory: A Journey into the Evangelical Subculture of America,* 3rd ed. (New York: Oxford University Press, 2000).

—Michele Rutledge

family life

During the latter half of the 20th century, the average size of the American family decreased significantly. By 2000, the average number of children per family was less than half what it was in 1900. This development, coupled with the decline of the prevalence of the nuclear family (mother and father and their children) since the 1960s and other social and cultural changes, has noticeably altered the nature and structure of the American family.

By the early 1960s there were indicators that the nuclear family was becoming threatened by the demands of modern life. Books such as Paul Goodman's *Growing Up Absurd* (1960) and Betty Friedan's *The Feminine Mystique* (1963) described widespread dissatisfaction among both men and women with modern life resulting from an increasing suburban isolation, a lack of meaningful work, and a loss of purpose. Friedan's book resonated so powerfully with American women that it is credited with helping to revive FEMINISM and justifying the entry of increasing numbers of women into the workforce. While Friedan emphasized the therapeutic nature of women's involvement in the world beyond the home, other critics faulted the family itself for women's dissatisfaction with family life. During the 1960s, numerous critics attacked the family as exploitative of women and children, unnecessarily hierarchical and authoritarian, narrow-minded, and capitalistic.

Perhaps the greatest instigator of change was the increasing demand for individual self-fulfillment, which became a significant influence on the family, and American society as a whole, from the 1960s to the end of the 20th century. This pursuit of self-fulfillment was enabled by a prospering economy in the 1960s and the introduction of the birth-control pill in 1957. The SEXUAL REVOLUTION, the human-potential movement, and the youth rebellion helped promote the individual's quest not only for physical pleasure, but for intellectual, emotional, spiritual, and material fulfillment. The women's rights movement along with the increasing acceptance of various forms of BIRTH CONTROL and family planning services contributed to the decreasing BIRTHRATES that reduced the average size of the American family.

Popular psychology during the 1970s further rationalized this behavior by insisting that failing to follow one's "growth curve" was psychologically unhealthy. In this environment, divorce represented an accomplished growth opportunity, a liberating experience dictated by the individual's need for self-fulfillment.

From the 1960s to the 1990s, statistics indicated that a major shift in the structure of the American family had occurred. The period showed increasing rates of divorce, number of single-person households, number of stepfamilies, number of single female parents, number of racially and ethnically mixed marriages, and the incidence of teenage pregnancies all skyrocketed. Although the final statistics showed a decrease over the final decade of the century, overall the statistics clearly indicated that the classic American family was slowly transforming itself. These developments, however, were noted by social scientists in both white and African-American families. Daniel Patrick Moynihan's famous 1965 report on African-American families, "The American Negro: The Case for National Action," documented high rates of illegitimacy, teen pregnancy, and divorce among black families and characterized what Moynihan called the pathological state of the black American family. The report continued to create controversy in the following decades. Anthropologist Carol Stack showed that it was more common among black families for women to be the backbone of the family, with an extended kinship network comprising the remainder of the family. In the late 1970s some black intellectuals insisted that the black family was indeed in trouble. Although these intellectuals received much criticism, their work began to resonate with many others, black and white, who realized that the problems formerly considered to affect only black families clearly pertained to the American family in general.

The contention that the nuclear family was beginning to dissolve prompted great debate during the 1980s and 1990s. The anxiety about the dysfunctional nature of the American family found its way into the political arena when the Republican Party, during the 1980s, campaigned on the notion of restoring "traditional family values." Changes in family structure, however, forced some observers to call such a defense of the traditional family a nostalgic reluctance to accept "progress." The increase of single-parent households, same-sex partnerships, group homes, extended kinship networks, and other replacements for incomplete nuclear families dictated a more broadly defined concept of "family." Many saw these new arrangements as positive indicators of increased personal freedom.

Another significant development was the increasing trend among two-parent families for both parents to work outside the home. The resulting problem of how to balance work and family responsibilities became a central issue and a major source of strain on the American family. Day care—once seen as a last resort—became a fact of life for those families who could afford it. Other options became available into the 1990s. Workplaces began offering "flex time," which allowed the worker to alter the starting or ending times of the usual shift, while some offered non-synchronous work schedules. In 1993 Congress passed the Family Leave and Medical Act, which allowed several weeks' leave from work for childbirth or illness. Traditional attitudes about gender responsibilities also began to change as fathers increasingly accepted a larger share of household and child-care duties.

Even where flexible arrangements made it possible to balance work and family, Americans often failed to take advantage of them. Some scholars claim that this is a result of Americans' inflated desire for material consumption, which impels both parents to work even when it is not really necessary. Others suggest that many workers actually prefer the ordered, calm, and civilized atmosphere of the workplace to the often chaotic environment of the home.

Even though the American family changed, the merits of its transformation remained a persistent issue in American public discourse, as signaled by the prevalent use of the "traditional family value" slogan. As the 20th century drew to a close, Americans began to demonstrate a certain discontentment with the belief that divorce constituted an act of personal liberation, and the unintended consequences of divorce came under closer scrutiny, although many mainstream religious denominations, state laws, family counselors, authors, and other Americans held that incompatible couples should not remain married. Nonetheless, the detrimental effects of divorce were also being noted. Family counselor Judith Wallerstein, in *The Unexpected Legacy of Divorce* (2000), argued that divorce significantly traumatized the children of separating parents. It appears that even though the traditional American family with its patriarchal order and gender-assigned roles has become a thing of the past, Americans still value the family as an integral social unit whose purpose is to enrich the lives of its members. How Americans will adapt family structure to the quickening pace of contemporary society remains to be seen.

See also ABORTION; ADVERTISING; BABY BOOMERS; CHRISTIAN COALITION; EDUCATION; FAMILY SUPPORT ACT OF 1988; FEMINISM; GENDER GAP; MARRIAGE; MORAL MAJORITY; RECREATION; WOMEN'S RIGHTS AND STATUS.

Further reading: Steven Mintz and Susan Kellogg, *Domestic Revolutions: A Social History of American Family Life* (New York: Free Press, 1988); Arlie Russell Hochschild, *The Time Bind: When Work Becomes Home and Home Becomes Work* (New York: Metropolitan, 1997).
—William L. Glankler

Family Support Act (FSA) (1988)

The Family Support Act was the culmination of a major 1987 congressional debate on welfare. The act provided for an extensive state-managed education and training program with transitional medical assistance, child-care benefits, and stronger child support enforcement.

Under the act, educators are provided opportunities to form linkages with other agencies to strengthen families and help them move toward self-sufficiency. Education is the pivotal goal of the FSA, to help families avoid long-term dependence on public assistance, and the act requires states to make educational services available to participants under the Job Opportunities and Basic Skills (JOBS) training program. Training and employment personnel and vocational and adult educators may join human services staff in providing education and training programs to JOBS clients.

Heralded as an "end of welfare," critics viewed the FSA as a failure. However, the act generated the expectation among voters that welfare recipients would and should be required to work. Despite the goals of the Family Support Act, the nationwide Aid to Families with Dependent Children (AFDC) caseload remained constant in the late 1980s, and then grew by more than a third between 1990 and 1994.

—Michele Rutledge

Farmer, James L. (1920–1999)

James Leonard Farmer was an American civil rights leader, born January 12, 1920, in Marshall, Texas, and educated at Wiley College and Howard University's School of Religion.

He helped found the Congress on Racial Equality (CORE) in 1942, was instrumental in its campaign of freedom marches and sit-ins, and served as its national director until 1966. He left CORE because he felt the organization was drifting away from its pacifist, nonresistance roots. Farmer also served as program director for the NATIONAL ASSOCIATION FOR THE ADVANCEMENT OF COLORED PEOPLE (NAACP) from 1959 to 1961, and was a professor of social welfare at Lincoln University in Pittsburgh in 1966 and 1967. In 1968 Farmer ran for a seat in the U.S. HOUSE OF REPRESENTATIVES from Brooklyn on the Liberty Party ticket but was defeated by Shirley Chisholm, an African-American Democrat. His political career did not end there, however. From 1969 to 1970 he served as assistant secretary of the Department of Health, Education, and Welfare during RICHARD M. NIXON's first administration.

Farmer retired from politics in 1971 but remained active in the public sector. He served on many organizational boards and, in 1976, became the associate director of the Coalition of American Public Employees, a group of labor and professional organizations. He also pursued a busy schedule of teaching and lecturing. His autobiography, *Lay Bare the Heart*, was published in 1985, and he received the Congressional Medal of Freedom from President WILLIAM J. CLINTON in 1998. James Farmer died July 9, 1999, in Fredericksburg, Virginia.

See also AFRICAN AMERICANS.

—William L. Glankler

Farrakhan, Louis A. (Louis Eugene Walcott)
(1933–)

As leader of the NATION OF ISLAM, Louis Abdul Farrakhan stresses personal responsibility, especially for black males, and advocates black economic self-sufficiency. His stance draws on a long history of black nationalist movements whose leaders sought to forge racial solidarity and self-reliance as their primary weapons against racial discrimination. He has often been criticized for appealing to black racism and anti-Semitism as means of promoting his views.

Farrakhan was born Louis Eugene Walcott in New York City on May 17, 1933. In 1955 he joined the Nation of Islam, adopted the name Abdul Haleem Farrakhan (later shortened to Louis Farrakhan), and rose to prominence in the organization on the strength of his speaking and singing abilities. In 1963, when a rift developed between Malcolm X and Elijah Muhammad, the leader of the organization, Farrakhan sided with Elijah Muhammad and publicly criticized Malcolm X for leaving the Nation of Islam. Farrakhan's severe denunciation of Malcolm X led many to suspect that he was responsible, either directly or indirectly, for the assassination of Malcolm X in 1965. Though Farrakhan denied complicity in the murder, he acknowledged that he may have fostered an atmosphere conducive to such an act.

After Wallace Muhammad, son of the deceased Elijah Muhammad, changed the organization's name to the World Community of Islam in the West and strayed away from the black nationalism of his father, Farrakhan formed a new organization under the original name, the Nation of Islam, and reasserted the principles of black separatism and self-reliance. Farrakhan's popularity rose during the 1980s, especially among young, urban AFRICAN AMERICANS who admired his willingness to stand up against a society they believed to be racist. Especially popular was his message to blacks that they assume moral and economic responsibility for themselves by avoiding drugs and crime, staying in school, providing for their children, and becoming involved in bettering their communities. Mixed with this message were open attacks on white society and anti-Semitic comments that were widely condemned by other black leaders.

Farrakhan's call for black self-reliance culminated in the Million Man March, organized in Washington, D.C., in October 1995. Hundreds of thousands of black men attended and renewed their commitments to family, community, and personal responsibility. Although such exposure renewed criticism of his rhetoric, the march was considered a successful display of African-American racial solidarity and his message, based squarely on "traditional values," moved Farrakhan closer to the political mainstream. This did not, however, remove his controversial status. He provoked further criticism by including Iran, Iraq, and Libya in his 1996 "world friendship tour" and for repeatedly criticizing the U.S. government during the tour.

See also AFFIRMATIVE ACTION; ISLAM IN AMERICA; POVERTY.

Further reading: Vibert White, *Inside the Nation of Islam: A Historical and Personal Testimony by a Black Muslim* (Gainesville: University of Florida Press, 2001).

—William L. Glankler

Federal Information Act (Privacy Act) (1974)

The Privacy Act of 1974 was enacted as a companion to the Freedom of Information Act (FOIA) of 1966, which established that government records must be accessible to the people. Before 1966 individuals had to show evidence to prove that they had sufficient right and necessity to gain access to records of any agency or department of the executive branch of government. After passage of the FOIA, the burden of proof shifted to the government, which now must present evidence to justify why private citizens should not view government documents. The FOIA does not open all documents to the public; certain critical exceptions apply, including documents related to elected officials of the federal government, private companies or individuals receiving federal contracts or grants, and documents from state and local governments. In addition, the FOIA permits affected agencies to reject information requests that might harm national DEFENSE and FOREIGN POLICY, or invade the privacy of individuals or businesses. The law, however, does provide individuals with a process by which to appeal such refusals.

The Privacy Act of 1974 was enacted in response to President RICHARD M. NIXON's IMPEACHMENT investigation. The public became concerned that politicians might abuse the power of the federal government to gather information on private citizens for their own benefit. The Privacy Act regulates the government's record keeping and disclosure practices, requiring each agency to gather information for individual files from the individuals directly, and not from spies or acquaintances. It also prohibits information gathered for one purpose from being used for another purpose, effectively prohibiting the government from creating secret files on its citizens. The Privacy Act also creates a mechanism by which individuals can examine, copy, and, if necessary, amend their personal records, which the federal government uses and maintains. As with the FOIA, the Privacy Act only applies to agencies and departments within the executive branch, and does not apply to state and local governments.

The Privacy Act of 1974 has been amended a dozen times since its initial passage; the most significant of the amendments occurred in 1988 and 1996. The Computer Matching and Privacy Protection Act of 1988 added new provisions to the Privacy Act to reflect the changes in computerized record keeping. Further changes were added in 1996 to account for the Internet and the implications of electronic indexing. As the Internet becomes a more prominent part of work, commerce, and daily routine, the issue of individual privacy becomes ever more important. So, the federal government will necessarily be forced to reconsider the balance between the rights of individual privacy and the necessities of national security and public order.

See also COMPUTERS; CRIME; GLOBALIZATION; INTERNET; WATERGATE SCANDAL.

—Aharon W. Zorea

federalism

Federalism is a political system in which two levels of government maintain jurisdiction over the same territories. The U.S. Constitution creates a federal authority to oversee peaceful relations between states through federal courts, provide for national security through federal armed forces and a diplomatic international corps, and manage interstate

and international relations involving trade and commerce. The Supremacy Clause in Article VI states that the federal Constitution retains priority in conflicts arising with any of the various state constitutions, except in instances when the state provides more individual protection than the federal government. The Tenth Amendment, however, guarantees that the states retain all rights not specifically mentioned in the Constitution. Taken together, the Supremacy clause and protection of state sovereignty guarantee individual liberty. State governments protect individuals from the possibility of an unconstitutional central government encroachment, while the federal government ensures that states provide at least a minimum level of individual protection.

In the late 19th century and early 20th centuries, the federal government demonstrated great restraint in matters of state sovereignty. In part, this was because federal involvement implied interference with local statutes involving race relations, which many southern states opposed under "states' rights."

During the Great Depression in the 1930s many state governments were forced to seek aid from the federal government in order to meet the demands arising from massive unemployment and agricultural depression. Though desegregation and AFFIRMATIVE ACTION programs during the 1960s and 1970s helped solidify public acceptance of enhanced federal authority, the largest single contributor to federal expansion arose from the increasing public demand for social services, public services, and educational funding, which provided the federal government with greater leverage over state authority. The Tenth Amendment prohibits direct legislative intervention in state autonomy, but Congress and the executive branch can still preempt state authority by attaching specific requirements to funds intended for social services. In 1974, for example, President RICHARD M. NIXON signed into law the Emergency Highway Energy Conservation Act, which mandated a national 55-mph speed limit. In order to encourage state compliance, the bill prohibited the federal Department of Transportation from approving any highway projects for states failing to adopt the new limit. The tactic succeeded; within three months each state legislature imposed 55-mph limits on all highways. The following year, President GERALD R. FORD signed the Federal-Aid Highway Amendments of 1974, making the 55-mph requirement permanent. Similar tactics were used to compel states to adopt a standard drinking age of 21 years.

Throughout the latter half of the 20th century, states lost a degree of their autonomy as they became increasingly dependent on federal money. In the late 1970s Governor RONALD W. REAGAN of California led a movement of "new Republicans" who emphasized a renewed commitment to federalism. As president, Reagan pushed for decentralization of the federal bureaucracy by devolution of responsibility for social services, including health care, income security, and job training, from the federal government to the states. In an effort to pull back federal involvement in commerce and communication, he also pushed for deregulation in the energy and finance industries. Critics argued that devolution placed undue burdens on state governments, depriving individuals of necessary social services, and that deregulation removed necessary safeguards from interstate enterprises. They believed the ideals of 19th-century federalism were outdated and the federal government necessarily assumed primacy in the area of social services, economic regulation, and national standards. Supporters asserted that local representatives better served individual needs, and that deregulation encouraged local entrepreneurialism.

In October 1987, during his second term, Reagan issued Executive Order No. 12612, titled "Federalism," calling for a new federal policy favoring state autonomy. The order required all federal agencies to issue Federalism Impact Assessments, in consultation with local authorities, on any new program involving the preemption of state autonomy. Since the order did not carry the weight of law, however, its effectiveness remains questionable. At the same time, Reagan tax reform eliminated state and local tax deductibility. Under the previous arrangement, states were seen to have first claim on tax money, and taxes paid to states were deductible from federal taxes. Under the new tax system, all federal taxes were assessed in addition to state and local taxes—in effect, allowing a significant reduction of state privilege. Reagan believed that this change compelled higher-tax states to reduce their tax burdens.

During President WILLIAM J. CLINTON's administration, the General Accounting Office reported that only five Federalism Impact Assessments were written for the 11,000 new federal rules issued during a three-year period. After assuming control of the Congress in 1994, Republican lawmakers promised to supplement the order with legislation designed to strengthen federalism, including the Personal Responsibility and Work Opportunity Reconciliation Act of 1996 and the Education Flexibility Partnership Act of 1999, both of which disbursed federal funding in block grants for state legislatures to distribute, and the Unfunded Mandates Reform Act (1995), which prohibited new federal mandates unless provided with necessary funding for implementation.

The U.S. SUPREME COURT reinforced the revival of federalism in several decisions during the 1990s. In *Judges v. Ashcroft, Governor of Missouri* (1991), the Court ruled that a state could set a mandatory retirement age for Missouri judges without involving the federal Age Discrimination and Employment Act of 1967, or the AGE DISCRIMINATION ACT OF 1975. The following year, *New*

York v. United States (1992) held that Congress violated state legislative autonomy when the Low Level Radioactive Waste Policy Amendments Act of 1985 compelled states to assume responsibility for waste treatment if they failed to adopt federal guidelines within a certain time period. Five years later, in *Printz v. United States* (1997), the Court struck down a provision in the Brady Handgun Violence Prevention Act of 1993 requiring background checks for all handgun purchases, because it compelled the cooperation of state law enforcement, which falls under the jurisdiction of state executives. During the same period, however, the Court also upheld the Supremacy Clause in several cases in which states tried to amend their constitutions so as to force term limits on federal representatives; in *U.S. Term Limits, Inc. v. Thornton* (1995) and *Cook v. Gralike* (2001), the Court ruled that state legislatures could not supersede Article I of the U. S. Constitution, which explicitly provides age, citizenship, and residency requirements for congressional service.

In May 1998 President Clinton issued Executive Order No. 13083, also titled "Federalism," which substantially revised Reagan's earlier executive order and altered federal policy. Though it retained the requirement of local consultation for programs that would preempt state and local law, the order also shifted the presumption of priority away from the states and toward the federal government. Republican lawmakers, as well as state and local officials, called for immediate withdrawal of the executive order. In 2001 President GEORGE W. BUSH affirmed his administration's commitment to new federalism through devolution and deregulation. The trend toward increased and more powerful federal authority has not significantly changed; states continue to lose their legislative autonomy. Since 1789, Congress has enacted 350 laws preempting state and local authority, half of which were passed between 1980 and 2000.

See also CONSERVATIVE MOVEMENT; NEOCONSERVATIVISM.

—Aharon W. Zorea

feminism

Feminism is a theory that women must share the same social, political, and economic rights and opportunities as men. Though feminism has had individual adherents throughout history, the first popular feminist movement in the United States focused on women's suffrage and began at the Seneca Falls Convention in 1848. It ended shortly after the passage of the Nineteenth Amendment to the Constitution in 1920. After women gained the right to vote, the movement lost much of its cohesiveness, and few women identified themselves as feminists. In 1963, feminism entered into its second incarnation after Betty

Friedan's book, *The Feminine Mystique,* helped reinvigorate popular support for a new women's movement. She argued that suffrage did not guarantee equality, and that American women had been taught to accept traditional, middle-class gender roles of homemakers and housewives, which kept them from pursuing self-fulfillment in the workplace. Her book came at a time when increasing numbers of educated women entering into the workforce experienced great frustration with gender discrimination. Employers often hired or promoted men over women on the theory that men had greater familial obligations, and that women were only working for supplementary incomes. In addition, the social pressures and fears of being labeled an "improper mother" caused many women to feel guilty about pursuing any career outside the home.

In 1961 enough women were complaining about their work conditions that President John F. Kennedy felt compelled to appoint a special commission to look into the way women were treated in the legal system, in the economy, and in the family itself. The Commission on the Status of Women, initially headed by former first lady Eleanor Roosevelt, helped to put women's issues back on the national agenda. It published a report in the same year that *The Feminine Mystique* appeared, and seemed to provide factual support for some of Friedan's conclusions; women faced employment discrimination, unequal pay, unequal protection under the law, and a general lack of social support for child care and other services that enable women to more easily pursue careers outside of the home. Congress responded by passing the Equal Pay Act, which required employers to pay the same rates to men and women for the same work. President Kennedy ordered the Civil Service Department not to discriminate on the basis of sex. Most historians point to the combination of these events in 1963 as a turning point in feminism in America. The legal protection was further bolstered the following year, when gender was included with race, creed, and national origin in the Title VII prohibition against employment discrimination in the 1964 Civil Rights Acts.

Many feminist leaders gained valuable experience as leaders in the civil rights and 1963 voter registration drives in the South. In 1966 feminist leaders developed their own civil rights organization when they formed the NATIONAL ORGANIZATION FOR WOMEN (NOW). It was modeled on the NATIONAL ASSOCIATION FOR THE ADVANCEMENT OF COLORED PEOPLE (NAACP), and set out to use existing tactics within the legal and political system to promote greater equality for women. They relied heavily on protections provided by Title VII's Equal Employment Opportunity Commission (EEOC) to file suits against employers and clubs that continued to discriminate on the basis of sex. Shortly thereafter, another group of feminists pursued a more radical approach outside the legal system to promote

equality. The "women's liberation" movement began in 1967 as independent women's groups in coffeehouses, bookstores, and college campuses in Chicago, New York, and Seattle. Borrowing ideas from the ANTIWAR MOVEMENT and student socialists, the groups challenged the dominant assumptions and stereotypes that may unnaturally bind women to subservient roles in society. In practice, these independent women's liberation groups engaged in "consciousness raising" wherein small groups of women would come together to systematically reconsider every assumption they had been taught while growing up; issues included marriage, religion, work, school, sexuality, and women's health. They then planned ways to publicize their new awareness to the society at large—usually by staging sensational public demonstrations that mocked traditional female roles by publicly throwing bras and girdles into a trashcan, or unfurling banners for "women's liberation" in unexpected places (like the 1968 Miss America Pageant).

These more radical groups complimented the more mainstream institutional organizations such as NOW and the Women's Equity Action League (WEAL), providing a broad spectrum for dynamic exchanges within the new feminism. This helped stimulate media attention, which attracted more popular support and brought feminist issues into the public forum. The success of the women's movement was demonstrated in 1970, when NOW called for a "women's strike for equality" to commemorate the 50th anniversary of the Nineteenth Amendment, and of women's right to vote in America. In New York City, the rally drew between 20,000 and 50,000 supporters; large numbers also came out in Boston, Berkeley, New Orleans, and more than 30 other cities. Though the movement reflected a diversity of tactics and priorities, it remained united on a number of issues, including ABORTION, child care, protection of women within the family, more inclusive education, greater opportunities in the workforce, and passage of the EQUAL RIGHTS AMENDMENT.

Laws restricting abortion had already begun to weaken throughout the 1960s, as family planning advocates worked to strike down laws that limited women's access to contraception; abortion was legal in 14 states before the SUPREME COURT ruled on *ROE V. WADE* in 1973. As early as 1968, the women's liberation forces became the "shock troops" for abortion rights. Rather than concentrate on lobbying or avenues of litigation, many feminists sought to intervene directly. The Chicago Women's Liberation Union counseled and referred interested women to doctors who were willing to perform illegal abortions. In 1971 these same women began performing the abortions themselves, totaling more than 11,000 in the two years between 1971 and 1973. In Austin, Texas, similar referral groups led to specialized research in legal precedents for abortion. The process eventually culminated with Sarah Weddington carrying the court case involving *Roe v. Wade* all the way to the Supreme Court.

The goal behind abortion rights advocacy was to limit the ties that bound women to the confines of a family unit. Access to abortion allowed women to decide when they wanted to start their family, but other issues, such as government-supported child care and crisis shelters for battered women, helped women escape abusive relationships. Washington, D.C. became the site of the first rape crisis hotline in 1972. In the following years, NOW helped establish more than 300 local rape crisis centers throughout the country. The first women's shelter formed in Saint Paul, Minnesota, in 1971. They not only provided a safe haven for battered women but also provided legal information and detailed handbooks on divorce to help women escape their situation. These types of institutions can now be found in most cities throughout the country.

While feminists explored new alternatives to the binding ties within the home, they remained equally committed to overcoming the obstacles out in the workplace. In March 1969 the Fifth Circuit Court of Appeals ruled in *Weeks v. Southern Bell* that employers could impose hiring restrictions based on sex only if it could be shown that "substantially all" women would be incapable of performing the required tasks. In 1970, Bernice Sandler, a professor at the University of Maryland, claimed that she was denied tenure because of her gender. Joining with WEAL, Sandler filed a complaint with the U.S. Department of Labor demanding a review of the promotion policies of more than 250 institutions of higher education. By 1971, more than 360 colleges and universities faced lawsuits for sexual discrimination. At the same time, along different lines, feminists also set out to change college curricula; Sheila Tobias compiled a collection of syllabi and bibliographies from existing, though unrelated, courses on feminism and female issues. The resulting "Women's Studies" program became a model for universities around the country. In the same year, a Chicago group of NOW members formed Women in Publishing, which codified guidelines for more inclusive language in textbooks and other educational materials. The guidelines sought to eliminate words that suggested natural gender roles: "firefighter" instead of "fireman," "police officer" instead of "policeman," "mail carrier" instead of "mailman," etc. Feminists pursued these efforts with the goal of educating women of all ages to transcend the psychological barriers to personal development that characterized more traditional ways of thinking. As more educated women entered into the workforce, they could force more far-reaching changes in the social infrastructure from within private corporations, public institutions, and the examples of day-to-day living.

More than any other single issue, the Equal Rights Amendment (ERA) became both a catalyst and a crucible, which influenced, motivated, and divided feminist groups of all varieties. By 1972, three main branches of feminism dominated the women's movement. Though all feminists considered themselves radical in that they opposed the dominant ideologies, not all pursued radical means. NOW, WEAL, and the National Women's Political Caucus (NWPC) focused on policy issues that would incorporate feminist principles into mainstream society. These groups were "liberal" in that they operated "within" the system, and advocated change through existing legal and political channels. In contrast, "radical" feminists sought to overturn all forms of oppression, including existing mechanisms that were inextricably linked to the existing social, political, and economic order. By 1975, the radical branch had split into two dominant forces—lesbian feminism and socialist feminism. Lesbianism arose as a feminist issue in 1969, as women challenged heterosexual norms because they grew out of patriarchal social orders. Linked closely with the concurrent sexual freedom and GAY RIGHTS MOVEMENTS, lesbian feminism eventually developed into a separate women's rights movement all its own. One of the more widely publicized of these groups was The Furies in Washington D.C. They argued that lesbian consciousness was the key to true women's liberation. In practice, these groups proved effective in promoting a feminist counterculture that emphasized female-centered leadership, institutions, and cultural events. Socialist feminists, however, criticized the lesbian emphasis on sex as the primary locus of oppression (which inevitably implied that men were "the enemy"). Instead, they argued that the key to women's liberation lay in radical egalitarianism, which could only be found in a more equitable economic system. Competition between the sexes was fueled by an overriding competition between private interests and could only be remedied with more enlightened public ownership and direction. Socialist feminists provided an intellectual foundation for later feminist scholars, long after the more economically oriented socialist organizations dissolved.

The ERA passed both houses of Congress in March 1972. Final ratification required passage by two-thirds of the state legislatures. By the end of the year, 22 of the necessary 38 states had ratified the amendment, and all three branches of feminists united to mobilize passage within the remaining states. Shortly thereafter, however, ERA advocates were met by a different kind of women's rights advocate under the leadership of PHYLLIS SCHLAFLY. Her Eagle Forum organization led the STOP ERA movement and succeeded in halting the progress of ratification within the states, eventually leading five states to rescind their earlier approval. Schlafly argued that the ERA actually deprived women of valuable rights by removing the protections that benefited their sex, including the right of a wife to be provided for by her husband, and the right to be excluded from national military drafts. Her movement was joined by Jerry Falwell's MORAL MAJORITY, and the National Right to Life Organization in arguing that the feminist promotion of abortion, government-supported child care, and liberal divorce laws undermined the sanctity of the family, and indirectly pressured women not to choose homemaking as their primary occupation.

Many feminist leaders were surprised by the effectiveness of Schlafly's organization, and struggled to find an appropriate countermeasure. In 1975 Congresswoman Bella Abzug (D-N.Y.) helped pass a $5 million appropriations bill to finance the International Women's Year (IWY) Conference in Houston, Texas. Delegates to the conference were chosen through 50 state conferences, though some were hand-selected by members of the conference commission. Two thousand delegates and another 18,000 observers arrived in Houston for a four-day convention in November 1977. At the same time, an alternative women's convention had convened on the other side of town; Phyllis Schlafly's movement gathered 10,000 pro-family supporters in an Anti-ERA rally. The two groups commanded widespread media attention and brought the issues of ERA, abortion, and lesbian rights to the national spotlight for almost a week. The IWY conference proved a mixed success for feminists. It led to a consolidation of many points of division between the liberal and lesbian feminist groups, and the massive, mostly favorable, media attention for the conference put pressure on Congress to extend the deadline for ERA ratification another three years to 1982. During the time between 1977 and 1982, membership in NOW, NWPC, the National Abortion Rights Action League (NARAL), and other feminist activist groups soared. At the same time, however, opponents of ERA gained wider popular support among mainstream liberals who felt apprehension with what seemed to be a new linkage between the ERA, homosexual entitlements, and abortion-on-demand. ERA failed to win any additional states after 1977, and the amendment officially died in 1982.

Many feminist historians point to the 1980s as a "backlash" against the women's rights movement. President RONALD W. REAGAN campaigned on a decidedly "pro-family" platform, and the Republican Party officially removed its endorsement of ERA in 1980. Reagan publicly courted the constituencies of both Phyllis Schlafly and Jerry Falwell, and after 1982, with ties severed to the administration, most feminist organizations declined in membership, and many radical action groups dissolved altogether. At the same time, however, while it appeared that Phyllis Schlafly and her supporters won their battle against the ERA, one could also argue that feminism actually won the war. Though the three Republican administrations between 1980 and 1992 proved hostile to radical feminism, the partisan identification actually opened more opportunities for feminists within the Democratic Party. GERALDINE FERRARO became the first female vice presidential nominee as a Democrat. In recent elections, 100 percent of political contributions from feminist lobby groups like NOW, NARAL, and Emily's List (an acronym for Early Money Is Like Yeast) has been given to the Democratic National Committee or to individual candidates within the party. When President WILLIAM J. CLINTON entered office in 1992, he appointed the first woman attorney general, JANET RENO, and the first woman secretary of state, MADELEINE ALBRIGHT. He also reversed the Republican policies regarding abortion, family planning, child care, and homosexual entitlements.

While few feminists would call themselves "radical" anymore, it seems that many of the issues that were of prime concern to radical feminists of the 1970s have become common realities in the 21st century. More women than men graduate from high school, and equal numbers earn college degrees. "Women's studies" departments are found on almost all campuses, and virtually all textbooks and reference materials adopt standards of inclusive language. Though there is some disagreement about pay equity, more women can be found in executive positions than ever before. Whether they adhere to the principles or not, most corporations proclaim their commitment to affirmative-action programs that encourage and cultivate greater numbers of women in fields that were traditionally dominated by men, such as MEDICINE, law, and the sciences. In addition, government-supported child care is available for low-income children as young as four and five, and tax credits are available for working parents of children of all ages. Contraception and abortion rights are taught in most secondary-school sex education classes, and although lesbianism and homosexuality remain minority sexual preferences, the media and entertainment centers and public institutions generally portray homosexuality with greater tolerance. Sexual activity outside the bounds of MARRIAGE is more common than abstinence, divorce rates are more than 50 percent, and the stereotype of the domesticated nuclear family represents an actual minority in American society. Most feminists would argue that there remains a long way to go toward true equality between the sexes, but clearly the effect of feminism on American society has been extraordinary over the past three decades.

See also AFFIRMATIVE ACTION; *AKRON V. AKRON CENTER FOR REPRODUCTIVE HEALTH;* AMENDMENTS TO THE U.S. CONSTITUTION; BIRTH CONTROL; GAY RIGHTS MOVEMENT; GENDER GAP; PRO-LIFE AND PRO-CHOICE MOVEMENTS; STEINEM, GLORIA; WOMEN'S RIGHTS AND STATUS.

Further reading: Sara Evans, *Personal Politics: The Roots of Women's Liberation in the Civil Rights Movement and the New Left* (New York: Knopf, 1979); Susan Hartmann,

The Other Feminists: Activists in the Liberal Establishment (New Haven: Yale University Press, 1998); Laura Kaplan, *The Story of Jane: The Legendary Underground Feminist Abortion Service* (New York: Pantheon, 1995); Ruth Rosen, *The World Split Open: How the Modern Women's Movement Changed America* (New York: Viking Books, 2000).

—Aharon W. Zorea

Ferraro, Geraldine A. (1935–)

Geraldine Ferraro became the first woman vice presidential candidate for a major political party when she received the Democratic nomination in 1984. Born in 1935 in Newburgh, New York, to Italian immigrant parents, Geraldine Anne Ferraro earned an undergraduate degree from Marymount College in Manhattan in 1956. While teaching in public schools in Queens, New York, Ferraro attended law school at night at Fordham University Law School, earning her degree in 1960. Deciding to stay home and raise a family, Ferraro became active in local Democratic politics.

In 1974 she accepted a job as assistant district attorney in the Investigation Bureau in Queens. In 1975 she transferred to the Special Victims Bureau, handling issues such as child abuse, domestic abuse, and rape. It was in this position that Ferraro came to believe that many crimes were rooted in poverty and social injustice. Ferraro quit her job at the district attorney's office in 1978 and ran for the vacant Ninth Congressional District seat. Running on a platform supporting law and order, the elderly, and neighborhood preservation, Ferraro won election to Congress and was reelected in 1980 and 1982.

In 1980 Ferraro was elected secretary of the Democratic caucus and served on the House Steering and Policy Committee. She also served on the House Budget Committee, the Public Works Committee, Post Office and Civil Service Committee, and the Select Committee on Aging. While in Congress, Ferraro headed efforts to pass the EQUAL RIGHTS AMENDMENT (ERA) and sponsored the Women's Economic Equity Act in 1984, which ended pension discrimination and enabled homemakers to open individual retirement accounts (IRAs).

In 1984 she was appointed chair of the Democratic platform committee, the first woman to hold the position. Her new responsibilities and past record attracted the attention of WALTER F. MONDALE. In July 1984, Mondale announced Ferraro as his vice presidential running mate, making her the first woman nominated for that position. Soon a scandal emerged concerning Ferraro's family over allegations that they owed more than $50,000 in back taxes. Although the ticket survived the scrutiny, it suffered a huge defeat in the election, with Mondale's opponent, RONALD W. REAGAN, garnering the highest electoral vote in history.

Ferraro ran unsuccessfully for the U.S. SENATE in 1992 and 1998 in New York. In 1993 she was appointed by President WILLIAM J. CLINTON to lead the U.S. delegation to the United Nations Human Rights Commission. She is a board member of the National Democratic Institute of International Affairs and is a member of the Council on Foreign Relations.

In 1999 Ferraro joined the public relations firm of Weber McGinn as president of the Women's Leadership Group, advising on women's issues such as education, health care, consumer products, and employment. On top of these responsibilities, Ferraro is a political pundit, appearing on television news programs and writing occasional newspaper columns.

See also ELECTIONS; POLITICAL PARTIES.

Further reading: Steve M. Gillon, *The Democrats' Dilemma: Walter F. Mondale and the Liberal Legacy* (New York: Columbia University Press, 1992).

—John Korasick

flag burning

The National Flag Conference adopted the first regulations governing the care and use of the U.S. flag on June 14, 1923. During World War II, Congress enacted a federal flag code establishing specific guidelines for its use and presentation, and included an explicit prohibition against acts of disrespect. The law empowered the president of the United States to make changes to the code as necessary, but empowered the states to determine the specific penalties for misuse.

The code remained largely unchallenged until the late 1960s, when protestors more frequently used the symbolism of flag desecration to dramatize their positions. In 1969, the U.S. SUPREME COURT chose to ignore the specific question of desecration in its first case on the subject, *Street v. New York,* finding that state legislation outlawing contemptuous speech against the flag violated the First Amendment. Five years later, in *Spence v. Washington,* the Court came closer to the issue when it ruled that state legislation prohibiting the defacement of the flag also violated protected forms of expression. It was not until 1989 that the Court addressed the specific question of flag burning; *Texas v. Johnson* concluded that flag burning was expressive conduct protected by the First Amendment. In his opinion, Justice WILLIAM J. BRENNAN, JR., wrote that "the government may not prohibit the expression of an idea simply because society finds the idea itself offensive or disagreeable." In response, Congress passed the Flag Protection Act of 1989, attempting to rectify the constitutional deficiencies of the original flag code; it imposed a fine and/or jail sentence of up to one year for knowingly muti-

Protesters burn an American flag in Washington, D.C., at the inauguration of President George W. Bush. *(Levine/Getty Images)*

lating, defacing, and physically defiling the flag. The following year, the Supreme Court, in *U. S. v. Eichman*, found the new language to be equally unconstitutional, concluding that neither the federal nor state legislatures were empowered to mandate special protections for the U.S. flag without a constitutional amendment.

Public sentiment on the question of flag burning overwhelmingly favored some form of constitutional protection. Opponents, including the American Civil Liberties Union, argued that a constitutional amendment might unintentionally compromise the First Amendment protection of expression. Supporters countered that the courts had already made exceptions to freedom of speech on issues such as libel, obscenity, and trademarks, and that the flag deserved such special protection. The first attempt to enact such an amendment passed the HOUSE OF REPRESENTATIVES with overwhelming support in 1990, and failed to pass the SENATE by only one vote. Similar bills were submitted every congressional session thereafter, coming within three votes of passing the Senate's required two-thirds majority in 1995 and again in 1999.

See also AMENDMENTS TO THE U.S. CONSTITUTION; ANTIWAR MOVEMENT; CENSORSHIP.

—Aharon W. Zorea

Foley, Thomas S. (1929–)

Stephen Foley, a longtime member of Congress representing the state of Washington, became Speaker of the House in 1989.

Born in Spokane, Washington, in 1929, Thomas Stephen Foley grew up in South Hill. Foley attended Gonzaga University before transferring to the University of Washington in his junior year. After graduating from the University of Washington Law School in 1957, Foley practiced law with his cousin, Henry Higgins, before moving on to become a deputy prosecutor with the Spokane County prosecutor's office and ultimately to the state level as an assistant state attorney general. In 1961 Foley joined U.S. senator Henry Jackson as a special counsel on the Senate Interior Committee.

Foley ran for a seat in the U.S. HOUSE OF REPRESENTATIVES as a Democrat from a predominantly Republican district in 1964. Foley would ultimately be reelected 14 times. Foley was a consistent liberal during his congressional career. Among the issues he faced during his 30 years in Congress, he favored a nuclear freeze, opposed Vietnam, and voted for the Civil Rights Act. In addition, he supported abortion as a constitutional right. Foley broke with the liberals on GUN CONTROL.

In 1974 in a major leadership shake-up, Foley became chairman of the Agriculture Committee, the first westerner to hold this position. In 1981 Foley became the House majority whip, and in 1987 the majority leader. And finally, in June 1989 Foley was elected the 49th Speaker of the House and the first from west of the Rocky Mountains. Foley replaced Jim Wright who resigned under criticism. Foley is credited with bringing civility back to the House. Seen by many as a conciliator, Foley opposed proposals to amend the Constitution to ban FLAG BURNING and opposed cutting the capital gains tax rate.

In 1992 the voters of Washington State passed a referendum imposing term limits on state and federal officeholders. Despite overwhelming support for the referendum, Foley sought a 16th term and challenged the referendum in federal court. In 1994 Foley was defeated by Republican challenger George Nethercutt, becoming the first incumbent Speaker to lose reelection since the Civil War.

Some election analysts attributed Foley's loss to general voter dissatisfaction with Foley's liberal stances on many issues, which were out of touch with his constituency. After leaving Congress, Foley became a partner in the law firm of Akin, Gump, Strauss, Hauer & Feld, L.L.P., specializing in international affairs. He also served on a number of private and public boards of directors. In 1997 Foley became U.S. ambassador to Japan.

—John Korasick

Ford, Gerald R. (1913–   )

Gerald Rudolph Ford was sworn in as the 38th president of the United States on August 9, 1974, after President RICHARD M. NIXON's resignation. He presided during a time when the public was still reeling from both the VIETNAM WAR and the WATERGATE SCANDAL. Though his administration achieved moderate successes in stimulating the ailing economy, Ford never managed to escape the long shadow of Nixon's resignation. He lost the 1976 election to JAMES EARL CARTER, JR., by only 57 electoral votes.

President Ford was born Leslie Lynch King, Jr., on July 14, 1913, in Omaha, Nebraska. His mother, Dorothy Ayer Garder, was the mayor's daughter in a small Illinois town, and his father, Leslie Lynch King, was a wealthy banker's son. Unfortunately, King was also alcoholic and physically abusive. Just days after his son's birth, the police

were called in to restrain him when he threatened to kill his wife, the new baby, and the nurse with a butcher knife. His wife left him, and an Omaha court later granted her a divorce, with custody of the baby, on the grounds of her husband's extreme cruelty. She and the baby moved in with her parents. Two years later, she married a paint salesman named Gerald R. Ford. Her two-year-old was renamed Gerald R. Ford, Jr. Dorothy Ford gave birth to three more sons, and the Ford household became a warm environment with strong family bonds. The oldest boy did not discover that his stepfather was not his biological father until he was 17 years old; he legally changed his name in 1935.

As a youth, Ford demonstrated a gift for athletics and went to the University of Michigan on a sports scholarship. An economics and political science major, Ford was also playing varsity football and was named most valuable player in 1934. After graduation, he accepted a position as boxing coach and assistant football coach for Yale. After a long wait, Ford was accepted to Yale Law School and earned his law degree in 1941. After the Japanese bombed Pearl Harbor, Ford enlisted in the navy. He served all four years of World War II, and was honorably discharged as a lieutenant commander in February 1946.

Upon returning to civilian life, Ford joined community organizations and made a name for himself as one of the "New Republicans." In 1948 Michigan senator Arthur H. Vandenberg urged Ford to challenge the incumbent Republican congressman, Bartel Jonkman, an isolationist, in the party primaries. After winning the primary, Ford went on to win the general election. Just a few weeks before the election during this first campaign, Ford married Elizabeth "Betty" Bloomer Warren; he even campaigned on his wedding day. Together they had four children: Michael Gerald (1950), John Gardner (1952), Steven Meigs (1956), and Susan Elizabeth (1957).

Throughout the 1950s, Ford focused on fiscal policy, though he continued to encourage a strong American presence in foreign affairs. He became a member of the House Appropriations Committee during his second term and later became a ranking member of the Defense Appropriations Subcommittee. Ford described himself as a "moderate in domestic affairs, an internationalist in foreign affairs, and a conservative in fiscal policy." Ford remained fairly consistently moderate throughout his service as legislator. Ford opposed efforts to federally subsidize education and housing as well as health care, and federal intervention in use of local lands through environmental protection strategies. He supported increases in defense spending and civil rights legislation.

Ford's ultimate goal was to become Speaker of the House. His first step toward national recognition came in 1961, when a group of younger, more progressive House Republicans known as the "Young Turks" revolted against the older leadership and elected Ford as the chairman of the House Republican Conference. Members of both parties liked Ford; he became known for his quiet honesty and political integrity. In 1963 this reputation led to his being named by President Johnson to serve on the Warren Commission, which was appointed to investigate the assassination of President John F. Kennedy. Two years later, Ford wrote a book on the subject, with John R. Stiles, called *Portrait of the Assassin*. With increasing national attention, the Young Turks rallied behind him in a bid to unseat Charles Halleck for minority leadership in 1965. Although Ford held the post of House minority leader for eight years, he never realized his dream of becoming Speaker of the House because the Republicans failed to win a majority during his tenure.

Ford rose to the office of president as a result of two separate scandals within his own party. Vice President SPIRO AGNEW resigned from office on October 10, 1973, after pleading no contest to charges of tax evasion, leaving the position vacant. The recently ratified Twenty-Fifth Amendment required Nixon to submit the name of a potential vice president for congressional approval. Since Agnew's resignation came just months after news broke about the break-in at the Watergate hotel, President Nixon feared a crash in public confidence. He invited Democratic leaders, Speaker CARL B. ALBERT and Senate Majority Leader Mike Mansfield, to the White House to discuss which nominee could win the fastest confirmation. Both men put Ford's name forward, and Nixon agreed. He

Gerald R. Ford   *(The Gerald R. Ford Library)*

announced the decision on October 11. This was not an entirely surprising move for Nixon or Ford, since the two had had a good relationship since the early 1950s. Ford accepted the appointment to help the party. After the most thorough background investigation in the history of the FBI, Ford was sworn in as vice president on December 6, 1973, becoming the first vice president appointed under the terms of the Twenty-Fifth Amendment.

Five months later, as Ford started his new appointment, the Watergate scandal erupted with new vigor. In March 1974 a grand jury indicted several members of Nixon's administration for their role in covering up the Watergate break-in, including U.S. Attorney General JOHN N. MITCHELL, White House Chief of Staff H. R. Haldeman, and White House Special Assistant on Domestic Affairs John Ehrlichman. President Nixon was referred to as an "unindicted co-conspirator." Following Nixon's resignation, Chief Justice WARREN E. BURGER swore Gerald Ford in as the 38th president of the United States on August 9, 1974. He became the only president to enter office without ever having faced a national election.

A month after his swearing-in ceremony, President Ford granted a "full, free and absolute pardon" to former president Nixon for all crimes "he committed or may have committed" while in office. Ford's first three news conferences had focused entirely on questions dealing with Watergate and Nixon, and he hoped to bring an end to the scandal with a full pardon. His administration needed to attend to other important issues, including increasingly high inflation, high unemployment, and a year-old ENERGY CRISIS. Historians' opinions are mixed as to whether Ford's tactic succeeded; the negative public reaction to the pardon surprised Ford, and some historians argue it was later responsible for his defeat in the 1976 election. Others give less importance to the public's reaction, arguing instead that both Nixon's and Agnew's separate resignations had tarnished the Republican Party, and that the public would have rejected Ford's reelection whether or not he pardoned Nixon. In either case, after September, President Ford conducted his administration with little reference to Watergate and President Nixon. He nominated New York governor Nelson Rockefeller for vice president and selected a cabinet of his own, retaining only HENRY A. KISSINGER as secretary of state, Earl Butz as secretary of agriculture, and William Simon as treasury secretary. The Democrats swept the 1974 Congress, and a special congressional hearing was called to investigate whether Ford's pardon had been prearranged with Nixon. Ford testified before the hearing committee and replied in person that, "There was no deal. Period. Under no circumstances." The matter was dropped, but the Congress grew increasingly suspicious of possible abuse of executive authority. Ford VETOed more than 50 bills during his two years in office because he felt they called for unnecessary, or overly costly, expenditures.

Ford's efforts to reduce inflation and stimulate the ECONOMY failed to overcome stagflation. Unemployment was higher than 9 percent in early 1975, but it dropped to just over 7 percent before Ford left office. Though industrial production had dropped significantly since 1972, Ford promoted a stimulus package that included a $16 billion corporate tax cut. He addressed the energy shortage by proposing an incentive program to reduce oil consumption and limit the nation's dependence on foreign oil. He called for cuts in federal programs to offset the reduction in revenue caused by the $16 billion tax cut.

In FOREIGN POLICY, Ford pulled out the remaining troops from Vietnam, and continued a cautious policy of DÉTENTE with China and the SOVIET UNION. Ford joined Soviet premier Leonid I. Brezhnev in signing the Helsinki Accords in 1975, which implicitly recognized the existing boundaries of Soviet-occupied territories in Eastern Europe and East Germany; he also entered into negotiations to return control of the PANAMA CANAL to Panama.

Both of these actions angered conservative Republicans, especially RONALD W. REAGAN, who used these issues to launch a strong challenge to Ford during the 1976 Republican primaries. Ford alienated the right wing of the GOP with his adamant support of the EQUAL RIGHTS AMENDMENT (ERA). Furthermore, his wife Betty's public support for the constitutional right to ABORTION further estranged Ford from the growing right wing within the Republican Party.

Ford managed to win his party's nomination on August 18, 1976, but the margin was so close that he was forced to include Ronald W. Reagan's more conservative positions on social issues and foreign policy in the Republican platform. He also changed running mates, substituting the more conservative Kansas senator ROBERT DOLE for Rockefeller. Ford eventually lost the 1976 election to Democratic challenger JAMES EARL CARTER, JR.

Upon leaving office in 1977, Ford lectured at colleges and universities, and briefly served as an adjunct professor of government at his alma mater, the University of Michigan. Ronald W. Reagan briefly considered him as a running mate in 1980, but Ford has since remained out of Republican Party politics. He has authored several books, including *A Time to Heal* (1979), and *Humor and the Presidency* (1987). President WILLIAM J. CLINTON awarded the nation's highest civilian honor, the Presidential Medal of Freedom, to Ford in 1999. Ford's presidential library is situated in Ann Arbor, Michigan.

See also CONSERVATIVE MOVEMENT; SCHLAFLY, PHYLLIS.

Further reading: James Cannon, *Time and Chance: Gerald Ford's Appointment with History* (New York: 1994); John Robert Greene, *The Presidency of Gerald Ford* (Lawrence: University of Kansas Press, 1995).

—Aharon W. Zorea

Foreign Corrupt Practices Act (1977)

Congress enacted the Foreign Corrupt Practices Act of 1977 to prevent corporate bribery by American businesses of foreign officials. During the mid-1970s, lawsuits revealed that a number of American corporations made questionable or illegal payments to foreign government officials. Federal officials decided that more direct prohibitions on foreign bribery, coupled with more detailed requirements concerning corporate record keeping and accountability, formed a method to deal effectively with the problem. Corporate bribery was seen as adversely affecting American FOREIGN POLICY, damaging the image of American democracy overseas, and impairing public confidence in the financial integrity of American corporations. Congress responded with the Foreign Corrupt Practices Act of 1977, composed of three major restrictions. First, it required corporations to keep accurate books, records, and accounts. Second, it required public companies registered with the Securities and Exchange Commission to maintain a responsible internal accounting control system. Finally, it prohibited bribery by American corporations of foreign officials.

The act attracted a great deal of criticism. Opponents argued the act held too many gray areas, and that many American companies would cease foreign operations rather than face the uncertainties in the Foreign Corrupt Practices Act. Furthermore, critics called for precise and specific guidelines to be enacted to ensure that American corporations acted within clearly defined guidelines set by the legislation. In addition, opponents of the act also sought the removal of the "reason to know" standard concerning liability for actions of a firm's agent in a foreign country. This would eliminate the legal responsibility of the management of a domestic firm over the unauthorized and undirected actions of an agent. Moreover, critics contended that the internal accounting controls required by the act were too costly and burdensome upon domestic firms. They instead wanted a standard for public record keeping, requiring a firm to report expenditures and outlays deemed relevant to the profits and revenues of the firm.

Congress responded to these criticisms by amending the act in 1988 and signing it into law as Title V of the Omnibus Trade and Competitiveness Act of 1988 on August 23, 1988. The amendments maintained the three major parts of the 1977 act, but removed criminal liability unless a person knowingly circumvented or knowingly violated the law. Another amendment stated that an issuer that holds 50 percent or less of the voting power of a domestic or foreign firm is required to use its influence only in good faith to cause the domestic or foreign firm to devise and maintain a system of acceptable accounting controls. As amended, the act defined "knowing" circumvention as "conscious disregard" and "willful blindness"—meaning a conscious effort to avoid learning the truth. Congress added amendments, so that antibribery provisions did not apply to any facilitating or expediting payment to a foreign official, political party, or party official if the purpose is to expedite or to secure the performance of a routine governmental action. The amended act also allowed an American business or individual to use one of the "affirmative defenses" in urging that no violation of the act occurred. The amendments also increased penalties for violations of the Foreign Corrupt Practices Act from a maximum of $1 million to $2 million for businesses and for individuals from $10,000 to $100,000.

—Leah Blakey

foreign policy

United States foreign policy underwent several major reevaluations after 1968 in response to changes abroad and at home. The emergence of strong economies in Japan and Western Europe diminished the economic clout of the United States. The Soviet Union achieved effective nuclear parity. China emerged as a major power and was hostile to the Soviet Union. At home, the VIETNAM WAR was becoming less popular and it appeared that the public would no longer support the deployment of troops to contain communism. In response to the public mood, Congress became increasingly partisan in foreign affairs—ensuring that no president would have a free hand. By the late 1980s the Soviet Union was declining in power, and the cold war was coming to a close. The resulting world order challenged U.S. conceptions of how the international system operated, and new challenges emerged.

The first shift occurred during the administration of RICHARD M. NIXON, when the president and his adviser HENRY A. KISSINGER worked to establish DÉTENTE—a policy to develop habits of restraint, coexistence, and cooperation—with the Soviet Union, and opened relations with the People's Republic of China. Nixon entered office in 1969 and quickly established the Nixon Doctrine. Nixon declared that the United States would provide a nuclear deterrent for the West and would honor its treaty commitments in the case of conventional attack. This policy pulled the United States back from its earlier stance of opposing the spread of communism wherever it emerged. Anticommunist ideology was replaced with a more rational assessment of national interest. With the changing economic and global political situation, a new system was necessary that was not predicated on a bipolar worldview, in which the United States and Soviet Union were the only important players. Nuclear parity diminished the threat of nuclear war; neither side was willing to destroy the world to win a war. The energy crisis, which emerged in 1973, showed that the Middle East, especially the Arab-Israeli conflict, required attention and presented problems of its own. By engaging the Soviet Union in détente and presenting the possibility that the United States would engage with China, Nixon and Kissinger attempted to create a system of rules that both sides would obey. The most visible result of détente was the Strategic Arms Limitation Treaty, which limited the development of antimissile systems and established temporary agreements to restrict offensive capabilities.

In addition to altering the relationship between the United States and the Soviet Union, Nixon oversaw the de-escalation of the war in Vietnam. Through a process known as "Vietnamization," the United States gradually turned the fighting of the war over to the South Vietnamese and withdrew troops. The United States intensified its bombing of North Vietnam and expanded into Cambodia. Determined to maintain U.S. prestige, Nixon refused to pull out of Vietnam until a settlement had been reached. In 1971 Nixon dispatched Kissinger to Paris to carry out secret negotiations with the North Vietnamese foreign minister, Le Duc Tho. In October 1972 an agreement was reached providing for a cease-fire, the establishment of a coalition government in South Vietnam, free elections, the withdrawal of American troops, and the release of all prisoners of war. South Vietnam initially refused to accept the plan, and negotiations broke down. After the 1972 elections, Nixon forced the North to return to the bargaining table with massive bombings. On January 22, 1973, Nixon announced that an agreement had been reached to end the war.

Critics argued that the war could have been ended much earlier and noted that more than half the Americans killed had died since Nixon had been elected. Critics of détente argued that the Soviet Union was not trustworthy and would not abide by the new ground rules. In addition, the new policies were seen as amoral, supporting right-wing dictators and repressive regimes in Iran, the Philippines, SOUTH AFRICA, Argentina, South Korea, Brazil, and Nigeria. Meanwhile, leftist regimes were subject to American intervention or overthrow, as in the case of Chile in 1973.

Nixon's successor, GERALD R. FORD, sought to maintain Nixon's initiatives. Ford was faced with the collapse of anticommunist resistance in Southeast Asia. In 1975 the Khmer Rouge seized control of Cambodia, and the North Vietnamese resumed hostilities and quickly conquered South Vietnam. The reluctance of the United States to intervene was interpreted by many at home and abroad as a sign of weakness. In addition, Ford's meetings with Soviet leader Leonid Brezhnev in 1974 on arms control and in 1975 on European borders and human rights drew criticism from his own party that he had surrendered too much for too little.

JAMES EARL CARTER, JR., broke with the Nixon-Kissinger realism policy and made human rights the focal point of his efforts. He pressured governments around the globe to address their human rights violations. A treaty ceding the PANAMA CANAL and Canal Zone to PANAMA was ratified. And he established full diplomatic relations with the People's Republic of China, thus concluding the transition begun by Nixon toward recognizing the most populous nation in the world. The most widely hailed accomplishment of the administration was the brokering of a peace treaty between Israel and Egypt.

The last year of Carter's administration bore witness to events that made the administration appear naively idealistic and weak. First, the SALT II treaty was submitted to the Senate, where it came under intense scrutiny and criticism that it would give the Soviets an advantage. When the Soviet Union invaded Afghanistan in 1979, Carter pulled the treaty from consideration and ordered a boycott of the 1980 Olympics in Moscow. In addition, in January 1979 the IRANIAN HOSTAGE CRISIS developed, and the United States's inability to rescue or gain the release of the hostages further eroded what had been a promising diplomatic reputation. Détente also came under increasing criticism. From the fall of Saigon in 1975 to communist advances in Africa and Central America, the United States had suffered numerous setbacks.

With the election of RONALD W. REAGAN in 1980, the cold war gained in intensity. Reagan preached that the nation had been left defenseless by post-Vietnam years of cuts in defense spending and the unwillingness of presidents to stand up to the Soviets. Reagan invoked the language of a moral crusade against communism used in the early years of the cold war. Charging that the Soviets had used détente to promote world revolution and dubbing the

Protesters jab a caricature of the Statue of Liberty during a protest in front of the U.S. embassy January 25th, 2002, in Manila. *(Calderon/Getty Images)*

Soviet Union the "evil empire," Reagan employed 1950s-style containment, reminiscent of the "liberation" and "roll-back" themes of the Eisenhower administration. Despite the rhetoric, Reagan was careful about the commitment of U.S. troops. After the deadly bombing of the marine barracks in Beirut, Lebanon, in 1983, U.S. troops were used only in small-scale operations such as the overthrow of the marxist government in Grenada. Reagan relied on covert operations and proxy wars. Through the CIA, money was funneled to the CONTRAS in Nicaragua, Afghan rebels, and anticommunist forces in Angola and Ethiopia.

His rhetorical comments aside, Reagan did not abandon détente. In 1983 he concluded the largest grain deal with the Soviets in history. In 1984 Reagan announced that new talks would commence with the Soviets on arms reduction and space weapons. With the rise of Mikhail Gorbachev to general secretary of the Soviet Union in 1985, détente had two figures who excelled at personal summitry and established a rapport. Each wanted to relax East-West tensions, and at four summits between 1985 and 1988, they significantly improved relations between the two nations and reached agreements on arms reductions.

A new and potent threat emerged in the 1980s. International terrorism exploded with more than 700 attacks around the world in 1985 alone. In 1986 pro-Libyan terrorists bombed military installations in West Germany. In response, the United States launched an air strike against Libya. Terrorists also kidnapped Americans overseas, hijacked airliners, and commandeered the cruise ship *Achille Lauro*. The official government position was that there would be no negotiations with terrorists.

In Central America, Reagan pursued his policy of rollback. To counter the Sandinistas, a marxist regime in Nicaragua, Reagan authorized the establishment of a counterrevolutionary army, the contras. When Congress later discontinued funding to the contras, a new plan emerged. White House aide OLIVER L. NORTH brokered a deal to sell arms to Iran in exchange for the release of American hostages held by terrorists in Lebanon. North funneled the proceeds to the contras. When it came to light in 1985, the IRAN-CONTRA AFFAIR prompted a congressional inquiry and the appointment of an INDEPENDENT COUNSEL. The affair damaged the credibility of the administration in the eyes of many.

In 1988 GEORGE H. W. BUSH assumed the presidency. The world Bush faced was changing rapidly. The cold war was coming to an end: communist governments in Eastern Europe crumbled, Gorbachev was attempting to reform the Soviet system, and the Sandinistas were voted out of office in Nicaragua. Bush wanted the renunciation of the Brezhnev Doctrine of 1968, which declared the right of the Soviet Union to intervene in the affairs of socialist states. In 1989 Bush and Gorbachev met for the first time. Bush urged further reforms and offered economic aid as an incentive. In 1991 the Strategic Arms Reduction Treaty was signed. Bush also took advantage of Soviet disarray to take actions against problematic former anticommunist allies, such as Manuel Noriega in Panama in 1989, and Saddam Hussein in Iraq in the PERSIAN GULF WAR in 1990–91.

Bush oversaw the end of the cold war, but did all he could to ensure that a reformed version of the Soviet Union would remain. Bush kept silent when the Soviets attempted to intimidate Lithuania into renouncing independence in 1990 and refused to recognize the republic until 1991. Also, Bush urged Ukraine not to secede from the Soviet Union. In response to the decline and partition of the Soviet Union, hard-line Communists staged an anti-Gorbachev coup in an attempt to restore 1970s-style communism. Russian president Boris Yeltsin led resistance to the coup, and after three days, it collapsed. But by the end of 1991, the Soviet Union had been dissolved and Ukraine and Belarus declared independent.

With the end of any traditional security challenge, U.S. foreign policy changed. Military security was de-emphasized, as pundits and politicians clamored for a "peace dividend." President Clinton advanced a free-trade foreign policy. In 1993 the NORTH AMERICAN FREE TRADE AGREEMENT (NAFTA) was approved by the United States, Mexico, and Canada, despite the objection of labor unions and human rights activists. The United States pursued broader trade regulations in the GENERAL AGREEMENT ON TARIFFS AND TRADE (GATT) and supported the creation of the WORLD TRADE ORGANIZATION (WTO) in 1995. In arms control, Clinton arranged for the dismantling of nuclear stockpiles in the former Soviet republics. In 1994 this initiative resulted in the Russian-Ukraine Trilateral Statement and Annex, which led to the dismantling of all nuclear weapons in Ukraine. In addition, Clinton and Yeltsin signed an agreement to de-target strategic missiles.

After embarrassments in Somalia in 1993, Clinton found his foreign policy focus. Following more than four decades of "containment," the cold war was over, and now U.S. policy would be dedicated to "democratic enlargement." This enlargement was based on four points: strengthening market democracies, fostering new democracies, countering the aggression of nations hostile to democracy, and aiding democracies in regions of humanitarian concern. The United States would encourage the development of democracy through capitalism. Clinton sought stability in the world. Relations were normalized with Vietnam. The United States provided economic assistance to Russia. Clinton took action to contain Saddam Hussein, and actively joined with NATO allies in preventing "ethnic cleansing" in the Balkans. Despite his successes, critics charged that he was an amateur who used military operations to draw attention away from scandals in his personal life.

The struggle for victory in the cold war had precluded policymakers from planning for the aftermath. When the conflict ended unexpectedly, presidents struggled to find the right course for the world's only superpower.

Less than a year after GEORGE W. BUSH came into office, U.S. foreign policy confronted its greatest challenge since the end of the cold war—a terrorist attack by Islamic militants on American home soil. On September 11, 2001, Islamic militants crashed two hijacked planes into the New York World Trade Center towers and another hijacked plane into the Pentagon, outside of Washington, D.C. A fourth plane crashed in western Pennsylvania when passengers attempted to seize control from the hijackers. Evidence revealed that the operation had been conducted through a militant Islamic terrorist group under the leadership of a Saudi religious fanatic, Osama bin Laden, who had taken refuge in Afghanistan. President Bush demanded that the government of Afghanistan turn over bin Laden. At the same time, President Bush declared a war against worldwide terrorism and any nation that supported terrorism. When the Afghanistan government, controlled by an Islamic religious sect, the Taliban, refused to turn over bin Laden, the United States launched an intensive bombing campaign to bring down the Taliban government and bin Laden's terrorist group, al-Qaeda. Military support was also given to Afghan rebel tribes, organized as the Northern Alliance. After an intensive bombing campaign, American ground forces assisted the Northern Alliance in bringing the downfall of the Taliban government. In early December 2001 the Taliban stronghold city, Kandahar, fell. Although bin Laden was rumored to have died in the bombing raids, Islamic terrorism remained a serious threat to American security. American advisers were sent to assist the Philippine government in its war against Islamic rebels. As the United States entered the 21st century, the war on terrorism had replaced the cold war, and the effects of this new war on American national security, foreign affairs, domestic policy, and politics remained uncertain.

See also STRATEGIC ARMS LIMITATION TREATIES.

Further reading: Stephen E. Ambrose and Douglas G. Brinkley, *Rise to Globalism: American Foreign Policy since 1938* (New York: Penguin, 1997); Alan P. Dobson and Steve Marsh, *U.S. Foreign Policy since 1945* (New York: Routledge, 2001).

—John Korasick

Fortas, Abe (1910–1982)

Abe Fortas was one of the most prominent attorneys during the New Deal era and served as an associate justice of the U.S. Supreme Court from 1965 to 1969. In 1968 President Lyndon Johnson nominated him to become chief justice, but his nomination failed, the first nomination to do so since 1795. One year later, Fortas became the first justice to resign under threat of impeachment.

Fortas was born June 19, 1910, in Memphis, Tennessee, and served as an associate justice of the U.S. Supreme Court from 1965–69. A son of immigrant Jews, Fortas excelled as a brilliant student at both Southwestern College and Yale Law School. He absorbed the influential contemporary doctrine of legal realism expounded by his professors, Thurman Arnold and William O. Douglas, while at Yale. Fortas graduated from Yale Law in 1933 at the top of his class. He immediately found employment as a lawyer with the Agricultural Adjustment Administration in Washington, D.C. He became a close friend of New Deal regulation enthusiasts in all three federal branches during the 1930s. Fortas's friends were a Who's Who of mid-20th-century liberalism: Hugo Black, Felix Frankfurter, William O. Douglas, Thurman Arnold, Thomas Corcoran, Benjamin Cohen, James Landis, and, most important for his career, young Lyndon Johnson.

In 1935 Fortas married Carolyn Agger, an aspiring lawyer. He gave up his government post and moved to New Haven, Connecticut, so his wife could also attend Yale Law School. Fortas taught the use of legal realism in practice at Yale Law, while commuting to Washington, D.C., to work for William O. Douglas, then chairman of another innovative New Deal agency, the Securities and Exchange Commission. After his wife graduated, the Fortases moved back to Washington. Fortas then became a close deputy of Secretary of the Interior Harold Ickes. Fortas served Ickes until World War II ended. While at Interior, Fortas opposed the internment of Japanese Americans and advocated civil rights for blacks. He then joined with friends Thurman Arnold and Paul Porter to found the prestigious Washington law firm, Arnold and Porter, after the war ended.

While managing partner of Arnold and Porter from 1945–65, Fortas became the epitome of the Washington lawyer. He wielded great influence through his formidable technical skills and awesome political connections. In 1965 Johnson, then president, rewarded Fortas for his friendship and counsel, with the Supreme Court seat vacated by retiring associate justice Arthur Goldberg. Fortas was easily confirmed. Three years later, however, Johnson's reputation was in ruins, and a conservative coalition of northern Republican and southern Democratic senators joined to wreck Fortas's nomination as chief justice. Fortas was attacked during confirmation hearings for both judicial liberalism and financial improprieties while serving on the Court. Enough opposition was aroused to launch a successful filibuster, and Fortas requested that Johnson withdraw his nomination. A year later, in 1969, Fortas resigned from the Court under fire, after his congressional critics threatened impeachment over allegations of impropriety.

Fortas's fall from power was so thorough that Arnold and Porter refused to rehire him after his resignation. So he formed his own firm and returned to representing corporate clients and performing pro bono work until his death on April 16, 1982.

—Christopher M. Gray

G

gay rights movement

The gay rights movement is the organized effort to combat all forms of prejudice and discrimination that is directed against homosexual men and women. It may be best understood as part of a broader cultural transformation that stresses self-realization and individuality rather than conformity to socially imposed patterns of behavior. Specifically within this cultural transformation, the women's movement that developed in the late 1960s and early 1970s generated a reevaluation of traditional male and female roles that, in turn, facilitated gay activism.

The primary impetus for the gay rights movement emerged from the Civil Rights movement in the postwar period. This movement for the rights of African Americans led to other movements that called for full civil rights for members of racial, ethnic, and religious minorities. Among the rights for which these groups agitated was the right to cultural diversity and self-determination. Gay activism coincided with a rise in international concern about overpopulation and with the SEXUAL REVOLUTION of the 1960s and 1970s, which together openly challenged the traditional procreative model of human sexuality. The gay rights movement, however, has not limited its activism to sexual freedom. While the freedom to be a homosexual has often served as a cornerstone of their political and legal challenges, it has symbolized for its supporters the overarching goal of achieving human rights and dignity.

Organizations for advocating and protecting the rights of homosexuals flourished in Germany and England from the 1860s through the 1920s. Not until the 1950s did similar organizations appear in the United States. The use of the term *gay activism* appeared in the early 1970s, primarily as a result of the Stonewall riots in New York City in June 1969. These riots marked the first time that patrons of a homosexual bar actively resisted police harassment. This incident sparked massive activity within the gay community. By 1972 the number of gay groups in the United States had grown from fewer than 20 to approximately 1,200.

These organizations sought primarily the passage of civil rights laws similar to those that forbade discrimination based on race, religion, ethnic origin, and sex. Essentially, gay activists began to define themselves as members of a group that was oppressed because of sexual orientation. Gay activists also worked for the repeal of all laws that criminalized any form of sexual behavior between consenting adults, a goal that, if achieved, would decriminalize the behavior that defined them as a separate group in American society.

In 1973 the American Psychiatric Association removed homosexuality from its list of disorders. This action significantly aided gay activists in their lobbying for civil rights. Homosexuals had made substantial institutional gains by the late 1970s, by forming gay caucuses within the major religious denominations and professional groups. Also, homosexual men and women had successfully created scores of gay political and legal organizations, some of which were national in scope. In the 1980s the gay rights movement focused much of its attention on the AIDS crisis by advocating more government funding of AIDS research, and by actively opposing discrimination against people suffering from AIDS. The AIDS epidemic provided a new focus for gay activism and helped unify the gay community, thus facilitating some initial successes.

The 1980s and 1990s witnessed the intensification of the legal battle over homosexual rights. Gay rights groups included Act Up, Lambda legal defense, and the Human Rights Campaign Fund, which face opposition over such issues as gay marriage and gays in the military. By 1986 over 50 county and local governments and the state of Wisconsin had enacted civil rights protections for homosexuals. In that same year, however, the U.S. SUPREME COURT essentially declared constitutional any state laws that criminalized homosexuality, by ruling that acts of homosexuality are not protected by the Constitution. Several events in the 1990s,

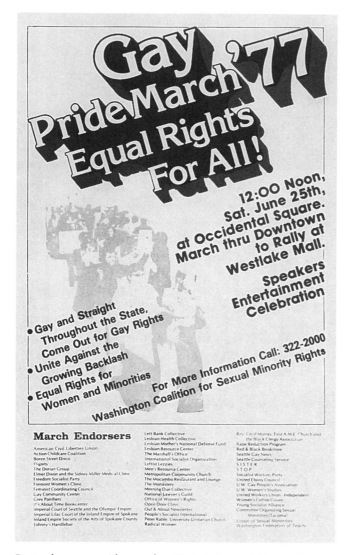

Poster for a gay pride parade, 1977 *(Library of Congress)*

however, demonstrated that the gay rights movement was making progress toward its goal of achieving equality under the law. In 1993 an anti-gay law passed by Colorado voters was declared unconstitutional by the state SUPREME COURT on the ground that "fundamental rights may not be submitted to a vote," thus establishing the right to be homosexual and declaring that right to be protected from any coercive will of the majority. Also in 1993, President WILLIAM J. CLINTON eased the ban on gays in the military. This compromise policy came to be known as the "Don't ask, don't tell" policy and allowed homosexuals to enlist in the military as long as they did not reveal their sexual orientation. Further advances were made in the political arena as several openly gay politicians were elected to offices ranging from city councils to the U.S. HOUSE OF REPRESENTATIVES. Moreover, individual homosexuals gained the right to adopt

children, to be ordained in some ministries, and to have legally recognized marriages in some states.

Concerns over a state court ruling in Hawaii led Congress to pass the Defense of Marriage Act by a vote of 342-67 in the House and 85-14 in the Senate. President Clinton signed the act into law on September 21, 1996. The act legally defined marriage as a "union between one man and one woman."

See also CONSERVATIVE MOVEMENT; MORAL MAJORITY; RELIGION.

Further reading: Barry D. Adam, *The Rise of a Gay and Lesbian Movement* (Boston: Twayne Publishers, 1987); John D'Emilio and Estelle B. Freedman, *Intimate Matters: A History of Sexuality in America*, 2d ed. (Chicago: University of Chicago Press, 1997); Jonathan Katz, *Gay American History: Lesbians and Gay Men in the U.S.A.* (New York: Crowell, 1976).

—William L. Glankler

gender gap

Gender gap was a term utilized by women's organizations in the early 1980s to draw attention to the important changes in voter choice, turnout, and partisanship occurring among women. The concept of the gender gap emerged concurrently with women voting in larger numbers than men. Even though there is evidence of the gender gap back to the 1950s, it was not until the 1980s that it began to emerge as a real and influential phenomenon in national politics. The transformation in the turnout of women was one of the most significant political changes of this time. Before 1980, the electorate was primarily influenced by white male voters. In the 1960s and 1970s, women were estimated to vote 10 percent less often than men, and even less frequently in previous decades. In the 1980 election, however, significant numbers of women participated in the presidential election, marking the first time that women voted at a higher rate then men. This is still the current trend in American electoral patterns. As women's roles in society changed through the 1970s, so did their party identification, from Republican to Democratic, while at the same time white male voters increasingly voted Republican. As of 1980, single women have consistently supported Democratic candidates at higher rates then men across all ranges of demographic categories including race, age, and education. The combination of more women voters, more women identifying themselves as Democrats, and more women supporting Democratic candidates in the 1980s has signified an important trend in voting that helped set the stage for the Democratic presidential victories of the 1990s.

See also WOMEN'S RIGHTS AND STATUS.

—Michele Rutledge

General Agreement on Tariffs and Trade (GATT)

The General Agreement on Tariffs and Trade, a treaty established after World War II, provided a forum for regulating international trade and negotiating tariffs. The treaty was signed by 23 nations, including the United States and Canada, in 1947, and became effective from January 1948. In a series of negotiations between 1947 and 1967, trade tariffs were progressively reduced and the rules of GATT refined. Two further rounds of negotiations, the Tokyo Round between 1973 and 1979, and the Uruguay Round between 1986 and 1994, expanded the provisions and scope of GATT. In 1994 GATT members, now numbering 110 countries, signed an agreement establishing the WORLD TRADE ORGANIZATION (WTO) to replace GATT.

The Tokyo Round, beginning in 1973, maintained GATT's steady reduction in tariffs, including an average one-third cut in customs duties in the nine major industrial markets, but failed to address major problems, especially with regard to farm trade. The Tokyo Round also produced a series of new agreements covering nontariff issues, and a new legal framework for international trade, including trade in civil aircraft, dairy and bovine meat, and arrangements governing the trade of developing countries. Countries were not bound, however, by all the agreements. Except for the agreements reached in "Text prepared by Group Framework," Tokyo Round agreements did not automatically bind all members, who could choose which codes to sign.

The Uruguay Round was first proposed in November 1982, at a meeting of GATT members in Geneva, but it took another four years of negotiations before the first round of talks, which were announced in September 1986, in Punta del Este, Uruguay. The United States insisted on enlarging the scope of GATT, and the talks included issues such as international investments, intellectual property, trade in textiles and clothing, and international trade in services. Agricultural trade barriers played a central role in these negotiations and raised bitter divisions between Europe and the United States. The negotiations concluded in 1993, and the United States ratified the agreement in December 1994. The new regulations included the establishment of the WTO to replace GATT.

Considerable criticism of the WTO has come from both the right and the left of the political spectrum. Generally, the right has expressed concern about maintaining American national sovereignty against what is seen as a "one-world" international agency, run by bureaucrats. Critics on the left have criticized the WTO for not doing enough to prevent the exploitation in developing nations of child labor, labor rights, and the environment by corporations, and that the WTO benefits the wealthy nations over poor ones.

See also ECONOMY; FOREIGN POLICY; GLOBALIZATION.

—Stephen Hardman

Gingrich, Newton L. (1943–)

Former Speaker of the U.S. HOUSE OF REPRESENTATIVES (1995–98), Newt Leroy Gingrich was born in Harrisburg, Pennsylvania, on June 17, 1943.

The son of a career soldier, Gingrich spent his youth on military bases in the United States and Europe, a formative experience to which he credits his adult political and career aspirations. After receiving his bachelor's degree in 1965 from Emory University, he went on to earn a doctorate in modern European history from Tulane University in 1971. During the 1970s he taught environmental studies and history at West Georgia College.

Long interested in politics, Gingrich joined the Republican Party and made two unsuccessful runs for the U.S. Congress in 1974 and 1976. In 1978 he was elected to the first of 11 terms as the Sixth District representative from Georgia before his resignation in 1999. Gingrich cofounded the Congressional Space Caucus and the Congressional Military Reform Caucus in 1981. Gingrich initiated ethics charges against Speaker of the House JIM WRIGHT in 1987 that ultimately led to Wright's resignation. In 1989 Gingrich succeeded Richard Cheney as minority whip of the HOUSE OF REPRESENTATIVES when the Wyoming representative became secretary of defense.

Gingrich's political career was dedicated to enacting conservative policies that engendered an intense dispute with his opponents, even as they helped unite conservatives. In his "Contract with America" (a 1994 Republican campaign platform), he supported reducing the scope of the federal government. Widely disseminated, this document contributed to the Republican victories of the 1994 elections. For the first time since 1954, Republicans controlled both the House and the SENATE. Gingrich replaced Democrat THOMAS FOLEY as Speaker of the House of Representatives, and was sworn in at the start of the 104th Congress in January 1995. The Republican "Contract with America" became the party's agenda for the first 100 days of the 1995 congressional session, during which bills related to crime, congressional term limits, welfare reform, the federal budget, social security, defense, illegal drugs, taxation, and other concerns were initiated. Although much of this agenda passed the House, many of the major items were stalled in the Senate. The presidential line-item veto became law in 1996, but congressional term-limit legislation was voted down. Issues such as tax cuts and social security became flash points between Congress and President WILLIAM J. CLINTON in the battle over the national budget for fiscal year 1996. This budget struggle led to two closures of the federal government, due to a deadlock between Congress and the president. Polls showed that the American electorate blamed Gingrich and the Republican-controlled Congress for the shutdowns. A compromise between Gingrich, the president, and other congressional leaders was reached in April 1996. Under Gingrich's leadership, Congress passed welfare reform, a balanced budget, and the first tax cuts in 16 years, but President Clinton, by supporting this legislation, gained equal credit in the eyes of the voters for these measures.

In 1996 Gingrich was reprimanded by the House Select Committee on Ethics for not registering his POLITICAL ACTION COMMITTEE (PAC) with the Federal Election Commission. In January 1997 Gingrich was reprimanded by the House of Representatives for ethics violations that included giving the Ethics Committee untrue information and using tax-exempt donations for political activities. Gingrich was fined $300,000. Although reelected Speaker later that month, he resigned from that position and from the House altogether following Republican losses in the November 1998 elections.

Currently Newt Gingrich is the CEO of an Atlanta-based communications and management-consulting firm known as "The Gingrich Group." He serves as a senior fellow at the American Enterprise Institute in Washington, D.C., and as a visiting fellow at the Hoover Institution at Stanford University. Gingrich also serves on the board of directors at the Internet Policy Institute. He serves on the bipartisan United States Commission on National Security/21st Century, which is charged with producing a series of reports to predict the nation's national security challenges through the year 2025, and is a member of the Senior Advisory Board of the Secretary of Defense's National Security Study Group. Gingrich has authored five books, including the fictional *1945* as well as the best-sellers, *Contract with America* and *To Renew America.*

See also CONSERVATIVE MOVEMENT.

Further reading: Elizabeth Drew, *Showdown: The Struggle between the Gingrich Congress and the Clinton White House* (New York: Simon & Schuster, 1996); Judith Warner, *Newt Gingrich: Speaker to America* (New York: Signet, 1995); Dan T. Carter, *From George Wallace to Newt Gingrich: A Race in the Conservative Counterrevolution, 1963–1994* (Baton Rouge: Louisiana State University Press, 1996).

—Michele Rutledge

Ginsburg, Ruth Bader (1933–   )

Born in 1933, Ruth Bader Ginsburg is the second woman and the first avowed feminist to sit on the U.S. SUPREME COURT. She received her B.A. from Cornell University and her LL.B. from Columbia Law School. After employment in the academic sector, with the American Civil Liberties Union (ACLU), and as a judge on the U.S. Court of Appeals, Ginsburg was appointed to the Supreme Court in 1993.

Despite graduating first in her law school class, Ginsburg was unable to secure anything more than a minor clerkship because she was female, pregnant, and Jewish. She finally secured a professorship at Rutgers University and pursued her three vocations of lawyer, wife, and mother. In 1972 Ginsburg became the first woman to achieve tenure at Columbia Law School. While visiting Sweden, she encountered a society that made her own country seem in need of rigorous reform. A year later, Ginsburg founded the Women's Rights Project of the ACLU. The project litigates against society's many gender inequities in American society by using the equal protection clause of the Fourteenth Amendment. As an advocate in gender inequity cases before the Supreme Court, Ginsburg won five of six cases. Many feminist jurists consider her "the legal architect of the modern women's movement."

In 1980 President Carter named Ginsburg to the most prestigious D. C. Circuit of the Federal Court of Appeals. Despite her ardent liberal feminist reputation, Ginsburg proved restrained as a circuit judge, and she forged a close friendship with conservative Justice ANTONIN SCALIA, while both served on the Circuit. In 1993 Ginsburg joined Scalia on the Supreme Court, filling the vacancy caused by Justice Byron R. White's retirement. President WILLIAM J. CLINTON selected her over STEPHEN BREYER, the candidate favored by Vice President ALBERT GORE, JR., and Senator EDWARD M. KENNEDY. The Senate confirmed her by a vote of 96-3.

Justice Ginsburg acknowledges seeing constitutional history as the process of extending original rights to formerly excluded groups. She opposes the original meaning of the judicial restraint position espoused by the conservative wing of the court, Justices Scalia and CLARENCE THOMAS, and to a lesser extent, Chief Justice WILLIAM REHNQUIST. According to Justice Ginsburg, she derives from the late Chief Justice Charles Evans Hughes her views that the courts should further national progress and social reform. She maintains that the "Supreme Court remains a vehicle for gradual, considered change, at least under the open-ended mandates of the Bill of Rights and similarly general statutes and the common law." She thinks dissent should be rare and hesitates to create new law outside of gender-related matters.

While voting to uphold ABORTION in *Stenberg v. Planned Parenthood* (2000), Ginsburg thinks the WARREN BURGER Court erred in *ROE V. WADE* (1973). She argues the Court should have firmly grounded abortion rights in gender differences. Ginsburg thinks the Court should have waited for legislatures to use the equal protection clause to gradually undermine state statutes regulating abortion. Her reservations on *Roe* have drawn criticism from some defenders of abortion rights.

Ginsburg's majority opinion in *Virginia v. United States* (1996) provided that women were to be admitted to the formerly all-male Virginia Military Institute. She used the equal protection clause to support her opinion. In *Romer v. Evans* (1996), Ginsburg voted with the majority to strike down a Colorado statute prohibiting discrimination favoring homosexuals. She based her vote on the equal protection clause.

On criminal cases, Ginsburg often joins Justice Stevens, considered by many a liberal on the court. In *Bush v. Gore* (2000), the Rehnquist Court's most political case, Ginsburg angrily dissented against the five-vote majority to stop the presidential ballot counting.

—Christopher M. Gray

glasnost

In the Russian language, *glasnost* means "openness." Glasnost, under the Soviet leader Mikhail Gorbachev, became a declared policy, in the 1980s, to dramatically enlarge individual freedom in the political and social life of Eastern European nations within the Soviet bloc. Initially, glasnost was intended to be limited in its scope, but it quickly expanded under pressure from dissidents in Eastern Europe and in the SOVIET UNION itself. As a result, citizens began to criticize party leaders in the U.S.S.R. and in Soviet-bloc countries. Within the Soviet Union, the brutality of the earlier Stalin regime was openly criticized, as was the corruption and stagnation of the Brezhnev era in the 1970s. This policy ultimately led to the overthrow of one-party control in the Soviet Union and in Eastern European nations under Soviet domination.

See also FOREIGN POLICY.

—Leah Blakey

globalization

"Globalization" refers to the increasing integration of global economics, finance, politics, technology, and culture, specifically since the early 1970s. The term has a second meaning as well: the ideology of globalization, meaning trade liberalization and the transnational integration of government economic policies. The difference between the two terms is at the center of an economic and political debate.

The term inspires considerable debate, not only among those who dispute the relative merits of the effects of globalization but also among those who argue that global integration of trade and politics has consistently been a feature of world history. The rapid development of technology and communications since the early 1970s and the concomitant surge in the volume of international trade, however, does indicate a distinct change in the pattern of international relations. James H. Mittelman, a prominent scholar of globalization, offers in *The Globalization Syndrome* (2000) a useful historical categorization of globalization, which takes into account these problems of location and definition. He suggests that the period before the 16th century may be referred to as "incipient globalization," the period until the early 1970s as "bridging globalization," and the period following the 1970s as "accelerated globalization."

One of the primary factors behind the recent developments in global relations has been the advances made in the development and sophistication of communication and information technology, as well as transportation technology, such as air freight. The impact of technological progress on international relations was predicted in the 1960s, when the academic Marshall McLuhan envisaged the dawning of what he referred to as a "global village." These developments, most notably the INTERNET, satellite communications, and COMPUTER technology, have had a profound impact on the speed and scope of personal, business, and political interaction, resulting in an unprecedented level of immediacy in the transfer of information.

Two manifestations of globalization have been the economic and political dominance of the United States, and the emergence of large multinational companies known as transnational corporations (TNCs). In 1999 the United States had a market value of $15.013 trillion, considerably ahead of Japan, the second-largest, with $4.244 trillion, and the United Kingdom, at $2.755 trillion. Most striking is the ranking of major corporations alongside national economies. As of 2000, Microsoft, with a market value of $546 billion, ranking 10th in world trade, and General Electric at 12th, with a market value of $498 billion, had a larger market value than countries such as Australia ($424 billion) and Spain ($390 billion). These transnational corporations have utilized the new conditions afforded by globalization to create business structures that increasingly cross national boundaries. Production can be transferred to more cost-efficient areas, increasingly in Third World countries, while finance, distribution, and sales can be coordinated globally to make effective use of financial markets and national economic conditions, as well as the flexibility of supplying disparate markets.

While such business structures enable more cost-effective products, critics have argued that the use of cheaper labor, and the production of standardized goods, stifle smaller competitors. The increasing power of these corporations is also perceived as a threat to the primacy of

Protesters march down Lexington Avenue, February 2, 2002, in New York City. Activists from around the nation came to protest the World Economic Forum, a meeting of corporate leaders from multinational conglomerates. *(McCollester/Getty Images)*

national governments, especially those with weaker economies. A 1994 report by the UNITED NATIONS identified 37,000 transnational corporations, 1 percent of which owned half the world's corporate assets, with over 40 percent based in England and the United States.

International institutions, such as the WORLD TRADE ORGANIZATION (WTO) and the International Monetary Fund (IMF), as well as international trade treaties, such as the NORTH AMERICAN FREE TRADE AGREEMENT (NAFTA), were in part developed to regulate the excesses of globalization. Their role has been troubled and ambiguous, however. Critics say these organizations represent the powerful interests of business and the wealthiest nations; that they supersede the autonomy of national governments; and that they provide tacit support for human rights abuses in countries such as China. These organizations have galvanized considerable opposition to globalization, as witnessed in the demonstrations at the Third Ministerial Conference of the WTO in Seattle in 1999. Nonetheless, the broad and disparate collection of demonstrators, including labor unions, environment groups, anarchists, and far-right con-

servatives, was indicative of the confusion and ambiguity surrounding the effects and structures of globalization.

The concentration of wealth and market share within a small number of multinational corporations and the increasing size of the U.S. economy have caused many to see globalization as synonymous with "Americanization." American hegemony across global markets has led to the development of what many people see as a form of economic and cultural imperialism. Corporations such as Nike, McDonald's, and Microsoft, as well as MEDIA organizations, such as AOL Time Warner, MTV, and the Hollywood film industry, arouse conflicting emotions. For supporters, these companies provide cost-effective quality goods and services as well as secure employment. Critics point to the loss of local cultural and economic autonomy, and the imposition of American market values and beliefs. Furthermore, globalization has raised concerns about illegal immigration, international terrorism, and the transnational crime syndicates.

Globalization, in its current manifestation, is in a formative stage of development. The structures and implications of these new global relations remain contentious and fraught with ambiguity.

See also BUSINESS; ECONOMY; GENERAL AGREEMENT ON TARIFFS AND TRADE; SCIENCE AND TECHNOLOGY.

—Stephen Hardman

Gore, Albert, Jr. (1948–)

Albert Gore, Jr., born in 1948, served as WILLIAM J. CLINTON's vice president (1993–2001) and, as the Democratic candidate for the presidency in 2000, became one of only three presidential nominees to lose the electoral vote while winning the popular vote.

The son of a Tennessee congressman and senator, Albert Gore, Jr., was born in Washington, D.C., where he was educated in elite private schools, graduating from St. Albans School for Boys. His father, Albert Arnold Gore, served in the House of Representatives, from 1934–44 and 1945–53, and in the U.S. Senate from 1953–71. As a consequence, the Gore household was quite political, and the elder Gore had his son sit in on meetings with the Kennedys, William Fulbright, and House Speaker Sam Rayburn. His father insisted, however, that his son return each summer to work on their farm in Carthage, Tennessee, to learn the value of hard work and become acquainted with the world outside the Washington, D.C., beltway. While in high school, he met his future wife, Mary Elizabeth "Tipper" Aitcheson. Gore graduated magna cum laude in government history from Harvard University in 1969, after writing a senior thesis on television and its impact on the presidency. Although he opposed the VIETNAM WAR, he joined the U.S. Army following graduation, and served in Vietnam as a reporter for *Stars and Stripes.* Following the war, he became a reporter for the *Nashville Tennessean* and attended Vanderbilt Law School.

Gore was elected to Congress in 1977 and served four distinguished terms in the HOUSE OF REPRESENTATIVES (1977–85) and in the SENATE (1985–93).

In Congress, Gore became an expert on defense and environmental issues.

Gore used congressional subpoena power to aggressively pursue consumer, environmental, and technological problems that were not hot-button issues. He mastered subjects like toxic waste and telecommunications. On social issues, Gore initially opposed federal funding of ABORTIONS, but later changed his position. He supported affirmative action.

On FOREIGN POLICY, he supported arms control efforts and some of RONALD W. REAGAN's defense spending. He became deeply knowledgeable about nuclear missile issues and was considered one of the handful of senators who were experts on defense policy. Gore followed the same moderate approach on Central America. He voted for food and

medical supplies to the CONTRAS but opposed any military assistance to them. Gore broke with the Democratic leadership, however, over the PERSIAN GULF WAR resolution in 1991, voting with 10 Democratic senators to back President GEORGE H. W. BUSH's policy against Iraq.

In 1988, at the age of 40, Gore made a run for the Democratic presidential nomination. Running as a "New Democrat," who wanted to return the party to the center, he won seven primaries and caucuses before he withdrew to allow Michael Dukakis to win the nomination. A near-fatal accident of his son led Gore not to make a run for the presidency in 1992. His selection by WILLIAM J. CLINTON as his running mate caught many by surprise, because it broke the cardinal rule of presidential elections to have regional balance. With the Clinton-Gore ticket, two southerners were running together. In a vigorous campaign, the Clinton-Gore ticket beat the incumbent ticket of Bush-Quayle.

Gore became one of the most powerful and influential vice presidents ever. Clinton recognized Gore's great understanding of foreign policy and congressional and technical issues, and put them under his deputy's portfolio. Gore influenced Clinton administration policy in a number of areas, including White House relations with Congress; foreign relations with Russia, Ukraine, Egypt, and South Africa; nuclear arms control and missile defense issues; environmental policy; the "reinventing government" initiative; and telecommunications.

Gore acted as President Clinton's liaison with Capitol Hill. He worked hard to pass Clinton's economic plan of tax increases, and cast the deciding Senate vote for it. He

Vice President Al Gore, with Senator Joseph Lieberman at his side, makes a statement to reporters, November 8, 2000, in Nashville, Tennessee. *(Wilson/Newsmakers)*

persuaded Clinton to fill a second U.S. SUPREME COURT vacancy with STEPHEN BREYER. The vice president encouraged the Clinton administration to maintain close ties with Russia's prime minister, Viktor Chernomyrdin, although many other administration officials had decided he was corrupt and incompetent. Gore opposed the developed of an anti-antimissile defense system because he thought it increased strategic instability. Gore supported arms control and nuclear proliferation policies in dealing with Russia.

As a result of Gore's efforts, the White House, through an executive order, closed much federal land to commercial development. He also played a role in regulation of oil exploration, and between 1993 and 2000, the number of oil rigs decreased by three-fourths nationally. In 1997 Gore also signed the international Kyoto Treaty aimed at reducing "global warming."

Although Gore did not "invent" the INTERNET, no politician did more to get the World Wide Web up and running than the vice president.

Gore's involvement in campaign fund-raising during the 1996 presidential election led to a Justice Department investigation, although he was later exonerated from allegations that he broke campaign finance laws. These allegations of impropriety continued to be raised in his presidential bid in 2000, when he was challenged in the Democratic primaries by former New Jersey senator Bill Bradley. Gore won the Iowa primary in January 2000, receiving more than 60 percent of the vote and then won the New Hampshire primary with 50 percent of the vote to Bradley's 46 percent. After Bradley's withdrawal, Gore won the Democratic Party nomination and selected Senator Joseph I. Lieberman (D-Conn.) as his vice presidential running mate, the first Jew to be nominated on a presidential ticket.

Although Gore had a reputation as a stiff and distant campaigner, he proved an adept candidate. Running on a message that was both centrist and populist, he emphasized the strength of the economy, the need to protect social security, and to expand health-care coverage.

On November 7 Gore narrowly won the popular vote with 50.2 percent, but a dispute over ballots in Florida appeared to give the state's electoral votes to Republican candidate George W. Bush, thereby providing him with the necessary electoral majority to win the White House. As the ballots were being recounted in four populous Florida counties, both campaigns took the issue to state and federal courts. In an unprecedented decision, the U.S. Supreme Court upheld Bush's victory in Florida by a vote of 5-4, in *Bush v. Gore*, by stopping further recounts of the Florida ballots. Following the decision, Gore made a statesman-like concession speech, declaring he would abide by the decision and calling for national unity.

Following the election, Gore taught a journalism class at Harvard University and continued to ponder another run at the presidency in 2004. He is the author of two books on the environment. He and Tipper Gore have four children.

See also CONSERVATION, ENVIRONMENTALISM, AND ENVIRONMENTAL POLICY; ELECTIONS; POLITICAL PARTIES.

Further reading: Jeffrey Toobin, *Too Close to Call: The Thirty Six Day Battle to Decide the 2000 Election* (New York: Random House, 2001; Bill Sammon, *At Any Cost: How Al Gore Tried to Steal the Election* (Washington, D.C.: Regnery Publishing, Inc., 2001).

—Christopher M. Gray

Gramm-Rudman-Hollings Act   (1985)

Officially known as the Balanced Budget and Emergency Deficit Control Act of 1985, Gramm-Rudman-Hollings (GRH) bears the names of its three principal sponsors— Senators Phil Gramm (R-Tex.), Warren Rudman (R-N.H.), and Ernest Hollings (D-S.C.). The law was intended to reduce the budget deficit that had been growing steadily since the 1960s. Various attempts had been made by Congress to impose fiscal discipline in the budgeting system. The Congressional Budget and Impoundment Control Act of 1974 was an effort to impose order, guidance, and discipline on fiscal budgeting. After 10 years of missed deadlines and increasing deficits, Congress adopted the Balanced Budget and Emergency Deficit Control Act, to rectify the problem.

GRH promoted deficit reduction through three mechanisms. First, annual deficit targets were established that were designed to create a balanced budget in six years. The act created an enforcement mechanism, called sequestration, that was triggered if both the Office of Management and Budget (OMB) and the Government Accounting Office (GAO) deficit estimates exceeded the target by $10 billion or more. If this occurred, the act required budget cuts to be made until the target was reached. One-half of the cuts would come from the discretionary defense budget, and the other half from the discretionary nondefense budget. Many nondefense programs—retirement, disability, and means-tested entitlement programs, as well as emergency defense funds, were exempted from sequestration, and cuts in programs like Medicare were limited. Finally, the act established a mechanism to change procedures to ensure that the law could be evaded.

In 1986 the Supreme Court found GRH unconstitutional, because it delegated executive authority to the comptroller general of the General Accounting Office, a legislative agency. Congress corrected this flaw in the Balanced Budget and Emergency Deficit Control Reaffirmation Act in 1987. This law made the OMB the sole deficit watchdog; it also somewhat relaxed deficit targets and moved the target date for a balanced budget from 1991 to 1993.

The GRH was largely a failure. It set targets for deficit reduction but provided no plan to achieve these targets. This emphasis on targets focused attention on the annual budget, and not on how to meet the long-term goal. Likewise, the act provided no incentive for responsible spending. Medicare, food stamps, and welfare were largely exempted from sequestration. Finally, the targets were too rigid to allow for emergencies and economic crises, which could not be predicted. Consequently, Congress, and Presidents RONALD W. REAGAN and GEORGE H. W. BUSH resorted to a variety of tricks to get around deficit targets.

The GRH provided a number of lessons. First, deficit reduction cannot be handled on an annual basis; it must be part of a long-range plan. Next, sequestration of large parts of the budget, upwards of 30 percent in the early 1990s, was unacceptable. Finally, the program needed to provide a measure of flexibility. These lessons were applied to the Budget Enforcement Acts of 1990 and 1993 and, combined with a booming economy, budget surplus was created in WILLIAM J. CLINTON's second term.

—John Korasick

Green Party

The international Green movement began in the 1970s with the Values Party in New Zealand. Heavily influenced by the national success enjoyed by Greens in Germany, American Greens met in 1984 in Saint Paul, Minnesota, and proceeded to adopt the 10 Key Values that Greens in the United States currently use as their basic political goals: "grassroots democracy, social justice and equal opportunity, ecological wisdom, nonviolence, decentralization, community-based economics and economic justice, feminism and gender equity, respect for diversity, personal and global responsibility, and future focus and sustainability."

By the 1980s several hundred Green chapters existed throughout the United States. In 1990 Alaska was the first state to achieve a recognized ballot line for the Green Party. In 1991 the Green Committees of Correspondence split, over issues related to political participation, into the Greens/Green Party USA (G/GPUSA). The group continued to organize during the 1990s, but numerous problems stunted its growth. After the 1996 ELECTIONS, the Association of State Green Parties (ASGP) was formed to fill the lack of national organization of Green politics, to create new state parties, and to facilitate the growth of existing state parties. RALPH NADER and Winona LaDuke ran as presidential and vice presidential candidates, and of the 82 party candidates, 19 were elected to positions including city council seats, a municipal judgeship, and a county commissioner.

Membership in the ASGP consists of state Green Parties, not individuals. The mission of the ASGP is to develop the Green Party into a viable political alternative in the United States, and its operating principle has been to present simple and straightforward goals. The party eschews a large budget in favor of keeping funds at the state and local level. The G/GPUSA still exists, however, and has approximately 1,200 members. The Green Party enjoyed more national visibility in the 2000 presidential election, putting forth Nader and LaDuke again as the party's candidates. Support for Nader's campaign is a likely factor in the loss of votes by Democratic nominee ALBERT GORE in the 2000 contest. Currently the party claims to have nearly 80 officeholders in local offices around the country.

See also POLITICAL PARTIES.

—Michele Rutledge

Grenada, invasion of

On October 25, 1983, United States military forces invaded the Caribbean island nation of Grenada, following the execution of prime minister Maurice Bishop, an avowed marxist who came to power in a coup in 1979. Bishop boasted good relations with Fidel Castro, which heightened U.S. apprehension about communist activity in the region. President RONALD W. REAGAN's administration sought to isolate the Bishop regime by cutting off aid to the government and isolating the country politically. In response, the Bishop government sought to improve its relations with the United States by distancing itself from Castro. Bishop's policy change prompted a military coup led by General Hudson Austin and Bishop's execution. The United States reacted immediately and launched an invasion of the island on October 25, ostensibly to protect American students enrolled at Saint George's University School of Medicine. Nineteen hundred U.S. troops coupled with forces from Barbados, the Dominican Republic, Jamaica, Saint Lucia, and Saint Vincent encountered three days of sporadic fighting. They were successful in establishing political order and removing a small Cuban military presence. After occupying the island, Americans oversaw elections in 1984 in which a centrist, Herbert A. Blaize, won a parliamentary majority.

See also FOREIGN POLICY.

—Leah Blakey

Griggs et al. v. Duke Power Company

This unanimous 8-0 U.S. SUPREME COURT decision is recognized as the most significant case in the development of employment discrimination law under Title VII of the Civil

Rights Act of 1964, which created equal opportunity in the workplace, because of its far-reaching implications.

Before Title VII became effective, Duke Power Company discriminated on the basis of race, in how it hired and assigned workers in its facility in Draper, North Carolina. The company traditionally had hired blacks into an all-black labor classification. In this classification, the highest-paying job paid less than the lowest paying job in the white labor classification. Additionally, blacks could only receive promotion along lines of progression within their segregated departments. On the date that Title VII became effective, July 2, 1965, the company began requiring a high school education and acceptable grades on two aptitude tests for any person applying for jobs traditionally classified as white. The district court found that the earlier practices were not under the purview of Title VII and that the newly instituted tests were not intentionally discriminatory.

The Supreme Court overruled this decision, holding in favor of the African-American plaintiffs. In doing so, the Court established a number of important precedents regarding employment discrimination. First, practices claimed to be neutral are unlawful if they uphold the effects of traditionally discriminatory practices. Second, regarding discrimination, the consequences of discriminatory practices are relevant, not the intent of the practices. Tests used for hiring and promotion must be job-related under the guidelines established by the Equal Employment Opportunity Commission. Finally, the Court invalidated practices that caused a disparate impact upon a group protected by the Civil Rights Act of 1964. By setting these precedents, the Court reaffirmed the act's intention of eliminating patterns of discrimination, and strengthened its ability to require the removal of obstacles that perpetuated white employees' advantages obtained at the expense of blacks.

See also AFFIRMATIVE ACTION; AFRICAN AMERICANS; NATIONAL ASSOCIATION FOR THE ADVANCEMENT OF COLORED PEOPLE; RACE AND RACIAL CONFLICT.

—William L. Glankler

Grove City College et al. v. Bell, Secretary of Education, et al.

Title IX of the Education Amendments of 1972 prohibits sex discrimination in programs that directly receive federal assistance. The federal government began in 1977 to require all institutions of higher learning to sign an assurance of compliance form. Grove City College, a private, coeducational, liberal arts college that did not participate in the regular disbursement system of the Department of Education on grounds of freedom from governmental control, refused to sign the form. The Department of Educa-

tion determined, however, that since enrolled students of Grove City received direct federal monies, the college was a recipient of federal financial assistance. Funds were cut off to the college until it agreed to comply, and the college and four of its students filed suit. The case was argued before the U.S. SUPREME COURT on November 29, 1983. The decision of February 28, 1984, placed federal governmental regulation only over the programs that accepted federal monies, not the entire institution. In addition, the Court decided that the federal Pell grants were considered federal aid, and therefore the school's financial aid office would be subject to federal regulation. The College subsequently withdrew from the Pell grant program and offered its students private programs to replace the federal grants. Congress responded to the Court's decision by passing the Civil Rights Restoration Act of 1988, which stated that any institution that receives any federal monies is subject as an institution to federal jurisdiction.

—Michele Rutledge

gun control

Control of handgun and automatic rifle sales has created fierce political and public debate.

Congress passed the National Firearms Act on June 26, 1934, during President Franklin D. Roosevelt's administration. The law arose as a response to the increasing rates of mob violence, which began in the 1920s and reached a peak in the early 1930s. Rates of violent overall CRIME had fallen to all-time lows during the 1950s and early 1960s, but jumped 25 percent between 1964 and 1967. The ASSASSINATIONS of Dr. Martin Luther King, Jr., on April 4, 1968, and Senator Robert F. Kennedy a month later on June 5, prompted a widespread public reaction, and in response, Congress enacted the Gun Control Act of 1968. The act banned interstate sales of firearms and required the licensing of most firearm dealers. It also barred felons, fugitives, minors, and the mentally ill from purchasing or owning firearms. In 1980, the U.S. SUPREME COURT upheld the 1968 law in *Lewis v. United States,* concluding that Congress could keep firearms away from "persons classified as potentially irresponsible and dangerous."

The push for the enactment of systematic gun control legislation arose in the 1970s, and became especially strong in the 1980s. On March 30, 1981, John Hinckley tried to assassinate President RONALD W. REAGAN, but succeeded only in wounding the president and paralyzing press secretary James Brady. After his recovery, Brady and his wife, Sarah, became vocal advocates for more stringent regulations on private firearms and formed Handgun Control, Inc. They helped rally numerous other state and local groups into a larger gun-control lobby and drew the attention of the national news MEDIA, and many film and TELE-

VISION celebrities. By the mid-1980s the issue of gun control polarized into two ideological positions: gun control versus gun rights.

Advocates of gun control contend that the need for public order requires close regulation of private access to firearms. Few activists seek total abolition of all firearms, nor has there been a call among activists for the repeal of the Second Amendment. Instead, most advocates seek federal legislation that would limit private access to only specific types of firearms, to be used only under specific conditions, and to be made available only to specific classes of people. Proponents of gun control argue that, with regulation of gun sales, handgun violence would decrease in the United States, and regulation would prevent access to guns through legal means for irresponsible and dangerous persons. Often, gun control activists make an analogy that just as driver's licenses are regulated, so too should guns be regulated.

In contrast, gun rights advocates argue that gun control legislation violates the Second Amendment, which specifically forbids infringement by the federal government of the people's right to "keep and bear arms." Gun rights advocates further argue that federal gun control legislation violates the Tenth Amendment, which forbids unnecessary intrusion of the federal government into the affairs of the states. Lastly, gun rights advocates argue that gun control legislation unduly interferes with noncriminal pursuits, such as hunting and competition shooting.

News coverage of firearm-related homicides and "drive-by" shootings in urban neighborhoods forced the issue into the forefront of public debate, making Handgun Control, Inc., the most vocal and popular advocate for gun control, and the NATIONAL RIFLE ASSOCIATION (NRA) the most well-known champion of gun rights. Though both sides cited national and international statistics, the correlation between gun ownership and crime is too tenuous for either side to claim empirical support.

During the 1980s, many efforts at gun control were aimed at state legislatures. President WILLIAM J. CLINTON, however, created an environment favorable to federal gun control, and signed the Brady Handgun Violence Prevention Act in November 1993, which was the first significant federal gun control law since 1968. It required a five-day waiting period and a background check on all persons seeking to purchase a handgun. Four years later, in *Printz v. United States* (1997), the Supreme Court struck down the provision requiring a mandatory background check as a violation of the Tenth Amendment, but upheld the provision requiring a five-day waiting period since it applied only to store owners and not state governments. *Printz* had no effect on the 27 states with gun control laws.

In 1994 Congress passed the Violent Crime Control and Law Enforcement Act, which, among other things

Columbine High School teacher Patty Nielson speaks at a Senate Policy Committee hearing on gun safety legislation, as Senator Tom Daschle looks on, May 15, 2000, in Washington, D.C. *(Smith/Newsmakers)*

made illegal the manufacture, sale, and importation of 19 different types of semiautomatic assault weapons and high-capacity ammunition magazines (holding 10 or more rounds). Several gun retailers tried to challenge the law in federal courts, but their cases were dismissed before reaching the Supreme Court. The following year, in *United States v. Lopez* (1995), the Supreme Court concluded that an earlier statute, Gun Free School Zones Act of 1990, was unconstitutional because the "zones" inevitably affect all classes of citizens who might live nearby. The courts have indicated tolerance for specific gun control legislation aimed at eliminating specific dangers to society, but have otherwise opposed general measures that limit access to firearms as a social good by itself.

In the late 1990s a series of school shootings again prompted a renewed effort to pass more stringent gun control legislation, including the Children's Gun Violence Prevention Act of 1998, which requires child-resistant safety devices on all new guns sold after 2002. The city of New Orleans became the first city to sue gun manufacturers, charging them with gross negligence for not including safety systems on all weapons. Chicago filed a similar suit, arguing that gun manufacturers contributed to illegal gun trafficking in the city. In addition, 17 other cities and counties filed similar suits. Later, nongovernment groups filed suits, including the NATIONAL ASSOCIATION FOR THE ADVANCEMENT OF COLORED PEOPLE (NAACP) and the parents of the students killed during the shooting at Columbine High School on April 28, 1999, in Littleton, Colorado. In March 2000, gun manufacturers Smith and Wesson settled their suits out of court by agreeing to include safety locks on all firearms, and to dedicate 2 percent of their profits toward the research and development of "smart" technology that would make it difficult for anyone but the owner to fire a handgun. The settlement angered many gun-rights advocates, and was not imitated by other manufacturers.

See also CONSERVATIVE MOVEMENT; FEDERALISM; MILITIA MOVEMENT; PROPERTY RIGHTS.

Further reading: William J. Vizzard, *Shots in the Dark: The Policy, Politics, and Symbolism of Gun Control* (Lanham, Md.: Rowman & Littlefield, Inc., 2000); Ted Gottfried, *Gun Control: Public Safety and the Right to Bear Arms* (Brookfield, Conn.: Millbrook Press, 1993).

—Aharon W. Zorea

H

Habib, Philip C. (1920–1992)

Philip Charles Habib was a career diplomat of Lebanese descent who served in various positions in the government for nearly four decades. From 1968 to 1971 he served as a U.S. delegate to the VIETNAM WAR negotiations in Paris. In 1969 he was named the acting head of the U.S. delegation because of his advanced skill and flexibility in the negotiations. Following the Vietnam War, Habib served as the U.S. ambassador to the Republic of Korea from 1971 to 1974 and then as assistant secretary of state for East Asian and Pacific affairs from 1974 to 1976. After those years abroad, he served as the under secretary of state for political affairs from 1976–78. During this time, he was instrumental in arranging the meetings that led to the Camp David Egyptian-Israeli peace accords in 1978.

He retired from government work in 1978 due to health reasons, but returned at the request of President RONALD W. REAGAN in the early 1980s. Habib served as President Reagan's personal representative to the Middle East from 1981–83, where he helped arrange a temporary cease-fire in the Lebanese civil war as well as a withdrawal of the Palestine Liberation Organization (PLO) from that country. In 1986 Habib served as a special presidential envoy to the Philippines, where he helped convince President Ferdinand E. Marcos to go into exile. Following his work in the Philippines, Habib once again retired from government service. He spent his last years working as a senior research fellow at the Hoover Institute at Stanford University. Philip Habib died on May 25, 1992, while on vacation in France.

See also CAMP DAVID ACCORDS; FOREIGN POLICY.

—Leah Blakey

Haig, Alexander M., Jr. (1924–   )

Born December 2, 1924, Alexander Meigs Haig grew up in Bala-Cynwyd, Pennsylvania, a suburb of Philadelphia. In 1943 Haig attended the University of Notre Dame and in 1944 he received an appointment to the United States Military Academy. After graduating in 1947, Haig was assigned to General Douglas MacArthur's staff during the occupation of Japan. He went on to serve in Korea and Vietnam before returning to the United States, and serving as deputy commandant at West Point.

In 1969 Haig was appointed military aide to National Security Advisor, HENRY A. KISSINGER. During this time, Haig cultivated a relationship with H. R. Haldeman, President RICHARD M. NIXON's chief of staff. In 1970 Haig became Haldeman's deputy, a position he held until 1973, when he replaced Haldeman because of the WATERGATE SCANDAL. When GERALD R. FORD became president, he appointed Haig as Supreme Allied Commander Europe (SACEUR), the commander of NORTH ATLANTIC TREATY ORGANIZATION (NATO) forces. While in Europe, Haig developed strong relationships with many European leaders. Also, Haig increased the combat effectiveness of NATO forces by staging maneuvers and war games with troops transported from the United States.

Haig resigned as SACEUR in 1979 over what he perceived as the weak and inconsistent FOREIGN POLICY of the Carter administration. These criticisms caught the attention of RONALD W. REAGAN, and Haig was invited to brief Reagan on Europe and military affairs. Haig's briefing led to his being named secretary of state in 1981. Haig proposed that an interagency group chaired by State Department officials should coordinate the foreign policy process.

Haig's push for control led to confrontations with Reagan's staff, when his critics accused him of being power hungry and, perhaps, dangerous. In order to blunt his advances, James Baker, Richard Allen, and EDWIN C. MEESE III limited Haig's role in the administration's crisis management team. Vice president GEORGE H. W. BUSH was appointed to head the team. This split within the administration was revealed to the public on March 30, 1981, after the attempted assassination of President Reagan. Haig's comments during a press conference that he was "in charge" until Vice President Bush arrived, struck many critics as high-handed and a revelation of Haig's ambition for power.

Haig's policy stances also generated friction. A strong supporter of NATO, he opposed sanctions against the Soviet Union after martial law was imposed in Poland in 1981. The Europeans feared sanctions would interfere with the natural gas pipeline being built from Siberia to Western Europe. Also, Haig was viewed as pro-British during the Falkland Islands war. The administration feared that his stance would imperil U.S. efforts to develop an anticommunist front among the Latin American governments. Finally, Haig strongly supported Israel during its invasion of Lebanon, an action deemed highly destabilizing and reckless.

His foreign policy disagreements contributed to his resignation on June 25, 1982. Haig ran unsuccessfully for the 1988 Republican presidential nomination, but pulled out due to lack of support. Since then, Haig has been active in various business enterprises, is president and became chairman of the board of Worldwide Associates, and is a trustee of the Hudson Institute.

—John Korasick

Haiti (U.S. intervention in 1993–1994)

In December 1990 the people of Haiti elected Jean-Bertrand Aristide as president. Shortly thereafter violence erupted, leading to a military coup on September 30, 1991. As a result of the coup, Aristide fled to the United States. On June 16, 1993, the UNITED NATIONS (UN) Security Council imposed an embargo on all petroleum and arms sales to Haiti. When trade sanctions failed to force reform in Haiti, the UN sent a contingent of 1,267 soldiers in late 1993, but when rioting and violence broke out, the UN troops withdrew from the island. Over the next several months, the situation worsened. On July 31, 1994, the UN Security Council authorized the use of force to restore Aristide to power. Under this mandate, U.S. Army forces were mobilized by President WILLIAM J. CLINTON on September 13, 1994, for deployment to Haiti. Shortly thereafter, former president JAMES EARL CARTER, JR., Senator Sam Nunn, and General COLIN L. POWELL went to Haiti and successfully negotiated the resignation and departure of the top military leaders from Haiti. On September 19, 1994, U.S. forces landed at the Haitian capitol of Port-au-Prince without resistance. Violence erupted on September 24 between a U.S. Marine patrol and Haitian forces, during which 10 Haitians were killed. Afterward the local military and police faded from sight. On October 15, 1994, Aristide arrived back in Haiti to resume his responsibilities as president. As he gained in power, Aristide repressed political opposition, thereby thwarting hopes of a democratic and prosperous Haiti.

See also FOREIGN POLICY; GLOBALIZATION; LATIN AMERICA; NICARAGUA (U.S. RELATIONS WITH).

—Leah Blakey

Helms, Jesse A., Jr. (1924–)

Born October 18, 1924, Jesse Alexander Helms served in the U.S. SENATE from 1973 to 2002 and is recognized as one of the leading conservative politicians in the late 20th century.

Born the son of the fire and police chief of Monroe, North Carolina, Helms embodies the rock-ribbed values of the rural and small-town Protestant South. He attended Monroe public schools, Wingate Junior College and Wake Forest College. Helms chose a life of journalism and politics while a teenager. During World War II, he served as a Navy recruiter from 1942 to 1945. Following the war, he became city editor of the *Raleigh* (North Carolina) *Times* and director of news and programs for Tobacco Radio Network and radio station WRAL in Raleigh. In 1951 he became a Senate aide to Willis Smith (D-N.C.), after working in his campaign against Senator Frank Porter Graham. Graham, president of the University of North Carolina, symbolized southern liberalism. Helms designed many of the confrontational anticommunist and pro-segregationist campaign tactics used in the 1950 campaign. In 1953 Helms became an aide to Senator Alton Lennon (D-N.C.). The previous year, Helms had directed the radio-television campaign for the unsuccessful presidential race of Senator Richard B. Russell of Georgia.

From 1953 through 1960, Helms was executive director of the North Carolina Bankers Association and served as editor of the *Tarheel Banker,* which became the largest state banking publication in the nation. He became a disciple of Austrian-born economist Ludwig von Mises, who asserted that socialist central planning was unsuitable for a modern economy.

From 1960 until his election to the Senate, Helms was an executive for the Capitol Broadcasting Company of Raleigh, North Carolina. He became known for his evening editorials during the tumultuous 1960s, in which he excoriated big government, big labor, the Soviet and Chinese Communist empires, sexual liberation, substance abuse, rioters, and civil rights activists. While Helms always supported the rule of law and opposed violence, he fiercely defended racial segregation and freely criticized Martin Luther King's civil disobedience. Helms endorsed Barry Goldwater's 1964 Republican presidential campaign. In 1970 he left the Democratic Party and joined the Republican Party. In 1972 he was drafted by powerful friends to run for the U.S. Senate.

President RICHARD M. NIXON's 1972 landslide helped sweep Helms to his first Senate victory. There, he joined with New York senator James Buckley to promote conservative policies. These two freshmen senators refused to play the humble understudy role traditionally assigned to freshmen. Both men championed Soviet dissident writer Alexander Solzhenitsyn and opposed DÉTENTE with the Soviet Union and legal ABORTION.

In the Senate Helms became known for his outspoken style and mastery of the Senate's arcane parliamentary rules. Helms mastered the tactic of forcing recorded roll call votes on controversial issues such as détente, FEMINISM, abortion, busing, and AFFIRMATIVE ACTION, and then using these recorded votes to political advantage. With his close friend PHYLLIS SCHLAFLY, Helms founded the New Right movement.

During 1976, Helms, Buckley, and Schlafly backed Ronald W. Reagan's insurgent challenge to GERALD R. FORD. Although Ford won the nomination, Reagan held a favorable position for 1980. During JAMES EARL CARTER, JR.'s presidency, Helms continued to play "Senator No." He harassed Carter's policies, especially the proposed Strategic Arms Limitation Treaty (SALT II), and violated Senate custom by campaigning against liberal Republicans.

Ronald W. Reagan's 1980 victory over Carter was especially sweet to Helms. It helped elect Helms's ally, John East, to the other North Carolina Senate seat and brought Helms a committee chairmanship. Helms continued to hew to his uncompromising conservative principles, criticizing members of the Reagan administration, especially Secretaries of State ALEXANDER M. HAIG, JR., and George Schultz, for being insufficiently hard-line. He warned repeatedly against Soviet advances in Central America. In 1984, in the most expensive Senate race to that time, Helms narrowly defeated North Carolina's governor Jim Hunt. During the Hunt race, Helms for the first time courted the support of AFRICAN AMERICANS.

Helms kept his conservative faith during the GEORGE H. W. BUSH and WILLIAM J. CLINTON presidencies. Since 1984, he served as the ranking Republican chairman of the Senate Foreign Relations Committee. Journalist Robert Novak accurately observed in 2001: "No single member of the U.S. Senate over the last generation has been so influential as Jesse Helms."

See also CONSERVATIVE MOVEMENT; ELECTIONS; POLITICAL PARTIES.

Further reading: Ernest Furgurson, *Hard Right: The Rise of Jesse Helms* (New York: Norton, 1986).

—Christopher Gray

Hill, Anita Faye (1956–)

Anita Hill is an African-American lawyer and educator, known for her controversial role in the SENATE confirmation hearings of U.S. SUPREME COURT nominee CLARENCE THOMAS in 1991. Born on July 30, 1956, in Lone Tree, Oklahoma, Hill was valedictorian of her high school class, received a bachelor's degree in psychology from Oklahoma State in 1977, and graduated from Yale Law School in 1980. In 1981 she took a position with the Washington, D.C., law firm Ward, Harkrader and Ross, and later that year became Clarence Thomas's assistant in the Office of Civil Rights at the U.S. Department of Education. In 1982 Hill left the Department of Education to work for Thomas when he became chairman of the Equal Employment Opportunity Commission (EEOC). She joined the faculty of Oral Roberts University as a law professor in 1983, and then accepted a position at the University of Oklahoma in 1986, where she achieved tenure in 1991.

In 1991 Anita Hill came into the national spotlight when she testified on October 11 in the nationally televised Senate confirmation hearings for Clarence Thomas's nomination to the U.S. Supreme Court. Hill was called to testify because she claimed that, while employed by Thomas at the EEOC, Thomas had sexually harassed her. Thomas denied the allegations and was later confirmed. Hill's testimony did increase public awareness of the issue of sexual harassment. This incident directly influenced the nature of sexual harassment litigation by broadening the definition to include the creation of an intimidating or uncomfortable environment as a prosecutable offense.

In 1991 *Glamour* magazine made Hill its Woman of the Year and she received the Ida B. Wells Award from the National Coalition of 100 Black Women. Hill details her professional relationship with Clarence Thomas and gives her account of her testimony and the Senate confirmation hearings in her 1997 book, *Speaking Truth to Power.*

See also AFRICAN AMERICANS; FEMINISM; WOMEN'S RIGHTS AND STATUS.

—William L. Glankler

Hispanic Americans

"Hispanic-American" refers to all people tracing their ancestry to Spanish-speaking areas of the Western Hemisphere. In the United States, most Hispanics trace their lineage to Mexico, followed by Puerto Rico and Cuba.

During the 1960s and 1970s, the Mexican-American civil rights movement emerged. During the 1960s, César Estrada Chávez worked as a labor organizer among migrant farm workers in California. Chávez organized Huelga, a 1965 strike directed against California grape growers to raise public awareness of unfair labor practices and poor working conditions in the vineyards. In 1970 the strike was won when the growers granted greater rights and higher wages to the workers.

The Chicano movement emerged from the Civil Rights and anti-war movements. Chicano students, especially in California, demanded that their language, culture, and ethnic contributions be recognized in schools. The Chicano movement included groups like the United Mexican Students (UMA) and the Movimiento Estudiantil Chicano de Aztlan (MECHA). In 1970 José Angel Gutiérrez established La Raza Unida (Mexican People United), a Mexican-American political party devoted to ending discrimination against Hispanics by gaining access to mainstream American politics and financial institutions. The group advocated bilingual and bicultural EDUCATION. The efforts of groups in the Chicano movement resulted in the establishment of Mexican-American studies programs in colleges and universities. Activist groups like the Young Lords advocated similar programs for Puerto Ricans. Unlike natives of other Hispanic nations, natives of Puerto Rico are American citizens by virtue of the 1920 Jones Act.

Most Cuban Americans immigrated to the United States in response to Fidel Castro's communist takeover of Cuba. Cuban Americans have become an important political group over the years, acting as a strong voting bloc. During the cold war, Congress passed a law granting asylum to all Cubans who reached American shores; that law was tested in 1980. A group of Cubans rammed the gates of the Peruvian embassy in Havana, seeking asylum because Castro had announced that all Cubans who wanted to leave should go to the embassy; 10,000 Cubans appeared. By the end of 1980, 125,000 Cubans had come to the United States. Some Americans charged that Castro was dumping Cuba's violent criminals and mentally ill on his northern enemy.

As of 1990 there were over 22 million Hispanic Americans in the United States, accounting for about 9 percent of the nation's population. This Hispanic population has grown steadily over the past 30 years. The Hispanic population increased by 61 percent in the 1970s and by 53 percent in the 1980s. The Mexican-American population grew by 92.8 percent in the 1970s and 54.4 percent in the 1980s. The Puerto Rican population increased 40.9 percent in the 1970s and 35.4 percent in the 1980s. The Cuban population increased 47.5 percent in the 1970s and 30 percent in the 1980s. Other Hispanic populations, primarily from Central and South America, increased 18.9 percent in the 1970s and 66.7 percent in the 1980s.

In 1990 Mexicans were the largest Hispanic group, representing 61 percent of the more than 22 million

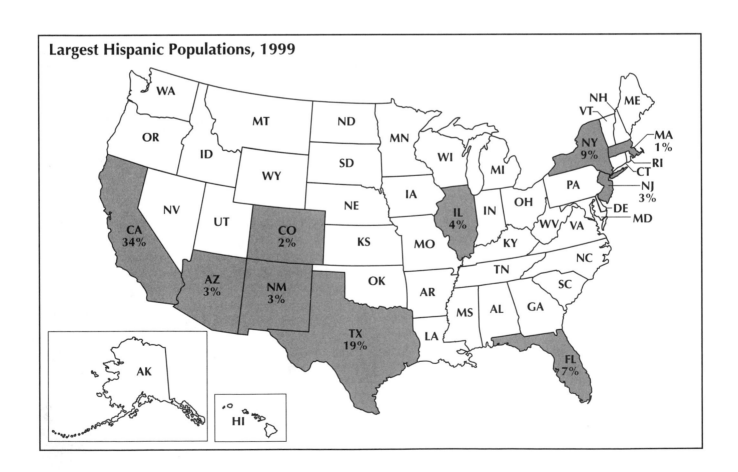

Largest Hispanic Populations, 1999

Hispanics; Puerto Ricans accounted for about 12 percent and Cubans made up 5 percent of the Hispanic population. Central Americans represented about 6 percent of Hispanics and South Americans account for nearly 5 percent.

In 1990 about half of the Hispanic population had at least a high school diploma and 1 in 11 earned a college degree. This was up from 3 in 10 finishing high school and 1 in 20 completing college in 1970. Broken down by national origin, high school diploma recipients made up about 44 percent of Mexican Americans; 53 percent of Puerto Ricans, 57 percent of Cuban Americans, about 46 percent of Central Americans, and 71 percent of South Americans had at least a high school diploma.

In 1990 nearly 8 million Hispanics were foreign born. Nearly three-quarters of the Hispanic population were native-born American citizens. Before 1960, about 20 percent of immigrants were from Latin America, increasing to 33 percent in the 1960s, 40 percent in the 1970s, and nearly 50 percent in the 1980s.

From 1990 to 2000 the Hispanic population in the United States increased 57.9 percent over the last decade. The 2000 census showed that the Spanish/Hispanic/Latino population, including Mexicans, Puerto Ricans, Cubans and others within this group numbered 35.3 million. In the entire population of 281.4 million in the country, Hispanics were 13.2 percent of the population. In the last decade Mexicans had increased 52.9 percent, from 13.5 million to 20.6 million; Puerto Ricans increased from 2.7 million to 3.4 million; and Cubans from 1 million to 1.2 million. Mexicans account for 58.5 percent of all Hispanic peoples in the United States.

Three-quarters of the Hispanic-American population live in the West or the South. Census data show that 43.5 percent of Hispanic Americans live in the West and 32.8 percent live in the South; 14.9 percent in the Northeast, and 8.9 percent in the Midwest. Of the total population in the West, Hispanics account for 24.3 percent; 11.6 percent in the South; 9.8 percent in the Northeast; and 24.3 in the Midwest.

Over half of Hispanic Americans live in two states, California (11 million, or 31 percent of the total population) and Texas (6.7 million, or 18.9 percent of the population). Moreover, more than 76.8 percent of Hispanics live in seven states (California, Texas, New York, Florida, Illinois, Arizona, and New Jersey). The state of New Mexico has the largest percentage of Hispanic Americans at 42.1 percent of the total population.

Census data revealed another interesting characteristic of Hispanic Americans. Of the total Hispanic-American population, 35 percent are under the age of 18 years. Moreover, while the median age of the entire population in the United States is 35.3 years the median age of Mexican Americans is 24.2.

Because of their youth and numbers, Hispanic Americans will play an important role in changing political and cultural life, especially in the western states. As a result, both the Democratic and Republican Parties have made conscious efforts to recruit Hispanic-American voters.

See also AFRICAN AMERICANS; ASIAN AMERICANS; IMMIGRATION; IMMIGRATION REFORM AND CONTROL ACT (1986); INTERMARRIAGE; POVERTY RATES.

Further reading: James D. Cockcroft, *Latinos in the Making of the United States* (New York: F. Watts, 1995); Nicolás Kanellos, *The Hispanic-American Almanac* (Detroit: Invisible Ink, 1993).

—John Korasick

homosexuality   See gay rights movement

Horton, Willie (campaign ad) (1988)

William R. Horton, an AFRICAN AMERICAN and convicted murderer, served as the centerpiece of a controversial political attack ad aired on TELEVISION during the 1988 presidential campaign waged between Republican candidate GEORGE H. W. BUSH and Democrat MICHAEL DUKAKIS. The ad attacked Michael Dukakis and the prison furlough system he had instituted while governor of Massachusetts.

Horton was serving a life term in Massachusetts for the murder of a convenience store clerk when, under the state's inmate rehabilitation program, he received a 48-hour unsupervised furlough on June 6, 1986. Horton failed to return from his furlough. In October 1987 Horton was convicted of assaulting a Maryland man and raping his fiancée, both of whom were white, and sentenced to two consecutive life terms plus 85 years by a Maryland judge, who refused to return him to Massachusetts.

In 1988 Citizens United, an independent POLITICAL ACTION COMMITTEE, produced a television ad that attacked Michael Dukakis and the prison furlough system he had preserved while governor of Massachusetts. The ad stated that George Bush supported the death penalty and that Michael Dukakis opposed the death penalty and allowed first-degree murderers to get weekend passes from prison. Featuring a picture of Willie Horton and detailing his furlough and convictions, the ad claimed Horton had received 10 weekend passes and concluded with the statement, "Weekend passes—Dukakis on crime."

The ad was both effective and controversial. Its effectiveness rested on the fact that the Democrats were unable to refute the facts underpinning the message in the ad; Tennessee senator ALBERT GORE, JR., had earlier criticized Dukakis on the issue during the Democratic primaries. Moreover, the visibility of the ad, and the issue addressed, spurred some state Republican committees to print anti-Dukakis pamphlets, like one in Illinois that claimed: "All the murderers and rapists and drug pushers and child molesters in Massachusetts vote for Dukakis. We in Illinois can vote against him." Controversy swarmed around the ad because many believed that it appealed to racial prejudices. Democrats accused Republicans of unearthing the old racial fears of black criminals being unleashed on white communities. Additionally, the ad was an early example of groups not affiliated directly with any political party affecting an election through the use of television ads. Finally, the ad demonstrated that television is a powerful medium with the ability to mold public political behavior through the manipulation of deeply embedded cultural symbols.

See also ADVERTISING; CAMPAIGN FINANCE; CRIME; ELECTIONS; MEDIA; POLITICAL PARTIES; RACE AND RACIAL CONFLICT.

—William L. Glankler

House of Representatives, U.S.

As a result of tremendous social and political pressures, the House of Representatives has undergone many changes since 1968, leading to greater influence for junior representatives, public decision making, ethics, oversight, and CAMPAIGN FINANCE reform.

Many of the reforms were initiated by the Democratic representatives elected in the 1960s and early 1970s. By 1975, 82 percent of members had been elected since 1960, and 61 percent had entered Congress since 1967. These junior members had no interest in maintaining the status quo seniority system, which placed all real power in the hands of senior members and ensured that junior members would receive stern rebukes if they did not play along. Many of these new representatives were political liberals and resented having to subordinate their beliefs to southern conservatives who dominated the House committees.

The reformers were fortunate in having Speakers who were more interested in passing legislation than in keeping backbenchers in line. These Speakers, John D. McCormack (D-Mass.), CARL ALBERT (D-Okla.), and THOMAS P. O'NEILL (D-Mass.), did little to help or hinder reform efforts. The Legislative Reorganization Act of 1970 brought about the first wave of reforms. This act required committees to have written rules, make public all votes, and make committee reports public at least three days before a bill was brought to the floor. The act also forced members to disclose their positions on legislative issues. In 1973 an electronic voting system was installed that indicated how each member voted instantaneously.

A second rule change in 1974, in the Democratic caucus, required that Democratic committee chairs be filled by secret ballot at the start of each new Congress. In 1975 the new rule resulted in the removal of three southern committee chairs, including Wright Patman (D-Tex.) of the Banking, Currency, and Housing Committee; F. Edward Hebert (D-La.) of the Armed Services Committee; and W. R. Poage (D-Tex.) of the Agriculture Committee.

The WATERGATE SCANDAL led to further reforms in the House as members sought to create more public transparency and greater influence among junior members. Following the death of House Speaker Carl Albert in 1972, Tip O'Neill of Cambridge, Massachusetts, became Speaker. O'Neill was disposed to work with insurgent Democrats, led by Phillip Burton of San Francisco, to undertake reforms in the House. In the midterm elections of 1974, the Democrats gained 46 seats over their 1972 total and controlled the House 290–145. One of the first steps in reform came when Congress adopted "sunshine" rules, requiring all committees and subcommittees to open all meetings to the public, unless a majority voted at an open session to close a hearing. Also, broadcast coverage of House committee hearings began. Public interest in the Judiciary Committee IMPEACHMENT proceedings against RICHARD M. NIXON created a drive for rule changes to allow television broadcasts. In 1979 gavel-to-gavel broadcasts of House sessions began with Tennessee representative ALBERT GORE delivering the first televised speech. In 1977 a new code of ethics was adopted. This required financial disclosures by members and aides, restricted outside income, and put limits on free mailing privileges.

When Republicans regained control of the SENATE in the 1980 election, the Democratic House became the center of opposition to RONALD W. REAGAN's policies. Early in the session, Republicans and conservative Democrats, known as the "Boll Weevils," passed Reagan's legislative program cutting taxes and appropriations, and increasing defense spending. This alliance quickly unraveled and partisanship increased.

Speaker O'Neill retired and was replaced in 1987 by JAMES WRIGHT. Wright proved himself to be resourceful and, potentially, very powerful. Wright resigned in 1989 after an ethics investigation alleged violations of House rules. Wright was replaced by THOMAS FOLEY. Foley attempted to restore bipartisanship and civility to the chamber. In the 1990 ELECTIONS, Democrats solidified their hold on the House, gaining eight seats. But the elections provided evidence of voter dissatisfaction. Fifteen incumbents were defeated and 110 members saw their winning margin decrease. In addition, several states began discussing term limits for members of Congress.

A number of scandals in the House of Representatives broke in the early 1990s. In 1991 the General Accounting Office disclosed that 325 current and former members had regularly overdrawn their accounts at the House bank without penalty. In 1992 a federal investigation into charges of embezzlement and drug dealing in the House Post Office uncovered a scam in which House members cashed campaign checks and expense vouchers through transactions made to look like stamp purchases. The most notable figure in this scandal was Dan Rostenkowski, chairman of the House Ways and Means Committee. Rostenkowski lost his reelection bid and pleaded guilty to mail fraud. He was sentenced to 17 months in prison and fined $100,000.

The 1992 elections brought a modest nine-seat gain for the Republicans, leaving the Democrats firmly in control. In 1994, however, the Republicans took control of the House for the first time in 40 years. Speaker Foley not only lost his leadership position, he became the first speaker to lose his seat since 1862.

In 1994 NEWTON L. GINGRICH became the first Republican Speaker from the South. The Republican plan was to reform government by reducing its size, power, and scope. The Republicans passed numerous reforms on their first day in power. They increased the power of the majority leader, made it easier to cut spending, and made it harder to raise taxes. Three committees were eliminated, committee staffs were cut, term limits were placed on committee chairs and the Speaker, and a three-fifths majority became the standard to raise taxes. The Republican "Contract with America" provided the agenda for the first 100 days. By April 1995, eight of the 10 planks had been passed in the House, although many of these bills failed to pass when they reached the Senate. Soon the Republican momentum faded, and the fiery conservatism of Republican House members ran up against the moderation of the Republican Senate, which blocked many of the House bills.

Partisanship remained a problem, and Speaker Gingrich was soon under fire. Gingrich had led the charge against Jim Wright and many Democrats questioned Gingrich's ethics. In December 1995 the ethics committee found Gingrich guilty of violating three House rules and imposed no punishment, but it did name an investigator to examine more serious charges. Gingrich's image was also injured by his role in government shutdowns in 1995 and 1996 when he attempted to force President WILLIAM J. CLINTON to compromise on a Republican budget plan. Public opinion was on the side of the administration, and Gingrich had to back down. In 1996 Gingrich admitted to an ethics violation: giving misleading information to the committee. Gingrich became the first sitting Speaker to receive a reprimand, and he was fined $300,000.

Gingrich stepped down after the 1998 election. The loss of five seats was blamed on the Speaker's drive to impeach President Clinton. Gingrich also announced his resignation from the House. As a replacement the Republicans chose J. Dennis Hastert in 1999. Hastert inherited a polarized House. In 1998 the House had approved two articles of IMPEACHMENT against President Clinton. The Democrats favored a censure, but the Republicans wanted Clinton removed from office. Following his acquittal, the House refused to endorse any action taken by the president. In April 1999, the House rejected a resolution endorsing NATO action against Serbia in KOSOVO.

The Republicans narrowly retained control of the House after the 2000 election. Intense partisanship continued to characterize congressional politics.

See also POLITICAL PARTIES.

—John Korasick

Human Genome Project

The Human Genome Project was a 13-year research effort coordinated by the U.S. DEPARTMENT OF ENERGY (DOE) Human Genome Project and the National Institutes of Health (NIH) National Human Genome Research Institute (NHGRI). Its goals included: identifying every gene in the human DNA (ca. 30,000); determining the sequence of each chemical base pair (ca. 3 billion); storing the information on publicly accessible electronic databases; developing tools for analyzing the information; transferring related technologies to the private sector; and providing specific policy recommendations regarding the ethical, legal, and social issues that might arise with respect to human genome research. Charles DeLisi of the Office of Health and Environmental Research is credited as the first government scientist to conceive and outline the feasibility, goals, and parameters of the Human Genome Project.

The DOE became interested in the project as a valuable resource for better studying the effects of radiation and certain energy-related chemicals on human health. They established the Human Genome Initiative with $5.3 million for initial research in 1986. The NIH became equally interested for the inevitable innovations that a human genome map would provide for health care in America. The two agencies formalized a long-term partnership in a 1988 agreement. After two years of development, they presented a five-year research plan to Congress. They received a congressional commitment of $200 million a year, for a projected 15-year project. Scientists argued that a complete, detailed map of the human genome would be "the source book for biomedical science in the 21st century," and would significantly advance scientific understanding of molecular medicine, waste control and environmental cleanup, biotechnology, energy sources, and risk assessment. Specific theoretical benefits might include improved diagnosis and early detection of diseases; more rational drug designs, leading to individually customized drugs, and effective gene therapy; better understanding of the vulnerabilities of specific genetic diseases; enhanced protection from biological warfare; more efficient bio-fuels;

and significantly improved forensics capabilities. Scientists even argued that a mature understanding of the human genome might provide historians and anthropologists with hard evidence for human migratory patterns, patterns of human mutation that may have had an impact on historical events, and an outline of genetic evolution.

Working in cooperation with 18 countries worldwide, the Human Genome Project surpassed its initial expectations early on and revised its initial five-year plan in 1993, bringing the project two years ahead of schedule. After announcing its third and final five-year plan in 1998, projecting a completion of a detailed map of the DNA sequence by 2003, the Human Genome Group faced its first competition from the private sector.

A private company, Celera Genomics, announced that it would complete its own sequencing in just three years—two years ahead of the publicly funded Human Genome Project. Politicians and the national news media voiced concerns that the private corporation might patent its findings before the Human Genome Project could make their research public. The risk of such a move was low, but the prospect was sufficiently shocking to force the project to the attention of the American public. Public sentiment strongly favored legislation forbidding private patents of human genetic information, and Celera finally announced that it would cooperate with the goals of the original public project. In May 2000 the International Human Genome Sequencing Consortium allayed fears by specifically reaffirming their opposition to patents, licenses, subscriptions fees, or other limitations on using information from the human genome database. The following month, on June 26, Celera and the Human Genome Project jointly announced that after mapping 90 percent of the DNA sequencing, they had both arrived at working rough drafts of the complete human genome, though a detailed map was still not expected until 2002.

The race between the Human Genome Project and Celera Genomics inspired public debate on the ethical implications of such easily accessible information. Scientists and other academics had long struggled with questions of privacy, fairness and discrimination, PROPERTY RIGHTS, and informed consent, as well as more mundane issues of how to incorporate the new information into mainstream clinical practice, and how to educate future generations in the field of genetic research. Other observers, however, noted that little or no attention was paid to governing how the human genetic information might be used in other research areas, including human cloning, stem cell research from human embryos, and custom cloning for organ harvesting. In 1998 the NHGRI issued an updated list of ethical questions to consider, including those dealing with the project's impact from philosophical, theological, and ethical perspectives. Religious leaders, including many within the Roman Catholic Church, continued to voice concerns that no effort was made to ensure that scientists were grounded by a reliable standard with which to judge their bioethical considerations. The project recommended that future students of genetics receive multidisciplinary training in biology, computer science, engineering, mathematics, physics, and chemistry, but no mention was made of the need for study in philosophy or theology. The full impact and consequences that the Human Genome Project will have on the direction of humanity, for good or ill, may not be understood by historians for another century or more; current predictions will most likely underestimate its future effects.

See also COMPUTERS; MORALITY; RELIGION; SCIENCE AND TECHNOLOGY.

—Aharon W. Zorea

I

immigration

Despite the fact that the United States is a nation of immigrants, immigration policy and aspects of American ideology have historically been ambiguous toward those seeking admittance into the country. As of 2000 an estimated 800,000 immigrants enter the United States legally each year, while roughly 300,000 overstay their visas or enter illegally. One out of every 10 Americans is foreign born—a demographic pattern not seen since the 1930s. An estimated 6 million illegal immigrants work low-skilled jobs in meat-packing plants; as farm labor; or in hotels, garment factories, and restaurants. This contrasts sharply with the decision made by Congress in 1999 to almost double the quota for highly skilled immigrants to fill labor shortages in high-tech industries.

The Immigration Act of 1965 eliminated the national origins standard, which had granted preferential quotas for those of Western European heritage. The most significant part of the Immigration Act of 1965 was that it restricted all nations to 20,000 immigrants annually, giving all countries equal standing. Under an amendment to this act, employers were allowed to hire undocumented workers without penalty. Continuing demand for low-wage labor throughout the 1960s led to an enormous increase in the number of undocumented workers.

By the 1970s, Congress realized that the 1965 act needed revision, especially as it related to illegal immigrants. Although Congress established a special committee to evaluate policies governing the admission of immigrants and refugees in 1979, the commission's findings were not implemented. Various bills were proposed through the 1980s, but divisions along party, regional, and class interests stopped their passage. Not until 1986 did Congress pass the IMMIGRATION REFORM AND CONTROL ACT (IRCA), commonly referred to as Simpson-Mazzoli. Under this act, employers are prohibited from knowingly hiring illegal aliens by requiring the verification of an applicant's eligibility for employment and identity prior to hiring. Illegal

aliens who entered the United States before January 1, 1982, and maintained continuous residence were given amnesty under the terms of this act. The act, however, had failed to stem the flow of illegal immigration as of 2001.

The Immigration Act of 1990 increased the number of immigrants allowed into the country. It provided additional visas for those having particular skills scarce in the American labor pool. Europeans were guaranteed approximately one-third of all visas, and the status of undocumented Irish was legalized. The bipartisan U.S. Commission on Immigration Reform, also known as the Jordan Commission, after its chair, Representative Barbara Jordan, was authorized by the Immigration Act of 1990. In particular, the commission examined the implementation and impact of provisions of the act related to employment-based immigration, family reunification, and the program to ensure diversity for the sources of U.S. immigration. The commission issued a total of four reports that focused on controlling illegal immigration, and presented recommendations on family and employment-based immigration, refugee admissions, and naturalization or Americanization. Subsequent immigration acts have sought international sanctions against the Castro government in Cuba, promoted antiterrorism, extended the authorized period of stay within the United States for certain nurses and religious workers, amended the Immigration and Nationality Act to exempt internationally adopted children 10 years of age or younger from immunization requirements, granted relief for torture victims, and extended into 1999 the visa processing period for "diversity applicants," whose processing was suspended during 1998 after the bombings of several American embassies.

Conflicting views of the place of immigrants abound. America is touted as the nation of immigrants, and the achievements of the hard-working citizen are lauded. At the same time, many American regard immigrants with mistrust, fearing economic competition will illegal aliens and terrorist infiltration. Penalties are in place for those

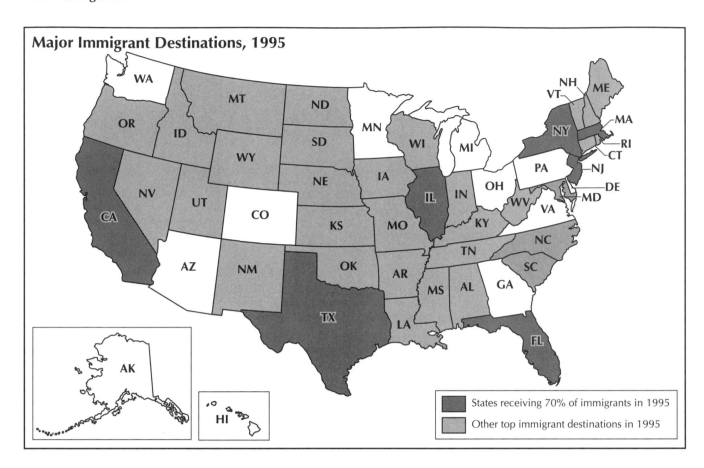

Major Immigrant Destinations, 1995

States receiving 70% of immigrants in 1995

Other top immigrant destinations in 1995

who hire undocumented workers, but enforcement is difficult, if not impossible. Business competition and lucrative profits make the risk of hiring illegal workers worthwhile.

Proponents of immigration argue that higher immigration levels increase the living standards of middle- and upper-income Americans. They argue that the post-1960s wave has contributed to urban renewal by providing low-wage labor, developing small businesses, and maintaining a population base necessary for economic growth. Despite the increase in technological jobs, unskilled and semiskilled labor is still in demand.

Critics charge that immigrants take jobs from native workers and drain social resources from impoverished citizens. American labor unions have historically viewed immigrants with suspicion, charging they drive wages down at the expense of native workers. Critics also assert that immigration erodes national identity and cultural cohesion. Governor Pete Wilson of California was reelected in 1994 after voicing his support of Proposition 187, which tried to bar illegal immigrants' children from public schools. Two years later, Congress approved bills that prohibited legal immigrants from receiving federal disability assistance and food stamps, and retroactively required the deportation of legal aliens convicted of a variety of offenses.

Attitudes toward immigrants and immigration are shaped by the ECONOMY, and attitudes regarding personal job security. A Gallup poll in 1990 revealed that 44 percent of the respondents thought immigrants mostly help the economy, while 40 percent felt they mostly hurt. Asked the same question by Gallop in 1993, 26 percent said immigrants helped and 64 percent said they hurt.

Both Republicans and Democrats have sought out foreign-born voters. GEORGE W. BUSH's election in 2000 marked the rise of the pro-immigrant wing of the Republican Party, which still has powerful anti-immigrant critics. Among Hispanic voters, immigration remains a salient issue. Bush drew 31 percent of the Hispanic vote, compared with 21 percent for Robert Dole in 1996. But he still fell a few points short of what RONALD W. REAGAN drew among Hispanics in 1980 and 1984, and barely beat his father, President George H. W. Bush, who registered 30 percent in 1988. The Democratic Party remains a pro-immigration party and continues to attract the Hispanic vote.

Under the WILLIAM J. CLINTON administration, lawmakers struck a compromise in 1999 to reunite 300,000 to 500,000 spouses and children with legal permanent residents. Clinton's broader proposals were rejected, including granting legal status to immigrants who fled political chaos and wars in El Salvador, Guatemala, Honduras, and HAITI. Whether this was a reflection of opposition to President Clinton in Congress, or the broader mood of the American people, time will tell.

See also ASIAN AMERICANS; HISPANIC AMERICANS.

Further reading: Debra L. DeLaet, *U.S. Immigration Policy in an Age of Rights* (Westport, Conn.: Praeger, 2000); ———— and David M. Reimers, *Unwelcome Strangers: American Identity and the Turn against Immigration* (New York: Columbia University Press, 1998); Thomas Muller, *Immigrants and the American City* (New York: New York University Press, 1993).

—Michele Rutledge

Immigration Reform and Control Act (1986)

In the late 1970s and early 1980s, with the influx of immigrants from Asia and increasing immigration, particularly illegal IMMIGRATION from Central America and Mexico, Congress enacted the Immigration Reform and Control Act (1986). Introduced by Alan Simpson (R-Wyo.) and Romano Mazzoli (D-Ky.) in 1985, the act granted temporary resident status to illegal immigrants who had lived in the United States prior to January 1, 1982, provided they had no criminal record and were not on welfare. By exhibiting a basic understanding of English and civics, these residents could achieve permanent resident status after 18 months. Over 1.7 million aliens applied for temporary residency under this program. In addition, illegal immigrants who had lived in the country for three years and were employed as agricultural workers could claim temporary resident status and could become permanent residents three years after the enactment of the law, provided they worked at least one more year in AGRICULTURE. Eventually 1.4 million illegal immigrants took advantage of this program.

To discourage further illegal immigration, Congress authorized over $800 million over two years for the Immigration and Naturalization Service (INS). Congress also increased the penalties levied on employers for hiring or smuggling illegal immigrants into the country. These penalties included fines of up to $10,000 for each illegal immigrant employed and the possibility of six months in jail for each immigrant employed. Also, the bill reduced the number of days' advance notice an employer must give to apply for a permit to hire foreign workers.

In terms of preventing illegal immigration, the law was largely a failure as illegal immigration, especially from the porous southern border of the United States, continued in the 1990s. In urban areas the INS could raid businesses employing illegal immigrants. Planters in Texas and Cali-

fornia applied pressure through their congressional representatives to restrain INS raids in their fields during harvest time. In addition, the people in these regions who served on juries proved many times that they would not convict farmers for hiring illegal immigrants.

—John Korasick

impeachment (of Richard M. Nixon; of William J. Clinton)

Two of the three presidential impeachment proceedings in the history of the United States occurred in the late 20th century. The first of the two was against RICHARD M. NIXON in 1974 for obstruction of justice, abuse of power, and contempt of Congress for his part in the WATERGATE SCANDAL. The second was against WILLIAM J. CLINTON in 1998–99 for perjury, obstruction of justice, and abuse of power in the Lewinsky affair.

On July 27, 1974, the House Judiciary Committee approved its first article of impeachment, charging Nixon with obstruction of justice. This article maintained that Nixon used the powers of the presidency to impede the investigations into the Watergate break-in (a burglary by Republican operatives into the Democratic campaign headquarters in the Watergate complex in Washington, D.C., during the 1972 election), and to protect those responsible. President Nixon was accused of making false statements, withholding relevant materials, approving the false statements of others, interfering in investigations by the Department of Justice and the FBI, misuse of the CIA, leaking information to suspects, and promising favors to defendants to remain quiet about executive involvement. This article was approved by a vote of 27-11.

The second article, abuse of power, was adopted on July 29, 1974 by a vote of 28-10. This article dealt with the Nixon administration's use of the Internal Revenue Service as a political tool, conducting audits against political enemies. In addition, it deemed as abuse Nixon's use of the FBI and Secret Service to conduct illegal electronic surveillance, and the concealment of records from this surveillance was deemed abuse. The use of the "burglars" to obtain information about Daniel Ellsberg, a former Pentagon official who had released documents concerning America's involvement in Vietnam, was another source for this charge. Finally, the second article charged that Nixon failed to take action against his subordinates when he learned of their participation, and that he used executive power to interfere with investigations. The final article, contempt of Congress, stemmed from his resistance to releasing to the Judiciary Committee White House tapes of his conversations in the Oval Office. This article was approved by a largely party-line vote of 21-17 on July 30, 1974.

The committee's articles never reached a full HOUSE OF REPRESENTATIVES vote and SENATE trial. On August 9, 1974, Nixon resigned the presidency, the only president ever to resign. Vice President GERALD R. FORD succeeded him and granted Nixon a full pardon for any crimes he may have committed.

The second impeachment proceeding led to the first impeachment of an elected president, Bill Clinton, since 1868. The beginning of the investigation concerned President Clinton's involvement in the Whitewater scandal, but the investigation of this affair led to an investigation of an obstruction of justice concerning Clinton's affair with a White House intern, Monica Lewinsky. The first article of impeachment held that the president had lied under oath about the intimate relationship with Monica Lewinsky. This article was approved 21-16 along party lines, with Republicans in the majority, by the House Judiciary Committee on December 11, 1998.

The second article charged that Clinton also perjured himself in a civil sexual harassment case brought against him by a former Arkansas state employee, Paula Jones. This article was approved 20-17 on December 11, 1998. The third article, relating to the Jones case, cited seven instances of obstruction of justice. The first two charged that Clinton had suborned (encouraged) perjury of a witness in the form of an affidavit and testimony. The third charged that Clinton had concealed evidence; the fourth charged that Clinton had found a job for a witness with harmful testimony; the fifth said that Clinton allowed his attorney to make false and misleading statements to a federal judge; the sixth was that Clinton recounted a false account of the events in question to a potential witness; and the seventh charge was that Clinton tampered with grand jury witnesses, causing them to give false information to the grand jury. This article was also approved 21-16 on December 11, 1998.

The final article of impeachment against Bill Clinton charged that he abused executive power by making perjurious statements to Congress in his answers to the 81 questions posed by the Judiciary Committee. It was approved 21-16 along party lines on December 12, 1998.

The full House of Representatives approved Articles One and Three, and the Senate began President Clinton's impeachment trial on January 7, 1999. For the president to be removed from office, 67 senators would have to vote against him. The prosecution argued that Clinton's perjury and obstruction of justice were grounds for impeachment, even though these actions occurred over "personal" matters. The defense argued that the entire case was circumstantial and did not rise to the constitutional standard to remove the president. After five weeks of testimony and deliberation, the Senate acquitted Clinton on both articles. The Senate was split along party lines, 55 Republicans and 45 Democrats. On Article One, 55 senators, including 10 Republicans, voted not guilty. On Article Three, the Senate split 50 for and 50 against, thereby ending the impeachment proceedings.

See also CRIME; EVANGELICAL CHRISTIANS; JUDICIAL WATCH; SUPREME COURT.

—John Korasick

independent counsel

The Independent Counsel Act was inspired by the investigation of the WATERGATE SCANDAL. Lawmakers, reflecting on the experience of ARCHIBALD COX, JR., and the memory of the Saturday Night Massacre, believed that a law creating a special prosecutor, not subject to the whims of the president, was necessary. A president should not have the power to fire the person investigating him or his administration.

The Independent Counsel Statute was originally enacted as Title VI of the Ethics in Government Act of 1978 and was reauthorized for five years in 1983 and 1988, before expiring in December 1992. It was reauthorized in June 1994 at the behest of President WILLIAM J. CLINTON. Under the terms of the act, the independent counsel can be called by Congress or the attorney general. Once appointed, the counsel can investigate allegations of any misconduct, with an unlimited budget and no deadline. Also, the counsel can only be dismissed by the attorney general or a panel of three federal judges.

The first independent counsel appointed under the new law was Arthur Christy in 1979. Christy was appointed to investigate President JAMES EARL CARTER, JR.'s chief of staff, Hamilton Jordan, for suspected cocaine use. This investigation resulted in no indictments. This would not be unusual; of the 20 independent counsels, 10 did not indict. Broken down by administration, there were two investigations of the Carter administration, eight of the Reagan administration, three of the Bush administration, and seven of the Clinton administration. The two highest-profile investigations were the IRAN-CONTRA AFFAIR under Reagan and Whitewater under Clinton.

In a 1988 U.S. SUPREME COURT decision, Justice ANTONIN SCALIA argued that the statute was a potential tool of partisan politics, and his words ring true. Both political parties have used the independent counsel, with limited success, to undermine the other party. LAWRENCE WALSH, the independent counsel for the Iran-Contra investigation, is credited with having led a successful investigation. Lasting six years and costing $52 million, none of the high-level suspects were indicted. Of the 14 indictments, eleven led to convictions, but two convictions were overturned on appeal. Robert B. Fiske and then KENNETH STARR were appointed to investigate Whitewater, which dragged on nearly as long as Iran-Contra. This investigation resulted in a number of related indictments and convictions. President Clinton was impeached, on other charges related to a sexual scandal that was included in the Starr investigation, but was not removed from office.

The questionable results and uses of the independent counsel have raised questions about its value. While reforms have been suggested, at present the act has expired, and the appointment of independent counsels is now in the hands of the attorney general as it was in 1973.

—John Korasick

Intermediate-Range and Shorter-Range Nuclear Forces Treaty (INF Treaty)

The Intermediate-Range and Shorter-Range Nuclear Forces (INF) Treaty was signed by President RONALD W. REAGAN and Soviet leader Mikhail Gorbachev on December 8, 1987, and took effect on June 1, 1988. The INF Treaty is distinguished from previous arms control agreements because it called for the ban and elimination of entire classes of weapons.

After World War II, the SOVIET UNION created a buffer zone of Communist states in Eastern Europe, and effectively closed the borders between the East and the West. The rise of the Berlin Wall in 1961, and the crisis in Czechoslovakia in 1968 prompted many in the West to fear for the safety of Europe in the event of Soviet expansion. The NORTH ATLANTIC TREATY ORGANIZATION (NATO) thus became an important source of security for Europe. The United States and the Soviet Union attempted to ease tensions by promising to limit certain classes of defensive-based weapons. These talks were generally ineffective, and throughout the 1970s, the Soviet Union continued to increase the size of its military arsenals. During his first term in office, President Reagan responded with a dual-track program, which promoted new efforts in NATO defense as well as new overtures for DÉTENTE. He deployed intermediate-range missiles to protect targeted European cities, and devoted considerable research to a space-based missile defense system intended to neutralize the threat of the Soviet Union's long-range nuclear missiles. At the same time, Reagan aggressively promoted a Strategic Arms Reduction Treaty (START), which called for deep cuts in land-based missile systems.

Talks between the United States and the Soviet Union began in 1982 but were broken off by the Soviets in 1983.

Premier Mikhail Gorbachev and President Ronald W. Reagan sign the Intermediate Nuclear Forces treaty *(Collection of the District of Columbia Public Library)*

Soon thereafter, however, the Soviet economy weakened from years of military buildup, and the new premier, Mikhail Gorbachev, was forced to pursue a reform agenda called GLASNOST, which included a new willingness to find agreement with the West. The United States responded accordingly, and after his reelection in 1984, President Reagan intensified efforts to reach a significant arms agreement that might end the COLD WAR. When talks resumed in 1985, both parties came to the table with a renewed commitment. In 1987 Reagan and Gorbachev met in person to discuss the issues. By December of that year, the two reached an unprecedented agreement, which eliminated all ground-launched ballistic and cruise missiles with ranges between 500 and 5,500 kilometers (310 to 3,415 miles). The agreement also called for the elimination of intermediate-range missile delivery systems; it banned the future production of intermediate-range missiles; and established strict limits on research and development in that technology. The parties also agreed to submit to on-site verification of missile disposal, and established the Special Verification Commission (SVC) to administer enforcement.

The INF Treaty marked the beginning of the end of the cold war. By eliminating INF-range missiles, the superpowers effectively removed Europe from the gambit of nuclear deterrence; the Soviets could not easily target European cities, and the United States could not use Europe as a base to launch its weapons. Immediately after signing the agreement, Reagan and Gorbachev began to work on reducing long-range missiles through the START treaties. They met twice in 1988, and after Reagan left office, President GEORGE H. W. BUSH continued the process throughout 1989, 1990, and 1991. Gorbachev and Bush agreed to reduce the size of conventional forces in Europe in 1990, and in 1991 they agreed to eliminate their stockpiles of chemical and biological weapons. They signed the START I treaty in July 1991, which reduced existing nuclear warheads by 25 percent. Six months later, the Warsaw Treaty organization dissolved, Gorbachev resigned from office, and the Soviet Union ceased to exist. START I was not ratified by the former Soviet states until November 1994. In appreciation for its ratification, and to help facilitate accelerated compliance, the United States agreed to provide Russia, Belarus, Kazakhstan, and Ukraine with $1 billion to help make the transition from a military to a civilian industrial complex.

See also ANTI-BALLISTIC MISSILE TREATY (1972); CATHOLIC BISHOPS' LETTER (THE CHALLENGE OF PEACE, 1983); DEFENSE POLICY; IRON CURTAIN; NUCLEAR FREEZE MOVEMENT; STRATEGIC ARMS LIMITATION TREATIES; STRATEGIC DEFENSE INITIATIVE.

—Aharon W. Zorea

Internet

As with many modern innovations, the origins of the Internet and the World Wide Web can be found in the COLD WAR. In 1957 the SOVIET UNION successfully launched Sputnik, the first artificial satellite, into space. Immediately, the United States responded with significant increases in funding for SCIENCE AND TECHNOLOGY. Congress reacted to a public fear that the nation was falling behind the Soviets in technology, thereby making it vulnerable to Soviet aggression. Along with the formation of the National Aeronautic and Space Agency (NASA), the Department of Defense also created a new sub-agency dedicated to advanced research, called simply the Advanced Research Projects Agency (ARPA). It was later renamed the Defense Advanced Research Projects Agency (DARPA).

At first, the agency's priorities were dominated by the space race and its subsidiary concerns—ballistic missile defense and nuclear test monitoring. As early as 1962, however, ARPA created the Information Processing Techniques Office (IPTO) to more specifically look into the wider implications of COMPUTERS and networking. At this point, computers had only just benefited from the invention of the integrated circuit, and thus still relied on vast commitments of space, energy, and manpower to operate. For the sake of efficiency, IPTO formally sponsored a study to look into the possibility of joining these huge computers through a network in order to take advantage of time-sharing and data transfers. By 1965 Lawrence G. Roberts of the Massachusetts Institute of Technology submitted the blueprints for a preliminary network design dubbed ARPANET. Shortly thereafter, ARPA awarded a $1 million construction contract to a then-small private corporation, Bolt Beranek and Newman, Inc. (BBN). It took four years to build ARPANET, but in 1969 the company had tied four computers together to form the first network, joining the National Measurement Center of the University of California at Los Angeles, the Stanford Research Institute, the University of California at Santa Barbara, and the University of Utah.

Throughout the 1970s, the ARPANET grew in both size and capabilities. In 1972 Ray Tomlinson wrote the first electronic messaging (E-mail) program, and Lawrence Roberts wrote the first E-mail managing software. E-mail not only increased communication between researchers, but also aided in shifting the network's purpose away from the time-sharing of resources, toward a new model of scientific collaboration. Within a year, there were more than 2,000 users of ARPANET, and E-mail made up 75 percent of all network traffic. In 1974 BBN opened the network to the public through Telenet. However, since personal computers were not commonly introduced until the early 1980s, Telenet remained primarily an academic and research tool. By 1981 a number of other nongovernment networks began to utilize the backbone of communication provided by ARPANET including THEORYNET, BIT-NET, CSNET, and USENET. These were independent networks, and could communicate with each other only indirectly. Nevertheless, the network became so popular that by 1983 DARPA divided itself into two separate entities: MILNET, which served its original intention as a safe and secure communication network for the government; and ARPANET, which remained the primary network for academic and research institutions. Almost two-thirds of the 113 existing nodes were dedicated to MILNET. With the rapid increase of personal computers in the public market, the demand rose dramatically and the ratio shifted. By 1984 there were more than 1,000 network hosts on ARPANET.

Through the early years of ARPANET, the federal government played a primary role in both planning and funding. The vast majority of users and developers were scientists and academics, even though the Department of Defense carried most of the financial support. In 1986 the National Science Federation (NSF) replaced the DARPA as the primary agency funding the network and created its own NSFNET. In 1987 NSF commissioned the management of the network to a private corporation, Merit Network, Inc. That same year, the first commercial network access provider, UUNET, also started. DARPA maintained its intimate relationship with the network through the formation of the Computer Emergency Response Team (CERT), which assumes responsibility for managing large-scale network problems (or virus attacks). The federal government continues to assert itself in the network in other less obvious ways, such as requiring government contractors to adopt specific network standards, which help promulgate network access. In 1987 there were 10,000 hosts, in 1988, there were 60,000, and in 1989 there were more than 100,000. By 1990, the success of commercially based Internet access providers allowed ARPANET to shut down, leaving NSFNET and private network hosts to support the existing network infrastructure. The following year, Congress passed the High Performance Computing Act of 1991, which provided considerable funding for the support of existing public networks, and encouraged the creation of additional private networks. The act also established the National Research and Education Network (NREN), which provides for separate high-speed networking for noncommercial research purposes. Senator ALBERT GORE JR. (D-Tenn.), sponsored the bill, which later led him to exaggerate his role in "inventing" the Internet. In fact, the networks upon which the World Wide Web relies had been in existence in one form or another since 1970. The additional federal support of the Computer Act of 1991 did, however, help to increase the number of Internet hosts to more than 1 million by 1992. Very quickly, private and commercial Internet access providers become the primary network carriers, and the

federal backbone, NSFNET, managed to revert back to a strictly academic resource by 1995.

The World Wide Web, or the Internet, as we know it today, officially began in March 1989 as a project led by Tim Berners-Lee of the European Laboratory for Particle Physics (Conseil Européen pour la Recherche Nucléaire, or CERN). They did not create a network, but instead invented a management system by which all existing networks might be more easily navigated. CERN's stated goal was to develop a software and hardware system that allowed researchers to quickly access existing collaboration projects and to leave lasting contributions before exiting. The project was executed in two phases: The first used existing hardware and software systems to implement simple browsers that could access each user's workstation; the second merely expanded the application area and allowed users to add their own material. The result was a management system that allowed users on one computer to automatically access information stored on another through existing international networks, without the need of special protocols. It was based on a system called "hypertext," which was originally conceived by Vannevar Bush in 1945, as an inevitable consequence of computerized archiving. He predicted that there would be so much data stored in national record banks that a computer based on nonsequential addressing would have to be developed to access it. Ted Nelson in 1960 coined the label "hypertext" to describe an interactive form of writing. The ideas of both Bush and Nelson served as the basis for CERN's management system, which links related pieces of information in a way that allows easy access to all types of files, regardless of their location. After three years, CERN released the World Wide Web (WWW) system to the public in 1992. It found immediate success, and the next year, Marc Andreessen, from the National Center for Supercomputer Applications at the University of Illinois, developed a graphical user interface to the WWW, called "Mosaic for X." Numerous entrepreneurs imitated the "browser," and the World Wide Web soon became a public property.

As of the middle of 1999, there were 56 million hosts on the Internet from 170 countries, with more than 300 million Web sites (an imprecise figure that rises at geometric rates). Though the U.S. federal government played a large role in the creation and establishment of the Internet, it is now an international phenomenon, larger than any single nation. Even U.S. governmental contributions relied heavily on academic initiative and outsourcing. In 1996, Congress passed its first wide-reaching regulation on the Internet with the Communications Decency Act (CDA), which intended to prohibit under-age access to PORNOGRAPHY by holding site owners criminally responsible for violations of decency. The following year, the U.S. SUPREME COURT struck down the CDA's Internet provision in *Reno v. ACLU,* concluding that it was an unconstitutional limitation on free speech, political discourse, and intellectual freedom. As of 2001, the decency provisions had not been revived, though they were often discussed in the public forum. Other attempts at government regulation have generally met with stiff resistance, though the issue of taxation remained an important topic of debate for 2001. Despite its critical role in the genesis of the Internet, the U.S. government is clearly unwelcome as the primary force in shaping its future evolution.

See also BUSINESS; CENSORSHIP; HUMAN GENOME PROJECT; MEDIA; PROPERTY RIGHTS; SCIENCE AND TECHNOLOGY.

—Aharon W. Zorea

Iran-contra affair

The Iran-Contra Affair occurred in 1986. In an attempt to evade congressional authority and aid anticommunist forces in Central America, and to gain the release of Americans held hostage in Lebanon, RONALD W. REAGAN's administration employed illegal means to achieve its FOREIGN POLICY goals. The ensuing scandal resulted in 14 indictments and 11 convictions, and made marine Lieutenant Colonel OLIVER NORTH a national personality.

Upon entering office in 1981, Reagan authorized the CIA to form a paramilitary force to harass the marxist Sandinista regime in NICARAGUA. This force became known as the CONTRAS. In the next three years more than $100 million in aid was funneled to the contras. When, in April 1984, it was revealed that the CIA had arranged to mine the harbors of Nicaragua, Congress reacted unfavorably. Responding to allegations of human rights violations and drug trafficking by the contras, Congress revoked military aid. Moreover, vocal public opposition to aiding the contras in any way developed across the country and in the universities. The BOLAND AMENDMENT, named for the chairman of the House Intelligence Committee, Edward Boland, banned all aid to the contras by the CIA, the Pentagon, or any other intelligence agency.

In an attempt to keep the operation running, despite the congressional directive, Oliver North, a White House aide, began recruiting agents to help the contras, in direct violation of the Boland amendment. Saudi Arabia pledged a total of $32 million, Taiwan pledged $2 million, and this money was used to pay for arms shipments from China, Poland, and other countries. North arranged these shipments and provided intelligence information and military advice to the contras.

Iran, a terrorist state, according to United States policy at the time, had been under an arms embargo since the IRANIAN HOSTAGE CRISIS in 1979. Also, it was believed that Iran controlled terrorist groups in Lebanon that were holding American citizens hostage. Officially, the United States would not negotiate with terrorists, but as time passed and pressure increased to bring the hostages home, Reagan looked for means of gaining their release. One possible way was presented by Israel in 1985. The Israelis wanted to sell American-made weapons to Iran for use against Iraq. Reagan approved the transfer, and North accordingly sold anti-tank missiles to Iran with the promise that hostages would be released. One American hostage, Reverend Benjamin Weir, held in Lebanon, was released. In November 1985 a shipment of anti-aircraft missiles was destined for Iran, but the deal went awry, and the CIA stepped in and delivered 18 missiles. Reagan later claimed that he did not approve the CIA activity, and Congress had not been informed of the Israeli shipments of U.S.-made weapons to Iran. In January 1986 Manucher Ghorbanifur, an Iranian exile, proposed financing the contras with profits from these Iranian arms sales. Admiral John Poindexter, the White House national security adviser, approved the plan, but later testified that he did not inform Reagan.

In April 1986 supplies financed by the arms sales were airdropped to the contras. Over the next six months, two more hostages were released—Reverend Lawrence Jenco and David Jacobsen. By October the arrangement began to unravel. First the Sandinistas in Nicaragua shot down a supply plane and captured Eugene Hasenfus, an American who claimed to be working under orders of the CIA. In November, a Lebanese newspaper reported on the U.S. arms sales to Iran. This revelation led to the resignations of Poindexter and North. As a response to the public and congressional outcry, the administration launched the Tower Commission. At the same time, Congress began hearings and subpoenaed Oliver North to testify. North came before the televised hearings dressed in full uniform. To the surprise of many, given the illegal and unconstitutional involvement in the affair, the general public responded positively to North, and Congress was flooded with letters and telegrams in his support. At the same time, INDEPENDENT COUNSEL LAWRENCE E. WALSH was appointed. The Tower Commission reported in February 1987 that Reagan had not properly supervised his aides and blamed the chief of staff, Donald Regan, for the chaos in the executive branch. Lawrence Walsh's investigation led to the indictment of 14 individuals, of which 11 were convicted. Later two of these convictions, including North's, were overturned on appeal.

The Iran-Contra affair provoked a constitutional crisis, and a number of newspaper editorials across the country called for the impeachment of Ronald W. Reagan. Ironically, Congress began supporting the contras again and in 1990 the Sandinistas were defeated in popular elections. The lasting legacy of Iran-Contra is the perilous topic of whether or not a democracy should conduct diplomacy in secret.

Further reading: Theodore Draper, *A Very Thin Line: The Iran Contra Affairs* (New York: Hill & Wang, 1991).
—John Korasick

Iranian hostage crisis

The Iranian Hostage Crisis came as a result of a revolution in Iran in 1979, which overthrew the shah, and led to the seizing of hostages when the American embassy in Tehran was overrun by revolutionary students. The United States has supported the shah prior to the revolution.

The shah of Iran, Mohammad Reza Pahlavi, was a Western-oriented ruler. The United States had given support to the shah in a variety of forms since the end of World War II, including a CIA operation that led to the assassination of a popular nationalist leader, Mohammed Mossadegh, in 1953, which reinstalled the royal family on the throne. Shiite Muslim dissidents opposed American influence in Iran because of its support of the shah, who had been placed on the throne with American covert support. As a result, Americans were targeted for violence throughout the 1970s. Dissidents made an unsuccessful kidnap attempt against the U.S. ambassador, Douglas MacArthur II. In the late 1970s the shah had been informed that he had cancer. In an effort to maintain his family's reign and create support for his teenaged heir, the shah began reforming his government. Public opinion turned against him, and numerous riots were staged in 1978 and 1979.

On January 16, 1979, the shah and his family fled Iran, and the Islamic fundamentalist leader, Ayatollah Ruholla Khomeini, returned from exile. For its years of support for the shah, the United States became a focus of the Iranian discontent. The United States lost access to Iranian oil and saw arms contracts cancelled, and on February 14, 1979, revolutionary forces overran the U.S. embassy in Tehran for a few hours. On February 26 the State Department evacuated the families of embassy personnel and urged Americans to leave the country.

An American hostage being paraded before cameras by his Iranian captors *(Hulton/Archive)*

The United States had not previously offered asylum to the shah, but in October, President JAMES EARL CARTER, JR., decided to reverse this policy and allowed the shah to enter the United States for medical treatment. Iranian students poured into the streets of Tehran, demanding the return of the shah and his fortune. On November 4, 1979, 3,000 dissidents stormed the U.S. embassy and took the 66 people inside hostage. News of the hostage-taking riveted the American public, and millions watched the nightly news footage of blindfolded Americans being paraded before television cameras, the burning of American flags, and the chanting of anti-American slogans. Protestors gathered in front of the Iranian embassy, demanding the release of the hostages. Iranian students in the United States held demonstrations in support of their country and faced a violent backlash, losing their jobs, and suffering vandalism and taunts.

Carter ordered preparations for a military rescue operation, ordered Iranian students to report to immigration offices, suspended arms sales, froze Iranian assets, and announced an oil embargo. Carter stressed the importance of the safety of the hostages. The Iranians released all non-American hostages, all of the African Americans, and most of the women. Also, six Americans managed to escape and made their way to the Canadian embassy. This brought the number of hostages down to 52.

In February 1980 the Iranians made their demands for the release of the hostages. The Iranian captors wanted the shah and his fortune returned, and an admission of guilt by the United States for its past actions, as well as an apology and a promise not to interfere in Iran again. Carter deemed these demands unacceptable, particularly since the shah had left the United States for Panama. On April 24, 1980, a rescue mission was staged, using helicopters to transport a rescue team outside of Tehran. Mechanical and weather difficulties resulted in all eight helicopters being lost. The public had been supportive of the president, though discouraged by the lengthy negotiation process, but this failed mission shattered the public's confidence in his ability to handle the situation.

On July 27, 1980, the shah died of cancer. In September, Khomeini presented four new conditions for the release of the hostages: cancel financial claims against Iran, free Iranian assets, and promise to never interfere in Iranian affairs. These were seen as acceptable starting points for negotiation, and the end of the crisis seemed to be near, especially with the invasion of Iran by Iraq.

Carter had more than just the hostage situation to deal with; 1980 was an election year. The Republicans were charging that Carter was engineering an "October Surprise" in which the hostages would be released so he would win the election. On November 4, 1980, the American people elected RONALD W. REAGAN. The nomination of Reagan, a hard-liner in foreign policy, appeared to give Carter an advantage in negotiations. Iranian prime minister Ali Rajai began negotiations, using Algeria as an intermediary. Tehran wanted the shah's fortune, but Carter had no authority to turn it over to them. For a period of three weeks the Iranians demanded first $24 billion, then $20 billion, and finally $8 billion to be deposited in Algeria. On Carter's last day in office, the Iranians agreed to a deal releasing $8 billion in Iranian assets, of which $5 billion was set aside to pay off Iran's American and European debts. In return, the Americans were released after 444 days as hostages.

See also FOREIGN POLICY; TERRORISM.

—John Korasick

Iron Curtain, collapse of

The Iron Curtain, a phrase coined in the late 1940s, by the former prime minister of Britain Winston Churchill, marked the line between East and West in Europe—or more important on a strategic level, the line between NORTH ATLANTIC TREATY ORGANIZATION (NATO) forces and those of the Warsaw Pact, a defense alliance organized by the Soviet Union in response to NATO. Its collapse resulted from the Soviet Union's withdrawal of its support and influence from its Eastern European satellites, and the subsequent political upheavals in those nations.

Shortly after coming to power in 1985, Soviet leader Mikhail Gorbachev announced plans for economic, political, and social reform in the Soviet Union. In December 1988, in a speech before the United Nations, Gorbachev announced his plan to unilaterally withdraw 500,000 troops and 10,000 tanks from the East European countries of the Warsaw Pact. Immediately after the withdrawal of Soviet support, the Communist regimes in Eastern Europe began to collapse. In Poland, the Solidarity movement won in parliamentary elections in June 1989. At the July 1989 Warsaw Pact meeting, Gorbachev told the Eastern European states that the Soviet Union would no longer work to control their economic and political policies. The newly elected Polish officials took office without Soviet interference. The success of the Polish dissident movement encouraged dissident resistance to the collapse of Communist regimes in other Eastern European countries. In the fall of 1989, the Hungarian Parliament dismissed the Communist Party as the official ruling institution. Hungarians throughout the nation responded by tearing down communist symbols. Czechoslovakia threatened to erupt in violence, as street demonstrations broke out demanding the release of Václav Havel, a leading dissident author, from prison. The tide turned on November 24, 1989, when Alexander Dubček, the leader in Prague, called for the ouster of Stalinists from the Czech government. The Communists responded with immediate resignations, and the people quickly named Havel to the presidency. The government of Erich Honecker sought to hold on to power in East Germany, despite numerous violent outbursts. On November 9, 1989, East Germany opened its border with its western neighbor. The following day, citizens from both East and West Germany began tearing down the Berlin Wall. One year later the two halves became one, after more than 40 years of separation, with the new united Germany instituted as a full member in NATO. In Romania, Nicolae Ceaușescu ruled for over 20 years as one of the harshest communist dictators, but in December 1989 opposition to him rose, along with a spirit of resistance. Most of the Romanian army turned against Ceaușescu. On December 25, 1989, he and his wife were tried by a military court and then executed on television.

The collapse of the Soviet Union came with an abruptness that took most people by surprise. In Eastern Europe, many of the nations were not prepared to make the political, economic, and social transition to democratic government and free-market economics. Yet in the following years, many of these nations created democratic governments and began to prosper economically. For the Soviet Union, the transition came less easily, as it continued to experience political corruption and a poor economy. As for the United States, policymakers were confronted with a new world in which the cold war had ended, but new international threats emerged, presenting challenges for the 21st century.

See also BUSH, GEORGE W. H.; COLD WAR; FOREIGN POLICY; REAGAN, RONALD.

—Leah Blakey

Islam in America

Economic changes and political upheavals in their own countries, as well as the desire to find new economic opportunities, spurred many Muslims from Asia and Africa to immigrate to the United States after World War II. Muslims live in every country in the Western Hemisphere, come from 60 different nations, and speak several Arabic dialects and various Turkic and Indo-European languages. Although the United States has not conducted a religious census since 1936, the Islamic Center of Washington, D.C., and the Federation of Islamic Associations estimate that there are more than 2 million Muslims in the United States. The Muslim population is ethnically diversified on the basis of national origin, language, and religious sect. Arabic-speaking Muslims constitute the largest and most differentiated Muslim group in the United States and are primarily from Lebanon, Palestine, and Yemen.

American Muslims have constructed many mosques that serve a wide variety of purposes. They function as the site of Friday and Sunday prayers, holiday celebrations, marriage and funeral rites, classes for children and adults, and informal social gatherings. Muslims have also established several national-level organizations. The Federation of Islamic Associations (founded in 1954) publishes *The Muslim Star* and has a scholarship fund for college-bound high school graduates. The Muslim Student Association (founded in 1963) promotes Islamic solidarity, helps to promote the Islamic way of life, and fosters friendship with non-Muslims.

Muslim communities in the United States reflect the backgrounds and social customs of their members. For example, Turkish families in Rochester, New York, emphasize their Turkish identity as well as their Muslim identity. They constructed a mosque as well as a social hall with a classroom where English language, Turkish history and heritage, and religious courses are taught. They hold weekly prayers led by a Turkish imam (priest), fast during Ramadan, hope to make the pilgrimage to Mecca, and avoid eating pork.

The flexibility of the Muslim religion has allowed its participants to adapt it to local customs that do not violate its tenets. American Muslims are developing revised standards of modesty for women in a society where the female body is highly exposed, viable guidelines for the interaction of men and women in an increasingly permissive cultural environment, social and marital relationships when wives work outside the home, and ways to transmit Islamic values to the next generation.

See also NATION OF ISLAM; RELIGION; WOMEN'S RIGHTS AND STATUS.

—William L. Glankler

Jackson, Jesse L. (1941–)

Jesse Louis Jackson, born October 8, 1941, in Greenville, South Carolina, appeared on the national scene following the assassination of Martin Luther King, Jr., in 1968. Jackson had a profound impact on the African-American community, as well as on national politics and race relations as a minister, as the founder of Operation PUSH and the National Rainbow Coalition, and as a two-time candidate for president of the United States.

A gifted athlete and student, Jackson won a football scholarship to the University of Illinois in 1959. When he was denied the quarterback position, he enrolled at North Carolina Agricultural and Technical State College, a historically black school. It was while attending this school that Jackson became involved in the Civil Rights movement by protesting the white-only local library system and agitating against segregation in public accommodations. After graduating in 1964, Jackson attended the Chicago Theological Seminary, where he distanced himself from local civil rights activities and focused on his theological training. His focus changed, however, when he participated in the historic civil rights march in Selma, Alabama, in 1965. There he met Martin Luther King, Jr., president of the Southern Christian Leadership Conference (SCLC).

Jackson recognized in this organization an opportunity for him to fulfill his leadership ambitions and his passion for civil rights. He left the seminary in 1966 to head the Chicago branch of Operation Breadbasket, a group committed to improving the economic situation of the local African-American community. He became the organization's national chairman in 1967. Through this organization, and because of his energy, and powerful oratory, Jackson was able to pressure several large Chicago corporations into hiring more African Americans, an achievement that garnered him much local fame. His strong personality and his claims of closeness with King caused friction between himself and the SCLC leadership after King's assassination. Despite the tension, Jackson remained with the SCLC. In

1971, however, Jackson left the SCLC to form Operation PUSH.

PUSH (People United to Serve Humanity) continued the theme of economic empowerment and operated under the motto: "I Am Somebody." PUSH weekly prayer meetings attracted large and enthusiastic crowds, and Jackson's influence and celebrity grew rapidly. He expanded the aims of PUSH to encompass education issues and voter registration drives. Jackson also became increasingly involved in politics, serving as a recognized voice for minorities and the poor, and appeared often in the national media supporting various political candidates.

Reverend Jesse L. Jackson *(Wong/Newsmakers)*

Jackson's boldest move came in 1983, when he declared himself as a candidate for the presidential nomination of the Democratic Party. His campaign emphasized his intense interest in the situation of America's poor and pledged a "rainbow coalition" committed to biracial political cooperation. During the campaign, however, he faced charges of anti-Semitism during the 1984 campaign, because of his association with the NATION OF ISLAM and his reference to New York City as "Hymietown." Lacking both an experienced national organization and the funds to operate it, Jackson never had a chance of winning the Democratic primary, although he won more delegates (384) than expected. In 1986 Jackson institutionalized his rhetoric by founding the National Rainbow Coalition, and he sought the Democratic nomination again in 1988. Although he lost this bid as well, he fared much better than in 1984, winning primaries in Alaska and Delaware and finishing second in 23 other states. Though Jackson failed to secure the Democratic nomination, his attempts were politically significant. Through these races, he mobilized unprecedented black political participation, inspired other blacks to seek political office, opened the way for future presidential challenges, and nationalized many social and racial issues.

Following his presidential bids, Jackson shelved his political aspirations but continued his leadership roles. He left PUSH in 1989 to lobby for the statehood of the District of Columbia in 1990. Jackson also resumed his role in unaligned diplomacy, a field in which he had success in 1983, when he negotiated the release of a black prisoner of war detained in Syria. In 1991 he was responsible for the release of hundreds of hostages held by Iraqi president Saddam Hussein. He resumed leadership of PUSH in Chicago but continued in his role as an unofficial, roving ambassador. In 1999 he secured the release from Slobodan Milosevic of three American members of United Nations peacekeeping forces, who had been captured on the border between Yugoslavia and Macedonia.

Jackson continued to play an important role in the Democratic Party, actively campaigning for ALBERT GORE in the 2000 election. In 2001 further controversy was created when he acknowledged he had fathered a child of one of his coworkers, but this did not affect his strong support among civil rights leaders.

See also AFFIRMATIVE ACTION; AFRICAN AMERICANS; FARRAKHAN, LOUIS; NATIONAL ASSOCIATION FOR THE ADVANCEMENT OF COLORED PEOPLE; POLITICAL PARTIES; RACE AND RACIAL CONFLICT.

Further reading: Marshall Frady, *Jesse: The Life and Pilgrimage of Jesse Jackson* (New York: Random House, 1996); Steven Lawson, *Running for Freedom: Civil Rights*

and Black Politics in America since 1941 (New York: McGraw Hill, 1997).

—William L. Glankler

Jackson State University

On May 13, 1970, approximately 150 protesters gathered at Jackson State College (now Jackson State University), an all-black college in Jackson, Mississippi, to protest the VIETNAM WAR. The demonstration quickly turned into a race riot, in which two black students were killed. The crowd was unusually hostile, their anger fueled by the killing of four white students at Kent State University nine days before, and by the racially motivated killing of six African Americans in Augusta, Georgia, just two days earlier. Most of the demonstrators were content to chant antiwar slogans, but many burned police barricades and threw rocks and bottles at passing white motorists. Alarmed local officials quickly alerted the National Guard. The next night, as the violence escalated, members of the Jackson police department and the Mississippi Highway Patrol fired into the crowd, killing two black students and wounding 12 others.

This incident took place in the midst of widespread antiwar activity centered on America's college campuses. The Jackson State incident, however, was not merely an antiwar protest. Jackson State students were agitating against President RICHARD M. NIXON's plans to invade Cambodia as well as the alleged racism of local police. Racial tensions between the students and local police had seethed for a decade, as had internal tensions resulting from the possibility that the school would lose its state funding if the campus turmoil did not abate. Neighborhood toughs had exacerbated the tensions in the community by harassing white motorists, actions that were invariably blamed on Jackson State students.

After the incident in 1970, local politicians and law enforcement agencies tried to blame students for the shootings by claiming that a sniper, not police, had fired shots into the crowd. Survivors of the incident and the victims' family members took the matter to court, but no members of the local police department, the Mississippi Highway Patrol, or the National Guard were ever indicted.

See also AFRICAN AMERICANS; ANTIWAR MOVEMENT—VIETNAM; RACE AND RACIAL CONFLICT.

—William L. Glankler

Jaworski, Leon (1905–1982)

Leon Jaworski is best known as the special prosecutor who replaced ARCHIBALD COX, JR., during the WATERGATE SCANDAL. The son of a Polish immigrant father and an Austrian immigrant mother, Jaworski was born in Waco, Texas, on September 19, 1905. After graduating from high school at the age of 15, Jaworski attended Baylor University, graduating from the law school in 1925. After joining the bar that year, Jaworski became the youngest person to practice law in Texas. Jaworski practiced in Houston, as a member of the firm of Dyess, Jaworski, and Strong, before joining the firm of Fulbright, Crooker, Freeman and Bate in 1935. During World War II, Jaworski served in the office of the army's judge advocate general as chief of the trial section of the war crimes branch. Jaworski personally tried two war crimes cases and left the army in 1945 with the rank of colonel.

In 1963 President Lyndon Johnson appointed Jaworski to positions on the President's Commission on the Causes and Prevention of Violence, the International Center for Settlement of Investment Disputes, and the International Court of Arbitration. Besides these appointments, Jaworski served as president of the American College of Trial Lawyers (1961–62), the State Bar of Texas (1962–63), and the American Bar Association (1971–72).

Jaworski's most significant appointment was as special prosecutor of the Watergate scandal, which began during the presidential election when Republican operatives broke into the Democratic campaign headquarters in the Watergate complex in Washington, D.C. Because the burglars were associated with the White House, questions were raised concerning President RICHARD M. NIXON's exact involvement in this crime. Nixon named Jaworski as the replacement for Archibald Cox in 1973, as a result of the public outcry following Cox's dismissal during the Saturday Night Massacre. As special prosecutor, Jaworski argued the case of *UNITED STATES V. NIXON* before the U.S. SUPREME COURT in 1974. Jaworski won a unanimous decision, and forced the administration to release Oval Office tapes in which Nixon's conversations had been taped by a White House recording system. The material on the tapes forced the resignation of the president and the conviction of several of his advisers. Jaworski's decision not to prosecute Nixon proved controversial, if not moot, given GERALD FORD's pardon of the former president. Jaworski maintained that Nixon could never receive a fair trial. Jaworski resigned as special prosecutor on October 25, 1974, and never argued another case after *United States v. Nixon*. In 1977 Jaworski served as special counsel to the U.S. House of Representatives Committee on Standards of Official Conduct. In what was dubbed "KOREAGATE," he assembled cases of misconduct in an influence-buying scandal involving members of Congress.

Jaworski returned to Texas and reassumed his duties as a managing partner at his law firm, now known as Fulbright and Jaworski. He retired in 1981 and died of a heart attack at his ranch on December 9, 1982.

—John Korasick

Jews and Judaism

Judaism is one of the most ancient religions still practiced in the world today. It has survived despite centuries of persecution that has lasted into the 20th century. Modern Judaism has evolved from trends of earlier centuries and the subsequent Diaspora, the displacement of Jews from ancient Israel. After the Holocaust, perpetrated under the Nazi regime during World War II, Jews located in three major geographic locations, which together include more than three-fourths of the Jewish population: Israel, the Slavic region of the former Soviet Union, and the United States.

Twentieth-century Judaism consists of Orthodox, Reform, and Conservative branches. In the 19th century Judaism separated into Orthodox and Reform bodies. For Orthodox Jews, both the written law (Scriptures) and the oral laws (commentaries on the legal portions of the Scriptures) are authoritative and derived from God. For Reform Jews, the Scriptures are not authoritative in any absolute sense, but binding only in their ethical content. While Orthodox Jews maintain the traditional practices, Reform Jews perform only those rituals that they believe can promote and enhance a Jewish, God-oriented life. In 1999 leaders of American Reform Judaism reversed century-old teachings by encouraging, but not enforcing, the observance of many traditional rituals. The Conservative moment, or "historical school," which emerged in the 20th century, seeks to formulate a middle position between Orthodox and Reform Judaism, which maintains most of the traditional rituals, while recognizing the need to make changes in accordance with contemporary deliberation. Conservative Jews believe that the history of Judaism proves that tradition and change occur together, and that what is central to Judaism and has remained constant throughout the centuries is the people of Israel, not the fundamentalism of Orthodoxy. Related to the Conservative movement is the Reconstructionism of Mordechai M. Kaplan, who maintains that Judaism is a human-centered rather than a God-centered religion.

Their differences are in ritual practices, which shade from one group into the other. Common to all is the role of the rabbi, no longer solely a Talmudic scholar but an administrator, spiritual leader, pastor, and preacher. Although there was some cooperation among the three major Jewish denominations—Orthodox, Reform, and Conservative—the real effort of organized Judaism in America in the late 20th century revolved around the individual synagogue and the branch to which it belonged.

Just as the Civil Rights movement led by Martin Luther King, Jr., marked a turning point in the civil rights history of AFRICAN AMERICANS and contributed to a sense of national pride, the Six-Day and Yom Kippur Wars, in which Israel defeated combined Arab armies, marked a turning point in the Jewish sense of self. There was a sharp rise in interest and pride in the embattled Jewish state of Israel that carried over to American Jewish culture generally. Of additionally political historical significance is the Democratic nomination of Senator Joseph Lieberman of Connecticut as vice presidential candidate in the 2000 election, the first Jew to be so nominated.

Jews followed the American norm, affiliating in greater numbers with synagogues, though often for ethnic or social, rather than religious, reasons. Although Jews constitute only a small fraction of the population of the United States (2 percent of the overall 1993 U.S. population), Judaism occupies a role far surpassing its numerical importance and is regarded, with Protestantism and Roman Catholicism, as one of the major American faiths.

See also RELIGION.

Further reading: J. L. Blau, *Modern Varieties of Judaism* (New York: Columbia University Press, 1966); A. Eisen, *The Chosen People in America* (New York: Dimensions, 1983); R. Seltzer, *Jewish People, Jewish Thought* (New York: Dimensions, 1980); Jack Wertheimer, *A People Divided: Judaism in Contemporary America* (New York: Basic Books, 1993).

—Michele Rutledge

Judicial Watch

Judicial Watch is a nonpartisan, nonprofit public interest foundation dedicated to "reforming the legal and judicial systems and fighting government corruption." It was established in 1994 by chairman and general counsel Larry Klayman, whose previous experience included 22 years as a trial attorney specializing in international trade. Though proclaiming itself nonpartisan, Judicial Watch promotes its mission as a conservative counterpoint to the American Civil Liberties Union (ACLU). Relying heavily on the Freedom of Information Act (FOIA), Judicial Watch typically makes requests of federal agencies for information related to instances where government corruption is suspected, and sues if its requests are denied.

Judicial Watch first received national attention in 1996 during its investigation into allegations that Commerce Secretary Ron Brown traded seats on overseas missions in exchange for major donations to the Democratic Party.

Brown was exonerated from these charges. In looking at fund-raising activities by the Clinton administration, Klayman subpoenaed Democratic fund-raiser John Huang just days before the 1996 presidential election, and eventually filed 11 civil lawsuits against President WILLIAM J. CLINTON's administration, relating to alleged misconduct in CAMPAIGN FINANCE.

In addition, Judicial Watch filed more than 50 lawsuits during Clinton's presidency, including cases related to "Filegate," when the White House accessed FBI files of former Republican employees; "Travelgate," when the White House retaliated against former travel office employees after an embarrassing gaffe; and allegations that the White House used the Internal Revenue Service (IRS) to engage in politically motivated tax audits. Judicial Watch also filed suits on behalf of several plaintiffs in sexual harassment suits against President Clinton, including those involving Paula Jones, Gennifer Flowers, and Juanita Broaddrick. In addition, the foundation directed several suits against Attorney General JANET RENO, for her failure to appoint INDEPENDENT COUNSELs to investigate numerous allegations of campaign finance corruption. Reno and others in the Justice Department were also sued for their role in the forcible removal of the Cuban boy, Elián Gonzáles, from the Miami home of his uncle in April 2000. Many of these suits, however, did not reach trial.

Judicial Watch has received considerable criticism for its aggressive use of pretrial rules of discovery, including lengthy depositions involving a wide range of questions, which critics decry as partisan "fishing expeditions" and a means of raising money for the organization. Judicial Watch continued to maintain a presence, even after President Clinton left office. In 2001 it conducted its own ballot inspection and recount in 67 Florida counties involved in the dispute over the 2000 Presidential election between Texas governor GEORGE W. BUSH and Vice President ALBERT GORE, JR.

The combative tactics by Judicial Watch, along with its aggressive fund-raising, has led to charges of partisanship and complaints by Democrats that this organization shows that "Clinton-haters" undertook a campaign to harass the administration at any cost. Supporters of Judicial Watch claim that these activities helped lead to Clinton's impeachment and revealed the Lewinsky scandal.

—Aharon W. Zorea

K

Kemp, Jack F. (1935–)

Born on July 13, 1935, in Los Angeles, California, Jack French Kemp became a professional football player and then went on to serve in Congress from 1971 to 1989. He became a leading proponent within the Republican Party for supply-side and free-market economics. He was selected by ROBERT DOLE as his vice presidential running mate in an unsuccessful campaign to defeat incumbent WILLIAM J. CLINTON in 1996.

Kemp graduated from Occidental College in 1957 and then enlisted in the U.S. Army Reserves from 1958–62 (active duty, 1958). He became a professional football player for 13 years. He was captain of the San Diego Chargers from 1960 to 1962 and also was captain of the Buffalo Bills, which he led to the American League championship in 1964 and 1965. He cofounded the American Football League Players Association, which elected him president five times. Following his football career he served as special assistant to California governor RONALD W. REAGAN in 1967 and then served on the staff of the Republican National Committee in 1969.

In 1970 former professional football quarterback Jack Kemp won a congressional seat representing suburban Buffalo, New York. The self-described conservative Republican held the seat for nine years and became known for his support of the VIETNAM WAR, increased defense spending, supply-side economics, and civil rights initiatives. Kemp questioned arms control agreements, such as the STRATEGIC ARMS LIMITATION TREATIES with the SOVIET UNION during the COLD WAR. He opposed school busing, federal subsidizing for abortions, increased aid to urban mass transit, strip-mining controls, and the creation of a consumer protection agency. In the 1970s Kemp was best known for his tax reform strategies, described in detail in his 1979 book, *An American Renaissance; A Strategy for the 1980s.*

Kemp sought the Republican nomination for president in 1988, but Vice President GEORGE H. W. BUSH prevailed. After Bush won the presidency, he named Kemp to head the Department of Housing and Urban Development (HUD). Kemp received bipartisan praise for his efforts at HUD. In 1996 Kemp was Robert Dole's running mate on the Republican presidential ticket, where Kemp's reputation as an advocate for programs supporting minorities and the poor made him a valuable addition, but the Democratic incumbents Clinton and ALBERT GORE, JR., once again claimed the White House. After the election, critics within the Republican Party concluded that the Dole-Kemp ticket was lackluster.

In 1993, with WILLIAM J. BENNETT and former UN ambassador Jeane Kirkpatrick, he cofounded Empower America, a conservative organization whose stated mission is to promote democratic capitalism and economic growth and through freedom and individual responsibility.

—Leah Blakey

Kennedy, Edward M. (Teddy) (1932–)

Senator Edward Moore Kennedy (D-Mass.) has had a long, active career in the U.S. SENATE, having been elected to this body in 1962. Ted Kennedy was born February 22, 1932, in Brookline, Massachusetts, the son of millionaire Joseph P. Kennedy and the youngest brother of John F. Kennedy and Robert Kennedy. After attending private schools, he received his college education at Harvard University and his law degree from University of Virginia in 1959. In 1960 he served as assistant district attorney to Suffolk County in Massachusetts, until 1962, when he was elected to the U.S. Senate to fill the unexpired term of his brother John F. Kennedy, who had become U.S. president.

Reelected in 1964, Kennedy gained the respect of his colleagues for well-researched promotion of social issues. With the escalation with the war in Vietnam, Kennedy became a leading dove. He worked to abolish the military draft and to aid the hundreds of thousands of refugees created by the war. Kennedy pressured the RICHARD M. NIXON administration to halt the bombing of North Vietnam and to withdraw the American forces. In 1969 he was elected by his colleagues as Senate majority leader. Many considered him the frontrunner for the U.S. presidency in 1972. A car accident in July 1969, in Chappaquiddick, Massachusetts, changed the trajectory of Kennedy's career. The accident occurred when Kennedy drove his car off a narrow bridge on Chappaquiddick Island, Massachusetts, and his only passenger, Mary Jo Kopechne, a staff member, drowned. Kennedy delayed reporting the accident for nine hours. Later, Kennedy was found guilty of leaving the scene of the accident, received a two-month suspended sentence, and lost his driver's license.

In 1971 ROBERT BYRD (D-W.V.) defeated him for Senate majority whip. In 1972 Kennedy asked his constituents if they wanted him to remain in office, and he received an overwhelming show of support. Despite the loyalty of locals, the Chappaquiddick incident plagued his national campaigns. He made a bid for the Democratic nomination in 1976, but withdrew from the race in 1974. In 1980 he challenged incumbent president JAMES EARL CARTER, JR., for the Democratic Party nomination, but ultimately failed his presidential bid.

In the 1970s Kennedy focused on a range of issues, including becoming a leading advocate of airline deregulation and sponsor of the Health Maintenance Organization Act of 1973. In the 1980s he became a leading critic of many of Reagan's initiatives—the defense build-up, Strategic Defense Initiative, cuts in children and mother welfare programs, and other reductions in social spending. In the 1990s he sponsored bills on IMMIGRATION, criminal code reform, fair housing, public education, health care, and AIDS research. He was instrumental in the enactment of the Insurance Portability and Accountability Act of 1997, which made it easier for employees to take their insurance plans to new jobs; and the Children's Health Act of 1997, which allowed broader medical coverage for children in all 50 states. On the Senate Judiciary Committee, he upheld liberal positions on ABORTION, CAPITAL PUNISHMENT, and racial busing. Among his most noted initiatives were crime reduction, labor laws, environmental protection, and the minimum wage. He has been a strong advocate of a national health system.

His activities in FOREIGN POLICY include warning Great Britain regarding their policies in Northern Ireland, condemning Pakistan for practicing genocide in Bangladesh, and meeting with Brezhnev privately in the SOVIET UNION in 1974.

Under the GEORGE W. BUSH administration, which came into office in 2000, Kennedy has worked closely with the White House for a Patients' Bill of Rights Act (2001) and education reform. Kennedy is currently the senior Democrat on the Labor and Human Resources Committee

and the Immigration Subcommittee. He is also a member of the Congressional Friends of Ireland and the Senate Arms Control Observer Group.

—Leah Blakey

Kent State University (protests at)

On April 30, 1970, President RICHARD M. NIXON announced to the American people that U.S. combat forces had launched an "incursion" into neutral Cambodia, in an effort to block North Vietnamese supply lines into South Vietnam. Nixon's announcement caused a storm of protest on college campuses throughout the country, but at Kent State University in Ohio, the four-day-long protests escalated into confrontation between students and the Ohio National Guard that resulted in the deaths of four students and injuries to nine others on May 4, 1970.

The National Guard, which had been ordered to Kent State University by Governor James Rhodes, resolved to disperse any assembly. As noon approached, a crowd of protesters and onlookers had grown to an estimated 1,500 people. Ohio's assistant adjutant general, Robert Canterbury, ordered the assembled students to disperse immediately. Students responded with taunts and chants. When the students refused, General Canterbury ordered the guardsmen to disband them. Approximately 116 men, equipped with loaded M-1 rifles and tear gas, formed a skirmish line toward the students. The guard advanced, firing tear gas and scattering the students into a wider area. Some students responded to the attack by throwing stones, and guardsmen also threw stones at the students; because of the distance, most stones from both parties fell far short of their targets. After most of the crowd dispersed, the guard appeared to retreat. Many students assumed the confrontation was over and began to walk to their next classes. As the guard reached the crest of the hill near a practice field, approximately 12 members of Troop G simultaneously turned around, aimed, and fired their weapons into the crowd in the Prentice Hall parking lot. (In 1975, civil trials proved that there was a verbal command to fire.) A total of 67 shots were fired in 13 seconds, killing four students and wounding nine others. The Kent State shootings sparked further demonstrations across the country, and only when Nixon withdrew American troops from Cambodia did the demonstrations subside.

See also ANTIWAR MOVEMENT—VIETNAM; JACKSON STATE; NIXON, RICHARD M.

—Michele Rutledge

Kissinger, Henry A. (1923–)

While acting as National Security Advisor and secretary of state in the 1970s, Henry Alfred Kissinger brought a new vision of international affairs to American foreign relations. Born Heinz Alfred Kissinger on May 27, 1923, in Fürth, Germany, Kissinger was the son of a local schoolteacher, Louis, and his wife, Paula Kissinger. The Kissingers were Jews, and soon after the Nazi Party came into power in Germany in 1933, Louis lost his teaching position, and Kissinger was obliged to attend a Jewish school. In 1938 the family left Germany for New York. Kissinger established himself as a superior student. After a year of high school in 1938, Kissinger was forced to take a job and attend school at night to help support his family. In 1942 Kissinger graduated from high school and entered the City College of New York to study accounting. After a year at City College, Kissinger was drafted into the United States Army.

Kissinger soon found himself attached to the 84th Infantry Division. A fellow German émigré, Fritz Kraemer, arranged to have Kissinger attached to U.S. Army intelligence as a driver and translator. In the following months, Kissinger became an administrator over occupied German towns, entered counterintelligence, taught at a military intelligence school, and entered Harvard University. In 1943, the year he was drafted, Kissinger had become a naturalized citizen.

Kissinger entered Harvard in 1947 as a sophomore and quickly gained a reputation as an outstanding student. He earned a B.A., M.A., and Ph.D. from Harvard before joining the faculty in 1954. During these years, Kissinger developed relationships with many future world leaders as the founder and director of the Harvard International Seminar. His *Nuclear Weapons and Foreign Policy* (1957), commissioned by the Council on Foreign Relations to study the concept of nuclear massive retaliation, became a surprise best-seller. Kissinger criticized the concept as a viable foundation for American foreign policy. He asserted that power politics is a constant, ongoing process that is sometimes peaceful and sometimes not. Permanent security, he argued, could never be achieved.

This study brought Kissinger to the attention of Nelson Rockefeller, governor of New York and a presidential aspirant. When Rockefeller ran for the Republican nomination in 1960, Kissinger was his main foreign policy adviser. Though Rockefeller lost the primary to RICHARD M. NIXON, Kissinger acted as an unofficial adviser to both President John F. Kennedy and President Lyndon Johnson.

During the presidential campaign of 1968, Kissinger acted briefly as an adviser to Nelson Rockefeller, before shifting his allegiance to Democratic candidate Hubert Humphrey. He then joined the Nixon campaign. Shortly after being sworn in as president, Nixon reorganized FOREIGN POLICY under the authority of his National Security Council, rather than the State Department, and appointed Kissinger as his National Security Advisor, which provided him with increased legitimacy in the eyes of many.

Secretary of State Henry Kissinger *(Library of Congress)*

Kissinger had impressive ties with the eastern wing of the Republican Party and academics, who remembered Nixon as a red-baiting congressman from the 1940s. The selection was surprising, because Kissinger and Nixon were virtual strangers, and Kissinger had supported candidates opposing Nixon.

Kissinger believed that the United States was suffering from a "crisis of power." He identified four areas in which American power had eroded since the end of World War II: nuclear arms power, economic power, international reputation, and domestic order. Kissinger's foreign policy was designed to bolster American strength in all these areas.

Kissinger also believed that the world lacked a stable order, and designed American foreign policy to try to establish such an order. For Kissinger, "order" did not necessarily mean "peace." Considering competition among nations natural, Kissinger regarded peace as an aberration because peace is at the mercy of any aggressive nation. For there to be order, he argued, there must be generally accepted rules of international conduct. Kissinger accordingly redefined U.S. national interest: The United States would no longer make the entire world vital to its security and would devise nonmilitary responses. The United States would no longer concern itself with foreign internal politics; it would work with nations pursuing similar international goals. The ideology of foreign countries would no longer be a vital factor in determining American national interest. In the old view, China had been part of the ideological problem of communism. In the new view, China became part of the solution to containing Soviet expansion. This same thinking led to renewed American partnerships with dictatorial regimes around the world. This focus on order led to arms control agreements with the Soviet Union, the Strategic Arms Limitation Treaty I, and the ANTI-BALLISTIC MISSILE TREATY in 1972.

In addition to arms control and the renewed relations with China, Kissinger negotiated the American withdrawal from Vietnam (he won a Nobel Peace Prize for his work), and a cease-fire between Israel and the Arab nations.

Kissinger became secretary of state in 1973, the first foreign-born person to hold the office. He remained in this position after GERALD R. FORD replaced Nixon as president. Kissinger came under increasing attack from members of Congress who charged that the SOVIET UNION was forging ahead of the United States militarily. At the end of Ford's presidency, Kissinger left the government and established the consulting firm Kissinger Associates. Since leaving government service, he has acted as an unofficial adviser to presidents, and as a pundit in print and television, and has written his memoirs and numerous books on diplomacy and international relations.

Further reading: Seymour Hersh, *The Price of Power: Kissinger in the Nixon White House* (New York: Summit, 1983); Walter Isaacson, *Kissinger: A Biography* (New York: Simon & Schuster, 1992); Henry Kissinger, *White House Years* (Boston: Little Brown & Company, 1979); ———, *Diplomacy* (New York: Touchstone, 1994).

—John Korasick

Koreagate

"Koreagate" was the name given to an influence-peddling scandal that came to light in 1977 between the South Korean Central Intelligence Agency (KCIA) and a number of American congressmen. The United States was committed to protecting the Republic of Korea (ROK), in South Korea, from North Korean aggression after the Korean War (1950–53). By the early 1970s, however, relations between Seoul and Washington, D.C., had begun to sour. In 1971 President RICHARD M. NIXON announced plans to withdraw one of the two divisions of American troops stationed in South Korea, and in 1972 ROK president Park Chung Hee began instituting authoritarian measures. In 1976, in an effort to relieve these growing tensions, the KCIA spent millions of dollars to fund a scheme they called "Intrepid." The primary goal was to reverse President Nixon's decision to withdraw American troops, and secondarily to smooth over general relations between the two countries.

The Intrepid plan involved inviting prominent American journalists to South Korea in order to "convert" them, and then sending them back to the United States to gather intelligence on sensitive high-level policies. At the same time, former ambassador Kim Dong-Jo worked with the flamboyant rice importer, Park Tong Sun, to peddle influence directly to American congressmen. Tong Sun became known for his lavish parties at his Georgetown home, where congressmen receiving anything from free trips and gifts to outright bribes.

The plan backfired when news of the influence peddling broke just before the 1976 election. The new president, JAMES EARL CARTER, JR., had campaigned on a promise to gradually withdraw the remaining division from South Korea, and news of the scandal further solidified that position. As promised, President Carter began withdrawing troops December 13, 1977, though he later suspended the withdrawal on June 29, 1979, after a three-day conference in Seoul with ROK president Park. In 1978 congressional investigations made by the Ethics Committee and the House Subcommittee on International Relation revealed that as many as 115 congressmen were implicated in the scheme, including the Speaker of the House, THOMAS O'NEILL (D-Mass.). Despite the widespread press coverage, the scandal gradually faded from the public view during Carter's term.

Carter later revisited the issue of U.S. troop commitments in South Korea, and on June 29, 1979, he suspended the withdrawal. The extent of American support was demonstrated four months later after President Park's assassination; American troops went on a DEFCON alert, and President Carter sent a powerful naval force into the Korean straits to prevent North Korea from taking any undue advantage of South Korea's temporary instability.

—Aharon W. Zorea

Kosovo

In 1995, Kosovo, an autonomous province of Yugoslavia, attracted world attention when ethnic conflict between Serbs and Albanians erupted, leading Yugoslavian president Slobodan Milosevic to intensify military operations against Albanian rebels. When an agreement brokered by President WILLIAM J. CLINTON failed to be honored by Milosevic, the United States, acting through NATO, launched a massive bombing campaign to prevent Milosevic from conducting "ethnic cleansing" against the Albanians. American intervention in Kosovo reflected a new role for the United States in the postwar world.

Slobodan Milosevic had come to power after Yugoslav leader Marshal Tito, who had presided over the country since World War II, died in 1980. Under Tito, the Kosovo region had been granted equal standing with other Yugoslavian states. With the collapse of communism in eastern and central Europe, Yugoslavia began to come apart, as various ethnic minorities called for independence in Croatia, Bosnia, and Kosovo. In 1981 ethnic Albanian students rioted in Pristina, the capital of Kosovo, demanding independence, and sparking a national movement. As tensions rose in Kosovo, Slobodan Milosevic sought to rally Serbian nationalists in Kosovo against the Albanians. In 1989 Milosevic revoked the autonomy that Tito had granted to Kosovo. At the same time, Milosevic imposed a police state that kept Serbs in control of all institutions and stripped Albanians of all power. He also expelled Albanians from universities, medical institutions, and schools. Ibrahim Rugova, an ethnic Albanian political leader, responded by creating a parallel system for Albanians in Kosovo, providing clinics, schools, and a university in Pristina.

By 1995 Albanian rebels had organized a guerrilla movement, operating under the auspices of the Kosovo Liberation Army (KLA). As fighting intensified between the KLA and Milosevic's Yugoslav army, the war spread to the civilian population. More than 200,000 ethnic Albanians, many of them women and children, took refuge in the hills near Kosovo. With the threat of war spreading to other Balkan countries, the international community sought to resolve the conflict.

In spring 1999 the Serbs once again attacked the Albanian population in Kosovo. NATO responded with a bombing campaign in March 1999, with the goal of protecting the ethnic Albanian population. In June 1999 NATO halted its bombing campaign in exchange for an agreement of Serb withdrawal from Kosovo, of the return of Albanian refugees, and the installation of a NATO-led multinational peacekeeping force in Kosovo. On June 20, 1999, the last of the 40,000 Serbian forces left Kosovo just before NATO's deadline for withdrawal. In the summer of 2001 the United Nations Court formally charged Slobodan Milosevic with crimes against humanity. Nonetheless, ethnic tensions continued in the region as ethnic Albanian nationalists unleashed violence against Serbian civilians in Kosovo and invaded the neighboring country of Macedonia, claiming part of the territory for Greater Albania.

See also FOREIGN POLICY.

Further reading: Miron Rezun, *Europe's Nightmare: The Struggle for Kosovo* (Westport, Conn.: Praeger, 2001).

—Leah Blakey

L

labor

After the 1955 merger of America's two largest labor unions, the American Federation of Labor (AFL) and the Congress of Industrial Organizations (CIO), organized labor's power was solidified. In the 1960s it called itself the "people's lobby," and lobbied for social causes like the Civil Rights Act and minimum wage and local labor laws. In 1970 its reach was still wide, with 25.7 percent of American workers belonging to a union. But by 1980, only 23 percent belonged to unions; in 1990, membership had dropped to 16.1 percent; in 2000, it was 13.5 percent. Forces behind this decline are complex, and involve many disparate elements, including technological advances that reduce need for employees, corporate relocation, the rise of a largely nonunionized service economy; and questions about the purpose of unions in a postindustrial global economy. How organized labor addresses these concerns will determine its role in the 21st century.

During the 1970s, internal upheaval and external social and government actions combined to erode organized labor's influence for the rest of the century. In 1970 came the death of Walter Reuther, the highly regarded, moderate, and powerful leader of the United Auto Workers (UAW) and head of the Congress of Industrial Organizations (CIO). Reuther was replaced by his partner in the union of the AFL and CIO, George Meany, a more inflammatory presence who mirrored the decade in labor relations.

During the early 1970s, many unions voiced protest through militancy and wildcat strikes: in 1974 alone there were 424 work stoppages, involving 1.8 million workers. Accounting for some strikes were public-sector union employees, whose rights were broadened in the 1960s by federal and local laws, and whose union representation tripled to 39 percent between 1960 and 1976. One public-sector strike, the 15-state-wide U.S. postal carriers strike in 1970, was the largest wildcat strike in U.S. history and resulted in 14 percent wage increases. Large-scale private-sector walkouts were held at General Motors and General Electric, among other companies.

While some strikes, such as the mail carriers' strike, were supported by the public, nonunion members came to view the increasing number of strikes as a reflection of union self-interest. This public mistrust was exacerbated by the high life and salaries of top union leaders and the high-profile criminal investigation of Teamsters leader Jimmy Hoffa.

At the same time, many union workers viewed George Meany's leadership as outdated. Meany supporters disagreed, causing widespread labor unrest. This dissent would help to weaken the union-supported Democratic Party, resulting in party defections and the 1968 election of Republican RICHARD M. NIXON. Upon Meany's death in 1979, Lane Kirkland was named head of the AFL-CIO. In the 1980s Kirkland took a diplomatic approach to mending fences within organized labor and countering antiunion forces.

One such force was the decreasing number of union-represented jobs. While major service industries and public-sector professions such as transportation workers, teachers, and the police were highly unionized, older sources of membership declined. Among them were construction, manufacturing, and mining trades, some of which were already facing downsizing through the introduction of labor-saving robots. Particularly on assembly lines, robots were successful in streamlining operations and reducing payrolls.

In the early 1980s union membership in the United States declined to its lowest level since the early 1930s. One reason was the lack of union funds devoted to recruiting new members: for the past two decades, only about 3 percent of union budgets were devoted to recruitment. Another problem was the ineffectiveness of union public relations. Unable to present their goals as being common to all workers, unions were instead seen as intrusive in or irrelevant to the workplace. Crystallizing these public views

Union members hold up signs at a rally against a trade agreement with China on Capitol Hill in Washington, D.C. (Elderfield/Liaison)

was the 1981 Professional Air Traffic Controllers Association (PATCO) strike.

In early August 1981 the 11,300 PATCO federal air traffic controllers voiced displeasure with their treatment by the Federal Aviation Administration (FAA), which ran the air-control towers, and staged a nationwide walkout. Among PATCO's grievances were long hours, persistent understaffing, and relatively low pay. President RONALD W. REAGAN declared the strike illegal, given their position as federal employees, and fired the controllers. The strike soon ended, nonunionized replacement controllers were hired, and in 1982 PATCO went bankrupt. Throughout the strike, some of the U.S. public supported the government's actions, which set the stage for future decades of private-sector strikebreaking. Over the next two decades, strikes were broken at Maytag, Greyhound Bus (both 1983); Continental Airlines (1984); Hormel and the *Chicago Tribune* (1985); TWA and Boise Cascade (1986); International Paper (1987); Eastern Airlines (1989); the *New York Daily News* (1990); and Caterpillar (1992); among others. As a result of these strikes, some 300,000 strikers, during the

1980s, lost their jobs to replacement workers. In light of the power shift from workers to employers, strikes decreased dramatically, from approximately 290 per year during the 1970s to approximately 35 during the 1990s. Additionally, beginning in 1979 and continuing into the mid-1990s, workers' real hourly wages decreased.

Another reason for decreased union membership was the growth of the international marketplace, which decreased demand for domestic goods and workers. Since the 1950s, the United States had been losing ground in manufacturing, and by the 1980s, countries such as Germany and Japan dominated markets for products including automobiles and electronics. International events also affected the labor market, particularly the unrest in the Middle East and actions of the Organization of Petroleum Exporting Countries (OPEC) that led to higher oil prices. As oil prices rose in the 1970s, demand for American-made cars with poor gas mileage decreased, which in turn eliminated jobs in the automotive industry.

Workers in the 1980s and 1990s also found their jobs jeopardized by corporate resettlement. To reduce overall operating costs, domestic manufacturing plants originally located in the Northeast and Southeast were relocated to less union-friendly southern and southwestern United States. Even more damaging to U.S. workers was the corporate employment shift abroad. In countries such as China, Mexico, India, or Hong Kong, workers were employed for dollars per day in manufacturing and specialized computer jobs, effectively eliminating thousands of U.S. union positions.

Another factor affecting the decline in union membership was the decades-long shift from a manufacturing to a nonunionized service economy. Continuing the shift that began in the 1970s, service industry jobs in the 1980s grew at a higher rate than jobs in basic industries, such as construction. Generally, appetite for union memberships in these previously nonunionized service professions, from fast-food worker to bank employee, is limited, in part because of the jobs' high turnover rates.

During this period, employers were also more active than they had been for decades in trying to keep companies from unionizing. Such efforts included promises to match union-level salaries if employees would remain ununionized. More aggressive tactics included antiunion campaigns aimed at convincing workers not to unionize; such "union avoidance" plans bloomed after the success of the PATCO strike, with corporations hiring over 7,000 law and planning specialists to persuade workers not to unionize.

The antiunion movement was complicated by the less-than-active union support from the National Labor Relations Board (NLRB). Months-long delays in ruling on illegal firings and demands for reinstatement left potential union organizers wary. Plans to streamline the NLRB and prohibit permanent replacements stalled in the House and Senate in the 1970s and 1990s.

Other antiunion government trends of the era include the deregulation of the airline and trucking industries in the 1970s; and the passage of the North American Free Trade Agreement (NAFTA) in 1993, which was strenuously fought by unions.

In 1995 John Sweeney, leader of the Service Employees International Union (SEIU), became leader of the AFL-CIO and declared the end of the postwar labor era. Sweeney then called to rebuild union strength by devoting more attention to organizing, a practice that proved fruitful in the United Steel Workers (USW) grassroots campaign against unfair labor practices at Bridgestone/Firestone in the mid-1990s, after an earlier strike had failed. Sweeney also called for developing new union procedures and bargaining strategies, to meet the needs of a more varied 21st-century workforce that included part-time and professional workers, and often, a more cooperative, less adversarial management. For example, unions would need to adapt to

represent autonomous professionals, such as doctors or engineers, now pressured by health-care conglomerates or public bureaucracies.

While manufacturing jobs and related union membership has declined over the past three decades, organized labor has experienced gains in areas of occupational growth, such as white-collar professions and the health-care industry. Union membership has increased substantially in many government-related professions, such as public school teaching, as well as private-sector arenas, such as health care, professional sports (players and nonplayers alike), and the arts. Among arts professionals now widely represented are members of ballet and opera companies, and symphony orchestras, specialized film professionals such as cinematographers and film editors, and musicians and studio engineers. University-based clerical and technical workers also improved wages and benefits or have become unionized during the 1980s and 1990s, often through grassroots initiatives that involved student or faculty support.

Despite years of government-related union setbacks and membership levels, the union remains a fixture in the American workplace. As of now, the union's collective bargaining power still delivers a higher paycheck: In 2000, the median weekly earnings for a nonunion person employed in a full-time job was $542; for a union member, it was $691.

For the future, however, U.S. labor is looking outward to the international community of workers. Just as corporations are making global business alliances, some labor leaders point to the need for global worker alliances to protect workers' rights. As AFL-CIO president John Sweeney told Mexican labor union members in 1998, "We want to . . . find practical ways to work together by seeking and developing coordinated cross-border organizing and bargaining strategies."

Further reading: Steve Babson, *The Unfinished Struggle: Turning Points in American Labor, 1877–Present* (Lanham, Md.: Rowman & Littlefield Publishers, 1999); John J. Flagler, *The Labor Movement in the United States.* (Minneapolis, Minn.: Lerner Publications, 1990); Nelson Lichtenstein et al., *Who Built America? Working People and the Nation's Economy, Politics, Culture & Society,* Vol. 2, *From the Gilded Age to the Present* (New York: Pantheon, 1992).

—Melinda Corey

Laffer curve

The Laffer curve is an economic model on the relationship between tax rates and revenue proposed by the economist Arthur Betz Laffer in 1974. Laffer had received an undergraduate degree at Yale University and a doctorate in international economics from Stanford University. He had served as chief economist for the Office of Management and Budget (1970–72). He attracted attention for supply-side economic theories that held reductions in federal taxes on business and individuals would lead to increased economic growth and ultimately increase government revenue. This model was highly influential among conservative policymakers and economists and was instrumental in the formation of RONALD W. REAGAN's tax policies in the 1980s.

Laffer developed what became known as the Laffer Curve, which showed that, starting from a zero tax increase, increases in tax rates will raise the government's tax revenue to the point at which, when rates become high enough, further increases in tax rates will decrease revenue, because such high rates create disincentives against earning more income. In other words, increased tax rates would discourage investment and act as a disincentive to enterprise, therefore leading to a reduction in government revenue. Laffer's model suggested a level of tax rates at which tax revenue could be maximized, and was illustrated graphically by the curve, whose peak marked an optimum balance between tax rates and government revenue.

Although Laffer was the first economist to emphasize its possible application to the U.S. income tax system, his main points were well known to public finance economists. His theory provoked controversy about where the American economy in 1981 should be located on the Laffer curve. He believed that conditions were right for cuts in tax rates, and this would lead to increased government revenues.

This model was attractive to conservative politicians in the 1970s and 1980s, as it underscored fiscal policies of lowering tax rates to stimulate the economy. The Laffer curve gave a theoretical basis for Reagan's 1981 economic plan, which called for cuts in marginal tax rates. Laffer served as an economic consultant to the U.S. Treasury and Defense Departments between 1972 and 1977, and as an economic adviser to President Reagan.

The effectiveness of Laffer's model created considerable criticism. President Reagan reduced tax rates significantly in 1981, and although an economic expansion occurred, there was a substantial increase in the budget deficit. Following the tax cuts, however, actual government revenue was less than had been projected. Supporters of the Laffer curve point to external economic pressures, especially in increased government spending for defense, as well as other areas, while critics argue that the Laffer curve has proven to be discredited.

See also ECONOMY; REAGANOMICS.

—Stephen Hardman

Latin America (U.S. relations with)

The complex relationship between Latin America and the United States began officially in 1823, with the assertion by President James Monroe of U.S. hegemony in the Western Hemisphere through the Monroe Doctrine. From the later 19th century to World War I (1914–18), U.S. influence increased southward through economic investments, military engagements, and hemispheric alliances. The First Pan-American Conference was held in 1889 in Washington, D.C., and from this emerged what would become the Organization of American States (OAS) in 1948. U.S. policies in the late 19th and early 20th centuries were supported by "gunboat" diplomacy and dollar democracies that served to protect growing U.S. investments and collect Latin American debts.

In Rio de Janeiro, Brazil, the 1947 Inter-American Treaty of Reciprocal Assistance was drafted. This treaty constituted the Latin American equivalent of the Truman Doctrine in Europe. The pact asserted that an attack by any state against an American state was considered an attack on all American states and would be countered by the assistance of the other American states. The Rio Pact circumvented the UNITED NATIONS and provided impetus for later U.S. covert and overt interventions against reformist democracies during the COLD WAR, in the name of combating communist aggression.

The VIETNAM WAR and the revolution in Cuba that brought Fidel Castro to power had a profound effect upon U.S. policymakers in Latin America during the 1960s and throughout the cold war. President John F. Kennedy's Alliance for Progress, which, among other things, promised increased U.S. economic aid on the condition that Latin American nations initiate land-reform programs, created a legacy that lasted until the end of the 20th century.

Lyndon Johnson continued Kennedy's Alliance and became determined to prevent the rise of any other Castros in the Western Hemisphere. The Johnson administration continued U.S. commitment to contain communism and was well aware of the political ramifications of the situation in Cuba. In the mid-1960s Johnson faced a crisis in PANAMA, when anti-American sentiment erupted into violence. In subsequent negotiations, the United States made a major concession that helped pave the way for the historic treaty of 1977 under President JAMES EARL CARTER, JR.

Named for its chair, Nelson Rockefeller, the *Rockefeller Report on the Americas* was released during the administration of RICHARD M. NIXON. The 1969 report asserted Latin American military forces to be the agents necessary to effect productive social change. It called for registering women to vote and preparing Latin America for limited democracy. The document indicated that direct U.S. investment in manufacturing industries had risen in the 1960s from one-fifth to one-third of all U.S. investments in Latin America. This began the era of the U.S.-based transnational corporation (TNC)—as well as growing criticism of these entities.

The Rockefeller Report called for regional implementation of policies articulated in the Nixon Doctrine and a Trilateral Commission Report. According to the Nixon Doctrine, the United States would share global police responsibilities with regional powers. The Trilateral Commission brought together political and business leaders from Japan, North America, and Western Europe to discuss and, where possible, coordinate long-range economic and governmental strategies. The economic recommendations of the report, which called for developing economic leadership in Latin America, were carried out through the expansion of the curriculum offered at the Inter-American Defense College, at Fort McNair in Washington, D.C., to include financial and industrial management in the Latin American officers' training.

Relations between the United States and Latin America, however, became strained when the United States supported a military coup against the socialist government of Salvador Allende in Chile in 1973. Later congressional investigations discovered that the Central Intelligence Agency had been involved in this coup against a democratically elected government. This involvement tarnished the image of the United States throughout Latin America.

The Linowitz Commission Report (named for its chair, Sol Linowitz) suggested a different perspective on U.S.–Latin American relations. Issued in 1976, the report highlighted a recent disclosure of U.S. involvement in human-rights violations by Latin American military regimes in the mid-1970s, and the detrimental effects those revelations were having on the United States. President Jimmy Carter resolutely followed the Linowitz Commission's recommendations. His administration brought together the Trilateralist advocacy of limited democracy with an emphasis on human rights. Carter directed U.S. policy toward his belief in global interdependence, and called on Americans not to succumb to unwarranted fear of communism. Carter successful negotiated a treaty with Panama to turn the Canal Zone over to Panamanian government control on December 31, 1999. The treaties indicated an effort in Washington to respond to the world of interdependence and Latin American nationalism, but they increased the American public's perception of Carter as weak and naïve. Moreover, the readiness of the president to transfer control to Panama implied to many observers a disengagement from Latin American affairs. It did not matter in opinion polls that the waterway had become practically obsolete and that American withdrawal was stretched out until the last day of the century.

The assumption of power by the Sandinista Front of National Liberation (FSLN), a guerrilla movement in NICARAGUA, posed yet another unwelcome challenge to the United States. In August 1978 the Sandinista Liberation Front, named after a 1930s revolutionary, overthrew the American-backed Anastasio Somoza regime. President Carter wanted to avoid the use of force and hesitated to counteract the instability within Nicaragua. In 1979 Carter proposed that the Organization of American States establish an alternative government and send a peacekeeping group, but only Argentina supported this. The OAS had taken this action in 1965 in the Dominican Republic, but this time the organization did not support the U.S. president.

The Sandinistas toppled the Somoza dictatorship, which had essentially been created and supported by the United States over many decades, although the United States had withdrawn its support of the regime shortly before its collapse. When RONALD W. REAGAN assumed the presidency in 1981, the United States moved to take direct action in Nicaragua and to strengthen the neighboring country of El Salvador, which was under extreme pressure from guerrillas supplied by Nicaragua and Cuba. The Reagan administration pressured Congress to lift its 1974 ban on police aid by requesting a $54 million police-training package for Central America, but Congress did not grant it because of its fear of human rights violations.

Also during the early 1980s, intelligence and satellite photos suggested that Cuba was building an airbase on the small island of GRENADA. This fell within striking distance of Venezuela's coastline and, in the COLD WAR context, was seen as a threat to U.S. security. Reagan's decision to invade the Caribbean island in 1983 demonstrated a new American willingness to use force.

HENRY A. KISSINGER was principal author of *The Kissinger Commission Report* (1984), a major political analysis of Latin America. The report maintained that the United States was seen as being associated with dictatorships in Latin America, which tarnished the U.S. international image.

Following this report, U.S. policy in Latin America sought to improve relations with its hemispheric neighbors by promoting democratic governments and free trade. Both President GEORGE H. W. BUSH's *Enterprise for the Americas Initiative*, backing free trade, privatization, and an eventual hemispheric common market, and President WILLIAM J. CLINTON's modified NORTH AMERICAN FREE TRADE AGREEMENT (NAFTA) used this approach.

Furthermore, the United States supported debt relief through government and U.S. bank loans when a number of Latin American countries, including Mexico and Brazil, faced a debt crisis. Policymakers understood that any long-term solution to debt problems would be found in Latin American governments imposing fiscal responsibility and economic development. In 1990 the Bush administration proposed a plan that called for bilateral free-trade negotiations and the establishment of a free-trade zone in the Americas. MEXICO had proposed such a free-trade agreement with the United States in the late 1980s. U.S. policymakers envisioned a Mexican arrangement as the initial step, to be followed by trade agreement with other countries. NAFTA resulted from this situation, but prompted American political concerns about environmental protection and labor conditions.

NAFTA went into effect in 1994. President WILLIAM J. CLINTON sought to advance hemispheric economic cooperation when he convened the 1995 Summit of the Americas in Miami. The meeting was called for the creation of a free-trade hemisphere to be established by 2005. Brazil created its own effective trading bloc, Mercado Comun del Sur tariff union (MERCOSUR) in 1995. MERCOSUR is comprised of Argentina, Brazil, Paraguay, Uruguay, and one year later, Chile. Bolivia also became an associate member of the South American bloc. MERCOSUR's success encouraged the revitalization of other trade groups. The long-term results may show not one Americas-wide organization, but eventually a number of competing groups.

In 1995 U.S. secretary of defense William Perry convened the first meeting of hemisphere defense ministers in Williamsburg, Virginia. The meeting emphasized Washington's desire for cooperative action in the Americas, except in the Caribbean basin, which the United States still considered vital to national security. The United States's continuing emphasis on political and security agreements, distinct from economic agreements, reemerged during the meeting. The American proposal to formulate a "Democratic Alliance for Cooperative Hemisphere Security" appeared to be a post–World War II and cold war–era version of the Good Neighbor policy.

Foreign policies of President GEORGE W. BUSH suggest a new direction of U.S. policy in Latin America. Mexican President Vicente Fox was the first official visited by the newly inaugurated Bush, and the stay was marked by promises to work with Mexico to build upon the 1994 NAFTA agreement, to review law enforcement policies on drug trafficking, and to police the U.S.–Mexican border in a way that ensures security and humane treatment of migrants.

See also CONTRAS; FOREIGN POLICY; IRAN-CONTRA AFFAIR; NORTH, OLIVER L.

Further reading: Robert A. Pastor, *Exiting the Whirlpool: U.S. Foreign Policy toward Latin America and the Caribbean* (Princeton, N.J.: Princeton University Press, 1992).

—Michele Rutledge

liberalism

Classical liberalism is a movement or philosophy that has as its objective the growth of individual freedom. Since the concepts of freedom or liberty vary in different historical eras, the specific agendas of liberalism have changed. The ultimate objective of liberalism, however, remains static, as does its characteristic belief not only in human rationality but also in essential human goodness. Liberalism assumes that individuals, having a rational intellect, have the ability to discern problems and solve them, and thus they can achieve systematic betterment in the human condition. Often opposed to liberalism is the doctrine of conservatism, which, in essence, maintains a belief in tradition and custom, while remaining suspicious of rapid change, human rationality, and centralized government.

In the early 20th century, theorists began to look to the state to prevent oppression and to advance the welfare of all individuals; the welfare state came into existence, and social reform became an accepted governmental role. Liberal thought came to accept the belief that society, through the state, should be responsible for providing the minimum conditions necessary for decent individual existence. This gained widespread acceptance in the United States during the depression of the 1930s and found expression in the New Deal of President Franklin Roosevelt. Unemployment insurance, minimum wage laws, and social security programs were all instituted as part of Roosevelt's adaptation of Keynesian economics, and remain today a large part of modern democratic government. Although most Americans appear to support such liberal programs as Social Security and an established minimum wage, there remained a strong antistatist impulse in the American political tradition that emphasized individual responsibility, community control, and shared power balanced between state and federal governments.

Although socialism promotes many similar liberal programs, liberalism does not support the socialist goal of complete equality prescribed by state control, and because it is rooted in the primacy of the individual, liberalism also resolutely opposes communism. In domestic politics, liberals have fought arbitrary power exercised over the individual by the state; restrictions that prevent people from rising out of a low social status; and barriers such as CENSORSHIP that limit free expression of opinion. In RELIGION, liberals have fought against attempts by religious pressure groups to influence public opinion and church interference in the affairs of the state. In economics, liberals have battled monopolies and mercantilist state measures that subject the economy to state control. Prevailing liberal goals in the United States include racial integration, the eradication of poverty, and sexual equality.

Modern liberalism accepts the idea that the principal function of the state is to protect the rights of the citizens.

These rights are often ascribed to nature and frequently affirmed in bills of rights, proclamations, declarations of the rights of man, petitions, and so on. Especially at the beginning of liberal movements, liberals are reformers, who go against customs, traditions, and entrenched institutions.

The word "liberal" is an ambiguous term. A classical liberal may believe in a minimalist state, and say that freedom is a matter for the individual alone, while the modern liberal believes that freedom is a concern of the state and that the state can and should be used as an instrument to advance freedom. In its extreme, classical liberalism tends toward minimum state involvement beyond protecting individual rights, the rule of law, and the nation's defense, while modern liberalism tends toward greater state intervention. In between lie innumerable gradations. As a consequence, the term "liberalism" is faced with great ambiguity. Nevertheless, liberalism has become identified with movements to change the social order through the further extension of individual and collective rights within a democracy.

Classical liberalism differs profoundly from modern-day American liberalism. Scholars have traced this change in liberalism to the Progressive Era, although a number of historians perceive a radical difference between the liberalism of the Progressive Era and liberalism in the second half of the century. These historians find the transformation of liberalism occurring in the 1960s and 1970s, as liberalism shifted from "opportunity liberalism" to "entitlement liberalism." Opportunity liberalism, as expressed in the New Deal, spoke of economic security using the rhetoric of opportunity and self-reliance. For example, Social Security was presented as a system that allowed individuals to save for their own retirement from funds that were earned by wage earners. In the 1960s, liberals such as Lyndon Johnson, some historians have argued, spoke in terms of the entitlement of economic security, medical care, work opportunities, and care for the aged and disabled. These "entitlements" were translated by liberals as "rights."

Critical to this transition from opportunity liberalism to entitlement liberalism was civil rights. Initially, the Civil Rights movement in post–World War II America focused primarily on "equal opportunity" and the end of racial segregation. The passage of the Civil Rights Act of 1964 made it unlawful to discriminate on the basis of race, age, national origins, religion, or gender. The Civil Rights Act of 1964, however, would provide a means of not only protecting equality under the law but of redressing social inequality imposed by years of discrimination. President Lyndon B. Johnson's 1965 Executive Order 11246 mandated that federal agencies actively "promote" employment of minorities. This program was strengthened in 1971 by President RICHARD M. NIXON's Revised Order No. 4, which

required government contractors to include AFFIRMATIVE ACTION programs that promoted minority hiring and included specific timetables by which specific goals of minority representation must be met. These guidelines not only affected all local and federal agencies and contractors but were also adopted by larger private corporations, which sought to demonstrate their tolerant culture. The goal was not simply to prohibit discrimination, but to promote preferential policies for minorities in employment, education, and other areas of society. From the 1970s through the 1990s, affirmative action guidelines have been used to promote greater equality for women, ethnic minorities, the physically challenged, and senior citizens, VIETNAM WAR veterans, the physically and mentally disabled, and homosexuals.

Following on the heels of the Civil Rights Act of 1964, President Johnson also launched a "war on poverty," aiming to bring about a "Great Society" in which the quality of life for all Americans was improved. As defined in his 1965 State of the Union address, Johnson's Great Society measures included Medicaid and Medicare, which extended health care benefits to the poor and elderly; direct federal aid to education and the arts; and the creation of the Department of Housing and Urban Development, which provided federal funding for public housing projects. The number of federally funded social programs rose from 45 in 1961 to 435.

The decades of the 1960s and 1970s gave rise to the so-called rights revolution. In the process, individual rights were translated into group and collective rights, as activists from various groups representing ethnic minorities, women, the aged, the disabled, homosexuals, and others argued that they were entitled to collective rights as distinct groups within society. Supporters of this "rights revolution" maintained that the extension of entitlement and the recognition of group rights represented the maturing of a democracy.

While the policies, programs, and court decisions that furthered this rights revolution enjoyed to varying degrees bipartisan support, entitlement liberalism became associated primarily with the Democratic Party. The rise of rights-based liberalism led liberals to take positions on a number of political, social, and cultural issues at times at odds with the majority of the American public, although not always. The Democratic Party's strong support of civil rights and affirmative action, even though many Republicans supported these policies as well, caused a wholesale desertion of white voters in the South and many white male voters in the North, thereby changing the political dynamics for both major parties. In addition, because liberals often supported civil rights and civil liberties issues such as ending prayer in school, gay rights, and reproductive rights, the Republican Party, especially as it moved to the right, was able to capture a political backlash, as many Americans felt that the rights revolution had gone too far and was undermining traditional morality and national identity in America.

Conservative critics argued that the rights revolution associated with entitlement liberalism had created a "cult of otherness," which envisioned a society made up of subgroups—African Americans, Hispanics, Asians, women, and homosexuals—who only identified with their own cultures and demanded collective rights to the detriment of individual rights and equal opportunity. Proponents of the rights revolution responded by arguing that American society needed to acknowledge and encourage existing diversity and to recognized that group rights enabled past injustices to be remedied.

Any resolution of this debate appeared to many to be intractable, yet underlying this apparent polarization was fundamental agreement by the majority of Americans on a range of issues, once only associated with modern liberalism: The vast majority of Americans accepted the end of racial segregation; most Americans accepted racial and gender equality; and most Americans accepted a greater role for the federal government in maintaining economic stability for the nation, and in ensuring the health, welfare, and education of the American people. Most of all, Americans remained an optimistic people, and while often skeptical of too much government interference in their daily lives, they continued to believe in the noble experiment, American democracy.

See also CONSERVATIVE MOVEMENT; LIBERTARIAN PARTY.

Further reading: A. Arblaster, *The Rise and Decline of Western Liberalism* (Oxford, U.K.: Blackwell, 1986); N. P. Barry, *On Classical Liberalism and Libertarianism* (New York: St. Martin's Press, 1987); Kenneth R. Minogue, *The Liberal Mind* (London: Methuen, 1963).

—Michele Rutledge and Aharon Zorea

Libertarian Party

The Libertarian Party was established in Westminster, Colorado, in 1971 and nominated its first candidate, University of Southern California philosophy professor John Hospers, for the presidency in the 1972 ELECTIONS. Hospers and his running mate, Tonie Nathan, although drawing less that 1 percent of the popular vote, each garnered one electoral vote that year. Thus Nathan became the first woman in U.S. history to win a vote in the electoral college. The party achieved its pinnacle of success in 1980 when it was on the ballot in all 50 states, and its presidential candidate, Edward E. Clark, received over 900,000 votes. Although totaling only about 1 percent of the national aggregate, it

was enough to make the Libertarian Party the third-largest political party in the United States.

The Libertarian Party has offered a wide slate of candidates at the local, state, and national levels in election years. Approximately 1,000 Libertarian candidates ran for local, state, and federal office in the 1996 general election. The party seems especially supportive of women and minorities. Of the presidential tickets in 1992 and 1996, only the Libertarian slate included women: Nancy Lord for vice president in 1992 and Jo Jorgensen for vice president in 1996. Over the years, AFRICAN AMERICANS, NATIVE AMERICANS, homosexuals, and members of several other racial and ethnic groups have held positions of influence and responsibility in the Libertarian Party by running for public office as Libertarians. In 1992, through the efforts of a massive grassroots volunteer effort, the Libertarian candidates for president and vice president were listed on all ballots in all 50 states, the District of Columbia, and Guam. The Libertarian Party achieved the same level of ballot access in 1996, a historic event marking the first time in U.S. history that the same third party has been listed on every state's ballot for two presidential elections in a row.

The Libertarian Party is devoted to the principles of libertarianism. Libertarians seek to maximize personal liberty and minimize the power of government. They are often described as being a combination of conservative and liberal. Like contemporary conservatives, they oppose taxation and the expansion of government. In the manner of modern liberals, they believe strongly in freedom of religion, press, and association; separation of church and state; and free speech. Libertarians support individual freedom, arguing that whatever consenting adults do with their bodies is their concern alone. The party supports the right to bear and keep firearms, defends ABORTION rights, and opposes CENSORSHIP. Arguing that "the initiation of force against others" constitutes a violation of fundamental rights, the Libertarian Party supports the prosecution of fraud and criminal violence, but also advocates the retraction of laws against such so-called victimless crimes as drug use, prostitution, and gambling.

The Libertarian Party opposes the traditional services and powers of federal, state, and local governments and advocates the rights of individuals to exercise singular authority over their lives. This is expressed through the contention that a completely free market is an essential economic condition for prosperity and liberty. For that reason, the party advocates the repeal of corporate and personal income taxes; replacing government-provided services (such as the post office and Social Security) with voluntary and private administration; the revocation of a wide range of regulations, including GUN CONTROL and minimum wage laws; and the breaking up of all regulatory bodies that do not explicitly encourage freely contracted trade. Libertarian Party ideals are incorporated into its platforms, which are established at semiannual conventions of delegates from state affiliates and national party officers. Convention delegates elect the Libertarian National Committee, composed of regional representatives, several at-large members, and a chairperson and other officers, to administer the ongoing functions of the party. Presidential candidates are elected by a simple majority of convention delegates. Libertarian candidates have run in every presidential election since 1972, and several members were elected to local and state office, particularly in the West. The party maintains a national office in Washington, D.C., and has affiliates in every state. The Cato Institute, a public-policy research organization, was founded in 1977 in part by prominent members of the Libertarian Party. The party publishes various kinds of literature in addition to brochures and newsletters, including the official party newspaper, the *Libertarian Party News.*

See also CONSERVATIVE MOVEMENT; LIBERALISM, POLITICAL PARTIES.

—Michele Rutledge

literature

The rise of the mass entertainment industry profoundly affected literature in the 20th century, especially in the last half of the century, with the emergence of huge MEDIA and entertainment conglomerates that combine movies, "blockbuster" fiction, and mass marketing of books. One major consequence has been a sharp distinction between "serious" literature that appeals to well-educated readers (often constituting a small readership) and "popular" fiction (usually for a mass audience.) Although there are occasional overlaps between serious literature and popular literature, a growing disparity between the two types became increasingly evident as Americans entered the 21st century. Witnessing this growing distance between audiences and the exhausted literature of a postmodernist world, some critics declared the "end of the novel." Serious literature often became more esoteric and, indeed, incomprehensible and unappealing, to most readers.

The one caveat to this generalization appeared in ethnic and regional writing that attracted both serious readers and a large audience. For example, Toni Morrison's novels, such as *The Bluest Eye* (1970) and *Beloved* (1970), appealed to a wide readership in its historical depictions of the African-American experience in the United States. Her books were found in assigned reading lists in literature classes in high schools and universities.

Other ethnic themes were found in Native American and Asian-American novels that began to appear in the late 1960s. Typical of Native American literature were such novels as N. Scott Momaday's *House Made of Dawn* (1968),

Leslie Marmon Silko's *Ceremony* (1977), and Louise Erdrich's *Love Medicine* (1984). Another Native American author, Sherman Alexie, also found a popular audience for his novels and short stories. Stories of the Asian-American experience were captured in best-selling novels by Maxine Hong Kingston, Amy Tan, and Gish Jen. The Chicano cultural experience in America was the focus of a number of Mexican-American writers, such as Sandra Cisneros.

Other authors attracted wide audiences with serious novels, including E. L. Doctorow, Richard Ford, Joan Didion, Joyce Carol Oates, Tom Wolfe, Mary Gordon, and Jane Smiley, among others. Novelists of an earlier, post–World War II generation including Norman Mailer, Saul Bellow, Philip Roth, Joseph Heller, and John Updike continued to produce novels that reached a popular audience, while being acclaimed by literary critics.

Yet a clear trend in literature appeared to place more emphasis on literary style and esoteric philosophical themes. In the mid-1970s a "minimalist" school of literature emerged. Minimalist writers sought to capture postmodern, alienated culture through spare, attenuated fiction that focused on the isolation of individuals in a mass, urban society. Sardonic in tone, spare in the use of words, deliberately avoiding grand themes and philosophical profundity, minimalist writers captured the disconnection of individuals in their personal lives. Closely associated with this minimalist fiction was short-story writer Raymond Carver, whose stories were collected in *Cathedral* (1984), and *What We Talk about When We Talk about Love* (1981). Frederick Barthelme's short stories, for example, are often set in shopping malls and apartment complexes, suggesting the "soullessness" of commercial culture. Novelist Thomas Pynchon wrote surrealist allegories of modern life in his well-received *The Crying of Lot 49* (1966), *Gravity's Rainbow* (1973), and *Vineland* (1990). Although minimalism became less fashionable in the 1980s, it continued to find expression in Ann Beattie's and Lorrie Moore's stories. For the most part, however, minimalist writers attracted a relatively small audience.

Symbolic of this bifurcation between serious literature and popular literature was the status of literary magazines in the late 20th century. As traditional literary magazines, such as *Saturday Review* and *Atlantic Monthly,* began to lose readers in the 1960s, literary reviews tended to become more academic, both in content and in their base of support. In the 1960s, small reviews such as *Tri-Quarterly, Salmagundi,* and *Field* were founded, all housed at universities. *Tri-Quarterly,* under the editorship of Charles Newman, found support from Northwestern University. *Salmagundi,* at Skidmore College, focused more on cultural issues than on literary themes. Edited by Robert and Peggy Boyers, *Salmagundi* published such distinguished cultural critics as Christopher Lasch, Gerald Graff, and

George Steiner. *Field,* housed at Oberlin College, remained devoted to contemporary poetry and the study of poetry. As a result, *Field* published every major American poet, and provided a forum for discussing new trends in poetry, from "confessional" poetry to contemporary poetry in Russia and South America. *Boundary 2,* started by faculty members at the State University of New York, emphasized experimental fiction and poetry, while promoting a literary POSTMODERNISM. Other college-based literary magazines, *The Chicago Review* (University of Chicago), the *Iowa Review* (University of Iowa), and the *Columbia Review* (Columbia University) also provided an outlet for aspiring young writers. These and other journals, as well as commercial magazines like the *New Yorker,* published leading short story writers such as Raymond Carver, William Taylor, Cynthia Ozick, and T. Coraghessan Boyle, as well as younger writers such as Amy Hempel, Mark Richard, and Rick Bass. While literary magazines introduced these writers to a larger public, most of them found limited audiences. For the most part, their market was confined to a relatively small audience of educated readers.

The publishing market itself changed, as established publishing companies underwent consolidation through mergers. In 1980 Harper and Row merged with J. B. Lippincott, for example, but in the late 1970s and early 1980s, large corporations such as Viacom and Time Warner began acquiring publishing houses to diversify their businesses. While W. W. Norton avoided amalgamation, other larger publishing enterprises, including HarperCollins, the Penguin Group, Simon and Schuster, and Random House, were absorbed by larger corporations. These mergers led to a greater emphasis on producing books with potential for large financial returns. Emphasis was placed on advertising, and on acquiring writers with potential for "celebrity" status. Although small independent publishing houses continued to survive, and occasionally published a best-seller, the new publishing corporations emphasized the "bottom line" in choosing the books they produced. Computer technology changed the publishing business, making it easier to write, edit, design, and print books, but the costs of books continued to increase for a variety of reasons, including the desire of large publishing houses to raise their marginal profits.

While the publishing business was changing, the distribution of books also changed. Independent bookstores were driven from business by mega-bookstores such as B. Dalton, Waldenbooks, and Barnes and Noble, that could afford store space in shopping malls. At the same time, wholesale book distributors, which provided the books to these stores, also consolidated. The development of the INTERNET provided another outlet for the distribution of books, as Amazon.com and Barnes and Noble sold books through their websites. Beneficiaries of the Internet, ironically, included used booksellers who used it to expand their markets.

In this new book market, publishers sought the "blockbuster" novel. This meant the acquisition of writers with established reputations in the marketplace. Romance novels (such as those published by Harlequin), westerns by authors such as Louis L'Amour, mysteries, and some science-fiction novels maintained a steady mass market. Older writers, such as Herman Wouk, Harold Robbins, and James Michener, remained popular as well. Female novelists, such as Danielle Steel and Jacqueline Susann, provided sexual drama to their fans. John Grisham's legal novels found a ready audience, while Stephen King's "horror" novels consistently reached the best-seller lists. The beauty of all these writers from the publishers' point of view was that their novels were easily adapted to movies for theaters and television, then released on videos, DVDs, and CDs.

Author Toni Morrison in September 1987 *(AP Photo)*

Yet the success of these novels, and movies made from them, suggested the great gap that had been created between serious fiction and popular fiction in the 21st century. This is not to say that the novels produced for the mass market were without literary merit; nonetheless, the market for fiction and literature had changed radically from the 19th century, when writers such as James Fenimore Cooper, Nathaniel Hawthorne, Herman Melville, Henry James, and Mark Twain were writing their novels. Still it is worth noting that the novels of these classic writers, too, found a place on the shelves of the mega-book chains. And Hollywood scriptwriters discovered that these classics sometimes made for good movies.

See also COMPUTERS; INTERNET; MEDIA; MOVIES; RECREATION.

Further reading: Dale M. Bauer, "Fiction," Robert S. Fogarty, "Literary Reviews and 'Little Magazines'" Paul Gutjahr, "Books," in *Encyclopedia of American Cultural and Intellectual History,* Vol. 3, eds. Mary Kupiec Cayton and Peter W. Williams (New York: Scribner, 2002), pp. 589–600, 317–323, 407–416; Emory Elliott, ed. *The Columbia History of the American Novel* (New York: Columbia University Press, 1991).

M

marriage

The institution of marriage experienced considerable change during the last three decades of the 20th century. In U.S. law, "marriage" refers to the legal action, contract, formality, or ceremony by which the conjugal union between a single man and a single woman is formed. In addition, many states accepted "common law" marriage, in which couples lived together for an extended period of time without having been "joined" together in a civil or religious ceremony. Though the legal definition of marriage remained relatively constant, the practices of cohabitation, premarital, and extramarital relations, and out-of-wedlock childbirth reflect the changing standards of sexual MORALITY in the United States.

In 1967 the U.S. Supreme Court, in *Loving v. Virginia*, overturned laws barring racial intermarriage (anti-miscegenation) in the South, concluding that states that bar marriages solely on the basis of race violate the equal protection and due process clauses of the Fourteenth Amendment. Beyond these civil rights considerations, however, the application requirements for marriage and divorce have remained under the discretion of state governments.

In 1969 California passed as "no-fault" divorce law. Prior to this, all states except Oklahoma and Maryland required proof of cruelty, desertion, or adultery before granting legal divorce. Women's rights advocates argued that such stringent divorce laws favored abusive husbands and restricted women's freedoms by binding them to unsatisfactory marriages.

The new "no fault" law in California was heralded as an advance for women's rights, and a movement to enact more lenient divorce laws spread like a wave throughout state legislatures; within five years, 44 states passed similar laws granting divorce on the basis of "incompatibility" or "irreconcilable differences" alone. The rate of marriages ending in divorce during these years from 1970 to 2000 increased from 35 percent to 52 percent. Opponents feared that permissive divorce laws encouraged divorce as a solution for marital difficulties; many predicted that rates would continue to climb, destroying the institution of the traditional two-parent family. Between 1972 and 1985, however, the rates remained relatively stable. Statistics suggest a slight decline in divorce rates during the late 1980s and early 1990s.

The most significant impact on the traditional definition of marriage came after the SEXUAL REVOLUTION of the 1960s and early 1970s, when the number of premarital relationships and out-of-wedlock births increased dramatically. In 1960 there was only one cohabiting couple for every 90 married couples, but by 1995 that ratio had increased to 1:12, with 50 percent of young adults in their 20s and 30s cohabiting. Likewise, a number of university studies revealed that the number of children engaging in sexual activity before 15 years of age rose from 4 percent in 1970 to 20 percent in 2001. The 2000 census showed that the number of out-of-wedlock births increased from 4 percent in 1950 to 35 percent in 2000. As a result of these changing patterns of sexual relations, marriage no longer served as the primary institution by which children are brought into the world and socialized in the United States. The 2000 census showed that six out of 10 children were born into homes in which the parents were either unmarried or divorced.

These changes in patterns of marriage and sexual mores precipitated a scholarly debate and spilled over into politics. Princeton University sociologist Kristin Luker argues that out-of-wedlock births should be seen as a common historical phenomenon and in itself not a social problem. Out-of-wedlock births, Luker maintains, reflect the changing nature of the family in contemporary America that allows women greater freedom to produce children outside the bounds of marriage. The problem of out-of-wedlock births is not a problem in itself, she concludes, but the real issue is poverty and society's commitment to taking care of the poor.

Others argue, however, that the breakdown of the traditional family and the increase in single-parent families has led to a social crisis in contemporary America that perpetuates poverty, juvenile delinquency, welfare dependency, child abuse, and other problems. Sociologist David Popenoe maintains that a divorce rate of 50 percent in first marriages, the rapid rise of nonmarital cohabitation, and out-of-wedlock births has eroded traditional family values and has led to social disaster. Citing a large body of social science evidence, he finds that children who grow up in single-parent homes are disadvantaged economically, educationally, and socially. Children from such families, he argues, are twice as likely to drop out of high school, 2.5 times as likely to become teen mothers, and 1.4 times as likely to become unemployed.

Social conservatives, such as Popenoe, maintained that sexual promiscuity resulted in out-of-wedlock births, and higher rates of abortion. Social conservatives saw the institution of marriage as the sole legitimate vehicle for the reproduction and education of the next generation; and argued that sexual activity outside the marriage contract risks depriving future children of the social framework necessary

for proper development. Such arguments found expression in the Republican Party, where social conservatives constituted an important faction within the party, although not a dominant force. As a consequence, the Republican Party was the first to include "family values" among its campaign issues, which encouraged abstinence education and condemned public funding for ABORTION counseling.

Opponents of this use of "family values" argued that this was only political rhetoric that failed to address the problem of poverty in American society. Such critics maintained further that the idealization of the traditional two-parent family only strengthened the ability of abusive husbands to maintain control over their wives. These critics, who began to call themselves "progressives," embraced a different concept of "family values" infused with the principle of moral tolerance, and not restricted to a two-parent home with children. This view defined the family as including childless couples caring for elderly relatives, single parents, nonmarried cohabiting parents, or any adult providing primary care for dependents.

The Democratic Party incorporated this version of family values into its campaign issues, emphasizing social

Gay rights protesters demonstrate for the right to obtain a marriage license *(Tim Boyle/Newsmakers)*

ideals, rather than moral or religious values. Democrats promoted increased government funding for contraception and abortion counseling to ensure proper family planning, and resisted laws requiring parental notification and consent for abortion services. Democrats also used the family values slogan to urge increased funding for day care, preschool, and after-school activities to help relieve working parents and assist them with some of their child-care responsibilities.

The conflict between moral conservatives and moral liberals over the redefinition of marriage often followed partisan lines with regard to the leadership of each party. Popular elections, however, indicate that the general constituency of each party tended to share more in common with each other than was typically represented by the political debates of their leaders. Nonetheless, sharp differences arose over same-sex marriages.

A public debate erupted during the 1990s over whether the legal definition of marriage should be changed to include noncontractual and same-sex unions. The first attempt to legalize same-sex marriages arose in 1972, after voters in the state of Hawaii passed a state-based EQUAL RIGHTS AMENDMENT (ERA) prohibiting discrimination on the basis of sex. In 1990 three same-sex couples applied for marriage licenses and were denied. They then sued the state of Hawaii, arguing that the state constitution prohibited discrimination on the basis of sex, and therefore prohibited the state from denying marriage licenses to same-sex couples. In *Baehr v. Miike* (1993), the state SUPREME COURT ruled in favor of the plaintiff, and ordered that licenses be granted to the couples unless the state could show a compelling interest in banning such marriages. The state legislature responded the following year with a bill explicitly stating that marriages could only be formed between a man and a woman. For five years, the state legislature and the state courts wrestled with the issue, while the public debated it on both the state and national levels.

Advocates for same-sex unions argued that the choice of a spouse was a fundamental human right of all persons, that homosexuality was determined by genetic predisposition, and that the prohibition of same-sex marriages discriminates against a recognized minority. More specifically, they argued that homosexual couples were denied the rights and benefits that heterosexual couples received from health and insurance beneficiary clauses.

Opponents argued in response that same-sex marriages would remove all obstacles to the adoption of children by homosexual couples, which they believed would have a negative impact on normal childhood development. Moreover, if same-sex unions are legalized on the basis of nondiscrimination, without considering traditional standards of morality, then other groups might also want legal

protection, including prostitutes, polygamists, and incestuous marriages.

In 1998, after five years of debate, the voters of Hawaii formally amended their state constitution, allowing the state legislature to explicitly forbid same-sex marriages.

The debate in Hawaii stimulated similar lawsuits in Alaska and Vermont. Between 1995 and 2000, widely publicized battles over this issue were fought through the ballot box in these and 29 other states. With the exception of Vermont, each state that voted on the issue eventually passed with overwhelming majorities laws barring more liberal definitions of marriage. In 1995, in an attempt to prevent similar suits in their state, Utah passed the first of what became a series of Defense of Marriage Acts (DOMA), which explicitly forbid same-sex marriages. Fourteen other states passed similar laws that year, and within five years, 31 states followed suit.

In 1996 Representative Steve Largent (R-Okla.) and Senator Don Nickles (R-Okla.) introduced the Defense of Marriage Act in the U.S. Congress, which was passed with an overwhelming majority, and WILLIAM J. CLINTON signed it into law, despite voicing opposition to it.

In 1998 Vermont became the only state to reject a Defense of Marriage Act. The Vermont Supreme Court ruled, in *Baker v. Vermont* (1999), that the state legislature had to either allow same-sex marriages, or create a new form of government-recognized relationship that permitted same-sex couples to receive the same benefits as heterosexual couples. In April 2000 the Vermont legislature passed by seven votes a law defining marriage as a legal union between a man and a wife, but which included a second classification allowing state-recognized "unions" between same-sex couples. As of 2001 Vermont had issued more than 2,600 licenses for same-sex unions.

During the 1990s, legislators in five states introduced bills intended to eliminate the no-fault divorce. Advocates of the bill argued that no-fault divorce destroys family more than any other factor. Since 80 percent of divorces are prompted unilaterally, they argued, the no-fault divorce laws unfairly favor the spouse intent on leaving the marriage. They further argued that divorce had a disproportionate impact on poor and minority communities, stranding many children in poverty. None of these measures came close to passing, however.

As Americans entered the 21st century, family structure was undergoing significant changes. The end result of these changes, however, remained unforeseen, and the social consequences unclear. Nonetheless, change was apparent, whether welcomed or not.

See also BIRTH CONTROL; BIRTHRATES; CONSERVATIVE MOVEMENT; FAMILY LIFE; FEMINISM; GAY RIGHTS MOVEMENT; MORAL MAJORITY; RELIGION; WOMEN'S RIGHTS AND STATUS.

Further reading: Edward O. Laumann, et. al., *The Social Organization of Sexuality* (Chicago: University of Chicago Press, 1994); Kristin Luker, *Dubious Conception: The Politics of Teenage Pregnancy* (Cambridge, Mass.: Harvard University Press, 1997); David Popenoe, *Life without Father: Compelling New Evidence That Fatherhood and Marriage Are Indispensable for the Good of the Child and Society* (New York: Free Press, 1996); Judith Wallerstein et al., *The Unexpected Legacy of Divorce* (New York: Hyperion, 2000).

—Aharon W. Zorea

McGovern, George S. (1922–)

George Stanley McGovern served in the U.S. SENATE from 1965 to 1981 and was the Democratic Party's presidential candidate in 1972. Born in Avon, South Dakota, in 1922, McGovern served as an air force pilot during World War II and as a history teacher at Dakota Wesleyan University (1949–53). He was active in Americans for Democratic Action. In 1956 he was elected to the U.S. HOUSE OF REPRESENTATIVES from South Dakota (1957–63), and, after a failed run for the Senate in 1960, he became director of the Food for Peace foreign aid program in the Kennedy administration from 1961 to 1964. He was elected to the U.S. Senate in 1964, where he emerged as an outspoken critic of the VIETNAM WAR.

McGovern played an important role in reforming the party national convention system, allowing more female and minority delegate representation, and weakening the influence of local party bosses. These reforms set the stage for his bid for the Democratic presidential nomination in 1972. In the primaries, he was challenged by the former vice president, Hubert Humphrey, and Alabama governor George Wallace. Calling for an immediate end of the war in Vietnam, McGovern attracted support in the left wing of the party, as well as among youth. He proclaimed that the war against communism was over and that it was time to peacefully coexist with the SOVIET UNION. While focusing primarily on the war in Vietnam, he also proposed heavy cuts in defense spending, increased spending for social programs, and a more progressive tax code. He also called for a $1,000-per-citizen tax rebate to stimulate the economy, which caused opponents to label his domestic program a "thousand-dollar giveaway." In addition, he called for amnesty for those young people who had evaded the military draft, state liberalization of ABORTION laws, and the reduction of penalties for marijuana drug use.

This liberal program drew heavy criticism from Humphrey. Although Humphrey lost the party nomination, his attacks damaged McGovern in the general campaign. Further difficulties emerged when it was revealed that McGovern's vice presidential running mate, Senator THOMAS F. EAGLETON (D-Mo.), had undergone electric shock treatment for mental depression. McGovern then selected SARGENT SHRIVER as his running mate.

McGovern's poll numbers began to fall immediately after the convention. They continued to fall as the Republican candidate, RICHARD M. NIXON, attacked McGovern for his proposals. On election day, Nixon won 60.7 percent of the popular vote, and McGovern only 37.5 percent. McGovern only carried the state of Massachusetts. Following his defeat, McGovern returned to the U.S. Senate, where he served until January 1981. During his many years in Congress, he served as the chairman of the Select Committee on Unmet Basic Needs (90th Congress) and on the Select Committee on Nutrition and Human Needs (91st through 95th Congress). McGovern unsuccessfully ran for reelection to the Senate in 1980, and then he made an unsuccessful bid for the Democratic presidential nomination in 1984. He currently resides in Washington, D.C., where he spends his time lecturing and teaching.

—Leah Blakey

media

The term "media" includes a wide variety of information delivery systems that, taken together, constitute a comprehensive system of bringing words and images to a mass population. During the last half of the 20th century, American media experienced profound change, primarily from the influence of TELEVISION and, in the 1980s and 1990s, COMPUTERS and the INTERNET. The result was a virtual explosion of information available to the American public, the content and presentation of which significantly influenced America's cultural, social, political, and economic development.

Because, in 2001, nearly 100 percent of American homes had at least one television set, television is the most powerful and pervasive form of media. In addition to being the primary source of home entertainment, it plays an overwhelming role in the selling of goods and services through ADVERTISING and, as such, has become the most desirable and expensive medium for advertising. Television also plays a significant role as educator. Although network broadcasting devotes little time to instructional programming, documentaries aired on the Public Broadcasting Service (PBS) and the proliferation of documentary-oriented stations offered by cable television provide a wealth of information, however simplified, on a wide range of topics, including science, history, and cultures of other countries. Television's educational contribution is its ability to provide live coverage of contemporary events. Coverage of the VIETNAM WAR, the upheavals of the Civil Rights movement during the 1960s and 1970s, and the Persian Gulf War in 1991, proved the capability of television to alter public beliefs and attitudes. Television is also the primary source from which Americans receive the news. During the 1980s, the networks began requiring their news departments to finance their own budgets and, as a result, entertainment value became as critical to the success of news programs as was the factual representation of the news. Thus, television has greatly contributed to Americans' relatively simplistic understanding of issues and events. Finally, by the end of the 20th century, television became the primary source of cultural, social, and political information for the American public.

Its preeminent status among the media made television the subject of a great deal of criticism. Debates over journalistic integrity followed the transformation of its presentation of the news. Its content invited criticism from minority and women's groups, who sought less stereotypical images in programming and greater representation of their memberships, both in programming and in industry management. Television became the target of various groups disturbed by the potential impact on children, because of the often violent and explicit nature of its content. Others argued that its rapid presentation of visual images inhibited viewers' ability to concentrate, and contributed to, if not caused, attention deficit disorder (ADD) among young children. Although the merits and shortcomings of television will be debated for years, its dominance in American media cannot be doubted. Its development over the last three decades was so significant that it forced the other media (books, newspapers, magazines, and radio) to change their formats to compete as information delivery systems.

Publishing did not immediately suffer from the advent of television. The number of new books published per year rose dramatically, from just over 6,000 in 1945 to 30,053 in 1966, 40,846 in 1974, 56,000 in 1987, and more than 120,000 in 2000. Although economic recession reduced the number to about 40,000 per year during the 1990s, the book business emerged as a $25 billion industry by 2000. The Book Industry Study Group estimates book publishing will be a $38 billion industry by 2004. During the 1990s, mass-market paperbacks held 30 percent of the book market, and fiction was the most popular reading. Despite the financial health of the book industry, Americans during the last third of the 20th century increasingly became less likely to read.

MOVIES, television, periodicals, and computers provided great competition for books as sources of information and entertainment. At the end of the 20th century, computer technology offered the potential for the creation of "virtual" libraries containing massive collections of fully digitized volumes. Book clubs and on-line bookstores like Amazon.com, however, have helped books maintain their position, but often at the expense of quality and substance.

Bookstore shelves were dominated by self-help books, "historical" romances, and various other genres of fiction designed for mass appeal. Similar transformations occurred with newspapers.

In 1969 there were 1,758 daily newspapers in the United States, competing with other media such as television and magazines; by 2000 there were 1,480 daily newspapers. The number of cities with more than one daily paper continued a downward trend, going from 55 in 1999 to 49 in 2001. A few, such as the *New York Times*, the *Washington Post,* and the *Los Angeles Times,* enjoyed strong national and international reputations for stressing foreign and national news, analysis and interpretation, politics, science, economics, and culture. Additionally, there were more than 8,000 nondaily newspapers, representing AFRICAN AMERICANS and other racial and ethnic groups, the military, university students, prison populations, and a wide variety of hobbyists. Cultural historian John Tebbell argues that television became the primary source of the news for most Americans, and as a result, most newspapers became primarily community bulletin boards in small towns and cities. Newspapers in large urban centers, Tebbell maintains, have been able to provide better indepth coverage and investigative reporting than television. The exposure of the WATERGATE SCANDAL by *Washington Post* reporters Carl Bernstein and Bob Woodward is perhaps the best example. Many other newspapers undertook investigative reporting on the state and local level as well. Two exceptions to the localization of newspapers are the *Wall Street Journal* and *USA Today.* Both achieved circulations of nearly 2 million during the 1990s and reached a national audience. The former represents the best in serious news reporting, with a focus on BUSINESS and the ECONOMY. The latter, while not as sensational as the popular *National Enquirer,* which thrives on rumor, innuendo, and fabrication, represents a transformation in newspapers in response to the primacy of television. With its wide variety of brief stories and its use of color and photographs, *USA Today* is a hybrid of television and newspaper.

The story of magazines since the 1960s has been one of specialization. Since the 1960s, the number of magazines devoted to very narrow areas of interest grew tremendously, so much so that by 1991 there were over 11,500 magazines and periodicals published in the United States. Industry surveys revealed that, by the mid-1990s, 80 percent of published periodicals were for specialized audiences. The growth in magazines reflected the rapid social changes occurring during the 1960s and 1970s. *Playboy,* first published in 1953, reflected the changing sexual mores of the time, while *Ms.* (founded in 1972) and others dedicated themselves to the changing status of women. *Ebony* (founded in 1945) and *Jet* (founded in 1951) echoed African-American pride. During the 1980s, magazines such

Television crews gather around a suspect in a murder case. *(McNew/Getty Images)*

as *Us* and *People* (founded in 1974) took advantage of Americans' obsession with movies, movie stars, and other celebrities, while *Sports Illustrated* and other sports-related magazines focused on Americans' passion for SPORTS and RECREATION activities. The last 30 years also witnessed an increase in the number of trade, scientific, technical, and academic journals and magazines. By the end of the 20th century, a magazine existed for virtually every activity undertaken by the American public.

Magazines, like newspapers, have been hurt by having to compete with television for advertising dollars. In the early 1990s advertisers bought about $7 billion in magazine advertising, which was only 5 percent of total advertising expenditures. This competition was the primary factor in the decline of large-circulation general magazines, as well as many smaller publications. Specialization allowed magazine publishers to target specific audiences, and thereby make their publications more appealing to advertisers. Moreover, magazines became primarily informational and directed at particular age, gender, ethnic, or income groups. For national photo magazines such as *Look* and *Life,* their failure was attributable to rising costs of production, especially paper and ink, and the trend toward

specialization that came with competition with television for advertising dollars.

Specialization also marked radio's response to the pervasiveness of television. Some stations broadcast news around the clock, while others specialized in talk shows, consisting of in-studio interviews or listener call-in formats. Most stations, both AM and FM, broadcast MUSIC and featured a specific musical genre such as rock and roll, country, jazz, urban contemporary, or classical. Many further specialize with formats, such as 1970s and 1980s "easy listening," album-oriented rock and roll, ethnic, or children's popular music. By 2000 there were 10,716 commercial radio stations in the United States, including 2,449 country; 1,557 adult contemporary; 1,426 talk, business, and sports; 1,135 oldies; 1,135 religion; 827 rock; 654 Spanish and ethnic music; 577 adult standards; 426 top-40; 426 urban rap; 71 jazz; 48 preteen; 36 classical; 35 variety; and a few scattered other formats. All of these depend on advertising for their survival and, because they compete with television for advertising dollars, they target specific audiences by region or age group. Television not only altered the business of radio; it altered its place in American culture by quickly replacing radio as the primary source of in-home entertainment. By 1990, over 60 percent of Americans listened to radio outside the home, primarily in their automobiles.

The role of movies in American culture has remained relatively unchanged throughout the 20th century. Despite the introduction of videotape in the 1980s and digital videodiscs (DVD) in the 1990s, Americans continued to go to theaters to see first-release movies in record numbers. In 1969–70, movie attendance was 200 million; in 2000, movie attendance had risen to 1.42 billion in the United States. Although movies are essentially an entertainment medium, the big-screen images are informational in that they continued to offer standards for the country's fashion, sense of morality, manners, and attitudes. In that sense, movies serve as a transmitter of ideas as well as information. Film can also be primarily informational, however. Business, industry, and government use film for training purposes, for selling products, and for general public relations.

As the 20th century came to a close, perhaps the most significant transformations in media were the result of rapidly advancing computer technology. New production techniques and storage systems made possible by computers helped print media survive in its competition with television for advertising dollars. The major development was the use by publishers of CD-ROMs for encyclopedias, dictionaries, and other reference works. Also, many magazines developed "E-zines," or electronic magazines that allowed publishers to more easily reach a wider readership at lower costs. Moreover, computer technology opened new avenues for the delivery of information, and is poised to revolutionize media in general. Chief among these developments is the growth of computer networks and the Internet. Networks make possible the storage and easy retrieval of vast amounts of information, and allow users to exchange information with each other, even from geographically remote locations. Various computer network systems provide interactive access to database, via computers or television sets, through subscription services such as Prodigy, Compuserve, and America Online. Subscribers can access information on the weather, news, attractions, or virtually any other matter of interest. An Internet "surfer" can view full-length movies, see up-to-date sports scores, or take a virtual tour of an Egyptian pyramid.

All the media—print, film, electronic, and computer—have played and continue to play a formative role in politics, economics, and social and cultural distinctiveness in the United States. Television, in particular, influences American political life by bringing people and events closer together and by providing the primary avenue of exposure for political candidates. However simplistic television's representation of the news is, it does make events, national and international, more immediate. The Internet, as well, makes available almost limitless information on issues and candidates. Media significantly influence the economy because, in all their forms, they are the principal vehicle for local and national advertising. Socially and culturally, the media both serve the nation's diverse intellectual need, and collectively reflect the identity of the American people who, at the beginning of the 21st century, are perhaps the most informed people on Earth.

See also CENSORSHIP; HORTON, WILLIE; LITERATURE; SCIENCE AND TECHNOLOGY.

Further reading: James L. Baughman, *The Republic of Mass Culture. Journalism, Filmmaking, and Broadcasting in America since 1941* (Baltimore: Johns Hopkins University Press, 1992); Herbert Schiller, *Mass Communications and the American Empire,* 2d ed. (Boulder, Colo.: Westview, 1992).

—William L. Glankler

medicine

Throughout the 20th century, the field of medicine enjoyed a constant rate of development. Though technological advances related to the computing revolution of the century's last three decades provided more sophisticated tools with which to further research and diagnosis, most of the midcentury innovations related to DNA, vaccination, and psychotropic medication remain unsurpassed as groundbreaking discoveries. But the single greatest breakthrough, the HUMAN GENOME PROJECT, may determine the direction of medical research far into the 21st century.

Americans enjoyed a gradual decrease in the death rate throughout the 20th century, with a marked improvement in the 1970s. Per 100,000 residents, the death rate fell from 760.9 in 1960 to 714.3 in 1970, after which the rate of decline almost tripled; 583.8 in 1980, and 479.1 in 1997. Although a variety of reasons unrelated to health care could explain the general decline, including fewer wars and safer working conditions, indicators such as maternal death rates and infant mortality rates reveal the impact of increased access to health care for a larger portion of the American public. In 1950, 2,960 women died giving birth, and the rate of infant mortality was 29.2 deaths for every 100,000 live births. Ten years later in 1960, the infant mortality rate had dropped only three points, but the number of maternal deaths dropped to 1,579, and to 803 in 1970. Throughout the 1980s and 1990s, the number fluctuated between 270 and 340 per year. In addition, the infant mortality rate dropped six points in the 1960s, and eight points in the 1970s. In 1990, there were only 9.2 deaths per 100,000 live births.

Generally speaking, medicine and health care gradually consumed a greater portion of the GDP, to become the nation's largest economic sector. The number of physicians nearly doubled between 1960 (260,484) and 1980

(467,679), and continued to grow to 756,710 in 1997, while the number of health service professionals grew from 76 million people in 1970 to 131 million in 1998. The amount of money spent on health research grew from $2.8 billion in 1970, to $13.5 billion in 1985, and $35.8 billion in 1995. As a percent of the gross national product (GNP), health expenditures grew from 5.1 percent in 1960, to 9.4 percent in 1980, and 13.5 percent in 1997.

As health care assumed a more prominent role in American society, it generally became more specialized, with greater support from the private sector, and financing from the public sector. Though all age groups tended to visit their doctors more frequently in the 1990s than they did in the 1960s, the number of contacts per person increased most for those Americans aged 65 and older, and for children aged 14 and younger. Also, those visits were more often made to a specialist than a general family practitioner. In 1970 less than 1 percent of active physicians were specialists, by 1980 the percentage increased to 3.5, and to 5 in 1990. In 1970, 63.4 percent of health professionals worked in hospitals, only 11.2 percent in offices and clinics, and 12 percent in nursing homes. The number of physicians working in hospitals plummeted to 44.5 percent in 1998. Improvements in medicine, techniques, and technologies have lessened the need for general hospital space; there were 1.4 million beds in 7,156 hospitals in 1975, and only a few more than 1 million beds in 6,097 hospitals in 1997. Yet, the percentage of occupied beds also fell from 76 to 65 during the same time span.

During the 1980s, the focus of health care and research shifted from government sponsorship to private sector. This privatization is less pronounced in the decline in hospitals; the number of privately owned, for-profit hospitals remained relatively constant (775 in 1975 as compared with 797 in 1997). During the same period, however, the number of state and federal hospitals declined by a third (2,143 to 1,545), and the number of private, nonprofit hospitals declined by 10 percent (3,339 to 3,000). The real growth in the private sector came in research; in 1970, private industry accounted for only $795 million, compared with $1.6 billion from the federal government. The relative ratio remained the same in 1980 ($2.4 billion to $4.7 billion), but changed dramatically in 1985, with private industry investing $5.3 billion compared with $6.7 billion by the federal government; by 1995 the ratio was reversed with $18.6 to $13.4 billion. The public money that had previously been devoted to research was reallocated to pay for increased insurance coverage. In 1970 the federal government paid $6.6 billion, while private insurance paid out $30.9 billion. In 1985 the federal government assumed a slightly larger share, paying $174.2 billion to $254.5 billion paid privately, and in 1997 the amounts paid were almost even; $507 billion to $585 billion, respectively.

The investment in health care was not without its benefits. After World War II, scientists redirected their attention toward another, longer war against disease. The subsequent development of effective vaccines not only impacted American health but also reduced select contagions on a global scale; diseases that had plagued society for centuries were all but eliminated in the following decades. Vaccines for diphtheria, whooping cough, and polio had a significant effect on the health of America. The annual number of diphtheria cases dropped from 5,796 in 1950 to 918 in 1960, 435 in 1970, and only three or four a year in the 1980s and 1990s. Whooping cough afflicted more than 120,000 people in 1950, but was reduced to 14,809 cases in 1960, 4,249 cases in 1970, and only 1,730 in 1980. Similarly, polio cases fell from 33,300 in 1950 to 3,190 in 1960, to only 33 in 1970, and less than a dozen a year in the 1980s and 1990s. The number of measles cases actually increased during the 1950s, jumping from 319,124 to 441,703 cases in 1960. A new vaccine, however, cut the rate by 90 percent; there were only 47,351 cases in 1970, and 13,506 cases in 1980. Another common childhood disease, mumps, also fell from 104,943 cases in 1970, to 8,576 cases in 1980, and 5,292 cases in 1990.

Vaccinations provide a better alternative to antibiotics, which have been linked to global increases in the number of drug-resistant pathogens. Antibiotics are designed to kill bacteria that cause illness. Unfortunately, bacteria evolve and adapt to their environment at a remarkable rate. Bacterial cells that survive antibiotic treatments can often acquire new genes that make them resistant to future doses of the same antibiotic. For example, in the late 1980s hospitals began seeing more frequent occurrences of vancomycin-resistant enterococci (VRE), which are only minimally responsive to existing antibiotics. Similarly, penicillin had near a 100 percent success rate against pneumococci in the 1960s, but by the 1990s, the rates of success had decreased to 70–80 percent, and in some parts of Europe, the rate had fallen to 50 percent. In 2001 the World Health Organization addressed the problem of bacterial resistance with the first Global Strategy for Containment of Antimicrobial Resistance. In contrast to antibiotics, vaccinations avoid the problem of resistance by offering protection for the human immune system before pathogens have a chance to adapt. In 1975 the possibility of side effects was significantly reduced by the discovery of monoclonal antibodies, which enabled doctors to target specific disease cells. This innovation allowed scientists of the 1990s to focus on vaccinations as a primary method of controlling disease. Initial trials include an experimental AIDS vaccine, announced in 1999, and other prototype vaccines for malaria, hepatitis C, and tuberculosis. Biomedical engineers are working on infusing vaccines in certain strains of potatoes, tomatoes, and bananas, so they will mature with vaccines present. Research arising from the full map of the human genome may lead to customized cancer-vaccines tailored to a patient's exact DNA makeup.

Over the course of the 20th century, life expectancy in the United States has increased by nearly 30 years, from 47.3 years to 76.5 years. While the numbers of all age groups grew steadily, older Americans became significantly more numerous after World War II than they had been in previous decades. In 1950, there were only 577,000 people over 85 years old; in 1960 the number had increased to 929,000 with similar increases every decade thereafter; 1.5 million in 1970, 2.2 million in 1980, and 3 million in 1990. The number of nursing home residents has similarly increased, jumping from 961,500 to 1.3 million over a 10-year period from 1974 to 1985. As the number of American seniors continued to grow, the number of prescribed drugs available to combat cardiovascular disease, high cholesterol, memory loss, and cancer similarly increased. Americans spent more than $12 billion on prescription drugs in 1980, nearly double that amount in 1985 ($21 billion), and

in 1993 the figure had reached $48 billion. The American Association of Retired Persons (AARP) lobbied heavily for reforming Medicare to include universal coverage for prescription medicine for senior citizens. Lawmakers responded and in December 2000, Congress passed an amendment to Title XVIII of the Social Security Act to provide coverage for outpatient prescription drugs under the Medicare program.

Mental health also became a priority in the postwar years. Psychotropic, or mind-altering, drugs were first used for therapeutic purposes during the 1950s and 1960s. The Food and Drug Administration (FDA) classified some experimental drugs under their Investigative New Drug (IND) regulations; some of these included lysergic acid diethylamide (LSD) and thalidomide. After a rash of birth defects around the world were linked to the use of thalidomide in 1962, the FDA tightened up its IND regulations and banned the use of thalidomide and LSD. Though the FDA has restricted experimental use of psychotropic, or mind-altering drugs, it did not altogether limit their use.

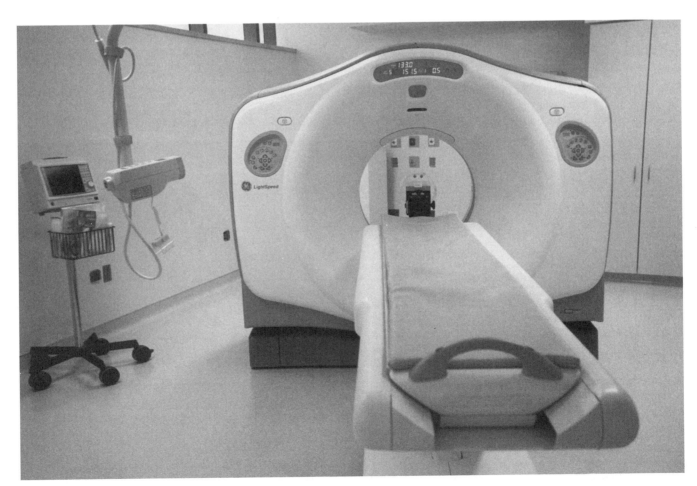

A high-speed CAT scan machine *(Darren McCollester/Getty Images)*

Psychiatrists had been relying on electroconvulsive therapy (ECT), more commonly known as electroshock, to treat symptoms of depression and mental illness. In the late 1960s and early 1970s, the public reacted to ECT as an example of the inhumane conditions of most mental hospitals, prompting most psychiatrists to pursue psychotropic alternatives, including antidepressants and antipsychotic drugs such as lithium, chlorpromazine, haldol, and clozapine. Chlorpromazine was so successful in treating hallucinations and delusions that it was championed as "the drug that emptied the state mental hospitals" during the 1970s and 1980s.

In 1980 public attention shifted from the state hospitals to childhood behavior, after the Diagnostic and Statistical Manual of Mental Disorders included Attention Deficit Disorder (ADD) and, later, Attention Deficit and Hyperactivity Disorder (ADHD) in their lists. Family counselors relied on methylphenidate, a derivative of amphetamine sold under the name of Ritalin, as the most commonly prescribed treatment for ADD and ADHD. Later in 1987, selective serotonin reuptake inhibitors (SSRI) were introduced under the name of Prozac and used as an antidepressant for both children and adults. Alternative varieties of these medications quickly followed, and many educators worked with doctors to promote medication as a popular solution for student behavior problems; between 1990 and 1997, 10 percent of children aged 6–14 years were using Ritalin, and 1 percent of preschool children aged 1–5. A third of those children were also prescribed SSRI treatments such as Zoloft, Luvox, and Paxil. Some parents and pediatricians became concerned about the side effects of these drug combinations, which can include mania, seizures, anorexia, toxic psychosis, and cardiovascular failure. Opponents were met with staunch opposition from education and counseling groups, many of which received funding from pharmaceutical corporations directly; one such lobbying group, Children and Adults with ADD (CHADD), received 10 percent of its funding from the makers of Ritalin. In 1998 and 1999, state school boards in Texas and Colorado passed resolutions discouraging educators from promoting the drugs, and in 2000 Connecticut passed legislation forbidding it. Proponents of psychotropic medication argued that the new drugs allow millions of people with chemical-based mental illness to lead normal lives in the mainstream of American society. Opponents argued that the prevalence of such licit drugs unavoidably promotes a large subculture of illicit drug use by training people to seek pharmaceutical solutions to problems that have social and interpersonal causes.

For internal medicine, innovative drug treatments permitted great advances in organ transplants. In 1959, scientists used the drug Imuran to suppress the human immune system, which allowed foreign organs to be transplanted into a host body. The first successful pancreas transplant occurred in 1966, and was followed the next year by the first successful heart and liver transplants. In 1981 doctors performed the first successful combination heart and lung transplant. Scientists developed a new anti-rejection drug, cyclosporine, which aided in the first successful lung transplant in 1983. Discoveries in microprocessing technologies during the same period permitted doctors to embark on the first artificial heart implant; although it only functioned for 112 days, it set a precedent for continued research in artificial organs. In 2001 doctors transplanted the first fully self-contained artificial heart in Robert Tools. Similar advances included artificial cochlear (inner ear) implants, eyes, muscle and blood, skin, kidneys, lungs, pancreas, and liver. Currently, artificial organs only provide a bridge to transplantation, which helps patients who may have to wait long periods before an acceptable donor organ becomes available. Pharmacologists of the 1990s focused on methods of preventing transplant rejection on the cellular and molecular level; their goal was to find a safe and cost-effective way to allow multiple transplants of natural or artificial organs for less than life-threatening reasons. The completion of the human genome map may lead to further innovations in this area.

Other aspects of internal medicine benefited from the COMPUTER revolution. In 1972 Godfrey Hounsfield recorded hundreds of X-ray images on a computer at slightly variant angles to produce a three-dimensional computer tomography (CT) scan. The procedure proved invaluable to doctors needing precise views of an area that would otherwise be too dangerous to access though invasive surgery. In 1984 Raymond Damadian augmented the CT scan when he invented magnetic resonance imaging (MRI), which provides more precise images of soft tissues; MRIs became especially useful in examining brain and spinal cord injuries. The later development of radioisotope tracers in the 1990s provided physicians with a means of tracking information about metabolism and the functions of enzymes and hormones through the injection of material that can be recorded by computerized sensors. Advances in medical techniques have decreased the time needed for recovery. During the 1990s, advances in minimally invasive laparoscopic surgery techniques, which use very small incisions, often reduced the length of hospital stays by 10 percent; in some cases, cutting the recovery time from 4 to 6 weeks to 2 to 7 days. Robotic lasers using computer-aided microscopes cut with near cellular precision; with these tools, physicians in the 1990s successfully performed surgery on neonatal arteries the size of a toothpick. When robotic surgery is combined with innovations in telecommunication, doctors can perform long-distance operations for patients who are unable to travel.

The human genome map promises a host of solutions for many common ailments, including cancer and congenital disorders. Though Oswald Avery discovered in 1943 that DNA carried genetic information, it took 30 years until 1972, for scientists Paul Berg, Stanley Cohen, and Herbert Boyer to develop a technique that allows researchers to decipher the information. By splicing fragments of DNA from one organism onto the DNA string of another, controlled experiments can isolate and reveal the functions of specific DNA segments. It took another 10 years before Eli Lilly & Company used the new technique to produce the first genetically engineered human insulin in 1982. Throughout the 1970s, researchers conducted ad hoc clinical trials, according to the specific needs of their research; a systematic mapping of the human genome seemed an impossible task. By the mid-1980s, however, with the advent of powerful information processors, Charles DeLisi of the Office of Health and Environmental Research felt convinced that a systematic map was possible. In 1990, after years of interagency discussion, the U.S. DEPARTMENT OF ENERGY joined the National Institutes of Health in a 15-year effort to identify each of the 30,000 genes in human DNA. The program was called the Human Genome Project, and Congress committed $3 billion toward its completion. The Human Genome Project completed a final draft of DNA sequencing in 2002, three years ahead of schedule. Scientists expect the specific benefits to include improved diagnosis and early detection of diseases; more rational drug designs leading to individually customized drugs and effective gene therapy; better understanding of the vulnerabilities of specific genetic diseases; enhanced protection from biological warfare; and significantly improved forensics capabilities. Already, significant advances have been made in the development of effective treatments for breast cancer, as well as improved gene therapy for cystic fibrosis, Duchenne's muscular dystrophy, and sickle cell anemia.

See also COMPUTERS; NARCOTICS; SCIENCE AND TECHNOLOGY.

Further reading: Edward I. Alcamo, *DNA Technology: The Awesome Skill* (San Diego, Calif.: Academic Press, 2001); John Duffy, *From Humors to Medical Sciences: A History of American Medicine* (Urbana: University of Illinois Press, 1993).

—Aharon W. Zorea

Meese, Edwin C., III (1923–)

Edwin Meese served as U.S. attorney general in RONALD W. REAGAN's administration from 1985 to 1988. Born in 1923, Meese received his B.A. from Yale University and his LL.B. from the University of California Law School. In 1967 he became deputy district attorney of Alameda County in northern California, where he undertook the successful prosecution of student protesters at the University of California at Berkeley, and Oakland Black Panthers. When Reagan was elected governor of California in 1966, he appointed Meese as executive assistant and chief of staff, a position Meese held from 1967 to 1974. From 1977 to 1981 Meese was a professor of law at the University of San Diego.

During the 1980 presidential campaign, Meese served as chief of staff and senior issues adviser for the Reagan-Bush committee and, following the election, headed the Reagan transition team. He served as counselor to the president from 1981 to 1985, functioning as chief policy adviser. As a member of the cabinet, Meese was responsible for the administration of the cabinet, policy development, and planning and evaluation.

As U.S attorney general, he tried to roll back some of the constitutional interpretations issued by the Earl Warren and WARREN E BURGER SUPREME COURT. He denounced judicial activism and called for a return to the "original meaning" of the Constitution as he believed the Founding Fathers understood it, a position Associate Justice WILLIAM J. BRENNAN, JR., criticized as "arrogance cloaked as humility." Meese disregarded such criticism, and he urged Reagan to appoint federal judges and Supreme Court judges who shared his views.

During his seven and a half years in the White House and the Justice Department, Meese was investigated on a number of ethics violations. In 1984, before he became attorney general, his failure to report reimbursements on more than 30 trips as White House counsel led the Office of Government Ethics to conclude that he had violated conflict-of-interest rules. A larger scandal emerged after he became U.S. attorney general, when independent prosecutor James C. McKay investigated Meese's efforts to help a friend, E. Robert Wallach, to secure U.S. government backing for an oil pipeline from Iraq to Jordan. As this scandal was breaking, Deputy Attorney General Arnold Burns and Assistant Attorney General William Weld resigned their positions at the Justice Department complaining that morale had plummeted under Meese because of the scandal. After 14 months of investigation, independent prosecutor McKay concluded in July 1988 that Meese had "probably violated criminal law" on four occasions, but he decided that Meese had not been motivated by "personal gain." Though Meese believed he had been vindicated by the investigation, the next month he resigned his office.

After leaving office, Meese worked briefly in the aerospace industry. Today he serves on a number of boards of conservative organizations.

See also INDEPENDENT COUNSEL.

Further reading: Lou Cannon, *President Reagan: The Role of a Lifetime* (New York: Simon & Schuster, 2000); Edwin Meese, *With Reagan: The Inside Story* (Washington, D.C.: Regnery, 1992).

Mexico (U.S. relations with)

Mexico lies across the southern border of the United States and shares a complex history with its northern neighbor. With 90 million inhabitants, it is one of LATIN AMERICA's most important countries. After Canada, Mexico is the United States's largest trading partner. Mexico is the number-two market and number-three supplier for the United States.

In 1964 Mexican president Adolfo López Mateos settled a long-standing border dispute between Mexico and the United States, concluding in 1964 a formal agreement with President Lyndon Johnson that gave Mexico sovereignty in territory near El Paso, Texas. Also during this time, Mexico successfully resisted the U.S. push for an anti-Cuban vote in the Organization of American States. Mexico was the only Latin American country never to break relations with Cuba.

In the late 1970s Mexico's economic system began to fall apart. Oil prices shot up, making Mexican reserves more valuable than before and providing collateral for international loans worth hundreds of millions of dollars. Institutions lent money on the assumption that Mexico's oil reserves and close relationship with the United States were good guarantees of repayment. This proved not to be the case, and Mexico defaulted on its outstanding debt in 1982. The International Monetary Fund (IMF) immediately stepped in to help renegotiate the defaulted loans. The effect of Mexico's fiscal crisis was to create social conditions that prompted the first swell of illegal IMMIGRATION to the United States. The IMMIGRATION REFORM AND CONTROL ACT OF 1986, known popularly as the Simpson-Mazzoli Act, was enacted in response, providing harsh penalties for U.S. employers who hire undocumented aliens, although migrant workers in California and the Southwest were exempted from this act. By the early 1990s, many believed this law was virtually ineffective.

Throughout the 1980s, although irritated by Mexico's recognition of the Sandinistas (the anti-U.S. government in Nicaragua), and condemnation of the U.S. invasion of PANAMA, both the RONALD W. REAGAN and GEORGE H. W. BUSH administrations negotiated debt, trade, and oil agreements that further integrated the two nations' economies. Mexican president Carlos Salinas took up the International Monetary Fund (IMF) and neo-liberal economic doctrines of the era, utilizing U.S.-trained policymakers and economists to implement a market-oriented strategy for the economy. Above all, Salinas pushed hard for the NORTH

Suspected illegal immigrants are searched by a U.S. Border Patrol agent. *(McNew/Getty Images)*

AMERICAN FREE TRADE AGREEMENT (NAFTA), with the intent to make Mexico an "export platform" like South Korea or TAIWAN. Some Mexican critics worried that NAFTA would reduce Mexico to a virtual colony of the United States, but Mexico's president insisted it was the only way to get the country out of its economic crisis. The NAFTA agreement of 1992 described a three-nation partnership among Mexico, the United States, and Canada, creating one of the largest trading blocs in the world. This agreement boosted Mexico to the world's eighth-largest exporter, moving from $42 billion in 1995 to $120 billion in 1999. Mexico's trade with the United States from the late 1990s into 2000 grew 113 percent, making the nation the number-two exporter to the United States after Canada. Bilateral Mexico-U.S. trade should exceed the commercial traffic between the United States and Europe by 2004.

Five major topics continue to dominate U.S.-Mexican relations: immigration, drugs, jobs, trade, and energy. One point of contention is the controversial annual certification and de-certification process, whereby Congress votes on whether to certify Mexico, making it eligible for aid from the United States. Mexican workers continue to migrate into the United States, because of lack of work in Mexico and the demand for workers in the United States. These workers generate roughly $28 billion a year to the U.S. ECONOMY and send $6 billion a year to Mexico. With the demand for electricity growing at an annual rate of 6 percent, energy cooperation between the two nations is a high priority in the United States in the 21st century.

The 2000 Mexican presidential election of Vicente Fox has also helped facilitate cordial relations between Mexico and the United States. Mexico was the first foreign country GEORGE W. BUSH visited as president, sending a strong message to the world that the United States intended on improving relations with its southern neighbor. Bush also promised early in his presidency to work with the Mexican president to build on the 1994 NAFTA agreement, to police the U.S.-Mexican border in a way that guarantees security and humane treatment of immigrants, and to review law enforcement policies on drug trafficking.

See also FOREIGN POLICY; HISPANIC AMERICANS.

Further reading: James Cockcroft, *Latin America—History, Politics, and U.S. Policy* (Palo Alto, Calif.: Wadsworth, 1996); David E. Lorey, *The U.S.-Mexican Border in the Twentieth Century. A History of Economic and Social Transformation* (Wilmington, Del.: Scholarly Resources, 1999).

—Michele Rutledge

militia movement

The militia movement is a host of small independent groups very loosely united under a common ideology of individualism, local autonomy, and separatism. They are organized along paramilitary command structures and most often found in isolated, rural U.S. communities.

The concept of limited government in the United States dates back to the American Revolution. Though the trend during the 20th century has been toward a larger and more powerful federal government, the ideal of local autonomy, free from interference by centralized government, continued to be held by many Americans. Although distrust of the federal government occurred in both the political left and the right wings, some groups on the far right came to believe that "subversive elements"—communists, Jews, international financiers—had gained control of the federal government.

The origins of the militia movement can be traced to the formation of the Minutemen, an extremist, right-wing group, organized by Missouri businessman Robert DePugh, in the early 1960s. Believing that a communist takeover of the United States was imminent, DePugh organized the Minutemen into secretive cells of 5 to 15 members, who were to stockpile weapons and train to defend the country. During the 1960s, there were a number of armed clashes between Minutemen and law enforcement officials. In October 1966, 19 New York Minutemen were arrested in raids and accused of planning to bomb three summer camps in the New York metropolitan area, which the Minutemen believed were being used by communists. Huge supplies of weapons were found in these raids. Charges against the Minutemen were dropped in 1977 after a lengthy trial, because the government had collected its evidence in improper searches. In 1968 DePugh went underground, but was arrested in the summer of 1969 and sentenced to 11 years in prison for firearm violations and fleeing bond. He was released in 1973. DePugh never regained his leadership position among far-right-wing groups, but the idea of forming militias gained adherents, although most of the groups remained law-abiding.

The militia movement of the 1980s and 1990s is best characterized as an extremists' reaction to federal encroachments on what members perceive as local autonomy and individual liberty. These groups often combined unrelated ideologies of racial supremacy and constitutional libertarianism. Though each militia group adheres to a unique set of principles, they share an unusually strong commitment to the Second Amendment, which they interpret to mean the right of American citizens to own firearms. They point to the opening clause of the amendment, which states that the "right of the people to keep and bear arms" is necessary to ensure "a well regulated militia," which is itself "necessary to the security of a free state." They argue that only a well-armed citizenry can check the growth of tyrannical government, because it represents the unspoken threat of revolution, if a dictator or aristocracy tries to usurp power. But other militia groups believe that the United States has already fallen into tyranny and that private militias must stockpile weapons to protect individual liberty.

Typical groups contend that current electoral processes have failed or are inoperable; that the political leadership is controlled by unseen forces, such as a global elite made up of powerful industrialists and Jews; and that, as a result, most current laws are unjust and are deliberately designed to deprive individuals of their liberty. Favorite examples used to support these claims include the introduction of federal income tax; the alleged sacrifice of American sovereignty to the UNITED NATIONS and the NORTH ATLANTIC TREATY ORGANIZATION (NATO); congressional efforts to strengthen GUN CONTROL laws; and federal involvement in desegregation and AFFIRMATIVE ACTION.

Many militia groups, though not all, find justification for their racist and political views through nonaffiliated churches made up of militia members. Militia groups are quite diverse; their charters differ considerably from group to group, often emphasizing entirely different priorities. Some unite around racism, others around hatred of taxation, and others around their fear of American cultural decay. Despite their reactionary rhetoric, most militia groups have never been involved in direct confrontations with the law. Some of the better-known groups include the Michigan Militia Corps, the Militia of Montana, and the Texas Constitutional Militia. The exact number of groups in the country is not known precisely, although those scholars who have studied these groups estimate their number to be only approximately 800 organizations.

The militia movement came to public attention during the early 1990s after three highly publicized events: the confrontations by federal officials with armed groups at Ruby Ridge in Idaho, and the BRANCH DAVIDIANS in Waco, Texas; and the bombing of the federal building in Oklahoma City, Oklahoma. The first occurred in April 1992 near a secluded homestead in Idaho. A team of six U.S. Marshals was preparing to execute a warrant against militia member Randy Weaver when they were discovered. The subsequent gunfire resulted in the deaths of Weaver's wife and 13-year-old son, and one U.S. Marshal. The second occurred 10 months later, in February 1993, on the Branch Davidian compound outside of Waco. Agents from the Bureau of Alcohol, Tobacco and Firearms (ATF) attempted to execute an arrest warrant against group leader David Koresh; gunfire erupted, killing four ATF agents and wounding 16 others. The Federal Bureau of Investigation immediately assumed control of the operation, leading to a six-week standoff between federal agents and more than 90 Branch Davidians, including 22 children. On April 19, 1993, the FBI launched teargas into the buildings in an effort to force the residents out. A fire erupted and killed 86 people inside the compound.

The Branch Davidians were an apocalyptic religious sect and did not fit the traditional profile of a typical militia group, except for their large stockpile of weapons, yet they won the sympathy of numerous groups who blamed the federal government for their deaths, portraying the incident as an example of a tyrannical government bent on disarming the population. Both the Ruby Ridge and Waco confrontations elicited sympathy from many Americans who did not otherwise relate to militia movement ideology.

This changed dramatically, however, when on April 19, 1995, two years after the anniversary of the Waco confrontation, a truck loaded with explosives detonated outside the Alfred P. Murrah Federal Building in Oklahoma City, killing 168 people including 19 children. The architects of the bombing, Timothy J. McVeigh and Terry L. Nichols, had long histories of militia activity. McVeigh later confessed that the bombing was planned as a reprisal against the federal government's involvement in Waco, which he viewed as an act of war. Other smaller standoffs between militia members and federal agents occurred in Texas, Idaho, Michigan, Missouri, and Illinois, but the public sympathy for the movement had dropped significantly. An estimated 300,000 people belonged to more than 800 militia groups in 1995, with 3 million supporters and sympathizers. By 2000, the estimated number of active members had dropped by half.

See also FEDERALISM; PROPERTY RIGHTS; TERRORISM.

Further reading: Richard Abanes, *American Militias: Rebellion, Racism & Religion* (Downers Grove, Ill.: InterVarsity Press, 1996); Vincent Coppola, *Dragons of God: A Journey through Far-Right America* (Atlanta, Ga.: Longstreet Press, 1996); Neil Hamilton, *Militias in America: A Reference Handbook* (Santa Barbara, Calif.: ABC-Clio, 1996).

—Aharon W. Zorea

Mitchell, George (John) (1933–)

George Mitchell is a Democrat from Maine who served in the U.S. SENATE from 1980 to 1995. He was elected Senate majority leader in November 1988, and served in that capacity until his retirement. While in the Senate, Mitchell actively supported liberal tax reform measures, as well as environmental legislation. He was noted for his skillful yet plainspoken interrogation of OLIVER L. NORTH during the Senate's investigation of the IRAN-CONTRA AFFAIR. He was respected, both inside and out of the Senate, for his instinct for compromise and sense of fair play.

Mitchell was born in Waterville, Maine, in 1933. Following graduation from Bowdoin College in 1954, he served as an officer in the U.S. Army Counterintelligence Corps until 1956. In 1960 he earned his law degree from Georgetown University.

When Maine's senator Edmund S. Muskie ran for vice president in 1968, he appointed Mitchell deputy director of the vice presidential campaign. After RICHARD M. NIXON won the election, Mitchell was named by the Democratic Party to the Commission on Party Structure and Delegate Selection. Mitchell again joined Muskie's team in 1972 when he ran for the Democratic presidential nomination. Muskie lost the nomination to GEORGE S. MCGOVERN.

In 1974 Mitchell was the Democratic gubernatorial candidate in Maine, where he lost to the Independent Party candidate, James B. Longley. That same year Mitchell was appointed to the executive committee of the Democratic National Committee. In 1977 President JAMES EARL CARTER, JR. appointed Mitchell as the U.S. attorney for Maine, and in 1979 he was appointed as judge of the U.S. District Court for Northern Maine. In 1980, when President Carter named Senator Muskie as secretary of state, Mitchell was appointed to serve out Muskie's term in the U.S. Senate.

In 1982 he beat the Republican challenger for the Senate seat by 61 percent to 39 percent. A staunch liberal Democrat, Mitchell opposed much of President RONALD W. REAGAN's agenda. He voted against the administration on prayer in public schools, limits on ABORTION, the balanced budget amendment, STRATEGIC DEFENSE INITIATIVE funding, MX missile deployment, resumption of chemical weapons production, aid to the CONTRAS in NICARAGUA, and confirmation of Justice WILLIAM H. REHNQUIST as chief justice of the U.S. SUPREME COURT, and he joined in the vote to override President Reagan's veto of sanctions on South Africa. Mitchell did cross party lines to work with the Republicans to construct the tax reform act of 1986.

Throughout Mitchell's stint in the Senate, though, his passion was for environmental issues. In 1981 Mitchell introduced the first bill regarding acid rain. He lobbied to convince senators from coal-producing states that sulfur dioxide from those businesses produced acid rain, which polluted drinking water, destroyed aquatic life, and corroded human lungs. Although repeated measures he sponsored to safeguard the environment failed, Mitchell remained dedicated to the issues throughout his terms in the Senate. He also supported the Maine Indian Land Claims Act of 1980, the Clean Water Act of 1981, and the Clean Air Act of 1990.

In 1984 Mitchell was named chairman of the Democratic Senatorial Campaign Committee, charged with putting the Senate back in Democratic hands in the 1986 election. Mitchell was instrumental in fund-raising and nurturing the candidates, winning a total of 54 Democratic Senate seats in the 100th Congress.

During the 1987 Iran-Contra hearings, Mitchell interrogated Lieutenant Colonel Oliver North in front of the world, through international television coverage. With hearing committee member and fellow Maine senator William Cohen, Mitchell wrote *Men of Zeal: A Candid Inside Story of the Iran-Contra Hearings.*

In 1988 Mitchell was elected Senate majority leader. Colleagues said they voted for Mitchell because he could work with the diversity of the Senate as well as be an effective national spokesman. Furthermore, Mitchell was a personal friend of newly elected president GEORGE H.W. BUSH, and Mitchell found the new administration easier to work with on several issues, such as budgetary measures and the environment.

In 1994 Mitchell announced he would not seek reelection to the Senate. President WILLIAM J. CLINTON proposed to nominate Mitchell to the U.S. Supreme Court to fill Harry A. Blackman's seat. Mitchell turned down the offer, telling the press he wanted to work for a health care initiative.

Clinton appointed Mitchell in 1995 as special adviser to the president for economic initiatives to Ireland. In January 1996, Mitchell issued a report calling for the Irish Republican Army (IRA) to give up guerrilla weapons and hold democratic elections prior to peace talks. In February 1996, the IRA, an opposition paramilitary force and political party, broke the 16-month cease-fire. On April 12, 1998, however, a multilateral peace agreement was signed by representatives of the United Kingdom and political parties in Northern Ireland. The peace agreement was approved by a public referendum in Northern Ireland on May 22, 1998.

In 2000 Clinton appointed Mitchell to head a similar peace effort to resolve the conflict between the Israelis and the Palestinians. Although this problem proved even more intractable than the Irish problem, Mitchell played a critical role in negotiating key agreements that allowed for Palestinian autonomy.

For his efforts in Ireland, Mitchell received the Medal of Freedom. Following the September 11, 2001, terrorist attack, Mitchell was appointed to chair the American Red Cross Liberty Fund. He continues to practice law in Washington, D.C., and serves on the boards of many corporations. He is the author of *Not for America Alone: The Triumph of Democracy and the Fall of Communism* and *Making Peace,* (1992).

—Leah Blakey

Mitchell, John N. (1913–1988)

Born in Detroit, Michigan, on September 15, 1913, John Newton Mitchell rose to prominence as RICHARD M. NIXON's campaign manager and attorney general before falling from grace during the WATERGATE SCANDAL. He was the first attorney general of the United States to be convicted of a crime.

Mitchell graduated from Fordham Law School in 1938 and joined the New York City law firm of Caldwell and Raymond, specializing in state and municipal bonds. During World War II, Mitchell served as a lieutenant in the navy, commanding John F. Kennedy's PT boat unit. During the war Mitchell won the Silver Star for bravery and was twice awarded the Purple Heart. After the war, Mitchell resumed his law practice in New York.

Mitchell met Richard M. Nixon in 1967, when the former vice president joined the firm of Mudge, Rose, Guthrie, Alexander and Mitchell. Nixon and Mitchell formed a close relationship, and Mitchell agreed to direct Nixon's 1968 presidential campaign, despite not having much experience. Following his election, Nixon appointed Mitchell U.S. attorney general, and he implemented anti-crime and civil rights policies, as well as assisting in the selection of U.S. SUPREME COURT nominees. Mitchell also collected information on the president's political rivals, through illegal wiretaps and investigations by the FBI.

In 1972 Mitchell resigned his office to head the Committee to Reelect the President (CREEP). Mitchell directed "dirty tricks" and espionage operations against Nixon's political opponents, the most famous of these being the break-in at the Democratic Party headquarters in the Watergate complex on June 16, 1972. The break-in was discovered, and five men were arrested. Investigations indicated that CREEP had directed the operation. In July Mitchell resigned, and it seemed that nothing was to come from the break-in. That November Nixon won one of the largest landslide elections in history.

Only through the efforts of two *Washington Post* investigative reporters, Robert Woodward and Carl Bernstein, did the full extent of CREEP's involvement become known. By 1973 the Watergate conspiracy was being uncovered by congressional investigations and special prosecutors. Mitchell, along with other high-ranking administration members including H. R. Haldeman, White House chief of staff, and John Ehrlichman, a Nixon adviser, was indicted for conspiracy, obstruction of justice, and perjury. During his trial, Mitchell remained loyal to Nixon, denying most of the charges and arguing that other actions were done for national security reasons.

On January 1, 1975, Mitchell was convicted on all counts and sentenced to 30 months to eight years in prison, making him the first attorney general sent to prison. Mitchell served 19 months in federal prison before being released in 1979. He was disbarred and lived quietly for the next nine years, dying of a heart attack on November 9, 1988. He was buried in Arlington National Cemetery, because of his military service and cabinet rank.

See also WATERGATE SCANDAL.

—John Korasick

Mondale, Walter F. (1923–)

Walter Frederick ("Fritz") Mondale has had a long and distinguished career as a public official. Born January 1, 1928, in Ceylon, Minnesota, the future senator, vice president, presidential candidate, and ambassador was politically active at an early age. As a freshman at Macalester College, Mondale was involved in the Democratic-Farmer-Labor (DFL) Party. He was a volunteer in Hubert Humphrey's Minneapolis mayoral campaign in 1947 and U.S. SENATE campaign in 1948. Mondale also organized a chapter of Students for Democratic Action (SDA), and in 1949, accepted the job of executive director of the SDA in Washington, D.C. In 1950 he resumed his college career at the University of Minnesota, graduating in 1951. After two years in the army, Mondale entered the University of Minnesota Law School, graduating in 1956. In 1955 he married Joan Adams; they had three children.

Mondale had resumed his political activities upon returning to Minnesota, supporting DFL candidates and actively participating in the attorney general and gubernatorial campaigns of Orville Freeman. By the late 1950s Mondale was a respected party tactician and was state financial director for the DFL. In 1960 Governor Orville I. Freeman, appointed him state attorney general, replacing Miles Lord, who had resigned. Mondale was elected to the position in November 1960, and reelected in 1962. During this time he demonstrated his commitment to the downtrodden, instituting antitrust, civil rights, and consumer protection actions. As attorney general of Minnesota, he wrote a amici curiae (friends of the court) brief in a case before the U.S. SUPREME COURT, urging reversal of the conviction of Clarence Earl Gideon for a noncapital crime in the state of Florida. In *Gideon v. Wainwright* (1963), the Supreme Court overturned the conviction, holding that a defendant must be provided legal counsel.

Mondale's emergence in Minnesota politics, legal expertise, and attachment to liberal causes earned him a role in the 1964 Democratic National Convention as a member of the convention credentials committee. He headed the committee that mediated the dispute between the black Mississippi Freedom Democratic Party and the Mississippi Democratic Party. Mondale orchestrated the compromise that kept the peace at the convention, though neither side was pleased. After the 1964 election, Mondale was appointed by Governor Karl F. Rovaag to fill the Senate seat of Hubert Humphrey, who had been elected Lyndon Johnson's vice president.

In 1966 Mondale was reelected to the Senate. He was a strong supporter of civil rights legislation, consumer protection, education reform, and campaign finance reform. He remained friendly with the LABOR movement. He was a supporter of Johnson's VIETNAM WAR policy until 1968. In 1972 Mondale refused GEORGE S. MCGOVERN's offer of the vice presidential spot and was reelected senator. In 1976 Mondale accepted JAMES EARL CARTER, JR.'s offer of the vice presidency. The Democratic ticket won in 1976 and Mondale, while often privately disagreeing with Carter, served as a close adviser and handled 13 foreign missions. He played a critical role in the CAMP DAVID ACCORDS (1979), which brought peace between Israel and Egypt. In 1980, Carter-Mondale lost their reelection bid to the Republican ticket of RONALD W. REAGAN and GEORGE H. W. BUSH. Mondale entered private law practice and made numerous speeches. By 1981 Mondale decided to run for president.

He ran in the 1984 campaign, choosing Representative GERALDINE A. FERRARO of New York as his vice presidential candidate and making her the first woman from a major party to run for executive office. Despite this, RONALD W. REAGAN was reelected in a landslide. In 1987 he became the chairman of the National Democratic Institute for

International Affairs, a position he held until 1993. That year President WILLIAM J. CLINTON named him U.S. ambassador to Japan, a position he held until 1996.

See also ELECTIONS; POLITICAL PARTIES.

Further reading: Steven M. Gillon, *The Democrats' Dilemma: Walter F. Mondale and the Liberal Legacy* (New York: Columbia University Press, 1992).

—John Korasick

Moral Majority

The Moral Majority was a conservative religious and political group founded by the Reverend Jerry Falwell and a group of Baptist pastors from large churches throughout the United States in 1979. The group's stated goal was to create a "nonpartisan political organization to promote morality in public life and to combat legislation that favored the legalization of immorality." It became visible on the national level when it supported Republican Party nominee RONALD W. REAGAN's bid for the 1980 presidential election. By 1981 the organization had chapters in each of the 50 states, local affiliates, and a Washington, D.C., office. The group claimed to represent the "moral majority" of the American people. Fundamentalist and EVANGELICAL CHRISTIANS provided the base of support. Paul Weyrich, president of Free Congress Foundation, coined the name "Moral Majority" and helped formulate its strategy as part of his three-decade effort to transform social and religious conservatives into political activists as part of the New Right movement.

Falwell graduated in 1956 from the Baptist Bible College in Springfield, Missouri, and was ordained by the Baptist Bible fellowship. Returning to his hometown of Lynchburg, Virginia, Falwell founded the Thomas Road Baptist Church, and soon after, began radio and television broadcasts of his popular "Old Time Gospel Hour." Falwell founded Lynchburg Baptist College in 1971. The Moral Majority, Inc., was founded eight years later. In its 10-year existence, the Moral Majority lobbied for prayer and the teaching of creationism in public schools and opposed the EQUAL RIGHTS AMENDMENT, homosexual rights, ABORTION, and the U.S.-Soviet STRATEGIC ARMS LIMITATION TREATIES. As a political action group composed of conservative, fundamentalist Christians, the Moral Majority played a role in helping to defeat the ERA. Furthermore, the Moral Majority helped mobilize Christian Evangelicals to become involved in politics. For the most part, these voters were conservative, born-again Christians, and the movement played a significant role in the 1980 elections through its strong support of New Right candidates.

On June 11, 1989, Reverend Falwell announced, "Our mission is accomplished." Falwell said that the Moral Majority would permanently close its doors on August 31. Contributing significantly to the movement's demise was the downfall of disgraced televangelists Jimmy Swaggart and Jim Bakker. Although Falwell himself was not engaged in the events that ruined Bakker and Swaggart, the fallout effects of the scandals dealt a hurtful blow to every national ministry, including Falwell's. In its final year, Moral Majority's annual revenue fell to barely $3 million from a peak of $11.1 million in 1984.

Many former supporters of the Moral Majority found other vehicles for conservative political expression in movements like the CHRISTIAN COALITION. Although clearly not representing the "majority" of American opinion, the Moral Majority sparked animated controversy among liberals, and was the catalyst that began the political activism of formerly inactive evangelical, fundamentalist Christians, who had begun to flex their political muscle and found they too could shape the legislative process.

See also CONSERVATIVE MOVEMENT; RELIGION; TELEVANGELISM.

—Michele Rutledge

movies

In the United States, movies have long been an entertainment staple as well as an artistic medium that reflected the nation's social and cultural trends. Powerful social movements, regulatory attitudes, and technological and commercial changes radically transformed the nature of American movies during the last 35 years of the 20th century.

The late 1960s witnessed what many called a Hollywood renaissance that extended well into the 1970s. Throughout this period American movies adapted themselves to various external forces that would shape the direction of the film industry. The national film audience had shrunk from 80 million to 20 million, while its members had become younger and more educated. The social movements of the 1960s had reconfigured social and sexual values. These developments, along with the need to accommodate itself to the competition of the world market, forced the film industry to alter its practices as well as the content of its products. Major Hollywood studios often became subsidiaries of huge conglomerates like Coca-Cola. In the 1980s some ownership moved overseas, when an Australian company bought Fox, and Japanese companies purchased Columbia and Universal. Studios began producing more fare for television audiences than for theatrical release, and increasingly, studios shot films on location outside Hollywood. For example, New York City recaptured its status as a movie-making center.

While many of the films of the period were produced strictly for entertainment value, the trend was toward films that commented on the state of society. Major directors such as Robert Altman, Francis Ford Coppola, Stanley Kubrick, and Martin Scorsese produced films that challenged the traditional norms and institutions of American life. Films like *Dr. Strangelove* (1964), *Bonnie and Clyde* (1967), *The Graduate* (1967), *Easy Rider* (1969), *Medium Cool* (1969), *The Godfather* (1972), and *Taxi Driver* (1976) searched for meaning in a society that had become entangled in the VIETNAM WAR and that many perceived had lost its way, becoming enamored of the merely material and suffocated by its institutions.

This artistic challenging of traditional norms was also instrumental in restructuring the way films were regulated. In 1968, the Motion Picture Rating System (MPRS) replaced the Hollywood Production Code that was established in 1930. The old code, essentially an industry-controlled CENSORSHIP program, was replaced by a series of ratings (G, PG, PG-13, R, and X) that indicated the level of audience maturity each film demanded. Once in place, this system allowed moviemakers to push the artistic envelope even further. The MPRS remained in effect at the end of the 20th century with one alteration. The X rating had proven unworkable and was replaced in 1990 by the NC-17 rating (no children under 17 allowed).

The late 1970s witnessed a radical change in both the content and the distribution of American films. While during the previous decade, films sought to challenge the myths of American life, beginning in the late 1970s and extending into the mid-1990s movies reaffirmed those myths and sought to create new ones. As many scholars of film history argue, mainstream films, with some exceptions, had become relatively conservative and predictable, unwilling to take artistic and political risks.

Star Wars (George Lucas, 1977) almost single-handedly effected this change. It renewed the old Hollywood genre of "good vs. evil" by offering unambiguous heroes and villains and provided an escape from social reality into a science fiction wonderland of myth and magic created by new visual technologies. Its pioneering use of Dolby NR (noise reduction) and the Dolby SVA (stereo variable area) soundtrack led many to herald it as a "second coming of sound." Lucas's use of COMPUTERS to control special-effect shots virtually computerized the industry; by the late 1980s, computers had become essential in every aspect of filmmaking. Further, *Star Wars* secured the viability of the sequel, and sequels, which made safe investments for both producers and audiences, began to dominate the industry with films such as *The Empire Strikes Back* (1980); *The Return of the Jedi* (1983); and *The Phantom Menace* (1999). Of course, sequels were not new, as evidenced in James Bond, Pink Panther, and Planet of the Apes films, but sequels came to dominate the industry.

Additionally, *Star Wars* earned so much money that it changed the way the industry did business. By the 1980s, studios concentrated on making blockbusters and reserved a few slots on the production schedule for low-budget and offbeat films. Other than that, they produced sequels and acquired independent films that they released under the studio logo. Because movies cost so much more to make and were capable of earning so much (Steven Spielberg's *Jurassic Park*, 1993, grossed almost $1 billion), studios considered it foolhardy to take chances on the public's taste. Finally, *Star Wars* and other movies such as *Close Encounters of the Third Kind* (Spielberg, 1977), *Raiders of the Lost Ark* (Lucas and Spielberg, 1981), and *Back to the Future* (Robert Zemeckis, 1985) combined the appeal to innocence with the appeal of special effects, and produced a cinematic world of spectacle and an unambiguous tribute to traditional values.

The unambiguous good-triumphs-over-evil myth and the childhood fascination with space and magic were not the only myths evoked by mainstream film, however. Films such as *Halloween* (1979), *Alien* (1979), and *Poltergeist* (1982) presented in a visually stunning way the darker myths of horror, terror, and the irrational and unknown menace. Many films investigated the dilemmas of real life in a comic way (*Ordinary People*, 1980; *The Big Chill*, 1983). Action heroes such as Clint Eastwood, Sylvester Stallone, and Arnold Schwarzenegger offered film series that affirmed the deeply rooted American value of assertive individualism. *Born on the Fourth of July* (1989) reasserted American patriotism, and *Saving Private Ryan* (1998) depicted the realities of war while venerating the incumbent heroism of its American participants.

In contrast to these relatively formulaic films stood many exceptions by artists who sought to explore the tragic aspects of American social history in films such as *Little Big Man* (1970) and *Heaven's Gate* (1980). Several AFRICAN AMERICANS directed their depictions of the realities of family and urban life for wide audiences: Charles Hughes (*Killer of Sheep*, 1970; *To Sleep with Anger*, 1990), Spike Lee (*Do the Right Thing*, 1989; *Malcolm X*, 1992), and John Singleton (*Boyz in the Hood*, 1991). John Sayles offered a realistic portrayal of baseball's 1919 Black Sox scandal (*Eight Men Out*, 1988), in which players conspired with gamblers to throw the World Series, but the film attracted a relatively small audience. In 1989, however, *Field of Dreams* was enormously successful because of its redemptive approach to the same scandal. In the typical late 20th-century American style, it suggested that the culture could heal itself by forgiving and erasing the troubles of the past. Redemption was complete when the ballplayers were welcomed back to the field of dreams, an action that rescued the financially stricken farmer who had built the field.

Director Steven Spielberg working with a camera on the set of his film *Close Encounters of the Third Kind* (Hulton/Archive)

Beginning in the 1980s, the film and TELEVISION industries became more interdependent, a result in large part of the growth of cable and satellite television and of the use of VHS videotape. Hollywood studios began to make movies for immediate release on network and cable TV. Some pay channels (HBO, Showtime) and basic cable channels (USA, TNT) started producing feature films in the 1990s for exclusive release on their network. At the end of the 20th century, most theatrically released movies were televised, usually on cable pay channels or cable pay-per-view, within a year after their initial release. This practice invited home viewers to make a videotape copy, thus diversifying the market for the film industry. Essentially, if a film did not fare well in theaters, a studio could recoup much of its losses in video sales and rentals. The video rental industry has also allowed film studios to market their entire library of films to the home-viewing public.

While providing a wide range of choices and increased accessibility, videotape lacks the quality of a celluloid film presentation. Additionally, editing, cropping (making the

film image fit the TV screen), and colorization (the process of adding electronic colors to black-and-white films) created a viewing experience quite different from viewing a film in its theatrical setting. Although many American movies increasingly rely on special effects to attract audiences, and the blockbuster and the predictability of its sequel drive the industry's success, theatrically released films still offer the *big* image, clear details, true colors, and state-of-the-art stereo sound all offered in a dedicated environment free of the distractions of home viewing. The uniqueness of the experience, as well as the content of the film, continues to make film a culturally important medium, while fostering the continued commercial success of Hollywood studios as integral parts of the American consumer economy.

See also MEDIA; POPULAR CULTURE; PORNOGRAPHY.

Further reading: Leonard Quart and Albert Auster, *American Film and Society since 1945* (Westport, Conn.: Greenwood Publishing Group, 1991); Robert Sklar, *Movie-*

Made America: A Cultural History of American Movies (New York: Vintage Books, 1994).

—William L. Glankler

multiculturalism

Multiculturalism, as Harvard University professor Nathan Glazer observes, is a term that describes the nature of American society, as well as an ideology and program. American society since 1968 has become increasingly multicultural as many people immigrated to the United States from different cultures to create a rich variety of subcultures that interacted with and influenced the general American culture.

The emergence of multiculturalism as an ideology and political program emerged from the Civil Rights movement in the 1960s. On college campuses, ethnic minorities, including African-American, Hispanic, Native American, and Asian-American students demanded the establishment of programs devoted to ethnic studies. At the same time, female student activists called for the creation of Women's Studies programs. These demands reflected a rising multicultural consciousness in society. By the 1990s, multicultural theory was extended to include homosexuals and lesbians. At the same time, traditional departments in colleges and universities, especially in the humanities and social sciences, established new courses or changed existing courses to incorporate a multicultural perspective.

In the 1980s and 1990s the United States experienced a significant influx of Hispanic and Asian immigrants. Hispanics became the fastest-growing ethnic group, as immigrants from Mexico settled not only in the Southwest and West but in eastern and midwestern cities. Puerto Rican people and Dominican people migrated to the East Coast, and Cubans made homes in Florida. Newcomers from Vietnam, Thailand, Korea, Hong Kong, Taiwan, and the Philippines created new communities, especially in California. Demographers predicted that by the year 2010, people of European ancestry would be a minority in California. During the 1980s, the number of residents for whom English was a foreign tongue jumped by a third to 31.8 million. As a result, about 14 percent of all residents grew up speaking a language other than English.

The result of this massive influx of new people of different races, religions, and cultures created a unique multicultural society in modern America. As these immigrant groups joined the existing minorities in the United States, some policymakers, educators, intellectuals, and activists called for a program to ensure cultural awareness and cultural sensitivity toward various subgroups. The ideology of multiculturalism maintained that the hegemonic white European culture excluded other ethnic, racial, and reli-

gious subcultures. American culture, proponents argued, was a rich tapestry composed of various elements, and claiming to define American culture simply as one derived from Europe was inaccurate, misleading, and politically destructive. Critics of multiculturalism promoted the importance of Judeo-Christian European culture as the foundation of American society and accused multiculturalists of trying to impose POLITICAL CORRECTNESS in public policy and education.

The term "multiculturalism" came into widespread use only at the end of the 1980s. In the 1990s, however, hundreds of books and journal articles appeared, discussing the meaning and implications of multiculturalism. The establishment of these new centers, programs, courses, and curriculum changes stirred great controversy within universities and colleges. In varying degrees, these new programs often were centers of advocacy as well as centers of scholarship. Some educators believed that such advocacy undermined academic standards of objectivity, while unnecessarily heightening racial, ethnic, and cultural difference.

For instance, Afrocentrism, a perspective that insisted on the importance of African culture to world civilization, sparked intense controversy. Afrocentrist scholars and educators held that African people had discovered fundamental concepts in mathematics and the sciences and contributed significantly to world history, but that often these discoveries and contributions were ignored and suppressed by white Europeans.

Moreover, these ethnic, women's, and gay studies programs often were staffed by faculty drawn from the various groups specific to these programs. When faculty members not of the group were excluded from appointment, controversy often followed, as seen in the 1990s in cases at Harvard, UC Berkeley, and Queens.

Multiculturalism also influenced elementary and secondary education. In the 1990s, many state education commissions mandated that curriculum and textbooks reflect multicultural perspectives by incorporating discussions of various cultures and peoples in American society. As established courses and textbooks in elementary and secondary education were replaced by multicultural ones, some parents, teachers, and politicians decried what they perceived as declining academic standards, racial divisiveness, and "political correctness." Conflicts erupted in California over standards for social studies textbooks and other texts selected by state committees seeking to introduce multiculturalism into the state education system. In the early 1990s, further controversy was created when a federally funded effort, cochaired by Gary B. Nash, a professor of American history at the University of California, Los Angeles, sought to create national history standards for American and world history.

Multiculturalism came under criticism by historians and other educators, including Arthur M. Schlesinger, Jr., C. Vann Woodward, and Diane Ravitch. These scholars argued that these efforts at "multiculturalism" overemphasized the role of minorities and women, thereby skewing history in the name of diversity. They also contended that the multicultural approach to the humanities and the social sciences failed to establish a solid base of knowledge for the further study of history and literature.

Supporters of multiculturalism maintain that education needs to develop within students a respect for and recognition of the wide range of subcultures and groups that compose American life and culture. This perspective reflects the changing nature of American society and culture. Although some advocates for multiculturalism seek a more "critical multiculturalism" or "transformative multiculturalism"—one that allows students to envision a reordering of culture and society—this view remains a minority among multiculturalists.

Multiculturalism, as a descriptive term for American society, accurately reflects the changing composition of the American population, as well as its changing cultural standards and attitudes. Multiculturalism as a theory has challenged the traditional vision of the American "melting pot," in which all groups are assimilated into one culture. Critics of multicultural theory maintain that its perspective promotes a "cult of otherness," which sees society made up of subgroups—African-American people, Hispanic people, Asian people, women, and homosexual people—who identify only with their own cultures. Proponents of multiculturalism respond by arguing that American society needs to acknowledge and encourage the existing diversity of cultures within the nation. These two immeasurable positions are not easily reconciled.

Further readings: Todd Gitlin, *The Twilight of Common Dreams* (New York: Metropolitan Books, 1995); Nathan Glazer, *We Are All Multiculturalists Now* (Cambridge, Mass.: Harvard University Press, 1997); Nathan Glazer, "Multiculturalism in Theory and Practice," in *Encyclopedia of American Cultural and Intellectual History*, Vol. 3, edited by Mary Kupiec Cayton and Peter W. Williams (New York: Houghton Mifflin, 2001), 253–262.

music

Throughout its history, American music has demonstrated the ethnic and cultural diversity of the United States as well as its penchant for commodification. Popular music in America, especially since the late 1960s, has been a product of both the country's cultural pluralism and its consumer ethic.

Late 20th-century American music reflected the political, economic, and racial outlooks of its audience. The classical tradition remained and continued to develop, although sales of recorded classical music in 1999 represented only 3.5 percent of all sales. (Rock constituted 25.2 percent; country, 10.8 percent; rap, 10.8 percent; R & B, 10.5 percent; pop, 10.3 percent; other, 9.1 percent; religious, 5.1 percent; jazz, 3.0 percent; and soundtracks, 0.8 percent.) Although most of its repertoire has remained European-focused, works by such American composers as Charles Ives, Aaron Copland, and George Gershwin are still performed in concert halls throughout the country.

The popularity of musical theater has increased, evidenced in shows such as *Cats* (more than 7,000 performances), *Chorus Line* (more than 6,000 performances), *Les Miserables* (more than 5,000 performances) and *The Phantom of the Opera* (more than 5,000 performances). Other shows, such as *The Lion King, Ragtime,* and *Bring in 'da Noise, Bring in 'da Funk* have attracted younger audiences to the theater. Although in the 1969–70 season, there were 62 new productions while in 1999–2000, there were only 37 new productions, attendance increased from 7.4 million to 11.4 million.

Symphonic and operatic performances also reached large audiences. By 2000 there were over 90 symphony orchestras in the United States with annual expenses reaching $2 million or more. Symphony orchestras were found not only in established cultural centers, such as New York, Boston, Chicago, Philadelphia, San Francisco, Los Angeles, Detroit, Saint Louis, Minneapolis, and Pittsburgh, but also in cities such as Knoxville, Tennessee; Dayton, Ohio; Spokane, Washington; Louisville, Kentucky; Grand Rapids, Michigan; and Raleigh, North Carolina. Furthermore, there are more than 60 opera companies with budgets of $1 million or more in cities across America. The classical and operatic tradition, however, remains for many a signifier of "high" culture and status, while popular music dominates both the music industry and the popular mind.

Popular music came to dominate the American music landscape because it more realistically reflected the everyday experiences of Americans. The racial boundaries that had marginalized popular music in the 1940s and 1950s slowly dissolved with the advent of early rhythm and blues, and rock and roll, both integrated forms of musical expression that developed from both black and white cultural influences. In the 1960s and 1970s, performers like James Brown ("I'm Black and I'm Proud") and Marvin Gaye ("What's Going On" and "Inner City Blues"), along with the influential and economically successful Motown Records, produced "soul" music recordings that reflected the growing sense of racial pride among AFRICAN AMERICANS. The 1960s also witnessed a popular music peppered with political messages that advocated racial and gender equality and an end to the VIETNAM WAR. Although such socially aware music continued to be produced throughout the 1970s 1980s, and 1990s, its prominence was eclipsed by the more commercially successful "British invasion," led by the Beatles and the Rolling Stones.

During the 1970s, disco music became the dominant popular musical form. The discotheque replaced the concert stage as the primary venue, and people danced to the sounds of performers such as The Village People, KC and the Sunshine Band, Donna Summer, and Kool and the Gang. Such a culturally diverse arena provided a musical platform for all ethnicities and sexual orientations.

The 1980s and 1990s signaled the end of one musical form's dominance and witnessed the splintering of popular music into several genres. Gone as well was the inclusive arena of the discotheque, produced by the cultural integration of the 1960s. Forms such as hard rock, rap, pop,

Bruce Springsteen *(Rick Diamond/Online USA)*

alternative, grunge, and rhythm and blues competed for audiences and consumers, and increasingly identified with geographical location as much as racial and economic status. The grunge movement, attributed largely to Kurt Cobain and his group, Nirvana, centered in Seattle, Washington, and gave voice to the undirected anguish of the white, pessimistic, twenty-something generation. The hip-hop movement reflected the African-American and Latino urban experience in America, and produced the enormously popular rap music, first made successful by Kurtis Blow in 1980 with "Christmas Rappin'" and "The Breaks." Rock music split into camps such as heavy metal, led by groups such as Poison and Motley Crüe, and alternative with such groups as Duran Duran and U2. Country and western music also experienced an increased popularity during the 1980s and into the 1990s, evidenced by the popularity of country and western dance halls and the crossover success of country and western bands like Alabama and Garth Brooks.

In the 1990s, Madonna, a female singer popular in the 1980s and well known for her risqué musical videos, sought a tamer, more mature image, while singers Britney Spears and the Spice Girls projected the sex kitten/bubble gum image (Britney Spears later sought to create a more explicitly sexy image in the 1990s). Also in the decade of the 1990s, the tradition of the male group sound with "boy bands," such as the Backstreet Boys and N'Sync, continued. These various genres clearly demonstrated the pluralism inherent in American culture, as each one enjoyed tremendous popularity but no one achieved dominance.

The diversity of music enabled performers and artists to more readily share the wealth generated by the recording industry. Propelled by technology and increased consumer activity, such performers as Michael Jackson, Whitney Houston, Bruce Springsteen, and Madonna amassed great fortunes and propelled the recording industry to its zenith while simultaneously defining popular culture with their hairstyles and fashion. Within a decade, total sales of recorded music, dominated by rock, country, rap, R & B, and pop rose from $7.834 billion, with 801 million in total unit sales in 1991, to $14.584 billion, with 1,660 in total unit sales in 1999.

The role of TELEVISION in the creation of the superstar cannot be overestimated. Dick Clark's *American Bandstand* and Don Cornelius's *Soul Train* (as well as popular variety shows such as Ed Sullivan's long-running Sunday evening program) established television's role in the music industry, by reinforcing the musical style heard on the radio and on record albums, as well as the cultural styles associated with the musical form. In the 1980s, the advent of music videos, and the cable music network, MTV, appeared to assure television's place as a conduit for the cultural influence of music. Initially, few artists used MTV and music videos for promotional purposes and the venue had only minimal impact.

By the late 1980s, however, performers realized the commercial power of short, two- to three-minute videos. These videos propelled artists like Madonna and Michael Jackson into superstardom, and recording companies began to pour millions of dollars into these short but powerful promotion tools. Record sales increased dramatically during the 1980s and early 1990s, as music videos became modifiers of public taste and style.

During the 1990s, technological developments boosted a recording industry that was undergoing both demographic and competitive changes. First introduced in 1980, the compact disc (CD) revolutionized the recording industry and almost eliminated the production and sale of vinyl record albums by the late 1990s. CDs allowed the production of more material on a single recording, greatly enhanced the quality of sound recordings, and increased the availability of music through INTERNET Web sites. The advent of MP3 files and rewriteable CDs increased the opportunities for listeners to customize their own recordings. Such technological developments also enhanced music's cultural influence by making it more easily attainable and flexible, a process that has complicated our understanding of music's role in cultural identity.

Although the racial and ethnic identities of many groups are still rooted in specific genres and styles of popular music, American popular music has come to reflect generational, economic, and political ideologies as much as racial or ethnic distinction. Hip-hop culture is no longer confined to the African-American and Latino communities. Rap music is a staple of suburban white teenagers and urban African-American youths alike. The increased Latino population and its incumbent influence have helped propel the popularity of salsa, samba, and Tejano music beyond its traditional ethnic audiences. Country and western, once confined to Nashville's Grand Ole Opry and the southern and midwestern white working class, has become one of America's most popular musical forms, with performers such as Faith Hill and Garth Brooks enjoying geographically, ethnically, and economically very diverse audiences.

Beyond ethnic, racial, geographical, and economic distinctions, American music has long served as a landscape in which American women could expand certain boundaries. During the late 1960s, Janis Joplin integrated women into the male-dominated world of rock music. Grace Slick (Jefferson Airplane), Cher, Pat Benatar, Joan Jett, and Tina Turner followed Joplin in the 1970s and 1980s and cultivated the image of the "rock chick." Cher and Turner went on to achieve superstardom, and demonstrated that women over the age of 20 could be successful in an industry governed by perceived notions of beauty and image. Loretta Lynn, Tammy Wynette, and Dolly Parton established a major place for women in country and western music, by bringing to life the realities of poverty and failed relationships. By the year 2000, women participated in all genres of popular music, and at all levels. The diversification of women's roles in the music industry was largely initiated by the advent of the Madonna age in the late 1980s. Many have become sought-after producers, such as Lauryn Hill and Missy Elliot. Sarah McLaughlin has sponsored and sustained Lilith Fair, an all-women music festival. Other women have dominated nominations for music industry awards, and have headed divisions and subsidiaries of major record companies (Madonna: Maverick Records; Tracy Edmonds: CEO of Yub Yum Records; Frances Preston: president of BMI).

American popular music during the last decades of the 20th century was but one manifestation of the history of the nation's developing cultural identity. Whether it is the latest Andrew Lloyd Webber musical, Lauryn Hill rap song, or Van Halen rock anthem, the very eclectic nature of American popular music reveals the nation's diverse cultural and artistic identity.

See also ADVERTISING; ANTIWAR MOVEMENT—VIETNAM; CENSORSHIP; COMPUTERS; MEDIA; MULTICULTURALISM; POPULAR CULTURE; RECREATION; WOODSTOCK.

Further reading: Richard Crawford, *The American Musical Landscape* (New York: W. W. Norton, 1993); H. Wiley Hitchcock, *Music in the United States: A Historical Introduction,* 4th ed. (Upper Saddle River, N.J.: Prentice Hall, 2000).

—William L. Glankler

N

Nader, Ralph (1934–)

American consumer advocate, author, lawyer, and GREEN PARTY presidential candidate Ralph Nader is credited with founding and leading the modern consumer rights movement.

Ralph Nader was born in Winsted, Connecticut, in 1934 to Lebanese immigrants Rose and Nathra Nader. Inspired at a young age by family discussions around the dinner table and by the writings of Progressive-era muckrakers Upton Sinclair, Lincoln Steffens, and Ida Tarbell, Nader embraced ideals of democracy and active citizenship. Graduating magna cum laude from Princeton University in 1955, Nader received a law degree from Harvard in 1958. It was there that Nader first began his exploration of the engineering design of automobiles, an unconventional legal topic at the time. His findings resulted in an article published in *The Nation* in 1959, "The Safe Car You Can't Buy," which asserted that automakers were sacrificing safety for cost, style, and calculated obsolescence.

Nader undertook the practice of law in Hartford, Connecticut, but left in 1963 to go to Washington, D.C. He moonlighted as a freelance writer for *The Christian Science Monitor* and *The Nation,* and worked for Assistant Secretary of Labor Daniel Patrick Moynihan as a consultant to the U.S. Department of Labor. Nader also acted as an unpaid Senate subcommittee adviser, examining what capacity the federal government might play in auto safety. His findings resulted in the 1965 best-selling book *Unsafe at Any Speed: The Designed-In Dangers of the American Automobile,* in which Nader criticized the American AUTOMOBILE INDUSTRY for its unsafe products and specifically denounced General Motors' Corvair model. Nader later sued GM for privacy invasion after the automaker attempted to discredit him. The case not only forced GM's president to go before a Senate committee and admit wrongdoing but also led directly to the passage of the 1966 National Traffic and Motor Vehicle Safety Act, which gave the government the power to enact safety standards for all automobiles sold in the United States. Nader used the money won in the settlement to initiate the modern consumer protection movement.

In 1969 Nader founded the Center for Study of Responsive Law and began to focus on other consumer safety issues, calling for new or stricter government regulation of industry and business in various product sectors. His associates, originally derided as "Nader's Raiders," presented numerous studies on such widely different items as pipeline safety, land use, baby food, mercury poisoning, pension reform, insecticides, and banking. He was credited with being the moving force in new legislation calling for stricter regulation of meat- and poultry-processing plants, radiation emissions from television sets, and coal mine health and safety. In 1971 Nader founded Public Citizen, a lobbying agency in Washington, D.C., that by 2001 involved more than 150,000 people in its six branches: Critical Mass Energy Project, Congress Watch, Global Trade Watch, Health Research Group, Litigation Group, and Buyers Up. Also in 1971, Nader and his "Raiders" began setting up a network of state-based Public Interest Research Groups (PIRGs) to investigate public policy and expose corporate and government misdeeds.

Nader's organizations have played a major role in the passage of such federal laws as the Safe Drinking Water Act and the Freedom of Information Act (FOIA), and in the creation of such regulatory agencies as the Occupational Safety and Health Administration (OSHA), Environment Protection Agency (EPA), and Consumer Product Safety Administration.

During the antiregulatory wave of the late 1970s and 1980s, Nader found himself mostly marginalized by the national policy debate. At the same time he found himself at odds with the political mainstream due to the increasing reliance of the Democratic and Republic Parties on corporate and special-interest funding, which ran counter to his lifelong advocacy of grassroots, participatory democracy. Charges of racial and gender bias in his hiring estranged Nader from the coalition of LABOR, FEMINISM, civil rights, and civil liberties advocates that formed in this era. President WILLIAM J. CLINTON's embrace of GLOBALIZATION and trade liberalization, and concomitant reassessment of traditional liberal views on antitrust and monopoly issues, further frustrated Nader.

In 1996 Nader put himself forward as a candidate for president on the GREEN PARTY ticket, but did not actively campaign. Four years later, Nader made a more vigorous bid on the same line, challenging Democrat ALBERT GORE, JR., Republican GEORGE W. BUSH, and Reform Party nominee PATRICK J. BUCHANAN. Nader's campaign message was centered on his belief that large corporations had usurped American democracy. He repeatedly insisted that there was no significant difference between Gore and Bush, and called for public financing of political campaigns; an end to what he termed "corporate welfare," including sweeping cuts in the defense procurement budget; universal health insurance; and numerous legal measures designed to move the balance of power away from private industry. Believing that victory was impossible because of the financial and legal disadvantages of a third-party challenge, Nader hoped to win 6 percent of the popular vote and exceed the 5 percent minimum threshold necessary to qualify the Greens for matching funds in future presidential elections.

Nader's 2000 campaign attracted a substantial level of interest on the left. But Nader failed in his goal of achieving public funding for the Greens, receiving only 2.7 percent of the vote. In two states (New Hampshire and disputed Florida), the official election results showed Nader garnering more votes than Bush's margin of victory, and exit polls in both states indicated that Gore would likely have prevailed had Nader not been a candidate. A shift in either state would have changed the outcome of the election and prevented the ascendancy of Bush, a vocal opponent of many of the regulations Nader fought for over the previous 35 years.

One result of Nader's role as a "spoiler" in the 2000 vote appears to have been a break between Nader and many of his former allies. According to both Nader and his critics, he has been ostracized within the public advocacy community that he did so much to shape in the 1960s and 1970s.

See also CONSERVATION; ENVIRONMENTALISM, AND ENVIRONMENTAL POLICY; POLITICAL ACTION COMMITTEE; POLITICAL PARTIES.

Further reading: Ralph Nader, *Crashing the Party: Taking on the Corporate Government in an Age of Surrender* (New York, 2002); David Sanford, *Me and Ralph: Is Nader Unsafe for America?* (Washington, D.C., 1976).

—Michele Rutledge

narcotics

Narcotics is the term used for opium and opium derivatives, and their synthetic substitutes that are commonly used under medical supervision to relieve intense pain and suppress coughs. The term is also used, however, as a reference to all illicit drugs, including opium, cocaine, morphine, heroin, codeine, and Demerol. Though not technically narcotics, marijuana, amphetamines, barbiturates, Benzedrine, and other psychotropics, such as LSD, psilocybin, and mescaline are often included under narcotics legislation and enforcement. Though unsupervised use of narcotics was first banned in the United States around the turn of the 20th century, special enforcement procedures were not adopted until widespread public use during the 1960s and 1970s required more systematic federal response. Recent trends reveal a decline in illegal drug use since its peak in the 1970s, though rates remain significantly higher than before 1960.

Throughout the first half of the century, illicit drug use and abuse carried harsh social condemnation and was associated mostly with poor immigrants and uneducated workers from urban centers. These trends changed dramatically in the late 1950s and 1960s, however, after a growing academic-based counterculture embraced illicit drug use as a statement of rebellion against the dominant culture of sobriety. Harvard professor Timothy Leary promoted the use of LSD as a medium for spiritual awakening, and other academic and cultural leaders promoted similar benefits for marijuana and opiate-related drugs. The new heroin and marijuana user of the late 1960s and 1970s was often a white, middle-class young adult who either was or had been in college. For many observers, the popularity of illicit drug use during the late 1960s and 1970s seemed a natural side-effect of the growing use of legal drugs for mood and behavioral disorders, including stimulants, tranquilizers, and antidepressants. Others argued that the promotion of narcotics by the counterculture represented a rising new moral order. The debates turned into swift government action, however, as the new counterculture became associated with dramatic increases in crime rates during the same period.

As a partial response to increases in drug-related crime, the Department of Education and Welfare during President Lyndon Johnson's administration supplemented the Treasury Department's Bureau of Narcotics with a new Bureau of Drug Abuse Control in 1966. The split administration, however, proved to be only a temporary solution, and in 1969, as part of President RICHARD M. NIXON's "war on crime" program, the two bureaus were consolidated under the Department of Justice (DOJ) with a new name, Bureau of Narcotics and Dangerous Drugs. Two years later, Congress passed a systematic drug policy with the Controlled Substance Act, Title II of the Comprehensive Drug

Abuse Prevention and Control Act of 1970, which consolidated the numerous laws regulating the manufacture and distribution of narcotics, stimulants, depressants, hallucinogens, anabolic steroids, and chemicals used in the illicit production of controlled substances. The Controlled Substance Act categorized all licit and illicit drugs into one of five schedules, ranging from Schedule I, for the most dangerous drugs that have no recognized medical use, to Schedule V, for the least dangerous drugs that still require federal regulation. Three years later, in 1973, the DOJ reorganized their drug task force for a final time, and renamed the new bureau the Drug Enforcement Agency.

The drug use of the late 1960s and early 1970s counterculture did not begin to taper off until parents joined together to lobby lawmakers for even greater enforcement measures. Congress passed the Comprehensive Crime Control Act in 1984, which provided especially stiff penalties for drug traffickers dealing near schools; it also included forfeiture penalties applicable to all property possessions related to the drug offense. While arrests for cocaine trafficking increased, the rate of gang-related violence in the urban centers appeared unaffected. Two years later, Congress added even more penalties to drug trafficking in the 1986 Anti-Drug Abuse Act, which addressed the gang-related violence with additional penalties for using juveniles to commit drug offenses. In one of his first addresses before a national audience, President GEORGE H. W. BUSH announced his intention to declare a "war on drugs" in 1989, which resulted in expanded efforts at drug-trafficking interdiction to control the supply side of drug abuse. Though the long-term effectiveness of the campaign is still undetermined, the immediate impact was significant.

The Federal Bureau of Investigation reports that arrests for abuse violations rose from 580,900 in 1980 to 1.532 million in 1999. Arrests for the sale and manufacture of illegal drugs rose from 135,200 for sale and manufacture of drugs, and 540,800 for possession in 1982, to 300,300 for sale and manufacture of drugs, and 1.231 million for possession in 1999. The U.S. Department of Justice crime surveys reveal that use of heroin and cocaine skyrocketed 750 percent from 1980 to 1988, before falling off just as dramatically from 1988 to 1992. Cocaine and heroin

A U.S. Coast Guard officer stands guard over some of the 13 tons of cocaine found hidden in secret compartments on a Belize-flagged fishing boat, May 14, 2001, in San Diego, California. *(McNew/Getty Images)*

use saw resurgence in the mid-1990s, before returning to their earlier 1992 levels. Marijuana use declined steadily from its peak in 1978 (37 percent usage) to its lowest rate in 1992 (12 percent), after which usage rose dramatically throughout the remaining 1990s. Observers noted a changing climate among high school students, favorable to marijuana; 78 percent perceived risks associated with marijuana use in 1991, while only 57 percent did so in 1999. The rate of American high school seniors who smoked marijuana during the previous month nearly doubled from 1992 to 2000 (12 percent to 22 percent), and nearly tripled for 10th graders (8 percent to 20 percent).

Some critics of the nation's drug policy contend that prohibition laws only encourage illegal narcotics use by eliminating government regulation, and forcing black market conditions to rule supply and demand. Critics also assert that drug use is a victimless crime that does not require government enforcement. Supporters of the drug war argue that prohibition laws do not create a demand, but rather reflect society's reactions to disturbing trends in drug use and drug-related crimes. They also argue that drug use damages individual judgment by reducing moral inhibitions, which make users more likely to engage in criminal and antisocial behavior. Advocates for drug legalization include the National Organization for the Reform of Marijuana Laws (NORML), founded in the mid-1970s, when it began its state-level campaigns to legalize marijuana. Their efforts met with limited success after 11 states decriminalized marijuana in the 1970s, though the victory was temporary. Almost every state repealed the decriminalization laws during the federal enforcement and public awareness campaigns of the 1980s. Legalization advocates earned a minor victory in 1996, after they succeeded in passing Proposition 215, which legalized the medicinal use of marijuana in California.

—Aharon W. Zorea

National Aeronautics and Space Administration
(NASA)   See space policy

National Association for the Advancement of Colored People (NAACP)

Founded February 12, 1909, as an interracial membership organization dedicated to civil rights and racial justice, the National Association for the Advancement of Colored People (NAACP) has played, throughout its history, an instrumental role in improving the legal, educational, and economic situation of AFRICAN AMERICANS. It has operated through the American legal system to reach its goals of full suffrage and other civil rights for African Americans, and also figured prominently in the struggle to end segregation

and racial violence. After the high tide of the Civil Rights movement, the influence of the NAACP waned, and it suffered declining membership, as well as a series of damaging internal scandals.

During the Civil Rights movement of the 1960s, the NAACP was criticized for its insistence on working within the system and seeking exclusively legislative and judicial solutions. The organization sought to apply its interracial, integrationist approach to the issues of increasing urban crime and poverty and of de facto segregation and job discrimination. This approach alienated many African Americans, whose sympathies began to shift toward more militant, even separatist, philosophies embodied in groups such as the Black Power Movement and the NATION OF ISLAM.

Although this shift in popular sentiment precipitated a decline in NAACP membership, the organization did not cease to be active in seeking legal and political solutions to the problems that confronted African Americans. In the 1970s, as the Civil Rights activist movement splintered politically and ideologically, the NAACP became less influential. To regain its momentum, the organization increased its focus on the doctrines of self-help, black pride, and moral and community values. The NAACP stepped up its attempts to register and organize black voters against the agenda of the RONALD W. REAGAN administration, which came into office in 1981, as well as lobby Congress to support affirmative action policies. Along with other organizations, the NAACP contributed to a 14 percent increase in black voter registration in the South between 1980 and 1984. The organization continued its push for black electoral activity by supporting JESSE L. JACKSON's "Southern Crusade" for voter registration during his 1984 bid for the Democratic presidential nomination. The group broke stride, however, with the majority of African Americans by opposing, on ideological grounds, CLARENCE THOMAS's nomination to the U.S. SUPREME COURT by President GEORGE H. W. BUSH in 1991. This failure to identify with the majority of African Americans, coupled with legislative setbacks and internal corruption in the 1980s and 1990s, further limited the organization's influence.

The NAACP faced major challenges during Benjamin Hooks's tenure as executive director (1977–95). In *REGENTS OF THE UNIVERSITY OF CALIFORNIA V. BAKKE* (1978), the U.S. Supreme Court upheld the state court's decision that racially exclusionary preferences in medical school admissions standards constituted a quota and, as such, were a denial of equal protection. This decision, made in favor of a white medical school applicant, seriously undermined the process of AFFIRMATIVE ACTION that the NAACP strongly supported. Concurrent with this setback, tensions between the executive director and the board of directors escalated into open hostility. Although such tension had always been present in the organization, this time it represented a serious threat to the stability of the NAACP. The tension and controversy intensified with the election of Benjamin Chavis as the director in 1993. In seeking to lead the NAACP in a new direction, Chavis reached out to LOUIS FARRAKHAN, leader of the Nation of Islam, and, in doing so, offended many liberals, black and white. He further undermined his position, and the credibility of the organization, by using NAACP funds to settle a sexual harassment lawsuit against himself, an error in judgment that forced his resignation in 1995. Chavis subsequently joined the Nation of Islam and changed his name to Chavis Muhammad.

Kweisi Mfume, former congressman and head of the Congressional Black Caucus, replaced Chavis as director of the NAACP. With Julian Bond as chairperson of the executive board, Mfume shifted the organization's focus to economic development and establishing educational programs for young African Americans, while also maintaining its function as legal advocate for civil rights issues. In 2001, the NAACP claimed a membership of more than half a million.

See also RACE AND RACIAL CONFLICT.

Further reading: Steven Lawson, *Running for Freedom: Civil Rights and Black Politics in America since 1941* (Philadelphia: Temple University Press, 1997); Warren D. St. James, *NAACP: Triumphs of a Pressure Group, 1909–1980* (Smithtown, N.Y.: Exposition Press, 1980).

—William L. Glankler

National Endowments for the Arts and Humanities (NEA; NEH)

Established through the National Foundation on the Arts and the Humanities Act of 1965, the National Endowment for the Arts (NEA) and the National Endowment for the Humanities (NEH) are independent agencies, whose chairperson reports directly to the president.

Both the NEA and NEH are organized along similar lines. Each has a chairperson appointed for four years, selected by the president and confirmed by the Senate. The respective chairs are advised by the National Council for the Arts and the National Council for the Humanities, panels of citizens recognized for their achievements and knowledge of the arts or humanities, and appointed by the president to six-year terms. These bodies meet quarterly to review grant applications and advise the chairs, who have the final word on policy and the awarding of grants.

During the 1970s the budgets for the two endowments grew quickly, each topping the $100 million level by the end of the decade. For much of the period the NEA was considered the more successful of the two. With well-known exhibits and strong administrative leadership, the NEA maintained a high profile.

During the Reagan administration, both endowments suffered major budget cuts, and the NEH came under harsh criticism from political conservatives, who questioned its accomplishments and economy. Reagan's first chairman, William Bennett, worked to focus the mission of the endowment with his report, *To Reclaim a Legacy,* calling for a return to a canon of great books in the Western tradition. Lynne Cheney, Reagan's second NEH chair, worked to encourage private donations to augment the remaining federal funding. Both of these endeavors proved successful in lessening some of the conservative criticism.

The NEA remained prominent during the 1980s, but also came under increasing attack from social conservatives as elitist. Opponents created an uproar by noting that NEA funded the homoerotic photography of Robert Mapplethorpe and the artwork of Andres Serrano, most notably *Piss Christ,* and conservatives lashed out at the "obscene" subject matter funded by the taxpayers. Actually, neither artist directly received any money from the NEA. A museum had received a grant to exhibit Mapplethorpe's work, and Serrano had received a grant from a local arts council, which had an NEA grant to use as it saw fit. Regardless, the public outcry against the NEA from the political right damaged its support. Meanwhile, the political left was questioning the NEA's grants as too narrowly distributed to "established" artists, thereby excluding artists from ethnic minorities.

During the 1990s, the NEA continued to come under fire. By extension, the NEH suffered from the NEA's controversy. Former NEH chairs Bennett and Cheney attacked both endowments and called for their abolition. When the Republicans gained control of Congress in 1994, there were serious threats against the endowments. Both endowments suffered major budget cuts. In 1997 the HOUSE OF REPRESENTATIVES voted to abolish the NEA, but the SENATE insisted that the endowment continue to receive funding. Congress has been less hostile to the endowments in the last few years, and their future seems more secure than it has for over a decade.

The NEA continues to receive federal funding. Of the thousands of grants it has made since 1966, only a handful have created any controversy. The NEA has encouraged the growth and democratization of the arts, grants are made to every state, and the number of artists in the United States has grown from approximately 700,000 in 1970 to 1.8 million in 2001. All of this has been accomplished at the cost, in 1995, of 64 cents for every American.

The NEH has provided more than $3 billion in fellowships and grants since its inception. In 1991, the NEH supplied 64 percent of funding to scholars in the humanities. In addition, the endowment has funded the publication of the papers of George Washington, Thomas Jefferson, Frederick Douglass, Mark Twain, Dwight Eisenhower, and

Thomas Edison, as well as sponsoring documentaries on the Adams family and the Civil War, along with many other projects.

See also ART AND ARCHITECTURE.

—John Korasick

National Environmental Policy Act (NEPA) (1969)

Rachel Carson's 1962 seminal work, *Silent Spring*, launched the modern environmental consciousness movement in the United States. As scientific evidence increasingly supported findings of unhealthy levels of toxins in human bodies and in the environment, a CONSERVATION, ENVIRONMENTALISM, AND ENVIRONMENTAL POLICY movement emerged in the late 1960s. The National Environmental Policy Act (NEPA) is the foundation for contemporary environmental policies. President RICHARD M. NIXON signed it into law on January 1, 1970, in response to polls that showed strong mainstream support for federal protection of the environment.

NEPA's mandate required all federal agencies to protect the environment. As part of this, the Council on Environmental Quality, and the Environmental Protection Agency (EPA) were created. During the course of the 1970s, important environmental legislation was enacted, including the Clean Air Act of 1970, the OCCUPATIONAL HEALTH AND SAFETY ACT (1970), the Water Pollution Control Act (1972), the Endangered Species Act (1973), the Safe Drinking Water Act (1974), and the Comprehensive Environmental Response Compensation and Liability Act (1980). The result of these laws was the addition of millions of acres to the federal wilderness system, the requirement of environmental impact assessments on major construction projects, the cleaning up of American lakes and streams, and the preservation of several species of wildlife native to the Americas.

Both the JAMES EARL CARTER, JR. and RONALD W. REAGAN administrations pursued a policy of deregulation of the economy, and making government more economical and efficient through agency reorganization. As a result, both the Carter and Reagan administrations unsuccessfully sought to disband the Council on Environmental Quality. The Reagan administration, in particular, sought to reorient environmental policy to favor business. In doing so, Reagan cut the EPA by a third. At the same time, the EPA pursued a policy of "voluntary compliance" by businesses in enforcing environmental regulations. While many conservatives called for the repeal or amendment of the National Environmental Policy Act, the Reagan administration was hesitant to undertake such action. It would have been unpopular in Congress, and moreover, the environmental movement had grown in power over the last decades. In 1960 there were approximately 150,000 members of envi-

ronmental organizations, whose budgets totaled $20 million; by the 1980s, environmental organizations claimed 8 million members with budgets totalling $500 million.

The WILLIAM J. CLINTON administration also called for a review of environmental policy. One result was that under Clinton, the Council on Economic Quality became the White House Office on Environmental Policy. In 1994 Republicans won the House with a platform called "Contract with America," which called for a reassessment of environmental regulation and enforcement. Although legislation was enacted that mandated economic impact studies of environmental enforcement, the Republican-controlled Congress did not repeal the Environmental Policy Act. The GEORGE W. BUSH administration eased environmental regulations in a number of areas, including standards of arsenic levels in drinking water. The administration insists that it remains committed to a pro-environmental policy, but one that seeks to promote economic growth, business development, and sound protection of the environment and natural resources.

—Michele Rutledge

National Organization for Women (NOW)

Founded in 1966, the National Organization for Women is an American activist organization that promotes equal rights for women.

Title VII of the 1964 Civil Rights Act, which prohibited discrimination in hiring or promotion based on race, color, religion, national orientation, or sex, led to the founding of NOW. To investigate discrimination complaints, the Equal Employment Opportunity Commission (EEOC) was established. In its early years, the EEOC focused its work on racial, rather than gender, discrimination. In response, Betty Friedan, author of the 1963 best-seller *The Feminine Mystique,* and others attending the Third National Conference of Commissions on the Status of Women in Washington, D.C., in 1966, formed the National Organization for Women. Initiated by President John F. Kennedy in 1961, the commission had been under the leadership of Eleanor Roosevelt, and three years had passed since its 1963 report, *American Women, The Report of the President's Commission on the Status of Women,* which asserted that, despite having won the right to vote, women were discriminated against in virtually every aspect of life. These findings had been reinforced by the reports of various state commissions on the status of women.

The 1966 conference delegates were prohibited from passing resolutions recommending that the Equal Employment Opportunity Commission (EEOC) enforce its legal mandate to end sex discrimination. In protest, Friedan invited a group of 29 women to her hotel room one night to discuss alternative strategies. Attendees decided that the only answer was to form a separate civil rights organization dedicated to achieving full equality for women. Kathryn Clarenbach, head of the Wisconsin Commission on the Status of Women, was named interim coordinator, and a statement of purpose was drafted, aimed at bringing women into full participation in equal partnership with men.

NOW's first organizing conference was held October 29–30, 1966, in Washington, D.C. More than 300 women and men gathered to put together an organizational structure and philosophy for what Friedan termed "the unfinished revolution." Kathryn Clarenbach was elected NOW's first chairperson and Betty Friedan, NOW's first president. NOW was incorporated officially in Washington, D.C., on February 10, 1967, after finalization of its national constitution and bylaws by an appointed committee.

In 1967 NOW filed suit against the EEOC to force it to comply with its own rules, and also sued the nation's largest 1,300 companies for sex discrimination. At its second national conference, NOW drew up a bill of rights for women, called for an EQUAL RIGHTS AMENDMENT (ERA) to the Constitution, and the repeal of laws restricting access to ABORTION and contraceptive devices. The issue of abortion created division within the organization, with dissenters believing NOW should avoid controversial issues and focus strictly on economic discrimination.

NOW focused on all aspects of sex discrimination, initiating task forces to deal with the problems of women in law, employment, RELIGION, EDUCATION, poverty, politics, and their image in the MEDIA. Committees were also organized to handle membership, finance, legislation and legal activities, and public relations.

While pursuing civil rights tactics of demonstrations and marches, NOW also became involved in legal suits involving gender equality. In 1969 NOW demonstrated for Women's Studies programs. In the spring of 1969, the first women's studies course was introduced at Cornell University, and the first full-fledged women's studies program was established at the University of California, San Diego. Also in 1970 NOW won an important case in *Week v. Southern Bell*, in which the courts ruled that, under Title VII of the Civil Rights Act of 1964, which made discrimination on the basis of sex unconstitutional, and removed the legal restriction on women lifting more than 30 pounds at their place of employment. On August 26, 1969, NOW organized the Women's Strike for Equality, although this demonstration had mixed success. That same year, NOW chapters began picketing newspapers to make "Help Wanted" ads gender neutral, a policy soon adopted by newspapers across the country.

In the 1970s, however, as ideological divisions within the feminist movement emerged, especially over political feminism and cultural feminism, these tensions spilled over into NOW. By the late 1960s and early 1970s, many feminists became increasingly militant, declaring that "equal opportunity" was not enough; instead, they called for a cultural and political revolution that empowered women. This became especially apparent in the New York NOW chapter headed by Ti-Grace Atkinson. Radical feminists also raised the call for gay and lesbian rights. In 1970, Betty Friedan led opposition to a NOW resolution calling for lesbian rights, but Friedan would be defeated by Aileen Hernandez, former EEOC commissioner, for the presidency. Friedan denounced this shift in NOW to supporting lesbian rights. She warned of a "lavender menace" within NOW, declaring that NOW should not be about sex, but about "equal opportunity in jobs." In 1971, NOW members, including Betty Friedan, Bella Abzug, and Gloria Steinem, formed the National Women's Political Caucus, a nonpartisan coalition of women in politics, but the divisions within the larger organization emerged in this group as well. The fight became particularly bitter between Gloria Steinem, founder of *Ms.* magazine, and Friedan.

NOW focused on three issues in the 1970s—reproductive rights, ERA, and lesbian rights. Lesbian rights was the focus of the 1975 convention, and the 1984–88 conventions. In 1979 NOW was involved in winning an important legal case for lesbian rights in *Belmont v. Belmont*, in which the court gave child custody to a lesbian mother and her gay partner.

Following the defeat of ERA in 1982, NOW sought to change its image as a militant feminist organization to a mainstream organization. NOW continued to struggle for reproductive rights and lesbian rights, but its strategy focused on political lobbying and legal battles. In 1994 NOW won another important case in *NOW v. Scheidler*, which applied the RACKETEER-INFLUENCED AND CORRUPT ORGANIZATIONS ACT against anti-abortion demonstrators.

With over 800 chapters across the country, NOW was the largest women's rights organization in the United States in 2001. Both men and women are part of the 250,000-membership base. The national offices are in Washington, D.C.

See also BIRTH CONTROL; FEMINISM; WOMEN'S RIGHTS AND STATUS.

Further reading: Leila Rupp and Verta Taylor, *Survival in the Doldrums* (Columbus: Ohio State University Press, 1987); Roslind Rosenberg, *Divided Lives: American Women in the Twentieth Century* (New York: Hill & Wang, 1992).

—Michele Rutledge

National Rifle Association (NRA)

The National Rifle Association (NRA) is an international, nonprofit organization dedicated to the promotion of firearms education and to the protection of an individual's right to bear arms for self-defense and sport. It was originally formed in 1871 by two Union officers who were disappointed in the marksmanship of their troops during the Civil War. Colonel William C. Church and General George Wingate formed the NRA to "promote and encourage rifle shooting on a scientific basis." For 30 years, the organization remained a small society based in the Northeast; it was not nationally recognized until after 1903, when it began actively promoting rifle clubs and shooting sports at all major high schools and universities. The NRA had little or no political aspirations during its early years, and focused instead on education and training. After Congress passed America's first federal GUN CONTROL act, the National Firearms Act of 1934, the NRA formed its Legislative Affairs Division; it did not lobby Congress directly, but instead used the office to mail out fact sheets and legislative analysis to its members. There was generally no need for direct lobbying, however, since gun control groups did not become prominent until much later, in the 1980s.

During World War II, the NRA provided the government with training materials and organized private firearm collections to aid British citizens against a homeland invasion. In 1949 the NRA worked with the state of New York to establish the first hunter-training program, which has since become a common supplement to almost every state fish and game department in the United States and Canada. In 1960, the NRA introduced the NRA Police Firearms Instructor certification program to become the only national trainer of law enforcement officers; it still certifies 10,000 police and security instructors each year. There was very little call for gun control during the 1940s and 1950s in America because guns seemed integral to post–World War II sports and hunting culture, and, as a consequence, the NRA limited its activities primarily to its first priority of education and marksmanship.

National Rifle Association president Charlton Heston raises a Revolutionary War-era musket above his head at the 130th NRA Annual Meeting in Kansas City, May 19, 2001. *(Collection of the District of Columbia Public Library)*

The NRA did not engage in direct lobbying until 1975, when it formed the Institute for Legislative Action (ILA). During the 1980s, the NRA became the leading voice for gun rights advocates, and its membership increased dramatically in response to growing efforts to pass more restrictive gun control legislation. In the 1990s, however, the organization drew strong criticism from Democrats and movie and television celebrities, who linked the rise in the number of school shootings with the availability of private firearms. Of particular concern was the apparent rise in the number of weapons used in American households, the use of high-powered, rapid-fire guns in urban-gang conflicts, and the increasing dangers of accidental deaths among children playing with unsecured handguns in the home. Gun control advocates portrayed the NRA's opposition to gun control as an unreasonable apathy toward crime. In 1999 and 2000, 19 city and county governments alleged the firearms industry was responsible for infractions ranging from gross negligence to outright conspiracy, and sued the five largest gun manufacturers in America. The confluence of the civil suits against large gun manufacturers and the NRA's vocal opposition to gun control stirred up old images of big businesses corrupting public government. This image was augmented with bitter insinuations during the 2000 presidential election; the NRA was the largest single-issue contributor throughout the 1990s, and donated more than $3 million to the Republican Party in 2000, nearly twice what it donated in the 1996 and 1992 elections. Many Democrats used the NRA as an example of why the nation needed stricter CAMPAIGN FINANCE laws. Both parties, however, received roughly the same amount of campaign contributions from various single-interest lobbying groups in the 2000 and 1996 presidential elections.

See also ELECTIONS; FEDERALISM; POLITICAL ACTION COMMITTEE.

—Aharon W. Zorea

Nation of Islam

The Nation of Islam (NOI) is a religious movement, based on black separatism, that was founded in Detroit, Michigan, in 1930 by Wallace D. Fard, an immigrant born in Mecca, Saudi Arabia. Its founding principles of economic self-sufficiency, racial self-determination, and the advocacy of a structured lifestyle emphasizing marriage, family, strict diet, and hygiene, still drive the organization. Concomitant with these beliefs is an explicit rejection of white society. In 1933 Fard passed control of the NOI to Elijah Muhammad who, by the 1950s, had transformed the movement into a military theocracy with a burgeoning membership. A year later, in 1934, Fard disappeared without a trace. Controversy over the NOI's place in the Civil Rights movement during the 1950s and 1960s, including the highly publicized criticism leveled by Malcolm X against the NOI, presaged the factionalism that would plague the movement in the 1970s.

Elijah Muhammad died in 1975 and his son, Wallace Dean Muhammad, assumed control of the movement. Almost immediately, he softened the NOI approach to whites, by claiming that whites were not necessarily evil, and by allowing whites to join the movement. Additionally, he moved the NOI toward the more widely accepted Sunni Islam. These actions alienated many followers and caused the Nation to splinter into several factions. In 1978 LOUIS FARRAKHAN resurrected the original vision of the Nation of Islam, and reasserted the teachings of racial separatism and black nationalism. Farrakhan's controversial persona earned him severe criticism, yet he has been credited with uniting, to some degree, non-Muslim black religious leaders and activists in an effort to effect positive change within urban African-American communities. Most representative of that effort was the Million Man March, orchestrated by Farrakhan in 1995. This event, held in Washington, D.C., brought together approximately 900,000 African-American men, representing various backgrounds and political viewpoints, to address the problems faced by black males, stressing their responsibilities to themselves and their families. In this way, the march reaffirmed the founding principles of the NOI, including its distinct emphasis on male responsibility.

The NOI continues to prosper economically, but it has not experienced a surge in membership since the early 1960s. There are no official sources on the membership of the NOI, and as a consequence, estimates of its membership by scholars and journalists vary from 10,000 to 100,000 members. These figures themselves might be too low, but there is no doubt that NOI emerged as an important force in the African-American community in many urban areas.

See also AFFIRMATIVE ACTION; AFRICAN AMERICANS; ISLAM IN AMERICA; NATIONAL ASSOCIATION FOR THE ADVANCEMENT OF COLORED PEOPLE; POVERTY; RACE AND RACIAL CONFLICT.

—William L. Glankler

Native Americans

Officially categorized as American Indians and Alaska Natives, Native Americans have organized, in the last 30 years, to claim, regain, or reassert rights to lands and have fought for more control over water, economic affairs, and education on native lands. During the 1960s, Native Americans borrowed the successful tactics of the Civil Rights movement to make their grievances public.

In the 1960s and 1970s a number of organizations and incidents promoted and illustrated the plight of Native Americans. One of the first successful Indian

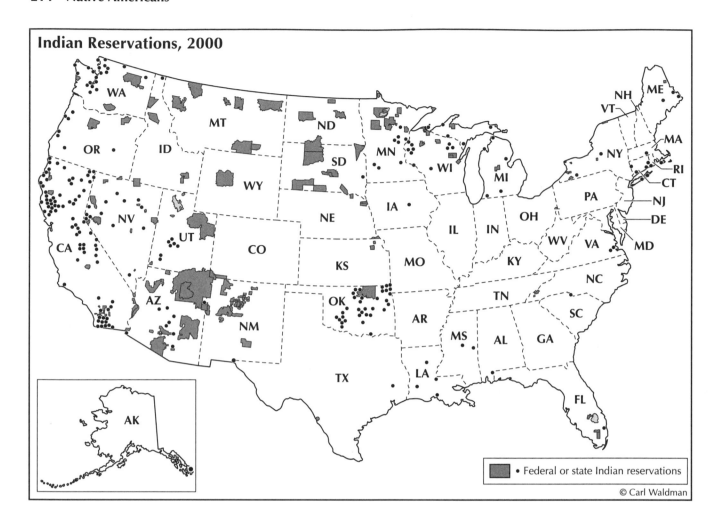

Indian Reservations, 2000

Federal or state Indian reservations

© Carl Waldman

protests was in the Pacific Northwest. Since the 1940s, native groups in Oregon and Washington had argued that the states were not living up to treaty obligations concerning fishing rights that had been ceded in the 19th century. Commercial fishers, with the support of the states, had taken control of the treaty waters. In 1964 the Survival of the American Indian Association organized "fish-ins" inspired by the sit-ins staged by the Civil Rights movement. By the late 1960s, the federal government became involved on the side of the Indians. In 1974 a federal district court ruled that non-Indians had only limited rights to fish in the treaty waters. The U.S. SUPREME COURT upheld this decision in 1979. This ruling spawned a reservation industry, as more natives began to fish, and this led to a number of related industries—fish buying, fish processing, and fish farming.

The late 1960s witnessed Native American activists occupying a number of sites. From November 1969 until July 1971, activists occupied Alcatraz, generating publicity by exposing the poor housing, health, education, and other issues faced by Native Americans. In 1972 the American

Indian Movement (AIM) and the National Indian Youth Council organized an occupation of the Bureau of Indian Affairs in Washington, D.C., to bring attention to the failure of the government to live up to its treaty obligations. In 1973 AIM took over the Pine Ridge Sioux reservation in Wounded Knee, South Dakota, for 71 days. The government reacted to these protests by arresting militant AIA leaders who broke the law, while at the same time enacting legislation to enhance the autonomy of Native Americans.

In 1971 the ALASKA NATIVE CLAIM SETTLEMENT ACT gave title to 44 million acres and cash compensation to Alaskan natives. The Maine Indian Settlement Act of 1980 provided $81.5 million for the purchase of 300,000 acres taken by the states of Maine and Massachusetts. It also established a $27 million trust fund for economic development.

Besides land concerns, Native American activists resented U.S. government control over education and the economy on native lands. These concerns were addressed in the Indian Education Act of 1972 and the Indian Self-Determination and Education Assistance Act of 1975, which allowed Indian-controlled school boards to help end the alienation of children from their culture.

Greater sensitivity emerged in the nation at large. Many colleges and universities ended the practice of using tribal names, or demeaning terms for Native Americans, for their athletic teams. Stanford and Dartmouth, to name just two, dropped the name "Indians." Some schools, like Florida State, received permission from specific Indian nations to use the name for their teams.

A number of laws have been passed to ensure greater sovereignty to Indian nations. In 1968 Congress passed the Indian Civil Rights Act, which guaranteed civil liberties on reservations. In 1978 the American Indian Religious Freedom Act was passed to encourage cultural preservation. In recent years the National Museum of the American Indian Act and the Native American Grave Protection and Repatriation Act were designed to promote the return of native artifacts and skeletal remains from museums and other agencies receiving federal funds.

Demographically, the Native American population increased from 827,000 in 1970 to over 1.9 million in 1990. Two-thirds of American Indians were high school graduates, up from 56 percent in 1980. Only 9 percent of American Indians had a college degree in 1990, up from 8 percent in 1980. The 2000 U.S. census showed that the Native American population had grown to 2.4 million, or 9 percent of the population. The median age was 27 years. Of the 500 recognized tribes, most had less than 10,000 members. Educational attainment since 1990 had still not been determined by the U.S. census as of 2001. The largest Indian nation in 1989 was the Cherokee, followed by the Navajo, Chippewa, and Sioux. In 2000 more than half the American Indian population lived in California, Oklahoma, Arizona, New Mexico, Alaska, and Washington. In Alaska 19 percent of the population reported themselves in 2000 as American Indian or Alaska Native alone. Alaska had the highest percentage of Native Americans, followed by Oklahoma and New Mexico, each at 11 percent, and South Dakota at 9 percent. The median household income for American Indians and Alaska Natives, based on a 1998–2000 average reported by the U.S. census, was $31,799, higher than African Americans ($28,679) and not statistically different from Hispanics ($31,703). The rate of poverty was 25.9 percent, similar to rates for African Americans and Hispanics. Census statistics also revealed that 26.8 percent of American Indians and Alaska Natives lacked health insurance coverage. In addition there was an 84 percent increase in Native American–owned firms between 1992 and 1997, compared to an increase for all U.S. firms over the same period of 40 percent.

See also AFRICAN AMERICANS; ASIAN AMERICANS; HISPANIC AMERICANS.

Further reading: Peter Iverson, "We Are Still Here," in *American Indians in the Twentieth Century* (Wheeling, Ill.: Harlan Davidson, Inc., 1998); Francis Jennings, *The Founders of America: America's First People from Their Beginnings* (New York: W. W. Norton, 1993).

—John Korasick

neoconservatism

Neoconservatism was an intellectual movement of COLD WAR liberals between 1968 and 1991 that opposed Black Power and gender-racial quotas.

"Neoconservatism" was the phrase coined by liberal Roman Catholic writer Peter Steinfels to characterize a group of formerly liberal and leftist intellectuals who opposed student radicalism in the late 1960s and the 1970s. The neoconservatives were defined by these common attributes: 1) they were all liberal Democrats who had supported Johnson in 1964 and Humphrey in 1968; 2) they all had opposed Joseph McCarthy but ardently supported the cold war; and 3) they all acquired prestigious establishment intellectual credentials before the rise of student radicalism and the New Left in the late 1960s. Their ethno-religious affiliation was mostly Jewish, with some Roman Catholics, and just a few Protestants. In contrast to other conservative intellectuals, that is, those who were conservative from a young age, the neoconservatives comprised no members from the South, few from the Midwest or West, and few who were religiously traditional. They tended to be urbane academics and writers from the Northeast metropolitan corridor.

The neoconservatives clustered around the following magazines and newspapers: *Commentary, The Public Interest, The National Interest, The American Scholar, The American Spectator, The New Criterion, The Wall Street Journal,* and the *Washington Times.* Occasionally neoconservatives authored articles for the conservative *National Review* and the neoliberal *New Republic.* Norman Podhoretz, editor of *Commentary,* and Irving Kristol, editor of *The Public Interest,* played important roles in shaping neoconservatism as it emerged in the late 1960s and early 1970s. A remarkably large proportion of the neoconservatives were disciples and friends of the émigré German formalist political philosopher Leo Strauss, and the COLD WAR liberal literary critic Lionel Trilling. Most were employed by the publications listed above or at Ivy League faculties.

The neoconservatives were shocked by the rise of political radicalism in the 1960s. Since many of the neoconservatives were Jewish, they were especially incensed by the New Left's embrace of the Palestine Liberation Organization. The neoconservatives used their formidable polemical skills to defend American society against these radical antinomian movements.

Irving Kristol, a New York University professor and former coeditor of *Commentary,* was the acknowledged "Godfather" of neoconservatism. Kristol used his contacts with Wall Street businessmen to create foundations that subsidized magazines and intellectuals promoting the neoconservative point of view. Kristol came to believe earlier than most neoconservatives that the Democratic Party had been captured by the New Left, and he became a Republican in 1970. He regularly advised RICHARD M. NIXON's administration. Kristol's friend, Evron Kirkpatrick, a Georgetown University political scientist and longtime adviser to Hubert Humphrey, also gave up on the Democrats, voting for Nixon in 1972 and Ford in 1976.

Despite Kristol's and Kirkpatrick's example, most neoconservatives remained Democrats. For example, Norman Podhoretz, the formerly leftist editor of *Commentary,* and his wife, Midge Decter, promoted their friend, political scientist and government official Daniel Patrick Moynihan as the man who would redeem the Democratic Party. Moynihan became ambassador to the UNITED NATIONS in 1975, and then used this position to win nomination as New York's U.S. Senate candidate in 1976. He faced incumbent conservative Republican Senator James Buckley, WILLIAM F. BUCKLEY, JR.'s brother. While Irving Kristol supported Buckley, other neoconservatives supported Moynihan. Despite Podhoretz's desperate urging, Moynihan declined to challenge JAMES EARL CARTER, JR.'s 1980 renomination.

Most neoconservatives voted for Jimmy Carter in 1976, soon broke with Carter and embraced the candidacy of Republican RONALD W. REAGAN in 1980. Neoconservatives enjoyed notable success in the Reagan administration. Jeane Kirkpatrick became UN ambassador; Richard Perle, an aide to Democratic senator Henry Jackson, served as a Pentagon official; William Bennett, a Kristol protégé, became secretary of education. With the end of the cold war, the neoconservatives split politically, most becoming Republicans, but a substantial plurality endorsed the election of Democratic president WILLIAM J. CLINTON in 1992.

See also CONSERVATIVE MOVEMENT; LIBERTARIAN PARTY.

Further reading: Gary Dorrien, *The Neoconservative Mind: Politics, Culture and the War of Ideology* (Philadelphia: Temple University Press, 1994); Irving Kristol, *Neoconservatism, Selected Essays, 1949–1995* (New York: Free Press, 1995).

—Christopher M. Gray

New Age movement

The New Age movement, although philosophically and theologically ambiguous, is based on a philosophy and theology that believes all forms of life are vitally affected by a sacred energy that exists throughout the universe. Often viewed as Gnosticism or resurgent paganism, the contemporary movement has its history in 19th-century spiritualism and in the 1960s counterculture, which cast aside materialism and embraced Eastern mysticism in its place. The movement emerged in the late 1960s and became an important force in Western civilization in the 1980s.

The New Age movement is a broad combination of divergent political, social, and spiritual elements with the shared ambition of transforming society and individuals through spiritual awareness. The movement is a utopian vision, encompassing an era of progress and harmony. It is comprised of individuals, businesses, professional groups, activist groups, and spiritual leaders and followers. Its message struck a chord in mainstream American thought during the 1980s, bringing ecological, human-potential, spiritual, and feminist concerns into the public domain. This in turn created a large market in the United States and elsewhere for audio- and videotapes, magazines, books, retreats, and workshops, as well as for meditation and healing aids, natural foods, and crystals.

Many disparate organizations make up the movement, and each differs in the kind of commitment it expects or requires from its adherents. Within New Age groups, one finds those who get involved via individual assimilation of New Age ideas through various sorts of media; those who regularly consult individual astrologers and/or channelers for counsel and instruction; and those who join highly organized movements.

Advocates of the coming of the New Age begin with the assumption that there is something wrong with the world as it is today. Many hold that science and materialism have choked the human spirit and stand in the way of humanity's ability to experience the holy. Humans, they believe, possess an innate desire for genuine spirituality, which organized religions appear to have systemized and possibly distorted. New Agers claim that changes that stress holistic values rather than individual desires for wealth and power must take place first on the individual level. Active participants in the New Age movement understand the human race as one family living and sharing the same planet, all linked in both common origin and destiny. The New Age is an era when people probe more deeply into the mysteries of the universe and self, and when they become more open to God's love and companionship in their daily lives. Believers assert that this new period will transform history as we understand it; people will acquire great psychic capabilities and become more spiritual, creative, and content.

The preparation for this new era centers on three practical concerns. First, there is a perceived need to disclose psychic powers believed inherent in human nature. Second, a grand desire exists to make contact with paranormal and supernatural dimensions of life. Last, many are unhappy with what the Judeo-Christian tradition has to offer and are seeking guidance and knowledge from other theologies and philosophies.

Those wishing to commence on a pilgrimage of self-transformation and the generation of a better world follow a program to heighten awareness. Believers emphasize that the world is not going through a paradigm shift or a radical revolution, but that a powerful and enormous association of people from all levels of society are striving to usher in a new consciousness that will lead to a regeneration of society. Because New Age is not a coherent movement or belief system, New Agers differ as to how they believe such awareness can be achieved: hypnosis; mutual help and self-help networks; magical and shamanic techniques; various kinds of meditation; seminars; mystical systems; and body disciplines like yoga and T'ai Chi. Some New Agers believe in creating new lifestyles and communities based on holistic healing and health; spirituality; yoga; astrology; or intuitive development/channeling. Fundamental to channeling is the belief that knowledge of others and self can be reached through some inner, higher aspect of their personality or through self-reflection. Channeling can be characterized as the transmission of information to or through a human being from paranormal sources, either other beings or the individual's innermost self.

The New Age relates to both practical and theoretical matters that affect peoples' lives. It offers a critique of traditional religions, particularly of Christianity, borrowing ideas from a variety of religions and reinterpreting them. Although not a formal organization, lacking central headquarters and other centralized institutions, its influence by century's end and into the next was still pervasive.

See also RELIGION.

Further reading: John Saliba, *Christian Responses to the New Age Movement* (London, U.K.: Cassell Academic Press, 1999); Steven Sutcliffe and Marion Bowman, eds., *Beyond New Age, Exploring Alternative Spirituality* (Edinburgh, Scotland: Edinburgh University Press, 2000).

—Michele Rutledge

New York City bailout

In 1974 New York City became financially insolvent due to years of budget deficits, a deteriorating middle-class tax base, and union contracts. For decades the city had borrowed money in order to meet its budget needs. Moreover, since 1965, the city's operating budget had more than tripled. In the fall of 1974 New Yorkers elected Democrats Hugh Carey to the governorship and Abraham Beame to City Hall. Faced with a fiscal crisis because of mismanage-

ment by their predecessors, New York governor Nelson Rockefeller and New York City mayor John Lindsay, both liberal Republicans, the newly elected Carey and Beame arranged to borrow millions of dollars in the tax-free municipal bond market. Still unable to meet its obligations, the city was told by several banks that it could no longer borrow in the market. Both Carey and Beame called upon the GERALD R. FORD administration for a $1 billion 90-day loan for the city. Ford felt the request was "ridiculous."

In the summer of 1974 the city created the Municipal Assistance Corporation to change the city's long-term debts into short-term ones. In September the aid increased, with the state approving a $2.3 billion aid package. By October, however, the city was facing default. New York senator James Buckley pleaded with the administration to provide federal aid to the city, but Ford declared in a speech on October 29 to the National Press Club that "the people of this country will not be stampeded" to any federal bailout of New York City. The next day's headline in the *New York Daily News* declared, "Ford to City: Drop Dead."

Faced with a crisis that had national ramifications, Ford finally relented and agreed to a modified form of bailout. On November 11 he announced his support of a plan by which the federal government would loan money to New York with the stipulation that the city impose certain fiscal disciplines. As a consequence, New York City improved its financial position and was able to pay back its debt.

—Leah Blakey

Nicaragua (U.S. relations with)

As with other countries in LATIN AMERICA, the United States has a controversial relationship with Nicaragua, whose origins began in the early 19th century and continued through the 20th. General Anastasio Somoza took power in Nicaragua in 1936 through a U.S.-backed military coup, establishing a dynasty supported by the United States, which lasted, through sons Luis and Tachito, until 1979.

The lack of representative organizations in Nicaraguan politics contributed significantly to the only apparently viable alternative—armed resistance to the Somoza regime. This opposition coalesced during the 1960s to become the Sandinista Front of National Liberation (FSLN), a guerrilla movement comprised of three primary groups. The first, organized in the early 1960s among rural, northern peasants, was known as the Prolonged Popular War (GPP). A second group, Proletarios, was an offshoot of the first, splintering in 1973 from the GPP to include urban dwellers like workers and intellectuals. The third was the Tercerista insurrectionists. The FSLN took its name from Augusto César Sandino, a guerrilla leader who fought against U.S. involvement in Nicaragua during the 1920s and early 1930s, until his murder in 1934 by Somoza's National Guard, a domestic police force created during the U.S. occupation in the 1920s. The Sandinistas set up a unified command structure in 1978 to coordinate the factions in the insurrection against Somoza. The following year, the United States proposed to the Organization of American States (OAS) that a peacekeeping force be sent to Nicaragua, but only Argentina supported this.

Tachito Somoza's regime collapsed in 1979 and he fled to Miami in exile. Somoza blamed an international communist conspiracy for his fall from power. He was later assassinated in Paraguay. The new government, the Provisional Junta of National Reconstruction, issued two broad administrative goals. The first called for implementing a foreign policy that separated Nicaragua from its reliance on the United States. The second anticipated the establishment of a "mixed economy" to effect broader socioeconomic balance.

In the aftermath of the conflict which left 5 percent of the population dead or wounded, one-third homeless, and unemployment rates at 50 percent, U.S. president JAMES EARL CARTER, JR. invited Nicaragua's new governmental leaders to the White House. The United States sent $8 million in emergency relief to Managua and secured authorization from Congress for an additional $75 million aid package. France, Spain, and West Germany also contributed financial assistance.

The Sandinista government sponsored programs to raise basic living standards among the Nicaraguan people. To assist them in their efforts, they engaged the support of some 2,500 Cuban sanitary engineers, schoolteachers, nurses, and doctors, an approach that conflicted with United States cold war policy of ostracizing the Cuban regime. A majority of the land and service sector remained under private ownership, and foreign multinationals continued to operate, but Sandinistas controlled nearly all executive officials, the police, and the military. Virtually all opposition media had been closed down, although opposition parties still functioned. The 1980 Republican Party campaign platform specifically decried "the Marxist Sandinista takeover of Nicaragua," and RONALD W. REAGAN's administration subsequently initiated a dogged campaign to undermine the Sandinista government. In May 1985 the United States launched a trade embargo against Nicaragua, and continued covert support of the CONTRAS, an exile army funded by the United States and commanded in part by former Somoza army officers, as well as several anti-Somocistas disillusioned with the Sandinista regime. The effect was to encourage greater dependence on Cuba and the Soviet Union by the Sandinista government. In 1986 the World Court in the Hague censured the United States on 15 counts of international law violations for acts of aggression against Nicaragua, including Central Intelligence Agency (CIA) involvement with the contras.

Although the contras put significant pressure on the Sandinista regime, they could not secure and hold major targets within Nicaragua. The contras did succeed in forcing the Sandinista government to spend a significant amount of its budget on defense and to disaffect Nicaraguans with wartime exigencies. In part, this contributed to a major recession and major economic decline. Inflation reached astronomical heights in 1988.

The 1990 elections saw Violeta Barrios de Chamorro, widow of a prominent Somoza opponent, nominated by the coalition party, the National Opposition Union (UNO), to run against Sandinista incumbent Daniel Ortega. Although Ortega was widely projected to win, the U.S.-backed Chamorro received nearly 55 percent of the vote. Former president Carter, present as an international observer, verified the legitimacy of the election results, and brokered an agreement for a peaceful transition of power—the first time a revolutionary government relinquished its power to its opponents by way of the ballot box. The Carter Center's Council of Presidents and Prime Ministers of the Americas was also present for the elections of October 1996, when Arnoldo Aleman was elected president. In 2001, Nicaragua elected Enrique Bolanos Geyer, a conservative from the Constitutional Liberal Party, easily defeating Daniel Ortega, who had attempted a political comeback.

See also FOREIGN POLICY; IRAN-CONTRA AFFAIR.

Further reading: Robert A. Pastor, *Exiting the Whirlpool: U.S. Foreign Policy toward Latin American and the Caribbean* (Princeton, N.J.: Princeton University Press, 1992); William Beezley and Colin MacLachlan, *Latin America, the Peoples and Their History* (Fort Worth, Tex.: International Thomason Publishing, 2000).

—Michele Rutledge

Nixon, Richard M. (1913–1994)

Richard Milhous Nixon, who was elected president in 1968 and reelected in 1972, became the first president of the United States to resign from office on August 8, 1974. Although his political career ended in disgrace, he had dominated Republican national politics for the previous three decades.

Nixon was born January 9, 1913, in Yorba Linda, California, to Francis (Frank) and Hannah Nixon. A lower-middle-class family, the Nixons owned a gas station and general store in Whittier, California. Young Richard M. Nixon spent much of his youth working part-time jobs to help support the family, including buying produce for the store, working as a janitor, and performing as a carnival barker.

The rest of Nixon's time was consumed with study. Nixon took great pride in his academic accomplishments and his skills as a debater. He graduated from Whittier High School in 1930, recognized as the "best all-around student," and then enrolled at Whittier College, which he could attend while living at home. Active in debate and drama, Nixon was president of the freshman class and student body president as a senior. He graduated second in his class with honors in history in 1934. After graduation he received a full-tuition scholarship to Duke Law School, where he graduated third in his class in 1937.

After being rejected by law firms in New York and by the Federal Bureau of Investigation, Nixon returned to California, joined the firm of Wingert and Bewley, and became a partner in 1939. During this time he served as deputy city attorney for Whittier. Nixon was active in the community, including the local theater group, the Whittier Community Players, where he met his future wife, Thelma Catherine Patricia (Pat) Ryan, whom he married in 1940.

In 1942 Nixon accepted a position with the Office of Price Administration in Washington. He was entitled to a draft deferment on two grounds—he was a Quaker, and he had a government job, but he joined the navy's Judge Advocate Corps. He resigned from the navy in October 1945, with the rank of lieutenant commander.

Nixon had not been particularly active in politics prior to 1940, the year he had registered as a Republican and supported Wendell Wilkie. One reason Nixon left the navy was to run in 1946 for the HOUSE OF REPRESENTATIVES from the 12th District of California against a five-term incumbent, Democrat Jerry Voorhis. Voorhis had been a Socialist, but had come to the Democrats and was a strong supporter of the New Deal. During the campaign, Nixon made much of Voorhis's Socialist past and accused him of being a communist or, at least, a "fellow traveler." Running as a "modern Republican," Nixon won 57 percent of the vote. In this election, Republicans gained control of the House of Representatives and SENATE for the first time since 1929.

During his first term Nixon served on the Education and Labor Committee, the House Un-American Activities Committee (HUAC), and the House Select Committee on Foreign Aid. Nixon was considered a political moderate, but he was a confirmed anticommunist. In 1948 Nixon won both the Republican and Democratic primaries and was easily reelected.

Nixon became a national political figure during HUAC's 1948–49 investigation of Alger Hiss. Hiss, a former State Department official, was accused by Whittaker Chambers, a senior editor at *Time* magazine and a confessed Soviet spy, of being a communist. Hiss denied knowing Chambers, but Chambers produced documents proving he had rented an apartment from Hiss. Hiss was convicted of perjury, disbarred, and sentenced to five years in prison. Nixon had been one of the few to believe Chambers and had been active in the investigation. On the heels of his triumph, Nixon ran for the Senate in 1950. While the campaign against Voorhis had been negative, the campaign against incumbent Democrat Helen Gahagan Douglas set new standards. Nixon suggested Douglas was a communist sympathizer and labeled her "pink right down to her underwear." In addition, Nixon supporters made phone calls pointing out the fact that Douglas's husband, actor Melvyn Douglas, was half Jewish, and mailed postcards urging voters to support Douglas, signed "the Communist League of Negro Women Voters." On election day Nixon won easily with 59 percent of the vote.

In 1952, just six years after entering politics, Nixon was picked as the Republican vice presidential candidate. During the campaign, Eisenhower stayed out of the fray, leaving Nixon to play the role of "attack dog." Nixon was adept at his new job, charging Democratic candidate Adlai Stevenson of having a Ph.D. from Secretary of State Dean Acheson's "College of Cowardly Communist Containment."

The Eisenhower-Nixon strategy was called, "formula K-1, C-3" (Korea, communism, corruption, and controls). Of special importance was the charge of corruption in the

Richard M. Nixon *(Library of Congress)*

Truman administration, and when the Democrats exposed a "slush fund" that donors had established for Nixon, questions were raised about him staying on the ticket. In an unprecedented appeal to the American public, Nixon went on television and gave what has since been dubbed the "Checkers" speech. He stated that he was not a rich man, and the only gift he had accepted was a puppy that he would refuse to surrender. Many pundits found the speech uncomfortable and saccharine, but it resonated with the American people. The flood of telegrams and letters that followed the speech ran overwhelmingly in favor of keeping Nixon. The Republicans won the White House in 1952 and 1956. Nixon played a minor role in the first term, primarily traveling and campaigning. In 1955, 1956, and 1957, various illnesses limited Eisenhower's ability to perform his duties, allowing Nixon an expanded role. Moreover, he played a central role in drafting and supporting the first civil rights legislation since Reconstruction, the Civil Rights Act of 1957.

As the time neared for considering the 1960 presidential election, Nixon found himself in the midst of two major FOREIGN POLICY confrontations that boosted his stature. In 1958, during a state tour of South America, he was confronted in Peru and Venezuela by violent anti-American mobs. Nixon was perceived to be cool under pressure, preventing a more serious confrontation. In 1959 was the famous "kitchen debate" with Soviet premier Nikita Khrushchev. Nixon's handling of the Soviet leader was impressive and he emerged as the Republican front-runner.

In 1960 Nixon faced Democratic challenger John F. Kennedy. The campaign featured the first televised debates. Nixon had recently been ill, and his appearance hurt him. Most viewers believed Kennedy had won the debate, but radio listeners favored Nixon. The election was one of the closest in history with Kennedy edging Nixon.

Nixon returned to California and ran for governor in 1962, losing to Edmund G. (Pat) Brown. Nixon then declared that he was through, and it appeared that his political career was over. In 1963 he moved to New York and joined the law firm of Mudge, Stern, Baldwin, and Todd.

In 1967 Nixon published an article in the journal *Foreign Affairs,* titled "Asia after Vietnam," in which he suggested that Communist China would someday become part of the international community. In 1968 Nixon won the Republican nomination and picked Maryland governor SPIRO AGNEW as his running mate. Agnew filled much the same role as Nixon had for Eisenhower. Nixon won a narrow victory, with 43 percent of the popular vote, to Democrat Hubert Humphrey's 42.7 percent, and Independent George Wallace's 13.5 percent of the vote.

Nixon followed a progressive domestic agenda. Nixon's administration expanded the food stamp program, in-creased construction of subsidized housing, lowered the voting age, ended the draft, and tied Social Security increases to the cost of living. In addition, the Environmental Protection Agency and the Occupational Safety and Health Administration were founded. Also, the practice of preferential hiring based on race or gender was begun. President Nixon worked closely with his National Security Advisor and later secretary of state, HENRY A. KISSINGER, to craft a new American foreign policy based on DÉTENTE with the SOVIET UNION, and opening diplomatic relations with mainland China. In 1972 Nixon made his trip to Communist China, paving the way for the renewal for diplomatic relations in 1978. The trip to China marked a shift in American policy away from treating communism as a monolithic block controlled by the Soviet Union. Nixon believed that by establishing relations with China, the United States could drive a deep wedge between China and the Soviet Union, even though both were controlled by communist regimes.

The policy of détente with the Soviet Union included the concept of diplomatic "linkage"—linking individual policies into a system of incentives and disincentives. Thus agricultural trade with the Soviet Union was linked to favorable agreements on arms reduction. Nixon inaugurated the Strategic Arms Limitation Talks (SALT) in 1969. These negotiations eventually resulted in two treaties, the first being signed by Nixon and Leonid Brezhnev in 1972, limiting antiballistic missiles. At the same time, Nixon offered agricultural trade with the Soviet Union that provided wheat to a distressed Soviet economy.

Nixon had claimed in the 1968 campaign that he had a plan to end the VIETNAM WAR. In fact he had no plan; his "honorable peace" philosophy meant that the United States would not abruptly pull out of Southeast Asia. During his first term, the conflict widened and intensified. The Paris Peace Accord, in 1973, ended American involvement in the war, and Nixon insisted, in later years, that had Congress lived up to American obligations, South Vietnam would not have fallen.

Nixon was reelected in November 1972. Despite his easy victory over the Democratic nominee, GEORGE S. MCGOVERN, Nixon was not able to enjoy his victory for long. In June 1972 the Democratic National Committee Headquarters in the Watergate office-apartment complex was broken into by five men employed by the Committee for the Reelection of the President, known derisively as CREEP. Their mission was to bug the office, tap the phones, and photograph confidential campaign strategy materials. In March 1973 Judge John J. Sirica extracted confessions from the burglars that implicated members of the White House staff, including former attorney general and Nixon campaign manager JOHN N. MITCHELL. Much of the next 17 months was spent investigating just how involved Nixon was in the break-in, and what else he had authorized. When it was discovered that there was a secret taping system in the Oval Office, subpoenas for the tapes were issued. In October, Special Prosecutor ARCHIBALD COX, JR., refused a compromise proposal from Nixon in which the White House would provide written summaries and paraphrases of the tape in return for a guarantee that Cox would seek no further presidential documents. In response, Nixon had Cox fired by ROBERT BORK, third in command in the Justice Department, after Attorney General ELLIOT RICHARDSON refused to fire Cox and resigned in protest, and Nixon fired Assistant Attorney General WILLIAM RUCKELSHAUS when he refused to fire Cox. Later, Bork's action was ruled illegal by the federal district court. Also in October 1973, Vice President Agnew resigned in the face of an unrelated set of indictments and House Minority Leader GERALD R. FORD was appointed as his replacement. On December 8 Nixon finally complied with the court orders, but produced only seven of the nine tapes sought. By now the scandal had grown beyond the initial break-in and attempted cover-up, and included revelations of a variety of misconduct related to Nixon's successful efforts to ensure his reelection through illegal campaign contributions. Public outcry forced Nixon to appoint a new special prosecutor, LEON JAWORSKI. In March 1974 a federal grand jury returned indictments against seven members of the administration and named Nixon as an unindicted co-conspirator. When Jaworski again subpoenaed Oval Office tapes needed for the trials, Nixon again offered transcripts. The transcripts were shown to be inaccurate and incomplete. The SUPREME COURT heard the case of *UNITED STATES V. NIXON* on July 8 and ruled on July 24, rejecting the administration arguments. That same month the House Judiciary Committee voted to recommend IMPEACHMENT on three charges: obstruction of justice, abuse of power, and defiance of congressional subpoenas. The disputed tapes were released on August 5, 1974. Facing certain impeachment, Nixon became the first president to resign from office on August 8, 1974. On September 8, 1974, President Ford pardoned Nixon for all crimes he "committed or may have committed or taken part in" while in office.

Nixon spent much of the rest of his life trying to rehabilitate his reputation. He was the author of nine books during his retirement, primarily memoirs and studies on foreign policy. Beginning with *RN: The Memoirs of Richard Nixon* in 1978 and continuing to *Beyond Peace* published just before his death in 1994, Nixon gradually regained some of his reputation and claimed his place as America's elder statesman. While he was not welcomed at Republican conventions until 1992, he was an occasional adviser to RONALD W. REAGAN, GEORGE H. W. BUSH, and WILLIAM J. CLINTON.

Nixon died in New York on April 22, 1994, after a severe stroke. He is buried next to his wife, Pat, who died in 1993, on the grounds of the Richard M. Nixon Library and Birthplace in Yorba Linda, California. The Nixon Library is the only presidential library erected without federal financing and the only one not housing original copies of presidential papers. The Nixon papers remain in the National Archives by order of Congress.

See also STRATEGIC ARMS LIMITATION TREATIES; WATERGATE SCANDAL.

Further reading: Stephen Ambrose, *Nixon: The Education of a Politician, 1913–1962, Nixon: The Triumph of a Politician, 1962–1972,* and *Nixon: Ruin and Recovery, 1973–1990* (New York: Simon & Schuster, 1987, 1989, 1991); Joan Hoff, *Nixon Reconsidered* (New York: Basic Books, 1994); Melvin Small, *The Presidency of Richard Nixon* (Lawrence: University of Kansas Press, 1999).

—John Korasick

North, Oliver L. (1942–)

Colonel Oliver North emerged as a central figure in the IRAN-CONTRA AFFAIR in 1985 in which the Reagan administration sold weapons to Iran and then illegally funneled funds to rebels seeking to overthrow an anti-American regime in Nicaragua.

Born on October 7, 1942, in San Antonio, Texas, Oliver Laurence North grew up in Philmont, New York. In 1961, North enrolled in the State University of New York at Brockport as an English major. While at Brockport, North joined the U.S. Marine Corps Reserve and in 1963 transferred to the United States Naval Academy.

After graduating in June 1968, Second Lieutenant North went to Vietnam in December 1968. During the following year, North received two Purple Hearts, a Bronze Star, a Silver Star, and a promotion to first lieutenant. In November 1969, he was rotated to the United States, where he spent much of the next six years training marines in guerrilla and jungle tactics, first at Quantico and then in Okinawa. During this period he was promoted to captain. In 1975 North was assigned to Marine Corps Headquarters in Washington, D.C., as a plans and policy analyst. In 1978 he was promoted to major and made battalion operations officer at Camp Lejeune, North Carolina.

In 1981 Secretary of the Navy John Lehman arranged for North to be assigned to the staff of the National Security Council (NSC) to lobby Congress for the sale of AWACs surveillance planes to Saudi Arabia. In 1983 North was promoted to lieutenant colonel.

North participated in the NSC's defense policies group, specializing in counterterrorism. While primarily concerned with Central America, North played a role in the planning of the GRENADA invasion and planned the interception of an Egyptian air liner carrying terrorists who had hijacked the *Achille Lauro* cruise liner in 1985. North helped plan the controversial mining of NICARAGUA harbors and tracked the right-wing "death squads" in El Salvador, but critics in Congress and human rights advocates charged that he and the CIA trained, equipped, and supported these groups.

In 1984 Congress enacted the BOLAND AMENDMENT, banning aid to the Nicaraguan contra rebels. North, unwilling to obey Congress's order, which meant abandoning the contras, began surreptitiously soliciting private donations and aid from other nations to circumvent the Boland law. In 1985 the Reagan administration decided to sell weapons to Iran in an attempt to facilitate the release of American hostages held in Lebanon, in direct contradiction of its own publicly stated policy. North was called in to handle the transfer, and he hit on the idea of funneling the excess profits to the CONTRAS. By 1986 the scheme had been ex-posed and North was dismissed. The "arms for hostages" arrangement was exposed in 1986, provoking intense public disapproval. When North's diversion was revealed, Congress opened criminal investigations, and President Reagan fired North.

Reagan appointed the Tower Commission to investigate the scandal. In its report, the Tower Commission noted that North had exercised unusually broad authority for an NSC aide and criticized the administration for not properly supervising its staff. During the joint congressional investigation, North was given limited immunity in exchange for his testimony. North's testimony in July 1987 was broadcast live on television, and his earnest appeals to patriotism and anticommunism transformed him into a hero in the eyes of many Americans. North testified that he had kept his superiors informed of his activities, and he assumed President Ronald W. Reagan knew about the operation. North's critics, however, noted that the testimony of others indicated North was less truthful and upright than he seemed. Witnesses reported that some of the funds had gone into North's pockets. President Reagan took full responsibility for the Iranian transactions, but insisted that he had not been informed of the contra connection.

In March 1988 North was indicted on 16 counts of conspiring to defraud the government and other charges. The trial lasted from February to May 1989 and ended with North's conviction on three counts: obstructing Congress, destroying classified documents, and accepting an illegal gratuity. North was sentenced to two years' probation and 1,200 hours of community service, and fined $150,000.

On July 20, 1990, a federal appeals court overturned the conviction on the grounds that witness testimony might have been influenced by North's immunized testimony to Congress. The Supreme Court upheld this ruling in 1991. Unable to prove that the testimony had not been tainted, independent counsel LAWRENCE E. WALSH was forced to drop all charges.

In 1990 North waged an expensive and high-profile challenge against incumbent U.S. senator Charles Robb of Virginia. The bid was notable for the opposition of the state's other U.S. senator, Republican John Warner, who actively campaigned against his fellow Republican as "morally unfit" to serve in the U.S. Senate. North narrowly loss the race. North remains in the public eye as a radio talk show host and television commentator.

Further reading: Ben Bradlee, *"Guts and Glory": The Rise and Fall of Oliver North* (New York: Donald I. Fine, 1988); Oliver L. North and William Novak, *Under Fire: An American Story* (New York: HarperCollins, 1991).

—John Korasick

North American Free Trade Agreement (NAFTA)

The leaders of Canada, Mexico, and the United States signed the North American Free Trade Agreement (NAFTA) on October 7, 1992. It came into effect on January 1, 1994. NAFTA calls for the lifting of trade barriers among the signatories over a 15-year time period. The treaty covered agreements on trade relations, labor relations, and environmental policy.

The three nations enjoyed strong trade relations before NAFTA went into effect. Nevertheless, the United States debated NAFTA's impact on labor and pollution extensively. People employed in manufacturing feared they would lose their jobs to the extremely cheap labor in Mexico. Labor unions in the United States spoke out often on the subject, fearing job losses as American companies relocated in Mexico. Critics cite the transformation of the *maquiladoras* area just over the U.S. border as an example of the negative impact of NAFTA. Deriving from the Spanish word *maquilar,* meaning to perform a task for another, the term refers to foreign-owned businesses located across the U.S. border in Mexico. The *maquiladoras* region includes the cities of Mexicali, Tijuana, and Ciudad Juarez, areas plagued with pollution problems, which many fear will worsen as more manufacturing moves into this area. Others criticized NAFTA because Mexico's environmental laws were lax and poorly enforced. Concerns over loss of American jobs, poor work conditions in Mexico, and environmental pollution kept Congress from voting on the treaty for more than a year before it was ratified.

The effects of NAFTA vary widely, but Mexico has seen the greatest impact. Proponents stress that impoverished Mexican cities have benefited greatly from the agreement. Ciudad Juarez has gained more than $4 billion in foreign investment and 150,000 manufacturing jobs since NAFTA went into effect. In contrast, a 1999 Labor University of Mexico study stated that, in the previous five years, the purchasing power of Mexican workers declined significantly. The study also describes increases in unemployment in the agricultural and small business sectors.

The effects of NAFTA on the American economy have been mixed. NAFTA has helped promote trade with Mexico and, in doing so, has improved the United States's relations with its southern neighbor. At the same time, American corporations have moved assembling plants to Mexico to avoid higher labor cost in the United States. Furthermore, critics charge that NAFTA has allowed increased access by drug smugglers to the United States through the increased traffic from Mexico entering the country. Finally, many critics charge that environmental and labor problems in Mexico have still not been addressed.

See also FOREIGN POLICY; GLOBALIZATION; WORLD TRADE ORGANIZATION.

Further reading: U.S. Congress. Senate Committee on Foreign Relations, Subcommittee on Western Hemisphere, *Lessons for NAFTA for U.S. Relations with the Americas* (Washington, D.C.: U.S. Government Printing Office, 2000).

—Leah Blakey and Michele Rutledge

North Atlantic Treaty Organization (NATO)

The North Atlantic Treaty Organization (NATO) is a collective security alliance among the United States, Canada, and several noncommunist countries of Europe, established in 1949. NATO was organized to ensure a just and lasting peaceful order in Europe, and this remains its primary objective in the post–COLD WAR world. Key to this objective is the transatlantic link between the security of North America and that of Europe.

On April 4, 1949, foreign ministers from 11 countries signed the North Atlantic Treaty in Washington, D.C. The signatory nations agreed to assist any member attacked by a hostile foreign nation, an agreement prompted by growing hostility between the Western wartime allies and the SOVIET UNION. The Vandenberg Resolution, passed by the U.S. SENATE on June 11, 1948, allowed the United States to enter into regional security pacts and set the stage for the United States to join NATO, the first defense alliance formed by the United States in peacetime. As of 1969, original NATO member nations included Belgium, France (political member only), Luxembourg, the Netherlands,

the United Kingdom, the United States, Canada, Denmark, Iceland, Italy, Norway, Portugal, Greece, Turkey, and West Germany. Spain was admitted in 1982. After the end of the cold war, NATO further expanded to include the former Warsaw Pact countries of East Germany (which combined with West Germany in 1990). Poland, Hungary, and the Czech Republic in 1999. The member nations are committed to sharing the risks and responsibilities, as well as the benefits of collective security. Member nations are further required not to enter into any other international commitment that might conflict with their NATO responsibilities.

Speculation at the end of the cold war centered on whether NATO was still necessary. It survived for three main reasons. First, Europeans had grown accustomed to a U.S. military presence. Second, even though the Warsaw Pact was gone, there were still many threats on the horizon. The Iraqi invasion of Kuwait, and the ethnic unrest in areas of the former Yugoslavia forced NATO units into action. Third, Eastern European nations desired its continuance and inclusion. These newly democratic states view alliance as a stabilizing factor in a very unstable world, as well as a hedge against Russian resurgence.

Security requirements of NATO member states changed fundamentally when the cold war ended. NATO adjusted by refocusing on the alliance's political role in providing security and stability in Europe. In 1991 the heads of state and government adopted a new strategic concept that outlined a broad approach to security, based on dialogue, cooperation, and the maintenance of a collective defense capability. It called for reduced dependence on nuclear weapons; reductions in force size and readiness, and improvements in their mobility, flexibility, and adaptability to different contingencies, as well as increased use of multinational formations.

NATO brought nonmember nations into some of their political and military actions through the North Atlantic Cooperation Council (NACC) and Partnership for Peace programs (PFP). The nonmember nations are from central and eastern Europe, and include Russia and many former Soviet republics. This increased interaction with its former enemies led to the enlargement of NATO in 1998, when Poland, Hungary, and the Czech Republic joined the alliance. The new members had to agree to all parts of NATO strategy and participate in NATO's integrated military structure. It was hoped that the enlargement would strengthen democracy in eastern Europe and promote good relations.

NATO's raison d'être shifted from confrontation with the Warsaw Pact to peacekeeping in the fragmenting areas of Central and Eastern Europe. NATO endorsed the Combined Joint Task Forces in 1994 as a means of facilitating contingency operations. NATO's new role as peacekeeper was tested on a political and military level in Bosnia, Kosovo, and the Middle East.

See also DEFENSE POLICY; FOREIGN POLICY.

—Leah Blakey

North Vietnam (U.S. relations with)

Following the end of the VIETNAM WAR and the take-over by North Vietnam of South Vietnam, unifying the country, the United States refused to establish diplomatic relations with Vietnam. Only in the 1990s, under the WILLIAM J. CLINTON administration, did the United States establish diplomatic relations with the unified nation of Vietnam.

On April 30, 1975, a helicopter lifted the last Americans off the embassy roof in Saigon, marking the final end of the Vietnam War, as victorious North Vietnamese troops marched into the South Vietnamese capital of Saigon, soon renamed Ho Chi Minh City. Relations between the United States and Vietnam remained strained until the late 1980s, as tensions between the two countries gradually eased with the end of the COLD WAR. When the Vietnamese-Soviet relationship ended, so did the $1.6 billion in annual aid from the USSR to Vietnam. Around the same time, the United States ceased to recognize the government of Cambodia under the Khmer Rouge, which had opposed the Vietnamese-supported government of Premier Hun Sen in Phnom Penh. Only in 1989 did the Vietnamese withdraw most of their forces from Cambodia under the new Khmer Rouge government. Two years later, in 1991, a UN-brokered settlement ended the Cambodian civil war. In 1991 President GEORGE H. W. BUSH authorized travel, and commercial sales of food and medicine, to Vietnam. Further progress in establishing relations with Vietnam came under the Clinton administration, starting in 1993. In his first year in office, President Bill Clinton authorized international lending to Vietnam and allowed American firms to agree to development projects. In 1994 President Clinton, with support from the U.S. Senate, lifted the trade embargo with Vietnam.

On July 11, 1995, President Clinton announced the normalization of diplomatic relations between the United States and still-Communist Vietnam. He named former Vietnam prisoner of war Douglas B. Peterson as America's first ambassador. The establishment of diplomatic relations between the two countries allowed for continued efforts to find and return the remains of 1,900 American servicemen still unaccounted for as of January 31, 2001.

—Leah Blakey

nuclear freeze movement

The nuclear freeze movement emerged in 1980, on both sides of the Atlantic, in response to America's defense build-up, which began under the JAMES EARL CARTER, JR., administration and accelerated under the RONALD W. REAGAN administration. American peace activist Randall Forsberg first introduced the proposal of a nuclear freeze that encompassed further nuclear testing, weapons production, and missile deployment. She maintained that the two superpowers had achieved parity regarding nuclear capability. She further contended that any additional increase in nuclear capability by either nation would increase the chance of nuclear war. Forsberg's proposal attracted peace activists in the United States and Europe. As the movement gained strength, a number of states passed "nuclear freeze" resolutions. In addition, the National Conference of Catholic Bishops endorsed a "nuclear freeze" in a pastoral letter on peace.

The proposal for a nuclear freeze gained little acceptance in Congress. In 1982 the HOUSE OF REPRESENTATIVES rejected a resolution calling for an immediate freeze on U.S. and Soviet nuclear weapons. In the next term, however, the House passed a resolution that called for negotiations between the Unites States and the SOVIET UNION to lead to a nuclear freeze, but the Senate refused to support this resolution. During the presidential election year of 1984, peace activists mobilized through the "Freeze Voter '84" campaign to endorse pro-freeze candidates. This activists' campaign had little influence on the elections. Arms control negotiations in Reagan's second term, as well as the eventual breakup of the Soviet Union, led the grassroots activist movement to decline. As a result, the nuclear freeze movement's influence on defense policy or arms control negotiations remained minimal.

See also ARMS RACE; CATHOLIC BISHOPS' LETTER.

Further reading: Douglas Waller, *Congress and the Nuclear Freeze: An Inside Look at the Politics of a Mass Movement* (Amherst: University of Massachusetts Press, 1987).

—Leah Blakey

Occupational Safety and Health Act (1970)

Also known as the Williams-Steiger Act, the Occupational Safety and Health Act established the Occupational Safety and Health Administration (OSHA), a federal regulatory agency that is responsible for workplace safety and health. The act was inspired by a 1968 West Virginia mining accident and agitation by organized labor for a federal presence in the workplace, to ensure health and safety standards. Congress proposed legislation in 1969 and President RICHARD M. NIXON signed the act into law December 29, 1970.

The new act emphasized the prevention of workplace accidents and illness. The act actually established three agencies, with OSHA being the most prominent. The other two, the National Institute for Occupational Safety and Health (NIOSH) was attached to the Department of Health, Education and Welfare (now the Department of Health and Human Services) to research occupational safety and health; and the Occupational Safety and Health Review Commission (OSHRC), an independent agency, was established to adjudicate employer challenges to OSHA enforcement actions.

OSHA began operations in April 1971. Its enforcement strategy has changed over the years. Initially OSHA targeted problem industries, primarily relying on voluntary compliance with standards set by the agencies. Inspections were limited to catastrophic accident scenes and workplaces deemed extremely dangerous. Over time this emphasis has shifted to target specific areas with high injury rates. These priorities led to an emphasis on workplace and worker safety in the 1970s, despite the fact that more workers died of occupational disease than occupational accidents. This emphasis on accidents was changed when Eula Bingham was appointed OSHA administrator in 1977. She focused the agency on health issues.

During the 1980s OSHA began requiring employers to provide information to employees on chemicals used in the workplace, and it instituted safety standards for agriculture and hazardous material handling. Also, OSHA inspectors would examine employer accident reports and injury rates at or below industry standards in industries exempt from inspection.

Entering its third decade in the 1990s, OSHA was not immune to the efforts to "reinvent government" and began to focus on reducing red tape, streamlining standards settings, and inspecting the most dangerous worksites. The emphasis was placed on achieving results. Standards were established covering protection from falls in construction work, electrical safety practices, and scaffolding. OSHA also began setting standards to address biological hazards, such as blood-borne pathogens, and issued rules protecting laboratory employees exposed to toxic chemicals. A new workplace threat was also recognized—the problem of violence in the workplace.

OSHA has been one of the most controversial regulatory agencies, with many in industry complaining its standards are too rigid. Recent OSHA attempts to establish federal standards for home offices met with fierce congressional resistance. Nevertheless, the agency has been successful in its mission. The occupational injury rate has decreased by 40 percent since OSHA began operations in 1971. Deaths due to workplace injury have fallen 60 percent. OSHA continues to act as a watchdog organization for the American worker, and now faces the challenge of setting the standards for the workplace of the future.

—John Korasick

O'Connor, Sandra Day (1930–)

Sandra Day O'Connor became the first female associate justice of the SUPREME COURT in 1981. O'Connor was born to Harry and Ada Mae Day, on March 26, 1930, in El Paso, Texas. She is the oldest of three children. Her parents owned a cattle ranch in southeastern Arizona, where O'Connor grew up. Life at the ranch was simple and isolated—the nearest neighbors lived 25 miles away, and the ranch itself did not have electricity or running water until O'Connor was eight years old. She was an avid reader and participated in many ranch activities, learning to shoot a rifle and ride horses before she was 10 years of age.

O'Connor was sent to El Paso to live with her grandmother for her school years, and she credits her grandmother's confidence in her ability for her later success. After completing high school, O'Connor went to Stanford University, graduating magna cum laude in 1950 with a baccalaureate in economics. While in law school, she met her future husband, a fellow student named John Jay O'Connor.

The O'Connors eventually settled in Phoenix, Arizona, to begin their family. After five years as a stay-at-home mother to the couple's three sons, O'Connor returned to work in 1965 as an assistant state attorney general in Arizona. The Arizona State Senate appointed her in 1969 to fill an unexpired term, and O'Connor was subsequently elected to three terms in the State Senate, serving as majority leader from 1973–74. O'Connor was elected in 1975 to the Maricopa County Superior Court and appointed to the Arizona Court of Appeals in 1979.

President Ronald W. Reagan nominated O'Connor on August 19, 1981, to the Supreme Court of the United States. She was opposed by antiabortion groups, because of her earlier support of a family planning bill in Arizona that would have repealed existing state laws banning abortion. Further, in the early 1970s, along with Richard Lamm, a Colorado state legislator (later governor), she had signed a statement that supported population control in the United States. In her nomination hearings, however, O'Connor refused to answer any questions on the issue. She easily won appointment to the court as its first female justice, in a 99-0 vote in the Senate.

Although viewed by many as a conservative, she occupied the center of the Court on abortion and civil rights decisions. In her first major abortion case on the Court, Justice O'Connor wrote a concurring dissent in AKRON V. AKRON CENTER FOR REPRODUCTIVE HEALTH (1981). In her dissent O'Connor claimed that Roe was "on a collision course with itself," because its trimester-based standard was "unworkable" in light of changing medical technology that increased viability. Later, in WEBSTER V. REPRODUCTIVE HEALTH SERVICES (1989), she used the doctrine of "undue burden" as a litmus test for judging the constitutionality of state abortion regulations. This view held that state regulations should not place an "undue burden" on women seeking to obtain an abortion. In *Webster*, she joined four of her colleagues in a concurring separate opinion that Missouri's abortion regulations did not unduly burden a woman's right to obtain an abortion.

One of her most significant votes came in the *Bush v. Gore* ruling, which resolved the legal and political deadlock

Associate Justice Sandra Day O'Connor *(United States Supreme Court)*

in the presidential election of 2000. In this case, disputes over the counting of ballots in the state of Florida had thrown the election into the state and ultimately the federal courts. Justice O'Connor sided with the 5-4 majority in stopping the hand recount of ballots in Florida. A 7-2 majority agreed that a recount could not be conducted in compliance with the requirements of equal protection and due process without substantial effort. This decision led to charges that the Court had usurped power and given GEORGE W. BUSH the presidency, although polls showed that the general public agreed with the decision.

—Michele Rutledge

Office of Management and Budget (OMB)

The Office of Management and Budget (OMB) is an agency located within the executive branch of the government and is primarily responsible for preparing presidential budget requests and supervising the executive agencies. The OMB was originally known as the Bureau of Budget and was created through the passage of the Budget and Accounting Act of 1921. In 1970 RICHARD M. NIXON reorganized the agency to make it more efficient, splitting it into two offices, the OMB and the Domestic Council. In

Nixon's view, the Domestic Council would be involved in choosing programs implemented by the government and the OMB would concern itself with how, and how well, the programs were implemented. This has resulted in a number of struggles between the two over who should have control. Besides preparing the budget and its role in domestic programs, the OMB also advises the president on legislation sent from Congress.

During the WATERGATE SCANDAL, Nixon critics charged that the OMB had taken over the daily operation of the White House, stepping out of its impartial advisory and supervisory role and into a partisan role implementing the Republican agenda. JAMES EARL CARTER, JR., attempted to restore the impartiality of the OMB, but with the election of RONALD W. REAGAN, it once again became a vehicle for furthering the president's agenda. A 1981 executive order created the Office of Information and Regulatory Affairs as part of the OMB, to oversee and review regulatory agencies. This was done as part of Reagan's "regulatory relief" plan, with the new office effectively eliminating further regulations. This practice was struck down in federal district court. The drive to reduce the size of government in the 1990s by

the WILLIAM J. CLINTON administration led to the Government Performance and Results Act in 1993, which requires federal agencies to submit plans to the OMB and to follow up these plans with progress reports, in an attempt to make government more efficient.

See also ENERGY; U.S. DEPARTMENT OF (CREATION OF).

—John Korasick

Oklahoma City bombing

Prior to September 11, 2001, the Oklahoma City bombing was the worst act of TERRORISM ever committed on American soil, and it remains the deadliest act of domestic terrorism. On April 19, 1995, a truck loaded with explosives made from fertilizer and diesel fuel ingredients exploded in front of the Alfred P. Murrah Federal Building in Oklahoma City, Oklahoma. The blast killed 169 people and injured more than 500, in addition to destroying the building and damaging more than 300 nearby businesses.

Federal agents arrested two men, Timothy J. McVeigh and Terry L. Nichols, and charged them with the crime. Both men had connections with the "patriot movement," a

Protective covering drapes part of the Alfred P. Murrah Federal Building in Oklahoma where a terrorist bomb killed 168 people *(Carter/Liaison)*

loose alliance of extremist groups advocating resistance to national laws and political institutions. McVeigh, a U.S. Army veteran of the PERSIAN GULF WAR, expressed solidarity with Randy Weaver, whose wife and son were killed during a shoot-out with federal agents in Ruby Ridge, Idaho, and with the BRANCH DAVIDIANS who died in a confrontation with federal agents in Waco, Texas. Both McVeigh and Nichols identified with the MILITIA MOVEMENT, especially with its fear that federal GUN CONTROL legislation was oppressive. In 1997 McVeigh was convicted of murder in the bombing and sentenced to death. At 8:14 A.M. (EDT), Monday, June 11, 2001, McVeigh was executed by lethal injection at the age of 33. Nichols was convicted in a separate trial of manslaughter and conspiracy, and was sentenced to life in prison in June 1998.

The ruins of the Murrah building were razed to make room for a memorial to those who died. The Oklahoma City National Memorial opened on February 19, 2001, with a dedication ceremony presided over by President GEORGE W. BUSH. The central element of the memorial is a 30,000-square-foot museum filled with photographs, testimonials, and interactive exhibits that tell the story of the bombing and its aftermath, and pay tribute to those who lost their lives in the tragedy. It also has 169 empty stone chairs to represent the dead.

—William L. Glankler

O'Neill, Thomas P., Jr. ("Tip") (1912–1994)

Thomas Phillip "Tip" O'Neill (D-Mass.) served as Speaker of the U.S. HOUSE OF REPRESENTATIVES from 1977–86. Born in North Cambridge, Massachusetts, he was first elected to the Massachusetts legislature as a Democrat in 1936, became Speaker of the state House in 1947, and was elected to Congress in 1952. For him, as he declared, "All politics is local."

He first participated in politics in 1928 when he campaigned for the Democratic presidential nominee, Al Smith. In 1936, the same year he graduated from Boston College, he won a seat in the Massachusetts state legislature. In 1941 he married Mildred Miller, with whom he had five children. In 1948 he became the first Democrat in 140 years to be named Speaker of the Massachusetts House. While in the Massachusetts House, he supported a series of social programs known as the "Little New Deal." In 1952 he was elected to the U.S. House of Representatives. In 1955 O'Neill was named to the House Rules Committee. O'Neill supported welfare, civil rights, housing, and education reform legislation proposals of President John F. Kennedy and President Lyndon B. Johnson. In 1968 he broke with the Johnson administration when he came out against the war in Vietnam. In 1971 O'Neill was elevated to majority whip, followed by an appointment to majority

leader in 1972, when Majority Leader Hale Boggs died in an airplane accident. While in this position, he voted to cut off funding of the air war in Vietnam. In 1976 he was elected as Speaker, the same year JAMES EARL CARTER, JR. came into the White House. From the outset, O'Neill experienced strained relations with the Carter administration. O'Neill wanted to focus on the economic problems of stagflation, and he felt Carter was too easily distracted by other issues, such as government reorganization, energy, and health and welfare reform. As a liberal Democrat, he opposed Carter's budget cuts.

When President RONALD W. REAGAN entered the White House, O'Neill unsuccessfully tried to form an alliance with aging House committee chairs and impatient young liberals who wanted to resist Reagan's conservative agenda. Although O'Neill opposed Reagan's budget cuts, many liberals within the House claimed that O'Neill caved in too easily to Reagan's other initiatives. O'Neill continued to serve as Speaker until he left office in 1986. After he retired, he cowrote *Man of the House: The Life and Political Memoirs of Speaker Tip O'Neill.* O'Neill died in Boston, Massachusetts, on January 5, 1994.

Further reading: Paul Clancy and Shirley Elder, *Tip: A Biography of Thomas P. O'Neill, Speaker of the House* (New York: Macmillan, 1980); Thomas P. O'Neill, with William Novak, *Man of the House: The Life and Political Memoirs of Speaker Tip O'Neill* (New York: Random House, 1987).

—Leah Blakey

Organization of Petroleum Exporting Countries (OPEC)

OPEC, an international organization of oil-exporting nations that coordinates the petroleum policies of its members, was formed on September 14, 1960, in Baghdad, and formally registered with the United Nations Secretariat on November 6, 1962. The five founding members—Saudi Arabia, Kuwait, Iraq, Iran, and Venezuela—were later joined by Algeria, Libya, Indonesia, Qatar, United Arab Emirates, and Nigeria. Ecuador and Gabon suspended their memberships in 1992 and 1994, respectively. Saudi Arabia, as the world's largest oil producer, has tended to dominate the organization.

The objectives of OPEC are to ensure the stabilization of oil prices on the international markets and to strike a balance between the security of the member nations' income and the availability of a regular and efficient supply to consuming nations. However, with the United States as the largest consumer of oil, and the precarious nature of Middle East politics, especially concerning the United States's support of Israel, the dividing line between economics and politics has not always been clear. As a result, the relationship between OPEC and the United States has often been an uneasy one.

The first major crisis occurred in the aftermath of the Yom Kippur War in 1973, in which the United States supported Israel. OPEC initially raised the price of oil, and then halted the supply to the United States as well as to Western Europe and Japan, from October 16, 1973, to March 18, 1974. This embargo caused severe economic problems in the United States, compounding an already weakening economy with high inflation and rationing of gasoline. OPEC continued to increase the price of oil throughout the 1970s and 1980s, including another severe hike in prices in 1979, the result of the civil war in Iran. From the mid-1980s, however, prices began to collapse, and despite a temporary increase during the Persian Gulf crisis in 1990 and 1991, prices remained relatively low, falling from over $50 per barrel in 1980 to around $10 per barrel in 1997. Throughout these years, the health and prosperity of the U.S. economy mirrored these fluctuations, with sudden price spikes causing recessions, and declining rates allowing recoveries.

In the late 1990s and early 2000s prices have begun to increase once again. In 2000 the price of oil rose to $38 per barrel. However, the impact of these increases has not been as severe as previous ones. In part this is due to the relatively weaker position of OPEC. Although the Middle East controls two-thirds of the world's proven oil reserves, it produces less than a third of the world's oil. The price increases of the 1970s and 1980s encouraged exploration for oil elsewhere, often in more inhospitable regions where it is more expensive to extract. As a result, the profits of OPEC members declined. Saudi Arabia, in particular, has suffered from a weak economic infrastructure, and the lower oil prices of the 1980s caused Saudi Arabia's debt to approach 100 percent of gross domestic product (GDP) in 1998.

Because of the shift in the United States from heavy industry toward high technology and service industries, the United States uses only half as much oil for every dollar of GDP as it did in the early 1970s. Still, the threat of higher energy costs continues to create concerns about economic instability. Moreover, many emerging economies, especially those in Asia, have substantially increased their dependency on oil, due to rapid industrialization and increased car ownership. The worldwide impact of a severe downturn in these economies could potentially damage the U.S. economy.

The political situation in the Middle East is also of concern. The tensions generated by U.S. foreign policy toward Iran and Iraq, and the continued unrest in Israel, still have the potential to politicize OPEC's attitude to the United States and lead to further economic crises. Environmental concerns, however, pose a serious threat to OPEC's position. Increased concern over global warming resulted in an agreement at the Kyoto summit in 1997 to reduce the emissions of "greenhouse" gases, which result from oil use. The consumption of oil remains high in the United States, and many worry about the environmental effects of this consumption. The development of more efficient and environmentally friendly sources of energy has the potential in the long term to render many of the economic and political problems between OPEC and the United States of relatively limited importance.

See also AUTOMOBILE INDUSTRY; ECONOMY; ENERGY CRISIS; FOREIGN POLICY.

—Stephen Hardman

organized crime   See crime

P

Panama (invasion)

At midnight on December 20, 1989, U.S. troops invaded and occupied Panama. The invasion, titled "Operation Just Cause," was triggered by a series of events that culminated in the shooting of an American soldier.

General Omar Torrijos Herrera ruled Panama for 13 years before he died in an airplane crash in 1981. Following his death, Panama underwent a series of crises, as three groups vied for political ascendancy. General Manuel Antonio Noriega successfully consolidated his power in 1984 in the National Guard, renaming it the Panama Defense Forces (PDF). Political reforms in 1983 called for a president, two vice presidents, and a National Assembly to be elected for five-year terms beginning in 1984. Noriega tampered with the election results, and the U.S.-backed candidate, Nicolas Ardito Barletta, won. After attempting to launch an investigation into Noriega's PDF, President Barletta was forced from office by Noriega. First Vice President Eric Arturo del Valle, regarded as a Noriega front, became president in 1985. General Noriega was reputed to be deeply involved in the corruption plaguing Panama. By 1986 the Panamanian economy had soured and underemployment and unemployment rates soared past 45 percent. In 1987 the Civil Crusade—an alliance of professionals, businesspeople, and opposition parties—demanded that del Valle and Noriega resign. The movement was endorsed by the Roman Catholic Church and had sympathizers in Washington, D.C. In response to the Civil Crusade, Noriega suspended opposition newspapers, declared a state of emergency, and sent troops into the streets, ostensibly to keep order. In response, the United States suspended economic and military aid to Panama and closed its embassy.

President del Valle discharged Noriega as PDF commander in 1988. Noriega, however, refused to leave his post, and the National Assembly instead voted to remove del Valle. RONALD W. REAGAN's administration condemned this action, and the United States imposed an embargo in an attempt to oust Noriega from power. Presidential elec-

tions were held in May 1989. Noriega nullified the results when it was determined that opposition leader Guillermo Endara Galimany was winning a majority of votes, and instead installed a figurehead president. In response, the United States suspended Panama Canal payments, tightened the economic sanctions, and intensified U.S. military strength in the Canal Zone to 12,000 troops.

In early October 1989 middle-ranking officers backed by the United States attempted a coup against Noriega and failed. On December 15, 1989, the Panamanian legislature declared Noriega president and stated that the United States and Panama were in a state of war. The shooting of a U.S. Marine caused Reagan's successor, President GEORGE H. W. BUSH, to take action, and on December 20, 1989, more than 25,000 troops were dispatched to eliminate the Noriega regime.

"Operation Just Cause" was controversial, due to the resulting loss of hundreds of Panamanian lives and the subsequent damage to both Panama City and El Chorillo. The military was able to quickly achieve its objective as Noriega surrendered on January 3, 1990. U.S. officials supervised the swearing in of President Endara and Vice Presidents Ricardo Arias Calderon and Billy Ford. Noriega was captured and extradited to Miami, tried and convicted for narcotics trafficking, and sentenced to a 40-year prison stay.

Officially, 23 Americans were killed during the conflict. Estimates of Panamanian deaths ranged from a low of 557 to several thousand (from the U.S. Southern Command) to between 2,000 and 4,000 (from the Association of Relatives of the Fallen of Over 6,000). The economic destruction of the invasion caused more than $2 billion in losses, of which the United States has paid $1 billion in aid. The invasion has left a strong undercurrent of anti-American sentiment in Panama.

Further reading: James Cockcroft, *Latin America—History, Politics, and U.S. Policy,* (Chicago: Nelson Hall,

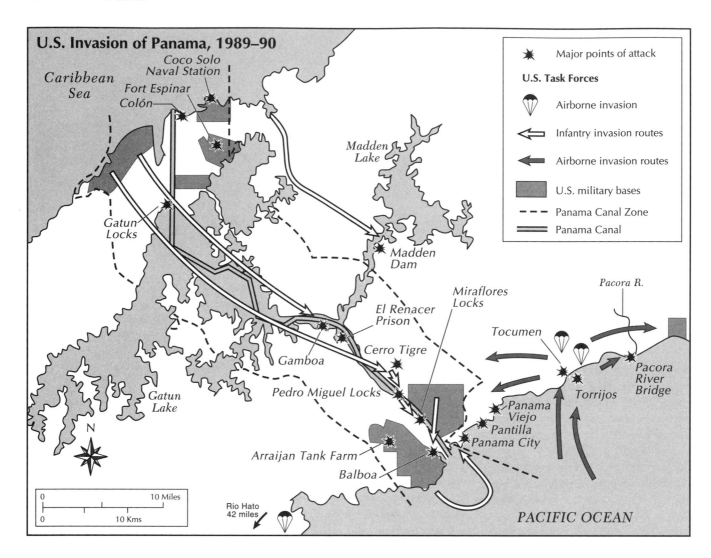

U.S. Invasion of Panama, 1989–90

Caribbean Sea

Coco Solo Naval Station
Fort Espinar
Colón

Madden Lake

Major points of attack

U.S. Task Forces

Airborne invasion

Infantry invasion routes

Airborne invasion routes

U.S. military bases

Panama Canal Zone

Panama Canal

Gatun Locks

Madden Dam

Pacora R.

Miraflores Locks

El Renacer Prison

Tocumen

Cerro Tigre

Gamboa

Pacora River Bridge

Gatun Lake

Pedro Miguel Locks

Panama Viejo
Torrijos

N

Pantilla
Panama City

Arraijan Tank Farm

Balboa

0   10 Miles

0   10 Kms

Rio Hato
42 miles

PACIFIC OCEAN

1996); Thomas Skidmore and H. Wayne Smith, *Modern Latin America* (New York: Oxford University Press, 1997).
—Michele Rutledge

Panama Canal (turnover)

In 1903 Panama became an independent nation. Two weeks later, the Hay-Bunau-Varilla Treaty was signed, granting the United States eminent domain throughout Panama and perpetual control over the future Canal Zone. A marvel of modern engineering, the 50-mile-long canal was completed in 1914 at a cost of some 22,000 human lives, and immediately became a major international waterway. The zone itself became a de facto U.S. colony, whose wealth and privilege stood in marked contrast to the local society.

The canal has been a source of controversy between the United States and Panama since its construction early in the 20th century. Numerous military interventions and treaty revisions have embroiled the United States in Panamanian affairs. Renegotiations of the treaty began in the 1950s, and while Panama received an increased annuity from the United States, the sovereignty question remained under discussion.

Tensions continued into the 1960s. In 1964 American high school students in the Canal Zone raised an American flag without the accompanying Panamanian colors; large-scale rioting followed, and diplomatic relations with Washington were severed by Panama. These "flag riots" ushered in a new political period for Panamanian politics and facilitated the rise to power of the National Guard. Under the leadership of General Omar Torrijos Herrera, the guard took power in 1968. As "Maximum Leader of the Revolution," Torrijos used the canal issue as a nationalist means to rally social classes. During his 13-year rule of Panama, Torrijos actively engaged in canal negotiations with the RICHARD M. NIXON, GERALD R. FORD, and JAMES EARL

CARTER, JR., administrations, with the United States accepting a treaty that called for Panamanian sovereignty over the canal by 1999.

American conservatives, such as PHYLLIS SCHLAFLY, denounced the negotiations as a sellout, supported by American corporate bankers seeking to guarantee their loans to Panama, but President Carter obtained the necessary Senate approval, and the United States and the Republic of Panama signed two treaties in 1977. The Panama Canal Treaty established a partnership between Panama and the United States until 2000, when Panama would take on full responsibility for the canal and provide for the immediate abolition of the Canal Zone. The Neutrality Treaty declared the canal permanently neutral, with U.S. and Panamanian ships having priority right-of-way in times of emergency and war.

Final control of the canal was given to Panama during ceremonies held in the closing days of December 1999. The official transition of the canal occurred at midday December 31st, with the focus of the ceremony on the raising of the Panamanian flag. A 21-gun salute and the sounding of ships' sirens completed the changeover.

Based on fears of computer breakdowns during the transition from the 1999 to 2000 (Y2K) calendar years, the Panama Canal Authority assumed control several hours before the changeover. The canal regularly handles 14,000 ships annually.

Further reading: James Cockcroft, *Latin America—History, Politics, and U.S. Policy* (Chicago: Nelson Hall, 1996).

—Michele Rutledge

penitentiaries   See crime

Pentagon Papers

The Pentagon Papers are a 47-volume study of U.S. involvement in Vietnam from 1945 through 1969. They were prepared by a team of analysts at the behest of Secretary of Defense Robert McNamara, beginning in 1967. In 1971 portions of the study were leaked to the *New York Times*, *Washington Post*, and other newspapers by Daniel Ellsberg, an analyst with the Rand Corporation. On June 13, 1971, the *Times* began publishing articles based on the information in the documents. Initially, RICHARD M. NIXON was pleased with the release of the documents because they cast the preceding Democratic administrations in an unfavorable light, showing that they had kept military and political decisions secret from Congress and the public, and had issued false or misleading statements.

Soon it became apparent that the release of the papers could also damage the current administration's war policies,

and the Justice Department requested a temporary restraining order to prevent the *Times* from publishing the entire set of papers. The administration argued that the legal standard cited to prevent publication should be national security, and the courts should defer to the administration's judgment in such matters. The newspaper asserted that blocking the publication of the papers violated the First Amendment of the Constitution and that the government was really trying to censor the news rather than protect national security. The *Times* lost and appealed to the U.S. Supreme Court. On June 30, 1971, the Supreme Court decided the case of *New York Times v. the United States*, ruling in favor of the newspaper, though every Justice wrote a separate opinion. The Justices asserted that the Constitution gave preference to freedom of the press, and that the government had failed to show that publication of the documents would have a negative impact on national security. This ruling left open the possibility that newspapers could be prevented from publishing classified documents, if they could be shown to directly threaten national security. The publication of the papers further intensified the debate over American involvement in Vietnam.

The general counsel for the newspaper, Jim Goodale, declared the result of the case a triumph for First Amendment rights. The government has never succeeded in preventing the publication of classified documents indefinitely.

After failing to prevent the publication of the papers, the Justice Department turned its attention to prosecuting Ellsberg for leaking the documents. Ellsberg was charged with treason, theft, and conspiracy. The trial lasted from January to May 1973. Ellsberg admitted that he had copied and released the documents, but he had the security clearance to view them. He also argued that the documents were released to bring them to the attention of Congress in an attempt to end the war.

On May 11, 1973, Judge William Byrne dismissed the charges against Ellsberg because of improper government conduct. A number of documents relating to the case had disappeared. Also, there was a break-in at Ellsberg's psychiatrist's office by a group known as the "plumbers," who worked out of the White House, looking for damaging information on Ellsberg. The plumbers would come into greater national prominence after their role in the WATERGATE SCANDAL was revealed. The break-in was listed under Article II of the Articles of IMPEACHMENT against President Nixon, under the heading of abuse of power.

See also VIETNAM WAR (END OF U.S. INVOLVEMENT).

—John Korasick

Perot, H. Ross (1930–)

A successful computer entrepreneur, H. Ross Perot ran for president in 1992 and 1996. In 1992 he received 19 percent of the vote, the best performance by a third-party candidate in 80 years. Henry Ross Perot was born on June 27, 1930, in Texarkana, Texas, and in 1948, he received an appointment to the U.S. Naval Academy, where he demonstrated leadership capabilities, serving as class president and head of the school's honor committee. While at the academy he met Margot Birmingham, whom he married in 1956. Perot graduated in June 1953 and served in the Navy until 1957. He and his wife moved to Dallas, Texas, where he accepted a position with International Business Machines (IBM).

In 1962 he left IBM and formed Electronic Data Systems Corporation (EDS), a computer management firm. The passage of Medicare legislation in 1965 suddenly increased the demand for computers, programmers, and storage. EDS secured government contracts in these areas and EDS experienced tremendous growth. EDS went public in 1968, and within two years, Perot's share of the company stock was worth $1.4 billion. EDS merged with General Motors (GM) in 1984, but disagreements between Perot and GM executive Roger Smith prompted Perot to publicly criticize GM. In 1986, GM bought out Perot's interest for $742.8 million.

Perot's business success made him highly visible and enabled him to become involved in international philanthropic efforts. In 1969, at the request of Secretary of State HENRY KISSINGER, Perot formed the United We Stand Committee to collect money and buy advertising to pressure the North Vietnamese into improving the conditions of their prisoner of war camps. Although Perot's efforts failed, he remained committed to locating and improving the condition of POWs. Perot became nationally known for his successful efforts to rescue two EDS employees from Iran. In 1978 revolutionary Iranian officials arrested the EDS manager and his assistant on charges that EDS had helped embezzle millions from the Iranian treasury. Diplomacy failed to gain their release, and Perot sent ex–Green Beret colonel Arthur D. Simons and a team of EDS executives to Iran in an effort to free them from prison. Although the executives were released before the rescue was attempted, Perot's team succeeded in removing them safely from the country. Ken Follett chronicled the effort in his 1983 nonfiction account, *On Wings of Eagles*.

On February 22, 1992, Perot appeared on the *Larry King Live* television show and stated that he felt America ought to be "fixed." He urged that the American people should "take back control of their government," and implied that he would run for president as an independent. He funded a campaign to have his name placed on the ballot in all 50 states before officially declaring himself a candidate. He removed his name from candidacy on July 17 based on his belief that WILLIAM J. CLINTON and the "New Democrats" had begun to address his concerns, but he con-

tinued to fund efforts initiated by United We Stand America to get his name on all state ballots. Stating that he wanted the campaign to focus more on economic issues, Perot reentered the campaign on October 1 and finished the election with 19 percent of the vote. This was the strongest showing by a third-party candidate since 1912 and many political analysts claimed that the three-way race contributed to GEORGE H. W. BUSH's loss to Bill Clinton.

Over the next three years, Perot continued to pressure both the Democrats and Republicans to consider his economic views. He became increasingly dissatisfied with both parties, and announced in September 1995 that he would be forming the independent REFORM PARTY for the 1996 election. He was overwhelmingly nominated to his party's candidacy but his campaign was severely damaged when he was not allowed to participate in the televised presidential debates. The 1996 campaign never gained the momentum of the 1992 campaign and he garnered only 8 percent of the vote. Although defeated, Perot vowed to continue his party's effort to pressure the government, but divisions within the Reform Party raised questions about its direction and leadership. These divisions led ultimately to an ugly conflict, when PATRICK J. BUCHANAN won the nomination for the Reform Party.

See also ECONOMY; ELECTIONS; IRANIAN HOSTAGE CRISIS; POLITICAL PARTIES; REAGANOMICS; TELEVISION; TERRORISM; VIETNAM WAR (END OF U.S. INVOLVEMENT).

Further reading: Ken Follett, *On Wings of Eagles* (New York: Morrow, 1983); Doron P. Levin, *Irreconcilable Differences: Ross Perot vs. General Motors* (Boston: Little Brown, 1989); Gerald Posner, *Citizen Perot: His Life and Times* (New York: Random House, 1996).

—William L. Glankler

Persian Gulf War

On August 2, 1990, Iraq, under the leadership of Saddam Hussein, a brutal dictator, invaded neighboring Kuwait, a major oil producer in the Middle East region. This invasion consolidated a large portion of the Persian Gulf oil supply under the control of an anti-American regime and threatened to disrupt the flow of oil from Saudi Arabia, which controlled more than a fifth of the world's proven oil supplies. President GEORGE H. W. BUSH declared, "This aggression will not stand." A 30-nation coalition, led by the United States, attacked Iraq and restored the Kuwaiti monarchy.

Iraq's invasion came after Kuwait unilaterally increased its oil production, which led to a drop in world prices. This drop in the value of its chief export came as Iraq struggled to repay loans borrowed from the Kuwaiti and Saudi regimes during the Iran-Iraq War of 1980–88. Kuwait and Saudi Arabia refused to forgive Iraq's debts. Ironically, many of Hussein's weapons had come through American aid when the United States supported the regime in the late 1980s. The RONALD W. REAGAN and Bush administrations had approved nearly $1 billion in economic and technical aid to the government of Hussein.

With the invasion of Kuwait, the UNITED NATIONS (UN) authorized a trade embargo on Iraq and sent a quarter of a million troops, mostly Americans, to defend Saudi Arabia, in a military operation called Desert Shield. General Norman Schwarzkopf headed the operation. Eventually the UN military force grew to 550,000 troops.

Congress debated at length the issue of using force to dislodge the Iraqi occupation of Kuwait. Congressional Democrats generally opposed military action and called for time to let the economic boycott work; Republicans called for military action. On January 12, 1991, Congress narrowly approved the use of American troops in the Persian Gulf. Only a few Democratic senators, including ALBERT GORE (D-Tenn.), supported military intervention. Four days later, Operation Desert Storm began.

Following weeks of air strikes, on February 23, 1991, General Schwarzkopf sent 200,000 troops into Iraq. Although coverage of the war was censured by the Pentagon, television carried much of the war live to American homes. Within five days after the invasion, Hussein accepted a cease-fire. As Iraq withdrew from Kuwait, it set fire to the oil fields and dumped huge quantities of crude oil into the gulf.

The United States lost only 148 Americans in the six-week conflict, while more than 100,000 Iraqi soldiers and citizens died. Bush's approval rating reached 90 percent, but he was later criticized for failing to remove Hussein from power. Still more criticism mounted when it was revealed that the administration had assisted several purported eyewitnesses to falsify their congressional testimony of accounts of Iraqi atrocities. Further criticism came when the administration encouraged the Kurdish minority in Iraq to revolt against the Hussein regime, which led to their brutal suppression by Iraqi soldiers.

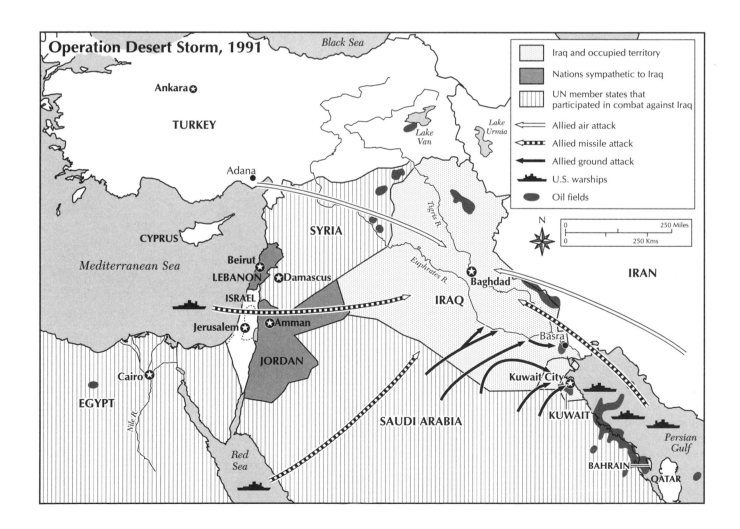

Following his defeat, Hussein continued to refuse to allow UN inspectors to search for weapons of mass destruction being built by Hussein's regime. This led the WILLIAM J. CLINTON administration to launch periodic air strikes against Iraq. Nonetheless, Hussein expelled the UN inspectors in 1998, which led to further American airstrikes. Hussein remained a thorn in the side of the United States, and many observers accused Hussein of continuing to develop biological and chemical weapons of mass destruction and continuing to harbor and train terrorists. As a consequence, the Middle East continued to be one of the world's most volatile regions as the United States entered the 21st century.

political action committee (PAC)

A political action committee (PAC) is an organization that raises money from individuals and distributes it to electoral candidates who meet a particular set of criteria. PACs solicit contributions either through individual businesses, consortiums, labor unions, associations, or directly from interested individuals; they then pool their resources to provide their contributors with a greater voice in the electoral process than they would have had separately through contributions to candidates. Their contributions can be made directly to their favored candidate or party, or indirectly in the form of paid advertisements supporting their candidate and political position.

PACs were legally recognized in the Federal Election Campaign Act of 1971, which authorized businesses, unions, and associations to sponsor third-party organizations that pooled voluntary political contributions of their members or employees. Individuals could also form PACs around sets of common interests or causes. The new statute intended to limit the influence of wealthy interests in federal elections by limiting individual contributions to $1,000 per candidate per election. In light of the representative nature of PACs, they were allowed also to contribute $5,000 to each campaign per election, and $15,000 to a national party committee.

Business and labor interests realized that multiple PACs working in alliance could channel even more money toward their preferred candidate. Later, members of single-issue and ideological organizations used PACs to get around the Federal Election Commission (FEC) limitations, by directly advertising their preferences in the media without actually contributing money to their preferred candidate. The SUPREME COURT concluded, in *Buckley v. Valeo* (1976), that this kind of "soft" money contribution was protected by the First Amendment guarantee of free speech.

Today, there are more than 4,000 PACs. Though nearly two-thirds represent business interests in the form of cor-

porations, industry consortiums, and professional groups, half of the largest PAC contributors in the 2000 election were labor unions, including the Teamsters Union, International Brotherhood of Electrical Workers, Laborers Union, Machinists and Aerospace Workers Union, and the United Auto Workers.

In 2001 Senator John McCain (R-Ariz.) and Representative Christopher Shays (R-Conn.) submitted a Bipartisan Campaign Finance Reform bill to the 107th Congress. Nine months later, it passed by a vote of 240-189 in the Republican-controlled House and by 60-40 in the Democratic-controlled Senate. President Bush signed it into law on March 27, 2002. On the same day, the National Rifle Association (NRA) and Senator Mitch McConnell (R-Ky.) filed separate suits challenging the soft-money provision, prohibiting independent organizations from advertising their interests during a campaign, as a violation of the First Amendment.

Critics of PACs contend that they corrupt the democratic process by giving well-funded special interests too much influence over politicians, thereby granting them an unfair advantage over individual voters. Supporters reply that PACs only pool the resources of the individual contributors that they represent; they do not influence candidates, but instead serve as an alternative means for individuals to support or oppose particular candidates.

See also CAMPAIGN FINANCE; ELECTIONS.

—Aharon W. Zorea

political correctness

Political correctness is the belief that language and practices that could offend political sensibilities should be eliminated or suppressed. A debate over political correctness emerged in the 1980s, and centered on the use of language that was perceived as derogatory toward minorities, or that displayed sexist or racist tendencies. However, the debate over individual phrases masks a much broader debate about culture and politics in the United States. The excesses of political correctness have been magnified to support political beliefs, and have entered the general culture, obfuscating real issues.

The first recorded use of the term "politically correct" was in the 1793 SUPREME COURT case *Chisholm v. Georgia* where it was used in its literal form to refer to a correct interpretation of the law. The first use in the 20th century was in the 1930s when American Communists used it to refer to the correct interpretation of the party line, frequently in a self-deprecating manner. The term gained further usage in the aftermath of the Civil Rights and feminist movements of the 1960s. During the 1970s, careful attention was paid to the use of language that signified an unequal balance of power or that contained implicit notions of racism. Advocates of social change argued that such terms should be replaced with less loaded ones. Words such as "Native American" or "chairperson" were to be preferred over more stereotyped ones such as "Indian" or "chairman."

In the 1980s and early 1990s political correctness exploded on the national scene. Articles in the *New York Times* and *Newsweek* in 1991 drew attention to fierce debates on college campuses and in the media, where attempts at rectifying gender and racial prejudices and discrimination, many believed, had led to the censuring of free speech. The cover of *New York* magazine on January 21, 1991, asked, "Are You Politically Correct?" and the article listed a range of terms from the obvious, such as African American, to the plainly ridiculous, such as "animal companion" rather than "pet." This debate, in essence, shrouded the CONSERVATIVE MOVEMENT criticism of what it perceived as leftist domination of many educational, religious, and cultural institutions in America. It was argued that leftist attempts to seek inclusivity and impose cultural diversity had led to the forced imposition of certain political values, thereby suppressing intellectual diversity and restricting free speech. Critics of this conservative complaint against political correctness charged that the debate was just a sensationalistic straw man designed to advance a conservative movement and its attacks on liberal notions of education, scholarship, and culture.

The debate has since expanded to include a wide range of cultural forms, from smoking in public, and the presentation of violence in movies and on TV, to sexually explicit lyrics of pop music. In some instances, "politically incorrect" served as a badge of authenticity for many conservative commentators and politicians. Critics of the conservative movement's critique have since charged that attacks on political correctness have become an excuse to indulge in inappropriate and offensive speech and behavior. The underlying debate continues over the extent of the ideological and political ramifications of language and culture in the United States.

See also AFFIRMATIVE ACTION; CONSERVATIVE MOVEMENT; FEMINISM; MULTICULTURALISM.

—Stephen Hardman

political parties

Within the American democratic system, a political party is a group of people organized to achieve and maintain political power through the electoral process. Parties are designed to help candidates win elections and operate government. Two parties, the Democratic and Republican, dominate contemporary government. (Although the Democrats are the older group, the Republicans are sometimes referred to as the "GOP" for "grand old party.") Each

of these major parties traditionally represent a broad and shifting coalition. In the latter half of the 20th century, the Republican Party has tended to be the ideologically right-of-center coalition and the Democratic Party the ideologically left-of-center coalition. Nevertheless, both parties have undergone significant changes in their platforms and constituencies as they have responded to the pressures of demographic, cultural, and technological change. Third parties have also been particularly active and influential since 1968, arguably shifting the outcome of presidential elections in 1968, 1980, 1992, and 2000.

American political parties, after 1968, have struggled with the changes brought about by demographic and social shifts. The New Deal democratic alliance of southern voters and the industrial and urban ethnic voters of the North began to unravel in the late 1960s as the party's embrace of civil rights alienated much of its base. Furthermore, divisions over FEMINISM, reproductive rights (ABORTION), the VIETNAM WAR, and the GAY RIGHTS MOVEMENT divided the coalition. The Republicans, under RICHARD M. NIXON, skillfully exploited these issues in 1968 and 1972. Indeed, the use of racial appeal and "wedge issues," such as abortion, characterized the GOP for the remainder of the century. The Republican Party also struggled with changes in America in those years. Led by RONALD W. REAGAN, the CONSERVATIVE MOVEMENT challenged the traditional Republicanism of Nixon and captured the GOP nomination and the presidency. Under Reagan's administration, the conservative movement was in control of the Republican Party. The election of WILLIAM J. CLINTON in 1992 represented a victory for "New Democrats," who sought to move the party back to the center. In 2000 Republicans once again regained the White House, when GEORGE W. BUSH took a softer approach than many conservatives within the party on education, affirmative action, and the environment.

Political parties in the United States are well organized and highly structured, operating on a local, state, and national level. Each party has a national chairman who directs recruitment and systematization. Presidential candidates are nominated every four years at a four-day-long national convention. Each state party apparatus sends delegates who cast votes for the party's nominee. State-by-state primary elections held before the convention determine which candidate's supporters are sent as delegates to the national convention. Delegates also select a running mate, but usually defer to the presidential nominee of the party in choosing a candidate.

Since 1852, every U.S. president has been either a Republican or Democrat. These two parties dominate the political process, organizing government at both the national and state levels. Roughly two-thirds of Americans consider themselves members of these parties; those claiming independent status still incline toward one or the other.

Less than 10 percent of Americans are strict independents. After the 1994 elections, there was a single independent representative in Congress, and less than 1 percent of state legislators elected were from minor parties.

American parties play a major role in shaping public policy. Indeed, since the mid-1990s both the Democrats and Republicans in Congress have shown sharp policy differences and exhibited fierce partisanship, especially in the House of Representatives. This opposition between parties is one of the political system's most enduring features, illustrating structural aspects of the political system as well as highlighting special characteristics of the parties themselves. National legislators in America are selected through the "single-member" district system—the candidate receiving a plurality of the vote is elected. Most states also use this system. This process allows only one party to win in any given district, thereby creating incentives to form two broadly based parties capable of winning legislative district majorities, and consigning minor parties to defeat. The presidential electoral procedure also drives the two-party system in the United States. Virtually every state allocates all its electors, selected by the parties, to the candidate who wins the plurality. This winner-take-all system makes it virtually impossible for minor parties to gain a majority of the vote, although they can change the outcome by taking votes away from the major parties. To become president requires an absolute majority of 538 electoral votes (270), making it extremely difficult for a third party to independently achieve the presidency.

The dominant parties have created electoral rules that work to their advantage. Most states have extensive barriers inhibiting the inclusion of a minor party on the ballot. Most smaller parties cannot qualify for benefits included in the Federal Election Campaign Act, which allocates public financing for national conventions, matching funds for candidates for presidential nominations, and public funding of presidential campaigns.

American parties are broad-based and include all income levels in their electoral support. With the exception of African-American voters, of whom nearly 90 percent back the Democratic Party, the major parties draw significant levels of support from virtually every major socioeconomic group in the society. For example, labor-union members, traditionally identified as Democrats, have tended to cast up to one-third of their ballots for Republican candidates in recent years. In addition, while allegiance to the Democratic Party historically has fallen as income levels rise, the current political trend shows both major parties enjoying substantial support from upper-middle-class voters, who were making their decisions on cultural rather than economic issues. Given the need to maintain their broad voter support to win elections, the two major parties have demonstrated much policy flexibility. This approach enables the Democrats and Republicans to accept ideological diversity within their organizations, as well as protest movements, and "third party" positions, when they have arisen.

Third parties and independent candidates have nevertheless intermittently appeared in American politics, usually in response to some issue or issues that the major parties were unwilling or unable to address. Most third parties have tended to last for a single election and then disappear, weaken, or join with one of the major parties. Only one new party since the 1850s, the Republican, has transitioned from a third party into a major party. Evidence suggests, however, that while third parties cannot compete against the entrenched parties, they can have a huge impact on election dynamics and outcomes.

Third party movements were significant in 1968, in 1980, in 1992, and in 2000. In 1968 Alabama governor GEORGE C. WALLACE pulled culturally conservative Democrats to his protest candidacy. Scholars continue to debate which party benefited from that year's whisker-thin election margin. Most of JOHN B. ANDERSON's 1980 votes, on the other hand, expressed a clear preference for Democratic incumbent JAMES EARL CARTER, JR., but nevertheless, not sufficient in number to have helped him surpass RONALD W. REAGAN's victory. Many of Reagan's voters later migrated to H. ROSS PEROT's 1992 campaign. Many observers believe that the independent's high-profile attacks shifted the momentum and dynamic of the race against Bush. By contrast, RALPH NADER's attraction for Democratic voters clearly contributed to ALBERT GORE, JR.'s narrow electoral defeat, demonstrably shifting the electoral votes of two states.

It is hardly surprising, therefore, that the leaders of both the Republican and Democratic Parties have been extremely concerned about third party or independent campaigns. This concern is not limited to presidential candidates; Vermont senator James Jeffords's defection from the Republican Party, shortly after the 2000 election, tipped the fragile majority of the Senate to the Democrats, causing a major realignment of the national political system. Imposing barriers exist to a third party's winning the presidency, or even electing a substantial number of representatives or senators. Many voters fear that a ballot cast for a third party candidate will be wasted. Savvy voters have strategically cast their ballots for their second choice when they sense that a third-party candidate has no chance of winning.

In 1980 independent candidate John B. Anderson gathered votes of only 57 percent of the voters who ranked him highest; in 1992 among voters ranking Ross Perot highest, 79 percent voted for him but 21 percent voted for the major parties' candidates. Third parties also face the phenomenon of "protest" voting for their candidates. In

1992 Gallup polls showed that 5 percent of the people who voted for Perot indicated they would not vote for him if they thought he could win.

Since the 1960s, campaign techniques have been changed by the increasing use of television advertisements and appearances. Media advisers became more prominent, often taking over the traditional party leaders' role. In addition, the function of party conventions in selecting candidates has been reduced by the growing prevalence of primary elections.

Although both major parties adopt a centrist pose in their election-year questions for the majority, significant differences exist between the Democratic and Republican Parties in terms of both ideology and base constituency. The Republican Party ideology is often viewed as one that wants a more limited and circumscribed government; advocates shifting more federal authority to state and local governments; opposes regulation of private industry and the economy, as well as social welfare programs, such as Social Security and Medicare; is more in favor of defense spending; and is against what it perceives as excessive gun control measures, as well as abortion rights, feminism, affirmative action, and preferential rights for gays. The Republicans nationally tend to draw suburban and rural voters; white male voters; and married white women. The Democrats are typically viewed as a party that works for the interests for the lower class by promoting progressive tax rates and programs to provide state assistance to those people. The Democrats get their most loyal support from African Americans, union workers, new immigrants, and single white women. On the national level, the Democrats tend to draw voters from large cities. Both parties have recently seen these "typical" supporters drift toward choosing individual candidates, rather than voting "party line."

Further reading: Malcolm E. Jewell and Sarah M. Morehouse, *Political Parties and Elections in American States* (Washington, D.C.: Congressional Quarterly, 2000); L. Sandy Maisel, *Parties and Elections in America: The Electoral Process* (Lanham, Md.: Rowman & Littlefield, 2002); ——— and John F. Bibby, *Two Parties—Or More? The American Party System* (Boulder, Colo.: Westview Press, 1998); Alan Ware, *Citizens, Parties and the State: A Reappraisal* (Princeton, N.J.: Princeton University Press, 1987).

—Michele Rutledge

popular culture

Since the mid-1960s, the popular culture has been directed by four forces: the youth market, technological advances, sophisticated marketing, and an increasingly diverse population. Film lost part of its audience to television until it rebuilt itself through the development of youth-oriented films, blockbuster movies, and commercial product tie-ins. Meanwhile, TELEVISION dealt with changes in delivery. The once-dominant three national networks (ABC, CBS, NBC) were joined by several dozen cable and satellite networks, often specialized by subject matter and demographic group. Television and MOVIES were affected by the availability of videocassette recordings. First introduced to the home market in 1977, VCRs opened the market to more sales but, in the case of movies, kept some people away from movie theaters. Theater was hampered by the increasingly high cost of mounting shows that began to rise dramatically in the 1970s, and by the effect of a modern society used to recorded, rather than live, performances. As it had for decades, popular MUSIC continued to be driven by youth, but after the breakup of the Beatles and other popular groups of the 1960s, it fragmented largely along demographic and ethnic lines. Technological advances included the commercially and technologically successful compact disc, first invented in 1969 by Klass Campann, a physicist with Philips Research, and introduced in 1972; the personal music player; and the expanding practice of Internet music transmission. Making a blockbuster that reaches a mass audience became the producers' aim in all the arts; serving a range of groups with rapidly changing tastes is the reality.

Movies

Beginning with 1960's *Psycho* and concluding with 1969's *Midnight Cowboy*, the 1960s in American film were marked by an increasing expression of adult issues and language. The movie *Who's Afraid of Virginia Woolf?*, a Warner Brothers film production, broke the language barrier by using the phrase "hump the hostess," although the word "screw" had been deleted from the final release. A few months later, Michelangelo Antonioni's *Blow Up* became the first film marketed by a major distributor (MGM) with nudity in it. In April 1968 the U.S. Supreme Court upheld the constitutional power of states and cities to prevent the exposure of children to books and films that could not be denied to adults. Officially marking that change was the replacement of the long-lived Production Code with a multitiered movie industry ratings system introduced in November 1968. The system included four ratings ranging from G (general audiences) to X (no one under 17 admitted).

The 1970s were marked by creative experimentation, the rise of the blockbuster movie, and the introduction of the videocassette recorder (VCR) in 1977. As the major studios foundered, young directors such as George Lucas, Martin Scorsese, and Steven Spielberg reinvigorated familiar genres and brought studios back to life. Francis Ford Coppola made the gangster movie a romantic tragedy with *The Godfather* (1972) and *The Godfather Part II* (1974).

This merchandise was produced as a "tie-in" to the release of the movie *Harry Potter and the Sorcerer's Stone*, based on the books of J. K. Rowling. Merchandise tie-ins are becoming more frequent in the movie industry, particularly with movies for children. *(Justin Sullivan/Getty Images)*

Stanley Kubrick continued his 1960s experimentation with the crime fantasy in *A Clockwork Orange* (1971); Robert Altman entered with *M*A*S*H* (1970) and *Nashville* (1975). But it was two summer movies that had the most lasting effects. Spielberg's shark thriller *Jaws* (1975) became one of the first films to top $100 million in rentals; Lucas's space spectacular *Star Wars* (1977) was even more popular. With them, the blockbuster was born.

During the 1980s, blockbusters and sequels dominated the box office. From *Star Wars* came two sequels, *The Empire Strikes Back* (1980), and *The Return of the Jedi* (1983). Spielberg directed two successes: the alien fantasy *E.T.* (1982) and the homage to afternoon serials, *Raiders of the Lost Ark* (1981). Other blockbusters included *The Terminator* (1984) and *Die Hard* (1988). Serious dramas included Scorsese's *Raging Bull* (1980).

The 1990s were marked by the refinement of Disney animation, the emergence of a new generation of filmmakers, and the top disaster film in movie history. Having already reinvigorated Disney animation in *Beauty and the Beast* (1991), Disney surpassed itself in visual creativity and box-office success with the 1994 film *The Lion King*. Director Quentin Tarantino presented the moral universe of the underworld in *Pulp Fiction* (1994); the Coen brothers set their crime drama *Fargo* (1996) in the snowy upper Midwest and featured as its sleuth a pregnant woman. Successful at the box office was James Cameron's *Titanic* (1997), which united the disaster movie with a star-crossed love story. It became the decade's top moneymaker.

The new millennium brought an increased interest in global productions, such as Ang Lee's martial arts saga *Crouching Tiger, Hidden Dragon* (2000), which was coproduced by companies in China, Hong Kong, Taiwan, and the United States. The Roman epic also made a comeback, this time secularized for modern audiences in Ridley Scott's *Gladiator* (2001).

Music

Although Frank Sinatra won a best-record Grammy as late as 1966, rock and roll dominated popular music by 1969. Its reach encompassed "British invasion" groups like the Beatles and Rolling Stones, the pop/soul Motown Sound, and the folk/rock/protest music of Bob Dylan and Simon & Garfunkel.

As the decade ended, many influential acts disbanded: Diana Ross and the Supremes in 1969, Simon & Garfunkel in 1970, and most famously, the Beatles in 1970. Further, by the early 1970s, some of the decade's defining figures died mysteriously or from drug overdoses: Jimi Hendrix in 1970, Janis Joplin in 1970, Jim Morrison in 1971.

During the 1970s, popular music was represented by subspecialties serving smaller audiences. Groups ranged from Tony Orlando and Dawn to Wings to the Jackson 5. Folk protest singers, such as Carole King and Joan Baez, mellowed into singer/songwriters. Outrageousness and/or political statement were offered by Kiss, the Village People, and the punk rock movement, epitomized by the Sex Pistols. Critical favorites included Stevie Wonder and Bruce Springsteen. For popularity, nothing beat disco music. Pounding and undulating, it bespoke sex and resurrected partner dancing. Leading purveyors were the Bee Gees and Donna Summer.

The 1980s began with a shock: the 1980 killing of Beatle John Lennon near his New York home. In 1981 the cable network Music Television (MTV) debuted and turned pop music into a visual as well as aural medium. Artists integrating original movement into their videos were able to rule the market. Among such video pioneers were Madonna and Michael Jackson; both reimagined dance as stylized self-expression. Another breakthrough, the compact disc, changed the way people listened to music. Small and clean-sounding, it made vinyl records obsolete. Other notable artists of the decade included Prince, the Police, and Culture Club.

The 1980s also witnessed the rise of the hypnotic, frank musical form, rap. By the 1990s, rap had a wide audience, with leading performers including Dr. Dre, Snoop Dogg, and Busta Rhymes. Gangsta rap was denounced for its link to crime, as seen in the 1996 killings of rap singers Tupac Shakur and Notorious B.I.G. Many of the rap performers were linked to urban gangs.

The 1990s revealed evidence of country music's crossover power, as Garth Brooks became a top-selling country and pop artist. Disaffected youth were drawn to the raw grunge music of Nirvana and Pearl Jam. Nirvana leader Kurt Cobain became the movement's dark icon, following his death by drug overdose in 1994. Hip-hop was informed by soul and reggae, with leading performers including Lauryn Hill. Preteens took to boy groups like 'N Sync and girl-woman singers like Britney Spears and Christina Aguilera, the latter illustrating another musical trend: the popularity of Latin music. Ricky Martin is among notable Latin performers.

The millennium in music begins with multiple musical subgenres pointing to both widespread demographic splintering and great creative variety. There is no single sound to American popular music.

Television

By 1960, over 90 percent of American homes had one or more television sets. By 1994, surveys showed that 99 percent of American homes have one or more televisions. Cable television reaches 58.5 percent of American homes with 60 million viewers.

In the 1960s the three major networks—ABC, CBS, and NBC—dominated programming, which was moving from the light comedies of the early decade (*Bewitched, Green Acres*) to shows more relevant to society. Among them were programs of political irreverence, such as *The Smothers Brothers Comedy Hour,* sexual liberation, like *The Mary Tyler Moore Show,* and social conflict, like *All in the Family.*

The 1970s were also notable for popularization of the miniseries. Setting the standard was the 1977 miniseries about American slavery, *Roots,* which ran for eight consecutive nights. Sports, broadcast during prime-time hours since 1946, gained new currency when *Monday Night Football* debuted on ABC in 1970. With commentary (after 1971) by Frank Gifford, Don Meredith, and Howard Cosell, the program blended sports and entertainment.

By the mid-1970s, networks faced competition brought by technological advances and cable television. These advances also provided consumers with greater access to trends in popular culture. In 1975 the videocassette player (VCR) was introduced, allowing viewers to record programming and play rental tapes. As of 2000, over 98 percent of U.S. households had at least one television set; 86 percent had a VCR; 69 percent received cable programming. In October 2000, Americans watched an average of 29.04 hours of television weekly.

In 1972 the cable network Home Box Office (HBO) began; it broadcast films and features, eroding network viewership. The 24-hour-per-day news channel, Cable News Network (CNN) began broadcasting in 1980, which eventually reconfigured news coverage. CNN revealed on audience for continuous news coverage, leading to expanded network news and the development of other cable news channels such as FOX NEWS and MSNBC. By 2002, Fox News dominated the cable news channels, while viewership of network news fell dramatically.

Prime-time programming during the 1980s was marked by larger-than-life soap operas, such as *Dallas,* and solid comedies, such as *Cheers* and *The Cosby Show.* The latter show was distinguished as an early example of an upper-middle-class family comedy starring AFRICAN AMERICANS.

In the 1990s and into the next millennium, cable programming has been seen as the forum for original programming. Cable series such as *The Sopranos* and *Sex and the City* won national awards and became part of the national currency. Overall cable viewing increased over the decade, with cable viewership surpassing network affiliate viewership for the first time in 2000. Dominating non-cable networks were the comedies *Seinfeld* and *Frasier,* as well as the game show, *Who Wants to Be a Millionaire?* and reality shows like *Survivor.* Reality shows featured average people put into extraordinary situations.

Responding to protest at the increasingly adult language and subject matter on television, the television industry instituted a set of TV parental guidelines in 1996. Modeled on the MPAA ratings, the guidelines encompassed several categories including TVY/All Children and TVMA/Mature Audience Only. Critics of violence and sex on television maintained that such programming was adversely affecting popular culture and indirectly promoting violence in the schools and lowering sexual mores among the youth. In response, television networks agreed that they had a responsibility to the public, and promised more self-regulation through labeling, but they also warned that censoring programs restricted "free speech."

Theater

Since the late 1960s, professional theater has been marked by conflicting impulses and realities. While sexually explicit 1968 Broadway works like *Hair* and *The Boys in the Band* were meant to appeal to a younger audience, the age of regular theatergoers during the era rose.

The success of the 1968 play *The Great White Hope,* which opened in Washington, D.C.'s Arena Stage, prefigured two movements in late-century theater. One was the introduction of works by and about African Americans, such as August Wilson's *Fences* (1987) and George C. Wolfe's *Jelly's Last Jam* (1992). The other trend was the use of regional theaters to provide Broadway offerings. Notable sites include Chicago's Goodman Theater.

Facing an unsure future in the socially relevant 1970s, Broadway was revived by the gutsy 1975 musical *A Chorus Line.* Other popular musicals of the era included *Annie* (1977), based on the Little Orphan Annie comic strip, and Bob Fosse's sensual *Chicago* (1975). Over the next quarter century, composer/lyricist Stephen Sondheim created complex works including *Company, Follies,* and *A Little Night Music.* In the 1990s the post-baby boom generation was represented by Jonathan Larson's musical, *Rent.*

The most successful purveyor of musicals during the last quarter century was British composer Andrew Lloyd Webber, who introduced the musical spectacle. His successes include *Joseph and the Amazing Technicolor Dreamcoat, Jesus Christ Superstar, Evita, Cats, The Phantom of the Opera,* and *Sunset Boulevard.* All were rich with effects and had lengthy runs.

Notable playwrights included Neil Simon, who continued his 1960s successes with the trilogy of *Biloxi Blues, Brighton Beach Memoirs,* and *Broadway Bound.* Wendy Wasserstein captured the complexities of women in the modern world in *The Heidi Chronicles* and *The Sisters Rosensweig.* Sam Shepard offered the unconventional dramas *Buried Child* and *True West.*

By the 1990–91 season, new Broadway productions hit a new low (28), and production costs continued to climb into the multimillions. This led producers to seek the predictable blockbuster that could attract a large audience and sustain a long run. They found their answer at the movies. A number of plays were adapted from movies, reversing a decades-old tradition of adapting plays for films. Among the lavish movie-based productions were the musicals *Beauty and the Beast, Big, Victor/Victoria,* and *The Producers,* which became the biggest theatrical success of the new century. *The Producers* was also distinguished for its record-breaking ticket prices of several hundred dollars for premium seating.

Further reading: Tim Brooks and Earle Marsh, *The Complete Directory to Prime Time Network TV Shows: 1946–Present,* 3rd ed. (New York: Ballantine Books, 1999); Gene Brown, *Movie Time: A Chronology of Hollywood and the Movie Industry from Its Beginnings to the Present* (New York: Macmillan, 1995); Michael Kammen, *American Culture, American Tastes: Social Change and the 20th Century* (New York: Knopf, 1999).

—Melinda Corey

population trends

The population of the United States rose steadily since 1970. In 1970 it stood at 203 million; in 2000, it totaled 281 million, an increase of 38.4 percent over the past three decades. The slowest growth rate was in the 1970s. The fastest growth rate was in the 1990s.

In each decade since 1970, the South has been the region with the greatest population growth in sheer numbers. With a total population of 100,236,820 in 2000, the South has more than 35 million more people than the next most populous region. The South is defined for census pur-

poses as having three divisions: the South Atlantic, the East South Central, and the West South Central. The most populous of these divisions, accounting for just over half of the total, is the South Atlantic, composed of Delaware, Maryland, the District of Columbia, Virginia, West Virginia, North Carolina, South Carolina, Georgia, and Florida. The second division, accounting for about one third of the total, is the West South Central, composed of Arkansas, Louisiana, Oklahoma, and Texas. The smallest division is the East South Central, composed of Kentucky, Tennessee, Alabama, and Mississippi.

The second most populous region, with a population of 64,392,776, is the Midwest, though its growth rate from 1970 to 2000 was the third slowest. In the 1970s the growth rate in the Midwest was 4 percent. During the 1980s it had a growth rate of 1.4 percent, before rebounding in the 1990s and posting a 7.9 percent increase. The Midwest is composed of the East North Central and the West North Central. The largest division, with over two-thirds of the population, is the East North Central, which includes the states of: Ohio, Indiana, Illinois, Michigan, and Wisconsin. The West North Central includes Minnesota, Iowa, Missouri, North Dakota, South Dakota, Nebraska, and Kansas.

The third most populous region is the fastest-growing in percentage terms. Prior to 1990, the West was the smallest region in terms of population. By 2000, with a population of 63,197,932, the West was just short of surpassing the Midwest. Thanks to an enormous population growth rate, the West will surpass the Midwest by 2010. The West grew 24 percent in the 1970s, 22.3 in the 1980s, and 20 percent in the 1990s. The West is composed of the Mountain and Pacific divisions. The Mountain division contains the states of: Montana, Idaho, Wyoming, Colorado, New Mexico, Arizona, Utah, and Nevada. The Pacific division includes Washington, Oregon, California, Alaska, and Hawaii.

The least populous region, and the one with the slowest growth rate, is the Northeast. Surpassed by the West in 1990, the Northeast had a population of 53,594,378 in 2000. The Northeast posted a growth rate of 1.6 percent in the 1970s, 3.4 percent in the 1980s, and 5.5 percent in the 1990s. The Northeast includes the New England and Middle Atlantic divisions. The larger of the two, the Middle Atlantic is made up of New York, New Jersey, and Pennsylvania. The New England division includes the states of Maine, New Hampshire, Vermont, Massachusetts, Rhode Island, and Connecticut.

According to the 2000 census, the five fastest-growing states in the 1990s, by percentage increase, are all in the West. Nevada's population increased 66.3 percent in the 1990s, Arizona by 40 percent, Colorado grew at 30.6 percent, Utah saw a 29.6 percent increase, and Idaho increased its population by 28.5 percent. The five slowest-growing states are: Maine (3.8), Connecticut (3.6), Pennsylvania (3.4),

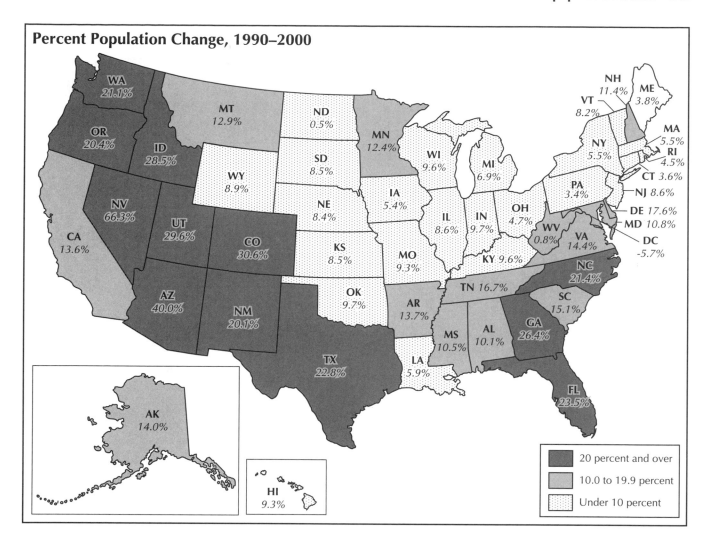

Percent Population Change, 1990–2000

WA 21.1%
OR 20.4%
ID 28.5%
MT 12.9%
ND 0.5%
MN 12.4%
NH 11.4%
ME 3.8%
VT 8.2%
NY 5.5%
MA 5.5%
RI 4.5%
CT 3.6%
NJ 8.6%
DE 17.6%
MD 10.8%
DC -5.7%
NV 66.3%
UT 29.6%
WY 8.9%
SD 8.5%
WI 9.6%
MI 6.9%
PA 3.4%
CA 13.6%
CO 30.6%
NE 8.4%
IA 5.4%
IL 8.6%
IN 9.7%
OH 4.7%
WV 0.8%
VA 14.4%
AZ 40.0%
NM 20.1%
KS 8.5%
MO 9.3%
KY 9.6%
TN 16.7%
NC 21.4%
SC 15.1%
OK 9.7%
AR 13.7%
MS 10.5%
AL 10.1%
GA 26.4%
TX 22.8%
LA 5.9%
FL 23.5%
AK 14.0%
HI 9.3%

20 percent and over
10.0 to 19.9 percent
Under 10 percent

West Virginia (.8), and North Dakota (.5). The District of Columbia lost 5.7 percent of its population in the 1990s.

Since 1970 the trend of more females than males in the nation has continued. Not since the 1940 census has there been more males than females. In 1970 women outnumbered men 104,300,000 to 98,912,000—a ratio of 105 women for every 100 men. By 1980 the ratio had grown to 106 women for every 100 men, and the population had increased to 116,493,000 females and 110,053,000 males. In 1990 the population of males was 121,239,000 to 127,470,000 females, bringing the ratio back to approximately 105 females to 100 males. By 2000 there were 138,054,000 males and 143,368,000 females, dropping the ratio to 103 females to every 100 males. This sudden drop in the ratio of females to males is accounted for by increased immigration and a falling death rate.

The period since 1970 has witnessed the continued urbanization of the nation. In 1970, 73.6 percent of the population lived in urban areas. This figure increased to 73.9 percent in 1980 and 75.2 in 1990. The urban/rural census data for 2000 was not available at the time of this article.

The policies established for the collection of racial statistics in the 2000 census have effectively eliminated any meaningful comparison with previous census data; respondents were given the choice of picking from multiple racial categories to indicate their racial identity. About 2.4 percent of the population picked multiple categories. Of the remaining population, 75.1 percent picked "White," 12.3 percent selected "African American," 0.9 percent picked "American Indian and Alaskan Native," 3.6 percent picked "Asian," 0.1 percent selected "Hawaiian and Other Pacific Islander," and 5.5 percent picked "Some other race." Among the Asians, 23 percent of respondents indicated their heritage to be Chinese, 18.1 percent were Filipino, and 16.4 percent were Indian. Information on Hispanics was collected under a separate question. Hispanic Americans accounted for 13 percent of the population.

The median age of the population has been increasing steadily for the past 40 years. The median age in 1970 was 28.1, increased to 30 in 1980, 32.9 in 1990, and 35.3 in 2000. The size of the 45-to-54 age groups increased 49 percent to 37.7 million. The 65 and over age group increased 12 percent to 35 million. The number of children 18 and under increased 14 percent to 72.3 million. The number of young adults 18 to 34 declined by 4 percent. This decrease in the number of working-age young adults is pointed to by some as evidence of the looming crisis facing the nation when the BABY BOOM generation retires and begins to collect Social Security and Medicare benefits.

—John Korasick

pornography

Pornography refers to any writings, images, and video deemed obscene, or contrary to public standards of morality. The pornography industry has become a big business. A 1972 government study estimated that the pornography industry made sales worth $5 million to $10 million; in 2000 the Forrester Research Group in Cambridge, Massachusetts, estimates that it is a $10 billion industry. Offline pornography sales account for $8 billion of this total.

Adult-video sales earn $4.2 billion and account for 32 percent of all video sales. Furthermore, pornographic movies have become available through cable and satellite television. The 8.7 million subscriber to DirecTV, a General Motors subsidiary, buy an estimated $200 million worth of hard-core pornography through pay-per-view television. The EchoStar Communications Corporation, the second-largest satellite provider, whose chief financial backers include Rupert Murdoch, makes more money selling graphic adult films through its satellite subsidiary than Playboy Enterprises makes from its magazine, cable, and Internet business. The AT&T Corporation, the nation's largest communication company, offers a hard-core sex channel called Hot Network to subscribers of its broadband cable. Nearly one in five of AT&T's broadband cable customers pay an average of $10 a film to see "real life" sex.

The Internet has also made pornography available to a large audience. Forrester Research estimates that sex sites on the Web generate at least $1 billion a year in revenue. There are 60,000 such sites. According to two Web rating services, about one in four regular Internet users, or 21 million Americans, visit one or more of these sites at least once a month—more people than go to sports or government sites. NetValue, a management company, reported that children spent 64.9 percent more time on pornography sites than they did on game sites in September 2000. Over one quarter (27.5 percent) of children age 17 and under visited an adult Web site, totaling 3 million underage visi-

tors. Of these minors, 21.2 percent were 14 years old or younger, and 40.2 percent were females.

Two of the most popular sites are owned by New Frontier Media, a Boulder, Colorado, company. It does business with several major companies, including EchoStar and In Demand, the nation's leading pay-per view distributor, which is owned in part by AT&T, Time Warner, Advance-Newhouse, Cox Communications, and Comcast.

Pornography has also become accessible through the cable and satellite television found in many chain hotels. Recently, the Omni Hotel chain announced it no longer would carry pay-per-view pornographic films in its hotels. This decision cost the chain an estimated $1.8 million per year, but the company received letters from 50,000 people supporting this decision. On the other hand, the Marriott hotel chain, whose owners have close associations with the Mormon Church, continues to provide direct-pay television showing pornographic films. One of the largest suppliers of sex video and other forms of room entertainment to hotels is LodgeNet, whose chairman, Scott C. Peterson, reports doing a $180 million annual business.

The SUPREME COURT has paid special attention to the definition of obscenity and pornography, because government regulation on the topics skirts so closely to constitutional protections of free speech and press. In 1957, the U.S. Supreme Court, in *Roth v. United States* ruled that obscenity does not fall within the First Amendment's guarantee of free speech, or the Fourteenth Amendment's due process clause. It also established a three-prong test for the legal definition of obscenity; 1) the dominant theme of the material taken as a whole appeals to a prurient interest in sex; 2) the material is patently offensive because it affronts contemporary community standards relating to the description or representation of sexual matters; and 3) the material is utterly without redeeming social value. *Roth* also explicitly noted that sex was not necessarily synonymous with obscenity, but was obscene only when it is dealt with in a wholly prurient manner. In 1966 the Supreme Court's decision in *Memoirs v. Massachusetts* overruled the *Roth* decision, arguing that there are no exceptions to the First Amendment's protection of speech, and that society has no interest in "overriding the guarantees of free speech and press and establishing a regime of CENSORSHIP." Seven years later, in 1973, the Supreme Court reversed itself again in *Miller v. California,* which ruled again that obscenity is outside the First Amendment's protections and reaffirmed the first two of *Roth's* original three-prong test for obscenity. It differed from the first two points, however, in that it left the determination of obscenity up to "local community standards," rejecting the necessity of national standards.

Though the Court has since refined its test for pornography, it has adhered to the underlying decision that obscenity lies outside the bounds of constitutional protection. This position has inspired criticism from a variety of groups. Some contend that the First Amendment protections of free speech and artistic expression prohibit any form of censorship. Such opponents argue that since the line dividing obscenity and serious art is subjective, restrictions infringe on personal liberty and freedom of thought. Some argue that since judgments regarding moral standards most often reflect religious heritages, then any form of governmental censorship necessarily violates the principle of separated church and state. Therefore, they argue the decision to access or not to access pornography involving consenting adults should depend on individual choice. This view is held by many political LIBERALS, as well as political LIBERTARIANS. A growing thread of radical feminist theory also defends pornography as a component of sexual liberation. Liberal feminists, however, reject this view, arguing that pornography amounts to the exploitation and objectification of women. Cultural conservatives and religious critics agree and argue further that pornography invariably undermines the institution of family, increases the rate of divorce, and desanctifies MARRIAGE. Many critics believe that pornography can become psychologically addictive, and may lead to depression or even manifest itself through sex crimes. These views are vigorously contested by censorship opponents and others.

Since the introduction of the World Wide Web in 1992, the debate over pornography has assumed an added dimension. Previous discussions of obscenity and pornography rested on the assumption that minors could be easily restricted from accessing offensive materials through physical barriers; for example, a door to an adult bookstore, or a teller at an adult movie house. Censorship opponents often argued that offended consumers could avoid pornographic materials by choosing not to enter the adult-oriented establishments. Pornography on the INTERNET, however, has no such physical barriers; minors, as noted above, can access obscene material in the privacy of their homes. Pornography flooded the Web almost as soon as it opened to the public, and indeed was a prime driver of the medium's growth and commercialization. In response, concerned lawmakers included the Communications Decency Act (CDA) within the widely supported Telecommunications Act of 1996. The CDA specifically prohibits the transmission of "obscene, lewd, lascivious, filthy, or indecent" material over a telecommunications device to a minor. Though the act applied to any telecommunications device, including telephones and cable television, the Internet promised to be most affected; any Web site administrator who knowingly published obscene materials in a manner that could be viewed by minors could be liable to prosecution. Since the World Wide Web is based on anonymous transactions, the CDA significantly complicated the business of providing pornography over the Internet.

The bill received overwhelming majorities in both houses (91 to 5 in the Senate; and 414 to 16 in the House), and President WILLIAM J. CLINTON signed it, despite his concerns that it was unconstitutionally broad. On that very day, anticensorship groups, including the American Civil Liberties Union (ACLU), the Electronic Privacy Information Center, and 18 other organizations, filed lawsuits against the government arguing that the CDA unfairly censored free speech. Many Internet promoters who consider "cyberspace" and the World Wide Web to be a kind of libertarian utopia joined the opposition.

On June 26, 1997, the Supreme Court ruled in *Reno v. ACLU* that the CDA violated the First Amendment because it failed to adequately define obscenity, and because it failed to provide any mechanism for parental consent, or for providers to prove socially redeeming value. The ruling, whether it intended to or not, was received by many as an endorsement of the idea that the Internet is immune to any form of censorship, other than child pornography. The following year, Congress passed the Child Online Protection Act (1998), which requires Web site administrators to put in place some form of electronic adult certification process to prohibit minor access of pornographic materials.

See also CENSORSHIP; FEMINISM; GAY RIGHTS MOVEMENT; MARRIAGE; SEXUAL REVOLUTION; SUPREME COURT.

Further reading: Gordon Hawkins, *Pornography in a Free Society* (Cambridge, U.K.: Cambridge University Press, 1988); Frederick S. Lane, *Obscene Profits: The Entrepreneurs of Pornography in the Cyber Age* (London: Routledge Press, 2000).

—Aharon W. Zorea

poverty

Poverty rates represent the proportion of American households and individuals whose annual income falls below a defined poverty threshold. In 2000 the poverty threshold for a family of four persons was approximately $13,000, and $7,000 for an individual. The 2000 Census showed that 11.3 percent of Americans lived below the poverty line, the lowest since 1979, when comprehensive poverty statistics began to be collected by the U.S. Census Bureau.

Analysis of the 2000 census reveals that poverty rates for those 65 years old and over, African Americans, people living in the South, and families headed by single women fell to an all-time low. Poverty rates among non-Hispanic whites and Hispanics fell to levels comparable to all-time lows, while the child poverty rate fell to 16.9 percent, its lowest since 1979. The U.S. Census Bureau also reports that the reduction in poverty in the nation's cities, as distinguished from the suburbs and non-metropolitan areas, dropped 81 percent between 1998 and 1999.

Census figures show some discouraging news, however. One in every two children under the age of six in 1999 lived in a female-headed family, and of these children 50.3 percent lived in poverty in 1999. Approximately one-third of African-American children (33.1) percent and nearly one-third of Hispanic children (30.3 percent) were poor in 1999. Moreover, while the overall percentage of Americans living in poverty fell since 1979, those who were poor in 1999, on average, grew poorer. That is to say that they fell farther below the poverty line than in any year since 1979, the first year that this data became available. Specifically, the average poor person fell $2,416 below the poverty line in 1999. Despite the drop of 3.4 million in the number of poor people from 1995 to 1999, those who remained poor grew poorer, which is to say that the "poverty gap" (i.e., the total amount by which the income of all poor households falls below the poverty line) grew. This should not be the case as the number of poor people declines. Yet in 1999 the "poverty gap" stood at $65 billion.

Census figures show that income disparity in the United States, which widened sharply between the mid-1970s and 1993, remained unchanged. While census income figures include most households, a substantial portion of the income in the highest income brackets is often missed, suggesting that this income gap might even be worse than the actual figures show.

The decline in the rate of poverty appears to be due to the vibrant economy between 1996 and 1999. The unemployment rate of 4.2 percent was the lowest since 1969. Furthermore, between 1996 and 1999, real wages (wages adjusted for inflation) increased. Wage increases were especially strong for very low-paid workers between 1996

and 1999. Low-paid male workers earning an hourly wage in the lowest 10th percentile saw their hourly wage increase 9.1 percent from 1996 to 1999, and for female hourly workers in this 10th percentile, hourly wages increased 9.7 percent in this same period.

A state-by-state breakdown of poverty rates showed that southern states had significantly higher poverty rates than northeastern states, most of which had poverty rates in the single digits.

For all U.S. families regardless of race, the poverty rate fell from 10.0 percent in 1968 to 8.6 percent with a spike in 1983 of 12.3 percent. Although the 2000 poverty rates for AFRICAN AMERICANS (19.1 percent) and HISPANIC AMERICANS (18.5 percent) remain well above those for white families (6.9 percent) and for all families regardless of race (8.6 percent), they showed significant improvement as well over the same time period. Hispanic-American families showed a slightly better improvement than all families, dropping from 20.6 percent in 1970 to 18.5 percent in 2000. The most dramatic decrease occurred between 1993 and 2000, a period that witnessed an increase in poverty rates from 8.0 percent in 1968 to 9.6 percent in 1982 and then a drop to 6.9 percent in 2000. African-American families experienced the most significant and most consistent decline in poverty rates. Poverty rates for African Americans rose from 29.4 percent to 33.0 percent between 1968 and 1982. They then steadily declined to 31.1 percent in 1992 and 19.1 percent in 2000. Finally, in large part as a result of high Social Security payments, elderly Americans experienced the most significant improvement in poverty rates.

This data demonstrates certain trends. All groups, with the exception of African-American families, experienced spikes in poverty rates in the early 1980s and the early 1990s. All enjoyed significant improvements during the economic boom of the 1990s. These improvements notwithstanding, the data also suggest a deepening of poverty for the poor and an increasingly unequal distribution of wealth over the same period.

See also ECONOMY; FAMILY SUPPORT ACT OF 1988; REAGANOMICS; RUST BELT; WAGE AND PRICE CONTROLS.

—William L. Glankler

Number of Poor and Poverty Rate, 1969–2000

Numbers in millions, rates in percent

31.1 million

Number in poverty

11.3 percent

Poverty rate

Recession

Powell, Colin L. (1937–)

General Colin Luther Powell is the first African-American secretary of state and was the first African-American chairman of the United States Joint Chiefs of Staff. Powell enjoyed immense popularity after his leadership role in the PERSIAN GULF WAR. He was born on April 5, 1937, in New York City and raised in the South Bronx by his parents, who had migrated from Jamaica. He began his military career in 1958 as a second lieutenant stationed in West

Germany. Powell served two tours of duty in Vietnam and earned two Purple Hearts and a Soldier's Medal. In 1969 Powell received a promotion to lieutenant colonel and, after receiving an M.B.A. from George Washington University in 1971, was assigned as a White House fellow in the Office of Management and Budget (OMB) in 1972. During his years with the OMB, Powell demonstrated the troubleshooting abilities that would propel his career. By 1979 he had achieved the rank of brigadier general and worked briefly as Charles Duncan's aide in his capacity as secretary of the Energy Department.

After commanding the Fourth Infantry Division and serving as senior military assistant to Secretary of Defense Casper Weinberger, Powell was promoted to lieutenant general in 1986 and given command of the Fifth Corps in Frankfurt, Germany. In 1987 he returned to Washington as National Security Advisor, advocating a strong military budget while opposing heavy spending on the space-based STRATEGIC DEFENSE INITIATIVE. In 1989 Powell became a four-star general and President GEORGE H. W. BUSH appointed him chairman of the Joint Chiefs of Staff. He was both the youngest person and the first African American ever to hold that position. During his four-year tenure, Powell planned the invasion of PANAMA to overthrow General Manuel Noriega and coordinated Operation Desert Storm with General Norman Schwarzkopf. Clear thinking and effective military strategy throughout the Persian Gulf War coupled with his comforting and capable demeanor gained for Powell immense public approval. During WILLIAM J. CLINTON's first year as president, Powell opposed an administration proposal to end the ban on gays in the military, and administration cuts in the military budget, which he had opposed in the previous administration as well.

Powell's retirement from the military in September 1993 sparked speculation that he would run for office in 1996. He never denied those rumors, but concentrated instead on promoting his autobiography, *My American Journey,* which appeared in 1995.

In 2001 Powell reentered public life when he accepted the post of secretary of state under newly elected president GEORGE W. BUSH. In this position, he has played a highly visible role in the war against terrorism, Middle East peace talks, and working with allies in Western Europe. Furthermore, he has undertaken diplomatic efforts to extend aid to African nations.

The ordinary duties of the secretary of state were transformed dramatically following the September 11, 2001, TERRORISM attacks on the World Trade Center and the Pentagon. As secretary of state, Powell's role was to build diplomatic support in the Arab world for the American-led "war on terrorism" declared by President Bush. To accomplish this, Powell pursued two strategies. First, he

U.S. Secretary of State Colin Powell *(Gabriel Mistral/ Getty Images)*

tried to win the support of the more moderate Arab states by suggesting that the United States would support the creation of a Palestinian state, something that Osama bin Laden, the mastermind of the September 11 attacks, used as justification for his and other terrorists' activities. Second, by assuring Pakistani president Pervez Musharraf that the United States would forgive certain debts owed it by Pakistan and remain committed to Pakistani interests in the long term, Powell sought to maintain ties with Pakistan and ensure their support for American military action in neighboring Afghanistan. Powell consistently sought to limit U.S. military involvement to Afghanistan alone and continued to stress the importance of coalition building in the Arab world.

See also AFRICAN AMERICANS.

—William L. Glankler

Powell, Lewis (1907–1998)
Lewis Franklin Powell, Jr., was appointed by President RICHARD M. NIXON to serve as the 99th associate justice to the SUPREME COURT in 1971. He replaced former Justice Hugo L. Black, was confirmed by the Senate with a vote of 89 to 1 and served until 1987.

Powell was born September 19, 1907, in Suffolk, Virginia. He earned a bachelor of science degree in 1929 and a law degree in 1931 from Washington and Lee University. He then spent a year at Harvard before returning to Virginia where he practiced law for nearly 40 years. He married Josephine Pierce Rucker in 1936; his family later grew to include three daughters and a son. Powell served as a colonel in an intelligence unit in the U.S. Army Air Force during World War II, and was a long-time member of state and local school boards (1950–69). He served as chairman of the Richmond (Virginia) School Board from 1952–61 and as president of the Virginia State School Board from 1968–69. His tenure on the school board came during a controversial time for southern schools battling over the issue of racial segregation, and most observers cited Powell's reasonable leadership as critical for Richmond's peaceful integration process.

Powell's first experience in national politics came in 1964 when he served as president of the American Bar Association. In 1965 he was appointed to serve on the President's Commission on Law Enforcement and Administration of Justice. He turned down an earlier appointment to the Supreme Court in 1969, citing his old age (he was 62 at the time), and served instead as president of the American College of Trial Lawyers from 1969–70. Two years later, he accepted President Nixon's second invitation and became the first Virginian to serve on the Court since the Civil War.

Before his appointment, Justice Powell was known as a moderate and lived up to his reputation as a consensus builder during his tenure. In 1977 the Supreme Court was strongly divided over REGENTS OF THE UNIVERSITY OF CALIFORNIA V. BAKKE, which dealt with AFFIRMATIVE ACTION. Powell cast the deciding vote that served as a compromise for both sides. He agreed with the opponents of affirmative action by arguing that a college's two-track admission policy violated the civil rights of white students. At the same time, he also agreed with the friends of affirmative action that colleges need not adopt rigid doctrines of color blindness, and that race could still be a factor in student selection. Justice Powell generally maintained his position in the center; he voted for ABORTION rights in the 1973 ROE V. WADE decision, but in *Maher v. Roe* (1977) he took the other side to argue that the state does not have to pay for abortions. He retired in 1987, and was replaced by Justice Anthony Kennedy. Justice Powell died August 25, 1998.

See also REHNQUIST, WILLIAM H.

—Aharon W. Zorea

pro-life and pro-choice movements

The pro-life and pro-choice movements arose during the late 1960s on either side of the debate over legalized ABOR-TION. There are sharp ideological and political differences between these groups, beginning with the definition of whether a pregnant women carries a "fetus" or an "unborn child." The terms "pro-life" and "pro-choice" are themselves politically loaded and did not come into wide usage until the late 1960s. Some activists on both sides of the issue prefer "anti-abortion" and "pro-abortion," but this nomenclature has not come into widespread use.

Pro-life advocates believe life begins at conception, and maintain that the unborn child is entitled to equal protections under the law guaranteeing life, health, and well-being. Comparing themselves to the abolitionists of the antebellum period, pro-life supporters argue that regardless of a court's decision, a mother has no more right to kill an unborn child than slave owners had to kill their slaves. Pro-choice advocates believe that abortion is not an issue of life, but involves a question of whether a woman has the right to control her body. They argue that any law that interferes with a woman's sovereignty over her body is a violation of her basic human rights and her constitutional right to privacy.

Both pro-life and pro-choice positions include larger, often unspoken, social implications. Pro-life groups argue that abortion harms the family because it deprives parents of the responsibilities inherent in marital relationships and in conception. Though not all pro-life advocates are religious, most believe that abortion is an offense against God's will. Pro-life advocates fear that abortion cheapens the value of human life. Pro-choice groups view abortion as one of a number of modern medical advances, including contraception, that have liberated women from the bonds of unwanted motherhood, allowing them to make considered choices about if and when to start a family. A few pro-choice adherents contend that abortion is necessary to curb the prospect of overpopulation, and thus represents a commitment to environmental conservation. This latter position, however, is not a major thrust of the pro-choice movement.

In the 1960s most states allowed "therapeutic" abortions to save the life of a mother, but these laws were restrictive. In 1969 members of Planned Parenthood of America formed the National Association for the Repeal of Abortion Laws (NARAL) as a political arm of the newly formed pro-choice movement. Only 16 states chose to legalize abortion in 1970; the remaining 33 chose to retain their prohibitions. (In 1967 the states of Colorado and California undertook reform of their abortion laws to allow easy access for legalized abortion.) In 1973 the SUPREME COURT's decisions in ROE V. WADE and *Doe v. Bolton* overrode law restricting abortion.

The pro-life movement solidified immediately, following the 1973 Court ruling, when the Catholic Conference of Bishops' Division on Family Life organized the National

Right to Life Committee. During the 1970s, pro-life groups directed their efforts toward passing a Right to Life Amendment to the federal Constitution, explicitly extending legal protection to what they see as unborn children, and thereby overturning the legal basis for *Roe* and *Doe*. Concurrently, many pro-choice groups, including Planned Parenthood, NARAL, and the NATIONAL ORGANIZATION FOR WOMEN (NOW), integrated abortion rights as a necessary component to feminism and the women's liberation movement, and began advocating the passage of the EQUAL RIGHTS AMENDMENT (ERA) as a further guarantee of existing abortion laws.

The deep polarization between the pro-choice and pro-life movements made any constitutional change on the issue of abortion impossible. The effort to pass a Right to Life Amendment died in Congress in 1981 and pro-life advocates were forced to focus their efforts toward alternative legislative restrictions on abortion in each state.

Both movements remained vital players in national politics, forcing candidates to declare their position on abortion, which often served as a litmus test for constituent support. The division over abortion began to follow partisan lines, after *Roe v. Wade*. Pro-choice organizations increasingly supported Democratic candidates and issues, while pro-life organizations, such as National Right to Life, American Right to Life, and National Pro-Life Alliance, supported Republicans.

The strongly pro-life Republican presidents RONALD W. REAGAN and GEORGE H. W. BUSH used their offices to VETO pro-choice legislation originating in the Democratic-controlled Congress. With tacit support from the administration, pro-life groups launched massive demonstrations in Washington, D.C., and in front of abortion clinics across the country, in an effort to support the rights of the unborn. During the late 1980s, a subset of pro-life supporters joined activist groups such as Operation Rescue and the Pro-Life Action League, which used nonviolent methods to block the entrances of abortion clinics, preventing women from access to abortion facilities. Thousands of Operation Rescue members were arrested for trespassing between 1986 and 1989. Abortion providers and pro-choice groups responded by suing the protestors under the RACKETEER INFLUENCED AND CORRUPT ORGANIZATIONS (RICO) ACT, which carries with it very harsh penalties, resulting in a dramatic decline in the number of intrusive demonstrations.

After the 1992 election of the strongly pro-choice WILLIAM J. CLINTON, most of the previous administrations' pro-life policies were reversed through a series of executive orders and legislation, including the National Institutes of Health Revitalization Act, which restored federal funding for abortions; and the Freedom to Access Clinic Entrances Act of 1994 (FACE), which provided heavy fines and jail terms for protestors who interfered with access to abortion clinics. The last measure was in response to increasing violence on the part of some pro-life activists, including violent assaults against abortion doctors and clinics and the murder of Dr. David Gumo by Michael Griffen in 1993. NOW and Planned Parenthood alleged that pro-life advocates, particularly Operation Rescue, were a violent radical movement, referring to them as the "pro-life mafia." The mainstream pro-life movement denounced acts of violence by what was seen as a small, unrepresentative, faction within the movement, while at the same time arguing that the movement's rights to peaceful protest and free speech were being violated by acts such as FACE.

See also ABORTION; *AKRON V. AKRON CENTER FOR REPRODUCTIVE HEALTH;* AMENDMENTS TO THE U.S. CONSTITUTION; BIRTH CONTROL; CAMPAIGN FINANCE; NATIONAL ORGANIZATION FOR WOMEN; POLITICAL PARTIES; *ROE V. WADE;* SCHLAFLY, PHYLLIS; *WEBSTER V. REPRODUCTIVE HEALTH SERVICES;* WOMEN'S RIGHTS AND STATUS.

Further reading: Donald T. Critchlow, *The Politics of Abortion and Birth Control in Historical Perspective* (New York: Oxford University Press, 1998); Cynthia Gorney, *Articles of Faith: A Frontline History of the Abortion Wars* (New York: Simon & Schuster, 1998).

—Aharon W. Zorea

property rights

Throughout the latter half of the 20th century, the expansion of federal authority and a new environmental awareness have forced the issue of property rights into the forefront of public debate. The property rights movement contends that the exercise of freedom rests with the individual, and unless the property is used for criminal purposes, it should be free of government supervision. Opponents of this view argue that government is duty-bound to curb individual liberty whenever it disrupts the greater good of society. The debate over property rights in the United States turns on a much larger debate over the nature of FEDERALISM, constitutional government, and individual liberty.

Property rights have a long history in English and American common law, but the rise of the environmental movement and subsequent environmental legislation in the 1970s intensified the issue of individual rights of property and governmental regulation of property and land-usage. In 1970 President RICHARD M. NIXON signed the National Environmental Policy Act, which established a federal interest in protecting the environment from the adverse effects of human development. Within a few years, Congress passed all of the laws that currently form the core of American environmental policy, including the Clean Water Act, the Clean Air Act amendments, and the Federal

Water Pollution Control Act amendments of 1972, which imposed progressively more stringent requirements on industries and cities to reduce pollution; the Endangered Species Act of 1973, which earmarked money for the Federal Wilderness Service for the purpose of saving plant and animals species listed as endangered, through research and, if necessary, regulatory injunction; and the Safe Drinking Water Act of 1974, which authorized the Environmental Protection Agency to specify federal standards for drinking water. At first, these laws provided only minor injunctions against violators, but after undergoing amendment throughout the 1970s, 1980s, and 1990s, they gradually assumed considerable powers of criminal enforcement, including heavy fines and prison terms. During the 1980s, Congress passed environmentally related acts, which designated certain significant sites as "green spaces"; the 1983 National Trails System Act permitted unused rail beds to be converted into trails pending possible resurgence of the railroad industry. Since the original rail leases included clauses returning the property to the owner, the "rails to trails" program angered many people who believed the land should revert to them.

In the late 1970s the courts experienced a surge of civil suits against the government by property owners, especially farmers, ranchers, and timber interests, claiming loss of property value as a result of federal regulatory interference. The SUPREME COURT created a legal framework with which to analyze the potential taking of property value through regulatory interference in the 1978 decision, *Penn Central Transportation v. New York City.* It established three considerations necessary to establish the threshold between compensatory and noncompensatory takings, including economic impact of the government action; the extent to which government action interfered with the reasonable expectations of investors; and the character of government action. Over the next decade, in more than two dozen cases, the Court held that even minor use of eminent domain required compensation. At the same time, the Court repeatedly concluded that the loss of economic value alone was insufficient to require compensation, unless the loss was 100 percent.

The combination of assertive environmental laws, and a series of unfavorable Court decisions inspired a property rights movement throughout the Midwest and West in the 1970s. Advocates included landowners who suffered federal takings directly, or those who feared they might in future; industries with direct economic interests tied to public and private lands, including real estate developers, farmers, ranchers, and extraction industries (timber, mining, and energy); and the CONSERVATIVE MOVEMENT and libertarians opposed to federal expansion in principle. In 1988 President RONALD W. REAGAN issued Executive Order No. 12630, titled "Government Actions and Interference with Constitutionally Protected Property Right," which ordered federal agencies to compensate landowners for any loss of value, whether through temporary or permanent occupation, or through regulatory interference.

During the 1990s, President WILLIAM J. CLINTON shifted administrative support away from property rights advocates, toward environmental concerns. In 1996 President Clinton used the Antiquities Act of 1906 to convert 1.7 million acres of federal land throughout Utah into the Grand Staircase-Escalante National Monument, the largest of its kind in the contiguous 48 states. The following year he announced the American Heritage Rivers Initiative, which had the potential to restrict development throughout millions of acres of public and private land along 250 rivers. In 1999 Clinton issued an Executive Order 13112, titled "Invasive Species" directing all federal agencies and their commercial partners to focus efforts on returning the biosphere to the condition it was believed to be in prior to 1492, including removing all plants that are not indigenous to North America. In 2000 Clinton announced plans to protect 750,000 acres of private forestland from development, while also designating 60 million acres of federal land off-limits to road building, logging, and mining.

Property rights advocates oppose the new environmental regulations because they see them as depriving landowners of substantial property value without compensating them for the loss. Conservationists and environmentalist groups argue that the definition of acceptable property use evolves over time, and that property owners should not expect compensation for rights they were never entitled to. Property rights advocates argue that the government's right should be extended to prevent an owner from using his property in a way that is injurious to his neighbor. They argue a neighbor is entitled only to that which belongs free and clear, such as peace and solitude, protection from noxious odors, noises, and particulate matter. The neighbor is not, they said, entitled to "aesthetic" comforts requiring cooperation from others outside his property, such as an unencumbered view. Society may elect to include scenic byways, heritage corridors, and wildlife reserves as important social goods, but the government must not use regulatory authority to take these goods without paying for them.

In contrast, the conservation and environmental movement views nature as an interconnected ecological system; individuals possess land, but they must use it in a way that is harmonious with the needs of society at large. No one, they argue, has a right to unlimited usage, and thus the government does not interfere with property rights when it restricts harmful usage. They further argue that compensating property owners for regulations that are necessary to preserve ecological integrity would not only be wasteful but would significantly hinder the survival of society—social reform would never advance if the state had to pay citizens not to engage in destructive behavior.

See also AGRICULTURE; CONSERVATION; CONSERVATIVE MOVEMENT; ENVIRONMENTALISM, AND ENVIRONMENTAL POLICY; FEDERALISM.

Further reading: Michael D. Klapowitz, *Property Rights, Economics, and the Environment* (Greenwich, Conn.: JAI Press, 2000); Robert Meltz, *The Takings Issue: Constitutional Limits on Land-Use, Control and Environmental Regulation* (Washington, D. C.: Island Press, 1999).

—Aharon W. Zorea

Quayle, J. Danforth (1947–)

J. Danforth Quayle was elected the 44th vice president of the United States in 1988 at the age of 41, when GEORGE H. W. BUSH won election to the White House. Quayle was known for his close relations with the CONSERVATIVE MOVEMENT and his support of family values.

Quayle was born on February 4, 1947, in Indianapolis, Indiana. After spending much of his youth in Arizona, where his family owned a leading Phoenix newspaper, he graduated from Huntington High School in Huntington, Indiana, in 1965. He matriculated at De Pauw University, where he received his B.A. degree in political science in 1969. Following graduation, Quayle joined the Indiana National Guard and served from 1969 to 1975. While serving in the guard, he earned a law degree from Indiana University in 1971. His service in the National Guard later led political opponents to accuse him of having avoided the draft during the VIETNAM WAR.

Quayle became an investigator for the Consumer Protection division of the Indiana Attorney General's Office in July 1971. That same year he became an administrative assistant to Governor Edgar Whitcomb. In November 1972 Quayle married Marilyn Tucker of Indianapolis. They have three children.

In 1976 Quayle was elected to Congress from Indiana's Fourth Congressional District, defeating an eight-term incumbent. He won reelection in 1978 by a landslide. In 1980, Quayle, at the age of 33, became the youngest person ever elected to the U.S. Senate from Indiana, defeating three-term Democrat Birch Bayh.

In the Senate, Quayle served on the Armed Services Committee, the Budget Committee, and the Labor and Human Resources Committee. In 1982 he coauthored with Senator EDWARD M. KENNEDY the Job Training Partnership Act. In 1986 Quayle won reelection to the Senate.

Quayle remained in the Senate until 1988 when vice president and Republican presidential candidate GEORGE H. W. BUSH chose him as his running mate. The Bush-Quayle ticket went on to win the November election by a convincing sweep of 38 states, capturing 426 electoral votes. Quayle became the 44th vice president of the United States.

Many consider Quayle to have also been one of the most active American vice presidents in the history of the United States. He made official state visits to 47 countries, discussing a multitude of issues. He led the administration deregulation efforts as chairman of the Council on Competitiveness, chaired the National Space Council, and worked as Bush's liaison with Capitol Hill.

Quayle's gaffes drew relentless criticism from the press and became comedy material for late-night television hosts. Some of his gaffes were not confirmed, however, such as his alleged remark about not knowing how to speak Latin before going to Latin America. Other of his gaffes were confirmed, such as when he corrected a young schoolgirl's spelling of "potato" by adding an "e" to the end of the word. His relations with the press did not get better when he gave a widely reported speech on May 19, 1992, to the Commonwealth Club in San Francisco in which he accused cultural elites of eroding family values. In the speech, he criticized the then-popular television sitcom, *Murphy Brown*, in which the main character was having a child out of wedlock. Quayle declared, "It doesn't help matters when prime-time TV has Murphy Brown, a character who supposedly epitomizes today's intelligent, highly paid women, mocking the importance of fathers by bearing a child alone and calling it just another lifestyle choice. We cannot be embarrassed out of our belief that two parents, married to each other, are better in most cases for children than one." These remarks drew heavy criticism from much of the press and news commentators, although polls showed, at the time, that the majority of the American public agreed with him. Nonetheless, the ridicule he took for his gaffes, and this statement, created a public image of Quayle that hurt his political career.

He left office when the Bush-Quayle ticket was defeated in the election of 1992.

Since his term as vice president, he has authored *Standing Firm* and *The American Family: Discovering the Values That Make Us Strong*, in addition to writing a nationally syndicated weekly newspaper column. Shortly after his move, Quayle also moved his political action committee to Arizona. In 1999 he unsuccessfully sought the Republican presidential nomination.

Further reading: David Broder and Bob Woodward, *The Man Who Would Be President: Dan Quayle* (New York: Simon & Schuster, 1992); Dan Quayle, *Standing Firm: A Vice-Presidential Memoir* (New York: HarperCollins Publishers, 1994).

—Leah Blakey

quotas (racial)   See affirmative action

R

race and racial conflict

Race and racial conflict have been dominant themes in U.S. history for almost 400 years, and their nature has changed dramatically over that time. Since the 1960s, discussions about race in America came to include HISPANIC AMERICANS and ASIAN AMERICANS, as well as other groups, and the inclusion of ethnicity in the debate over racism further complicated both public and private discourse. Yet, regardless of these added complexities, discussions of race and racism, and episodes of racial conflict, remained firmly grounded in the relationship and conflicts between AFRICAN AMERICANS and European Americans, as black and white Americans continued to struggle with a 400-year legacy of racial conflict that fundamentally informed their attempt to define their relationship to one another and to the nation.

The year 1968 was a pivotal year in the history of American race relations. The country was at the end of a long and bitter struggle over African-American civil liberties. The struggle culminated in the passage of the Civil Rights Act of 1964 and the 1965 Voting Rights Act. Along with these victories, however, came defeats. In 1968 Americans witnessed the ASSASSINATIONS of Martin Luther King, Jr., the most prominent of the civil rights leaders, and of Robert F. Kennedy, candidate for the Democratic Party's presidential nomination and a champion of civil rights and racial reconciliation. In the 1960s racial riots erupted in many major cities. The violence prompted many white supporters of the Civil Rights movement to turn away from active participation. At the same time, violence divided African-American civil rights leaders. These events set the stage for a subtler, and in many ways more divisive, form of racial conflict as both African Americans and white people became more separated from one another. Even though the general conditions of life greatly improved for African Americans, most perceived the work of the Civil Rights movement as unfinished, and the subsequent unrest manifested itself in various forms.

The most dramatic form of racial conflict is the race riot. Although race riots have been numerous in American history, their nature changed during the years following World War II. The insurrection type of riot first manifested itself in 1935 and in 1943 in Harlem, but became fully established during the riots of the 1960s that exploded in the inner cities of many American metropolises. Insurrection riots differed from the communal riots prior to World War II, in that they generally did not involve clashes between black and white citizens. Generally they involved African-American inner-city ghetto residents and police, typically set off by real or alleged acts of police brutality. Confined to the ghetto, these riots specifically targeted white-owned businesses and property. Major riots occurred in Harlem (1964), the Watts section of Los Angeles (1965), and Chicago (1966). The country experienced racial disorders in 128 cities in 1967 that required the services of 59,000 National Guard and federal troops to restore order. The assassination of Martin Luther King, Jr., spurred riots in Memphis, Tennessee; Cleveland, Ohio; Washington, D.C.; Chicago; Baltimore, Maryland; Detroit, Michigan; and Newark, New Jersey.

The incidence of race riots declined after 1968, but occurrences in Miami in 1980 and in Los Angeles in 1992 indicated that violent racial conflict remained a part of the American experience. When five white policemen, accused of beating a black motorist to death, were acquitted, black residents of Liberty City, a predominantly African-American neighborhood of Miami, began throwing bricks, rocks, and bottles at white motorists. The violence escalated as a crowd attacked the Dade County Department of Public Safety headquarters, as well as many white-owned businesses. The violence resulted in the deaths of eight whites and 10 blacks, the arrest of 855 people, and $80 million in property damage. Attacks upon white civilians during the riot marked a divergence from the insurrection-type pattern witnessed during the 1960s, as did the Los Angeles riot of 1992.

255

Just as in Miami, the acquittal of four white police officers (by an all-white jury) accused of brutally and unnecessarily beating a black motorist, Rodney King, in Los Angeles, spawned a riot that was the largest and deadliest since the end of the 19th century. By the time 13,000 local and federal officers had restored order, 54 people were dead, and 2,383 were injured. Property damage was estimated to be $800 million. This riot contained elements unseen since the communal riots of the pre–World War II era. Widespread attacks on white civilians by African-American and, later, Hispanic rioters, clashes between black and Hispanic rioters and Asian-American merchants, the spread of looting and arson outside the ghetto area, and the wholesale use of firearms indicated that future riots might entail even more widespread intergroup violence. These riots also involved Hispanic Americans, Asian Americans, and whites in looting and rioting, and demonstrated that racial tension was not and is not simply a black-white issue.

Violence, however, was not the hallmark of racial conflict during the last three decades of the 20th century. Racism became less overt and, as a result, racial conflict pursued more traditional paths and manifested itself in less spectacular ways. Much of it found voice in the political and legal system. In cities across the nation, black activists organized to elect black officials in an attempt to have their needs addressed on the local level. The first such success was the election of Carl Stokes in 1967 in Cleveland, as the first black mayor of a major American city. While Stokes was able to assemble a coalition that included some white supporters, other cities required the unification of a majority black population to achieve the same goal. For example, Memphis, with a majority black population since the mid-1970s, was unable to elect a black mayor until 1991, although it was a goal of many black leaders. On the national level, black congressmen formed the Congressional Black Caucus in 1971, to function as a lobbying group for black interests in the legislative branch. Also, spurred by reparations paid in 1988 to Japanese families for internment during World War II, several groups, such as the National Coalition of Blacks for Reparations in America, undertook political activity in the late 1990s to gain monetary reparations as a way of righting the wrongs of slavery. By insisting on separate interests based on race and by demanding present accountability for past actions, these developments, and others, prepared the way for further political conflict drawn exclusively along racial lines at the local, state, and national levels.

The most recognizable battles were those joined by the U.S. SUPREME COURT on the issues of AFFIRMATIVE ACTION and school desegregation. Affirmative action refers to policies used to increase opportunities for minorities by favoring them in the awarding of government contracts, college admissions, and hiring and promotion with the express purpose of helping to eliminate the effects of past discrimination. President RICHARD M. NIXON first implemented federal affirmative action policies in 1969, and the Supreme Court decision in GRIGGS ET AL. V. DUKE POWER COMPANY (1971), along with the Equal Opportunity Act of 1972, further encouraged the hiring and admission of minorities, and the establishment, in some cases, of racial quotas. In the 1980s and 1990s an increasingly conservative Supreme Court eliminated some affirmative action programs deemed unfair. As a response to these conservative rulings, Congress passed the CIVIL RIGHTS ACT OF 1991, which strengthened antidiscrimination laws. In 1996 California voters approved Proposition 209 that ended all state-sponsored affirmative action programs. Affirmative action remained an arena for racial conflict into the 21st century, as critics called it legalized reverse discrimination, and supporters maintained that it was the only feasible way to integrate society and to atone for the effects of past discrimination.

Increasing residential segregation, coupled with the desire to end the detrimental effects of educational segregation, made school desegregation a prominent racial, legal, and political battlefield during the last third of the 20th century. The attempt to create racially balanced schools began with the Supreme Court's decision in *Brown v. Board of Education* (1954), which ordered the immediate desegregation of Little Rock's Central High School. In the 1970s, the debate centered on the method of desegregation. The Court set the precedent for busing in *Swann v. Charlotte-Mecklenburg Board of Education* (1971), in which it upheld a district court's order that mandated the achievement of racial balance in a southern, urban school district by busing. Similar rulings demanded busing in northern and western cities as well. The central criticism of busing, voiced primarily by white suburbanites, was that it prevented families from sending their children to the neighborhood school of their choice. Supporters claimed that busing was the only feasible way to provide a quality education to inner-city youths, who had been previously denied such by racial discrimination. The racial divisiveness of this issue was tempered somewhat during the 1980s and 1990s, as blacks began to criticize the impracticality of school desegregation in the face of irreversible residential segregation, and turned their energies toward receiving better funding for schools in predominantly black neighborhoods. Regardless, education remained a racially charged and divisive issue as the 20th century came to a close.

The integration-segregation debate attained new complexity in the 1990s, as many blacks and whites sought to identify themselves racially, and looked to the other as the source of social problems. Yet polls show overwhelming support among all racial groups for racial justice in America, including the end of racial segregation and equal opportunity under the law for all racial groups. Only on the fringes did some black and white leaders call for racial separation. Black nationalism achieved new life in the person of LOUIS FARRAKHAN and his group, the NATION OF ISLAM. In often vituperative language, Farrakhan advocated racial solidarity and economic and social self-reliance, as the primary weapons against racial discrimination. Appeals for racial purity and solidarity also arose on the fringe of mainstream white America, as pseudo-military militia groups and various white supremacist organizations, such as the Aryan Nations and the Ku Klux Klan, preached a gospel of hate that declared America a "white man's country," and often advocated the violent overthrow of the government for its role in mongrelizing the nation.

It is clear that, as America entered the 21st century, race mattered and could not be discounted when considering almost any political, social, or cultural issue. For example, it figured prominently in the murder trial of O. J. Simpson in 1995. Simpson, a former professional football player and movie star, was acquitted of murdering his ex-wife and her male friend, by a jury of nine blacks, two whites, and one Hispanic. The significance of this trial lies in the fact that hundreds of millions of people watched it on TELEVISION, and that Simpson's lawyer argued that, in spite of a significant amount of evidence against his client, racism on the part of the police had resulted in Simpson's indictment. Public opinion clearly split along racial lines, with whites overwhelmingly supporting Simpson's conviction, and African Americans supporting his acquittal. Episodes like this demonstrated that the racial antagonism present in American society remained a valuable political and cultural tool.

Throughout American history, however, racial conflict has had more than a purely negative effect. It made possible political equality for all groups of Americans, and offered the possibility of social integration for those who wished to pursue it, however undesirable some groups believed it to be. Moreover, inasmuch as racial conflict divided, it also fused. Out of conflict came what historian Charles Banner-Haley calls integrative cultural diversity. As blacks and whites sought to define themselves as both racial groups and Americans, they, along with the wide variety of America's other ethnic and racial groups, forged a unique American culture that synthesized the artistic, literary, and intellectual talents of all groups. What remains for the 21st century is the challenge of continually defining a coherent American identity, in the face of increasingly complex definitions of race and ethnicity.

See also ADVERTISING; BILINGUAL EDUCATION ACT; CIVIL LIBERTIES ACT; EDUCATION [ALL ENTRIES]; HORTON, WILLIE; IMMIGRATION; IMMIGRATION REFORM AND CONTROL ACT; MILITIA MOVEMENT; MULTICULTURALISM; NATIVE AMERICANS.

Further reading: Donald Kinder, *Divided by Color: Racial Politics and Democratic Ideals* (Chicago: University of Chicago Press, 1996); Paul Sniderman and Edward Carmines, *Reaching beyond Race* (Cambridge, Mass.: Harvard University Press, 1997).

—William L. Glankler

Racketeer Influenced and Corrupt Organizations Act (RICO)

The Racketeer Influenced and Corrupt Organizations Act (RICO) became law in 1970 as a means of targeting organized crime in America. RICO proved to be one of the most powerful tools law enforcement has to combat organized crime. It is not a criminal statute because it does not criminalize any act that is not already recognized as illegal. Instead, it enhances the normal punishments and penalties of certain crimes when they are committed by organizations, usually providing prison sentences and fines that are three times the norm. RICO also provides civil remedies for the victims of organized crime, which includes trebled damages plus reasonable attorney's fees and court costs. Though most observers have welcomed the criminal provisions, many jurists fear that the civil provisions have been abused.

Originally, RICO was only a minor part of the much larger Organized Crime Control Act (OCCA) of 1970. Following on the heels of the 1967 *Report of the President's Commission on Law Enforcement and Administration of Justice*, OCCA was intended to provide the government with the necessary tools to combat organized crime, which many observers believed was overtaking New York and other large urban centers. Some of its points included special provisions for grand juries, and use immunity, as well as special procedures to deal with contempt, false statements, and depositions. At the time, the criminal forfeiture provision inspired the most controversy; it ordered law enforcement to seize all property used in the commission of a crime. Forfeiture was an innovation in criminal justice and, though advocates claimed precedence for it in old English common law, it had never been used in the United States. Much of the congressional debate focused on this element alone.

Although RICO has since been heralded as a major step forward in the war against organized crime, initially the Department of Justice (DOJ) hesitated for almost a decade before exploiting its full potential. This was largely a result of its vague language. Modern RICO prohibits any person from using income derived from a pattern of racketeering activity to acquire or maintain interest in an enterprise; from conducting the affairs of an enterprise through racketeering activity; and from conspiring with others to do so. The authoring Congress did not know how to define organized crime in a way that would not violate the free association clause of the Constitution, and was instead left with having to list crimes that are commonly associated with organized criminal behavior, including murder, kidnapping, arson, gambling, robbery, bribery, extortion, drug dealing, and mail and wire fraud. Without a strict definition of organized crime, the "pattern of racketeering" necessary to trigger the RICO statute was broadly defined. The law also provided a broad construction clause to ensure that law enforcement agencies would be able to apply the statute to unforeseen circumstances as needed. Despite this added precaution, the courts still found significant ambiguity in the definitions of "enterprise," "pattern," and "person." Until the courts arrived at some consensus on these terms, the DOJ used the statute infrequently, and only in conjunction with other, better defined laws. The civil component was used even less frequently, usually because true victims of organized crime were typically too intimidated to pursue civil recovery, preferring instead to let the FBI assume the risks of prosecution for them. This also added to the reasons why the criminal side of RICO received limited use; legitimate businesses were often too frightened to file a complaint with law enforcement.

One solution to this problem was to redefine the nature of "enterprise" in a way that would permit law enforcement to use RICO against the mob without involving legitimate businesses. Throughout the 1970s, the law professor who drafted the original language for the 1970 Senate committee, G. Robert Blakey, toured the Northeast, giving seminars to law enforcement officials urging them to reconsider the object of RICO. In 1981, however, the SUPREME COURT decided in *United States v. Turkette* that RICO's broad construction clause justified a reinterpretation of "enterprise" that included both legal and illegal organizations. From that point on, the DOJ has depended on RICO as the prime tool in their war against organized crime and drug dealing.

During the mid-1980s, certain corporations tested the legal waters by attaching civil RICO complaints to their standard breach-of-contract suits. After years of lower-court debate, the Supreme Court ruled in *Sedima, S.P.R.L. v. Imrex Co.* (1985) that the liberal construction clause prevented the Court from distinguishing civil RICO from "garden variety" contract disputes. Congress made numerous attempts during the late 1980s and early 1990s to reform the RICO statute to prevent civil RICO abuse. They were successfully blocked by consumer advocate groups who feared that weaker language would bar victims of white-collar crime from appropriate remedies, particularly in light of the savings-and-loan and insider-trading scandals of

the later 1980s. Advocates of reform claimed that consumer-protection remedies already existed at the state level, and, under the auspices of the Securities and Exchange Commission (SEC), they argued that RICO abused principles of federalism by imposing federal remedies for offenses that could be better addressed locally. Despite years of debate and compromise, Congress failed to pass any measures seeking to reform the civil provisions of the RICO statute. On the criminal side, however, Congress passed numerous laws adding additional predicate offenses, including child pornography, black-marketing, and terrorism. In the 1990s, RICO stirred further controversy when it was used as the basis for numerous civil lawsuits against pro-life protesters, gun manufacturing, and tobacco companies.

—Aharon W. Zorea

Reagan, Ronald W. (1911–)

Ronald Wilson Reagan became the 40th president of the United States in 1981 and served two terms in the White House. His election marked the ascension of conservatism to political power in postwar America. Reagan spent his early life as a liberal Democrat. His mother, Nellie, was an evangelical Protestant who stressed religious values; his father, John Reagan, was a salesman and a liberal Democrat.

After working as a radio sports announcer, Reagan became a movie actor with Warner Brothers' studio in Hollywood. Reagan performed in well-received films, including *Kings Row, The Hasty Heart,* and *The Winning Team.*

He was elected to five terms as president of the Screen Actors Guild (SAG), the movie actors' union, by his fellow actors. As SAG's president, Reagan worked to secure better benefits and working conditions from studio executives. A New Deal Democrat, who enthusiastically voted and campaigned for both Franklin Delano Roosevelt and Harry Truman, Reagan struggled with Communist Party members in SAG, and developed a permanent loathing for communism and socialism in general, and the Soviet Union in particular. Reagan slowly turned away from the New Deal liberalism of his youth, voting for Republican Dwight Eisenhower in the 1952 presidential election. In 1962, after being a Democratic endorser of Eisenhower and Nixon, Reagan finally registered as a Republican.

Reagan's nationwide television speech in October 1964 for Republican presidential nominee Barry Goldwater inspired rich, conservative California businessmen to back the former actor for governor of California in 1966. Reagan's campaign featured forceful uncompromising attacks against student protesters at the University of California, African-American urban rioters in Los Angeles, welfare cheaters, and taxes created by Democratic governor Pat

Brown. Reagan promised to restore order. He was easily elected by more than 1 million votes.

As governor, Reagan cut the rate of budgetary growth in California. Reagan's long experience with television, movies, and radio enabled him to appeal directly to voters in simple language over the appeals of legislators and bureaucratic experts, winning him the sobriquet, "The Great Communicator." To Reagan's later embarrassment, in 1967 he became one of the first three governors to sign an abortion rights bill. In one year, California abortions jumped from 517 to over 100,000. A divorced man himself, Reagan also became the first governor to sign a no-fault divorce bill in 1970. He was reelected that year.

Reagan made an unsuccessful bid for the 1968 Republican presidential nomination, but lost to RICHARD M. NIXON. Nixon's WATERGATE SCANDAL, mismanagement of the economy, and détente with the communist Soviet Union and People's Republic of China, revived Reagan's presidential hopes. Nixon's successor, GERALD R. FORD, continued Nixon's policies. After the SUPREME COURT's *ROE V. WADE* (1973) pro-abortion ruling, the CONSERVATIVE MOVEMENT discovered another reason to oppose traditional Republicanism. Reagan publicly converted to an antiabortion position, supported prayer in the public schools, and promised to rein in what he viewed as "federal judicial activism." He allied himself with New Right leaders Senator JESSE HELMS and PHYLLIS SCHLAFLY, and challenged Ford for the 1976 Republican nomination. Reagan denounced détente and called for a tougher stance against the Soviet Union. At the convention, Reagan lost the contest by a handful of delegates. It appeared his political career might be over.

As JAMES EARL CARTER, JR.'s presidency confronted stagflation, Soviet expansionism, and the seizure of the Iranian embassy hostages, Reagan solidified his position in the Republican Party, and won its presidential nomination in 1980. He selected GEORGE H. W. BUSH as his vice presidential running mate. Reagan told the American people he would "get the government off our backs," that is, shove liberal bureaucratic experts aside, so he could renew prosperity, control crime, and regain respect for the country overseas.

On election day 1980, Reagan won in a landslide, taking 50 percent of the popular vote to Carter's 41 percent, while third-party candidate JOHN B. ANDERSON won 9 percent. Reagan won 44 states, helping the Republicans to win the Senate (for the first time in 16 years) with a net gain of 12 seats, and to attain a working majority in the House with a net gain of 33 seats.

Despite being wounded in an assassination attempt in March 1981, Reagan carried through many of his 1980 campaign promises during his first term. Federal income taxes were cut 25 percent over a three-year period with

President Ronald W. Reagan *(Ronald W. Reagan Library)*

the Economic Recovery Tax Act of 1981. Nondefense spending was cut sizably. Some welfare administration was shifted to the states. Federal regulations were slashed. Federal Reserve chairman Paul Volcker aided Reagan's program to suppress inflation with a tight money supply policy. Although unemployment rose to more than 10 percent in late 1982, losing the Republicans 26 House seats and their working majority, the American economy rebounded, and Reagan and Volcker's policies were widely credited with beginning a seven-year-long boom in 1983, the longest peacetime expansion in the country's history to date.

However, Reagan failed to deliver on balanced-budget or entitlement-reform promises. His huge defense spending increases combined with entitlement mandates to balloon federal deficits, despite his cheery campaign promises. However, Democratic legislators confined him to procedural changes. In 1986, during his second term, Reagan managed to work with House Democrats to reform the federal tax structure by lowering tax rates, eliminating tax shelters, and expanding the earned-income tax credit for working people. Nonetheless, because of demographic trends, entitlements continued to expand.

Reagan's 1980 promises of what he called a "moral revival" enjoyed less success than his economic policy. He enacted executive orders forbidding federal subsidies for abortion. But the SUPREME COURT continued to uphold *Roe v. Wade*. Reagan named SANDRA DAY O'CONNOR in 1981 as the first woman U.S. Supreme Court justice. O'Connor disappointed the conservative movement by becoming a swing vote. Reagan's first-term attorney general, William French Smith, was replaced by Edwin Meese, who declared culture war on what he perceived as liberal policies toward crime, sexuality, affirmative action, and federalism. Under Meese, the Justice Department systematically appointed judicial conservatives to federal district and appellate courts. Meese also persuaded Reagan to name conservatives WILLIAM H. REHNQUIST and ANTONIN SCALIA to be chief justice and associate justice, respectively, on the Supreme Court in 1986. However, the Democratic majority in the Senate blocked the appointment of conservative judge ROBERT BORK in 1987. Instead, Anthony Kennedy won appointment to the Court. The Rehnquist Supreme Court rolled back criminal rights, reinterpreted property rights, and began whittling down affirmative action rulings. However, it continued to uphold reproductive rights and free speech precedents.

In face of opposition, Reagan's presidency did not roll back environmental regulation much. Interior secretary JAMES WATT received harsh criticism, as did EPA administrator Anne Gorsuch Burford. Both were pressured to resign.

Despite his failure to deliver a balanced budget, Reagan achieved most of his domestic policy aims. Tax cutting, deregulation, and tax reform changed American society. Critics charged Reagan administration officials with corruption, and in the case of Michael Deaver, a presidential aide, an investigation led to his conviction on criminal charges.

In 1984 Reagan was reelected in an electoral landslide against Democratic opponent WALTER F. MONDALE, winning 49 states and a 59 percent popular vote. The Republicans retained control of the Senate. Reagan's Democratic critics called him "a Teflon president."

Reagan restored American military power. He persuaded Congress to almost double defense spending from $171 billion in 1981 to $300 billion in 1985. The bulk of these increases financed military pay increases, spare parts, the new Intermediate Nuclear Force, or INF, and MX missile systems, and a 600-ship navy. Reagan eschewed nuclear arms control measures in his first term. Instead, he advocated building a space-based ballistic missile defense system, known as the STRATEGIC DEFENSE INITIATIVE, or SDI. Reagan fought skeptics among the Pentagon command, the scientific establishment, diplomatic circles, NATO, and Democratic opposition, who derided SDI as "Star Wars," to champion SDI as the solution to Soviet nuclear missile superiority.

Reagan acted to prevent American high-technology exports, or "technology transfer," from being sent to the USSR or countries friendly to it. No presidency had ever policed technology transfer so stringently. These policies helped to delay Soviet development of a computer revolution. William Clark, Reagan's second National Security Advisor, issued orders denying the USSR access to American financial resources, plugging a gap previously left open during the COLD WAR. Clark also assisted the Solidarity labor resistance movement in the Soviet satellite of Poland. Reagan denounced Soviet totalitarianism, labeling it "an empire of evil." While avoiding direct military confrontation with the Soviets, Reagan did assist anti-communist insurgencies in the Third World. This so-called Reagan Doctrine used the CIA to aid anticommunist military movements in Afghanistan, Nicaragua, Angola, and Cambodia. The Afghan resistance, especially, took a bloody toll of Soviet troops and lowered Soviet morale.

Reagan's diplomatic initiatives in the Middle East proved more problematic. The first involved Lebanon. Reagan dispatched a marine brigade to "keep peace" between Israeli-backed and Muslim militia forces there. A Muslim suicide truck bomber killed 241 marines in October 1983. Reagan withdrew. The second failure was the selling of arms to Iran in an attempt to free American hostages held by Iranian-backed Muslim terrorists in Lebanon. Americans were indignant to discover in late 1986 that their hard-line president, who had declared Iran a terrorist state, had negotiated with Iran's fundamentalist leaders. Further revelations that the proceeds from these arms sales were used to fund the contras, anticommunist insurgents in Nicaragua, in direct violation of U.S. law, deepened the scandal. The IRAN-CONTRA AFFAIR seriously weakened Reagan's presidency.

Reagan extended military and financial assistance to El Salvador in its war with Nicaraguan-sponsored communist guerrillas. The campaign resulted in repeated reports of atrocities on both sides of the civil war. Two days after the 1983 massacre of the marines in Lebanon, Reagan ordered marines and army troops to invade the Caribbean island nation of Grenada to remove its communist government, which had close ties to Cuba.

Reagan's presidency enjoyed good relations with British prime minister Margaret Thatcher, an ideological soulmate. Reagan persuaded NATO members to deploy INF missiles for defense against Soviet invasion, to acquiesce in SDI, and to support antiterrorist measures.

Reagan showed little faith initially in arms control negotiations with the Soviet Union. Following his reelection in 1984, Reagan surprised his leading advisers—as well as his critics—by resuming negotiations with the Soviets. In late 1985 Reagan traveled to Geneva to meet with the new Soviet leader, Mikhail Gorbachev, for a three-day summit meeting. At the meeting, Reagan insisted on America's right to develop SDI. This position precluded any major agreements being reached, but Reagan and Gorbachev pledged to accelerate arms control negotiations in future meetings.

Finally, in 1987 Gorbachev flew to the United States to sign the historic Intermediate Nuclear Forces Treaty (INF), the first major arms control agreement that called for the destruction of deployed nuclear weapons systems. The treaty provided that inspectors from both nations would observe the destruction of intermediate-range missiles. Soviet and American leaders also announced that they would seek further arms reductions through the Strategic Arms Reduction Treaty (START), which had been suspended in Reagan's first term. Gorbachev also began to withdraw Soviet troops from Afghanistan, to end support to the Sandinista government in Nicaragua, and to reduce commitments to Cuba and Vietnam. Moreover, Gorbachev urged Soviet-backed governments in Eastern Europe to undertake political and economic reform. This last policy set the stage for opposition forces in Eastern European bloc nations to overthrow their communist regimes, leading to the eventual breakup of the Soviet Union during the GEORGE H. W. BUSH administration. As Reagan's administration drew to a close, the COLD WAR appeared to have ended.

Following his presidency, Reagan retired to his ranch in California. In 1994 he revealed he suffered from Alzheimer's disease. His public appearances since then have been limited by his illness.

See also REAGANOMICS.

Further reading: Michael Barone, *Our Country: America from Roosevelt to Reagan* (New York: Free Press, 1990); Steven Hayward, *The Age of Reagan: The Fall of the Old Liberal Order, 1964–1980* (San Francisco: Prima Publishing, 2001); Peter Rodman, *More Precious than Peace: Fighting and Winning the Cold War and the Struggle for the Third World* (Boston, Mass.: Scribner, 1994).

—Christopher M. Gray

Reaganomics

The term "Reaganomics" describes the economic policies of RONALD W. REAGAN's administrations between 1981 and 1988. More broadly it has been used to identify the economic, political, and social approaches to government associated with what has been termed the CONSERVATIVE MOVEMENT since the 1980s, closely identified with the policies of Margaret Thatcher in the United Kingdom.

Reagan set out his economic policies in his 1981 Program for Economic Recovery. Referred to as "supply-side economics," the major objectives were to reduce taxes, to limit federal spending and the level of government regulation, and to balance the budget. The rationale was that the economy would be stimulated by increased consumer spending and improved business confidence, and that reductions in government regulation would initiate a competitive and more efficient economy. The Reagan administration maintained that it had achieved its objectives in the lowering of inflation from 10.4 percent in 1980 to 4.2 percent in 1988, while unemployment fell from 7 percent in 1980 to 4.2 percent in 1988, and marginal tax rates were reduced. However, federal spending was not reduced and the budget not balanced, primarily due to a large increase in defense spending.

Critics contend that the inflation rate fell as a result of the ongoing strict "monetarist" policies of the independent Federal Reserve Board and not "supply-side" fiscal policies. They further argue that Reaganomics' cuts in taxes and social spending were short-sighted. Proponents credit it with the revival of the American economy in the 1980s and 1990s.

—Steve Hardman

recreation

During the last third of the 20th century, the economy of the post–World War II years greatly increased the amount of time Americans had available for recreational activities. The extension of the paid vacation, increased income, the introduction of more efficient labor-saving devices in the home, and the enhanced mobility provided by the proliferation of automobiles all combined to provide more leisure time for most Americans. Moreover, the ethic of pleasure, and the concern for personal self-fulfillment that became legitimate during the 1960s and 1970s served to focus attention on filling the newfound leisure time with an ever-increasing variety of recreational activities.

During the last half of the 20th century, family incomes increased dramatically. The median family income before payment of taxes rose from $3,031 in 1947 to $31,241 in 1993, and in 1993 almost 60 percent of American families had incomes of $25,000 or more. More important, Americans experienced substantial growth in their disposable income. Income after taxes averaged more than $18,000 per person in 1994. Increasingly, Americans spent this income on consumer goods and recreational activities.

Recreational sports remained a popular activity. As both participants and spectators, Americans throughout the 20th century avidly involved themselves in sports activities. As spectators, they continued to loyally support their local teams, either by attending games in person or viewing them on TELEVISION. Cities built stadiums that seat crowds of 50,000 to 100,000 for their football teams and smaller arenas for their baseball, basketball, or hockey teams. In

People walk through Disney-MGM Studios, at Disney World theme park in Orlando, Florida. *(Raedle/Getty Images)*

ifornia, and other states, and the ever-growing number of participants made skiing an integral part of their social lives. Tennis experienced increased participation during the 1960s and 1970s because of high-profile professionals such as Billie Jean King, Chris Evert, and Jimmy Connors. Golf, once reserved for the members of country clubs, began to grow as a popular sport during the 1960s and 1970s, when players such as Arnold Palmer and Jack Nicklaus helped turn golf into a major spectator sport. During the late 1990s, Tiger Woods's immense popularity revived golf as a spectator sport and helped make it the most-played sport in America.

Female professional and amateur sports became increasingly popular in the 1970s. Led by Billie Jean King, women's tennis grew in popularity and gained respect and equal treatment in the world of professional tennis. Similarly, women's professional golf grew. The Ladies Professional Golf Association (incorporated in 1950) grew rapidly in the 1960s, under the leadership of Lenny Wirtz, and the rise of television brought women's golf into the American home with the first televised broadcast of the U.S. Women's Open Championship in 1963. In the 1970s women's professional golf took off when David Foster, the chairman and CEO of Colgate-Palmolive Company, began sponsoring several worldwide tournaments throughout the next decade. Nancy Lopez became a sports hero for her excellent play, and the Lopez phenomenon set off a golf fad among women. As a result, as more amateurs played golf, the popularity of professional women's golf grew as well. By 1980, LPGA-tour prize money totaled $4.4 million. In the 1990s prize money grew from 17.1 million in 1990 to more than 36.2 million in 1999, while television coverage increased from 15 events in 1990 to 35 in 1999.

These sporting activities—along with others, such as hunting, fishing, boating, and swimming—were often incorporated as essential elements in another major American recreational activity: the family vacation. Made possible by increased income, the paid vacation, more leisure time, and the mobility offered by the automobile, the family vacation contributes significantly to the U.S. tourism industry that is a considerable component of the overall U.S. economy. Indeed, the economies of some states, such as Florida, are largely dependent on tourist dollars. Yearly, millions of Americans pack up their families and venture off to secluded or exotic locations.

Although getaways are still immensely popular, technological advancements during the 1980s and 1990s made home entertainment an increasingly popular form of passive recreation. Increased ease of consumption also contributed to the presence of television and, by the end of the century, nearly 100 percent of American homes had at least one television set. (In 1960, 80 percent of homes had television.) The technology also made possible the

the 1990s, through the innovations of cable television and pay-per-view subscription services, fans could watch any major sports competition they chose. Americans spent ever-larger amounts to attend games. By the end of the century, the average cost of a ticket to a National Football League game was $51 and it cost more than $300 to take a family of four to a game. Even at these prices, fan support remained strong for most professional sports; in contrast, Major League baseball experienced depressed attendance figures throughout the 1990s. Americans loved their professional sports heroes and continued to make this a major component of their recreational activities.

Other recreational sports became popular during the last three decades of the century, largely from the fame of associated television and famous sports personalities. Snow skiing became popular during the 1950s, largely stimulated by the Olympic skiing competitions. The sport swept across the country to new sites in Colorado, Wyoming, Utah, Cal-

introduction of video games into the home during the 1980s and 1990s, with systems such as the Sony Playstation. During the late 1990s, WebTV made it possible to connect to the INTERNET through the television, thus opening numerous information and entertainment options to the entire family.

Perhaps the most significant impact of television was on the traditional American recreational activity of going to the MOVIES. At the end of the 20th century Americans still went in droves to the local multiple-screen theater to view the latest movie with its lavish production values and state-of-the-art special effects, and they paid as much as $10 per ticket to do so. Television, however, made it easy, affordable, and enjoyable to watch movies at home. Throughout the 1980s and 1990s, cable television allowed Americans to view movies soon after they had ended their theatrical run. The pay-per-view service shortened that time considerably, often showing movies within a few weeks after they left the theaters. The introduction of videotape in the 1980s and digital video discs (DVD) in the 1990s allowed the rental or purchase of movies that could be watched at one's leisure. Movies remained an essential element of American recreation, yet the setting in which Americans viewed movies changed radically as viewing options increased.

Another development in American recreation at the end of the 20th century was the proliferation of gambling casinos and the tremendous popularity they enjoyed. In 1969 legal gambling was essentially limited to Las Vegas and Reno, Nevada. The 1980s and 1990s saw the growth of casino gambling in areas as diverse as Tunica, Mississippi; St. Louis, Missouri; and on Native American reservations in the West, Northeast, and Florida. The gambling craze was further fueled by the increasing accessibility of gambling on the Internet. Critics of the spread of gambling argued that legalized gambling did not help local economies and exploited the most desperate people seeking a "quick fix."

Americans also hike, listen to music, read, surf, and enjoy family cookouts. They indulge in a culture driven by consumerism and aimed at maximizing the quality of leisure time. The postwar trend of a shortening workweek began to reverse itself in 1970, and Americans found themselves working more and more hours, the most among industrialized nations. This transformation made leisure time an increasingly valuable commodity and strengthened the bond between consumption and recreation, as Americans sought to participate in activities that demanded more expertise, higher ticket prices, more specialized equipment, and more remote locales. Americans began to pour as much, if not more, effort into their recreation as they did into their work. As this process developed over the last half of the century, it spawned an industry that became firmly entrenched in the consumer economy.

See also ART AND ARCHITECTURE; COMPUTERS; FAMILY LIFE; LITERATURE; MEDIA; POPULAR CULTURE; SCIENCE AND TECHNOLOGY; SEXUAL REVOLUTION.

Further reading: Elliot J. Gorn and Warren Goldstein, *A Brief History of American Sports* (New York: Hill & Wang, 1993); James D. Hunter, *Culture Wars: The Struggle to Define America* (New York: Basic Books, 1991).

—William L. Glankler

Reform Party

The Reform Party emerged as a challenge to the two major parties, Republican and Democratic, in the late 1990s when it appeared many voters were alienated from "politics as usual."

Although the Reform Party was officially founded November 2, 1997, at a convention held in Kansas City, Missouri, it began with the presidential election of 1992. As a guest on the *Larry King Live* show February 20, 1992, H. ROSS PEROT, a Texas billionaire, declared that if citizens would get him on the ballots in all 50 states he would run for president. The following day, his office was inundated with phone calls pledging support, and volunteers began to organize in each of the 50 states. By the middle of summer, United We Stand America (UWSA) had been organized to coordinate the Perot campaign; in early fall Perot announced his candidacy with Admiral James Stockdale, retired, as his vice presidential candidate. Although Perot received no electoral votes in the 1992 election, he did gather nearly 19 percent of the popular vote.

By 1995 the ineffectiveness of UWSA lobbying elected officials from the two major parties had members calling for the formation of a new political party. On September 25, 1995, Ross Perot announced that he would help create the Reform Party. One by one, the states worked to form their own Reform Party organizations for the presidential election of 1996. For this election, Perot selected Pat Choate, a Vietnam War hero, as his vice presidential running mate. When the election votes were tallied, Ross Perot got just under 8.5 percent of the popular vote.

Since Perot had received the requisite number of popular votes, the Reform Party of the United States of America was qualified to receive federal funding in presidential elections. A national organizing convention was held in Nashville, Tennessee, in January 1997, and the National Reform Party was officially formed at a convention in Kansas City in November. At the Kansas City convention Russ Verney was elected chair and Patricia Benjamin was elected vice chair.

Party members pledged to reform the American political system. Founding principles included setting high ethical standards for the White House and Congress; balancing the federal budget; effecting CAMPAIGN FINANCE reform; term limits; creating a new tax system; addressing the anticipated needs of Medicare, Medicaid, and Social Security; promoting jobs; and initiating lobbying reform. The party's platform elaborates these details.

In the hotly contested 2000 presidential election between GEORGE W. BUSH and ALBERT GORE, JR., Reform candidates Patrick Buchanan and Ezola Foster were not able to collect even a half million popular votes (.42 percent of the popular vote). The party itself was wracked with discord and split, with some members forming the American Reform Party.

See also REGENTS OF THE UNIVERSITY OF CALIFORNIA V. ALLAN BAKKE (SEE UNDER BAKKE).

—Michele Rutledge

Rehnquist, William H. (1924–)

William H. Rehnquist became a justice of the United States SUPREME COURT in 1971 and then was appointed chief justice of the Court in 1986. He was one of only two chief justices to preside over a presidential impeachment.

Rehnquist was born in Milwaukee, Wisconsin, October 1, 1924, and grew up in the suburb of Shorewood in a strongly Republican family. He served in the army air corps during World War II, which enabled him, following the war, to attend Stanford University on the G.I. Bill. He received both his B.A. (Phi Beta Kappa) and his M.A. in political science. He received a second M.A. in government from Harvard in 1950, and then completed Stanford Law School, where he graduated first in his class in 1950. He clerked for Associate Supreme Court Justice Robert Jackson in 1951, and the following year he married Natalie Cornell, and the couple had a son and two daughters. He went to work for a law firm in Phoenix, Arizona, where he became a Republican Party official and an outspoken critic of busing to achieve school integration. While campaigning for Goldwater in 1964 he became friendly with Richard Kleindienst, another Phoenix attorney. When Kleindienst became deputy attorney general in the RICHARD M. NIXON administration, he invited Rehnquist to become assistant attorney general for the Justice Department's Office of Legal Counsel. When Justice Marshall Harlan retired from the Supreme Court, Rehnquist was appointed to fill his seat. At the same time, LEWIS POWELL was appointed to the Court.

Powell became a "swing" justice, while Rehnquist emerged as the Court's rightist dissenter. Rehnquist's early law clerks dubbed him "the Lone Ranger," as he strongly dissented against majority court rulings on abortion, affirmative action quotas, church-state relations, criminal procedure, free speech, and the death penalty. Rehnquist's dissents constructed a persistent critique of the majority "constructionist" philosophy of the Court.

Rehnquist thought the Warren and Burger Courts erred by nullifying what he viewed as true federalism in order to mandate radical egalitarian change in the states and localities. His interpretation of the Fourteenth Amendment's equal protection clause held that it applied to racial discrimination, not to abortion, sexual discrimination, or public assistance rights. He also claimed that the judicial opinions of the other justices exceeded judicial authority, and usurped the legislative and executive functions. In a 1976 speech espousing "originalist" judicial restraint, he argued that the Constitution's framers desired the Congress and the presidency to "furnish the motive power for the solution of the numerous and varied problems that the future would bring."

Chief Justice Burger retired in 1986. President RONALD W. REAGAN nominated Rehnquist to replace Burger as chief justice and conservative judge ANTONIN SCALIA to fill the associate justice vacancy. Although this nomination caused much controversy, Rehnquist was confirmed by the Senate in a 65-33 vote. He conducted Court business in a collegial, disciplined, and expedited manner. He deliberately compromised his own leanings on certain cases to help the Court achieve unanimity. He fulfilled the demanding administrative duties of the chief justice in a manner pleasing to his colleagues. Rehnquist thus reduced the number of cases the Court decided, despite the docket's increasing by one-fourth at the time.

The Rehnquist Court experienced mixed success in curbing the most famous rulings by the Warren and Burger Courts. It rolled back the rulings restricting the death penalty and weakened the exclusionary rule on criminal evidence, but upheld the procedural protections of the Miranda decision. Federal court power over state and local government was restricted. Rehnquist created slender majorities narrowing affirmative action quotas in the *Ward's Cove Packing Co. v. Antonio* (1989) and *Adarand Constructors Inc. v. Pena* (1995) cases.

Rehnquist sought to overrule ROE V. WADE (1973), the abortion case that underlay abortion rights, but ambivalent opposition by his longtime friend, Justice SANDRA DAY O'CONNOR prevented him. In the WEBSTER V. REPRODUCTIVE HEALTH SERVICES (1989) and *Planned Parenthood v. Casey* (1992) cases, Rehnquist wrote the opinions for 5-4 and 6-3 majorities, respectively, in whittling down abortion rights. In *Stenberg v. Carhart* (2000), on the other hand, Rehnquist joined the minority in a 5-4 ruling upholding the substance of *Roe*.

The chief justice enjoyed more success for his interpretative agenda with cases involving euthanasia. In *Cruzan v. Missouri* (1990), Rehnquist spoke for a 5-4 majority refusing to allow Nancy Cruzan's parents to withdraw her life support on the basis of the Fourteenth Amendment. In *Washington State v. Glucksberg* (1997), Rehnquist managed to persuade some wavering justices to unanimously support his 9-0 majority opinion upholding Washington State's statute banning physician-assisted suicide.

In 1997 Rehnquist ruled for a unanimous 9-0 court in the Paula Jones sexual harassment case that civil suits could proceed against a standing president of the United States. Rehnquist led a bitterly divided 5-4 Court in settling the Florida election case and thereby the 2000 presidential election in *Bush v. Gore* (2000).

Further reading: Kermit Hall, ed., *The Oxford Companion to the Supreme Court* (New York: Oxford University Press, 1992); William H. Rehnquist, *The Supreme Court,* 2d ed. (New York, Knopf, 2001); ———, *Grand Inquests* (New York: Knopf, 1992); David Savage, *Turning Right: The Making of the Rehnquist Supreme Court* (New York: John Wiley & Sons, 1992).

—Christopher M. Gray

religion

American religion reflects the diversity of the population of the United States. Historically America is a nation of immigrants who brought both Protestant and Catholic Christianity; Judaism; Buddhism; and Islam—and continues as a nation of the faithful, innovating new faiths such as Mormon, Christian Scientist, Jehovah's Witness, Seventh-Day Adventist, and NEW AGE adherents.

Americans cherish their constitutional right prohibiting state-sponsored religion. Despite the varieties and variances of the religions practiced in the United States, most Americans focus more on the shared characteristics and commonalities of their respective faiths. Christianity, Judaism, and Islam have the largest number of practitioners and are the dominant religions in the United States: Jews represent 5.6 million Americans; Muslims, 4.1 million; Buddhists, 2.4 million; and Hindus, 1 million. The rapid growth of evangelical Protestant congregations and more charismatic, less hierarchical faiths like the Church of Jesus Christ of Latter-day Saints (Mormon), the Pentecostals, and Jehovah's Witnesses contrast with the shrinking overall membership of Episcopalians, Presbyterians, Lutherans, Methodists, and other mainline Protestant groups. Some sociologists claim that American faith groups have entered a post-denominational era, citing as evidence the growth of 5,000-plus-member megachurches complete with coffee bars and fast food restaurants. However, 62 percent of all U.S. congregations have strong denominational loyalties. In the

1950s newly organized Roman Catholic parishes represented about 10 percent of all new churches; by the beginning of the 21st century, that figure dropped to 5 percent.

In the past 50 years, Americans have changed little in eight key religious practices and beliefs, as measured by the Gallup Index of Leading Religious Indicators. These include church or synagogue membership; weekly attendance at religious services; the value Americans place on religion; confidence in organized religion; the proportion who give a religious preference; the percentage who say religion can answer the problems of the era; belief in God; and belief in the honesty and ethics of the clergy. Ninety percent of Americans assert a belief in God, and six out of 10 Americans claim that religion is "very important" in their lives. More than half of the American population are members of a faith community.

Americans express overall confidence in the church and "organized religion," although this confidence was shaken by TELEVANGELISM scandals of the late 1980s. Correspondingly, the clergy's ethics and honesty ratings on opinion polls have consistently been among the highest of any field or profession tested, with 60 percent of Americans giving them a high score, although these numbers too have fluctuated. Clergy members have not been invulnerable to the effects of adverse publicity: positive ratings of their honesty and ethics fell from 67 percent to 55 percent between 1984 and 1989. A consistent majority of Americans continue to believe in the ability of religion to answer today's problems, although this belief has varied widely over the decades, from a high of 81 percent in 1955 to a low of 56 percent in 1984.

Since 1950, roughly nine out of 10 Americans have consistently given a religious preference. The percentage of Protestants and Jews has declined sharply since then, while the percentage of Catholics has remained at approximately the same level. Among Jews there has been a shift from Reform Judaism to Conservative and Orthodox Judaism. Paralleling these trends has been a growth in the proportion of those who name other religions, or do not give a preference. At the close of the century, religion in the United States is broadly ecumenical and increasingly tolerant, reflecting a multicultural and pluralistic American society.

See also MULTICULTURALISM.

Further reading: Martin Marty, *Modern American Religion* (Chicago: University of Chicago Press, 1986); M. A. Meyer, *Response to Modernity: A History of the Reform Movement* (New York: Oxford University Press, 1988); Robert Wuthnow, *Christianity in the Twenty-First Century* (New York: Oxford University Press, 1993).

—Michele Rutledge

Religious Freedom Restoration Act

Enacted in 1993, the Religious Freedom Restoration Act (RFRA) required governments to refrain from the limitation of religious freedom, unless there was a compelling societal reason to do so. It also required the selection of the least intrusive method, if the need to restrict religious freedom did arise.

A series of U.S. SUPREME COURT decisions during the 1960s and 1970s upheld the individual's religious freedom and limited government's ability to pass restrictive legislation. During the 1980s, however, the Court's position shifted in the direction of allowing governments to restrict religious freedom, as long as the limitations were applied equally to all faiths. For example, in *Employment Division v. Smith* (1990) the Court ruled that the religious use of peyote (a hallucinogenic drug) was not a constitutionally protected religious right, despite its centuries-old use by some Native American tribes. The RFRA specifically reversed that decision and restored the original balancing test set forth in Warren and Burger Court decisions such as *Sherbert v. Verner* (1963) and *Wisconsin v. Yoder* (1972).

More than 60 religious groups and civil liberties organizations united to form the Coalition for the Free Exercise of Religion to promote the RFRA. The group represented religious liberals and conservatives and included Native American spiritual groups and Christian, Jewish, Muslim, Scientology, and Sikh religious organizations. It also included more secular organizations such as the American Civil Liberties Union, Americans United for Separation of Church and State, and the Traditional Values Coalition. The group continues to exist and includes over 72 different organizations, many with sharply opposing viewpoints on other issues. American Atheists were one of the few organizations that actively opposed the RFRA. They believed the law gave special rights to churches, mosques, temples, synagogues, and other sectarian organizations.

The House of Representatives unanimously approved the legislation on October 27, 1993, and the Senate passed it 97 to 3 on November 3. President WILLIAM J. CLINTON signed the RFRA into law on November 16. The U.S. Supreme Court declared the RFRA unconstitutional on January 25, 1997. A number of similar laws have been enacted on the state level. On the federal level, the Religious Land Use and Institutionalized Persons Act, was signed into law on September 22, 2000. This law restricts government interference with the religious use of land and guarantees religious freedom for inmates of institutions.

—William L. Glankler

Reno, Janet (1938–)

Janet Reno served as Florida's first female state attorney general and as the first woman attorney general of the United States. During her tenure in these positions, she focused on reorienting crime policy toward prevention first and then punishment. She hoped to accomplish this reorientation by implementing programs to change the social and personal conditions that lead people to crime. As attorney general she also oversaw a rapid expansion of offenses punishable by the DEATH PENALTY.

Reno was born July 21, 1938, in Coconut Grove, Florida, and attended public schools. She received a bachelor's degree in chemistry from Cornell University in 1960 and a law degree from Harvard in 1963. Her first political appointment came in 1971 as staff director of the Judiciary Committee of the Florida House of Representatives. She lost a bid for a seat in the Florida state legislature in 1972. In 1973 she joined the state attorney's office in Dade County, Florida, where she was assigned the task of organizing a juvenile division within the prosecutor's office. It was in this capacity that she began to form her views about preventive crime fighting by providing services to children and rehabilitating delinquent youths.

Reno became Florida's first female state attorney general in 1978 when she accepted the position for Dade County. She was elected to this post five times on her beliefs that a prosecutor's first objective was to ensure that innocent people were not charged and that the guilty were convicted according to due process. During her tenure as state attorney, Reno undertook several programs designed to reform and reorient public views about fighting crime.

She began by reforming the juvenile justice system and began to aggressively prosecute child abuse cases. She also established a domestic violence intervention program geared toward prevention by relying heavily on counseling for both victims and abusers. This orientation toward prevention manifested itself most prominently when, in the mid-1980s, she espoused a new approach to the traditional mission of the prosecutor. This new approach is best described as preventive crime-fighting and hinged on getting at the root causes of crime. Coupled with high rates of recidivism, this viewpoint resulted in an emphasis on rehabilitation. She believed that incarceration was not the solution to most crime, but advocated life imprisonment of the most violent offenders.

Reno's new approach led to several effective programs in Dade County. She developed a community policing team that helped clean up a crime-ridden housing project in Miami. In 1989 she established Miami's innovative drug court. This system offered first-time drug offenders a chance to expunge their record if they completed a year-long treatment program. Almost 60 percent of those enrolled in the program finished, and of those who finished 90 percent were trouble-free a year later. Such success made the Miami drug court a model for other cities around the country. In 1990 she extended the drug court idea fur-

Former U.S. attorney general Janet Reno *(Smith/Newsmakers)*

ther to encompass other young, nonviolent offenders. Such offenders could avoid imprisonment and a criminal record if they undertook a rehabilitation program that included, among other things, making restitution to their victims. These successes and her commitment to law and order caught the attention of the president-elect, WILLIAM J. CLINTON, in 1992.

On March 12, 1993, Janet Reno became the 78th attorney general of the United States, the first woman ever to hold that position. Her two terms as attorney general (the longest ever) under Clinton witnessed success as well as controversy—controversy that began only one month after her swearing-in. In April 1993, she ordered the Federal Bureau of Investigation (FBI), along with agents of the Bureau of Alcohol, Tobacco, and Firearms (ATF), to launch an assault on the BRANCH DAVIDIAN compound outside Waco, Texas. The FBI and ATF had been in a standoff with the cult group for several weeks; Reno believed that the children inside the compound were being physically

abused. During the assault, a fire broke out in the compound killing 86 people, including 17 children. Reno took full responsibility for the assault amid criticism that the FBI had acted irresponsibly and had indeed started the deadly fire. An investigation in 2000 by former senator John C. Danforth (R-Mo.) found that members of the cult had started the fire within the compound.

Reno brought her new vision of law enforcement to the attorney general's office by encouraging federal, state, and local government agencies to work together to combat the root causes of crime. She advocated beginning with proper prenatal care and continuing to ensure that all children have adequate health care, education, supervision, jobs, and job training. She also called for comprehensive programs that provided a balance between punishment and prevention, and stated her belief that society's resources should be directed toward better schools, housing, and health care, rather than toward more jails. However, she did not waver from her conviction that the most violent criminals should be permanently imprisoned, and she oversaw the expansion of the federal death penalty statute to cover dozens of new offenses.

Reno's dedication to law and order could not protect her from charges of having politicized her office. Democrats criticized her for appointing numerous INDEPENDENT COUNSELS, and Republicans criticized her for not pursuing charges connected to those counsels' reports. She ended investigations into Vice President ALBERT GORE, JR.'s fund-raising activities on two separate occasions, much to the Republicans' chagrin. Yet she did not back down when pursuing the president's alleged misconduct. Her appointment of KENNETH STARR to investigate the allegations led to a critical moment in U.S. history—the impeachment of President Clinton.

After leaving office, she returned to Florida where she ran unsuccessfully for the governorship of the state.

See also CAMPAIGN FINANCE; CRIME; MILITIA MOVEMENT; OKLAHOMA CITY BOMBING; RACKETEER INFLUENCED AND CORRUPT ORGANIZATIONS ACT; TOBACCO SUITS; WHITEWATER.

Further reading: Paul Anderson, *Janet Reno: Doing the Right Thing* (New York: Wiley, 1994).

—William L. Glankler

Richardson, Elliot L. (1920–1999)

Richardson devoted his life to public service and gained great renown when he resigned as RICHARD M. NIXON's attorney general in 1973 rather than fire special prosecutor ARCHIBALD COX, JR. Elliot Lee Richardson was born in Boston, Massachusetts, on July 20, 1920, to a prominent New England family. Richardson attended Harvard University, graduating in 1941. During World War II he was a lieutenant in the army and participated in the Allied invasion in Normandy. During the war, Richardson was awarded the Bronze Star and two Purple Hearts. After the war, Richardson attend Harvard Law School, graduating in 1947. Richardson had an impressive early legal career, working as a law clerk for Judge Learned Hand at the United States Court of Appeals from 1947 to 1948 and for Supreme Court Justice Felix Frankfurter from 1948 to 1949.

Richardson's political career began during the Eisenhower administration, first as an assistant secretary of health, education and welfare (HEW) from 1957 to 1959 and then as United States attorney to Massachusetts from 1959 to 1961. During the 1960s, Richardson became active in Massachusetts politics, serving as lieutenant governor from 1965–67, and as attorney general from 1967–69. He was recalled to federal service by Richard M. Nixon, serving as undersecretary of state from 1969 to 1970 before becoming secretary of HEW, a post he held until 1973. After a brief stint as secretary of defense, Richardson was appointed attorney general in February 1972, replacing JOHN MITCHELL who had resigned to head the Committee to Reelect the President.

Richardson served until October 20, 1973, when he resigned rather than fire Archibald Cox. In May 1973 Richardson had named Cox as special prosecutor to investigate allegations that President Nixon had authorized the break-in at the Watergate, and other illegal activities aimed at gaining confidential Democratic Party strategies for the 1972 election. Cox demanded tapes of secret conversations held in the Oval Office. Nixon offered a compromise proposal, which Cox refused. Angered, Nixon ordered Richardson, and then William Ruckelshaus, to fire Cox. Richardson held firm on the grounds that he had specified that Cox would have full authority to contest Nixon's assertion of executive privilege. After Richardson resigned, Robert Bork accepted the order. The episode provoked a national outcry and became notorious as the "Saturday Night Massacre."

During the GERALD R. FORD administration, Richardson served as ambassador to Great Britain from 1975 through 1976. He then served as secretary of commerce from 1976 to 1977. During JAMES EARL CARTER, JR.'s administration he served as ambassador-at-large to the international law of the seas conference from 1977 to 1980. Richardson authored two books, *The Creative Balance* (1976) and *Reflections of a Radical Moderate* (1996). Richardson died December 30, 1999.

—John Korasick

Roe v. Wade (1973)

This was the landmark United States SUPREME COURT decision in 1973 that established a woman's right to have an ABORTION the first two trimesters of pregnancy. The plaintiff, Norma McCorvey (the case listed her as "Jane Roe"), was unable to receive an abortion legally under restrictive Texas law. She sued the state of Texas, and her case, essentially a challenge to all state abortion laws, eventually appeared before the Supreme Court. The Court ruled 7-2 in favor of Roe and thereby extended the right to personal privacy in sexual matters that was originally established in *Griswold v. Connecticut* (1965). The *Griswold* decision held that severe restrictions on the availability of contraceptives violated a woman's implied constitutional right to privacy. Justice Harry Blackburn wrote the majority opinion in *Roe v. Wade*, with Justices William Rehnquist and Byron White dissenting.

The decision solidified the divisions within an electorate already polarized by the abortion debate and ensured that abortion would remain a highly contentious and extremely visible political issue. The Court's decision led to the emergence of an organized antiabortion movement. Supported by the Christian Coalition, the Roman Catholic Church, and many conservative politicians, the "pro-life" movement began to agitate for a constitutional amendment that would prohibit abortion except for therapeutic reasons and in cases involving rape and incest. The decision also galvanized those wanting to expand abortion rights. Groups such as the NATIONAL ORGANIZATION FOR WOMEN (NOW) and other "pro-choice" activists took the view that *Roe v. Wade* had established constitutional protections for women's rights to reproductive control. Although the Court's decision did not explicitly deal with issues of women's rights and gender equality, advocates see the "right to choose" as a fundamental human right, and *Roe v. Wade* continues to serve as a touchstone for the debate revolving around such issues.

The decision handed down by the Court in *Roe v. Wade* has survived several challenges since 1973 without being overturned. By the late 1990s, the abortion debate shifted toward the regulation of abortion, as opponents sought to erect practical barriers to the exercise of abortion rights. With the legality of abortion standing on a firm constitutional ground, the opposing groups struggled locally and nationally over the extent and legality of abortion restrictions.

See also BIRTH CONTROL; FAMILY LIFE; POPULATION TRENDS; WOMEN'S RIGHTS AND STATUS.

—William L. Glankler

Ruckelshaus, William D. (1932–)

William Doyle Ruckelshaus gained a national reputation for his service to government as head of the Federal Bureau of Investigation and the Environmental Protection Agency. He was born in Indianapolis, Indiana, on July 24,

1934, and graduated from Princeton University in 1957. He entered his family's law firm in 1960 after graduating from Harvard Law School. Named deputy state attorney general in Indiana during his first year out of school, three years later he became chief counsel in the state attorney general's office. Three years after this appointment, Ruckelshaus was elected to the Indiana House of Representatives.

In 1968 President RICHARD M. NIXON's administration named Ruckelshaus assistant attorney general. When President Nixon created the Environmental Protection Agency (EPA) in 1970, he named Ruckelshaus its first director. In 1973 Ruckelshaus moved to the Federal Bureau of Investigation (FBI), where he became acting director. While in this position, Ruckelshaus uncovered the government wiretaps of news media and political opponents of President Nixon. Later that year, Ruckelshaus was named deputy attorney general. On October 20, 1973, Attorney General ELLIOT L. RICHARDSON resigned rather than carry out President Nixon's order to fire Watergate special prosecutor ARCHIBALD COX, JR., who was investigating the president's alleged involvement in the WATERGATE SCANDAL. Ruckelshaus, now the acting U.S. attorney general, also resigned, and his successor, ROBERT BORK, complied with the order to dismiss Cox. The resignations and firing became known as the Saturday Night Massacre.

After several years of serving as senior vice president of corporate affairs for the Weyerhauser Corporation, Ruckelshaus became director of the EPA. He resigned one year later in 1983. In 1988 he went to Browning-Ferris Industries, becoming chief executive officer, a position he held until 1995. Ruckelshaus served as the chairman of the board of Browning-Ferris, principal owner of Madrona Investment Group, and as chairman of the University of Wyoming Institute for Environment and Natural Resources, as well as on the boards of several other nonprofit organizations.

—Leah Blakey

rust belt

The economic decline of heavy industry during the 1970s led many critics to refer to the manufacturing centers in the Northeast and Middle West as the rust belt, usually including the states of Ohio, Michigan, Illinois, Indiana, and Pennsylvania.

During the recessions of the 1970s, key manufacturing industries such as steel, automotive, mining, and shipbuilding struggled to maintain their competitive base and failed to sustain their capital investment programs. Moreover, increased competition from abroad, especially in the automotive and steel industries, and the development of high technology and service industries, resulted in massive factory closures, large-scale redundancies, and severe economic repercussions for the region. As a result, cities such as Detroit, Cleveland, and Pittsburgh were especially hard hit, with high unemployment and rapid population emigrations. The high cost of public subsidies in keeping open major factories and the loss of tax revenues forced many cities to the brink of bankruptcy, such as Cleveland in 1978. Increased technological innovation also compounded the difficulties of sustaining the competitiveness of heavy industry, as the major companies drastically reduced their workforces. With the development of high technology and increased communication networks, many manufacturers relocated out of the rust belt to the less expensive South, or abroad, and newer industries began to develop in California.

However, during the 1990s, a sustained effort was made to reverse this decline. Many cities initiated inner-city renewal programs, focusing on attracting high technology, financial, and research companies to the regions. Cities such as Pittsburgh and Detroit, in particular, have focused on marketing themselves as centers of research and development, in order to complement their traditional industries.

See AUTOMOBILE INDUSTRY; CHRYSLER CORPORATION LOAN GUARANTEE ACT .

S

Scalia, Antonin (1936–)

Born March 11, 1936, in Trenton, New Jersey, Scalia became an associate justice of the U.S. SUPREME COURT in 1986. Scalia's outlook owes much to his father, Eugene Scalia, a devout Roman Catholic, Italian immigrant, and distinguished romance languages professor at Brooklyn College. His mother was a schoolteacher. When he was five, the family moved to Queens, New York, where Scalia attended public school and St. Francis Xavier, a military prep school. He received his B.A. in history from Georgetown University in 1957, where he was class valedictorian. He graduated from Harvard Law School. At Harvard, he married Maureen McCarthy in September 1960, and had nine children.

Scalia began his legal career at a firm in Cleveland, Ohio, before becoming a law professor at the University of Virginia in 1967. In 1971 he entered government, becoming general counsel for the Office of Telecommunications Policy. In 1972 he served as chairman of the administrative Conference of the United States, an independent agency charged with improving the effectiveness of the administrative process. From 1974 to 1977 he served President GERALD FORD as assistant attorney general for the Office of Legal Counsel in the Justice Department.

After he left government he returned to teaching, at the Georgetown Law Center, and then at the University of Chicago, from 1977–82. From 1981 to 1982 he served as chairman of the American Bar Association's section on administrative law. In 1982 President RONALD W. REAGAN appointed Scalia to the U.S. Court of Appeals in the D.C. Circuit. He served in this position for four years. On June 17, 1986, Reagan nominated him to the Supreme Court to fill the seat of WILLIAM H. REHNQUIST, who had become chief justice of the Court. During his confirmation hearing, he said that the most important part of the Constitution was its "checks and balances."

The first Italian American on the Court, Scalia received unanimous Senate confirmation after President Reagan's nomination. He immediately began applying his legal philosophy to the Court's docket. Scalia wrote a vitriolic lone dissent in *Morrison v. Olson* (1988), shunning all the case law on INDEPENDENT COUNSEL and terming his friend Chief Justice Rehnquist's majority opinion "an exercise in folly" for overlooking the independent counsel statute's clear separation of powers violation. Congress ended up agreeing with Scalia's prophetic dissent. It refused to renew the independent counsel law 11 years later.

Scalia displayed his libertarian leaning in free speech and PROPERTY RIGHTS cases. He joined narrow liberal majorities in the flag burning cases, *Texas v. Johnson* (1989) and *U.S. v. Eichman* (1990). In *R.A.V. v. City of St. Paul* (1992), Scalia wrote a broad majority opinion excoriating laws aimed at racist "hate speech." In *Lucas v. South Carolina Coast Council* (1992), he authored a landmark majority opinion, upholding "just compensation" for a property holder suffering a state government "taking" under the Fifth and Fourteenth Amendments. This opinion overruled many decades of case law justifying government expropriations of private property. Scalia encountered much less success discarding state decisions on abortion. In *Bush v. Gore* (2000), Scalia wrote a concurring opinion explaining why the Court stopped the Florida vote count, while also criticizing two of his concurring and four of his dissenting colleagues.

Further reading: Richard Brisbin, *Justice Antonin Scalia and the Conservative Revival* (Baltimore, Md.: Johns Hopkins University Press, 1997).

—Christopher M. Gray

Schlafly, Phyllis (1924–)

As a CONSERVATIVE MOVEMENT activist, author, and spokesperson for the "pro-family" movement and conservative cultural values, Phyllis Schlafly played a critical role in the transformation of the political right wing in America from isolated groups in the 1950s into a powerful movement that elected a president in 1980 and continues to exert considerable influence in local and national politics. As head of the Eagle Forum, a grassroots activist organization that promotes pro-family opinion, Schlafly continues to head a powerful grassroots movement of women involved in state and local politics. She has authored 11 books. Schlafly was instrumental in defeating ratification of the EQUAL RIGHTS AMENDMENT in 1982. Schlafly was born August 15, 1924, in Saint Louis, Missouri, and educated at the Convent of the Sacred Heart. Her father lost his job in 1930, and her mother, a librarian, had to support the family throughout the Depression. Schlafly grew up in a loving Roman Catholic family where she saw women treated with respect. She was valedictorian of her high school class and received a full scholarship to a local Catholic college but, believing she was not getting the education she needed, she transferred to Washington University in Saint Louis. To pay for tuition, she took a full-time night job in a local ordinance plant, testing ammunition. She graduated from Washington University in 1944, where she was admitted to Phi Beta Kappa, an honorary society. Following graduation, she accepted a graduate fellowship at Radcliffe College, where she earned an M.A. in government in 1945. (Later, at the age of 54, while heading the anti-ERA movement, she enrolled in law school and received a degree from Washington University.)

After leaving Radcliffe, she moved to Washington, D.C., where she worked at the American Enterprise Institute, and then returned to Saint Louis to manage at the age of 24 a successful campaign for a Republican congressional candidate in Saint Louis, while working full time as a research assistant and librarian at a local bank. In 1949, she was, as she later put it, "rescued from the life of a working girl" when she married 39-year-old-bachelor John F. Schlafly, scion of a prominent family in Saint Louis and a conservative Republican. After their move to Alton, Illinois, across the river from St. Louis, she became active in the YWCA and the Community Chest. They had six children in the following years.

While raising her family in Alton, Illinois, she became involved in local civic affairs, grassroots anticommunist education, and Republican politics. She ran for Congress in 1952 and 1970, as a conservative Republican, but lost both races. During these campaigns, reporters invariably referred to her as "the good-looking blonde candidate" or the "powder-puff candidate." She served as a delegate or alternate to Republican national conventions in 1956, 1960, and 1964, and ran for president of the National Federation of Republican Women in 1967, but was defeated in a hotly contested national election. She became a celebrity in 1964 with the publication of her best-selling book, *A Choice, Not an Echo,* in support of Republican BARRY GOLDWATER's candidacy for the presidency.

In the 1970s Schlafly gained further national attention for her active opposition to the Equal Rights Amendment (ERA), which declared, "Equality of rights under the law shall not be denied or abridged by the United States or by any State on account of sex." She founded and was chairperson of STOP ERA, and she was president of the Eagle Forum, a conservative political-activist organization. She argued that the ERA would force women into combat and mean the abolition of laws protecting women as workers and wives. While she did not deny that discrimination toward women occurred, she argued that legislation already on the books should be enforced to prevent illegal discrimination toward women. Furthermore, she argued that ERA would "liberate" husbands from obligations toward their wives and children. In addition, she maintained that ERA, if ratified, would allow abortion on demand. Feminists, she charged, wanted to "brainwash" women into believing that there was something wrong with being "just a housewife." She went on to say, "The claim that American women are downtrodden and unfairly treated is the fraud of the century," given the special status that women enjoyed in the United States compared with other countries in the world and with past history. While critics often accused her of being a hypocrite who wanted to keep women at home, while she built a successful career as a national spokesperson for conservative causes, Schlafly was not opposed to women working outside the home. After all her own mother had worked as a professional librarian. Instead, Schlafly argued that the primary responsibility of mothers should be toward their children and family, and not their professional careers.

Schlafly rallied opposition to the ERA and through years of hard work, speeches, and debates, the Equal Rights Amendment fell short of ratification in 1982. Schlafly was the single most influential person in preventing the ratification of the ERA. As Illinois Republican congressman Henry Hyde said, "Without her, I can say without a twinge of doubt, ERA would be part of the Constitution—unquestionably." Together with her Eagle Forum, she continues to crusade on the social issues of pornography and abortion, literacy, immigration reform, and big government.

See also ABORTION; CONSERVATIVE MOVEMENT; AMENDMENTS TO THE U.S. CONSTITUTION; EQUAL RIGHTS AMENDMENT.

Further reading: Carol Felsenthal, *The Sweetheart of the Silent Majority: The Biography of Phyllis Schlafly* (New York: Doubleday, 1981).

—Elizabeth A. Henke and Donald T. Critchlow

science and technology

Since the 1970s, personal technology has transformed America with what many have called a "COMPUTERS revolution." There were thousands of small electronic innovations that contributed to the technological advances in the 1970s and 1980s, but some of the most important arose from discoveries made in electricity and light.

In 1958 Jack Kilby invented the smaller, more durable "integrated circuit," and 13 years after that, Marcian E. Hoff combined hundreds of integrated circuits on small silicon "chips," which he called "microprocessors." These inventions serve as the basis for all subsequent computing and electronic technologies. During this same period, scientists at Columbia University invented the "maser" in 1954, which used ammonia to produce coherent microwave radiation. In 1960 Theodore H. Maiman, of Hughes Research Laboratories, built the first laser (Light Amplification by Stimulated Emission of Radiation). Lasers have since been adapted and enhanced for a multitude of applications, including nuclear physics, MEDICINE, guidance systems, and mass storage. By the 1970s, the basic components were ready for a technological revolution in home appliances, information processing, and communication.

By the 1960s many consumers already had high-fidelity phonograph systems, but by the 1970s the list of common electronic equipment included magnetic tape–based eight-track and cassette decks, transistor-based stereo receivers, color televisions, and digital alarm-clock radios. Sony introduced the first Betamax home-use VCR in 1975, which inspired JVC to introduce the competing VHS format a year later. As prices dropped, the units became so widespread that the SUPREME COURT was called in to decide on whether home recordings of televised programming constituted a copyright violation; in *Sony v. Universal* (1984), they held that it did not.

The prevalence of electronics in the home encouraged a similar trend in specialty appliances for the family kitchen; Mr. Coffee introduced the first automatic drip coffee maker in 1972. Though Percy Spencer, of Raytheon Corporation, invented the Radar Range microwave in 1946, it was not until 1967 that Amana introduced the first countertop model for home use. By 1975, sales of microwave ovens exceeded the sale of gas ranges, to become, by the end of the decade, more commonly owned than dishwashers. Throughout the 1980s and 1990s, appliances based on microprocessor chips appeared for the American home, including compact disk (CD) players, introduced in 1982, and digital video disk (DVD) players in 1997. Other common devices include analog and digital video cameras, 5.1-channel Dolby Surround Sound speaker systems, and satellite cable connections. Digital thermostats, smoke and carbon dioxide detectors, and alarm systems have transformed even the home's infrastructure. Many of these advances are only decades old, and yet most have become so common that few Americans notice their presence.

Advances in information processing first developed in the late 1960s among government agencies and large corporate BUSINESSES; computers often filled entire rooms and required large staffs of programmers to operate. By the 1980s, however, personal computers entered the home, and by 2000 more than half of American households owned at least one. The first home computer, the Altair 8800, was sold through hobby magazines starting in January 1975. Two years later, Stephen Wozniak and Steve Jobs introduced the Apple II computer, which legend says they first built in Wozniak's garage. In 1981 IBM introduced the IBM PC (for personal computer), which was so successful that the computer industry adopted the PC moniker and it became the generalized term for all subsequent computers, no matter who produced them. New companies arose to augment existing computing systems with peripherals that have since become standard attachments, including the hard disk drive system, graphics and sound cards, inkjet and laser printers, and combination fax and modem cards.

Throughout the 1980s, the rate of innovation in computing technology grew so fast that many consumers feared purchasing lest their model become obsolete before year's end. The resulting struggle for common standards forced some of the initial pioneers of home computing, like Tandy, Commodore, and Texas Instruments, to redesign their product lines to ensure 100 percent IBM compatibility, because consumers relied on the PC standard to judge the quality of their software and hardware purchases. Despite these fast changes, some standards emerged based on the Microsoft Windows operation system and the Intel-compatible microprocessor. Apple computers remained the only significant alternative, with a market share hovering between 3 and 5 percent. The consolidation of standards made the introduction of new peripherals much easier, and by 2000, common peripherals included rewritable CD and DVD players, full-page color scanners, video-capture cards, and digital cameras. With so many options for capturing information, in the 21st century there will be very little that will pass undocumented.

The prevalence of home computers during the 1980s paved the way for similar advances in communication. Bell Laboratories invented fiber optics in 1977, when it experiment with thin strands of glass to transmit pulses of light between telephone exchange centers. Fiber optic connections permit digital transmission with greater bandwidth at much faster rates than traditional analog connections. Though telephone companies installed fiber optic connections throughout the 1980s, private consumer demand remained limited because there was little need for large

Satellite dishes and the satellites they communicate with have revolutionized the flow of information around the world. *(Boyle/Getty Images)*

bandwidth at home. This changed, however, after the World Wide Web (WWW) was released over the Internet in 1991.

Though the entry of powerful personal computers during the 1980s made private access to these networks more feasible, the lack of simple navigation software inhibited widespread public access. The situation improved, however, when Tim Berners-Lee developed information management software called the World Wide Web, while working at Conseil Européen pour la Recherche Nucléaire (CERN). It stored information using random associations called "links," based on Hyper Text Markup Language (HTML), to provide an easier and more systematic way of accessing the various information threads over the Internet. The following year, Marc Andreessen, a 22-year-old student at the University of Illinois, developed the Mosaic browser, which attached a graphical interface to the Web, allowing visitors to navigate using a few mouse clicks. Shortly thereafter, the popular version, called Netscape Navigator, was released to the public creating an immediate demand for Internet access.

In 1992 there were only 50 pages on the Internet; by 1993 the number had grown to 341,000, and within three years, the number of pages had grown so great that accurate figures were no longer possible. The consumer demand for Internet access produced an equally great demand for faster communication from home, including fiber optic connections and even cable and satellite options. Americans quickly grew accustomed to instant communication with relatives, friends, and colleagues around the world through e-mail, and later, through instant messaging.

Not surprisingly, the demand for portable communications grew by similar proportions. The Federal Communications Commission repealed restrictions on mobile phones in 1983, which allowed Bell Telephone to introduce the first one later in the year, though the high price initially restricted mobile phones to businesses. The 1996 Telecommunications Act deregulated local telephone service, opening the market to increasing competition between telephone providers. By 1995, 32 million Americans made up more than a third of the mobile phone users worldwide. By 2001, the number had increased to 115 million.

As personal technology becomes more common in American homes, the size of the nation and the world appears to shrink. When Boeing introduced the 747 jumbo jet on January 21, 1970, observers reacted with a mixture of confidence and awe at the extent of human achievement; the *New York Times* wrote, "The 747 will make it possible for more and more people to discover what their neighbors are like on the other side of the world." The new jet could travel 4,600 nautical miles without refueling and could carry 490 people, almost four times that of its closest rival, the Boeing 707. It also forced existing airports to modernize their runway and terminals to accommodate the giant aircraft, which had the positive effect of improving safety throughout the airline industry. Unfortunately, the jumbo jet also made accidents much more tragic; one of the worst aviation disasters in history occurred when two 747s collided on a runway on March 27, 1977, killing more than 570 people. Despite these singular incidents, air travel remains the safest form of transportation in the United States, and the 747 significantly improved traffic between coasts and overseas; it also provided farmers and manufacturers with a fast alternative to trucking, thereby expanding their available market base to a global scale. Though the basic style of the jumbo jets has remained unchanged since 1970, the interior has been routinely adapted to reflect the advances in information processing and communication. By 2000, most American jets included telephones and entertainment consoles for each passenger.

More traditional forms of transportation have tried to maintain relative parity with airlines. Though the United States has lagged far behind European and Asian nations in its high-speed railroads, automobiles have benefited greatly from the computing revolution. As early as 1966, William Lear, founder of the Lear Jet Aviation Company, invented the eight-track tape deck as an option in luxury cars. By the mid-1980s automobile electronics expanded far beyond the stereo system. As fuel efficiency became a growing concern for consumers, most cars included microprocessors to regulate fuel management and suspension systems. Later innovations included computer-monitored airbags, digital speedometers, and complex alarm systems. In 1996, Cadillac introduced the OnStar system, which provided motorists with remote access to their vehicle, emergency roadside assistance, and a computerized navigation system that used Global Positioning System (GPS) technology to pinpoint the vehicle's exact location. By 2000, CD players, keyless entry, and automatic door lifts became common options, while some minivans included miniature televisions, with VCR and DVD players, and laser-guided reverse warning systems. Though no company has introduced a driverless automobile, many of the necessary components are already in production.

One of the most directly relevant applications of computing technology occurred in the field of medicine. Computer-aided microscopes with attached robotic lasers that cut with near-cellular precision enabled physicians in the 1990s to successfully perform surgery on neonatal arteries the size of a toothpick. In 2001 AbioCor used microprocessors with long-lasting power sources in the first fully contained artificial heart, which Dr. Gary Laman of Jewish Hospital in Louisville, Kentucky, implanted in Robert Tools; its success promises a future where artificial organs will be cheaper and more commonly used. Researchers involved in nanotechnology work with tiny machines that can be as small as three atoms wide; some of the projected applications include projects involving information gleaned from the complete map of the human genome, which might enable scientists to develop a direct interface between computer technology and human biology. The prospect of cybernetic organs or "intelligent" plastic surgery promises to expand the lifespan of humans.

Some technology advocates hope that science will provide solutions for some ancient social problems, such as disease, old age, poverty, and even crime. Others, however, are not as optimistic; some religious leaders fear that an influx of technology, without an equivalent emphasis on philosophical and religious values, may result in a breakdown of familial and personal relationships, which form the basis for civic responsibility. Other social critics worry that the continuous introduction of new technology creates an artificial demand that only encourages a materialistic society. One point, however, seems clear—the true impact of the computer revolution will not be fully understood for many decades to come.

See also COMPUTERS; HUMAN GENOME PROJECT; INTERNET; SPACE POLICY.

Further reading: Edward Nathan Singer, *20th Century Revolutions in Technology* (Boston, Mass.: Nova Science Publishers, 1998); Charles Flowers, *A Science Odyssey: 100 Years of Discovery* (New York: Morrow, 1998).

—Aharon W. Zorea

Senate, U.S.

Since 1968 the U.S. Senate as an institution has become increasingly partisan and given less to reform than the U.S. HOUSE OF REPRESENTATIVES. In the period from 1968 through 2002, neither major party has held control for an extended period. Procedural reforms in the Senate were less far-reaching than in the House, because the Senate was already more accessible and less structured.

The most important reform in the Senate centered on the filibuster. Unlimited debate is a method used by senators to obstruct legislation. Under Senate rules, a filibuster could be ended by a vote of two-thirds of the members present. In 1975 this was changed to two-thirds of the full Senate. A second reform was on post-cloture filibusters (after the Senate has voted to end a filibuster), which had been used to get around the 1975 rules had tried to reform the use of a filibuster. The Senate also adopted a new ethics code.

The 1970s saw each party change its leadership. Democratic majority leader Mike Mansfield (D-Mont.) and Republican minority leader Hugh Scott (R-Pa.) each announced their retirement in 1977. Succeeding Mansfield was ROBERT BYRD (D-W.V.) and succeeding Scott was Howard Baker (R-Tenn.). Both men effectively downplayed their individual political views and succeeded at bringing the parties to a common ground through persuasion. Bipartisanship flourished in the Senate.

In 1980 the Republicans gained control of the Senate, and Baker and Byrd exchanged places. Initially the Republicans fell into line behind RONALD W. REAGAN's policies, and many conservative Democrats crossed the aisle to support the Republicans. By 1982, moderate Republicans and Democrats began to rebel against further cuts in social programs and the growing budget deficit. In 1983, despite a Republican majority, the Senate Budget Committee passed a Democratic-inspired budget plan calling for $30 billion in new taxes.

The difficulties experienced by Baker in exercising leadership were in part due to the Senate's composition. Virtually every member was a leader—89 percent were chairmen or ranking members of a committee or subcommittee. Baker retired in 1985 and was replaced by ROBERT DOLE (R-Kans.). Dole proved to be a charismatic and resourceful leader. Using a combination of negotiation, compromise, arm-twisting, and humor, he brought competing interests into line. Dole gained passage for a 1985 budget that would reduce the deficit by cutting both defense and domestic spending. Dole oversaw the passage of the GRAMM-RUDMAN-HOLLINGS ACT. He also helped to gain authorization for televising the Senate proceedings.

The Democrats regained control of the Senate in 1986. The new Democratic Senate witnessed some sharp partisan divisions over appointments and legislation. In 1987 the nomination of ROBERT BORK to the Supreme Court led to a lengthy debate on Bork's philosophy before he was rejected. In 1991 the nomination of Clarence Thomas created more controversy, as Anita Hill accused Thomas of sexually harassing her years before.

Majority Leader George Mitchell (D-Maine) instituted a number of "quality of life" reforms after he replaced Byrd. Mitchell limited late-night sessions, scheduled no roll call votes after 7 P.M., except on Thursdays. Most votes were scheduled for the middle of the week, so senators could visit their home districts. Mitchell continued the practice begun by Byrd—scheduling Senate sessions for three weeks with the fourth week off so members could tend to home-state business.

The Senate was not immune to the ethics scandals that plagued the House. Senator Harrison Williams (D-N.J.) resigned his seat in 1982 in the face of an expulsion threat after a federal grand jury found him guilty of bribery and conspiracy. The Senate reprimanded Dave Durenburger (R-Minn.) in 1990 for attempting to exceed honoraria limits. Overshadowing Durenburger was the "Keating Five." The five were senators who had used improper influence on behalf of savings and loan executive Charles Keating. The senators—Alan Cranston (D-Calif.), Dennis DeConcini (R-Ariz.), John Glenn (D-Ohio), Donald Riegle (D-Mich.), and John McCain (R-Ariz.)—were accused of acting after receiving $1.3 million in campaign contributions from Keating. In 1991 the Ethics Committee exonerated all but Cranston who was formally reprimanded. Later, two senators faced accusations of sexual misconduct—Brock Adams (D-Wash.) and Bob Packwood (R-Oreg.).

In 1994 the Republicans regained control of the Senate. Bob Dole resumed his mantle of majority leader. The Senate never endorsed the "Contract with America" and was less than enthusiastic about the tactics of the House Republicans. Dole resisted the Republican euphoria, but eventually succumbed to pressure to take advantage of the House victories. In 1996, Dole resigned from the Senate after winning the Republican presidential nomination. Dole lost to WILLIAM J. CLINTON in 1996, but the Republicans gained two seats. This margin was maintained in 1998.

The new majority leader became Trent Lott (R-Miss.). In 1999 the Senate sat in judgment of an impeached president. Forced to deal with the House's actions, the Senate was sworn to impartiality in January 1999. In February the Senate acquitted Clinton on all charges.

After the 2000 election the Senate was evenly split. With Vice President Dick Cheney able to cast the deciding vote, the Republicans retained control of the Senate until James Jeffords (R-V.) left the Republican Party and declared himself an Independent, closely aligned with the Democrats. As a result, Tom Daschle (D-S.D.) became head of the Senate. This intensified partisanship in the Senate and imparted greater influence to the moderate Republican wing. The terrorist destruction of the World Trade Center and attack on the Pentagon in September 2001 appeared to lessen partisanship, but it soon revived over legislation and judicial appointments in the closely divided body.

Further reading: Congressional Quarterly, *Guide to Congress* (Washington, D.C.: Government Printing Office, 2000).

—John Korasick

sexual revolution

During the 1960s a sexual revolution occurred in the United States that reshaped Americans' understanding of sexuality, the acceptance of artificial contraception and premarital sex, and the increased visibility of the gay and lesbian community. These trends combined to cultivate a wide-ranging ethic of sexual pleasure by further complicating the relationship between sexuality and reproduction, pleasure, and identity.

Sexual behavior became more associated with pleasure than with reproduction. Growing access to BIRTH CONTROL reinforced the message that sex and reproduction were not necessarily connected. By the early 1950s a significant number of women used the diaphragm, the method most widely recommended by birth control advocates. The availability of oral contraceptives in 1960, and the U.S. SUPREME COURT's decision that legalized the sale of contraceptives nationwide in *Griswold v. Connecticut* in 1965 precipitated a contraceptive revolution. By the 1970s, the birth control pill, diaphragms, voluntary sterilization, and, in 1973, legalized ABORTION were widely available to most women regardless of race or class.

Another development that brought the ethic of pleasure into prominence was the youth rebellion of the late 1960s. As the baby boomers filled the college campuses, they fomented a COUNTERCULTURE centered on cultural radicalism, political and social protest, and a challenge to traditional sexual mores. They joined the Civil Rights and ANTIWAR MOVEMENTS and advocated such practices as the distribution of contraceptives by university health services and the institution of coed dorms. Some young Americans rallied around their guru, Timothy Leary, a Harvard University research psychologist, who promoted a drug-oriented, sexually free, and antimaterialistic lifestyle. A clear manifestation of the relationship between youth and the ethic of sexual pleasure occurred in August 1969 when several hundred thousand young adults gathered near WOODSTOCK, New York, for a three-day festival to enjoy popular music, drugs, nudity, and sexual encounters. The reorientation of sexual attitudes also found expression on Broadway, where musicals such as *Hair* and *Oh! Calcutta* that contained nudity and sexually explicit language proved hugely popular.

The increased visibility of the gay and lesbian community during the 1960s and into the 1990s contributed to the restructuring of American sexuality in two ways. First, it underscored the message of the contraceptive revolution that sex was not necessarily linked to reproduction. More important, the homosexual community legitimated the possibility of constructing an identity predicated on one's sexual preferences rather than just one's race, class, or gender. In the 1950s public displays of homosexuality were repressed, and in many states homosexual sexual relations were illegal. Some gays and lesbians actively resisted the discrimination that threatened their livelihood and even their lives. Gay men formed the Mattachine Society and lesbians formed the Daughters of Bilitis. With the Civil Rights movement in the 1960s, some gays began demanding equal rights and treatment. In the summer of 1969, patrons of the Stonewall Inn, a gay bar in Greenwich Village, resisted a police raid and touched off demonstrations in New York City. The Stonewall Riot, as it became known, served as the touchstone for the GAY RIGHTS MOVEMENT that received much media attention and made "coming out of the closet" a more realistic possibility for many homosexuals.

The contraceptive revolution and the emergence of the gay and lesbian community as a powerful cultural force emphasized the declining power of the reproductive ideal. Concurrently, the mass media stepped up its promotion of the ethic of sexual pleasure and desire and helped make sexuality a central component of public discourse. Advertisers used sexual images and innuendo to sell their products. In the late 1960s MOVIES showed nudity and couples having sexual relations, although these depictions were not graphic. In the wake of the sexual revolution, the sex industry expanded enormously, with PORNOGRAPHY entering the realm of mainstream entertainment during the 1970s with such films as *Deep Throat* (1972) and *Behind the Green Door* (1973). In the 1980s and 1990s videotape and the INTERNET helped make pornography a multibillion-dollar industry. TELEVISION programs also became increasingly explicit. In the 1970s television programs showed couples sleeping in the same bed. By the 1990s, such prime-time shows as *NYPD Blue* contained glimpses of partial nudity, and virtually all prime-time shows were rife with sexual innuendo.

In the 1960s and 1970s sexual manuals appeared on the best-seller lists. Such titles as *The Sensuous Man* and *The Sensuous Woman* were sold in significant numbers. By the end of the 20th century, most women's magazines contained some information on how to improve one's sex life in virtually every issue.

The emergence of the ethic of sexual pleasure from the sexual revolution of the 1960s seriously complicated the question of transgression. Much of what Americans had previously considered immoral, illegal, or abnormal, late 20th-century Americans viewed as acceptable or even desirable. American society began to celebrate the public expression of sexuality and the boundaries of acceptable sexual behavior expanded well beyond marriage and reproduction. The AIDS epidemic of the 1980s helped rein in the unmitigated pursuit of sexual pleasure and forced the drawing of ethical lines for those who subscribed to the pleasure ideal. This applied not only to the gay and lesbian communities, who, with intravenous drug users, experienced the terrors of AIDS first, but to all sexually active Americans. Although some moralists claimed that AIDS was divine retribution for the sin of homosexuality and sexual promiscuity, this view was not widely accepted. Gays and lesbians, however, focused on the responsibility they had to one another and mobilized to care for those who had contracted the disease and to increase awareness of the disease among mainstream American society. Within the context of the pleasure ideal and the specter of sexually transmitted diseases, transgression was defined as failing to care for oneself or for one's partner. A cross section of American society, from college students to the federal government, initiated efforts to educate sexually active Americans about the importance of using protection and being responsible to their partners.

Largely as a result of the sexual revolution of the 1960s and of the continued evolution of Americans' understanding of sexuality, the meaning of sexuality and the parameters of sexual behavior continued to be the focus of highly contentious debate. Americans disagreed, essentially, about the relationship between sexuality and reproduction, identity, and pleasure. Through the legal system, the media, and sometimes by violence, Americans attempted to promote their particular view on issues such as abortion, homosexual marriage, and pornography. America's diversity necessarily produced ambivalence about sexuality that continued to exist alongside the traditional, but still present, uneasiness with sexuality. It is true that at the end of the 20th century sexual imagery was pervasive in American public discourse, a fact that presents a distorted image of American culture as "oversexed." However, sexuality in behavior, and in its representation, continues to be regulated and controlled, thus creating a conflicted environment in which *NYPD Blue*, a popular television show, is more criticized for portraying sexual intercourse between two people in a relationship than for very graphically depicting a police officer being shot in the head. If any conclusion can be made, it is that the sexual revolution enabled an explosion of discourse about sexuality that has catapulted the debate over sexual attitudes and behavior into one of the most prominent positions in American culture and society.

See also ADVERTISING; BIRTHRATES; CENSORSHIP; FEMINISM; MORAL MAJORITY; WOMEN'S RIGHTS AND STATUS.

Further reading: John D'Emilio and Estelle Freedman, *Intimate Matters: A History of Sexuality in America*, rev. ed. (Chicago: University of Chicago Press, 1997); Sharon Ullman, *Sex Seen: The Emergence of Modern Sexuality in America* (Berkeley: University of California Press, 1997).

—William L. Glankler

Shriver, Robert Sargent, Jr. (1915–   )

Sargent Shriver is best known for his work in the Lyndon Johnson administration and its War on Poverty, and his selection as a vice presidential candidate for the Democratic Party in 1972.

Shriver was born in Westminster, Maryland, in 1915. A graduate of Yale University (1938) and Yale Law School (1941), Shriver went on to serve in World War II as a naval officer. Shriver briefly worked as an editorial assistant at *Newsweek* magazine after concluding his military career. He then joined the management of the Chicago Merchandise Mart, owned by Joseph P. Kennedy. In 1953 he married Eunice Kennedy, a sister of John F. Kennedy. The couple had five children.

Shriver was politically active, heading the National Conference on Prevention and Control of Juvenile Delinquency, in Washington, D.C., serving as president of the Chicago Board of Education, assisting his brother-in-law in his presidential campaign efforts. His most notable activities were his work with the Peace Corps, Volunteers in Service to America (VISTA), and Head Start. From 1961 to 1966, Shriver served as the organizer and first director of the Peace Corps, where he developed and coordinated volunteer activities in more than 50 countries in Latin America, Asia, and Africa. In 1964 Shriver created Head Start and VISTA, under President Lyndon Johnson's Great Society program. In 1972 Shriver was nominated by the Democratic Party as a candidate for vice president with Senator GEORGE S. MCGOVERN in the presidential race against RICHARD M. NIXON and SPIRO AGNEW. In 1994, President WILLIAM J. CLINTON awarded the Presidential Medal of Freedom to Shriver.

—Michele Rutledge

Souter, David (1939–   )

Justice Souter replaced retiring associate justice WILLIAM J. BRENNAN, JR., the liberal driving force on the WARREN E. BURGER and WILLIAM H. REHNQUIST Courts. Born in Melrose, Massachusetts, on September 17, 1939, Souter grew up in New Hampshire on a farm left to his parents by his grandparents. His father was a banker in Concord, New Hampshire, and there David Souter attended public school before entering Harvard University, where he would graduate magna cum laude in 1961. He received a Rhodes scholarship to Oxford University, and while there, he completed another B.A. and an M.A. degree. He returned to New Hampshire to take up private practice and become involved in civic affairs. In 1968 he was asked by the new state attorney general, Warren Rudman, to serve as his assistant, which he did from 1968 to 1976. When Rudman left the position, Souter was appointed state attorney general by Republican governor Meldrum Thompson. As attorney general, Souter opposed legalized gambling and protests at Seabrook, a local nuclear plant.

From 1978 to 1983 Souter served on the state superior court, before John Sununu appointed him to the state supreme court. In 1990 Souter was appointed to the U.S. Court of Appeals by GEORGE H. W. BUSH. Five months later, William J. Brennan, Jr. retired from the U.S. SUPREME COURT, and Souter was nominated for his seat. He was confirmed by the Senate on October 2, 1990, by a 90-9 vote.

From the outset, Souter assumed a moderate position on the Court. This was reflected in his first major decision, *Planned Parenthood of Southeastern Pennsylvania v. Casey* (1992). Writing with SANDRA DAY O'CONNOR and Anthony Kennedy, Souter's opinion permitted several state regulations on abortion to stand, but declined to overturn *ROE V. WADE*. His concurrence in *Stenberg v. Carhart* (2000), the so-called "partial birth abortion" case, reaffirmed his defense of abortion. In *Lee vs. Weisman* (1992), Souter was the swing vote resisting changes in public school prayer.

In other areas Souter gained a reputation for his independence. In 1992 he wrote the majority opinion for *Norman v. Reed,* invalidating on constitutional grounds portions of the Illinois election law that unduly burdened access to the ballot by new political parties. He also concurred with a decision in a capital case, concluding that information about a murder victim can be presented to a sentencing jury.

Until the election of 2000, O'Connor, Kennedy, and Souter formed what appeared to be a centrist block on the court, but in *Bush v. Gore* (2001), Souter joined the minority in the 5-4 decision ending the ballot count in Florida. Souter wrote a passionate dissent and in doing so, joined what most people perceive as the liberal block on the Court. This decision might prove to be this Court's legacy, as well as Souter's.

See also BUSH, GEORGE W.; GORE, ALBERT, JR.

—Christopher M. Gray

South Africa (U.S. relations with)

American relations with South Africa became a source of tremendous controversy in the 1970s and 1980s over the South African policy of apartheid. Apartheid was a policy of strict racial segregation imposed by the South African National Party after its election in 1948. Playing on the fears of the white minority of losing control to and being dominated by the black majority, the National Party narrowly defeated the less extreme United Party. Between 1949 and 1960 a series of laws were passed implementing apartheid, guaranteeing the separation of the races and limiting black mobility and associations.

The United States government tended to downplay apartheid in the 1950s and early 1960s. The South Africans were strongly anticommunist and possessed the most developed economy on the African continent. The United States took the position that apartheid was strictly a South African internal issue.

Following the SUPREME COURT decision in *Brown v. Board of Education* (1954), the apartheid issue in South Africa was less easy to ignore without giving the appearance that the United States was supporting the apartheid regime. By 1958, the United States began moving away from the position that apartheid was just a domestic issue. In the wake of the Sharpeville massacre in 1960, when South African police killed 69 antiapartheid protestors, the United States recalled its ambassador and for the first time participated in a UNITED NATIONS vote condemning the action.

During the RICHARD M. NIXON administration, a concerted effort was made to bring the nations closer. Nixon embraced the idea that closer relations would allow the United States to have more influence with the South African government concerning its racial policy than it could exert by isolating the nation. In addition, Nixon wanted to push aside racial concerns in favor of strategic and commercial concerns with international reach.

With the election of JAMES EARL CARTER, JR., in 1976, there was a significant shift in American policy from the COLD WAR to international human rights. Carter's ambassador to the UN, Andrew Young, hinted that sanctions against South Africa were a possibility and charged that the white minority government was illegitimate. In this increasingly hostile atmosphere, the death of Stephen Biko, a South African civil rights activist who was murdered in 1977 in police custody, moved the UN to impose an arms embargo on South Africa. While the United States supported this embargo, it did not sever commercial relations. As a result, an activist movement in the United States began demanding that American corporations and universities divest stock holding in South Africa. Carter continued to oppose mandatory economic sanctions on South Africa.

The election of RONALD W. REAGAN in 1980 resulted in yet another U.S. policy shift. Reagan's approach to South Africa was called "constructive engagement" and had four objectives: to encourage the abandonment of apartheid; to preserve American access to strategic minerals; secure the sea lanes; and counter communist activity in southern and central Africa, especially in Angola. American companies were encouraged to use their influence to improve conditions for blacks. In 1984 South Africa adopted constitutional changes granting political rights to Indians and

"Coloureds," citizens of mixed race. These reforms, however, did not address the central problem of the disenfranchisement of black Africans. The U.S. Congress called for sanctions and initiated legislation to impose economic sanctions. Public protests against South Africa demanded sanctions and divestment by American firms.

In mid-1985 Reagan, under congressional pressure, imposed limited sanctions—ending nuclear cooperation, banning new loans, and banning the export of computers and technology and the importation of South African gold coins. Further, American banks refused to roll over short-term loans to South Africa.

In 1986 Congress passed and overrode Reagan's veto of the Comprehensive Anti-Apartheid Act (CAAA). The CAAA imposed wide-ranging economic sanctions, banning new U.S. investment and trade. It required six actions from the South Africans to get the sanctions lifted—political prisoners must be freed, opposition parties legalized, and the state of emergency lifted; discriminatory legislation must be repealed; political freedom must be granted to blacks; and the government must enter into negotiations with black leaders to dismantle apartheid.

The end of the cold war in 1989, and the rise to power of the reform-minded South African president F. W. De Klerk, helped change the course of South African history. No longer could opposition parties like the African National Congress (ANC) be credibly charged with being communist fronts. In 1990, De Klerk released jailed ANC leader Nelson Mandela. He also legalized opposition groups and called for negotiations to end apartheid. U.S. president GEORGE H. W. BUSH lifted some of the CAAA sanctions in 1991 and began economic and development programs aimed at South African blacks to educate them to participate in a democracy. American policy during this period focused on keeping the negotiations on track.

President WILLIAM J. CLINTON maintained much of the Bush program. In November 1993 an agreement ending apartheid was reached, and Congress passed legislation repealing the remaining CAAA sanctions, and authorized further development assistance. In 1994 Mandela was elected president of South Africa in the nation's first all-race election. Clinton subsequently announced a three-year, $600 million aid package, giving South Africa more aid than all of the other African countries combined. By the later 1990s, South Africa had become an important American trading partner in Africa.

See also AFRICAN NATIONS.

Further reading: A. M. Thomas, *The American Predicament: Apartheid and United States Foreign Policy* (Brookfield, Mass.: Dartmouth Publishing Company, 1997); Kema Irogbe, *The Roots of United States Foreign Policy toward Apartheid South Africa, 1969–1985* (Lewiston, N.Y.: Edwin Mellon Press, 1997).

—John Korasick

Soviet Union (breakup)

The breakup of the Soviet Union, which had been established following the Bolshevik Revolution in 1917 and grew in subsequent years until World War II, occurred in 1991 under the strain of economic failure.

In 1985 Mikhail Gorbachev became general secretary of the Communist Party of the Soviet Union. He believed that his nation could no longer compete with the United States economically or militarily, due to the supremacy of U.S. technological abilities and the extremely poor condition of the Soviet economic system. Furthermore, he felt that the continuous military buildup of Soviet defenses had sapped the industrial and economic resources of the country. Gorbachev worked to reduce tensions with the United States and establish better relations with President RONALD W. REAGAN. The two superpower leaders met in autumn of 1985 in Geneva, Switzerland, with the expectations of defusing tensions between the two nations that had worsened in the last years of JAMES EARL CARTER, JR.'s administration and Reagan's first term in office.

Within the Soviet Union, Gorbachev proposed modest economic reforms to allow a rudimentary market economy to develop, while reducing government price subsidies on some basic goods. He called his plan to reinvigorate the Soviet economy "perestroika" (restructuring), which was meant to streamline production and management. Gorbachev also proclaimed a policy of GLASNOST (openness) by which he intended to allow Soviet citizens new rights of free speech.

At the same time, Gorbachev instituted economic change and decreased the Communist Party's control on the political system. Nonetheless, Soviet citizens continued to face soaring prices, unemployment, and a scarcity of goods. On August 19, 1991, a clique within the Soviet government attempted to oust him because the imminent signing of the Union Treaty promised to provide limited autonomy to the 15 Soviet republics.

Russian president Boris Yeltsin, a supporter of reform, called for mass resistance to the coup. Thousands of supporters rallied to his cause. The heads of the other republics also declared their support for Yeltsin and Gorbachev. By August 21, the coup had failed and the Communist Party's grip on the Soviet Union had ended. Citizens responded by tearing down statues of former Soviet leaders, including Lenin and Stalin.

By the end of 1991, the Soviet Union no longer existed. In its place was the Commonwealth of Independent States (comprising 12 republics of the former Soviet Union) and the 15 independent nations of Russia, Kazakhstan, Kyrgyzstan, Tajikistan, Uzbekistan, Azerbaijan, Armenia, Georgia, Ukraine, Moldova, Belarus, Turkmenistan, Lithuania, Latvia, and Estonia.

After the collapse of the Soviet Union, it became obvious that its economy was in even worse shape than formerly believed. Conversion from the state-controlled market to a free-market economy proved to be difficult. Leaders of all the new independent nations turned to the West for economic assistance. The United States and its Western allies responded slowly to the requests and sent money and experts to help ease the transition, but corruption, bureaucratic regulations, and economic inefficiency prevented quick or easy recovery.

See also BUSH, GEORGE W.; FOREIGN RELATIONS.

—Leah Blakey

space policy

The United States first developed its space program during the COLD WAR with the goal of promoting military technology, while also reinforcing public confidence in the superiority of American SCIENCE AND TECHNOLOGY. After the United States won the space race, however, the program gradually evolved from a military application into a more civilian-oriented, commercial enterprise.

The American space program started after President Dwight D. Eisenhower signed the National Space Act on July 29, 1958, creating the National Aeronautics and Space Administration (NASA). Throughout the decade of the 1960s, NASA received almost $35 billion in funding for the purpose of safely transporting a manned vehicle to the Moon and back. By the 1970s, the influx of resources created five program offices within NASA, including: Aeronautics and Space Technology, which develops necessary equipment; Space and Science Applications, which researches the origin, structure, and evolution of the universe; Space Flight, which includes direction of all manned and unmanned space transportation; Space Tracking and Data, which gathers information on existing space objects; and Space Station, which facilitates NASA's long-term goal of a manned space station. With its headquarters in Washington, D.C., NASA has affiliated programs at the Goddard Space Flight Center (Greenbelt, Maryland), Jet Propulsion Laboratory (Pasadena, California), Lyndon B. Johnson Space Center (Houston, Texas), Kennedy Space Center (Cape Canaveral, Florida), and Langley Research Center (Hampton, Virginia).

The Apollo space program began in 1966 as the final phase of NASA's race to the Moon. Though the first Apollo mission resulted in three fatalities after a malfunction on the launch pad, the 11th mission succeeded in sending Neil Armstrong and Edwin "Buzz" Aldrin to the Moon's surface in July 1969. Over the six years of the Apollo program, NASA sent 17 missions into space, six of which successfully landed on the Moon, during which 12 men actually touched the surface. After its goals had been achieved, and American superiority demonstrated in that field, the increasingly large collection of moon rocks no longer seemed to justify the massive expense of each launch, and the Apollo program ended after its final mission in December 1972. Federal funding for NASA dropped as a percentage of the federal budget every year until 1987; the largest cuts came immediately following Armstrong's successful leap for mankind.

Critics charged the space program with being an expensive symbol of cold war braggadocio, which diverted federal funds from necessary social programs. Supporters replied that NASA and the space program represented America's commitment to scientific discovery, which influenced the values of modern society. By the mid-1960s, 80 percent of all funding came from government research and development sources, 90 percent of which are devoted to the Department of Defense, NASA, and the Atomic Energy Commission. The operations budget of NASA doubled every year between 1959 and 1964, reaching a peak in 1966 with a budget of $5.93 billion, which was almost 6 percent of the federal budget. Other major powers like China, Japan, France, and especially the Soviet Union tried to approximate American spending levels even though their gross national products (GNP) were significantly less. The result was a major leap forward in science and technology not only in the United States but also for the world in general.

Society has benefited from the direct products of space technology, such as telecommunication satellites, advanced Doppler radar for meteorological forecasting, global positioning systems, and the vastly improved accuracy of digital mapping. Society also benefits from the spill-over technologies that arise when private corporations use the technical discoveries they learned from fulfilling government contracts and apply them to other, related innovations with strictly commercial applications; for example, medical researchers now use the techniques NASA developed to extract data from satellite images. In addition, private corporations routinely sell and rely on freeze-dried foods, which were originally developed for the Apollo program, while the protective insulation used by super tankers carrying liquefied natural gas came from technology used in the Saturn V launch vehicle.

NASA responded to budget cuts of the 1970s by focusing on other areas of exploration that were not so closely tied to cold war competition, including developing unmanned space probes, a space station, and a reusable space shuttle. NASA's probes stimulated public interest by investigating science fiction's most popular planet; starting

Billows of steam and smoke rise as space shuttle *Endeavor* lifts off at Kennedy Space Center, Florida. *(NASA/Newsmakers)*

in 1972, the Mariner program sent numerous probes past Mars to map out and investigate the planet's surface, resulting in the transmission of more than 7,000 surprisingly clear pictures. By 1975, the Viking program sent two satellites accompanied by remote landers, which descended to the surface to take soil samples and panoramic photographs that were relayed back to Earth from the orbiting satellites. At the same time, the Pioneer and Voyager programs' probes went beyond the red planet to study Jupiter, Saturn, Neptune, and Uranus. *Pioneer X* became the first spacecraft to travel beyond the asteroid belt, and after 12 years in space, *Voyager II* became the first man-made object to leave the solar system in 1989. *Pioneer X*'s weak signal continues to be tracked, and *Voyager II* is expected to continue transmitting data until 2025.

Not all NASA projects, however, were as successful as these programs. *Skylab,* the first American space station, was launched in 1973 and eventually housed nine astronauts over three missions during a 10-month period. After February 1974, the $2.9 billion *Skylab* remained vacant for five years until it prematurely fell into a decaying orbit, which the onboard boosters failed to correct. To NASA's great embarrassment, the station fell into a sparsely populated region of western Australia after only six years in orbit.

NASA's most successful program, the space shuttle, received its first funding in 1972 when President RICHARD M. NIXON signed a bill providing a $5.5 billion six-year commitment. Originally, the shuttle was intended to serve as an auxiliary to the space station by providing a relatively inexpensive form of transportation to the Earth's high atmosphere, but *Skylab* had already crashed two years before the shuttle's first launch in 1981. The space shuttle program eventually outgrew *Skylab* to become the pride of NASA; the agency built six shuttles over a 10-year period, including *Enterprise, Columbia, Challenger, Endeavor, Atlantis,* and *Discovery.* In 1986, after 24 successful missions, however, the space shuttle *Challenger* exploded, killing all seven passengers on board, including Sharon McAuliffe, who was the first civilian passenger to ride into space. The explosion stunned the public; NASA had not suffered any casualties since the *Apollo 1* mission in 1966, and the public had largely taken the risks of space travel for granted. The immediate effect was a general halt to all future shuttle missions until NASA determined the causes for the explosion and implemented necessary safeguards to prevent it from occurring again. As a result, the space program remained in relative stasis for two years while it reassessed its position.

At the same time, however, the possibility that budget cuts may have led to the tragedy forced Congress to reconsider its funding allocation; though NASA has yet to even come close to the budgets it enjoyed during the 1960s, the agency received significant increases relative to the total budget for every year between 1987 and 1993, bringing funding back to the same relative position it had in 1975.

During the 1990s, NASA refocused its energies toward a more cost-effective exploration of the solar system, in cooperation with nations around the world, including its former competitor, Russia. On one of the first missions after the explosion, the *Galileo* craft hitched a ride on the space shuttle *Atlantis* before beginning its trip to Jupiter, where it arrived in 1995 and transmitted hundreds of thousands of pictures before being deliberately plunged into the Jovian atmosphere in 1999. In 1990, the *Hubble Space Telescope* was set in orbit 370 miles above Earth, where it takes pictures of the universe without the distorting effects of the Earth's atmosphere. After an initial flaw in the optics was repaired in 1993, *Hubble* amazed the scientific community with its clear images. NASA upgraded the telescope in 2000, and plans to launch the "*Next Generation* space telescope" in 2008. In 1997 NASA deployed the *Mars Pathfinder* mission as part of its Discovery program aimed at providing faster and less expensive exploration missions. The lander, which was named *Sojourner,* was developed and produced for a 10th of the cost of its predecessors from the Mariner and Viking programs; the lander sent back 16,000 images over a three-month period, which helped reinvigorate public support for NASA. Unfortunately, in 1999 both vehicles in the *Mars Surveyor* were lost in space; including the *Deep Space 2* probes and the *Mars Polar Lander* (December); the *Mars Climate Orbiter* (September) failed when engineers forgot to properly convert specifications from English to metric units.

Other programs, including the Deep Space I, Lunar Prospector, and the Mars Global Surveyor were successful, and NASA still has plans for several manned missions to Mars during the first decade of the 21st century. NASA's greatest achievement, however, has been the *International Space Station,* which it developed in cooperation with Russia, Canada, Japan, and 11 members of the European Space Agency. Conceived in 1983, the station underwent numerous design changes; the final station will weigh a million pounds, extend 100 yards in length with an internal volume roughly that of a Boeing 747 jumbo jet. It is expected to cost $98 billion over 15 years of construction. The first modules were launched by the United States and Russia in 1998. The station's six laboratories are expected to serve as a platform for scientific experiments and space research.

See also ARMS RACE; COLD WAR; COMPUTERS; SCIENCE AND TECHNOLOGY.

Further reading: Walter McDougall, *The Heavens and Earth: A Political History of the Space Age* (Baltimore, Md.: Johns Hopkins University Press, 1997).

—Aharon W. Zorea

sports

The history of professional sports in the United States since 1969 is a story of further expansion, commercialization, entertainment, and celebrity, thanks mainly to the role played by TELEVISION.

Professional baseball is the oldest organized sport in America, dating to 1867. Major League Baseball, composed of the National League and the American League, expanded from 20 teams in 1962 to 30 teams in 1998, two of which play in Canadian cities, Montreal and Toronto. Another change occurred in 1970, when voting for players in the annual All-Star game was restored to the fans. Little changed in the functioning of the leagues until 1994 when the two leagues were reconfigured into three divisions —the Eastern, Central, and Western Divisions. This prompted a new playoff format in 1995 that consisted of the three division winners in each league and a wild card team, a team other than the division winners with the best record. Two playoff series would be held in each league to determine the representative that would play in the World Series, baseball's national championship.

The most significant change in professional baseball occurred because of the increasing revenue generated by the sport for the team owners. Early in the sport's history, owners created a "reserve clause" that prevented players from freely moving from team to team, to the highest bidder. This clause remained in effect until 1973 when the Players Association, the players' trade union, negotiated an agreement with the team owners that allowed veteran players of six years or more to become "free agents" by not signing a new contract during the final year of their current contract. Free agency led to dramatic increases in player salaries with the average increasing from $45,000 in 1975 to $450,000 in 1988. By the end of the 20th century, players like Mannie Ramirez and Alex Rodriguez commanded salaries in excess of $100 million over the term of their contract. High salaries, guaranteed contracts, and no-trade clauses became common throughout professional baseball and made baseball players the highest paid professional athletes.

While helping the players enormously, the exorbitant salaries damaged baseball's popularity. Players' strikes in 1980, 1981, and 1985 and an owners' lockout in 1990, combined with the demand for increasingly higher salaries, caused many fans and sports writers to complain. Rebounding popularity was dashed by the players' strike in mid-August of 1994 that caused the cancellation of the World Series for the first time since 1904. Fan support began to return in 1995 when Cal Ripken, Jr., broke Lou Gehrig's streak of consecutive games played and rebounded further in 1998 as fans watched Mark McGwire break Roger Maris's record of 61 home runs in a single season. Baseball continued to draw large crowds, although fan support varied. In 1969 professional baseball stadiums drew 27 million fans (1.1 million per team); in the 1999 season professional baseball drew 70 million fans to its games or 2.3 million per team. In addition, baseball was watched by millions on network and cable television channels like ESPN or Fox Sports Net, except on Saturday when the Fox network broadcast one game.

Professional football increased continuously in popularity since 1969, growing in stadium attendance from 9.5 million in 1970 to 16.4 million in 2000. The National Football League (NFL), founded in 1922, enjoyed enormous growth during the last four decades of the 20th century, thanks in large part to the efforts of its commissioner, Pete Rozelle, who served in that capacity from 1960 until 1989. Under his tutelage, professional football became America's most popular spectator sport and franchises that once cost $100 were worth millions by the late 1960s. During the 1960s, the NFL experienced stiff competition from the American Football League (AFL) for television contracts and player talent. In 1966, the merger of the two leagues was announced and became official in 1970 under the name of the NFL. The new league contained 26 teams divided into two 13-team conferences, the American Football Conference and the National Football Conference. In an effort to curtail skyrocketing player salaries, the league instituted a draft of college players. They also started a national championship game in 1967, renamed the Super Bowl in 1969. The NFL expanded to 28 teams in 1976 and to 30 in 1995.

The NFL's reign over professional football was challenged in the 1970s by the World Football League (WFL) which began competition in 1974. The WFL experienced widespread financial difficulties and disbanded in 1975. Another challenger appeared in 1983. The United States Football League (USFL) began with 12 teams and offered competition during the spring and summer months. In 1986, the USFL announced plans for a fall-winter season to compete directly with the NFL. In an antitrust suit filed by the USFL, a federal court found the NFL to be a monopoly, but awarded the USFL only one dollar in damages. This defeat-in-victory, along with the league's existing financial difficulties, forced the USFL to suspend operations in 1986.

Professional football experienced criticism similar to baseball's regarding high player salaries. Despite this, professional football remains the most popular spectator sport in the country. On any weekend during the football season, there are at least five games broadcast on the major networks and ESPN between Sunday afternoon and Monday night. Players command multimillion-dollar salaries, although not as high as baseball players', and receive lucrative contracts from advertisers to endorse a variety of products. The Super Bowl telecast commands in excess of $200 million per spot for advertising.

While not nearly as popular as either baseball or football, professional basketball enjoys great popularity and its players, as well, command multimillion-dollar salaries and endorsement contracts. The National Basketball Association (NBA) formed in 1949 with 17 teams. By the early 1960s, the NBA had franchises from coast to coast, annual attendance exceeded 3 million, and star players earned $100,000 or more. The American Basketball Association (ABA), formed in 1967, and merged with the NBA in 1976, creating a 22-team NBA. By 1985 there were 23 franchises, an 82-game regular season, a lengthy playoff series, and a national championship. Also, players earned an average salary of $300,000 and many had multimillion-dollar contracts. Yet NBA attendance failed to experience the growth of other professional sports, even though the association expanded. By 1995 the NBA consisted of 29 teams, including two Canadian teams, in Toronto and Vancouver. In 1980, average game attendance was approximately 10,000 per game; 20 years later in 2000, attendance per game stood at 17,000 per game, leading many basketball team owners and sports commentators to express concern about the health of professional basketball in the future.

Professional basketball became the first major sport to have a black coach when Bill Russell was appointed as a player-coach of the Boston Celtics in 1966, and the first to have a black ownership group in 1989. Basketball is also the first major sport to support a successful women's league. After two failed attempts to sustain a women's league in the 1980s, the increased popularity of the sport at the college level helped make possible the formation and survival of the Women's National Basketball Association (WNBA) in 1993.

During the 1980s and 1990s, other sports enjoyed increased popularity both on the amateur and professional levels. Soccer experienced a boom in the 1970s and by the mid-1980s almost 9 million young people were playing soccer in the United States in school and community leagues. Such popularity spurred nominal growth in professional soccer, but not enough to sustain it at the level of professional baseball, football, and basketball. Soccer received a much-needed boost in 1999 when the U.S. Women's National Team beat China before a crowd of over 100,000 for the World Cup title. Another sport that experienced a phenomenal growth in popularity was stock car racing. Long a favorite in the South, NASCAR (National Association for Stock Car Auto Racing) became the nation's largest sports entertainment industry.

One of the most significant developments in professional sports during the last half of the 20th century was the rise of star athletes to celebrity status. Aside from multimillion-dollar salaries and endorsement contracts, professional athletes became icons and role models. Michael Jordan and Tiger Woods are examples of this phenomenon.

Chicago Bulls's Michael Jordan makes a layup against the opposing team. *(Allen/Getty Images)*

Jordan, a player for the NBA's Chicago Bulls, is known as perhaps the best to have ever played professional basketball. He won numerous scoring titles during the late 1980s and 1990s and led his team to six national championships in seven years during the 1990s, taking a year off to play minor league baseball. Such performances reinvigorated basketball's lagging popularity. His salary was modest compared with other players but he commanded hundreds of millions of dollars in advertising endorsements and could sell virtually everything. The slogan from one of his popular ad campaigns, "If I could be like Mike," became ingrained in popular discourse. He encouraged children to stay in school (although he left college early to join the NBA), while he simultaneously pitched athletic shoes that the same children were unable to afford. He became the most recognizable athlete in the world and a cultural icon of wealth and celebrity, an exemplar of success through hard work and dedication.

Tiger Woods eclipsed Jordan's premier status, however. Rigorously encouraged by his father from the time he was a toddler to excel at the game, Woods breathed new life into professional golf. Golf has always been hugely popular as a participant sport, but the popularity of professional golf waned after players such as Arnold Palmer and Jack Nicklaus retired to the Senior PGA (Professional Golfers Association) tour in the 1980s and early 1990s. Tiger Woods entered the PGA tour in 1997 at the age of 21 and promptly became the first African American to win a major golf tournament when he convincingly won the 1997 Masters, breaking several long-standing records in the process. By the end of the 2000 tour, in addition to his three U.S. Amateur titles, he had won six major championships, more than 20 other professional titles in the United States, and more than a dozen titles in Europe and Asia. He, like Michael Jordan, was crowned as the greatest to have ever played his sport. He turned his fame into huge endorsement contracts and started a foundation to promote the game of golf among primarily inner-city youths. His fortune and celebrity quickly made him the most recognizable athlete in the world, and created huge new audiences for professional golf.

While professional sports became new forms of mass entertainment, and professional athletes became celebrities, participant sports reached new heights. Commercial fitness and RECREATION became multibillion-dollar businesses. Both boys and girls participated in organized sports in record numbers, as parents hoped sports would provide wholesome activity and the possibility of future financial rewards in the form of college scholarships and perhaps professional contracts. The possibility of financial success only partly explains the extreme popularity of professional sports and the position that its star participants hold in American society. Spectator sports provide both a distraction and a vicarious experience for the audience. Moreover, they represent a metaphor for human existence and the struggles it contains as well as the desires to succeed and be the best that are embedded in American culture. Finally, professional sports represent both the fulfillment and the excesses—the best and the worst things—to which a consumer-driven society is directed. Both despite this and because of this, sports continue to provide mass entertainment and recreation, and contribute to the social structure of an increasingly diverse nation.

See also AARON, HENRY; ECONOMY; MEDIA.

Further reading: Elliot J. Gorn and Warren Goldstein, *A Brief History of American Sports* (New York: Hill & Wang, 1993).

—William L. Glankler

Starr, Kenneth (1946–)

A distinguished attorney and former solicitor general of the United States (1989–93), Kenneth Starr served as INDEPENDENT COUNSEL for the Whitewater investigation from 1994–99. In the course of his investigation he recommended to Congress that President WILLIAM J. CLINTON be impeached for perjury and obstruction of justice. The intense controversy surrounding Starr's actions led directly to the demise of the office of Independent Counsel in 1999.

Starr's appointment on August 5, 1994, was a departure from previous independent counsels. Starr was known as a distinguished Washington appellate lawyer, who had served as counsel to the attorney general in the administration of RONALD W. REAGAN, and solicitor general in the administration of GEORGE H. W. BUSH. Starr was also well known as a former Republican SENATE candidate and a critic of President Clinton and his wife, HILLARY RODHAM CLINTON. When a federal judicial panel appointed Starr to replace Robert Fiske in the Whitewater investigation, it baffled many observers who knew that Starr lacked trial experience. Perhaps most surprising was the fact that Starr had been a leading critic of the independent counsel concept, warning that it violated the separation of powers.

Within the Clinton administration, Starr was accused of having a partisan agenda from the outset of his investigation. Its slow pace and what was seen as its expansion into matters unrelated to the original Whitewater controversy, however, led Clinton's supporters to accuse Starr of abusing his mandate to conduct a partisan witch-hunt. Starr refused to respond to these charges, maintaining it inappropriate for an independent counsel to engage in partisan debate. His supporters were quick to defend Starr, arguing that the slow pace of the investigation reflected a careful perusal of a complex set of allegations and potential improprieties. They further laid the blame for the delays on the administration. Arguing that Clinton had refused to cooperate, these critics speculated that members of the administration engaged in an attempt to cover up illegal activities and accused them of trying to smear and discredit Starr's investigation. Furthermore, the two sides argued very different views of the role of the independent counsel, with Starr's critics insisting that his mission was only to present a full accounting of the facts surrounding the Whitewater development, and Starr's supporters maintaining that his role was essentially prosecutorial.

Starr's investigation led to the conviction of Arkansas's governor Jim Guy Tucker and Associate U.S. Attorney General Webster Hubbell on criminal charges unrelated to the Whitewater allegations. Starr announced his intention to resign his office February 17, 1997. After a barrage of criticism, Starr agreed to stay. On May 27, the SUPREME COURT unanimously rejected Clinton's request to have

Jones's sexual harassment civil suit delayed until the end of his presidential service, and on June 25, the *Washington Post* reported that Starr had begun to investigate charges that Clinton had sought to influence testimony in the Jones suit. On January 12, 1998, Linda Tripp, who had befriended and secretly recorded the confidences of former White House intern Monica Lewinsky, approached Starr with tapes on which Lewinsky described a series of intimate relations with the president. Jones's attorneys had sought to show that Clinton had a pattern of sexual harassment. On January 16 Starr was given authority by the grand jury to investigate Tripp's charges that Clinton had encouraged Lewinsky to lie under oath in the Jones case. In his own testimony the next day before the grand jury, Clinton relied on narrow definitions and legal technicalities to deny that he had engaged in sexual relations with Lewinsky. Whether Clinton's hair-splitting constituted perjury, or the clever avoidance of it, became a central issue in the IMPEACHMENT controversy.

Starr believed that Clinton's testimony was perjury. Further, he believed that Clinton had been guilty of obstruction of justice both in attempting to influence Lewinsky's testimony and in resisting the independent counsel's investigation. On September 9 Starr submitted a 445-page report detailing the charges to Congress, along with supporting evidence. The Starr Report became notorious for its salacious sexual detail about Clinton's personal life.

Critics accused Starr of reveling in Clinton's sex life, seeking to criminalize private sexual behavior and conspiracy due to Starr's close ties to the Jones suit. Even Republican congressmen supporting Clinton's impeachment grumbled that Starr should have obtained more evidence about Clinton's alleged abuse of federal power. In his defense, Starr argued that the explicit details were necessary to make the legal case and pointed out that the decision to release the report to the public was made by the House Republican leadership and not him.

Starr appeared in person before the House Judiciary Committee, urging Clinton's impeachment on the basis of the evidence. The House, divided along partisan lines, followed through on Starr's recommendations. Clinton was acquitted of all charges on February 12, 1999, after a Senate trial. Starr resigned as independent counsel on October 18, 1999. The existing independent counsel investigation nevertheless continued under Starr's aide, Robert W. Ray, until March 20, 2002. No charges were brought against President Clinton or his wife in connection with the Whitewater real estate development. Because of his testimony before the grand jury, however, the U.S. Supreme Court barred Clinton from practicing before it, and the Arkansas Bar Association suspended Clinton's license to practice law for five years. Congress allowed the renewable independent counsel statute to lapse in 1999.

Further reading: Richard Posner, *An Affair of State: The Investigation, Impeachment, and Trial of President Clinton* (Cambridge, Mass.: Harvard University Press, 1999); David Schippers, with Alan Henry, *Sellout* (Washington, D.C.: Regnery, 2000).

—Christopher M. Gray

Steinem, Gloria (1934–)

The second daughter of Leo Steinem and Ruth Nuneviller Steinem, Gloria Marie Steinem was born in Toledo, Ohio, on March 25, 1934. Steinem endured a difficult childhood, marred by her mother's poor health and the departure of her father. Steinem was confronted with many personal and professional hurdles early in her career, but in the 1970s emerged as a leader and spokesperson for the women's liberation movement.

Her father worked as a traveling antiques dealer and moved his family regularly. Because of Steinem's unsettled home life, her mother, who had a college degree, provided much of her early education. Steinem's mother was prone to bouts of depression, and the severity of these bouts worsened over time, leaving her increasingly bed-ridden. In 1944 Steinem's parents separated, and her older sister left for college, leaving Steinem and her mother to fend for themselves. The two settled in Toledo, and Steinem was finally able to attend school regularly, but the health of her mother placed a great deal of strain on Steinem, who found herself, increasingly, in charge of the household.

Upon graduation from high school, Steinem entered Smith College. While at Smith, she majored in government and wrote for the student newspaper. Steinem also became a political activist, volunteering to work in the presidential campaign of Adlai Stevenson. During these years, Steinem discovered that her grandmother had been a suffragist and her mother had been a journalist. Steinem's mother had been a columnist and reporter for a Toledo newspaper, but had given up her career when she married. Steinem believed that her mother's mental and physical problems could be traced directly to society's unwillingness to allow women to have both a career and a family.

Steinem graduated with honors from Smith in 1956 and won a two-year fellowship to study in India. Before leaving, however, Steinem discovered that she was pregnant. Steinem found a doctor to approve and perform an abortion and then left for India. On her return, Steinem moved to New York to find a job as a journalist. A guidebook she wrote about India received a lukewarm reception from publishers. Her efforts to find a job as a reporter were met with skepticism about the ability of an attractive young woman to be a serious journalist. Eventually, Steinem accepted a job as an editorial assistant with *Help!* magazine and began to freelance as a journalist. In 1962 *Esquire* magazine published her first article, "The Moral Disarmament of Betty Coed." The publication of this story led to more assignments, and in a short time, Steinem was earning enough to become a full-time freelance journalist.

Steinem remained unhappy with the types of stories she was assigned, however. She wanted to cover politics and major social issues, but found herself relegated to celebrity interviews and woman-focused stories. In 1963 Steinem gained notoriety for an exposé she wrote on New York's Playboy Club in which she went undercover as a Playboy bunny. Her article focused on sexual discrimination and harassment, but her editors continued to dismiss her ability as a serious journalist.

In 1968 Steinem got her chance to cover politics, as she followed the presidential campaign of George McGovern. Also that year, Steinem became a founding staff member of *New York* magazine. As a contributing editor, Steinem had the freedom to write about what she wanted. Among the stories Steinem covered were the assassination of Martin Luther King, Jr., and the organization of migrant workers by César Chávez. She also became politically active in antiwar protest marches and other social causes, including the women's movement.

In 1970 her article, "After Black Power, Women's Liberation" won the Penney-Missouri Journalism Award. That same year Steinem helped organize the Women's Strike for Equality, a national strike organized by the NATIONAL ORGANIZATION FOR WOMEN (NOW). While participating in the strike, Steinem became friends with Dorothy Pitman Hughes, an African-American feminist who urged Steinem to devote herself entirely to the feminist cause. The two undertook a national lecture tour, speaking on such issues as legalized abortion, equal pay for women, and the EQUAL RIGHTS AMENDMENT. Through this tour, Steinem emerged as a national leader of the women's liberation movement, which was becoming more radical as the movement's focus increasingly shifted from the issue of equal opportunity for women to sexual politics. Representing this shift, Steinem found herself at odds with Betty Friedan, the founder of NOW.

Trouble between the two occurred when Steinem, at a news conference in 1971 speaking in favor of lesbian rights, declared, "We all are lesbians." Friedan opposed what she perceived as radicals taking over the women's rights struggle for equal opportunity, and shifting the focus toward gay rights. At the 1973 National Women's Political Caucus (NWPC) convention, Friedan openly challenged Steinem by running as an independent for the national steering committee. In the election, the final ballots disappeared and Friedan lost the race. Friedan believed that she had won the election and accused Steinem of engineering the election. Friedan refused to have any contact with Steinem for years afterward. As a consequence of this fight, Friedan

became marginalized in NOW, NWPC, and the antiabortion movement, and Steinem helped lead the shift in the women's movement in a more militant direction.

In 1972 Steinem founded *Ms.* magazine, devoted to women's issues. Also in 1972 Steinem attended the Democratic Party convention to lobby for an abortion plank in the party platform and protest the underrepresentation of women at the convention. That same year, Steinem publicly announced that she had undergone an abortion. For her work on behalf of the feminist movement, Steinem was named Woman of the Year by *McCall's* magazine.

Throughout the remainder of the 1970s, Steinem kept up the drive for equal rights. She was a strong supporter of the Equal Rights Amendment, which failed ratification. Steinem pressured politicians to support women's issues and participated in high-profile events to keep women's issues and the leaders of the women's movement in the public eye. Steinem is still regularly sought out to provide the feminist position on various issues.

In 1989 *Ms.* went bankrupt. In 1990 the magazine was restarted with new investors, In 1999 another group of investors bought the magazine, with the full support of Steinem. In 2000 Steinem, who had once, in reference to marriage, said, "I do not breed well in captivity," married for the first time. This caused a rift within the feminist movement, especially among some radical feminists who accused Steinem of having betrayed the feminist cause.

Steinem is the author of a number of books including a collection of her essays, *Outrageous Acts and Everyday Rebellions* (1989). Steinem has also authored a biography of Marilyn Monroe and two other books, *Revolution from Within: A Book of Self-Esteem* and *Moving beyond Words* (1992). Steinem is a member of the Women's Hall of Fame (1993) and the American Society of Magazine Editors Hall of Fame (1998).

See also NATIONAL ORGANIZATION FOR WOMEN; SCHLAFLY, PHYLLIS; WOMEN'S RIGHTS AND STATUS.

Further reading: Carolyn Daffron, *Gloria Steinem* (New York: Chelsea House, 1988) ; Carol G. Heilbrun, *The Education of a Woman: The Life of Gloria Steinem* (New York: Dial Press, 1995); Sydney Ladensohn Stern, *Gloria Steinem: Her Passion, Politics, and Mystique* (Secaucus, N.J.: Carol Publishing Group, 1997).

—John Korasick

Strategic Arms Limitation Treaties (SALT I; SALT II) (1972, 1979)

The Strategic Arms Limitation Treaties (SALT I and SALT II) were the end result of negotiations between the United States and the Soviet Union to slow the nuclear arms race. For decades, the two superpowers devoted many resources to researching and deploying improved rockets and more powerful warheads. By the mid-1960s, the arsenals of the two nations were more than sufficient to guarantee the destruction of the world. Talks commenced in 1969 to set limits on nuclear weapons. Gerard Smith, of the Arms Control and Disarmament Agency, led the official U.S. delegation, but much of the negotiations occurred between national security adviser HENRY A. KISSINGER and Soviet ambassador Anatoly Dobrynin. After 30 months of negotiations, an agreement was reached, and President RICHARD M. NIXON traveled to Moscow in 1972 to sign SALT I.

SALT I was comprised of two distinct agreements. The first was the Interim Agreement on Strategic Offensive Arms. During the negotiations, the two sides could not agree on absolute limits, but both sides agreed to continue negotiations, while abiding by temporary force level and development limitations. The Interim Agreement was set to expire five years after it was adopted. It created a great deal of controversy during ratification because the raw numbers indicated that the Soviets could maintain a larger force than the Americans. The second part of the agreement was the ANTI-BALLISTIC MISSILE TREATY (ABM). This agreement placed limits on ballistic missile defense deployment, development, and testing. The ABM treaty was to last indefinitely with reviews every five years.

There were a number of flaws in the ABM treaty. First was the issue of verification. The Soviets would only agree to space and aerial reconnaissance and other less indirect means of checking. This made it virtually impossible to track mobile weapons systems, and to determine the number of warheads on a missile, the number of bombs on a plane, or if a missile silo even contained a missile. Although on-site inspection was deemed appropriate only for verification of treaty-mandated weapon destruction, there was considerable political pressure in the United States to reach an agreement.

The second round of talks commenced in November 1972. These talks spanned the remainder of the Nixon administration, the administration of GERALD R. FORD, and into the administration of JAMES EARL CARTER, JR. After seven years, SALT II was signed in 1979. The treaty was viewed as a step toward arms reduction, and in that spirit was due to expire in 1985. The agreement contained a protocol limiting the testing and deployment of specific weapons systems, and a statement to guide the next round of talks.

Because it specifically outlined what was denied, loopholes opened in SALT II could be exploited by advances in engineering and technology. SALT I, on the other hand, outlined what was permissible, and anything not listed was prohibited. SALT II was never ratified. In August 1979 the Senate refused to consider the treaty after the disclosure of the presence of Soviet troops in Cuba. When the Soviet Union invaded Afghanistan in December, President Carter withdrew the treaty from consideration.

Though it was not ratified, both nations abided by the SALT II provisions. During the presidency of RONALD W. REAGAN, a new series of talks was initiated—the strategic arms reductions talks (START).

Further reading: John Newhouse, *Cold Dawn: The Story of SALT* (Washington, D.C.: Brasseys, 1989); Strobe Talbott, *Endgame: The Inside Story of SALT II* (New York: HarperCollins, 1980).

—John Korasick

Strategic Defense Initiative (SDI)

Dubbed "Star Wars" by the media, the Strategic Defense Initiative (SDI), first proposed by President RONALD W. REAGAN in a televised address on March 23, 1983, is a research program designed to explore the technical feasibility of defense against enemy missiles using satellites and laser technology.

The public announcement of SDI created a furor over whether the development of such a weapon technology was feasible in the immediate future, and if such a system was permitted under the ANTI-BALLISTIC MISSILE TREATY. Proponents, such as physicist Edward Teller, argued that the basic technology had existed for 30 years and that the ABM treaty did not apply to new technologies (i.e., lasers) that had emerged since its ratification. Furthermore, proponents argued such a system would reduce the likelihood of war because any enemy would hesitate to attack us. Opponents charged that a "missile shield" was technologically impossible, that such a system would cause the Soviets to increase their offensive capabilities, and that the United States had always followed the letter of treaties. In this case, opponents argued, the ABM treaty prevented the development of any antimissile system by either party.

By the early 1990s, concerns over the spread of missile technology and the proliferation of nuclear, chemical, and biological weaponry caused President GEORGE W. H. BUSH to shift the focus of the program from intercepting a massive Soviet attack to the new threat of isolated attacks from rogue states. In his 1991 State of the Union Address, Bush announced that SDI would be directed to providing protection from limited attacks. By the end of the Bush administration, SDI development had cost over $30 billion.

During the administration of WILLIAM J. CLINTON, the project was downgraded and the focus of research became the interception of short-range missiles. The director of the program no longer reported directly to the secretary of defense; instead, reports were made to the undersecretary for acquisition and technology. The budget was cut nearly in half, from $6.8 billion to $3.8 billion. While the program survived, it was no longer a centerpiece of American strategic policy. With the election of GEORGE W. BUSH, the debate was rekindled with the president's announcement that he plans to implement a missile defense system.

See also ANTI-BALLISTIC MISSILE TREATY; DEFENSE POLICY; REAGAN, RONALD W.; STRATEGIC ARMS LIMITATION TREATIES.

Further reading: Frances Fitzgerald, *Way Out There in the Blue: Reagan, Star Wars, and the End of the Cold War* (New York: Simon & Schuster, 2000).

—John Korasick

Sunbelt

The Sunbelt refers primarily to the southern tier of the United States, including the states of Florida, Texas, Arizona, and California. The term "Sunbelt" came into wide use in the 1970s as the population's shift to the South and West became evident, having profound political and economic consequences. The growth and affluence of the sunbelt contrasted with the sharp decline in population and industry in the RUST BELT.

The tremendous growth in population of the Sunbelt came from internal migration from the Northwest and Midwest regions of the United States, as well as immigration across the Mexican border. While the economic and political changes became more pronounced in the 1970s, as the rust belt declined, the growth of Sunbelt states began after World War II. By 1990, Los Angeles, San Diego, Phoenix, Houston, Dallas, and San Antonio were among the 10 largest cities in the United States. While many cities in the Northeast and Midwest experienced declining or stagnant population growth, Sunbelt cities boomed.

The Sunbelt attracted population because of its warm climate and low cost of living, making Sunbelt states ideal for retirees. Florida and Arizona benefited especially from the growth of an aging American population, as retirement communities in these states sprang up. In addition, the birthrate in the Sunbelt was about 10 percent greater than in the rest of the nation.

Business was attracted to the Sunbelt for a variety of reasons, including the relative lack of labor unions and the prospect of cheaper labor. Following World War II, manufacturing companies began to relocate in the Southeast. Aerospace firms and defense contractors also moved to the Sunbelt states, often near large military bases in Southern California and throughout the Southwest. Moreover, the rise of oil prices in the 1970s benefited oil and natural gas–producing states such as Texas, Louisiana, and Oklahoma. The climate of these states also encouraged growth of a tremendous tourist industry, especially in Florida, California, and Arizona.

The regions' economic prosperity has been uneven. Of the 25 metropolitan areas with the lowest per capita income in 1990, 23 were in the Sunbelt. The oil boom of the 1970s crashed in the early 1980s, hurting cities in oil-producing states. Cities such as Houston, which had been overbuilt in the 1970s, crashed in the 1980s with the decline in oil prices and the savings and loan failures.

In the 1990s Sunbelt cities experienced problems related to their rapid growth—air pollution, clogged highways, high crime rates, and unskilled immigrants. Politically, the Sunbelt has been viewed as advantageous to the Republican Party, although Florida voted Democratic in the presidential elections in 1992 and 1996, and was barely won in a contested vote by the Republicans in 2000. Arizona voted, albeit narrowly, Democratic in 2000, and California is now considered a Democratic stronghold. Texas remains solidly Republican.

See also POPULATION TRENDS.

Further reading: Carl Abbott, *The New Urban America* (New York: Oxford University Press, 1987); B. L. Weinstein and R. E. Firestine, *Regional Growth and Decline in the United States: The Rise of the Sunbelt and the Decline of the Northeast* (New York: Praeger, 1978).

Supreme Court

Since 1969 the Supreme Court shifted gradually in a more conservative direction from what many saw as the liberal activism of the Warren Court. Under Chief Justice Earl Warren, the court championed civil rights and limited police powers, and restricted the power of states over such issues as birth control. President RICHARD M. NIXON vowed to change the course of the Court when he came into the White House in 1969.

When Chief Justice Warren retired in June 1969, Nixon responded by nominating WARREN E. BURGER, the first of four nominees to the Court, including Harry Blackmun, LEWIS POWELL, and WILLIAM H. REHNQUIST. Though Nixon expected the Court to become more conservative, it initially continued the liberal direction established by Warren. In 1972 the Court struck down the arbitrary application of capital punishment, especially for ethnic inmates, and prevented the administration from using electronic surveillance without a court order. In 1973 the other controversial decisions continued. Much to the dismay of some conservatives, the Court legalized abortion; upheld desegregation in northern schools; upheld the use of property taxes to support schools; and broadly defined obscenity. During the WATERGATE SCANDAL the Court ruled against the president in *UNITED STATES V. NIXON* (1974), forcing him to release tapes to the special prosecutor that ultimately led to Nixon's resignation.

In 1975 GERALD R. FORD named John Paul Stevens, a moderate, to the Court. In 1976 the Court began to turn in a more conservative direction, striking down campaign spending limits; rejecting the power of Congress to force wage rates on state and municipal employees; and reinstating capital punishment. In the *University of California Regents v. BAKKE* (1978), the Court ruled in a 5 to 4 decision that race could not be the sole factor in university admissions policies to law school.

When Jimmy Carter left the presidency in 1981, he became the first full-term president to not name a Supreme Court justice. In 1981 RONALD W. REAGAN became president. Reagan saw the federal judiciary as too intrusive in the lives of Americans, deciding matters that should be decided by voters. Early in his first term Reagan named the first female justice, SANDRA DAY O'CONNOR. In 1986 Chief Justice Burger announced his retirement, and Reagan named Justice Rehnquist as his successor, and ANTONIN SCALIA to Rehnquist's seat. At the end of 1986, Justice Powell retired and Reagan nominated ROBERT BORK, who was rejected by the SENATE after a vicious confirmation process. Reagan then nominated Anthony Kennedy, who was quickly confirmed.

Twice during his administration, Reagan pushed the court to overturn *Roe v. Wade*. Both times *Roe v. Wade* was reaffirmed, but the Court shifted under Sandra Day O'Connor's leadership, away from a trimester standard to an "undue burden" standard for regulating abortion. The Court upheld affirmative action, in general, and relaxed its view on the separation of church and state.

The appointment of Justice Kennedy marked a definite shift in the direction of the Court. Kennedy, along with Justices Scalia, O'Connor, BYRON R. WHITE, and Rehnquist established a moderate to conservative majority on the Court, although O'Connor and Kennedy often proved to be swing votes on the Court. In 1989 the Court struck down a set-aside plan from Virginia that required 30 percent of city construction funds to go to black-owned firms. By a 6-3 margin, the Court found the plan too rigid and not justified.

During this period the Court sought to balance the needs of employer and employee. In criminal law, the Court adopted a tougher stance, allowing the execution of criminals who were juveniles at the time of their offense and of convicted murderers who were judged mentally retarded. The Court approved the drug testing of some workers. The Court allowed states to regulate abortions. These were considered conservative positions, but the Court ruled that the state of Texas could not punish an individual for burning an American flag in protest. Citing the First Amendment, the Court argued that such a law violated freedom of expression. This decision sparked a movement for a constitutional amendment to reverse the decision.

In the 1990s four justices retired, including William J. Brennan, Jr., Thurgood Marshall, Byron White, and Harry A. Blackmun. Brennan and Marshall retired during the presidency of GEORGE W. H. BUSH. Bush named DAVID SOUTER and CLARENCE THOMAS to the bench. The Thomas nomination was highly controversial, and he was confirmed despite allegations he had sexually harassed a former employee. White and Blackmun retired under President WILLIAM J. CLINTON who replaced them with RUTH BADER GINSBURG and STEPHEN BREYER. As a consequence, the Court became divided between liberal and conservative justices, which imparted greater weight to the swing votes of O'Connor, Kennedy, and Souter. As a consequence, the Court did not follow a clear ideological direction in the 1990s.

In the 1990s the Court limited the ability of Congress to regulate interstate commerce by striking down a law banning the possession of guns near schools. The Court reduced the authority of Congress to subject states to federal lawsuits for failure to enforce federal rights. In a series of decisions, the Court struck down electoral districts created solely to ensure the election of minority candidates. The Court restricted the ability of federal judges to order desegregation programs. The Court rejected state-imposed term limits for members of Congress. And in one of the most sensational cases of the decade, it nullified a Colorado constitutional amendment that barred local governments from protecting homosexuals from discrimination.

During the 2000 presidential election, the Court put itself in the position of determining the winner of the election. The controversial decision in *Bush V. Gore* (2000) in a 5-4 decision awarded the election, in effect, to GEORGE W. BUSH over Democratic challenger Albert Gore. Gore had involved the judiciary when he challenged vote counts in Florida. Critics of the decision charged the Court with partisanship and having overstepped its judicial powers by interfering with a Florida Supreme Court decision. This controversial decision might be the lasting legacy of this Court.

See also *ROE V. WADE*.

Further reading: Robert G. McCloskey, *The American Supreme Court* (Chicago: University of Chicago Press, 2000).

—John Korasick

Taiwan (U.S. relations with)   See China, U.S. relations with

technology   See science and technology

televangelism

Televangelism refers to evangelical religious television programming that depends on viewers for direct financial support. By the 1980s there were more than 220 religious television stations and three Christian networks that broadcast to nationwide audiences 24 hours a day. According to Nielson and Arbitron rating services, during the period from 1980 to 1987, eight leading televangelists were watched by 85 percent of the total national religious television audience. These televangelists were Robert Schuller, Jimmy Swaggart, Oral Roberts, Rex Humbard, Jerry Falwell, Jim Bakker, Pat Robertson, and James Robison.

Although the televangelists differ theologically, they share common elements within the Protestant tradition. Most notably, they emphasize the importance of Christian conversion. In their evangelistic tradition, conversion is a key to salvation and forms the central message that the televangelists bring to their audiences.

Another critical element is the charismatic leadership of the televangelist, whose power resides in his or her ability to preach, teach, and heal through the intervention of the Holy Spirit. Television allows televangelists to project their charismatic personalities and to admonish their viewers to confess sins, repent, convert, and contribute.

Politically oriented televangelists, such as Pat Robertson, tend to simplify complex social, political, and economic issues and offer their viewers a categorical choice between right and wrong. These preachers, generally associated with the "Religious Right," oppose abortion, advocate prayer in public schools, and deplore what they depict as the moral degeneration of America. They most often identify sins of the flesh—drug and alcohol addiction, sexual infidelity, and homosexuality—as evidence of cultural decay in American society caused by what they perceive as failed LIBERALISM.

Another common theme is the apocalyptic interpretation of world events that televangelists use to prophesy the final days and the coming of the millennium. They enlarge the warfare metaphor to a cosmic scale and describe the imminent end of history with detailed scenarios of the conflict between Christ and the Antichrist. Pat Robertson, for example, is known for reporting a particular world crisis as a news story and then making that story a point of departure for speculation and apocalyptic prophecy.

Televangelists also share a view that Scripture is without flaw in matters of science and history as well as in

Franklin and Billy Graham   *(Billy Graham Center Museum)*

morality and theology. Along with biblical literalism, they preach the necessity for direct personal encounters with Scripture through Bible reading and personal interpretation. The total rejection of critical methods of biblical interpretation harbors an anti-intellectualism that dissipates the strength of scholarly traditions of most mainline Protestant denominations.

Finally, televangelists succeeded by developing support through the solicitation of funds from their viewers. Although some televangelists have local churches, most head independent organizations that cannot rely on local or denominational support for the continuation of their ministries. The use of computerized mailing and contributor lists and telephone systems for viewers to call in for counseling and prayer or to make donations form the structure of televangelists' fund-raising activities. Because there is no larger denomination to supervise fund-raising activity, the issue of accountability has been raised by critics of televangelism. For many, the financial and organizational autonomy has enabled them to diversify their evangelical activities while for others it has led to scandal and disgrace.

Oral Roberts, Jerry Falwell, and Pat Robertson have been the most successful at building influential evangelical organizations. Roberts began his television ministry in 1955 and its success, along with his ability to avoid mixing politics and religion, enabled him to establish the Oral Roberts Evangelical Association that includes Oral Roberts University as a major component. Falwell's program, *The Old-Time Gospel Hour*, delivers a fundamentalist message that speaks out against issues such as abortion, pornography, homosexuality, and the decline of morality and family values. He heads the Liberty Baptist Theological Seminary in Lynchburg, Virginia, and wielded political influence in the late 1970s and early 1980s as spokesman of the Moral Majority during the 1980s. Robertson, the preeminent televangelist, heads the Christian Broadcasting Network (CBN) and hosts *The 700 Club*, a talk/news program centered on revealing the power of God in people's lives. On these programs he offers detailed analysis of world issues through a conservative Christian perspective.

Jimmy Lee Swaggart and Jim Bakker, both ordained ministers in the Assemblies of God, have not experienced such success. Best known for his exuberant, emotional preaching, Swaggart created one of the largest television ministries in the United States with a worldwide organization worth an estimated $141 million. In 1987 the revelation that Swaggart regularly visited a prostitute severely damaged his credibility and cost him his Assemblies of God pulpit. He returned to his ministry, however, as an independent minister.

Jim Bakker, with his wife Tammy Faye, developed the Praise the Lord (PTL) Club in a multimillion-dollar televi-

sion ministry consisting of a cable network and a real estate venture known as Heritage USA, a "Christian Disneyland" in Fort Mill, South Carolina. He preached the "gospel of prosperity," claiming that material prosperity was a sign of God's love. The couple's personal lifestyle and extravagant spending made them stereotypical targets in the secular popular media. Jim Bakker was accused of sexual misconduct with former church secretary Jessica Hahn in 1987 and convicted of federal wire and mail fraud charges in 1989. This scandal led to a reduction in financial support for all televangelists and to major changes in televangelism as a whole.

Televangelism is still a viable part of American evangelical Protestantism, but most television ministries have been forced to scale down their organizations and decrease the amount of airtime they purchase. Televangelism, in context, represents the adaptation of religious ritual to a technological and media-oriented society through the electronically transmitted celebration and renewal of common values.

See also RELIGION.

Further reading: John K. Hadden and Anson Shupe, *Televangelism, Power, and Politics* (New York: Henry Holt, 1988).

—William L. Glankler

television

At the beginning of the 21st century, television has become unquestionably the single most influential media form in American society and, as such, is perhaps society's best cultural storyteller. Largely because of the social movements of the 1960s, the advent of cable television in the late 1970s, and deregulation in the 1980s, television programming offered viewers choices ranging from animated children's shows to pay-per-view PORNOGRAPHY.

Congress has regulated television programming under the auspices of the Federal Communications Commission (FCC) since television's inception. Before the advent of cable television in the late 1970s, the FCC promulgated regulations designed to moderate the power of the three major networks and to encourage diverse programming. The 1980s witnessed major deregulation in the broadcasting industry as the FCC cut many record-keeping regulations, relaxed limitations on the number of stations one company could own, and revoked the fairness doctrine, which required stations to provide response time from community members opposed to broadcasters' editorial opinions. In 1984 Congress passed the Cable Communications Policy Act that effectively created an unregulated monopoly by allowing cable companies to hold exclusive franchises over their service areas. Complaints led to the re-regulation of cable television in 1992, then present in 67 percent of American homes.

In addition to the FCC, the broadcast industry has its own organ of self-regulation, the National Association of Broadcasters (NAB). Its "Code of Good Practices" banned obscenity, nudity, and programs that might encourage violation of the law from either network programming or basic cable programming. This code does not apply to programming on premium cable channels, like HBO, or on pay-per-view offerings. The NAB also limited the number of commercials a station could run, but a federal judge ruled such limitations unlawful restrictions of trade in 1981. The NAB remains the chief lobbyist and advocate for the broadcast industry.

Regardless of the shifting levels of regulation, the categories of television programming have remained virtually unchanged. The nature of the programs within the categories has changed, however, and reflects changes in American society and culture.

By the late 1960s, filmed series shot on location rather than in the studio had replaced live television drama. Such programs also began to deal with more relevant social issues and to appeal to the younger, urban, more upscale audiences courted by television advertisers. For example, ABC's *The Mod Squad* (1968–73) was a police drama that featured three youthful, "hippie" police officers and plots that addressed social issues. Much slicker and more realistic crime dramas followed with *Hill Street Blues* and *Miami Vice* in the 1980s and *N.Y.P.D. Blue* in the 1990s. The latter graphically depicted someone being shot in the head in its premiere episode.

Legal dramas experienced a renaissance in the 1980s and 1990s. Although the popular *Perry Mason,* a legal drama, had been off the air since 1966, viewers welcomed a series of television movies featuring the popular lawyer in the late 1980s and early 1990s. *L.A. Law* aired in the 1980s and featured yuppie lawyers facing personal as well as professional crises. It also began to address the issue of ethics in the legal profession. The weekly series, *Family Law,* continued the exploration of controversial issues and legal ethics in the late 1990s with episodes on topics such as child custody and high school violence. A similar evolution took place with medical dramas. The sterile and "feel-good" shows like *Marcus Welby, M.D.* gave way to shows in the 1990s like *E.R.*, which realistically portrayed life in an emergency room.

Cable television extended the dramatic envelope even further with programs that unabashedly addressed some of the most poignant issues of the late 20th century. HBO's *The Sopranos* told the story of a contemporary Mafia family. Showtime's *Queer as Folk* is about the gay community and *Resurrection Boulevard* centers on a Hispanic family in the inner city.

Comedy series also adapted to the changing culture by portraying a more realistic and relevant, yet still humorous, picture of American life. The show that changed the situation comedy from universally cheery, homey stories of families headed by warm, insightful parents was *All in the Family* (premiering in 1971). It brought a sense of hard reality as the outspoken, narrow-minded, bigoted Archie Bunker continually clashed with his liberal son-in-law. During the 1970s and 1980s, situation comedies began to feature black casts, most notably *The Jeffersons* and the enormously successful *Cosby Show.* Many of the most popular situation comedies—including *Seinfeld* and *Friends*—began in the 1990s and reflected the concerns, tastes, and neuroses of the baby-boom generation. Cable television added to the flavor of television comedy programming by adding uncensored shows that featured prominent comics, like George Carlin, Eddie Murphy, and Robin Williams, on the premium channels.

Reality programming is a relatively new genre, although its roots could be traced back to *You Asked For It* from the 1950s and *That's Incredible* from the 1980s. It blossomed, however, during the 1990s when network budgets demanded shows that were cheap to produce. *America's Most Wanted,* which re-created crimes and sought viewer help in apprehending criminals, and *America's Funniest Home Videos,* which featured amateur videotapes, were both very popular in the late 1980s and early 1990s. By the late 1990s reality programming introduced the element of competition by producing shows like *Survivor, Big Brother,* and *The Race.* These shows ostensibly observed "real people," not actors, in a competition that required cooperation but, ultimately, betrayal in order to win a large cash prize.

The talk show at the end of the 20th century, at least on the major networks, still serves as an avenue for exposure for celebrities, authors, and other entertainers. The late-night audience can choose from either *The Tonight Show,* hosted by Jay Leno, or *The Late Show* with David Letterman. During the 1980s, however, the talk show became more than just an informal interview show containing the occasional comedy skit. Phil Donahue, Oprah Winfrey, Geraldo Rivera, and others hosted shows that emphasized current events rather than celebrities. Because many of these shows addressed the more controversial issues and, like *The Jerry Springer Show,* went to great lengths to present the most bizarre participants, this genre came to be called "tabloid TV." Cable's premium channels offered talk shows as well. *Dennis Miller Live* (HBO), for example, is a mixture of uncensored stand-up comedy, caustic and humorous social criticism, and a celebrity interview.

Full-length motion pictures have always been an important part of television programming. By the end of the 1960s there were as many as nine network MOVIES on each week. The networks primarily showed theatrical movies sold to them by Hollywood studios, but ABC pioneered the made-for-television movie during the 1970s with its *Movie of the Week*. The advent of cable movie channels and home video during the 1980s made theatrical movies available to the public long before they would appear on network television. This prompted the networks to turn more to movies produced specifically for television. The increased popularity of cable movie channels and home video not only changed the nature of television programming; it reflected the growing desire for realism in entertainment by offering uncensored films to a much wider audience.

The influence of cable was also widely felt on documentary programming. Until the 1980s the major networks featured documentaries that examined complex and often taboo subjects. Such programs served as a source of prestige for the network news departments, but low ratings and cost-consciousness pushed most documentaries off the air by the end of the 1980s. Most were replaced by "news magazine" shows like *48 Hours, Dateline NBC,* and *20/20.* Cable filled the documentary void in two ways. First, it offered an array of channels that exclusively produced documentaries, including the Arts and Entertainment Network, the History Channel, and the Discovery Channel. Additionally, the premium cable channels regularly offered uncensored, gritty documentaries on contemporary issues in a series format, including HBO's *America Undercover.*

SPORTS programming has remained prominent since the 1950s, perhaps because sports is perceived as the one truly real, unrehearsed televised event. In 1970 *Monday Night Football* premiered and quickly went to the top of the ratings in its time slot. Since the late 1970s the National Football League's annual Super Bowl has usually attracted the largest audience of the year and demanded the highest price for a commercial spot. The Olympics, baseball's World Series, the National Basketball Association championship, the NCAA basketball championship, and college and professional football games continue to draw large audiences. Even professional golf, with the arrival of Tiger Woods on the PGA tour in the late 1990s, has begun to draw very large audiences for its major events. By the 1990s cable had become saturated with sporting events, and network audiences and advertising revenues dramatically declined. At the end of the 20th century, it is possible, with cable television, pay-per-view, and satellite television, to view literally hundreds of major sporting events on any given day.

Quiz and game shows were relegated to daytime television beginning in the early 1960s, until the mid-1980s when *Wheel of Fortune* and *Jeopardy!* became major hits in syndication. Game shows did not break back into prime time, however, until the late 1990s. The desire to see "real people" win $1 million made possible the phenomenal success of *Who Wants to Be a Millionaire?* In 2000 this game show, which aired three nights per week, occupied five places in the top 20 most viewed programs.

Because of its power as a medium, television is considered by the American public as its primary source of news and has been since the early 1970s. Network news anchors have achieved the status of celebrity and news became the kind of programming in which networks and local affiliates could compete against one another for audience share. News programs began to exhibit more entertainment value during the 1980s, as cost-consciousness prompted the networks to put more pressure on their news divisions to become more profitable. In addition, network evening news programs experienced sharp competition with the advent of cable news programs such as Cable Network News (CNN) and the later establishment of Microsoft National Broadcasting Corporation (MSNBC), a joint venture formed in 1996, with Microsoft and NBC linking Internet news with cable news. A short time later, in October 1996, media mogul Rupert Murdoch launched the Fox News Channel, under the slogan, "fair and balanced news," thereby implying that the other news channels were biased toward the political left. By 2000 Fox News had become the most-watched news cable channel and had cut into network evening news programs on ABC, NBC, and CBS. In 1979–80, 75 percent of all TV sets tuned in to either ABC, NBC, or CBS. By 2001 only 43 percent of Americans with television sets were watching network evening news programs. While ABC and NBC nightly newscasts fell in viewership, *CBS Evening News* was particularly hurt. When Walter Cronkite retired in 1981, *CBS Evening News* held first place for viewers, but 20 years later, this news program with Dan Rather as its anchor had fallen by more than half in viewership.

Until the advent of cable in the 1980s, children's programming consisted generally of Saturday morning cartoons and programs offered by the Public Broadcasting Service (PBS). PBS began broadcasting children's and educational programming in 1970. It is operated by the Corporation for Public Broadcasting, created in 1967, and is funded by public memberships, grants, corporate underwriters, and the federal government. It pioneered the broadcast of such shows as *Sesame Street* and *Mister Rogers* in the late 1960s and early 1970s. PBS also offers documentaries, dramatic series, and performing arts presentations. Cable television during the 1980s took advantage of the relative lack of children's programming by offering entire networks, including the Disney Channel and Nickelodeon, devoted entirely to children's educational and entertainment programming.

The power and pervasiveness of television in American society and culture at the end of the 20th century has caused a complex array of criticism to be leveled against it.

The shift in programming content toward relevance and realism demonstrates that television has become an integral part of American culture. But many critics argue that the electronic depiction of reality is distorted. The increased depiction of violence and sexuality, critics contend, has desensitized the American public to the reality of violence and sexuality. These critics raise important questions about CENSORSHIP by placing television as a critical player in the shaping of American society. Still other critics claim that television networks have failed to have proper minority representation on the screen and within the industry. The questions raised by these critics suggest that television as a medium, and its role in American culture and society, will continue to be debated and criticized, but its significance is indisputable.

See also ADVERTISING, ANTIWAR MOVEMENT, BABY BOOMERS; FAMILY LIFE; MEDIA; POPULAR CULTURE; RECREATION; SCIENCE AND TECHNOLOGY; TELEVANGE-LISTS; VIETNAM WAR (END OF U.S. INVOLVEMENT).

Further reading: Erik Barnouw, *The Tube of Plenty: The Evolution of American Television* (New York: Oxford University Press, 1990); Bernard Goldberg, *Bias: A CBS Insider Exposes How the Media Distort the News* (Washington, D.C.: Regnery Publishing, 2002).

—William L. Glankler

terrorism

Terrorism involves illegal acts of violence or intimidation by persons seeking to coerce or influence the conduct or policy of a government or civilian population. These acts often take the form of kidnapping, beating, or murder and are applied either individually, as in the case of hostage taking and ASSASSINATION, or collectively through the hijacking of aircraft, or indiscriminate bombing. For most of the 20th century, the physical territory of the United States has been largely untouched by acts of international terrorism and only rarely touched by incidents of domestic terror, and its defense strategy has reflected this relative peace. The devastation wrought by the attacks on the twin World Trade Center towers of New York, and on the Pentagon in Washington, D.C., on September 11, 2001, forced the United States to dramatically rethink its homeland defense.

Most of the acts of terror inflicted on American soil during the early to mid-1970s came from domestic radicals, such as the Black Panthers, the WEATHER UNDERGROUND, and the Symbionese Liberation Army. These groups undertook criminal actions that included burglary, bank robbery, assassination of police officers, and bombings. Though members of these groups viewed themselves as radicals organized against the government, federal authorities generally treated them as they would criminal

organizations. As a result, throughout most of the 1970s, the United States policy for homeland defense involved enacting new laws such as the Gun Control Act of 1968 and the Organized Crime Control Act (OCCA) of 1970, although these measure were aimed more against criminals than radical terrorists.

International terrorism was addressed only indirectly through a policy of economic sanctions against nations believed to harbor terrorist organizations or who gave asylum to hijackers. This response changed, however, in 1979, after Islamic fundamentalists overthrew the shah of Iran, Mohammed Reza Pahlavi, and installed an Islamic revolutionary government. On November 4, with tacit approval from the new authorities, Iranian students stormed the American embassy in Tehran and held 52 hostages for 444 days. President Carter failed to win their release during his term, even after halting oil imports from Iran and freezing more than $8 billion in Iranian assets. The hostage crisis had two results; it emboldened other Arab nations to use terrorist groups to take hostages with relative impunity, and it forced American lawmakers to reassess their counterterrorism strategies. In addition to existing sanctions, Congress provided special funding for the Federal Bureau of Investigation (FBI) and the Department of Defense (DOD) for new special forces units and antiterrorism assistance programs. It also required the administration to establish specific protocols in the event of future attacks on Americans abroad.

In March 1984 Central Intelligence Agency (CIA) station chief William Buckley was kidnapped by Iranian-backed Islamic Jihad in Beirut, Lebanon, and was later tortured and executed. The following month, 18 servicemen were killed and 83 injured in a bomb attack by Hezbollah terrorists near a U.S. Air Force base in Torrejon, Spain. Beginning in 1983, dozens of journalists, academics, and businessmen were taken hostage in a series of abductions throughout the mid 1980s, including Associated Press bureau chief Terry Anderson; Joseph Cicippio and Thomas Sutherland of American University in Beirut, Lebanon; and American businessman Edward Tracy. Anderson was held hostage for more than six and a half years, and many others were held more than five years in captivity. In addition to taking hostages, terrorists used suicide bombers to attack American installations; twice in Beirut in 1983, including the U.S. embassy in April (17 dead), the marine barracks in October (299 dead), and the U.S. embassy in Kuwait in December (5 dead). The U.S. embassy annex in Beirut was bombed again in September 1984, killing 16. American citizens became special targets even when the installation was not American in origin; a navy diver aboard a TWA flight was killed after terrorists hijacked the plane and forced it to land in Beirut in 1985. They held 39 Americans for more than two weeks, awaiting their demanded release of 700

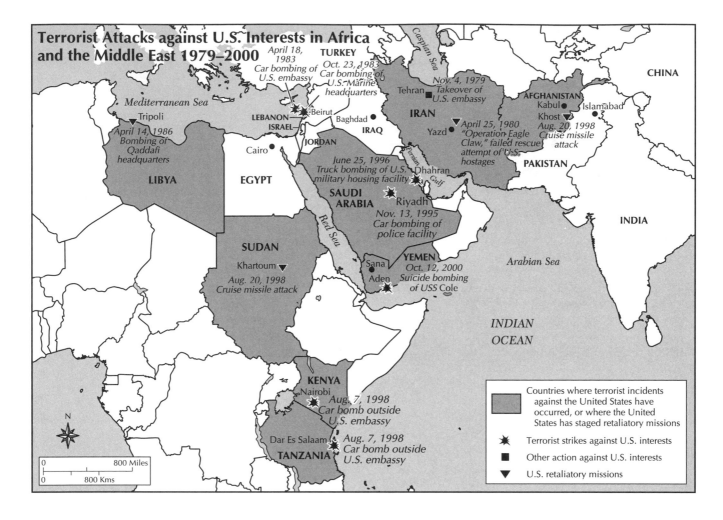

Terrorist Attacks against U.S. Interests in Africa and the Middle East 1979–2000

Arabs held in Israel. In October of that same year, Palestinian militants killed crippled American Leon Klinghoffer after they seized the Italian cruise liner *Achille Lauro*. The wave of terrorism culminated in December 1988, when Pan Am flight 830 exploded over Lockerbie, Scotland, killing 270 people.

The United States responded with a flurry of legislation including the Act to Combat International Terrorism (1984), which established rewards for the capture of terrorists; a call for a civil aviation boycott of terrorist states in 1985, and the Anti-Terrorism Act (1987), which specifically prohibited trade with or recognition of agents of the Palestine Liberation Organization. In addition, President RONALD W. REAGAN authorized the bombing of terrorist bases in Libya in April 1986. These efforts eliminated the more obvious vulnerabilities of American installations in the Middle East, but were largely ineffective in rescuing hostages. President Reagan came under criticism when he became associated with a CIA scheme to trade arms for hostages in the IRAN-CONTRA AFFAIR. For many Americans, however, terrorism remained a foreign problem asso-

ciated with the Mideast peace process; the solution to future terrorism seemed to depend on peace treaties between Israel and Arab nations. Congress continued to address homeland security indirectly with the Biological Weapons Anti-Terrorism Act of 1989 prohibiting transfer of relevant hazardous materials outside U.S. borders; an amendment to the Immigration and Naturalization Act (1990) providing safeguards against terrorist immigration; and the Anti-Terrorism Act of 1990, which provided civil remedies for American victims of international terrorist assault.

By 1990 the frequency of terrorist attacks declined by a third from its average of 630 attacks a year during the mid-1980s. A period of relative peace followed the first years of the 1990s, until a surprise attack on the World Trade Center in February 1993 left six people dead and wounded more than 1,000 others. A bomb exploded in the parking garage, but it failed to bring the towers down. Six Islamic radicals were caught, tried, and imprisoned by American authorities. Despite the ambitious scope of the attack, the United States did not significantly alter its policies with regard to terrorism, and the attack was largely viewed as a singular incident. Two years later in Tokyo, Japan, the Aum Shinrikyo cult placed containers of Sarin nerve gas in the Kasumigaseki subway station, killing 12 and injuring thousands. Some lawmakers became increasingly concerned that American cities were similarly vulnerable to attacks using weapons of mass destruction.

The following month their fears were confirmed when a massive truck bomb destroyed the Alfred P. Murrah Federal Building in Oklahoma City on April 19, 1995, killing 166 people and injuring more than 500. The tragedy was the largest terrorist attack on American soil up to that date. After initial speculation that it was the work of Middle Eastern terrorists, authorities soon discovered that it was in fact the work of two American domestic terrorists, Timothy McVeigh and Terry Nichols, acting in retaliation for the BRANCH DAVIDIAN disaster two years earlier. The Oklahoma City bombing, therefore, was not seen as an act of terrorism per se, but rather as the result of radical militia elements within the nation. This view was compounded when a militia group called the Montana Freemen entered into a two-month standoff with federal authorities in March 1996, followed six months later by a bomb explosion in Centennial Square during the 1996 Atlanta Olympic Games, which killed one person, and injured 111 others. Again, in January 1997, two bombs exploded outside an abortion clinic in Atlanta, Georgia, which many believed to be related to the Olympic bombing. Congress responded by establishing the Domestic Counter-Terrorism Center in 1995, which monitored the sale and distribution of materials that might be used to make weapons of mass destruction; and the Anti-Terrorism and Effective Death Penalty Act of 1996, which allowed the federal government to seek the death penalty for crimes of terrorism, and included provisions for easier information-gathering by law enforcement. Timothy McVeigh was sentenced to death, and was executed on June 11, 2001. Terry Nichols was convicted on federal charges and sentenced to life in prison.

While the American public became preoccupied with domestic terrorism, the most serious threats continued to originate with international terrorists. In November 1995 a car bomb exploded outside a U.S. military headquarters in Riyadh, Saudi Arabia, killing five American servicemen. The news came so close on the heels of the Oklahoma City bombing that it elicited little public response. Similarly, there was little public reaction after a truck bomb exploded outside the Khobar Towers in Dhahran, Saudi Arabia, killing 19 Americans and wounding hundred of others the following year. Congress passed a resolution that the United States should declare war against any nation that commits terrorist acts against American properties, but the law had little force and was soon forgotten. In August

Smoke billows from the World Trade Center's twin towers after they are struck by commercial airliners that had been hijacked by terrorists. *(Shaw/Getty Images)*

1998 two car bombs exploded simultaneously outside American embassies in Nairobi, Kenya, and Dar es Salaam, Tanzania, killing 224 people and wounding thousands of others.

Congress responded by passing the Global Military Force Policy (1998), which established a Coordinator for Counterterrorism under the Office of the Secretary of State. President WILLIAM J. CLINTON retaliated by sending 70 Tomahawk cruise missiles against a suspected terrorist stronghold in Afghanistan, and destroyed a pharmaceutical factory in the Sudan. Since the attacks came on the same day he was scheduled to testify before Congress concerning a scandal related to Monica Lewinsky, many Americans feared the reprisal was intended only to distract from the president's domestic problems. In October 2000, terrorists bombed the American warship USS *Cole* while it was refueling at a port in Yemen, killing 17 sailors

An F/A-18 Hornet prepares for launch November 14, 2001, while aboard the USS *Kitty Hawk*. The ship was supporting bombing missions over Afghanistan in Operation Enduring Freedom. *(Woods/U.S. Navy/Getty Images)*

and permanently disabling the ship. The *Cole* attack was viewed as an example of poor safeguards in American naval procedure, and not as evidence of an increasingly dangerous threat of international terrorism.

American policy with regard to both international and domestic terrorism changed significantly after the events of September 11, 2001. Nineteen members of the al-Qaeda terrorist network hijacked four separate commercial jets; two were crashed into the twin towers of the World Trade Center in New York City, a third struck the Pentagon, and a fourth was prevented from reaching its destination in Washington, D.C., by a passenger uprising. The resulting explosions and fires brought down both of the World Trade Center's towers and inflicted serious damage to a section of the Pentagon, with a resulting death toll of nearly 3,000.

The horror of the events united America unlike anything the recent generation had experienced. Thousands of volunteers donated blood in Red Cross centers around the country and showed their support with a flurry of American flags and financial gifts of nearly $2 billion to help the families of those lost in the tragedy. On the day of the attacks, President GEORGE W. BUSH announced the

new direction the United States would take in its policy against international and domestic terrorism; the United States would "make no distinction between the terrorists who committed these acts and those who harbor them." Earlier partisan conflicts disappeared almost immediately as the president received unqualified support from the entire Congress who passed a series of emergency response bills at the president's request, including the Combating Terrorism Act of 2001, which appointed a deputy attorney general for combating domestic terrorists and a national director for homeland security; and the USA Patriot Act of 2001. The latter law provided substantial funding increases to the FBI and DOD for their counterterrorism divisions; empowered the FBI, CIA, and Immigration and Naturalization Service (INS) with greatly enhanced surveillance powers to use against individuals and institutions suspected of terrorist activities; and tripled the personnel for the border patrol, customs service, and INS. It also provided law enforcement with stronger tools to investigate and prosecute money-laundering schemes used to finance terrorist activities. The new "war on terrorism" included an immediate attack on Taliban forces in

Afghanistan that were linked to Osama bin Laden's al-Qaeda network. In what is expected to last at least a generation, the United States redirected its FOREIGN POLICY, reoriented its domestic priorities, and has mobilized a major portion of its military and intelligence resources toward a new effort to destroy the sources of international terrorism throughout the world.

See also ASSASSINATIONS; BRANCH DAVIDIANS; CRIME; IRAN-CONTRA AFFAIR; IRANIAN HOSTAGE CRISIS; MILITIA MOVEMENT.

Further reading: Steve Emerson, *American Jihad: The Terrorists Living among Us* (New York: Simon & Schuster, 2002); Mark Juergensmeyer, *Terror in the Mind of God: The Global Rise of Religious Violence* (Berkeley: University of California Press, 2000).

—Aharon W. Zorea

think tanks

Think tanks are policy-oriented research organizations that provide expertise to government. By the year 2000 there were an estimated 1,200 nongovernment think tanks of various descriptions, various focuses on social and economic issues, and various sources of funding, at work in the United States. Of the major think tanks, only the Brookings Institution (1916) and the Carnegie Endowment for International Peace (1910) were founded before World War II. The American Enterprise Institute was founded during the war in 1943.

Although think tanks are ostensibly nonpartisan, in many instances they function as extensions of state power, coming into and falling out of influence with changes in governments, and shifts in the ideological climate of the country. In other cases, think tanks function more independently, questioning and monitoring state strategies and structures. (For example the Rand Corporation, founded in the aftermath of World War II, was created to monitor and evaluate air force programs, before it became an independent research organization in the 1950s.)

The course of the Brookings Institution reflects the kinds of changes that can occur in shifting ideological currents. In 1965 it represented mainstream Keynesian economic thinking, and its growing influence was reflected in renewed foundation support, especially from the Ford Foundation. Under its president, Kermit Gordon, Brookings' reputation as a liberal Democratic think tank was well entrenched. Under Gordon, the Brookings Institution became a major center for policy innovation in welfare, health care, education, housing, and taxation policy.

In 1976 the board of trustees appointed Bruce MacLaury to head the institution. A former regional Federal Reserve banker and treasury official, MacLaury suc-

cessfully courted business support, increased corporate representation on the board of trustees, and moved the institution toward a more moderate ideological stance. By the 1970s, the Brookings Institution confronted competition from other major policy research institutions, especially the American Enterprise Institute and the Heritage Foundation, both viewed as conservative research institutions close to the Republican Party.

The American Enterprise Institute (AEI), which was founded in 1943 as the American Enterprise Association (AEA), illustrates the experience of a conservatively oriented research institution that expressed deep ambivalence about the post–World War II policy consensus. The key figure behind the establishment of the AEA was Lewis Brown, chairman of Johns-Manville Corporation. From the start, the AEA reflected a conservative bias.

In 1954, A. D. Marshall, head of General Electric, assumed the institution's presidency and immediately hired William Baroody, Sr., and W. Glenn Campbell, both staff economists at the U.S. Chamber of Commerce, to head the research program. Under their guidance, AEA was gradually built into a modern research institute under its new name, the American Enterprise Institute. Principal support came from the Lilly Endowment, the Scaife Fund, and the Earhard and Kresge Foundations, as well as major corporate sponsors. The institution's reputation was enhanced when the Nixon administration called upon a number of AEI associates for government positions. The AEI also emerged as a successful proponent of economic deregulation.

In 1977 William Baroody, Sr., retired and his son, William Baroody, Jr., took over the presidency of the institution. To improve its standing in the academic community, the AEI assembled an impressive staff, including Melvin Laird, William Simon, Robert Bork, Michael Novak, and Herbert Stein. The tenure of William Baroody, Jr., however, ended abruptly in the summer of 1986, when an increasingly restive board of trustees forced his resignation because of cost overruns and declining revenues. Baroody's successor, Christopher DeMuth, bolstered the conservative orientation of the institute by bringing on board several former Reagan administration officials with strong rightist reputations.

The founding of the Heritage Foundation in 1973 revealed a new ideological climate in the analysis of public knowledge. Founded by Edwin Feulner and Paul Weyrich to provide rapid and succinct legislative analysis on issues pending before Congress, the Heritage Foundation sought to promote conservative values and demonstrate the need for a free market and a strong defense. The Heritage Foundation's articulation of conservative values in social policy, education, and government activities placed it at the forefront of New Right activity. The Heritage Foundation remained relatively small in its early years, but the election of Ronald W. Reagan to the presidency in 1980 enhanced the institution's prestige. By the mid-1980s the Heritage Foundation had established a solid place in the Washington world of think tanks as a well-organized, efficient, and well-financed research organization that called for the turning over of many government tasks to private enterprise, a strong defense, and a cautious approach to the Soviet Union and China.

During these years, a myriad of other think tanks emerged in Washington representing a range of ideological positions and specialized policy interests, including the left-oriented Institute for Policy Studies (1963) and the libertarian-oriented Cato Institute (1977). Think tanks concerned with national security including the Center for Strategic and International Studies (1962) and the Center for National Security Studies (1962), affiliated with the American Civil Liberties Union. The Urban Institute (1968) focused on domestic social, welfare, and family policy, while the National Women's Law Center (1972) worked on policies that affect women, especially reproductive rights, employment, and education. The Institute for International Economics (1981) became a major center for international economic and monetary policies, especially from a free-trade perspective. The traditionalist-oriented Ethics and Public Policy Center provided analysis of public policies related to religious issues.

Further reading: David Ricci, *The Transformation of American Politics: The New Washington and the Rise of Think Tanks* (New Haven: Yale University Press, 1993); James Allen Smith, *The Idea Brokers: Think Tanks and the New Policy Elite* (New York: Basic Books, 1991).

—Donald T. Critchlow

Thomas, Clarence (1948–)

Appointed to the United States SUPREME COURT in 1991, Clarence Thomas became the second African American to serve on the Court. Born the son of a poor laborer in Pin Point, Georgia, on June 23, 1948, Thomas was abandoned by his father before the age of two. Thomas's maternal grandparents then raised him and his brother. As a young man, Thomas considered becoming a Roman Catholic priest and entered Conception Seminary from 1967 to 1968, and then Holy Cross College, where he graduated in 1971. After abandoning his plans to become a priest, Thomas entered Yale Law School, graduating in 1974.

After law school, Thomas was hired as an assistant attorney general by Missouri's Republican attorney general, John Danforth, later U.S. senator. Renowned for his personal probity (he was an ordained Episcopal minister as well as an attorney), Danforth motivated Thomas to become a Republican.

When Danforth was elected to the Senate in 1978, Thomas became his legislative assistant. In 1981 Thomas became assistant secretary for civil rights in the Department of Education, and then chairman of the U.S. Equal Employment Opportunity Commission (EEOC) from 1982 to 1990. In 1990 President GEORGE H. W. BUSH nominated Thomas to the Federal Court of Appeals, D.C. Circuit. Eighteen months later, GEORGE W. BUSH nominated Thomas to fill the seat of Thurgood Marshall, the Supreme Court's only African American, who had retired. Immediately, Thomas faced opposition from liberals in the Senate because of his well-known judicial conservatism. Further troubles arose when accusations were raised by a former colleague at the EEOC, ANITA FAYE HILL, who accused him of sexual harassment.

The Senate Judiciary Committee reconvened to hear testimony from Hill that Thomas had harassed her with verbal obscenities. Thomas replied by denying her accusations. He also denounced his opponents for conducting "a high-tech lynching" of an African American man determined to think for himself on controversial issues. Distinguished witnesses testified for both sides. Public opinion polls sided two-thirds with Thomas's version of events, since Professor Hill had apparently kept in close touch with her former boss long after the supposed sexual harassment occurred. Thomas was narrowly confirmed, 52-48, along partisan lines, with 11 Democratic senators supporting his confirmation. On October 23, 1991, Thomas joined the Court.

On the Court, he constructed a rigorous jurisprudence based on natural law, historical context, and a strict interpretation of the Constitution. Thomas often votes with Justice ANTONIN SCALIA. Although Thomas has voted 90 percent of the time with Scalia, Thomas places more emphasis on historical analysis and national law, as seen in his extensive historical arguments in *U.S. Term Limits v. Thornton* (1995) and *U.S. v. Lopez* (1995). In *Bush v. Gore* (2000), Thomas voted with the five-justice majority. Unlike Justices SANDRA DAY O'CONNOR and Kennedy, though, Thomas agreed with WILLIAM H. REHNQUIST and Scalia that Article II of the Constitution, not the Fourteenth Amendment's Equal Protection Clause, should be the basis of the ruling on Florida's ballots. Thomas consistently argues the Equal Protection Clause should only apply to racial discrimination.

Further reading: Scott Douglas Gerber, *First Principles: The Jurisprudence of Clarence Thomas* (New York: New York University Press, 1999); Andrew Peyton Thomas, *Clarence Thomas: A Biography* (New York: Encounter Books, 2001).

—Christopher M. Gray

Thurmond, James Strom (1902–   )

Strom Thurmond, a U.S. senator from South Carolina, is best known for his strong support of state's rights and adherence to strict constitutional principles. He is also the oldest person ever to serve in Congress, an achievement he reached on March 8, 1996, at the age of 93 years and 94 days. On May 25, 1997, he set the record for the longest service in the Senate—41 years, nine months, 30 days.

Thurmond was born in Edgefield, South Carolina, on December 5, 1902. He received his bachelor's degree from Clemson University in 1923, became a state senator in 1933, and was elected governor of South Carolina in 1947. He was first elected to the U.S. Senate in 1954.

Thurmond's early political career was defined by a strong support of racial segregation and a fear of federal intrusion into the duties of state government. In 1948 he withdrew from the Democratic Party because of its civil rights plank in the party platform and ran as president on the newly formed State's Rights Party, nicknamed the "Dixiecrats." Although he received only 9 percent of the popular vote he had established himself as a leading proponent of state's rights. In 1956 he drafted the "Southern Manifesto" against the 1954 SUPREME COURT school desegregation ruling, singed by 19 U.S. senators and 81 representatives. In 1956 Thurmond filibustered 24 hours and 18 minutes against the 1957 civil rights bill.

Yet, after passage of the 1965 Voting Rights Act, Thurmond was the first southern senator to hire black staff members and appoint blacks to high positions. In 1964, Thurmond switched from the Democratic Party to the Republican Party to support Barry Goldwater in his unsuccessful bid for the presidency against Lyndon Johnson. He was also instrumental in shaping the "southern strategy" that helped capture the White House for RICHARD M. NIXON in 1968.

During RONALD W. REAGAN's administration, Thurmond served on the President's Commission on Organized Crime and as chairman of the Judiciary Committee, and was president pro tempore of the Senate from 1981 to 1987. He also became a member of the Labor and Human Resources Committee in 1984. In 1995 he was elected again as the president pro tempore of the Senate and today serves as the senior member of the Judiciary Committee and the Veterans Affairs Committee and is chairman of the Armed Services Committee. Thurmond is also the author of *The Faith We Have Not Kept* (1968). He announced he will retire from the Senate in 2002.

Further reading: Nadine Cohodas, *Strom Thurmond and the Politics of Southern Change* (New York: Simon & Schuster, 1991).

—William L. Glankler

tobacco suits

During the late 1990s, almost every state attorney general in the nation filed a suit against the tobacco industry to recover health-care costs of tobacco-related illnesses. American tobacco companies eventually resolved the suits in one of the largest settlement agreements in history, amounting to more than $300 billion over a 25-year period. These suits on tobacco-related products have been heralded by some as a victory for health and condemned by others as a gross violation of government authority.

It was not until the mid-1960s that the U.S. government took an active role in discouraging smoking. In 1964 the Surgeon General's office released a 387-page report entitled "Smoking and Health," which stated explicitly, "cigarette smoking is causally related to lung cancer in men." The following year, Congress passed the Federal Cigarette Labeling and Advertising Act, requiring tobacco companies to include the Surgeon General's warnings on all cigarette packages. By 1971 Congress further banned all broadcast ADVERTISING for cigarette products.

Private lawsuits were filed against individual tobacco companies as early as 1954 based on legal theories involving product liability and negligent breach of implicit warranty, though none of them succeeded. The first serious challenge came in 1983 after lung-cancer patient Rose Cipollone sued the nation's fifth-largest cigarette manufacturer, the Liggett Group, for failing to warn her about the dangers of its products. She was awarded a $400,000 judgment, but it was later overturned on appeal. The tobacco industry typically countered these types of charges by emphasizing the role of individual choice and consumer responsibility. Furthermore, tobacco lawyers claimed that it was "common knowledge," a legal term, that tobacco smokers realized the health consequences of tobacco use before they started smoking. They maintained that smokers made a voluntary decision to smoke and made a voluntary decision not to quit, and therefore voluntarily assumed any risks associated with the habit. Relying heavily on the 1965 imposition of warning labels on cigarettes, the tobacco industry successfully argued that the public was well informed of the reputed risks of smoking when they started. More important, the plaintiffs were never able to produce any direct causal links between smoking and various diseases, such as lung cancer and emphysema.

Opponents of the tobacco industry argued that the health consequences of smoking and chewing were not fully known to the public, but had become known to the tobacco industry, which continued to promote tobacco through massive advertising campaigns, often aimed at youth, and publicly denying research that showed a relation of tobacco use to cancer and emphysema, and other diseases. Furthermore, opponents of tobacco used public documents as well as industry memorandums that, they alleged, showed that the tobacco companies were covering up the serious, indeed, lethal effects of tobacco use.

On May 23, 1994, the legal attack on tobacco took an entirely new turn when Mississippi state attorney general Mike Moore filed a lawsuit against the entire industry in an attempt to recoup health costs of indigents' smoking-related illnesses paid for by the state. This approach allowed plaintiffs to avoid the question of consumer responsibility; the state was forced to pay a portion of smoking-related health costs, regardless of whether private citizens made informed decisions about smoking. Mississippi sued the tobacco industry for selling a defective product that carried with it known risks to individual and public health. Two and a half months later, on August 17, Minnesota attorney general Hubert H. Humphrey III filed a similar suit based on new arguments of fraud; he charged the tobacco industry with knowingly exploiting and manipulating the addictive characteristics of cigarettes to compel continued consumption. Furthermore, competing compa-

nies violated antitrust laws to conspire to conceal this information from the general public. Both states employed arguments that circumvented the issue of consumer responsibility. In addition, both cases emphasized the societal damage brought about by teen smoking, and charged tobacco companies with deliberately marketing to underage consumers. They maintained that tobacco companies needed teen smokers in order to facilitate new addictions in each succeeding generation. Tobacco companies rejected all claims, and responded with a countersuit arguing that the state attorneys general had no standing to file suit because they were not directly affected.

West Virginia followed Mississippi's example and filed a similar suit the next month; Florida joined in four months later. Though attracted by the new approach, most other states remained reluctant to file until after the question of standing had been answered. The hesitation ended, however, after the Liggett Group settled its claims with four states in 1995 for a total of $38 billion. The sign of vulnerability on the part of the tobacco industry resulted in an immediate action; 14 states filed

Antismoking demonstrators in front of the Philip Morris companies headquarters July 25, 2001, in New York City. *(Platt/Getty Images)*

suits in 1996 and another 20 filed during the first months of 1997. Each state requested multibillion-dollar judgments.

By early 1997 the federal government attempted to mediate a settlement between the states and the five major tobacco companies, R. J. Reynolds, Lorillard Tobacco, Philip Morris, Brown & Williams, and American Tobacco. Considering the scope of the pending litigation, the tobacco companies were persuaded to settle quickly; they reached an agreement on June 20, 1997, which required congressional approval and a presidential signature because it involved changes in federal law.

Initially, the settlement asked tobacco companies to pay $368.5 billion over 25 years; the states would receive an average of $5 billion a year, while the federal government would receive close to $6 billion a year to fund national antismoking campaigns through the Food and Drug Administration, which would be newly empowered to establish minimum federal standards for public smoking, regulate the production and manufacture of tobacco products, and enforce suspected violations. The agreement included specific provisions banning all outdoor advertising of cigarettes and the use of cartoon characters in printed media. The settlement also prohibited tobacco companies from sponsoring sporting events that cater to children and ordered the industry to set aside $750 million over 10 years to aid those programs affected by the loss of sponsorship. Most important, the agreement measured tobacco company compliance according to declining rates of teen smoking; if the rate did not follow established guidelines, the tobacco companies would be forced to pay additional money. Lastly, $25 billion set aside in a public health trust fund would be used to pay individual claims. In exchange, the tobacco industry would be protected from all future civil suits levied by public agencies, and would be limited in liability for individual suits to a total of $25 billion.

The tobacco industry signed the 1997 agreement because it promised to end all public litigation and set specific limits on the extent of private suits. The federal government would have benefited because it received more than half the award even though it was not party to any suit. Congress rejected it altogether in early 1998. Lawmakers claimed that the agreement was based on tobacco lobbyist groups, but the opposition actually stemmed from deeper concerns of justice and constitutionality. Opponents of the argument said that the government should never use civil litigation to effect social change; if tobacco products were in fact contrary to the public good, then they should be outlawed directly. Furthermore, government involvement in civil suits represented a clear conflict of interest, since it received annually, on both the state and federal levels, hundreds of millions of dollars in tax revenue from the sales of cigarettes.

In total, 52 pieces of legislation were submitted in both houses of Congress related to the tobacco settlement; none of them passed. Throughout 1998, tobacco industry representatives continued to meet separately with the state representatives suing the industry. By November, a new master settlement agreement required tobacco companies to pay out $250 billion to each of the plaintiff states over a 25-year period; each state legislature could choose to use the money in any way they deemed appropriate. They were also required to spend $2 billion to develop independent antismoking programs for youth and teens; ban all outdoor ads; provide athletic sponsorships; and create retailer education programs to halt the sales of cigarettes to teens. The states agreed to drop their suits, though no limitations were placed on civil suits filed by private plaintiffs.

In 1999 President WILLIAM J. CLINTON announced that the federal government would continue to pursue federal suits against the industry. On September 22, 1999, the U.S. attorneys general filed suit under the RACKETEER INFLUENCED AND CORRUPT ORGANIZATIONS (RICO) ACT, the first time the government had used civil RICO against an entire industry.

The following year, in September 2000, a District Court judge ruled that the federal government had no standing to sue because the government suffered no losses from tobacco industry practices. Janet Reno's office immediately submitted revised claims, but in July 2001, the same judge dismissed these suits as well. The federal response prompted some observers to question whether the state suits would have survived court consideration. As of 2001, Attorney General John Ashcroft continued prosecuting the remaining RICO claim against the tobacco industry.

The tobacco suits introduced a new approach to civil litigation in American jurisprudence. During the final years of the 20th century, state and local governments filed similar class-action suits against gun manufacturers and pharmaceutical companies. The future viability of this approach remains to be seen.

See also ADVERTISING; PROPERTY RIGHTS.

Further reading: Martha Derthick, *Up in Smoke: From Legislation to Litigation in Tobacco Politics* (Washington, D.C.: Congressional Quarterly Press, 2001); David A. Kessler, *A Question of Intent: A Great American Battle with a Deadly Industry* (Washington, D.C.: Public Affairs Press, 2001).

—Aharon W. Zorea

Tower Commission

John Goodwin Tower (1925–91), a former Republican senator from Texas was appointed to head RONALD W. REAGAN's President's Special Review Board (the Tower Commission) on November 6, 1986, to investigate the IRAN-CONTRA AFFAIR. Tower chaired the three-member, bipartisan panel that included former national security adviser Brent Scowcroft, and former secretary of state Edmund Muskie.

In February 1987 the commission issued a report chastising the Reagan administration and the president's advisers for their lack of control over the National Security Council (NSC). The Congressional Joint Investigative Committee, in 40 days of public hearings, listened to 28 witnesses, conducted more than 500 interviews and depositions, and amassed more than 300,000 documents. Although the report suggested the NSC should be overseen by Congress, it did not call for legal action or major institutional changes. In November 1987 the committee reported that the president bore the ultimate responsibility for the implementation of his administration's policies, but found no firm evidence that he had known of the diversion of funds to the contras.

Democrats in Congress criticized the Tower Commission's findings, asserting that since the commission did not have subpoena power and the assistance of the special prosecutor, it did not explain the entire affair. Republicans largely felt the matter closed, and commended the commission's findings.

—Michele Rutledge

Twenty-sixth Amendment

This amendment declares that the right of citizens age 18 years or older to vote "shall not be denied or abridged by the United States or by any state on account of age." In effect, this amendment gave the right to vote to all citizens of the United States 18 years and older.

The Twenty-sixth Amendment to the U.S. Constitution is the fourth amendment to specify voting rights (others include the Fifteenth, the Nineteenth, and the Twenty-third Amendments).

The passage of this amendment in June 1971 was encouraged by large-scale protests in the 1960s by students and others regarding the VIETNAM WAR. The amendment responded to the argument that citizens old enough to fight and die for their country should be able to vote. It reduced the voting age from 21 to 18 years, and allowed the opportunity for younger people to have a voice in the affairs of government and to share in the political process.

The Voting Rights Act of 1970 lowered the voting age only in national elections. In extending the Voting Rights Act of 1965 in 1970 Congress included a provision lowering the age qualification to vote in local, state, and federal elections to 18. In a divided decision, the SUPREME COURT held that Congress was authorized to reduce the age qualification in federal elections, but revoked the application of the provision in other elections as outside congressional authority. Facing the imminent possibility that the states might have to maintain dual registration records as well as bear the expense of running separate federal and state election systems, the states were responsive to Congress's proposal to establish a minimum age qualification of 18 for all elections, and quickly ratified the constitutional amendment.

See also AMENDMENTS TO THE U.S. CONSTITUTION.

—Michele Rutledge

U

United Nations (U.S. participation since 1968)

Since 1969 the United States has played largely a defensive role in the United Nations (UN), although occasionally it has emerged as a leading force within this body. In general, opposition to American leadership in the body had been found in the General Assembly; as a result, the United States has been most active in exerting its power in the UN Security Council, where it is a permanent member with a veto.

During the 1960s most of the European colonial possessions were granted independence, most notably in Africa. This influx of new states shifted the balance of power in the General Assembly. No longer were the Americans and their allies the dominant force, as had been the case since the United Nations was first established following World War II. African states became the largest single group of UN members. In the mid-1960s African, Asian, and Latin American states joined together to form the Group of Seventy-Seven, which became the dominant force in the assembly. Over time, the Group of Seventy-Seven came to include more than 100 states and constituted a solid voting bloc.

Being comprised of so many former colonies, the group often assumed a decidedly anti-Western stance and adopted positions on world economics, the Middle East conflict, and SOUTH AFRICA that were often at odds with American foreign policy. During the 1980s the United States became increasingly confrontational, not just arguing for liberal democracy, but acting in protest against UN agencies and policies. In 1985 the United States withdrew from the United Nations Educational, Scientific, and Cultural Organization (UNESCO) over disagreements on the nature of UNESCO activities, which were seen as being anti-Israel. That same year the United States refused to pay its assessed contribution to the UN Issues such as UN support for abortion counseling and the decided anti-Western posturing of the General Assembly prompted the U.S. Congress to withhold UN dues payments. The Americans were pledged to contribute 25 percent of the UN budget, not including special UN programs and peacekeeping operations. The United States did not alter its position on paying the UN until the 1990s, but it still withheld a substantial portion of its overdue payments.

Prior to 1989 the United States conducted most of its foreign policy largely outside of the United Nations. The United States established its own agencies to deliver humanitarian and foreign aid, participating only marginally with UN humanitarian agencies, compared with funding to its own organizations. In the COLD WAR period, it should be noted, the Soviet Union largely conducted its foreign policy outside the UN as well.

As the cold war came to an end, policymakers in the United States expressed greater interest and hope in the UN as an international peacekeeping organization. In 1991 the United States tested this new disposition toward the UN when Iraq invaded Kuwait. The United States exerted leadership in pressing for a UN resolution condemning Iraq's invasion of Kuwait, and in mobilizing a coalition army, with the support of the UN, to remove Iraqi forces from Kuwait in the PERSIAN GULF WAR. The resulting military operations successfully liberated Kuwait and marked the beginning of a very active period of UN peacekeeping activities. Peacekeepers were deployed to the Balkans, Mozambique, Somalia, El Salvador, Rwanda, and Angola. In 1999 the UN deployed new missions to Kosovo and East Timor, and expanded a long-term mission in Sierra Leone. As of March 2000, there were 765 Americans participating in peacekeeping operations, though none of these personnel were members of the U.S. military. Indeed, Americans accounted for less than 3 percent of UN peacekeepers.

In the period since 1968, 19 people have represented the United States at the United Nations. Lyndon Johnson appointed three ambassadors between 1968 and his leaving office in 1969 including Arthur Goldberg, George W. Ball, and James Russell Wiggins. RICHARD M. NIXON named

U.S. secretary of health and human services Tommy Thompson, with UN secretary general Kofi Annan, center, and U.S. secretary of state Colin Powell, before a meeting at a special United Nations General Assembly session on AIDS June 25, 2001, in New York City *(Platt/Getty Images)*

three ambassadors: Charles Yost, GEORGE H. W. BUSH, and John Scali. GERALD R. FORD retained Ambassador Scali until 1975 when he appointed Daniel Patrick Moynihan. William Scranton replaced Moynihan. JAMES EARL CARTER, JR., named two ambassadors: Andrew Young and Donald McHenry. RONALD W. REAGAN named just two ambassadors in eight years including Jeane Kirkpatrick and Vernon Walters. George Bush named just two ambassadors: Thomas Pickering and Edward Perkins. WILLIAM J. CLINTON named four persons to the post including MADELEINE K. ALBRIGHT, Bill Richardson, A. Peter Burleigh, and Richard Holbrooke. In 2001 GEORGE W. BUSH appointed John D. Negroponte UN ambassador.

Further reading: John Allphin Moore and Jerry Pubantz, *To Create a New World? American Presidents and the United Nations* (New York: Peter Lang, 1999); Edward C. Luck, *Mixed Messages: American Politics and International Organization, 1919–1999* (Washington. D.C.: Brookings Institution Press, 1999).

—John Korasick

United States v. Eichman   See flag burning

United States v. Nixon (1974)

This case occurred during the Watergate scandal and involved the issue of executive privilege and congressional power.

During the investigations of the WATERGATE SCANDAL, information came to light that President RICHARD M. NIXON had secretly taped conversations in the Oval Office that possibly were relevant to the investigation. In March 1974 a federal grand jury indicted White House officials H. R. Haldeman, John Ehrlichman, John Mitchell, Robert Mardian, Charles Colson, Gordon Strachan, and Kenneth W. Parkinson for participating in a cover-up of the Watergate burglary. President Nixon was named as an unindicted co-conspirator.

Following Nixon's firing of Special Prosecutor ARCHIBALD COX, JR., in April 1974 a new special prosecutor, LEON JAWORSKI, subpoenaed 64 tapes needed for the trials resulting from the indictments. Nixon refused to comply with the subpoena, offering instead edited transcripts in place of the actual tapes. The 1,254 pages of transcripts contained embarrassing material, including a large number of presidential deleted expletives, and they were also inaccurate and incomplete. The inaccuracies were exposed when the House Judiciary Committee released its version of the tapes.

U.S. District Court judge John Sirica, who had issued the original subpoena, rejected the transcripts as unacceptable and reissued an order for the original tapes. James St. Clair, the head of Nixon's Watergate defense team, appealed Sirica's ruling to the Court of Appeals. Jaworski, wishing to expedite the process, appealed directly to the Supreme Court. The Court agreed to hear the case on July 8, 1974.

Nixon's case rested on two issues. First, the administration questioned the judiciary's jurisdiction in subpoenaing the tapes, citing separation of powers. Second, the administration cited executive privilege, the need for the protection of communication between high government officials and their advisers. The Court unanimously rejected both claims in a ruling on July 24, 1974. On the first point, the court cited *Marbury v. Madison* (1803), which affirmed the power of judicial review. As for the second point, Chief Justice Warren Burger argued that neither separation of powers nor the need for confidential communication allowed for presidential privilege of absolute immunity from the judicial process.

On August 5, 1974, the transcripts were released, including one particularly damaging to Nixon, in which he discussed using the CIA to obstruct the FBI investigation of the Watergate break-in. Facing a congressional vote on IMPEACHMENT, Nixon announced his resignation on the evening of August 8, 1974.

—John Korasick

V

veto (presidential)

While no president since 1968 rivals Franklin Roosevelt's 635 vetoes, or even Harry S. Truman's 250 vetoes, vetoes invoked by all of the presidents from RICHARD M. NIXON through WILLIAM J. CLINTON account for 12 percent of all the vetoes in U.S. history. RONALD W. REAGAN vetoed the most legislation with 78, and Clinton vetoed the fewest bills with 30.

GERALD R. FORD, facing a Congress controlled by Democrats, vetoed 66 bills during his brief term, the most per year of any president except Franklin Roosevelt. GEORGE W. BUSH, also facing a Democratic-controlled Congress, vetoed 44 bills with only one veto being overturned, giving him a 98 percent success rate. JAMES EARL CARTER, JR., vetoed 31 bills and had two overturned and shares the second most successful veto rate with Clinton at 99 percent. Reagan had nine vetoes overturned for a success rate of 88 percent. Nixon had seven of his 43 vetoes overturned for a success rate of 84 percent. Ford was the least successful president having 12 vetoes overturned leaving him with a success rate of 82 percent.

Broken down by type of veto (either a regular veto, which can be overturned by Congress, or a pocket veto which cannot) 37 percent of vetoes since 1968 have been pocket vetoes. Clinton accounts for zero pocket vetoes. Fifty-eight percent of Carter's vetoes were pocket vetoes. Half of Reagan's vetoes were pocket vetoes. Nixon refused to sign 17 bills, or 40 percent. George H. W. Bush held 15 bills—34 percent of his vetoes. Ford only pocketed 18 of his 66 vetoes, 27 percent.

—John Korasick

Vietnam War (end of U.S. involvement)
(1969–1973)

The Vietnam War, America's longest war, which began in 1965 under the Johnson administration (although the United States had assigned military advisers to South Viet-

nam earlier), ended in 1973. America's involvement in Vietnam divided the nation, leading to a reevaluation of American foreign policy during the COLD WAR and America's place in the world.

When he came into the White House in 1969, President RICHARD M. NIXON sought to end America's involvement in the war in Vietnam through a negotiated settlement that would save as much face as possible for the United States. In order to pressure the North Vietnamese to accept an agreement, he intensified air strikes, while withdrawing American ground troops. By the time Nixon came into office, the war in Vietnam had become for many Americans a moral issue as to whether the United States should be involved in an "internal" war between North Vietnam and South Vietnam. As a pragmatist, Nixon sought to get the United States out of Vietnam as expeditiously as possible with the minimal cost to American prestige. In order to accomplish this, he decided to upgrade South Vietnam's military capacity through a policy of "Vietnamization."

When HENRY A. KISSINGER, his National Security Advisor, reported that North Vietnamese soldiers were using a trail through Cambodia as a supply route, while at the same time using Cambodia as a sanctuary, Nixon decided to launch a U.S. ground offensive and air raids into Cambodia on April 30, 1970. The Cambodian invasion unleashed a fury of angry protests on American college campuses. As a result of these demonstrations, Nixon withdrew American troops from Cambodia, declaring that their mission had been achieved.

In February 1971 the South Vietnamese army invaded Laos to cut off supplies flowing to communists in the south. The North Vietnamese army routed the invaders, who fled in disarray back to South Vietnam. Meanwhile, negotiations to end the war which were being conducted in Paris between Kissinger, the U.S. representative, and Le Duc Tho, the North Vietnamese representative, dragged on. Nixon sent Kissinger to Paris to negotiate secretly with North Vietnam's foreign minister.

American prisoners of war, most of them downed American pilots, were released from North Vietnam prison camps beginning on February 12, 1973, two weeks after the signing of a cease-fire agreement. *(United States Army)*

The war entered its final phase in 1972. By October 1972, with the American presidential elections fast approaching, Kissinger and Le Duc reached a secret agreement. This agreement provided for a cease-fire, the formation of a coalition government in South Vietnam, free elections, the withdrawal of the remaining American troops, and the release of all prisoners. When the South Vietnamese refused to accept the peace plan, the North Vietnamese angrily broke off further negotiations. Following his reelection in November, Nixon put additional pressure on North Vietnam to renew negotiations, by launching a massive bombing campaign from December 18 to December 29. The campaign, the "Christmas bombing," brought Le Duc Tho back to the table.

Finally, on January 22, 1973—the day Lyndon Johnson died of a heart attack on his Texas ranch—Nixon announced that a cease-fire agreement had been signed in Paris, which would allow U.S. troops to withdraw. Kissinger and Le Duc Tho won the Nobel Peace Prize for their efforts. Nearly 60,000 Americans had been killed—more than half during Nixon's presidency, 300,000 were wounded. In April 1975 the war ended in a communist victory, when the North Vietnamese captured Saigon, renaming it Ho Chi Minh City, and quickly absorbed South Vietnam into a single communist country of Vietnam.

The consequences of the American defeat in Vietnam left the nation traumatized. The war had polarized American politics as the Democratic Party swung to the left and the Republican Party swung to the right. Moreover, in the aftermath of the Vietnam War, defense budgets would be reduced and the United States appeared to lose confidence in its own place in international affairs. Only in the 1980s would the United States begin to regain its confidence as the world's leading power.

See also CONSERVATIVE MOVEMENTS; FORD, GERALD R.; FOREIGN POLICY; POLITICAL PARTIES, LIBERALISM; REAGAN, RONALD.

—Leah Blakey and Donald T. Critchlow

W

wage and price controls (Nixon)

Following the VIETNAM WAR, the economy in the United States experienced rising inflation that began in the late 1960s and continued into the early 1980s. President RICHARD M. NIXON sought to control rising prices by imposing wage and price controls in 1971, shortly before the 1972 election.

Nixon entered office in 1969 hoping to fight inflation, which had begun during the war in Vietnam, through spending cuts and tight monetary policy, while holding unemployment at 4 percent. Nixon's efforts failed, and by 1970 inflation had risen to six percent and unemployment had risen from 3.6 percent in 1968 to 4.9 percent. The rise in unemployment was partially due to the influx of servicemen returning home from Vietnam. In an effort to deal with these economic pressures, Congress passed the Economic Stabilization Act of 1970. This legislation granted the president the authority to impose wage and price controls. Nixon signed the act into law in June 1970, but was hesitant to impose wage and price controls, an economic measure he had criticized throughout his political career. As conditions worsened, however, Nixon was pressured by Congress, his own party, and the general public to take action. On August 15, 1971, wage and price controls were imposed under a policy Nixon called the "New Economy Policy."

Nixon implemented the New Economic Policy in four phases: Phase I froze wages, prices, and rents for 90 days. Phase II created a pay board and price commission to limit inflation to 3 percent and wages to 5.5 percent per year. In January 1973 Phase III relaxed the controls, and Phase IV replaced controls with commitments from business to limit price and wage increases for one year, beginning in July 1973. Finally, in April 1974 all controls were lifted when Congress refused to extend presidential authority further.

Initially the controls were successful and generally popular. Consumer prices rose by just 3.3 percent in 1972 and unemployment fell from 5.9 to 4.9 between 1971 and 1973. Problems soon surfaced in the form of consumer shortages, as businesses exported goods to more profitable foreign markets. More important, the oil-producing states in the Middle East, organized into a consortium called OPEC, imposed an oil embargo on the United States in October 1973. The cost of a barrel of oil rose from $3.00 in 1973 to $14.00 by 1974. As a consequence, inflation rose from 6.2 percent in 1973 to 11 percent in 1974.

Later, GERALD R. FORD and JAMES EARL CARTER, JR. tried to cajole business and labor into voluntary wage and price controls, but these measures failed as well.

—John Korasick

Wallace, George C. (1919–1998)

George Corley Wallace emerged as a powerful political leader in the late 1960s and early 1970s, running unsuccessfully for president three times in 1968, 1972, and 1974. He was elected governor of Alabama four times, in 1962, 1970, 1974, and 1982. He first gained national attention in the early 1960s for his opposition to school integration, but in his runs for the presidency he expanded his appeal to some northern white ethnic voters, upset with the VIETNAM WAR, antiwar demonstrators, and federal social programs.

Wallace was born in the small town of Clio, Alabama, in 1919. Although slight in stature, the young Wallace gained a reputation as a fierce amateur boxer. After matriculating at the University of Alabama, he graduated from the University of Alabama Law School in 1942. After serving in the army Air Corps during World War II, he entered politics, first serving as a Democratic representative in the Alabama legislature from 1947 to 1953, and then as a state judge from 1953 to 1958. In these years he earned a reputation for being a liberal on the "race" question. In 1958, however, he lost a race for governor when he was baited by his opponent as being too soft on the issue of segregation. This marked a turning point in Wallace's political outlook.

Four years later he ran for governor, declaring himself a proponent of states' rights and segregation. He won.

As the Civil Rights movement heated up across the country, Wallace declared at his inauguration in 1963, "Segregation now, segregation tomorrow, and segregation forever." He promised to "stand in the doorway" at the University of Alabama in 1963 to prevent the admission of two black students under a court order. After intense negotiations with the Kennedy administration, Wallace was allowed to stand blocking the doorway to the university administration office, and then step away when confronted by federal marshals, thereby allowing the university to be integrated. Wallace's symbolic act made him a hero to opponents of integration. Nonetheless, the public schools in Alabama were integrated during Wallace's first term.

Unable to serve a third consecutive term as governor, Wallace engineered his wife Lurleen's election to the governor's mansion in 1966. Already stricken with cancer during the campaign, Lurleen died in office in 1968. After failing to win the Democratic Party presidential nomination that year, Wallace organized the American Independent Party and ran on a third ticket. Although he ran a distant third behind RICHARD M. NIXON and Hubert Humphrey, he receive 10 million votes and carried five states to receive 46 electoral votes. His running mate was retired air force general Curtis LeMay.

In 1971 Wallace married Cornelia Ellis Snively. Shortly afterward, he began his race for the presidency as a Democrat. (The rumor was that Richard M. Nixon had pressured Wallace into running as a Democrat, instead of with a third party, in order to split the Democrats. The Wallace administration was under federal investigation for corruption.) During the campaign, Wallace was shot and left paralyzed by Arthur H. Bremer, a deranged 21-year-old man from Milwaukee, who was sentenced to 53 years in prison for the assassination attempt. In 1981 Wallace's marriage to Cornelia ended in divorce. Later he married country music singer Lisa Taylor, but this marriage ended in divorce in 1987. He made another race for the presidency in 1976, but was forced to withdraw.

In 1982 Wallace made a fourth bid for the governorship of Alabama. He declared himself to be a "born again" Christian and asked forgiveness from the African-American people of Alabama for his defense of segregation, which had led to violence across the South. He won election, receiving strong support from the black voters. He retired from politics in 1987 and died 11 years later in 1998.

See also POLITICAL PARTIES.

Further reading: Michael Barone, *Our Country: The Shaping of America from Roosevelt to Reagan* (New York: 1990); and Dan Carter, *The Politics of Rage: George Wallace, the Origins of New Conservatism, and the Transfor-* *mation of American Politics* (Baton Rouge: Louisiana State University Press, 1995).

Walsh, Lawrence E. (1912–)

Lawrence Walsh had a long and distinguished career as a lawyer before coming to national prominence in the 1980s as the independent counsel investigating the IRAN-CONTRA AFFAIR. Born January 8, 1912, in Port Maitland, Nova Scotia, Walsh and his family moved to New York City in 1914 and became naturalized in 1922. Walsh graduated from Flushing High School in 1928 and enrolled in Columbia University as a pre-law student. Walsh graduated from Columbia University Law School in 1935, and was admitted to the New York Bar in 1936.

Upon graduating from law school, Walsh worked on the staff of special prosecutor Hiram Todd's investigation of corruption in Brooklyn. In 1938 Walsh became one of District Attorney Thomas Dewey's "bright young men," charged with attacking the New York underworld. In 1941 Walsh quit the district attorney's office to join the Wall Street law firm of Davis Polk and Wardwell, but this foray into private practice was short-lived. In 1943 Governor Thomas Dewey named Walsh his assistant legal counsel and in 1953 appointed him general counsel of the Waterfront Commission of New York Harbor. In 1954 President Dwight Eisenhower appointed him federal judge for the southern district of New York. In 1957 Walsh became deputy attorney general and helped to coordinate the integration of the Little Rock, Arkansas, schools.

Walsh left public service in 1961, rejoining the Davis Polk and Wardwell law firm. During this time Walsh became a prominent corporate attorney with clients such as General Motors, ATT, and General Mills. In 1975 Walsh was elected president of the American Bar Association, where he advocated improved legal assistance for the poor; the elimination of jury trials in civil cases; and the decriminalization of gambling, prostitution, and marijuana possession. In 1981 Walsh resigned from Davis Polk and Wardwell, relocating to Oklahoma City and joining the firm of Crowe and Dunlevy.

Walsh returned to public service when he was selected as the independent counsel investigating the Iran-contra affair in December 1986. Within the first year, Walsh was under fire from critics, who charged that his investigation was taking too long. Walsh's job was made more difficult when Congress insisted on holding hearings and immunizing the testimony of key figures involved in the scandal. Walsh's team tried to gather as much evidence as possible before the hearings, and submit the results of his investigation to the courts before any testimony was immunized. In March 1988 Walsh indicted OLIVER L. NORTH, John

Poindexter, Richard Secord, and Albert Hakim on 12 criminal counts, including trying to deceive Congress. In June 1988, Judge Gerhard Gesell ruled that each defendant must be tried separately.

In May 1989 a jury convicted North of three of the 12 criminal counts; and in July the court fined him $150,000 and gave him a three-year suspended sentence. On April 7, 1990, Poindexter was convicted on five counts of deceiving Congress and sentenced to six months in prison. Both the North and Poindexter convictions were subsequently set aside on the grounds that their immunized congressional testimony had been unfairly used against them. In 1992 former defense secretary Caspar Weinberger was indicted on five counts of lying to Congress. On December 24, 1992, President GEORGE H.W. BUSH pardoned all the principals charged in the scandal. Walsh's eventual report, released in 1994, scored presidents Reagan and Bush for their roles in events related to the scandal but did not charge either with criminal wrongdoing. In July 1990 an appeals court overturned one and set aside North's other two convictions until Walsh could prove that his immunized testimony to Congress had not been a factor in the convictions. The SUPREME COURT upheld this decision in 1991. Unable to prove to the court's satisfaction that North's conviction was legitimate, Walsh was compelled to drop all charges in September 1991.

Walsh, a lifelong Republican, became a pariah to many in his party because of his dogged pursuit of justice, which many deemed a "witch hunt." Democrats criticized him for the length of the investigation, and the few convictions it produced.

See also IMPEACHMENT; INDEPENDENT COUNSEL.

—John Korasick

War Powers Act

The War Powers Resolution, generally known as the War Powers Act, was passed by Congress in 1973 over President Nixon's veto. The purpose of the act is to constrain presidential powers in involving American military troops in foreign interventions. This act was a direct consequence of the VIETNAM WAR.

The resolution stated that the president as commander in chief could only introduce and engage U.S. troops in hostilities following a declaration of war, specific statutory authorization, or an attack upon U.S. territory or against its armed forces. The resolution also required that after U.S. forces were involved, it was the president's responsibility to consult regularly with Congress throughout the duration of the forces' involvement. The resolution required congressional oversight by setting goals and deadlines for military "policing" actions. After U.S. armed force

involvement is approved, the commitment is limited to 60 days unless the Congress has declared war or has given special authorization for continued use of U.S. forces, or has extended by law the allotted 60-day period, or is physically unable to meet due to an attack on U.S. territory. The extension is limited to 30 days.

This resolution was a clear reaction following American intervention in Vietnam under the administrations of Eisenhower, Kennedy, Johnson, and Nixon. The *Interpretation of Joint Resolution* states, "Nothing in this joint resolution . . . shall be construed as granting any authority to the President with respect to the introduction of United States Armed Forces into hostilities or into situations wherein involvement in hostilities is clearly indicated by the circumstances which authority he would not have had in the absence of this joint resolution."

After the enactment of this law, presidents have generally ignored the strict limits set by this legislation as shown in a number of military interventions ordered by the president. In December 1982 Congress, concerned with American support for the CONTRAS in Nicaragua, amended the War Powers Act through the BOLAND AMENDMENT. Congressional opponents of President WILLIAM J. CLINTON's military intervention in Kosovo attempted to invoke the War Powers Act, but to little avail.

—Leah Blakey

Watergate scandal

The Watergate scandal was one of the worst political scandals in American history. It resulted in the resignation of the president, RICHARD M. NIXON, under threat of IMPEACHMENT and the conviction of several high-ranking members of his administration. Watergate takes its name from the break-in at the Democratic National Committee (DNC) headquarters in the Watergate apartment and office complex in Washington, D.C., in June 1972, but the scandal spread, as other illegal activities were made public.

The activities that would fall under the umbrella term "Watergate" began early in the Nixon administration. In 1969, Nixon approved wiretaps on the phones of government officials and reporters in an attempt to discern the source of news leaks about activities in Vietnam. In 1971 a special investigations unit was formed to plug news leaks. Dubbed the "plumbers," they broke into the office of Dr. Lewis Fielding looking for information to be used in the espionage trial against the psychiatrist of Daniel Ellsberg, the Rand Corporation analyst who had leaked the PENTAGON PAPERS to the *New York Times*. Also in 1971, Attorney General JOHN MITCHELL and John Dean, counsel to the president, met to discuss the need to obtain political intelligence for the Committee for the Re-Election of the

A demonstration outside the White House in support of the impeachment of President Nixon following the Watergate revelations *(Hulton/Archive)*

President. In 1972 Mitchell resigned as attorney general to accept the position as director of the committee. Shortly thereafter a plan was approved to break into the DNC headquarters to secure campaign strategy documents and other materials. The deputy director of the committee, Jeb Magruder, later testified that Mitchell had approved a plan developed by G. Gordon Liddy, the chief plumber, to break into the Watergate complex. Mitchell denied this. It has never become clear who ordered the operation or what the conspirators hoped to find.

On June 17, 1972, five men were arrested at the DNC headquarters, including the security coordinator for the committee, James McCord. The burglars were adjusting surveillance equipment they had installed in May when they were caught. Immediately a cover-up began. Magruder destroyed documents and gave false testimony to investigators. The White House blocked an FBI inquiry, declaring that it was a national security operation undertaken by the CIA. Mitchell resigned from his post on July 1, 1972, citing personal reasons. From the original investigation only the five burglars, plus Liddy and E. Howard Hunt, were indicted. In January all seven were convicted,

but the cover-up was beginning to unravel. In March 1973 U.S. District Court judge John Sirica received a letter from McCord charging that witnesses had committed perjury at the trial. He went on to implicate Dean and Magruder. Dean and Magruder broke under questioning and offered testimony that implicated White House and Nixon campaign officials. Dean testified that Mitchell had approved the break-in with the knowledge of White House domestic adviser John Ehrlichman and chief of staff H. R. Haldeman.

In May 1973 Senator Sam Ervin (D-N.C.) opened a special Senate committee investigation into the affair. At the same time, Attorney General ELLIOT RICHARDSON appointed ARCHIBALD COX as special prosecutor to investigate the entire affair. Cox soon uncovered widespread evidence of political espionage, illegal wiretaps, and influence peddling. In July 1973 it was revealed that Nixon had secretly recorded conversations in the White House since 1971. Cox sued to obtain the tapes. On October 20, 1973, Nixon ordered Richardson to fire the special prosecutor. Richardson refused and resigned; his assistant, William Ruckelshaus, refused and was fired. Finally, Solicitor General Robert Bork fired Cox. This became known as the "Saturday Night Massacre." It led to calls for Nixon's impeachment and the House of Representatives began an impeachment investigation.

Following Nixon's firing of Special Prosecutor Archibald Cox, in April 1974 Nixon appointed a new special prosecutor, LEON JAWORSKI. Upon assuming office, Jaworski subpoenaed 64 tapes needed for the trials resulting from the indictments. Nixon refused to comply with the subpoena and proposed a compromise in which he offered to provide edited transcripts in place of the actual tapes. The 1,254 pages of transcripts contained embarrassing material, including a large number of presidential deleted expletives; they were also inaccurate and incomplete. The inaccuracies were exposed when the House Judiciary Committee released its version of the tapes.

U.S. District Court judge John Sirica, who had issued the original subpoena, rejected the transcripts as unacceptable and reissued an order for the original tapes. James St. Clair, the head of Nixon's Watergate defense team, appealed Sirica's ruling to the Court of Appeals. Jaworski, wishing to expedite the process, appealed directly to the Supreme Court. The Court agreed to hear the case, *UNITED STATES V. NIXON*, on July 8, 1974.

Nixon's case rested on two issues. First, the administration questioned the judiciary's jurisdiction in subpoenaing the tapes, citing separation of powers. Second, the administration cited executive privilege, the need for the protection of communication between high government officials and their advisers. The Court unanimously rejected both claims in a ruling on July 24, 1974. On the first point, the Court cited *Marbury v. Madison* (1803) which affirmed the power of judicial review. As for the second point, Chief Justice Warren Burger argued that neither separation of powers nor the need for confidential communication allowed for absolute presidential privilege of immunity from the judicial process.

On August 5, 1974, the transcripts were released, including one particularly damaging to Nixon, in which he discussed using the CIA to obstruct the FBI investigation of the Watergate break-in. These tapes led to the indictments of Haldeman, Ehrlichman, Mitchell, Charles Colson, Robert Mardian, and Kenneth Parkinson for conspiring to cover up the Watergate scandal. Colson pleaded guilty to charges stemming from the Fielding break-in and the cover-up charges were dropped. Ultimately Haldeman, Ehrlichman, and Mitchell were found guilty.

Facing a congressional vote on IMPEACHMENT, Nixon announced his resignation on the evening of August 8, 1974, to be effective the next day at noon.

Further reading: Carl Bernstein and Bob Woodward, *All the President's Men* (New York: Simon & Schuster, 1974); Stanley I. Kutler, *The Wars of Watergate: The Last Crisis of Richard Nixon* (New York: W. W. Norton, 1990).

—John Korasick

Watt, James G. (1938–)

During his career in both public and private sectors, James Gaius Watt earned a reputation as an opponent of environmentalism and an advocate of business and industrial development. Watt was born January 31, 1938, in Lusk, Wyoming. He attended public schools, earned a B.A. and law degree at the University of Wyoming, then went to Washington, D.C., to work. Watt's nomination to lead the Interior Department was opposed by conservation and environmental groups. Nonetheless, appointed in 1981 by President RONALD W. REAGAN Watt served as secretary of the interior until his resignation in 1983.

As secretary of the interior, Watt narrowed the scope of the wilderness preserves, opened federal lands to coal and timber production, and sought to make a million acres of offshore land available for oil drilling. He raised the entrance fees to national parks, invoking more waves of protest. These policies, in addition to off-color remarks toward women, Jews, blacks, and Native Americans, encouraged the Reagan administration to accept Watt's resignation.

See also CONSERVATIVE MOVEMENT; ENVIRONMENTAL POLICY.

—Michele Rutledge

Weather Underground

The Weathermen emerged in the late 1960s as one of the most militant revolutionary organizations in the United States. Frustrated by their perceived failure to start a revolution in the United States, the Weathermen went underground to undertake a terrorist campaign against the country.

The Weather Underground emerged as a split within the student radical group, the Students for a Democratic Society (SDS), at its convention in June 1968. The split involved a Maoist faction, the Progressive Labor Party, and another Marxist-Leninist faction, the Revolutionary Youth Movement (RYM). Out of this RYM faction, the Weathermen (later changed to the gender-neutral "The Weather Underground") emerged, led by student revolutionaries, including Bernadine Dohrn, Mark Rudd, and Bill Ayers. Taking its name from a Bob Dylan lyric, "You don't need a weatherman to know which way the wind blows," the Weathermen called for guerrilla warfare to aid the communist North Vietnamese in their war against South Vietnam and the United States. The revolutionary group issued a "Declaration of War against Amerikkka," extolling violence. In 1969 the leaders of the Weathermen, including

Dohrn and Ayers, traveled to communist Cuba to meet with representatives from North Vietnam. At these meetings the Weathermen pledged themselves to aid the victory of North Vietnam in its war with the United States. In 1969 the Weathermen staged four days of rioting in Chicago, in the so-called Days of Rage. Organizers predicted the demonstrations would involve thousands, but only about 700 people actually participated. As a result of these violent days, other antiwar organizations denounced the Weathermen's actions and cut all ties with them.

The Weathermen decided to go "underground" and strike out at the government with a coordinated program of bombings. Shortly after the Chicago "Days of Rage," a townhouse in Manhattan exploded as bombs were being prepared by one cell of Weathermen for a planned terrorist attack at a dance at the nearby military base, Fort Dix. Other bomb attacks were more successful. Bill Ayers, as he describes in his memoir *Fugitive Days* (2001), bombed a New York City police station, the Capitol building, and a Pentagon men's room. Another member of the revolutionary terrorist group, Kathy Boudin, was involved in a robbery of a Brinks armored car that left two police officers and a guard dead. Another member of the Weather Underground, Linda Evans, was arrested for transporting 740 pounds of dynamite to be used to bomb the U.S. Capitol, the National War College, Israeli aircraft industries, and other sites. The Weather Underground established relations with other domestic and international terrorists, and throughout the next decade, terrorist bombings occurred throughout America.

By 1975, internal fighting caused factional divisions within the organization. In 1977 several Weather Underground leaders and members were arrested. Other activists turned themselves in to the police following President JAMES EARL CARTER, JR.'s partial amnesty for draft resisters. In 1980 Bernadine Dohrn and her husband Bill Ayers turned themselves in and were given probation. Dohrn became director of a law program at Northwestern University in Chicago, although she was disbarred from practicing in Illinois. Linda Evans was pardoned by President WILLIAM J. CLINTON in 2000. The organization is no longer active, but left a reputation for violence and terrorism in modern America.

Further reading: Ron Jacobs, *The Way the Wind Blew: A History of the Weather Underground* (New York: Verso Books, 1997).

—Leah Blakey

Webster v. Reproductive Health Services

In a 5-4 decision, the Supreme Court ruled in *Webster v. Reproductive Health Services* (1989) that states can impose limited restrictions on abortions services, and that mothers do not have a right to publicly funded abortions.

In June 1986 Missouri governor John Ashcroft signed a law requiring physicians to perform viability tests prior to abortions if they had reason to believe the pregnancy was 20 weeks advanced. The Missouri law also prohibited the use of public funds or public facilities or employees for abortion counseling if it was not necessary to save the life of the mother. Abortion rights advocates were especially upset by the statute's preamble, which explicitly declared that the "life of each human being begins at conception" and that "unborn children have protectable interests in life, health, and well-being."

Shortly after passage, representatives of the abortion industry sued the state of Missouri in federal district court, claiming that every provision of the statute, including the preamble, violated federal constitutional protections as interpreted by *Roe v. Wade* (1973). The district court ruled against Missouri. Upon appeal, however, the Supreme Court reversed the ruling, concluding, "nothing in the Constitution requires States to enter or remain in the abortion business."

Specifically, the Court considered two larger questions in the case: whether states can make value judgments favoring childbirth over abortion; and whether states can promote the state's interest in potential human life when viability is possible. On the first point, the Court ruled that due process clauses in the Constitution do not confer affirmative rights to government aid. Therefore no one has a right to publicly funded abortions. As such, states may establish their preference for childbirth by withholding public funds and public facilities for nontherapeutic abortions. Furthermore, the preamble to Missouri's statute does not compel legal action, but merely explicates the state's preference for childbirth. On the second point, the Court reiterated *Roe*'s finding that recognized a state's right to regulate or proscribe abortions to protect unborn children after the point of viability. The *Roe* Court created bright-line rules of viability based on an artificially created trimester system. In *Webster*'s majority opinion, Chief Justice William Rehnquist wrote that *Roe*'s "rigid trimester analysis has proved to be unsound in principle and unworkable in practice . . . Thus, the *Roe* trimester framework should be abandoned." As Justice Sandra Day O'Connor noted, *Webster* did not overturn *Roe* because it did not allow for the complete prohibition of all abortions. It did, however, recognize the state's interests and right to impose some limitations.

Webster was the first of a number of Court cases that recognized the state's right to regulate or proscribe nontherapeutic abortions within a limited scope, while at the same time upholding *Roe v. Wade*, which made abortion a constitutional right. Two years later in *Rust v. Sullivan* (1991), the Court upheld a federal policy prohibiting health care providers who receive federal funding from counseling or encouraging abortion as a method of family planning.

In *Planned Parenthood of Southeastern Pennsylvania v. Casey* (1992), the Court upheld a Pennsylvania law requiring women to wait 24 hours before procuring an abortion, and requiring abortion providers to give women state-developed information kits detailing the risks and consequences of an abortion.

In the end, the *Webster* decision did not satisfy either abortion proponents or opponents. Pro-choice advocates disliked the decision because it upheld state regulations that they felt restricted the right to abortion, while pro-life advocates maintained that the decision had upheld *Roe*.

See also ABORTION; AKRON V. AKRON CENTER FOR REPRODUCTIVE HEALTH; PRO-LIFE AND PRO-CHOICE MOVEMENTS; ROE V. WADE; SEXUAL REVOLUTION; SUPREME COURT.

—Aharon W. Zorea

White, Byron R. (1917–2002)

Byron R. White served as associate justice of the U.S. Supreme Court from 1962 to 1993. Justice White was a renowned civil rights liberal when he joined the Court. He adhered to judicial restraint for three decades on all cases, except those involving reapportionment and minority civil rights.

Born in Fort Collins, Colorado, White attended public schools and then went to the University of Colorado, where he became an All-American football player and valedictorian of his graduating class in 1937. In 1938 he signed with the Pittsburgh Steelers professional football team for the largest NFL contract at that time. In 1938 he accepted a Rhodes scholarship to study in England at Oxford University. In 1940 he returned to the United States to play for the Detroit Lions, leading the league in rushing before he retired in 1941. During World War II, White served as a naval intelligence officer in the Pacific from 1942–45. While attending Oxford and serving during World War II in the Pacific, White became friendly with young John F. Kennedy.

White graduated at the top of his class at Yale Law School in 1946 and then clerked for Chief Justice Fred Vinson from 1946 to 1947, before returning to private practice in Colorado from 1947 through 1961. During the 1960 presidential campaign, he supported John F. Kennedy, and following the election, he was appointed Attorney General Robert Kennedy's deputy at the Justice Department. White's experiences working against legalized segregation and prosecuting violent civil rights violations influenced him to be a lasting supporter of voting rights, reapportionment, desegregation, and affirmative action. In 1962 Kennedy nominated him to fill a seat on the SUPREME COURT vacated by Charles Evans Whittaker. He was easily confirmed by the Senate on April 11, 1963.

On the Court, White became known as a moderate, often siding with liberals on civil rights cases, though on personal liberty and criminal justice cases he usually sided with the conservatives. For example, in *Robinson v. California* (1962), White dissented from the majority ruling that states could not make narcotics addiction a crime. He accused the majority of importing "into the Constitution [their] own abstract notions of how best to handle the narcotics problem." Also, White authored a dissent in *Miranda v. Arizona* (1966), which stated that it was a constitutional right to have the right to counsel after an arrest.

White's reading "of the long-range interest in the country" led him to be skeptical of rights to protect confidential sources, and protests against lawful authority. He upheld subpoena powers against reporters' confidentiality in various cases. In *Cohen v. California* (1971), *Texas v. Johnson* (1989), and *U.S. v. Eichman* (1990), White joined minority dissenters in opposing obscene political speech and burning of the American flag.

White also dissented from majority decisions in the Warren and Burger Courts' decisions concerning contraceptive and abortion rights, based on a loosely constructed definition of "privacy" in the U.S. Constitution. In a case involving the constitutionality of prohibiting the sale of contraceptives, *Griswold v. Connecticut* (1965), White concurred with the majority that this Connecticut statute regulating contraceptives was unenforceable, but he dissented from Justice William Douglas's use of the legal concept, "right to privacy." In *Roe v. Wade* (1973), the Court declared abortion was a constitutional right, based on the "right to privacy" standard. White was one of two justices to dissent from this decision, arguing that he could find "no constitutional warrant for imposing such an order of priorities on the people and legislatures of the states."

White continued to oppose *Roe* in later abortion decisions that came before the Court, most notably in WEBSTER V. REPRODUCTIVE HEALTH SERVICES (1989) and *Planned Parenthood v. Casey* (1992). He wrote the majority opinion in *Bowers v. Hardwick* (1986) upholding the Georgia statute criminalizing homosexual sodomy.

White stepped down from the Court in 1993 because of illness. He died April 17, 2002.

Further reading: Dennis J. Hutchinson, *The Man Who Once Was Whizzer White* (New York: Free Press, 1998).

—Christopher M. Gray

women's rights and status

American women have experienced dramatic changes in their economic status, social roles, and cultural place since

1969. More women attend college, work outside the home, earn more income, and remain single than ever in American history. In 2000, 60.3 percent of women participated in the labor force, compared with 43.1 percent participation in 1970. In 1970 the median income for women employed full-time was $21,470 compared to a median income of $36,247 for full-time male workers; in 1998, the medium income for women was $26,855 compared with a median income of $36,252 for male full-time workers. Furthermore, more women remain single; the proportion of women, age 30–34, who had never married increased from 6.2 percent in 1970 to 21.6 percent in 1998. For men, it rose from 9.4 percent to 29.2 percent.

Life expectancy for women has increased steadily throughout the 20th century. While life expectancy differs by race, life expectancy for women of all races exceeds that of men. African-American males' life expectancy increased from 60 years to 68 years between 1970 and 2000. African-American women significantly outlive African-American men, with a life expectancy in 1970 of 68 years increasing to 74 years in 1990. White women's life expectancy has grown less, from 76 to 79 years. White men's expected span increased from 68 to 73.

In 2000 men and women were earning high school diplomas at a higher rate than in 1970. In 1970, 53 percent of women over 25 years of age had earned a high school diploma compared with 52 percent of men. By 2000, 84 percent of women and 88 percent of men over 25 years were high school graduates. The same period, 1970–2000, saw an increase in the percentage of college graduates. In 1970 only 8 percent of women or women over 25 had college degrees. This had grown to 24 percent by 2000. In 1970 women received 43 percent of the bachelor's degrees conferred; this had increased to 56 percent by 2000.

The increase in educational achievement parallels changes in marriage status for women. In 1990, 79 percent of women over the age of 15 and over 24 had never been married. This figure increased to 31 percent of women in 2000. Divorce became more common between 1970 and 2000, increasing from 4 to 10 percent of women. The percentage of families maintained by women has increased steadily between 1970 and 2001, from 11 to 17 percent.

These families maintained by women have earned considerably less than married-couple families. Female householder families earned $15,616 in 1969 compared with $32,136 for married couple families. The gap widened significantly by 1989 with female householder families earned $17,414 compared with $39,584 with married couple families.

Women have increasingly entered the workplace. In 1980, 50 percent of all women worked outside the home. This increased to 60 percent in 2000. Despite the increasing numbers of women entering the workforce and the increased education of women, the labor market is still largely segregated by sex.

Women have made inroads into managerial and professional positions, with 42 and 54 percent of these occupations being represented by women in 2000. Still, in 2000 women tended to be overrepresented in "female" occupations such as administrative support/clerical and services occupations, 77 and 63 percent. In 2000 women were underrepresented in farming, forestry, fishing, craft, transportation, and labor occupations.

These statistics indicate an improvement in the status of women over the past 30 years. The emergence of the women's movement in the 1960s benefited from the successes of the Civil Rights movement and contributed to the social upheaval of the period. The women's movement of the 1960s and 1970s, championing equal rights for women, was the "second wave" of feminism, which had begun in the 19th century with the struggle over women's right to control property, be educated, work outside the home, and vote. In *The Feminine Mystique* (1963), Betty Friedan gave voice to American homemakers unhappy in their roles of wives and mothers. Friedan challenged the notion that women could and should only find fulfillment in these domestic roles. Friedan became one of the founders of the NATIONAL ORGANIZATION FOR WOMEN (NOW) in 1966. In *Sexual Politics*, feminist author Kate Millet defined politics as a power relationship with one group controlling another, and applied this to marriage, a patriarchal institution. This view of marriage politicized issues like the division of labor in the household. By embracing this position, feminism quickly became labeled as antifamily.

Women have benefited from national legislation. The Equal Pay Act of 1963 and the Civil Rights Act of 1964 were major steps forward in terms of women's rights in the workplace. The Education Act of 1972 is also hailed as a landmark piece of legislation. Title IX of the Civil Rights Act prohibited sex discrimination in educational programs that received federal funds and opened the door for women to participate more fully in colleges and universities. In addition to legislation, the U.S. SUPREME COURT decision in *Roe v. Wade* (1973) guaranteed the right to abortion, making abortion an issue of privacy and giving women more control over their bodies.

During the 1970s, the Equal Rights Amendment surfaced as a major political issue. Originally proposed in the 1920s and voted on periodically in the 1940s and 1950s, it had never been passed. In 1972 the ERA passed the House of Representatives and the Senate and was sent to the states for ratification. By 1973, 30 states had ratified the ERA. Backlash against the amendment coalesced into a formal movement in 1973, led by PHYLLIS SCHLAFLY, a conservative activist. Despite an extension of the ratification deadline from 1978 to 1982, the STOP-ERA movement succeeded in blocking ratification.

Women play an important role in politics, although women held only 71 seats (13.3 percent of the total) in both houses of Congress in 2000. As of 2000, 3 of the 50 state governors were women, including Jane Dee Hull (R-Ariz.); Christine Todd Whitman (R-N.J.), later appointed to head the Environmental Protection Agency in the GEORGE W. BUSH administration, and Jeanne Shaheen (D-N.H.). On the state level in 2000, 1,670, or 22.5 percent, of state legislators were women. In 1969, 301 or 4 percent of state legislators were women. The Supreme Court has two women, SANDRA DAY O'CONNOR and RUTH BADER GINSBURG.

Women's participation in high school and collegiate sports increased following the passage of Title IX of the Education Amendments Act, prohibiting discrimination against women by schools receiving federal aid. In 1971, before Title IX, fewer than 300,000 girls in the United States took part in high school sports, compared with 3.6 million boys. By 1998, 2.5 million girls and 3.7 million boys participated in high school athletics.

The changing roles and status for women from 1969 to 2000 is arguably one of the most significant social changes in this period of America's history.

Further reading: Jo Freeman, *Women: A Feminist Perspective* (Mountain View, Calif.: Wadsworth, 1995); Nancy Woloch, *Women and the American Experience: A Concise History* (Boston: McGraw Hill, 2002).

—John Korasick

Woodstock (music festival)

The Woodstock Music and Art Fair marked the largest counterculture gathering of the 1960s and has come to symbolize hippie values and youthful excess. Taking place over three days, August 15–17, 1969, on a farm near Bethel, New York, over 400,000 people gathered to hear the music of many of the greatest acts in rock 'n' roll history, including Creedence Clearwater Revival; Crosby, Stills, Nash, and Young; the Grateful Dead; Jimi Hendrix; Janis Joplin; and the Who.

Woodstock was the idea of four young men: John Roberts, Joel Rosenman, Artie Kornfeld, and Michael Lang. In March 1969 the four formed a corporation, Woodstock Ventures, Inc., and the idea for the world's largest rock 'n' roll show was born. Originally, the plan was for a concert for 50,000 people, but gradually the number increased to 200,000. No one was prepared for the number of people who actually arrived. There was a severe lack of water, food, and sanitation facilities. Because the concert was held in the open, and the organizers did not erect fences, thousands of people showed up without paying and with no intention of paying. The numbers of people trying to reach the festival closed the New York State Thruway and created a horrendous traffic jam.

The concert was sold as "Three Days of Peace and Music," to provide a link to the antiwar movement and to prevent any violence. The campaign was successful; the concert was remarkably nonviolent given the size of the crowd and the lack of amenities.

Two subsequent "Woodstock" concerts were held in the 1990s. The first, in 1994, commemorated the 25th anniversary of the original event, and was successful enough that another concert was planned. The second "Woodstock" of the 1990s was held in 1999 and rapidly degenerated into a riot, becoming more famous for arson, assault, rape, and looting.

–John Korasick

World Trade Organization (WTO)

The WTO was formed during the Uruguay Round of the GENERAL AGREEMENT ON TARIFFS AND TRADE (GATT) and codified in the signing of the "Marrakesh Protocol to the General Agreement on Tariffs and Trade 1994." The WTO was to replace GATT's informal negotiating role with a permanent organization to implement and promote international trade practices. The WTO has the authority to enforce trade agreements, oversee disputes and provide an international legal framework for trade. The rules of the WTO are legally binding on all member states. The scope of the WTO is far greater than GATT and includes trade in services and intellectual property. The headquarters of the WTO were established in Geneva, Switzerland, and came into operation on January 1, 1995. The 128 nations of GATT became members and by 2000 the WTO had 136 members, with others, including China and Russia, applying for membership. The United States approved China's entry in 2000, China was admitted in late 2001. The WTO is headed by a biennial Ministerial Conference, in which each country has one equal vote. There is a director-general, who heads the Secretariat, and a General Council, composed of representatives of each member state, which meets as required to take action on issues brought forward by either the Trade Policy Review Body or the Dispute Settlement Body (DSB).

The WTO has attracted a great deal of attention in the fierce debate over globalization. Supporters point to the achievement of free-trade policies and the extension of the global economy. Critics cite the great disparities in global wealth and argue that the WTO disproportionately favors the wealthiest nations. Furthermore, critics on the right, such as PATRICK BUCHANAN, have charged that the WTO infringes on the national sovereignty of the United States. The United States, as the leading economy, draws particular criticism, as was evident at the third ministerial meeting of the WTO in Seattle, Washington, in November and December 1999. More than 30,000 protesters descended on the city to protest against the WTO and the subsequent media coverage ignited a debate over its role, and its relationship to large business interests in the United States. The American people, generally, became aware of the opposition to the WTO during the Seattle conference, as a variety of groups, including radical fringe groups, seized the national spotlight by demanding that the WTO become a more socially conscious institution, focused on improving the living and working conditions in developing nations.

Subsequent protests in Europe and Washington, D.C., in 2000 and the debate over the entry of China and Russia highlighted the problems faced by the WTO in defining its role and in its relationship to national governments.

See also ECONOMY; GLOBALIZATION.

—Stephen Hardman and John Korasick

Wright, James C., Jr. (1922–)

James Wright (D-Tex.) served as a member of the U.S. Congress from 1954 to 1989, and he became Speaker of the House in 1987 until he resigned from office. James Claud Wright was born in Fort Worth, Texas, on December 22, 1922. After attending public schools in Dallas and Fort Worth, Wright went on to study at Weatherford College and the University of Texas. In December 1941 he enlisted in the U.S. Army Air Corps, was commissioned in 1942, and flew combat missions in the South Pacific. Following World War II, Wright was a Texas state representative (1947–49), mayor of Weatherford, Texas (1950–54), and served as president of the League of Texas Municipalities in 1953. He was elected to the U.S. House of Representatives from Texas in 1954, served as a delegate to the Democratic National Conventions held in 1956, 1960, 1964, and 1968, and convention chairman in 1988. A moderate Democrat, he became House majority leader in 1976 and was designated by his colleagues as the most respected member of the House in 1980.

In 1987 Wright became House Speaker, but within two years he became embroiled in allegations of financial impropriety involving a sweetheart deal on a privately published book with royalties of 55 percent compared to the normal 10–15 percent in most contracts. Leading the campaign against him was Newt Gingrich (R-Ga.), who with a group of other conservatives had seized on ethical problems of his colleagues, particularly but not exclusively when cases involved a Democrat. In April 1989 the House Ethics Committee issued a five-count indictment against Wright. Shortly afterward, newspapers revealed that Wright's right-hand man, House Democratic whip Tony Coelho (D-Calif.) had been involved in a questionable junk-bond deal, leading to his resignation from his seat on Memorial Day. On May 31, 1989, Wright, under public pressure, announced he was resigning from his seat. Thomas Foley (D-Wash.) became Speaker of a partisan-charged House. The defeat of Wright marked the first step in a campaign under Gingrich for the Republican Party to become the majority party in the House, finally doing so in the 1994 midterm elections.

—Michele Rutledge

Chronology

1969

California passes the first "no-fault" divorce law, which permits dissolution of marriages on the basis of incompatibility or irreconcilable differences; previously adultery, cruelty, and desertion were the only legal grounds.

Abe Fortas resigns from the U.S. Supreme Court after conservative senators call for his impeachment.

Warren Burger succeeds Earl Warren as chief justice of the Supreme Court.

Patrons of the Stonewall Inn, a gay bar in New York City, resist a routine police raid. The resulting Stonewall Riot spurs the gay rights movement in the United States.

Neil Armstrong becomes the first man to walk on the moon during the *Apollo 11* mission.

More than 400,000 people attend the Woodstock Music and Art Fair.

A domestic terrorist group known as the Weathermen tries to spark a socialist revolution, staging the four-day "Days of Rage" riots in Chicago.

The Nixon administration implements the Philadelphia Plan, which requires contractors on federally funded projects to set specific goals for hiring minorities.

The "Chicago Eight" are tried in a highly publicized trial. They are charged with inciting a riot outside the 1968 Democratic National Convention.

President Nixon's "Silent Majority" speech announces his intention to end the war in Vietnam.

A protest group called Indians of All Tribes occupies Alcatraz Island in San Francisco Bay for 19 months.

1970

U.S. Congress passes the National Environmental Policy Act of 1970, which requires federal agencies to include an environmental impact statement in every recommendation or proposed federal action that will significantly affect the U.S. environment. That same year the Environmental Protection Agency is established to evaluate the impact of waste and pollution and to enforce standards.

The first Earth Day is celebrated on March 21.

Kate Millet's *Sexual Politics* is published; the best-selling book analyzes female oppression.

American troops invade Cambodia. Protests sweep American college campuses; Ohio National Guardsmen fatally shoot four students while dispersing a demonstration at Kent State University.

U.S. Congress passes the Organized Crime Control Act of 1970, which strengthens laws used to fight crime syndicates. Among its provisions is the Racketeer Influenced and Corrupt Organizations (RICO) Act of 1970, which defines penalties for racketeering.

U.S. Congress passes the Controlled Substance Act, which consolidates numerous laws regarding the manufacture and distribution of legal and illegal drugs.

U.S. Congress passes the Occupational Safety and Health Act of 1970, which gives the Secretary of Labor the authority to establish safety standards for all workers engaged in interstate commerce.

U.S. Congress passes the Clean Air Act of 1970, which sets national ambient air quality standards.

1971

In *Gillette v. United States,* the U.S. Supreme Court limits conscientious-objector status to those who oppose all wars, not just a particular war.

The U.S. Supreme Court decision *Swann v. Charlotte-Mecklenburg Board of Education* upholds the constitutionality of court-imposed desegregation plans, such as busing students to schools outside of their neighborhoods.

Bury My Heart at Wounded Knee by Dee Brown is published; it provides inspiration to the burgeoning Native American protest movement.

The Twenty-sixth Amendment to the U.S. Constitution establishes a uniform voting age of 18 years for national elections.

In *New York Times v. United States; United States v. Washington Post,* the U.S. Supreme Court limits the constitutional right of the federal government to prohibit the publication of certain material considered vital to national security.

U.S. Congress bans all broadcast advertising for tobacco products.

The silicon chip is invented.

President Nixon freezes prices and wages to control inflation, unemployment, and international monetary speculation.

U.S. Congress passes the Federal Election Campaign Act of 1971, which provides public funding for presidential election campaigns through a voluntary one dollar income tax check-off.

1972

Nixon visits the People's Republic of China; this is a major step in normalizing relations between the two nations.

Congress approves the proposed Equal Rights Amendment (ERA) to the U.S. Constitution, originally proposed in 1923, which explicitly stipulates "equality of rights under the law shall not be denied or abridged by the United States or by any State on account of sex."

U.S. Congress enacts the Equal Employment Opportunities Act of 1972, which encourages racial quotas in hiring and education and marks the beginning of affirmative action.

The Trail of Broken Treaties, a protest march to Washington, D.C., culminates in the takeover of the Bureau of Indian Affairs building.

U.S. president Richard Nixon and Soviet general secretary Leonid Brezhnev negotiate the Strategic Arms Limitation Treaty (SALT I), which mandates a reduction in U.S. and Soviet strategic offensive weapons launch vehicles.

The Democratic Party's national headquarters at the Watergate Hotel is burglarized by agents of the Nixon White House.

In *Branzburg v. Hayes,* the U.S. Supreme Court rules that the First Amendment to the U.S. Constitution does not grant journalists the right to withhold the identities of their sources.

In *Furman v. Georgia,* the U.S. Supreme Court declares the death penalty to be "cruel and unusual punishment" and in violation of the Eighth and Fourteenth Amendments to the U.S. Constitution.

U.S. Congress passes the Clean Water Act of 1972 with the principal goal of eliminating all water pollution discharges by 1985.

President Richard Nixon is reelected, defeating Democratic challenger George McGovern.

Nixon's "Vietnamization" policy leads to the withdrawal of many U.S. troops from South Vietnam.

1973

In *Roe v. Wade,* the U.S. Supreme Court rules that the Fourteenth Amendment to the U.S. Constitution gives an adult woman the right to terminate her pregnancy during the first trimester without any government interference. The decision stipulates that a woman's right to privacy includes her reproductive organs and draws a distinction between utter dependency and human viability.

Members of the American Indian Movement (AIM) occupy the site of the Wounded Knee Massacre of 1890 for 71 days. The protestors make a wide range of demands, including an investigation into the treatment of Native Americans. The demonstration ends in an armed confrontation between AIM activists and government officials.

The United States signs the Paris Accord, which pledges to end U.S. involvement in the Vietnam War.

President Nixon announces the end of the draft.

The American Psychiatric Association removes homosexuality from its list of disorders.

The Senate conducts an investigation of the Watergate affair under Senator Sam Ervin.

Vice President Spiro T. Agnew resigns after an investigation reveals that he had accepted bribes while governor of Maryland; Representative Gerald R. Ford of Michigan succeeds him.

In retaliation for U.S. support of Israel during the Yom Kippur War, the Organization of Petroleum Exporting Countries (OPEC) begins an oil embargo; the resulting gas shortage leads many Americans to question the nation's dependence on fossil fuels in general, and on imported oil in particular. The embargo and a subsequent fourfold increase in oil prices drive inflation higher and prompt worldwide recession and fuel shortages.

President Nixon refuses to cooperate with the Watergate investigation of Special Prosecutor Archibald Cox and orders Cox's dismissal. Attorney General Elliot Richardson and Deputy Attorney General William Ruckelshaus resign rather than carry out the illegal order. These resignations and Cox's eventual firing come to be called the "Saturday Night Massacre."

U.S. Congress passes the War Powers Act of 1973; it requires the president to consult with Congress before and during any direct involvement of U.S. forces in hostilities abroad.

The Endangered Species Act of 1973 provides greater protection for fish and wildlife that are in danger of becoming extinct.

Responding to U.S. business interests in Chile, the United States assists General Augusto Pinochet in a military coup against the democratically elected government of Salvador Allende. Pinochet's regime remains in power until 1990.

1974

Hank Aaron breaks Babe Ruth's home run record when he hits his 715th home run in Atlanta.

The Congressional Budget and Impoundment Control Act of 1974 standardizes the federal budget process.

Riots break out in Boston, Massachusetts, in reaction to the busing of black students into white neighborhoods.

Under threat of impeachment and with his administration discredited by the Watergate scandal, President Nixon resigns; Gerald Ford becomes president.

The Federal Election Campaign Act of 1974 provides public financing of presidential primaries and elections, and sets limits on contributions and spending in House, Senate, and presidential campaigns.

President Gerald Ford preemptively pardons Richard M. Nixon for Watergate and related charges.

U.S. Congress passes the Trade Reform Act, which significantly reduces tariffs and, in some circumstances, eliminates them altogether.

U.S. Congress passes the Privacy Act of 1974, which prohibits the executive branch of government from using information gathered for one purpose to be used for another purpose.

Facing bankruptcy, New York City receives loan guarantees from the federal government.

U.S. Congress passes the Equal Credit Opportunity Act, which outlaws the refusal of credit due to discrimination by sex or marital status.

1975

Led by Pol Pot, Communist rebels known as the Khmer Rouge seize Cambodia's capital, Phnom Penh. Communist leaders in nearby Laos likewise gain power.

After the last U.S. forces withdraw from Saigon, South Vietnam falls to North Vietnam. An influx of Southeast Asian refugees to the United States begins.

1976

America holds its bicentennial celebration in recognition of the anniversary of the signing of the Declaration of Independence.

Alex Haley publishes *Roots*, which is later adapted to television and viewed by millions; Haley receives a special Pulitzer Prize for the novel in 1977.

In *Runyon v. McCrary et al.*, the U.S. Supreme Court prohibits private schools from denying admission based on race.

Barbara Jordan delivers a keynote address at the Democratic National Convention in New York City; she is the first African American ever to do so.

Gerald Ford loses the presidential election to Democrat Jimmy Carter, former governor of Georgia.

1977

President Carter pardons Vietnam draft evaders.

Tip O'Neill of Massachusetts becomes Speaker of the House, a position he holds for 10 years.

President Carter's human rights speech at Notre Dame University outlines his foreign policy framework of championing the cause of human rights around the world.

The movie *Star Wars,* directed by George Lucas, is released. With cutting-edge special effects and sound, the film draws huge audiences and revolutionizes the movie industry, prompting a shift to fewer, more expensive blockbusters.

U.S. Congress enacts the Foreign Corrupt Practices Act of 1977 to deter bribery of foreign officials by American businesses.

The Panama Canal Treaties grant Panama control of the isthmian canal in 1999.

Bell Labs invents the fiber optic cable, which permits high-speed digital data transmission for telephone and, later, Internet connections.

1978

President Carter helps to negotiate the Camp David accords formalizing an end to hostilities between Israel and Egypt.

In *Regents of University of California v. Allan P. Bakke,* the U.S. Supreme Court upholds the use of factors of race, gender, and ethnicity in evaluating applicants but declares unconstitutional the use of rigid quota systems.

1979

A potential nuclear disaster is averted at the Three Mile Island nuclear power plant in Pennsylvania. The scare prompts a nationwide "anti-nuke" movement.

The Israeli-Egyptian Peace Treaty of 1979 ends the state of war that had existed between the two nations since 1948.

U.S. president Jimmy Carter and Soviet president Leonid I. Brezhnev sign the Strategic Arms Limitation Treaty (SALT II), which reduces the number of U.S. and Soviet nuclear weapons. U.S. Congress never ratifies the treaty.

The U.S.-supported shah of Iran is deposed; Iranian militants seize the U.S. embassy, trapping 52 Americans inside.

The Sandinista National Liberation Front (FSLN) overthrows the U.S.-backed dictatorship of Anastasio Somoza in Nicaragua.

U.S. Congress approves $1.5 billion in loan agreements to the Chrysler Corporation to stabilize the foundering U.S. automaker.

1980

The United States boycotts the 1980 Olympic Games in Moscow to protest the Soviet invasion of Afghanistan.

Eight U.S. servicemen are killed in an abortive attempt to free the American hostages in Iran.

Inflation reaches 13.5 percent.

Cuban leader Fidel Castro permits the emigration of 125,000 Cubans by way of the port city of Mariel. Some Americans charge that Castro used the Mariel boatlift to "dump" undesirable immigrants on the United States.

Republican Ronald Reagan, former governor of California, is elected president over incumbent Democrat Jimmy Carter and National Unity Party candidate John B. Anderson. In the same election, Republicans gain control of the U.S. Senate for the first time since 1958. The "gender gap" is evident at the polls: For the first time, more women than men vote.

1981

On President Carter's last day in office, the hostages in Iran are freed.

Sandra Day O'Connor is appointed to the U.S. Supreme Court; she is the first female Supreme Court justice.

President Reagan is wounded in an assassination attempt.

The cable channel Music Television, or MTV, debuts.

The human immunodeficiency virus (HIV), which causes acquired immune deficiency syndrome (AIDS), is first identified in the United States.

IBM introduces the personal computer (PC); its operating system becomes the standard used by a variety of manufacturers.

In August, 11,300 federal air traffic controllers strike to protest hours, understaffing, and pay. President Reagan declares the strike illegal and replacement workers soon break the strike—and, consequently, the Professional Air Traffic Controllers Association—setting the stage for future decades of private-sector strike-breaking.

1982

The Census Bureau reports that the poverty level in the United States is at its highest point since 1967.

The space shuttle *Columbia* makes its first successful flight.

The United States sends marines into Beirut, Lebanon, as a peacekeeping force.

U.S. Congress passes the Boland Amendment, prohibiting further U.S. aid in support of the U.S.-organized rebel forces that are fighting against Nicaragua's Sandinista government.

The deadline for states to ratify the Equal Rights Amendment (ERA) as part of the U.S. Constitution expires.

1983

U.S. Congress makes the birthday of Dr. Martin Luther King, Jr., a national holiday; the bill takes effect in 1986.

Astronaut Sally Ride becomes the first U.S. woman to travel in space.

In *Immigration and Naturalization Service v. Chadha*, the U.S. Supreme Court restricts Congress's ability to veto immigration and deportation rulings.

Unemployment reaches its highest rate, 11 percent, since the Great Depression.

A terrorist bomb kills 239 U.S. marines in Beirut, Lebanon.

U.S. and Caribbean troops invade the island of Grenada after an anti-U.S. coup.

1984

In *Lynch v. Donnelly,* the U.S. Supreme Court decides that a Christmas Nativity display that had been sponsored and funded by a city did not necessarily violate the First Amendment doctrine of separation of church and state.

Democratic presidential candidate Walter Mondale, a former vice president, is defeated by incumbent Ronald Reagan; Mondale's running mate is Geraldine Ferraro, the first woman to be nominated for vice president by a major party.

U.S. Congress passes the Comprehensive Crime Control Act of 1984, which includes forfeiture provisions for all drug offenses.

The U.S. Supreme Court rules in *Sony v. Universal* that home recordings of televised programming do not constitute a copyright violation.

1985

President Reagan meets with Soviet leader Mikhail Gorbachev in Geneva to discuss human rights, regional conflicts, and arms control.

With the deficit at nearly $2 trillion and rapidly rising, U.S. Congress passes the Gramm-Rudman-Hollings Act of 1985, which requires the president and Congress to eliminate the budget deficit by 1991.

1986

The space shuttle *Challenger* explodes seconds after take-off, killing all seven members on board.

The United States bombs suspected terrorist bases in Libya.

The Iran-contra affair is exposed; funds from the clandestine sale of U.S. arms to Iran have been secretly and illegally funneled to anticommunist rebels in Nicaragua by members of the Reagan administration.

In *Bowers v. Hardwick,* the U.S. Supreme Court rules that an 1816 Georgia state law prohibiting sodomy does not violate an individual's constitutional right to privacy.

U.S. Congress passes the Tax Reform Act of 1986 to lower tax rates and eliminate some tax loopholes.

The Immigration Reform and Control Act of 1986 creates a process for legalizing the status of many illegal aliens and requires employers to verify applicants' eligibility for employment.

U.S. Congress overrides President Reagan's veto of the Comprehensive Anti-Apartheid Act, which imposes wide-ranging economic sanctions on South Africa and prohibits U.S. trade and investment.

William Rehnquist succeeds Warren Burger as chief justice of the Supreme Court.

1987

The U.S. Senate refuses to confirm U.S. Supreme Court nominee Robert Bork.

The Dow Jones Index drops severely; many express concern over the growth of the federal deficit.

The United States and the Soviet Union sign the Intermediate Nuclear Forces Treaty (INF); the accord calls for both countries to remove many midrange nuclear weapons from Europe.

1988

U.S. Congress passes the U.S.-Canada Free-Trade Agreement Implementation Act of 1988, which provides for the elimination of most remaining tariffs.

U.S. Congress passes the Medicare Catastrophic Coverage Act of 1988, which protects the elderly against medical bankruptcy in case of severe illness.

Jesse Jackson receives strong support in Democratic presidential primaries, the first African-American candidate to win such contests.

The Civil Liberties Act of 1988 authorizes reparation payments to all Japanese Americans and Alaskan Aleuts who were interned, relocated, or evacuated during World War II.

The Fair Housing Amendments Act of 1988 prohibits discrimination against the disabled and families with children in public and private housing.

Republican vice president George Bush is elected president over Governor Michael Dukakis of Massachusetts, the Democratic candidate.

A bomb set by Islamic fundamentalists explodes in Pan Am flight 803 over Lockerbie, Scotland; 270 die in the terrorist attack.

1989

The United States sends 24,000 troops into Panama to depose the government of General Manuel Antonio Noriega.

General Colin Powell is appointed chairman of the Joint Chiefs of Staff; he is the youngest person and first African American to hold the position.

The *Exxon Valdez* oil tanker strikes a reef in Alaska's Cape William Sound, causing one of the largest oil spills in history.

The U.S. Supreme Court decision in *Texas v. Johnson* holds that burning the American flag as a form of symbolic speech is protected by the First Amendment to the U.S. Constitution.

In *Webster v. Reproductive Health Services,* the U.S. Supreme Court rules that a Missouri state law restricting the availability of abortions is constitutional.

Euphoric crowds demolish the Berlin Wall, symbol of Soviet control in Eastern Europe.

1990

The Hubble Telescope is set into orbit 370 miles above the Earth where it transmits images of the universe without the distorting effects of the Earth's atmosphere.

U.S. Congress passes the Americans with Disabilities Act of 1990, barring discrimination against the handicapped.

The United States sends troops and warplanes to the Persian Gulf to restore the Kuwaiti regime after its ouster by Iraq.

East and West Germany, Britain, France, the United States, and the Soviet Union sign the Treaty on the Final Settlement with Respect to Germany, which begins the process of restoring full sovereignty to Germany upon reunification.

The Clean Air Act of 1990 tightens federal air pollution standards in order to curb acid rain, urban smog, and the release of toxic chemicals into the atmosphere.

The Conventional Armed Forces in Europe Treaty formally ends the tension between NATO and the Warsaw Pact countries.

U.S. Congress passes the Immigration Act of 1990, which allows more immigrants into the United States, especially skilled workers and immediate relatives of U.S. citizens.

1991

The United States and its allies defeat Iraq in the Persian Gulf War.

The General Accounting Office discloses that 325 current and former U.S. representatives have regularly overdrawn their accounts at the House "bank" (actually a check-cashing office) without penalty, effectively receiving free overdraft insurance. Voters react angrily, replacing many of those implicated.

A coup d'état in Haiti leads to the migration of thousands of refugees to Florida.

The Senate approves Clarence Thomas as a Supreme Court justice. Sexual harassment charges brought against Thomas by law professor Anita Hill spark a nationwide controversy.

U.S. Congress passes the Civil Rights Act of 1991, which makes it easier for employees to sue employers in job discrimination cases.

After the collapse of an anti-Gorbachev coup, the Soviet Union renounces communism and splinters into an array of affiliated and independent nations.

1992

A *New York Times* article by Jeff Gerth implies wrongdoing by presidential candidate Bill Clinton relating to a real-estate development called Whitewater.

Riots and looting break out in Los Angeles after an all-white jury acquits four policemen on all but one count in the beating of motorist Rodney King. The attack had been videotaped and shown on television.

Democratic governor Bill Clinton of Arkansas defeats Republican incumbent George Bush and independent H. Ross Perot in the presidential election.

The United States sends 28,000 troops to Somalia to restore civil order.

1993

U.S. Congress passes the Family and Medical Leave Act of 1993, which requires businesses employing 50 or more people to grant their employees up to 12 weeks of unpaid leave annually for family and medical emergencies.

A terrorist bomb explodes in New York's World Trade Center, killing six and injuring 100. The event sets off a decade-long escalation of U.S. antiterrorism efforts.

Janet Reno becomes the first female U.S. attorney general.

After a 51-day standoff, federal agents storm the Waco, Texas, compound of the Branch Davidians, a fundamentalist Christian sect wanted for the murder of federal law-enforcement agents, child abuse, and possession of illegal firearms. The Davidians set fire to the compound; 86 of its occupants die.

In *Shaw v. Reno*, the U.S. Supreme Court rules that U.S. congressional districts that were deliberately created to elect minority candidates violate the rights of white voters.

The U.S. Senate ratifies the North American Free Trade Agreement (NAFTA), which limits trade barriers between the United States, Canada, and Mexico.

U.S. troops on a humanitarian mission in Somalia encounter unexpected resistance. In a two-day battle with local warlord Muhammad Farah Aideed, 30 American soldiers are killed and the bodies of two of them are dragged past cheering crowds through the streets of the capital, Mogadishu.

The Brady Handgun Violence Prevention Act requires a five-day waiting period and a background check on all persons seeking to purchase a handgun.

1994

Responding to continuing rumor and charges of impropriety concerning President Clinton's investment in the Whitewater real-estate development, Attorney General Janet Reno appoints Robert B. Fiske in January to investigate the matter. In August a three-judge panel appoints conservative movement activist and former U.S. solicitor general Kenneth Starr to take over the investigation.

An earthquake strikes Los Angeles, killing 61 people and causing heavy damage.

In response to North Korea's threatened invasion of South Korea, the United States promises full-scale war and begins military buildup. Former president Jimmy Carter negotiates a compromise averting armed conflict.

Major League baseball players go on strike, forcing the cancellation of the World Series for the first time since 1904.

U.S. Congress passes the Crime Act of 1994, which authorizes $30.2 billion in federal spending over the next six years for a wide range of anticrime measures.

More than 300 Republican House candidates, including about 150 incumbents, sign the Contract with America, which promises a balanced budget amendment, tax cuts, and more defense spending.

The Health Care Security Act, the most ambitious federal proposal in 30 years, is defeated after a fierce nationwide debate.

The United States issues an ultimatum to the government of General Raoul Cedras in Haiti, threatening military action if the U.S.-negotiated Governor's Island Accords are not implemented. Cedras capitulates and agrees to leave the country, permitting democratic elections.

In November elections, Republicans take control of the House of Representatives for the first time in 40 years. Thomas Foley, a Democrat, becomes the first Speaker of the House since 1862 to lose his seat.

A conference of 128 countries develops the General Agreement on Tariffs and Trade (GATT), which advances globalization by cutting international trade barriers and creating the World Trade Organization to administer trade laws.

1995

Researchers in Scotland successfully replicate an adult animal, raising concern over the possibility of creating human genetic clones.

The Glass Ceiling Commission Report reveals that women and minorities are extremely underrepresented in senior management posts.

A terrorist bomb explodes outside the federal office building in Oklahoma City, killing 169 people. Right-wing activist Timothy McVeigh later confesses to the crime.

In *U.S. Term Limits, Inc. v. Thornton,* the U.S. Supreme Court strikes down an Arkansas state law that imposes term limits on U.S. senators.

The United States reestablishes full diplomatic ties to Vietnam for the first time since the Vietnam War.

Following a long and controversial trial in which athlete and actor O. J. Simpson's defense argues that he had been the victim of a police conspiracy, he is acquitted on charges of killing his ex-wife and a bystander.

Hundreds of thousands of African-American men converge on Washington, D.C., for the "Million Man March," organized by Nation of Islam minister Louis Farrakhan.

Serbia, Croatia, and Bosnia sign the U.S.-negotiated Dayton Peace Agreement, which ends the Bosnian civil war.

Service Employees International Union leader John Sweeney is elected head of the AFL-CIO. He declares the end of the postwar labor era and calls for an innovative national organizing campaign.

1996

U.S. Congress passes the Telecommunications Act of 1996, which enacts legal and regulatory reform of telephone service, radio and television broadcasting, and online computer services.

In *Bush v. Vera* and *Shaw v. Hunt,* the U.S. Supreme Court prohibits the creation of race-based electoral districts.

The U.S. Supreme Court decision *United States v. Virginia et al.* orders the Virginia Military Institute (VMI), a state-funded, all-male military academy, to admit women.

U.S. Congress passes a major welfare reform bill that shifts the responsibility for welfare to state governments and imposes lifetime limits on benefits.

President Bill Clinton wins reelection, defeating Republican senator Bob Dole and independent candidate H. Ross Perot.

California voters approve Proposition 209, which eliminates state affirmative action programs in public employment and education.

1997

To correct a military omission, seven African-American soldiers are awarded the Medal of Honor for heroism in World War II.

The House of Representatives reprimands the Speaker of the House, Newt Gingrich, and fines him $300,000 for official misconduct.

Madeleine Albright becomes the first female U.S. secretary of state.

NASA's *Pathfinder* mission successfully lands a mechanical probe on Mars.

President Clinton apologizes on behalf of the United States for the Tuskegee Experiment, which took place between 1932 and 1972. The study denied medical attention to 412 African-American men suffering from syphilis while pretending to treat them.

In *Romer, Governor of Colorado, et al. v. Evans et al.,* the U.S. Supreme Court invalidates a Colorado law that excludes homosexuals from civil rights protections.

Timothy McVeigh is found guilty for his role in bombing the Alfred P. Murrah Federal Building in Oklahoma City, Oklahoma, and is sentenced to death.

Five U.S. cigarette producers agree to compensate state governments for the billions of dollars spent on health care for tobacco-related illnesses.

In *Kansas v. Hendricks,* the U.S. Supreme Court validates the authority of the states to confine violent sex offenders to mental institutions after they have completed prison terms for their crimes.

In *Reno v. ACLU,* the U.S. Supreme Court finds that the Communications Decency Act of 1996 violates the constitutional guarantee of free speech.

In a set of related cases, the U.S. Supreme Court upholds state laws prohibiting euthanasia.

In *Printz v. United States* the U.S. Supreme Court rules that the Brady gun control law's background check requirement is an unconstitutional intrusion on states' rights.

At the Kyoto Summit, 160 leading industrial nations, including the United States, agree to reduce the emissions of greenhouse gases, which promote global warming.

1998

U.S. district court justice Susan Weber Wright dismisses Paula Corbin Jones's sexual harassment suit against President Bill Clinton as without merit.

The United Nations creates an international tribunal to investigate war crimes committed in the former Yugoslavia.

The U.S. Department of Justice files an antitrust lawsuit against the Microsoft Corporation, contending that the mandatory inclusion of its Internet Explorer program with the Windows 98 operating system amounts to a monopoly.

In *National Endowment for the Arts v. Finley,* the U.S. Supreme Court upholds a congressional mandate requiring the National Endowment for the Arts to consider "general standards of decency" when deciding which projects receive federal funding.

The federal budget produces the first sustained federal surpluses in two centuries.

On August 7, bombs explode at the U.S. embassies in Nairobi, Kenya, killing 213 people, and in Dar es Salaam, Tanzania, killing 11. Over 4,500 people are injured. In response, the United States bombs suspected terrorist strongholds in Afghanistan and the Sudan.

Independent Counsel Kenneth Starr delivers his report to Congress on President Clinton's intimate relationship with former White House intern Monica Lewinsky. The report alleges perjury in Clinton's testimony in the Jones suit.

In a fierce party-line vote, the House of Representatives votes to impeach Clinton for obstruction of justice and perjury related to the Jones lawsuit.

1999

The U.S. Senate acquits President Clinton on both articles of impeachment.

In response to the Serbian government's campaign of ethnic cleansing in Kosovo, U.S. and NATO forces begin air strikes against military targets in Serbia. After 11 weeks of bombing, the Serbians withdraw and agree to peace talks.

On April 20, Eric Harris and Dylan Klebold, students at Columbine High School in Littleton, Colorado, go on a shooting rampage at the school, killing one teacher and 12 students before committing suicide.

Four police officers shoot and kill Amadou Diallo, an unarmed African immigrant, near his home in New York City. They fire 41 shots in total, striking Diallo 19 times. All four officers are later acquitted of criminal charges, leading to massive protests in New York and Washington, D.C.

The International Criminal Tribunal indicts Serbian president Slobodan Milosevic and four of his government officials for "crimes against humanity."

Justin Volpe, a 27-year-old New York City police officer, pleads guilty to sodomizing Abner Louima in a police precinct bathroom in 1997. He receives a fine and a 30-year prison sentence. A second officer, Charles Schwarz, is found guilty of violating Louima's civil rights. Three other officers are later found guilty of obstructing justice.

Riots erupt in Seattle, where more than 30,000 activists for consumers, workers, and the environment protest WTO policy.

Control of the Panama Canal is transferred from the United States to Panama on December 31.

2000

In April, the Microsoft Corp. is found to have violated U.S. antitrust laws. Federal appeals court judge Richard Posner recommends the corporation be split into two companies.

U.S. agents return seven-year-old Elian Gonzales to the custody of his father. The boy had been the sole survivor when a small boat carrying a group of Cuban refugees sank off the coast of Florida. Elian's repatriation sparks virulent protests within the Cuban-American community.

The U.S. Supreme Court strikes down the Violence against Women Act. The act had been used by female victims of sexual violence to sue their attackers in federal court.

In June, U.S. and U.K. scientists announce that they have decoded the human genome.

The U.S. Supreme Court rules in *Boy Scouts of America v. Dale* that the First Amendment to the U.S. Constitution protects the right of the Boy Scouts to bar gays from serving as adult scout leaders.

The U.S. Supreme Court rules in *Stenberg v. Carhart* that a Nebraska law prohibiting "late-term" or "partial-birth" abortion is an unconstitutional infringement on a woman's right to reproductive choice.

The House of Representatives votes in July to ease the 38-year-old embargo on the trade of food and medicines to the island nation of Cuba. The vote also eases existing travel restrictions for U.S. citizens. The embargo had repeatedly been criticized for contributing to Cuba's lower standard of living in the post–cold war era.

Napster, a website that allows its customers to download popular music for free on-line, is sued by the Recording Industry Association of America (RIAA) for copyright infringement. A U.S. District Court orders Napster to shut down, but the controversy continues over the meaning of copyright laws on the Internet.

President Clinton hosts peace talks at Camp David to attempt to resolve the conflict between Israel and Palestine. Some progress is made as Israel, for the first time, considers sharing limited sovereignty in Jerusalem with Palestine, and Palestine considers, also for the first time, allowing Israel to keep the lands it captured in the 1967 Middle East war. The talks break down before a solution can be reached, however, when both governments refuse to compromise on sovereignty in the eastern section of Jerusalem, an area with sites sacred to both Jews and Arabs.

The United States normalizes trade relations with China.

The U.S. Food and Drug Administration approves the sale of mifepristone, commonly known as RU-486 or the abortion pill, a drug that would enable women to perform safer, non-surgical abortions in the first seven weeks of a pregnancy.

Vermont becomes the only state to legalize same-sex civil unions, which grant gay couples the same legal rights as heterosexual married couples.

On October 12, two Islamic fundamentalists bomb the USS *Cole*, a U.S. warship stationed in Yemen, killing 17 sailors. Officials believe Saudi billionaire Osama bin Laden is behind the explosions.

Hillary Rodham Clinton is elected U.S. senator of New York. She is the first First Lady to be elected to political office.

More than a month after voters cast their ballots in the closest election in U.S. history, the presidential election of 2000 is decided by the Supreme Court decision *Bush v. Gore*. The Court finds in favor of Republican candidate George W. Bush, who had successfully sought to prevent a recount of contested Florida ballots called for by Democratic candidate Al Gore.

2001

The 10-year expansion of the U.S. economy ends and a recession begins.

Colin Powell becomes the first African American to be named secretary of state.

A U.S. spy plane makes an emergency landing on Hainan island, China, after colliding with a Chinese fighter jet. Tensions mount between the United States and China as China searches the plane and holds both it and its crew for nearly a week before dismantling the plane and sending it back to the United States.

On January 31, at a trial held in the Netherlands, Abdel Baset Ali Mohmed Al Mehrahi is found guilty of 270 counts of murder in the bombing of Pan Am flight 103 over Lockerbie, Scotland in 1988. A second Libyan defendant, Al Amin Khalifa Fhimah, is acquitted.

The state of California begins "rolling blackouts" to deal with an energy crisis brought about by its botched deregulation of the industry and the profiteering of energy companies such as Enron.

In May, Senator Jim Jeffords of Vermont withdraws from the Republican Party to become an independent. The Senate, which had been split 50-50 between Democrats and Republicans, swings to Democratic control.

In June, a U.S. Court of Appeals reverses the ruling made in April 2000 that the Microsoft Corp. be split into two separate companies. By the end of the year both sides are negotiating to settle the case.

President Bush refuses to submit the Kyoto Protocol, an international treaty committed to reducing carbon dioxide, for Senate ratification because of fears that ratification could negatively impact the U.S. economy. Most of the rest of the signatories remain committed to the protocol.

President George W. Bush bans the creation of new stem cell lines for medical research.

On September 11, Islamic fundamentalists hijack four commercial airliners. Two hijacked planes crash into the twin towers of the World Trade Center. A third plane is crashed into the Pentagon. The fourth plane crashes in a deserted area of Pennsylvania when passengers foil the terrorists. More than 3,000 die in the attacks, which shock and rally the nation.

The United States accuses Saudi billionaire Osama bin Laden of directing the terrorist attacks of September 11 and demands that Afghanistan's Taliban regime extradite him for prosecution. The Taliban refuse.

On October 5, Robert Stevens, a photo editor in Boca Raton, Florida, dies of inhalation anthrax. Within days media outlets in New York City announce anthrax exposure by some employees. Letters sent to media figures and politicians, including Senate majority leader Tom Daschle, are also found to contain anthrax. Postal workers in Washington, D.C., and New Jersey contract the disease due to contact with contaminated mail. By December a total of 18 people have been infected and five people have died from inhaling the spores.

On October 7, the United States strikes strongholds of Osama bin Laden's al-Qaeda terrorist network in Afghanistan. Two months after the initial strikes the Taliban surrender most of their control of Afghanistan but Taliban leader Mullah Omar and al-Qaeda leaders, including bin Laden, elude capture.

The U.S. unemployment rate for November, 5.7 percent, is the highest in six years.

Enron, a large energy company based in Houston, declares bankruptcy in December. Its stock price has fallen from a high of $83.00 to $0.26 per share. Nearly 4,500 employees lose their jobs.

On December 11, Federal Reserve chairman Alan Greenspan cuts interest rates for the 11th time this year.

On December 13, President George W. Bush announces that the United States will pull out of the Anti-Ballistic Missile Treaty of 1972.

Documents

"Silent Majority" Speech (1969)
President Richard M. Nixon

Public Papers of the Presidents of the United States,
Richard Nixon, 1969, pp. 901–909

The White House, Washington, D.C.
November 3, 1969

. . . We have faced other crises in our history and have become stronger by rejecting the easy way out and taking the right way in meeting our challenges. Our greatness as a nation has been our capacity to do what had to be done when we knew our course was right.

I recognize that some of my fellow citizens disagree with the plan for peace I have chosen. Honest and patriotic Americans have reached different conclusions as to how peace should be achieved.

In San Francisco a few weeks ago, I saw demonstrators carrying signs reading: Lose in Vietnam, bring the boys home."

Well, one of the strengths of our free society is that any American has a right to reach that conclusion and to advocate that point of view. But as President of the United States, I would be untrue to my oath of office if I allowed the policy of this Nation to be dictated by the minority who hold that point of view and who try to impose it on the Nation by mounting demonstrations in the street.

For almost 200 years, the policy of this Nation has been made under our Constitution by those leaders in the Congress and the White House elected by all of the people. If a vocal minority, however fervent its cause, prevails over reason and the will of the majority, this Nation has no future as a free society.

And now I would like to address a word, if I may, to the young people of this Nation who are particularly concerned, and I understand why they are concerned, about this war.

I respect your idealism. I share your concern for peace. I want peace as much as you do.

There are powerful personal reasons I want to end this war. This week I will have to sign 83 letters to mothers, fathers, wives, and loved ones of men who have given their lives for America in Vietnam. It is very little satisfaction to me that this is only one-third as many letters as I signed the first week in office. There is nothing I want more than to see the day come when I do not have to write any of those letters.

I want to end the war to save the lives of those brave young men in Vietnam. But I want to end it in a way which will increase the chance that their younger brothers and their sons will not have to fight in some future Vietnam someplace in the world. And I want to end the war for another reason. I want to end it so that the energy and dedication of you, our young people, now too often directed into bitter hatred against those responsible for the war, can be turned to the great challenges of peace, a better life for all Americans, a better life for all people on this earth.

I have chosen a plan for peace. I believe it will succeed.

If it does succeed, what the critics say now won't matter. If it does not succeed, anything I say then won't matter.

I know it may not be fashionable to speak of patriotism or national destiny these days. But I feel it is appropriate to do so on this occasion.

Two hundred years ago this Nation was weak and poor. But even then, America was the hope of millions in the world. Today we have become the strongest and richest nation in the world. And the wheel of destiny has turned so that any hope the world has for the survival of peace and freedom will be determined by whether the American people have the moral stamina and the courage to meet the challenge of free world leadership.

Let historians not record that when America was the most powerful nation in the world we passed on the other side of the road and allowed the last hopes for peace and freedom of millions of people to be suffocated by the forces of totalitarianism.

And so tonight—to you, the great silent majority of my fellow Americans—I ask for your support.

I pledged in my campaign for the Presidency to end the war in a way that we could win the peace. I have initiated a plan of action which will enable me to keep that pledge.

The more support I can have from the American people, the sooner that pledge can be redeemed; for the more divided we are at home, the less likely the enemy is to negotiate at Paris.

Let us be united for peace. Let us also be united against defeat. Because let us understand: North Vietnam cannot defeat or humiliate the United States. Only Americans can do that.

Fifty years ago, in this room and at this very desk, President Woodrow Wilson spoke words which caught the imagination of a war-weary world. He said: "This is the war to end war." His dream for peace after World War I was shattered on the hard realities of great power politics, and Woodrow Wilson died a broken man.

Tonight I do not tell you that the war in Vietnam is the war to end wars. But I do say this: I have initiated a plan which will end this war in a way that will bring us closer to that great goal to which Woodrow Wilson and every American President in our history has been dedicated—the goal of a just and lasting peace.

As President I hold the responsibility for choosing the best path to that goal and then leading the Nation along it.

I pledge to you tonight that I shall meet this responsibility with all of the strength and wisdom I can command in accordance with your hopes, mindful of your concerns, sustained by your prayers.

Thank you and goodnight.

The Clean Air Act of 1970

United States Statutes at Large, 1970,
pp. 1,676–1,713

December 31, 1970

Sec. 7401. —Congressional findings and declaration of purpose

(a) Findings

The Congress finds—

(1) that the predominant part of the Nation's population is located in its rapidly expanding metropolitan and other urban areas, which generally cross the boundary lines of local jurisdictions and often extend into two or more States;

(2) that the growth in the amount and complexity of air pollution brought about by urbanization, industrial development, and the increasing use of motor vehicles, has resulted in mounting dangers to the public health and welfare, including injury to agricultural crops and livestock, damage to and the deterioration of property, and hazards to air and ground transportation;

(3) that air pollution prevention (that is, the reduction or elimination, through any measures, of the amount of pollutants produced or created at the source) and air pollution control at its source is the primary responsibility of States and local governments; and

(4) that Federal financial assistance and leadership is essential for the development of cooperative Federal, State, regional, and local programs to prevent and control air pollution.

(b) Declaration

The purposes of this subchapter are—

(1) to protect and enhance the quality of the Nation's air resources so as to promote the public health and welfare and the productive capacity of its population;

(2) to initiate and accelerate a national research and development program to achieve the prevention and control of air pollution;

(3) to provide technical and financial assistance to State and local governments in connection with the development and execution of their air pollution prevention and control programs; and

(4) to encourage and assist the development and operation of regional air pollution prevention and control programs.

(c) Pollution prevention

A primary goal of this chapter is to encourage or otherwise promote reasonable Federal, State, and local governmental actions, consistent with the provisions of this chapter, for pollution prevention . . .

Title IX – Prohibition of Sex Discrimination

Erik Bruun and Jay Crosby, eds. *Our Nation's Archive:
The History of the United States in Documents*
(New York: Black Dog & Leventhal
Publishers, 1999), p. 790

Sec.901(a) No person in the United States shall, on the basis of sex, be excluded from participation in, be denied the benefits of, or be subjected to discrimination under any education program or activity receiving Federal financial assistance, except that:

in regard to admissions to educational institutions, this section shall apply only to institutions of vocational education, professional education, and graduate higher education, and to public institutions of undergraduate higher education;

in regard to admissions to educational institutions, this section shall not apply (A) for one year from June 23, 1972, nor for six years after June 23, 1972, in the case of an educational institution which has begun the process of changing from being an institution which admits only students of one sex to being an institution which admits students of both sexes, but only if it is carrying out a plan for such a change which is approved by the Secretary of Education or (B) for seven years from the date an educational institution begins the process of changing from being an institution which admits only students of only one sex to being an institution which admits students of both sexes, but only if it is carrying out a plan for such a change which is approved by the Secretary of Education, whichever is the later;

this section shall not apply to an educational institution which is controlled by a religious organization if the application of this subsection would not be consistent with the religious tenets of such organization;

this section shall not apply to an educational institution whose primary purpose is the training of individuals for the military services of the United States, or the merchant marine; andin regard to admissions this section shall not apply to any public institution of undergraduate higher education which is an institution that traditionally and continually from its establishment has had a policy of admitting only students of one sex;

Nothing contained in subsection (a) of this section shall be interpreted to require any educational institution to grant preferential or disparate treatment to the members of one sex on account of an imbalance which may exist with respect to the total number or percentage of persons of that sex participating in or receiving the benefits of any federally supported program or activity, in comparison with the total number or percentage of persons of that sex in any community, State, section, or other area: Provided, That this subsection shall not be construed to prevent the consideration in any hearing or proceeding under this chapter of statistical evidence tending to show that such an imbalance exists with respect to the participation in, or receipt of the benefits of, any such program or activity by the members of one sex.

For purposes of this chapter an educational institution means any public or private preschool, elementary, or secondary school, or any institution of vocational, professional, or higher education, except that in the case of an educational institution composed of more than one school, college, or department which are administratively separate units, such term means each such school, college, or department.

Roe v. Wade (1973)
United States Supreme Court

93 *Supreme Court Reporter,* pp. 705–763
410 U.S. 113, 35 L.ED.2D 147
JANE ROE, ET AL., APPELLANTS, V. HENRY WADE.
Argued Dec. 13, 1971; Reargued Oct. 11, 1972; Decided Jan. 22, 1973; Rehearing Denied Feb. 26, 1973

Mr. Justice Blackmun delivered the opinion of the Court.

This Texas federal appeal and its Georgia companion, *Doe v. Bolton,* 410 U.S. 179, 93 S.Ct. 739, 35 L.Ed.2d 201, present constitutional challenges to state criminal abortion legislation. The Texas statutes under attack here are typical of those that have been in effect in many States for approximately a century. The Georgia statutes, in contrast, have a modern cast and are a legislative product that, to an extent at least, obviously reflects the influences of recent attitudinal change, of advancing medical knowledge and techniques, and of new thinking about an old issue.

We forthwith acknowledge our awareness of the sensitive and emotional nature of the abortion controversy, of the vigorous opposing views, even among physicians, and of the deep and seemingly absolute convictions that the subject inspires. One's philosophy, one's experiences, one's exposure to the raw edges of human existence, one's religious training, one's attitudes toward life and family and their values, and the moral standards one establishes and seeks to observe, are all likely to influence and to color one's thinking and conclusions about abortion. In addition, population growth, pollution, poverty, and racial overtones tend to complicate and not to simplify the problem.

Our task, of course, is to resolve the issue by constitutional measurement, free of emotion and of predilection. We seek earnestly to do this, and, because we do, we have inquired into, and in this opinion place some emphasis upon, medical and medical-legal history and what that history reveals about man's attitudes toward the abortion procedure over the centuries. We bear in mind, too, Mr. Justice Holmes' admonition in his now vindicated dissent in *Lochner v. New York,* 198 U.S. 45, 76, 25 S.Ct. 539, 547, 49 L.Ed. 937 (1905):

"[The Constitution] is made for people of fundamentally differing views, and the accident of our finding certain opinions natural and familiar, or novel, and even shocking, ought not to conclude or judgment upon the question whether statutes embodying them conflict with the Constitution of the United States." . . .

II

Jane Roe, a single woman who was residing in Dallas County, Texas, instituted this federal action in March 1970 against the District Attorney of the county. She sought a declaratory judgment that the Texas criminal abortion statutes were unconstitutional on their face, and an injunction restraining the defendant from enforcing the statutes.

Roe alleged that she was unmarried and pregnant; that she wished to terminate her pregnancy by an abortion "performed by a competent, licensed physician, under safe, clinical conditions"; that she was unable to get a "legal" abortion in Texas because her life did not appear to be threatened by the continuation of her pregnancy; and that she could not afford to travel to another jurisdiction in order to secure a legal abortion under safe conditions. She claimed that the Texas statutes were unconstitutionally vague and that they abridged her right of personal privacy, protected by the First, Fourth, Fifth, Ninth, and Fourteenth Amendments. By an amendment to her complaint Roe purported to sue "on behalf of herself and all other women similarly situated." . . .

1. *Ancient attitudes.* These are not capable of precise determination. We are told that at the time of the Persian Empire abortifacients were known and that criminal abortions were severely punished. We are also told, however, that abortion was practiced in Greek times as well as in the Roman Era, and that "it was resorted to without scruple." The Ephesian, Soranos, often described as the greatest of the ancient gynecologists, appears to have been generally opposed to Rome's prevailing free-abortion practices. He found it necessary to think first of the life of the mother, and he resorted to abortion when, upon this standard, he felt the procedure advisable. Greek and Roman law afforded little protection to the unborn. If abortion was prosecuted in some places, it seems to have been based on a concept of a violation of the father's right to his offspring. Ancient religion did not bar abortion. . . .

[10] This right of privacy, whether it be founded in the Fourteenth Amendment's concept of personal liberty and restrictions upon state action, as we feel it is, or, as the District Court determined, in the Ninth Amendment's reservation of rights to the people, is broad enough to encompass a woman's decision whether or not to terminate her pregnancy. The detriment that the State would impose upon the pregnant woman by denying this choice altogether is apparent. Specific and direct harm medically diagnosable even in early pregnancy may be involved. Maternity, or additional offspring, may force upon the woman a distressful life and future. Psychological harm may be imminent. Mental and physical health may be taxed by child care. There is also the distress, for all concerned, associated with the unwanted child, and there is the problem of bringing a child into a family already unable, psychologically and otherwise, to care for it. In other cases, as in this one, the additional difficulties and continuing stigma of unwed motherhood may be involved. All these are factors the woman and her responsible physician necessarily will consider in consultation.

On the basis of elements such as these, appellant and some *amici* argue that the woman's right is absolute and that she is entitled to terminate her pregnancy at whatever time, in whatever way, and for whatever reason she alone chooses. With this we do not agree. Appellant's arguments that Texas either has no valid interest at all in regulating the abortion decision, or no interest strong enough to support any limitation upon the woman's sole determination, are unpersuasive. The Court's decisions recognizing a right of privacy also acknowledge that some state regulation in areas protected by that right is appropriate. As noted above, a State may properly assert important interests in safeguarding health, in maintaining medical standards, and in protecting potential life. At some point in pregnancy, these respective interests become sufficiently compelling to sustain regulation of the factors that govern the abortion decision. The privacy right involved, therefore, cannot be said to be absolute. In fact, it is not clear to us that the claim asserted by some *amici* that one has an unlimited right to do with one's body as one pleases bears a close relationship to the right of privacy previously articulated in the Court's decisions. The court has refused to recognize an unlimited right of this kind in the past. *Jacobson v. Massachusetts*, 197 U.S. 11, 25 S.Ct. 358, 49 L.Ed. 643 (1905) (vaccination); *Buck v. Bell,* 274 U.S. 200, 46 S.Ct. 584, 71 L.Ed. 1000 (1927) (sterilization).

We, therefore, conclude that the right of personal privacy includes the abortion decision, but that this right is not unqualified and must be considered against important state interests in regulation. We note that those federal and state courts that have recently considered abortion law challenges have reached the same conclusion. A majority, in addition to the District Court in the present case, have held state laws unconstitutional, at least in part, because of vagueness or because of overbreadth and abridgment of rights . . .

In the recent abortion cases, cited above, courts have recognized these principles. Those striking down state laws have generally scrutinized the State's interests in protecting health and potential life, and have concluded that neither interest justified broad limitations on the reasons for which a physician and his pregnant patient might decide that she should have an abortion in the early stages of pregnancy. Courts sustaining state laws have held that the State's determinations to protect health or prenatal life are dominant and constitutionally justifiable. . . .

X

In view of all this, we do not agree that, by adopting one theory of life, Texas may override the rights of the pregnant woman that are at stake. We repeat, however, that the State does have an important and legitimate interest in preserving and protecting the health of the pregnant woman, whether she be a resident of the State or a non-resident who seeks medical consultation and treatment there, and that it has still *another* important and legitimate interest in protecting the potentiality of human life. These interests are separate and distinct. Each grows in substantiality as the woman approaches term and, at a point during pregnancy, each becomes "compelling." [13,14] With respect to the State's important and legitimate interest in the health of the mother, the "compelling" point, in the light of present medical knowledge, is at approximately the end of the first trimester. This is so because of the now-established medical fact, referred to above at 725, that until the end of the first trimester mortality in abortion may be less than mortality in normal childbirth. It follows that, from and after this point, a State may regulate the abortion procedure to the extent that the regulation reasonably relates to the preservation and protection of maternal health. Examples of permissible state regulation in this area are requirement as to the qualifications of the person who is to perform the abortion; as to the licensure of that person; as to the facility in which the procedure is to be performed, that is, whether it must be a hospital or may be a clinic or some other place of less-than-hospital status; as to the licensing of the facility; and the like.

This means, on the other hand, that, for the period of pregnancy prior to this "compelling" point, the attending physician, in consultation with his patient, is free to determine, without regulation by the State, that, in his medical judgment, the patient's pregnancy should be terminated. If that decision is reached, the judgment may be effectuated by an abortion free of interference by the State.

[15] With respect to the State's important and legitimate interest in potential life, the "compelling" point is at viability. This is so because the fetus then presumably has the capability of meaningful life outside the mother's womb. State regulation protective of fetal life after viability thus has both logical and biological justifications. If the State is interested in protecting fetal life after viability, it may go so far as to proscribe abortion during that period, except when it is necessary to preserve the life or health of the mother.

[16] Measured against these standards, Art. 1196 of the Texas Penal Code, in restricting legal abortions to those "procured or attempted by medical advice for the purpose of saving the life of the mother," sweeps too broadly. The statute makes no distinction between abortions performed early in pregnancy and those performed later, and it limits to a single reason, "saving" the mother's life, the legal justification for the procedure. The statute, therefore, cannot survive the constitutional attack made upon it here.

This conclusion makes it unnecessary for us to consider the additional challenge to the Texas statute asserted on grounds of vagueness. See *United States v. Vuitch,* 402 U.S., at 67–72, 91 S.Ct., at 1296–1299.

XI

To summarize and to repeat:

1. A state criminal abortion statute of the current Texas type, that excepts from criminality only a life-saving procedure on behalf of the mother, without regard to pregnancy stage and without recognition of the other interests involved, is violative of the Due Process Clause of the Fourteenth Amendment.

(a) For the stage prior to approximately the end of the first trimester, the abortion decision and its effectuation must be left to the medical judgment of the pregnant woman's attending physician.

(b) For the stage subsequent to approximately the end of the first trimester, the State, in promoting its interest in the health of the mother, may, if it chooses, regulate the abortion procedure in ways that are reasonably related to maternal health.

(c) For the stage subsequent to viability, the State in promoting its interest in the potentiality of human life may, if it chooses, regulate, and even proscribe, abortion except where it is necessary, in appropriate medical judgment, for the preservation of the life or health of the mother.

[17] 2. The State may define the term "physician," as it has been employed in the preceding paragraphs of this Part XI of this opinion, to mean only a physician currently licensed by the State, and may proscribe any abortion by a person who is not a physician as so defined. In *Doe v. Bolton,* 410 U.S. 179, 93 S.Ct. 739, 35 L.Ed.2d 201, procedural requirements contained in one of the modern abortion statutes are considered. That opinion and this one, of course, are to be read together.

This holding, we feel, is consistent with the relative weights of the respective interests involved, with the lessons and examples of medical and legal history, with the lenity of the common law, and with the demands of the profound problems of the present day. The decision leaves the State free to place increasing restrictions on abortion as the period of pregnancy lengthens, so long as those restrictions are tailored to the recognized state interests. The decision vindicates the rights of the physician to administer medical treatment according to his professional judgment up to the points where important state interests provide compelling justifications for intervention. Up to those points, the abortion decision in all its aspects is inherently, and primarily, a medical decision, and basic responsibility for it must rest with the physician. If an individual practitioner abuses the privilege of exercising proper medical judgment, the usual remedies, judicial and intra-professional, are available.

XII

[18] Our conclusion that Art. 1196 is unconstitutional means, of course, that the Texas abortion statutes, as a unit, must fall. The exception of Art. 1196 cannot be struck down separately, for then the State would be left with a statute proscribing all abortion procedures no matter how medically urgent the case.

Although the District Court granted appellant Roe declaratory relief, it stopped short of issuing an injunction against enforcement of the Texas statutes. The Court has recognized that different considerations enter into a federal court's decision as to declaratory relief, on the one hand, and injunctive relief, on the other. *Zwickler v. Koota,* 389 U.S. 241, 252–255, 88 S.Ct. 391, 397–399, 19 L.Ed.2d 444 (1967); *Dombrowski v. Pfister,* 380 U.S. 479, 85 S.Ct. 1116, 14 L.Ed.2d 22 (1965). We are not dealing with a statute that, on its face, appears to abridge free expression, an area of particular concern under *Dombrowski* and refined in *Younger v. Harris,* 401 U.S., at 50, 91 S.Ct., at 753.

We find it unnecessary to decide whether the District Court erred in withholding injunctive relief, for we assume the Texas prosecutorial authorities will give full credence to this decision that the present criminal abortion statutes of that State are unconstitutional. . . .

Resignation Speech (1974)
President Richard M. Nixon

Public Papers of the Presidents of the United States, Richard Nixon, 1974, pp. 626–629.

Good evening:

This is the 37th time I have spoken to you from this office, where so many decisions have been made that shaped the history of this Nation. Each time I have done so to discuss with you some matter that I believe affected the national interest.

In all the decisions I have made in my public life, I have always tried to do what was best for the nation. Throughout the long and difficult period of Watergate, I have felt it was my duty to persevere, to make every possible effort to complete the term of office to which you elected me. In the past few days, however, it has become evident to me that I no longer have a strong enough political base in the Congress to justify continuing that effort. As long as there was such a base, I felt strongly that it was necessary to see the constitutional process through to its conclusion, that to do otherwise would be unfaithful to the spirit of that deliberately difficult process and a dangerously destabilizing precedent for the future.

But with the disappearance of that base, I now believe that the constitutional purpose has been served, and there is no longer a need for the process to be prolonged.

I would have preferred to carry through to the finish, whatever the personal agony it would have involved, and my family unanimously urged me to do so. But the interests of the Nation must always come before any personal considerations.

From the discussions I have had with Congressional and other leaders, I have concluded that because of the Watergate matter, I might not have the support of the Congress that I would consider necessary to back the very difficult decisions and carry out the duties of this office in the way the interests of the Nation will require.

I have never been a quitter. To leave office before my term is completed is abhorrent to every instinct in my body. But as President, I must put the interests of America first. America needs a full-time President and a full-time Congress, particularly at this time with problems we face at home and abroad.

To continue to fight through the months ahead for my personal vindication would almost totally absorb the time and attention of both the President and the Congress in a period when our entire focus should be on the great issues of peace abroad and prosperity without inflation at home. Therefore, I shall resign the Presidency effective at noon tomorrow. Vice President Ford will be sworn in as President at that hour in this office.

As I recall the high hopes for America with which we began this second term, I feel a great sadness that I will not be here in this office working on your behalf to achieve those hopes in the next $2\frac{1}{2}$ years. But in turning over direction of the Government to Vice President Ford, I know, as I told the Nation when I nominated him for that office 10 months ago, that the leadership of America will be in good hands.

In passing this office to the Vice President, I also do so with the profound sense of the weight of responsibility that will fall on his shoulders tomorrow and, therefore, of the understanding, the patience, the cooperation he will need from all Americans.

As he assumes that responsibility, he will deserve the help and the support of all of us. As we look to the future, the first essential is to begin healing the wounds of this

Nation, to put the bitterness and divisions of the recent past behind us and to rediscover those shared ideals that lie at the heart of our strength and unity as a great and as a free people.

By taking this action, I hope that I will have hastened the start of that process of healing which is so desperately needed in America.

I regret deeply any injuries that may have been done in the course of the events that led to this decision. I would say only that if some of my judgments were wrong—and some were wrong—they were made in what I believed at the time to be the best interest of the Nation.

To those who have stood with me during these past difficult months—to my family, my friends, to many others who joined in supporting my cause because they believed it was right—I will be eternally grateful for your support.

And to those who have not felt able to give me your support, let me say I leave with no bitterness toward those who have opposed me, because all of us, in the final analysis, have been concerned with the good of the country, however our judgments might differ.

So, let us all now join together in affirming that common commitment and in helping our new President succeed for the benefit of all Americans.

I shall leave this office with regret at not completing my term, but with gratitude for the privilege of serving as your President for the past $5\frac{1}{2}$ years. These years have been a momentous time in the history of our Nation and the world. They have been a time of achievement in which we can all be proud, achievements that represent the shared efforts of the Administration, the Congress, and the people.

But the challenges ahead are equally great, and they, too, will require the support and the efforts of the Congress and the people working in cooperation with the new Administration.

We have ended America's longest war, but in the work of securing a lasting peace in the world, the goals ahead are even more far-reaching and more difficult. We must complete a structure of peace so that it will be said of this generation, our generation of Americans, by the people of all nations, not only that we ended one war but that we prevented future wars.

We have unlocked the doors that for a quarter of a century stood between the United States and the People's Republic of China.

We must now ensure that the one quarter of the world's people who live in the People's Republic of China will be and remain not our enemies, but our friends.

In the Middle East, 100 million people in the Arab countries, many of whom have considered us their enemy for nearly 20 years, now look on us as their friends. We must continue to build on that friendship so that peace can settle at last over the Middle East and so that the cradle of civilization will not become its grave.

Together with the Soviet Union, we have made the crucial breakthroughs that have begun the process of limiting nuclear arms. But we must set as our goal not just limiting but reducing and, finally, destroying these terrible weapons so that they cannot destroy civilization and so that the threat of nuclear war will not longer hang over the world and the people. We have opened the new relation with the Soviet Union. We must continue to develop and expand that new relationship so that the two strongest nations of the world will live together in cooperation, rather than confrontation.

Around the world—in Asia, in Africa, in Latin America, in the Middle East—there are millions of people who live in terrible poverty, even starvation. We must keep as our goal turning away from production for war and expanding production for peace so that people everywhere on this Earth can at last look forward in their children's time, if not in our own time, to having the necessities for a decent life.

Here in America, we are fortunate that most of our people have not only the blessings of liberty but also the means to live full and good and, by the world's standards, even abundant lives. We must press on, however, toward a goal, not only of more and better jobs but of full opportunity for every American and of what we are striving so hard right now to achieve, prosperity without inflation.

For more than a quarter of a century in public life, I have shared in the turbulent history of this era. I have fought for what I believed in. I have tried, to the best of my ability, to discharge those duties and meet those responsibilities that were entrusted to me.

Sometimes I have succeeded and sometimes I have failed, but always I have taken heart from what Theodore Roosevelt once said about the man in the arena, "whose face is marred by dust and sweat and blood, who strives valiantly, who errs and comes short again and again because there is not effort without error and shortcoming, but who does actually strive to do the deed, who knows the great enthusiasms, the great devotions, who spends himself in a worthy cause, who at the best knows in the end the triumphs of high achievements who at the worst, if he fails, at least fails while daring greatly."

I pledge to you tonight that as long as I have a breath of life in my body, I shall continue in that spirit. I shall continue to work for the great causes to which I have been dedicated throughout my years as a Congressman, a Senator, Vice President, and President, the cause of peace, not just for America but among all nations—prosperity, justice, and opportunity for all of our people. There is one cause above all to which I have been devoted and to which I shall always be devoted for as long as I live.

When I first took the oath of office as President 5½ years ago, I made this sacred commitment: to "consecrate my office, my energies, and all the wisdom I can summon to the cause of peace among nations."

I have done my very best in all the days since to be true to that pledge. As a result of these efforts, I am confident that the world is a safer place today, not only for the people of America but for the people of all nations, and that all of our children have a better chance than before of living in peace rather than dying in war.

This, more than anything, is what I hoped to achieve when I sought the Presidency. This, more than anything, is what I hope will be my legacy to you, to our country, as I leave the Presidency. To have served in this office is to have felt a very personal sense of kinship with each and every American. In leaving it, I do so with this prayer: May God's grace be with you in all the days ahead.

Remarks on Taking the Oath of Office (1974)
President Gerald R. Ford

Public Papers of the Presidents, Gerald R. Ford, 1974,
Vol. III, pp. 1–3

August 9, 1974

Mr. Chief Justice, my dear friends, my fellow Americans:

The oath that I have taken is the same oath that was taken by George Washington and by every President under the Constitution. But I assume the Presidency under extraordinary circumstances never before experienced by Americans. This is an hour of history that troubles our minds and hurts our hearts.

Therefore, I feel it is my first duty to make an unprecedented compact with my countrymen. Not an inaugural address, not a fireside chat, not a campaign speech—just a little straight talk among friends. And I intend it to be the first of many.

I am acutely aware that you have not elected me as your President by your ballots, and so I ask you to confirm me as your President with your prayers. And I hope that such prayers will also be the first of many.

If you have not chosen me by secret ballot, neither have I gained office by any secret promises. I have not campaigned either for the Presidency or the Vice Presidency. I have not subscribed to any partisan platform. I am indebted to no man, and only to one woman—my dear wife—as I begin this very difficult job.

I have not sought this enormous responsibility, but I will not shirk it. Those who nominated and confirmed me as Vice President were my friends and are my friends. They were of both parties, elected by all the people and acting under the Constitution in their name. It is only fitting then that I should pledge to them and to you that I will be the President of all the people. Thomas Jefferson said the people are the only sure reliance for the preservation of our liberty. And down the years, Abraham Lincoln renewed this American article of faith asking, "Is there any better way or equal hope in the world?"

I intend, on Monday next, to request of the Speaker of the House of Representatives and the President pro tempore of the Senate the privilege of appearing before the Congress to share with my former colleagues and with you, the American people, my views on the priority business of the Nation and to solicit your views and their views. And may I say to the Speaker and the others, if I could meet with you right after these remarks, I would appreciate it.

Even though this is late in an election year, there is no way we can go forward except together and no way anybody can win except by serving the people's urgent needs. We cannot stand still or slip backwards. We must go forward now together.

To the peoples and the governments of all friendly nations, and I hope that could encompass the whole world, I pledge an uninterrupted and sincere search for peace. America will remain strong and united, but its strength will remain dedicated to the safety and sanity of the entire family of man, as well as to our own precious freedom.

I believe that truth is the glue that holds government together, not only our Government but civilization itself. That bond, though strained, is unbroken at home and abroad. In all my public and private acts as your President, I expect to follow my instincts of openness and candor with full confidence that honesty is always the best policy in the end.

My fellow Americans, our long national nightmare is over.

Our Constitution works; our great Republic is a government of laws and not of men. Here the people rule. But there is a higher Power, by whatever name we honor Him, who ordains not only righteousness but love, not only justice but mercy.

As we bind up the internal wounds of Watergate, more painful and more poisonous than those of foreign wars, let us restore the golden rule to our political process, and let brotherly love purge our hearts of suspicion and of hate.

In the beginning, I asked you to pray for me. Before closing, I ask again your prayers, for Richard Nixon and for his family. May our former President, who brought peace to millions, find it for himself. May God bless and comfort his wonderful wife and daughters, whose love and loyalty will forever be a shining legacy to all who bear the lonely burdens of the White House. I can only guess at those burdens, although I have witnessed at close hand the tragedies that befell three Presidents and the lesser trials of others.

With all the strength and all the good sense I have gained from life, with all the confidence my family, my friends, and my dedicated staff impart to me, and with the good will of countless Americans I have encountered in recent visits to 40 States, I now solemnly reaffirm my promise I made to you last December 6: to uphold the Constitution, to do what is right as God gives me to see the right, and to do the very best I can for America.

God helping me, I will not let you down.

Thank you

"Malaise" Speech (1979)
President Jimmy Carter

Public Papers of the Presidents of the United States,
Jimmy Carter, 1979, Vol. II, pp. 1,235–1,241

July 15, 1979

Good evening.

This is a special night for me. Exactly 3 years ago, on July 15, 1976, I accepted the nomination of my party to run for President of the United States. I promised you a President who is not isolated from the people, who feels your pain, and who shares your dreams and who draws his strength and his wisdom from you.

During the past 3 years I've spoken to you on many occasions about national concerns, the energy crisis, reorganizing the Government, our Nation's economy, and issues of war and especially peace. But over those years the subjects of the speeches, the talks, and the press conferences have become increasingly narrow, focused more and more on what the isolated world of Washington thinks is important. Gradually, you've heard more and more about what the Government thinks or what the Government should be doing and less and less about our Nation's hopes, our dreams, and our vision of the future.

Ten days ago I had planned to speak to you again about a very important subject—energy. For the fifth time I would have described the urgency of the problem and laid out a series of legislative recommendations to the Congress. But as I was preparing to speak, I began to ask myself the same question that I now know has been troubling many of you. Why have we not been able to get together as a nation to resolve our serious energy problem?

It's clear that the true problems of our Nation are much deeper—deeper than gasoline lines of energy shortages, deeper even than inflation or recession. And I realize more than ever that as President I need your help. So, I decided to reach out and listen to the voices of America. I invited to Camp David people from almost every segment of our society—business and labor, teachers and preachers, Governors, mayors, and private citizens. And then I left Camp David to listen to other Americans, men and women like you. It has been an extraordinary 10 days, and I want to share with you what I've heard.

First of all, I got a lot of personal advice. Let me quote a few of the typical comments that I wrote down.

This from a southern Governor: "Mr. President, you are not leading this Nation—you're just managing the Government."

"You don't see the people enough any more."

"Some of your Cabinet members don't seem loyal. There is not enough discipline among your disciples."

"Don't talk to us about politics or the mechanics of government, but about an understanding of our common good."

"Mr. President, we're in trouble. Talk to us about blood and sweat and tears."

"If you lead, Mr. President, we will follow."

Many people talked about themselves and about the condition of our Nation. This from a young woman in Pennsylvania: "I feel so far from government. I feel like ordinary people are excluded from political power."

And this from a young Chicano: "Some of us have suffered from recession all our lives."

"Some people have wasted energy, but others haven't had anything to waste."

And this from a religious leader: "No material shortage can touch the important things like God's love for us or our love for one another."

And I like this one particularly from a black woman who happens to be the mayor of a small Mississippi town: "The big-shots are not the only ones who are important. Remember, you can't sell anything on Wall Street unless someone digs it up somewhere else first."

This kind of summarized a lot of other statements: "Mr. President, we are confronted with a moral and a spiritual crisis."

Several of our discussions were on energy, and I have a notebook full of comments and advice. I'll read just a few.

"We can't go on consuming 40 percent more energy than we produce. When we import oil we are also importing inflation plus unemployment."

"We've got to use what we have. The Middle East has only 5 percent of the world's energy, but the United States has 24 percent."

And this is one of the most vivid statements: "Our neck is stretched over the fence and OPEC has a knife."

"There will be other cartels and other shortages. American wisdom and courage right now can set a path to follow in the future."

This was a good one: "Be bold, Mr. President. We may make mistakes, but we are ready to experiment."

And this one from a labor leader got to the heart of it: "The real issue is freedom. We must deal with the energy problem on a war footing."

And the last that I'll read: "When we enter the moral equivalent of war, Mr. President, don't issue us BB guns."

These 10 days confirmed my belief in the decency and the strength and the wisdom of the American people, but it also bore out some of my long-standing concerns about our Nation's underlying problems.

I know, of course, being President, that government actions and legislation can be very important. That's why I've worked hard to put my campaign promises into law—and I have to admit, with just mixed success. But after listening to the American people I have been reminded again that all the legislation in the world can't fix what's wrong with America. So, I want to speak to you first tonight about a subject even more serious than energy or inflation. I want to talk to you right now about a fundamental threat to American democracy. I do not mean our political and civil liberties. They will endure. And I do not refer to the outward strength of America, a nation that is at peace tonight everywhere in the world, with unmatched economic power and military might.

The threat is nearly invisible in ordinary ways. It is a crisis of confidence. It is a crisis that strikes at the very heart and soul and spirit of our national will. We can see this crisis in the growing doubt about the meaning of our own lives and in the loss of a unity of purpose for our Nation. The erosion of our confidence in the future is threatening to destroy the social and the political fabric of America.

The confidence that we have always had as a people is not simply some romantic dream or a proverb in a dusty book that we read just on the Fourth of July. It is the idea which founded our Nation and has guided our development as a people. Confidence in the future has supported everything else—public institutions and private enterprise, our own families, and the very Constitution of the United States. Confidence has defined our course and has served as a link between generations. We've always believed in something called progress. We've always had a faith that the days of our children would be better than our own.

Our people are losing that faith, not only in government itself but in the ability as citizens to serve as the ultimate rulers and shapers of our democracy. As a people we know our past and we are proud of it. Our progress has been part of the living history of America, even the world. We always believed that we were part of a great movement of humanity itself called democracy, involved in the search for freedom, and that belief has always strengthened us in our purpose. But just as we are losing our confidence in the future, we are also beginning to close the door on our past.

In a nation that was proud of hard work, strong families, close-knit communities, and our faith in God, too many of us now tend to worship self-indulgence and con-sumption. Human identity is no longer defined by what one does, but by what one owns. But we've discovered that owning things and consuming things does not satisfy our longing for meaning. We've learned that piling up material goods cannot fill the emptiness of lives which have no confidence or purpose. The symptoms of this crisis of the American spirit are all around us. For the first time in the history of our country a majority of our people believe that the next 5 years will be worse than the past 5 years. Two-thirds of our people do not even vote. The productivity of American workers is actually dropping, and the willingness of Americans to save for the future has fallen below that of all other people in the Western world.

As you know, there is a growing disrespect for government and for churches and for schools, the news media, and other institutions. This is not a message of happiness or reassurance, but it is the truth and it is a warning.

These changes did not happen overnight. They've come upon us gradually over the last generation, years that were filled with shocks and tragedy.

We were sure that ours was a nation of the ballot, not the bullet, until the murders of John Kennedy and Robert Kennedy and Martin Luther King, Jr. We were taught that our armies were always invincible and our causes were always just, only to suffer the agony of Vietnam. We respected the Presidency as a place of honor until the shock of Watergate.

We remember when the phrase "sound as a dollar" was an expression of absolute dependability, until 10 years of inflation began to shrink our dollar and our savings. We believed that our Nation's resources were limitless until 1973, when we had to face a growing dependence on foreign oil.

These wounds are still very deep. They have never been healed.

Looking for a way out of this crisis, our people have turned to the Federal Government and found it isolated from the mainstream of our Nation's life. Washington, D.C., has become an island. The gap between our citizens and our Government has never been so wide. The people are looking for honest answers, not easy answers; clear leadership, not false claims and evasiveness and politics as usual.

What you see too often in Washington and elsewhere around the country is a system of government that seems incapable of action. You see a Congress twisted and pulled in every direction by hundreds of well-financed and powerful special interests. You see every extreme position defended to the last vote, almost to the last breath by one unyielding group or another. You often see a balanced and a fair approach that demands sacrifice, a little sacrifice from everyone, abandoned like an orphan without support and without friends.

Often you see paralysis and stagnation and drift. You don't like, and neither do I. What can we do?

First of all, we must face the truth, and then we can change our course. We simply must have faith in each other, faith in our ability to govern ourselves, and faith in the future of this Nation. Restoring that faith and that confidence to America is now the most important task we face. It is a true challenge of this generation of Americans.

One of the visitors to Camp David last week put it this way: "We've got to stop crying and start sweating, stop talking and start walking, stop cursing and start praying. The strength we need will not come from the White House, but from every house in America." We know the strength of America. We are strong. We can regain our unity. We can regain our confidence. We are the heirs of generations who survived threats much more powerful and awesome than those that challenge us now. Our fathers and mothers were strong men and women who shaped a new society during the Great Depression, who fought world wars, and who carved out a new charter of peace for the world.

We ourselves and the same Americans who just 10 years ago put a man on the Moon. We are the generation that dedicated our society to the pursuit of human rights and equality. And we are the generation that will win the war on the energy problem and in that process rebuild the unity and confidence of America.

We are at a turning point in our history. There are two paths to choose. One is a path I've warned about tonight, the path that leads to fragmentation and self-interest. Down that road lies a mistaken idea of freedom, the right to grasp for ourselves some advantage over others. That path would be one of constant conflict between narrow interests ending in chaos and immobility. It is a certain route to failure.

All the traditions of our past, all the lessons of our heritage, all the promises of our future point to another path, the path of common purpose and the restoration of American values. That path leads to true freedom for our Nation and ourselves. We can take the first steps down that path as we begin to solve our energy problem.

Energy will be the immediate test of our ability to unite this Nation, and it can also be the standard around which we rally. On the battlefield of energy we can win for our Nation a new confidence, and we can seize control again of our common destiny.

In little more than two decades we've gone from a position of energy independence to one in which almost half the oil we use comes from foreign countries, at prices that are going through the roof. Our excessive dependence on OPEC has already taken a tremendous tool on our economy and our people. This is the direct cause of the long lines which have made millions of you spend aggravating hours waiting for gasoline. It's a cause of the increased inflation and unemployment that we now face. This intolerable dependence on foreign oil threatens our economic independence and the very security of our Nation.

The energy crisis is real. It is worldwide. It is a clear and present danger to our Nation. These are facts and we simply must face them.

What I have to say to you now about energy is simple and vitally important.

Point one: I am tonight setting a clear goal for the energy policy of the United States. Beginning this moment, this Nation will never use more foreign oil than we did in 1977—never. From now on, every new addition to our demand for energy will be met from our own production and our own conservation. The generation-long growth in our dependence on foreign oil will be stopped dead in its tracks right now and then reversed as we move through the 1980's, for I am tonight setting the further goal of cutting our dependence on foreign oil by one-half by the end of the next decade—a saving of over $4\frac{1}{2}$ million barrels of imported oil per day.

Point two: To ensure that we meet these targets, I will use my Presidential authority to set import quotas. I'm announcing tonight that for 1979 and 1980, I will forbid the entry into this country of one drop of foreign oil more than these goals allow. These quotas will ensure a reduction in imports even below the ambitious levels we set at the recent Tokyo summit.

Point three: To give us energy security, I am asking for the most massive peacetime commitment of funds and resources in our Nation's history to develop America's own alternative sources of fuel—from coal, from oil shale, from plant products for gasohol, from unconventional gas, from the Sun.

I propose the creation of an energy security corporation to lead this effort to replace $2\frac{1}{2}$ million barrels of imported oil per day by 1990. The corporation will issue up to $5 billion in energy bonds, and I especially want them to be in small denominations so that average Americans can invest directly in America's energy security.

Just as a similar synthetic rubber corporation helped us win World War II, so will we mobilize American determination and ability to win the energy war. Moreover, I will soon submit legislation to Congress calling for the creation of this Nation's first solar bank, which will help us achieve the crucial goal of 20 percent of our energy coming from solar power by the year 2000.

These efforts will cost money, a lot of money, and that is why Congress must enact the windfall profits tax without delay. It will be money well spent. Unlike the billions of dollars that we ship to foreign countries to pay for foreign oil, these funds will be paid by Americans to Americans. These funds will go to fight, not to increase, inflation and unemployment.

Point four: I'm asking Congress to mandate, to require as a matter of law, that our Nation's utility companies cut their massive use of oil by 50 percent within the next decade and switch to other fuels, especially coal, our most abundant energy source.

Point five: To make absolutely certain that nothing stands in the way of achieving these goals, I will urge Congress to create an energy mobilization board which, like the War Production Board in World War II, will have the responsibility and authority to cut through the redtape, the delays, and the endless roadblocks to completing key energy projects. We will protect our environment. But when this Nation critically needs a refinery or a pipeline, we will build it.

Point six: I'm proposing a bold conservation program to involve every State, county, and city and every average American in our energy battle. This effort will permit you to build conservation into your homes and your lives at a cost you can afford.

I ask Congress to give me authority for mandatory conservation and for standby gasoline rationing. To further conserve energy, I'm proposing tonight an extra $10 billion over the next decade to strengthen our public transportation systems. And I'm asking you for your good and for your Nation's security to take no unnecessary trips, to use carpools or public transportation whenever you can, to park your car one extra day per week, to obey the speed limit, and to set your thermostats to save fuel. Every act of energy conservation like this is more than just common sense—I tell you it is an act of patriotism.

Our Nation must be fair to the poorest among us, so we will increase aid to needy Americans to cope with rising energy prices. We often think of conservation only in terms of sacrifice. In fact, it is the most painless and immediate way of rebuilding our Nation's strength. Every gallon of oil each one of us saves is a new form of production. It gives us more freedom, more confidence, that much more control over our own lives.

So, the solution of our energy crisis can also help us to conquer the crisis of the spirit in our country. It can rekindle our sense of unity, our confidence in the future, and give our Nation and all of us individually a new sense of purpose.

You know we can do it. We have the natural resources. We have more oil in our shale alone than several Saudi Arabias. We have more coal than any nation on Earth. We have the world's highest level of technology. We have the most skilled work force, with innovative genius, and I firmly believe that we have the national will to win this war.

I do not promise you that this struggle for freedom will be easy. I do not promise a quick way out of our Nation's problems, when the truth is that the only way out is an all-out effort. What I do promise you is that I will lead our fight, and I will enforce fairness in our struggle, and I will ensure honesty. And above all, I will act.

We can manage the short-term shortages more effectively and we will, but there are no short-term solutions to our long-range problems. There is simply no way to avoid sacrifice. Twelve hours from now I will speak again in Kansas City, to expand and to explain further our energy program. Just as the search for solutions to our energy shortages has now led us to a new awareness of our Nation's deeper problems, so our willingness to work for those solutions in energy can strengthen us to attack those deeper problems.

I will continue to travel this country, to hear the people of America. You can help me to develop a national agenda for the 1980's. I will listen and I will act. We will act together. These were the promises I made 3 years ago, and I intend to keep them.

Little by little we can and we must rebuild our confidence. We can spend until we empty our treasuries, and we may summon all the wonders of science. But we can succeed only if we tap our greatest resources—America's people, America's values, and America's confidence. I have seen the strength of America in the inexhaustible resources of our people. In the days to come, let us renew that strength in the struggle for an energy-secure nation.

In closing, let me say this: I will do my best, but I will not do it alone. Let your voice be heard. Whenever you have a chance, say something good about our country. With God's help and for the sake of our Nation, it is time for us to join hands in America. Let us commit ourselves together to a rebirth of the American spirit. Working together with our common faith we cannot fail.

Thank you and good night

Remarks at the Brandenburg Gate (1987)
President Ronald Reagan

*Public Papers of the Presidents of the United States,
Ronald Reagan*, Vol. 1 (Jan.–July 1987),
pp. 634–637

June 12, 1987

Thank you very much. Chancellor Kohl, Governing Mayor Diepgen, ladies and gentlemen: Twenty four years ago, President John F. Kennedy visited Berlin, speaking to the people of this city and the world at the city hall. Well, since then two other presidents have come, each in his turn, to Berlin. And today I, myself, make my second visit to your city.

We come to Berlin, we American Presidents, because it's our duty to speak, in this place, of freedom. But I must confess, we're drawn here by other things as well: by the feeling of history in this city, more than 500 years older than our own nation; by the beauty of the Grunewald and the Tiergarten; most of all, by your courage and determination. Perhaps the composer, Paul Lincke, understood something about American Presidents. You see, like so many Presidents before me, I come here today because wherever I go, whatever I do: *"Ich hab noch einen koffer in Berlin."* [I still have a suitcase in Berlin.]

Our gathering today is being broadcast throughout Western Europe and North America. I understand that it is being seen and heard as well in the East. To those listening throughout Eastern Europe, I extend my warmest greetings and the good will of the American people. To those listening in East Berlin, a special word: Although I cannot be with you, I address my remarks to you just as surely as to those standing here before me. For I join you, as I join your fellow countrymen in the West, in this firm, this unalterable belief: *Es gibt nur ein Berlin.* [There is only one Berlin.]

Behind me stands a wall that encircles the free sectors of this city, part of a vast system of barriers that divides the entire continent of Europe. From the Baltic, south, those barriers cut across Germany in a gash of barbed wire, concrete, dog runs, and guardtowers. Farther south, there may be no visible, no obvious wall. But there remain armed guards and checkpoints all the same—still a restriction on the right to travel, still an instrument to impose upon ordinary men and women the will of a totalitarian state. Yet it is here in Berlin where the wall emerges most clearly; here, cutting across your city, where the news photo and the television screen have imprinted this brutal division of a continent upon the mind of the world. Standing before the Brandenburg Gate, every man is a German, separated from his fellow men. Every man is a Berliner, forced to look upon a scar.

President von Weizsacker has said: "The German question is open as long as the Brandenburg Gate is closed." Today I say: As long as this gate is closed, as long as this scar of a wall is permitted to stand, it is not the German question alone that remains open, but the question of freedom for all mankind. Yet I do not come here to lament. For I find in Berlin a message of hope, even in the shadow of this wall, a message of triumph.

In this season of spring in 1945, the people of Berlin emerged from their air-raid shelters to find devastation. Thousands of miles away, the people of the United States reached out to help. And in 1947 Secretary of State—as you've been told—George Marshall announced the creation of what would become known as the Marshall plan. Speaking precisely 40 years ago this month, he said: "Our policy is directed not against any country or doctrine, but against hunger, poverty, desperation, and chaos."

In the Reichstag a few moments ago, I saw a display commemorating this 40th anniversary of the Marshall plan. I was struck by the sign on a burnt-out, gutted structure that was being rebuilt. I understand that Berliners of my own generation can remember seeing signs like it dotted throughout the Western sectors of the city. The sign read simply: "The Marshall plan is helping here to strengthen the free world." A strong, free world in the West, that dream became real. Japan rose from ruin to become an economic giant. Italy, France, Belgium—virtually every nation in Western Europe saw political and economic rebirth; the European Community was founded.

In West Germany and here in Berlin, there took place an economic miracle, the *Wirtschaftswunder.* Adenauer, Erhard, Reuter, and other leaders understood the practical importance of liberty—that just as truth can flourish only when the journalist is given freedom of speech, so prosperity can come about only when the farmer and businessman enjoy economic freedom. The German leaders reduced tariffs, expanded free trade, lowered taxes. From 1950 to 1960 alone, the standard of living in West Germany and Berlin doubled.

Where four decades ago there was rubble, today in West Berlin there is the greatest industrial output of any city in Germany—busy office blocks, fine homes and apartments, proud avenues, and the spreading lawns of park land. Where a city's culture seemed to have been destroyed, today there are two great universities, orchestras and an opera, countless theaters, and museums. Where there was want, today there's abundance—food, clothing, automobiles—the wonderful goods of the Ku'damm. From devastation, from utter ruin, you Berliners have, in freedom, rebuilt a city that once again ranks as one of the greatest on Earth. The Soviets may have had other plans. But, my friends, there were a few things the Soviets didn't count on— *Berliner herz, Berliner humor, ja, und Berliner schnauze.* [Berliner heart, Berliner humor, yes, and a Berliner *schnauze.*] [*Laughter*]

In the 1950's, Khrushchev predicted: "We will bury you." But in the West today, we see a free world that has achieved a level of prosperity and well-being unprecedented in all human history. In the Communist world, we see failure, technological backwardness, declining standards of health, even want of the most basic kind—too little food. Even today, the Soviet Union still cannot feed itself. After these four decades, then, there stands before the entire world one great and inescapable conclusion: Freedom leads to prosperity. Freedom replaces the ancient hatreds among the nations with comity and peace. Freedom is the victor.

And now the Soviets themselves may, in a limited way, be coming to understand the importance of freedom. We hear much from Moscow about a new policy of reform and openness. Some political prisoners have been released. Certain foreign news broadcasts are no longer being jammed. Some economic enterprises have been permitted to operate with greater freedom from state control. Are these the beginnings of profound changes in the Soviet state? Or are they token gestures, intended to raise false hopes in the West, or to strengthen the Soviet system without changing it? We welcome change and openness; for we believe that freedom and security go together, that the advance of human liberty can only strengthen the cause of world peace. There is one sign the Soviets can make that would be unmistakable, that would advance dramatically the cause of freedom and peace. General Secretary Gorbachev, if you seek peace, if you seek prosperity for the Soviet Union and Eastern Europe, if you seek liberalization: Come here to this gate! Mr. Gorbachev, open this gate! Mr. Gorbachev, tear down this wall!

I understand the fear of war and the pain of division that afflict this continent—and I pledge to you my country's efforts to help overcome these burdens. To be sure, we in the West must resist Soviet expansion. So we must maintain defenses of unassailable strength. Yet we seek peace; so we must strive to reduce arms on both sides. Beginning 10 years ago, the Soviets challenged the Western alliance with a grave new threat, hundreds of new and more deadly SS-20 nuclear missiles, capable of striking every capital in Europe. The Western alliance responded by committing itself to a counterdeployment unless the Soviets agreed to negotiate a better solution; namely, the elimination of such weapons on both sides. For many months, the Soviets refused to bargain in earnestness. As the alliance, in turn, prepared to go forward with its counterdeployment, there were difficult days—days of protests like those during my 1982 visit to this city—and the Soviets later walked away from the table.

But through it all, the alliance held firm. And I invite those who protested then—I invite those who protest today—to mark this fact: Because we remained strong, the Soviets came back to the table. And because we remained strong, today we have within reach the possibility, not merely of limiting the growth of arms, but of eliminating for the first time, an entire class of nuclear weapons from the face of the Earth. As I speak, NATO ministers are meeting in Iceland to review the progress of our proposals for eliminating these weapons. At the talks in Geneva, we have also proposed deep cuts in strategic offensive weapons. And the Western allies have likewise made far-reaching proposals to reduce the danger of conventional war and to place a total ban on chemical weapons.

While we pursue these arms reductions, I pledge to you that we will maintain the capacity to deter Soviet aggression at any level at which it might occur. And in cooperation with many of our allies, the United States is pursuing the Strategic Defense Initiative—research to base deterrence not on the threat of offensive retaliation, but on defenses that truly defend; on systems, in short, that will not target populations, but shield them. By these means we seek to increase the safety of Europe and all the world. But we must remember a crucial fact: East and West do not mistrust each other because we are armed; we are armed because we mistrust each other. And our differences are not about weapons but about liberty. When President Kennedy spoke at the City Hall those 24 years ago, freedom was encircled, Berlin was under siege. And today, despite all the pressures upon this city, Berlin stands secure in its liberty. And freedom itself is transforming the globe.

In the Philippines, in South and Central America, democracy has been given a rebirth. Throughout the Pacific, free markets are working miracle after miracle of economic growth. In the industrialized nations, a technological revolution is taking place—a revolution marked by rapid, dramatic advances in computers and telecommunications.

In Europe, only one nation and those it controls refuse to join the community of freedom. Yet in this age of redoubled economic growth, of information and innovation, the Soviet Union faces a choice: It must make fundamental changes, or it will become obsolete. Today thus represents a moment of hope. We in the West stand ready to cooperate with the East to promote true openness, to break down barriers that separate people, to create a safer, freer world.

And surely there is no better place than Berlin, the meeting place of East and West to make a start. Free people of Berlin: Today, as in the past, the United States stands for the strict observance and full implementation of all parts of the Four Power Agreement of 1971. Let us use this occasion, the 750th anniversary of this city, to usher in a new era, to seek a still fuller, richer life for the Berlin of the future. Together, let us maintain and develop the ties between the Federal Republic and the Western sectors of Berlin, which is permitted by the 1971 agreement. And I invite Mr. Gorbachev: Let us work to bring the Eastern and Western parts of the city closer together, so that all the inhabitants of all Berlin can enjoy the benefits that come with life in one of the great cities of the world. To open Berlin still further to all Europe, East and West, let us expand the vital air access to this city, finding ways of making commercial air service to Berlin more convenient, more comfortable, and more economical. We look to the day when West Berlin can become one of the chief aviation hubs in all central Europe.

With our French and British partners, the United States is prepared to help bring international meetings to Berlin. It would be only fitting for Berlin to serve as the site of United Nations meetings, or world conferences on human rights and arms control or other issues that call for international cooperation. There is no better way to establish hope for the future than to enlighten young minds, and we would be honored to sponsor summer youth exchanges, cultural events, and other programs for young

Berliners from the East. Our French and British friends, I'm certain, will do the same. And it's my hope that an authority can be found in East Berlin to sponsor visits from young people of the Western sectors.

One final proposal, one close to my heart: Sport represents a source of enjoyment and ennoblement, and you many have noted that the Republic of Korea—South Korea—has offered to permit certain events of the 1988 Olympics to take place in the North. International sports competitions of all kinds could take place in both parts of this city. And what better way to demonstrate to the world the openness of this city than to offer in some future year to hold the Olympic games here in Berlin, East and West?

In these four decades, as I have said, you Berliners have built a great city. You've done so in spite of threats—the Soviet attempts to impose the East-mark, the blockade. Today the city thrives in spite of the challenges implicit in the very presence of this wall. What keeps you here? Certainly there's a great deal to be said for your fortitude, for your defiant courage. But I believe there's something deeper, something that involves Berlin's whole look and feel and way of life—not mere sentiment. No one could live long in Berlin without being completely disabused of illusions. Something instead, that has seen the difficulties of life in Berlin but chose to accept them, that continues to build this good and proud city in contrast to a surrounding totalitarian presence that refuses to release human energies or aspirations. Something that speaks with a powerful voice of affirmation, that says yes to this city, yes to the future, yes to freedom. In a word, I would submit that what keeps you in Berlin is love—love both profound and abiding. Perhaps this gets to the root of the matter, to the most fundamental distinction of all between East and West. The totalitarian world produces backwardness because it does such violence to the spirit, thwarting the human impulse to create, to enjoy, to worship. The totalitarian world finds even symbols of love and of worship an affront. Years ago, before the East Germans began rebuilding their churches, they erected a secular structure: the television tower at Alexander Platz. Virtually ever since, the authorities have been working to correct what they view as the tower's one major flaw, treating the glass sphere at the top with paints and chemicals of every kind. Yet even today when the Sun strikes that sphere—that sphere that towers over all Berlin—the light makes the sign of the cross. There in Berlin, like the city itself, symbols of love, symbols of worship, cannot be suppressed.

As l looked out a moment ago from the Reichstag, that embodiment of German unity, I noticed words crudely spray-painted upon the wall, perhaps by a young Berliner, "This wall will fall. Beliefs become reality." Yes, across Europe, this wall will fall. For it cannot withstand faith; it cannot withstand truth. The wall cannot withstand freedom.

And I would like, before I close, to say one word. I have read, and I have been questioned since I've been here about certain demonstrations against my coming. And I would like to say just one thing, and to those who demonstrate so. I wonder if they have ever asked themselves that if they should have the kind of government they apparently seek, no one would ever be able to do what they're doing again.

Thank you and God bless you all.

"Thousand Points of Light" Speech (1988)
Vice President George Bush

Bush Presidential Materials Project, College Station, Texas
Republican National Convention,
New Orleans, Louisiana

August 18, 1988

Thank you. Thank you very much.

I have many friends to thank tonight. I thank the voters who supported me. I thank the gallant men who entered the contest for the presidency this year, and who have honored me with their support. And, for their kind and stirring words, I thank Governor Tom Kean of New Jersey—Senator Phil Gramm of Texas—President Gerald Ford—and my friend, President Ronald Reagan. I accept your nomination for President. I mean to run hard, to fight hard, to stand on the issues—and I mean to win.

There are a lot of great stories in politics about the underdog winning—and this is going to be one of them.

And we're going to win with the help of Senator Dan Quayle of Indiana—a young leader who has become a forceful voice in preparing America's Workers for the labor force of the future. Born in the middle of the century, in the middle of America, and holding the promise of the future—I'm proud to have Dan Quayle at my side.

Many of you have asked, "When will this campaign really begin?" I have come to this hall to tell you, and to tell America: Tonight is the night.

For seven and a half years I have helped a President conduct the most difficult job on earth. Ronald Reagan asked for, and received, my candor. He never asked for, but he did receive, my loyalty. Those of you who saw the President's speech this week, and listened to the simple truth of his words, will understand my loyalty all these years.

But now you must see me for what I am: The Republican candidate for President of the United States. And now I turn to the American people to share my hopes and intentions, and why—and where—I wish to lead.

And so tonight is for big things. But I'll try to be fair to the other side. I'll try to hold my charisma in check. I reject the temptation to engage in personal references. My approach this evening is, as Sergeant Joe Friday used to say, "Just the facts, ma'm."

After all, the facts are on our side.

I seek the presidency for a single purpose, a purpose that has motivated millions of Americans across the years and the ocean voyages. I seek the presidency to build a better America. It is that simple—and that big.

I am a man who sees life in terms of missions—missions defined and missions completed. When I was a torpedo bomber pilot they defined the mission for us. Before we took off we all understood that no matter what, you try to reach the target. There have been other missions for me—Congress, China, the CIA. But I am here tonight—and I am your candidate—because the most important work of my life is to complete the mission we started in 1980. How do we complete it? We build on it.

The stakes are high this year and the choice is crucial, for the differences between the two candidates are as deep and wide as they have ever been in our long history.

Not only two very different men, but two very different ideas of the future will be voted on this election day.

What it all comes down to is this:

My opponent's view of the world sees a long slow decline for our country, an inevitable fall mandated by impersonal historical forces.

But America is not in decline. America is a rising nation.

He sees America as another pleasant country on the U.N. roll call, somewhere between Albania and Zimbabwe. I see America as the leader—a unique nation with a special role in the world. This has been called the American Century, because in it we were the dominant force for good in the world. We saved Europe, cured polio, we went to the moon, and lit the world with our culture. Now we are on the verge of a new century, and what country's name will it bear? I say it will be another American century.

Our work is not done—our force is not spent.

There are those who say there isn't much of a difference this year. But America, don't let 'em fool ya.

Two parties this year ask for your support. Both will speak of growth and peace. But only one has proved it can deliver. Two parties this year ask for your trust, but only one has earned it. Eight years ago I stood here with Ronald Reagan and we promised, together, to break with the past and return America to her greatness. Eight years later look at what the American people have produced: the highest level of economic growth in our entire history—and the lowest level of world tensions in more than fifty years.

Some say this isn't an election about ideology, it's an election about competence. Well, it's nice of them to want to play on our field. But this election isn't only about competence, for competence is a narrow ideal. Competence makes the trains run on time but doesn't know where they're going. Competence is the creed of the technocrat who makes sure the gears mesh but doesn't for a second understand the magic of the machine.

The truth is, this election is about the beliefs we share, the values we honor, the principles we hold dear.

But since someone brought up competence . . .

Consider the size of our triumph: A record high percentage of Americans with jobs, a record high rate of new businesses—a record high rate of real personal income.

These are facts. And one way you know our opponents know the facts is that to attack the record they have to misrepresent it. They call it a swiss cheese economy. Well, that's the way it may look to the three blind mice. But when they were in charge it was all holes and no cheese.

Inflation was 12 percent when we came in. We got it down to four. Interest rates were more than 21. We cut them in half. Unemployment was up and climbing, now it's the lowest in 14 years. My friends, eight years ago this economy was flat on its back—intensive care. We came in and gave it emergency treatment: Got the temperature down by lowering regulation, got the blood pressure down when we lowered taxes. Pretty soon the patient was up, back on his feet, and stronger than ever.

And now who do we hear knocking on the door but the doctors who made him sick. And they're telling us to put them in charge of the case again. My friends, they're lucky we don't hit them with a malpractice suit!

We've created seventeen million new jobs in the past five years—more than twice as many as Europe and Japan combined. And they're good jobs. The majority of them created in the past six years paid an average of more than $22,000 a year. Someone better take 'a message to Michael': Tell him we've been creating good jobs at good wages. The fact is, they talk—we deliver. They promise—we perform.

There are millions of young Americans in their 20's who barely remember the days of gas lines and unemployment lines. Now they're marrying and starting careers. To those young people I say, "You have the opportunity you deserve—and I'm not going to let them take it away from you."

The leaders of the expansion have been the women of America—who helped create the new jobs, and filled two out of every three of them. To the women of America I say "You know better than anyone that equality begins with economic empowerment. You're gaining economic power—and I'm not going to let them take it away from you."

There are millions of older Americans who were brutalized by inflation. We arrested it—and we're not going to let it out on furlough. We're going to keep the social security trust fund sound, and out of reach of the big spenders. To American's elderly I say, "Once again you have the security that is your right—and I'm not going to let them take it away from you."

I know the liberal democrats are worried about the economy. They're worried it's going to remain strong. And they're right, it is. With the right leadership.

But let's be frank. Things aren't perfect in this country. There are people who haven't tasted the fruits of the expansion. I've talked to farmers about the bills they can't pay. I've been to the factories that feel the strain of change. I've seen the urban children who play amidst the shattered glass and shattered lives. And there are the homeless. And you know, it doesn't do any good to debate endlessly which policy mistake of the '70's is responsible. They're there. We have to help them.

But what we must remember if we are to be responsible—and compassionate—is that economic growth is the key to our endeavors.

I want growth that stays, that broadens, and that touches, finally, all Americans, from the hollows of Kentucky to the sunlit streets of Denver, from the suburbs of Chicago to the broad avenues of New York, from the oil fields of Oklahoma to the farms of the great plains.

Can we do it? Of course we can. We know how. We've done it. If we continue to grow at our current rate, we will be able to produce 30 million jobs in the next eight years. We will do it—by maintaining our commitment to free and fair trade, by keeping government spending down, and by keeping taxes down.

Our economic life is not the only test of our success. One issue overwhelms all the others, and that is the issue of peace.

Look at the world on this bright August night. The spirit of democracy is sweeping the Pacific rim. China feels the winds of change. New democracies assert themselves in South America. One by one the unfree places fall, not to the force of arms but to the force of an idea: freedom works.

We have a new relationship with the Soviet Union. The INF treaty—the beginning of the Soviet withdrawal from Afghanistan—the beginning of the end of the Soviet proxy war in Angola, and with it the independence of Namibia. Iran and Iraq move toward peace.

It is a watershed.

It is no accident.

It happened when we acted on the ancient knowledge that strength and clarity lead to peace—weakness and ambivalence lead to war. Weakness tempts aggressors. Strength stops them. I will not allow this country to be made weak again.

The tremors in the Soviet world continue. The hard earth there has not yet settled. Perhaps what is happening will change our world forever. Perhaps not. A prudent skepticism is in order. And so is hope. Either way, we're in

an unprecedented position to change the nature of our relationship. Not by preemptive concession—but by keeping our strength. Not by yielding up defense systems with nothing won in return—but by hard cool engagement in the tug and pull of diplomacy.

My life has been lived in the shadow of war—I almost lost my life in one.

I hate war.

I love peace.

We have peace.

And I am not going to let anyone take it away from us.

Our economy is strong but not invulnerable, and the peace is broad but can be broken. And now we must decide. We will surely have change this year, but will it be change that moves us forward? Or change that risks retreat?

In 1940, when I was barely more than a boy, Franklin Roosevelt said we shouldn't change horses in midstream.

My friends, these days the world moves even more quickly, and now, after two great terms, a switch will be made. But when you have to change horses in midstream, doesn't it make sense to switch to the one who's going the same way?

An election that is about ideas and values is also about philosophy. And I have one.

At the bright center is the individual. And radiating out from him or her is the family, the essential unit of closeness and of love. For it is the family that communicates to our children—to the 21st century—our culture, our religious faith, our traditions and history.

From the individual to the family to the community, and on out to the town, to the church and school, and, still echoing out, to the county, the state, the nation—each doing only what it does well, and no more. And I believe that power must always be kept close to the individual—close to the hands that raise the family and run the home.

I am guided by certain traditions. One is that there is a God and He is good, and His love, while free, has a self imposed cost: We must be good to one another.

I believe in another tradition that is, by now, imbedded in the national soul. It is that learning is good in and of itself. The mothers of the Jewish ghettoes of the east would pour honey on a book so the children would know that learning is sweet. And the parents who settled hungry Kansas would take their children in from the fields when a teacher came. That is our history.

And there is another tradition. And that is the idea of community—a beautiful word with a big meaning. Though liberal democrats have an odd view of it. They see "community" as a limited cluster of interest groups, locked in odd conformity. In this view, the country waits passive while Washington sets the rules.

But that's not what community means—not to me.

For we are a nation of communities, of thousands and tens of thousands of ethnic, religious, social, business, labor union, neighborhood, regional and other organizations, all of them varied, voluntary and unique.

This is America: the Knights of Columbus, the Grange, Hadassah, the Disabled American Veterans, the Order of Ahepa, the Business and Professional Women of America, the union hall, the bible study group, LULAC, "Holy Name"—a brilliant diversity spread like stars, like a thousand points of light in a broad and peaceful sky.

Does government have a place? Yes. Government is part of the nation of communities—not the whole, just a part.

I do not hate government. A government that remembers that the people are its master is a good and needed thing.

I respect old fashioned common sense, and have no great love for the imaginings of social planners. I like what's been tested and found to be true.

For instance:

Should public school teachers be required to lead our children in the pledge of allegiance? My opponent says no—but I say yes.

Should society be allowed to impose the death penalty on those who commit crimes of extraordinary cruelty and violence? My opponent says no—but I say yes.

Should our children have the right to say a voluntary prayer, or even observe a moment of silence in the schools? My opponent says no—but I say yes.

Should free men and women have the right to own a gun to protect their home? My opponent says no—but I say yes.

Is it right to believe in the sanctity of life and protect the lives of innocent children? My opponent says no—but I say yes. We must change from abortion—to adoption. I have an adopted granddaughter. The day of her christening we wept with joy. I thank God her parents chose life. I'm the one who believes it is a scandal to give a weekend furlough to a hardened first degree killer who hasn't even served enough time to be eligible for parole.

I'm the one who says a drug dealer who is responsible for the death of a policeman should be subject to capital punishment.

I'm the one who won't raise taxes. My opponent now says he'll raise them as a last resort, or a third resort. When a politician talks like that, you know that's one resort he'll be checking into. My opponent won't rule out raising taxes. But I will. The Congress will push me to raise taxes, and I'll say no, and they'll push, and I'll say no, and they'll push again. And all I can say to them is no new taxes, period.

Let me tell you more about the mission.

On jobs, my mission is: 30 in 8. Thirty million jobs in the next eight years.

Every one of our children deserves a first rate school. The liberal democrats want power in the hands of the federal government. I want power in the hands of the parents. I will increase the power of parents. I will encourage merit schools. I will give more kids a Head Start. And I'll make it easier to save for college.

I want a drug free America—and this will not be easy to achieve. But I want to enlist the help of some people who are rarely included. Tonight I challenge the young people of our country to shut down the drug dealers around the world. Unite with us, work with us. "Zero tolerance" isn't just a policy, it's an attitude. Tell them what you think of people who underwrite the dealers who put poison in our society. And while you're doing that, my administration will be telling the dealers: whatever we have to do we'll do, but your day is over, you're history.

I am going to do whatever it takes to make sure the disabled are included in the mainstream. For too long they've been left out. But they're not going to be left out anymore.

I am going to stop ocean dumping. Our beaches should not be garbage dumps and our harbors should not be cess pools. I am going to have the FBI trace the medical wastes and we are going to punish the people who dump those infected needles into our oceans, lakes and rivers. And we must clean the air. We must reduce the harm done by acid rain.

I will put incentives back into the domestic energy industry, for I know from personal experience there is no security for the United States in further dependence on foreign oil.

In foreign affairs I will continue our policy of peace through strength. I will move toward further cuts in the strategic and conventional arsenals of both the United States and the Soviet Union. I will modernize and preserve our technological edge. I will ban chemical and biological weapons from the face of the earth. And I intend to speak for freedom, stand for freedom, and be a patient friend to anyone, east or west, who will fight for freedom.

It seems to me the Presidency provides an incomparable opportunity for "gentle persuasion." I hope to stand for a new harmony, a greater tolerance. We've come far, but I think we need a new harmony among the races in our country. We're on a journey to a new century, and we've got to leave the tired old baggage of bigotry behind.

Some people who are enjoying our prosperity have forgotten what it's for. But they diminish our triumph when they act as if wealth is an end in itself.

There are those who have dropped their standards along the way, as if ethics were too heavy and slowed their rise to the top. There's graft in city hall, the greed on Wall Street; there's influence peddling in Washington, and the small corruptions of everyday ambition.

But you see, I believe public service is honorable. And every time I hear that someone has breached the public trust it breaks my heart.

I wonder sometimes if we have forgotten who we are. But we're the people who sundered a nation rather than allow a sin called slavery—we're the people who rose from the ghettoes and the deserts.

We weren't saints—but we lived by standards. We celebrated the individual—but we weren't self-centered. We were practical—but we didn't live only for material things. We believed in getting ahead—but blind ambition wasn't our way.

The fact is prosperity has a purpose. It is to allow us to pursue "the better angels," to give us time to think and grow. Prosperity with a purpose means taking your idealism and making it concrete by certain acts of goodness. It means helping a child from an unhappy home learn how to read—and I thank my wife Barbara for all her work in literacy. It means teaching troubled children through your presence that there's such a thing as reliable love. Some would say it's soft and insufficiently tough to care about these things. But where is it written that we must act as if we do not care, as if we are not moved?

Well I am moved. I want a kinder, gentler nation.

Two men this year ask for your support. And you must know us.

As for me, I have held high office and done the work of democracy day by day. My parents were prosperous; their children were lucky. But there were lessons we had to learn about life. John Kennedy discovered poverty when he campaigned in West Virginia; there were children there who had no milk. Young Teddy Roosevelt met the new America when he roamed the immigrant streets of New York. And I learned a few things about life in a place called Texas.

We move to west Texas 40 years ago. The war was over, and we wanted to get out and make it on our own. Those were exciting days. Lived in a little shotgun house, one room for the three of us. Worked in the oil business, started my own.

In time we had six children. Moved from the shotgun to a duplex apartment to a house. Lived the dream—high school football on Friday night, Little League, neighborhood barbecue. People don't see their experience as symbolic of an era—but of course we were. So was everyone else who was taking a chance and pushing into unknown territory with kids and a dog and a car. But the big thing I learned is the satisfaction of creating jobs, which meant creating opportunity, which meant happy families, who in turn could do more to help others and enhance their own lives. I learned that the good done by a single good job can be felt in ways you can't imagine. I may not be the most eloquent, but I learned early that eloquence won't draw oil from the ground. I may sometimes be a little awkward, but there's nothing self-conscious in my love of country. I am a quiet man—but I hear the quiet people others don't. The ones who raise the family, pay the taxes, meet the mortgage. I hear them and I am moved, and their concerns are mine.

A President must be many things.

He must be a shrewd protector of America's interests; And he must be an idealist who leads those who move for a freer and more democratic planet.

He must see to it that government intrudes as little as possible in the lives of the people; and yet remember that it is right and proper that a nation's leader take an interest in the nation's character. And he must be able to define—and lead—a mission.

For seven and a half years I have worked with a President— and I have seen what crosses that big desk. I have seen the unexpected crises that arrive in a cable in a young aide's hand. And I have seen problems that simmer on for decades and suddenly demand resolution. I have seen modest decisions made with anguish, and crucial decisions made with dispatch.

And so I know that what it all comes down to, this election—what it all comes down to, after all the shouting and the cheers—is the man at the desk. And who should sit at that desk.

My friends, I am that man.

I say it without boast or bravado; I've fought for my country, I've served, I've built—and I will go from the hills to the hollows, from the cities to the suburbs to the loneliest town on the quietest street to take our message of hope and growth for every American to every American. I will keep America moving forward, always forward—for a better America, for an endless enduring dream and a thousand points of light.

That is my mission. And I will complete it.

Thank you. God bless you.

The Americans With Disabilities Act, 1990

United States Statutes at Large, 1990, Vol. 104,
Part 1, pp. 327–378

July 26, 1990

Sec. 2. Findings and Purposes

(a) Findings.—The Congress finds that—

(1) some 43,000,000 Americans have one or more physical or mental disabilities, and this number is increasing as the population as a whole is growing older.

(2) historically, society has tended to isolate and segregate individuals with disabilities, and, despite some improvements, such forms of discrimination against individuals

with disabilities continue to be a serious and pervasive social problem;

(3) discrimination against individuals with disabilities persists in such critical areas as employment, housing, public accommodations, education, transportation, communication, recreation, institutionalization, health services, voting, and access to public services;

(4) unlike individuals who have experienced discrimination on the basis of race, color, sex, national origin, religion, or age, individuals who have experienced discrimination on the basis of disability have often had no legal recourse to redress such discrimination;

(5) individuals with disabilities continually encounter various forms of discrimination, including outright intentional exclusion, the discriminatory effects of architectural, transportation, and communication barriers, overprotective rules and policies, failure to make modifications to existing facilities and practices, exclusionary qualification standards and criteria, segregation, and relegation to lesser services, programs, activities, benefits, jobs, or other opportunities;

(6) census data, national polls, and other studies have documented that people with disabilities, as a group, occupy an inferior status in our society, and are severely disadvantaged socially, vocationally, economically, and educationally;

(7) individuals with disabilities are a discrete and insular minority who have been faced with restrictions and limitations, subjected to a history of purposeful unequal treatment, and relegated to a position of political powerlessness in our society, based on characteristics that are beyond the control of such individuals and resulting from stereotypic assumptions not truly indicative of the individual ability of such individuals to participate in, and contribute to, society;

(8) the Nation's proper goals regarding individuals with disabilities are to assure equality of opportunity, full participation, independent living, and economic self-sufficiency for such individuals; and

(9) the continuing existence of unfair and unnecessary discrimination and prejudice denies people with disabilities the opportunity to compete on an equal basis and to pursue those opportunities for which our free society is justifiably famous, and costs the United States billions of dollars in unnecessary expenses resulting from dependency and nonproductivity.

(b) Purpose.—It is the purpose of this Act—

(1) to provide a clear and comprehensive national mandate for the elimination of discrimination against individuals with disabilities;

(2) to provide clear, strong, consistent, enforceable standards addressing discrimination against individuals with disabilities;

(3) to ensure that the Federal Government plays a central role in enforcing the standards established in this Act on behalf of individuals with disabilities; and

(4) to invoke the sweep of congressional authority, including the power to enforce the fourteenth amendment and to regulate commerce, in order to address the major areas of discrimination faced day-to-day by people with disabilities.

Sec. 3. Definitions

As used in this Act:

(1) Auxiliary aids and services.—The term "auxiliary aids and services" includes—

(A) qualified interpreters or other effective methods of making aurally delivered materials available to individuals with hearing impairments;

(B) qualified readers, taped texts, or other effective methods of making visually delivered materials available to individuals with visual impairments;

(C) acquisition or modification of equipment or devices; and

(D) other similar services and actions.

(2) Disability.—The term "disability" means, with respect to an individual—

(A) a physical or mental impairment that substantially limits one or more of the major life activities of such individual;

(B) a record of such an impairment or

(C) being regarded as having such an impairment.

(3) State.—The term "State" means each of the several States, the District of Columbia, the Commonwealth of Puerto Rico, Guam, American Samoa, the Virgin Islands, the Trust Territory of the Pacific Islands, and the Commonwealth of the Northern Mariana Islands . . .

A) In general.—The term "employer" means a person engaged in an industry affecting commerce who has 15 or more employees for each working day in each of 20 or more calendar weeks in the current or preceding calendar year, and any agent of such person, except that, for two years following the effective date of this title, an employer means a person engaged in an industry affecting commerce who has 25 or more employees for each working day in each of 20 or more calendar weeks in the current or preceding year, and any agent of such person.

(B) Exceptions.—The term "employer" does not include—

(i) the United States, a corporation wholly owned by the government of the United States, or an Indian tribe; or

(ii) a bona fide private membership club (other than a labor organization) that is exempt from taxation under section 501(c) of the Internal Revenue Code of 1986 . . .

8) Qualified individual with a disability.—The term "qualified individual with a disability" means an individual

with a disability who, with or without reasonable accommodation, can perform the essential functions of the employment position that such individual holds or desires. For the purposes of this title, consideration shall be given to the employer's judgment as to what functions of a job are essential, and if an employer has prepared a written description before advertising or interviewing applicants for the job, this description shall be considered evidence of the essential functions of the job.

(9) Reasonable accommodation.—The term "reasonable accommodation" may include—

(A) making existing facilities used by employees readily accessible to and usable by individuals with disabilities; and

(B) job restructuring, part-time or modified work schedules, reassignment to a vacant position, acquisition or modification of equipment or devices, appropriate adjustment or modifications of examinations, training materials or policies, the provision of qualified readers or interpreters, and other similar accommodations for individuals with disabilities.

(10) Undue hardship.—

(A) In general.—The term "undue hardship" means an action requiring significant difficulty or expense, when considered in light of the factors set forth in subparagraph (B).

(B) Factors to be considered.—In determining whether an accommodation would impose an undue hardship on a covered entity, factors to be considered include—

(i) the nature and cost of the accommodation needed under this Act;

(ii) the overall financial resources of the facility or facilities involved in the provision of the reasonable accommodation; the number of persons employed at such facility; the effect on expenses and resources, or the impact otherwise of such accommodation upon the operation of the facility;

(iii) the overall financial resources of the covered entity; the overall size of the business of a covered entity with respect to the number of its employees; the number, type, and location of its facilities; and

(iv) the type of operation or operations of the covered entity, including the composition, structure, and functions of the workforce of such entity; the geographic separateness, administrative, or fiscal relationship of the facility or facilities in question to the covered entity.

Remarks to the Fourth World Conference on Women: Ambassador Madeleine K. Albright, U.S. Permanent Representative to the United Nations

U.S. Department of State, Washington, D.C.

Beijing International Convention Center Beijing, China September 6, 1995

Honored guests, fellow delegates and observers, I am pleased and proud to address this historic conference on behalf of the United States of America.

My government congratulates the thousands who have helped to organize the conference, to draft the Platform for Action, to inform the world about the subjects under discussion here and to encourage wide participation both by governments and NGO's. We have come here from all over the world to carry forward an age-old struggle: the pursuit of economic and social progress for all people, based on respect for the dignity and value of each. We are here to promote and protect human rights and to stress that women's rights are neither separable nor different from those of men.

We are here to stop sexual crimes and other violence against women; to protect refugees, so many of whom are women; and to end the despicable notion—in this era of conflicts—that rape is just another tactic of war.

We are here to empower women by enlarging their role in making economic and political decisions, an idea some find radical, but which my government believes is essential to economic and social progress around the world; because no country can develop if half its human resources are de-valued or repressed.

We are here because we want to strengthen families, the heart and soul of any society. We believe that girls must be valued to the same degree as boys. We believe, with Pope John Paul II, in the "equality of spouses with respect to family rights." We think women and men should be able to make informed judgments as they plan their farrulies. And we want to see forces that weaken families—including pornography, domestic violence and the sexual exploitation of children—condemned and curtailed.

Finally, we have come to this conference to assure for women equal access to education and health care, to help women protect against infection by HIV, to recognize the special needs and strengths of women with disabilities, and to attack the root causes of poverty, in which so many women, children and men are entrapped.

We have come to Beijing to make further progress towards each of these goals. But real progress will depend not on what we say here, but on what we do after we leave here. The Fourth World Conference for Women is not about conversations; it is about commitments.

For decades, my nation has led efforts to promote equal rights for women. Women in their varied roles—as mothers, farm laborers, factory workers, organizers and community leaders helped build America. My government is based on principles that recognize the right of every person to equal rights and equal opportunity. Our laws forbid discrimination on the basis of sex and we work hard to enforce those laws. A rich network of nongovernmental organizations has blossomed within our borders, reaching out to women and girls from all segments of society, educating, counseling and advocating change.

The United States is a leader, but leaders cannot stand still. Barriers to the equal participation of women persist in my country. The Clinton Administration is determined to bring those barriers down. Today, in the spirit of this conference, and in the knowledge that concrete steps to advance the status of women are required in every nation, I am pleased to announce the new commitments my government will undertake:

First, President Clinton will establish a White House Council on Women to plan for the effective implementation within the United States of the Platform for Action. That Council will build on the commitments made today and will work every day with the nongovernmental community.

Second, in accordance with recently-approved law, the Department of Justice will launch a six-year, $1.6 billion initiative to fight domestic violence and other crimes against women. Funds will be used for specialized police and prosecution units and to train police, prosecutors and judicial personnel.

Third, our Department of Health and Human Services will lead a comprehensive assault on threats to the health and security of women—promoting healthy behavior, increasing awareness about AIDS, discouraging the use of cigarettes, and striving to win the battle against breast cancer. And, as Mrs. Clinton made clear yesterday, the United States remains firmly committed to the reproductive health rights gains made in Cairo.

Fourth, our Department of Labor will conduct a grassroots campaign to improve conditions for women in the workplace. The campaign will work with employers to develop more equitable pay and promotion policies and to help employees balance the twin responsibilities of family and work.

Fifth, our Department of the Treasury will take new steps to promote access to financial credit for women. Outstanding U.S. microenterprise lending organizations will be honored through special Presidential awards; and we will improve coordination of federal efforts to encourage growth in this field of central importance to the economic empowerment of women.

Sixth, the Agency for International Development will continue to lead in promoting and recognizing the vital role of women in development. Today, we announce important initiatives to increase women's participation in political processes and to promote the enforcement of women's legal rights.

There is a seventh and final commitment my country is making today. We, the people and government of the United States of America, will continue to speak out openly and without hesitation on behalf of the human rights of all people.

My country is proud that, nearly a half century ago, Eleanor Roosevelt, a former First Lady of the United States, helped draft the Universal Declaration of Human Rights. We are proud that, yesterday afternoon, in this very hall, our current First Lady—Hillary Rodham Clinton—restated with memorable eloquence our national commitment to that Declaration.

The Universal Declaration reflects spiritual and moral tenets which are central to all cultures, encompassing both the wondrous diversity that defines us and the common humanity that binds us. It obliges each government to strive in law and practice to protect the rights of those under its jurisdiction. Whether a government fulfills that obligation is a matter not simply of domestic, but of universal, concern. For it is a founding principle of the United Nations that no government can hide its human rights record from the world.

At the heart of the Universal Declaration is a fundamental distinction between coercion and choice. No woman—whether in Birmingham, Bombay, Beirut or Beijing—should be forcibly sterilized or forced to have an abortion. No mother should feel compelled to abandon her daughter because of a societal preference for males. No woman should be forced to undergo genital mutilation, or to become a prostitute, or to enter into marriage or to have sex. No one should be forced to remain silent for fear of religious or political persecution, arrest, abuse or torture.

All of us should be able to exercise control over the course of our own lives and be able to help shape the destiny of our communities and countries.

Let us be clear. Freedom to participate in the political process of our countries is the inalienable right of every woman and man. Deny that right, and you deny everything. It is unconscionable, therefore, that the right to free expression has been called into question right here, at a conference conducted under the auspices of the UN and whose very purpose is the free and open discussion of women's rights.

It is a challenge to us all that so many countries in so many parts of the world—north, south, west and east—fall far short of the noble objectives outlined in the Platform for Action. Every nation, including my own, must do better and do more—to make equal rights a fundamental principle of law; to enforce those rights and to remove barriers to the exercise of those rights.

That is why President Clinton has made favorable action on the Convention to Eliminate Discrimination Against Women a top priority. The United States should be a party to that Convention. And it is why we will continue to seek a dialogue with governments—here and elsewhere—that deny to their citizens the rights enumerated in the Universal Declaration.

In preparing for this conference, I came across an old Chinese poem that is worth recalling, especially today, as we observe the Day of the Girl- Child. In the poem, a father says to his daughter:

> We keep a dog to watch the house;
> A pig is useful, too;
> We keep a cat to catch a mouse;
> But what can we do
> With a girl like you?

Fellow delegates, let us make sure that question never needs to be asked again—in China or anywhere else around the world.

Let us strive for the day when every young girl, in every village and metropolis, can look ahead with confidence that their lives will be valued, their individuality recognized, their rights protected and their futures determined by their own abilities and character

Let us reject outright the forces of repression and ignorance that have held us back; and act with the strength and optimism unity can provide. Let us honor the legacy of the heroines, famous and unknown, who struggled in years past to build the platform upon which we now stand. And let us heed the instruction of our own lives.

Look around this hall, and you will see women who have reached positions of power and authority. Go to Huairou, and you will see an explosion of energy and intelligence devoted to every phase of this struggle. Enter any community in any country, and you will find women insisting—often at great risk—on their right to an equal voice and equal access to the levers of power.

This past week, on video at the NGO Forum, Aung San Suu Kyi said that "it is time to apply in the arena of the world the wisdom and experience" women have gained.

Let us all agree; it is time. It is time to turn bold talk into concrete action. It is time to unleash the full capacity for production, accomplishment and the enrichment of life that is inherent in us—the women of the world.

Second Inaugural Address (1997)
President Bill Clinton

The White House, Office of the Press Secretary

THE PRESIDENT: My fellow citizens: At this last presidential inauguration of the 20th century, let us lift our eyes toward the challenges that await us in the next century. It is our great good fortune that time and chance have put us not only at the edge of a new century, in a new millennium, but on the edge of a bright new prospect in human affairs—a moment that will define our course, and our character, for decades to come. We must keep our old democracy forever young. Guided by the ancient vision of a promised land, let us set our sights upon a land of new promise.

The promise of America was born in the 18th century out of the bold conviction that we are all created equal. It was extended and preserved in the 19th century, when our nation spread across the continent, saved the union, and abolished the awful scourge of slavery.

Then, in turmoil and triumph, that promise exploded onto the world stage to make this the American Century.

And what a century it has been. America became the world's mightiest industrial power; saved the world from tyranny in two world wars and a long cold war; and time and again, reached out across the globe to millions who, like us, longed for the blessings of liberty. Along the way, Americans produced a great middle class and security in old age; built unrivaled centers of learning and opened public schools to all; split the atom and explored the heavens; invented the computer and the microchip; and deepened the wellspring of justice by making a revolution in civil rights for African Americans and all minorities, and extending the circle of citizenship, opportunity and dignity to women.

Now, for the third time, a new century is upon us, and another time to choose. We began the 19th century with a choice, to spread our nation from coast to coast. We began the 20th century with a choice, to harness the Industrial Revolution to our values of free enterprise, conservation, and human decency. Those choices made all the difference. At the dawn of the 21st century a free people must now choose to shape the forces of the Information Age and the global society, to unleash the limitless potential of all our people, and, yes, to form a more perfect union. When last we gathered, our march to this new future seemed less certain than it does today. We vowed then to set a clear course to renew our nation.

In these four years, we have been touched by tragedy, exhilarated by challenge, strengthened by achievement. America stands alone as the world's indispensable nation. Once again, our economy is the strongest on Earth. Once again, we are building stronger families, thriving communities, better educational opportunities, a cleaner environment. Problems that once seemed destined to deepen now bend to our efforts: our streets are safer and record numbers of our fellow citizens have moved from welfare to work.

And once again, we have resolved for our time a great debate over the role of government. Today we can declare: Government is not the problem, and government is not the solution. We—the American people—we are the solution.

Our founders understood that well and gave us a democracy strong enough to endure for centuries, flexible enough to face our common challenges and advance our common dreams in each new day.

As times change, so government must change. We need a new government for a new century—humble enough not to try to solve all our problems for us, but strong enough to give us the tools to solve our problems for ourselves; a government that is smaller, lives within its means, and does more with less. Yet where it can stand up for our values and interests in the world, and where it can give Americans the power to make a real difference in their everyday lives, government should do more, not less. The preeminent mission of our new government is to give all Americans an opportunity—not a guarantee, but a real opportunity—to build better lives. Beyond that, my fellow citizens, the future is up to us. Our founders taught us that the preservation of our liberty and our union depends upon responsible citizenship. And we need a new sense of responsibility for a new century. There is work to do, work that government alone cannot do: teaching children to read; hiring people off welfare rolls; coming out from behind locked doors and shuttered windows to help reclaim our streets from drugs and gangs and crime; taking time out of our own lives to serve others.

Each and every one of us, in our own way, must assume personal responsibility—not only for ourselves and our families, but for our neighbors and our nation. Our greatest responsibility is to embrace a new spirit of community for a new century. For any one of us to succeed, we must succeed as one America.

The challenge of our past remains the challenge of our future—will we be one nation, one people, with one common destiny, or not? Will we all come together, or come apart? The divide of race has been America's constant curse. And each new wave of immigrants gives new targets to old prejudices. Prejudice and contempt, cloaked in the pretense of religious or political conviction are no different. These forces have nearly destroyed our nation in the past. They plague us still. They fuel the fanaticism of terror. And they torment the lives of millions in fractured nations all around the world.

These obsessions cripple both those who hate and, of course, those who are hated, robbing both of what they might become. We cannot, we will not, succumb to the dark impulses that lurk in the far regions of the soul everywhere. We shall overcome them. And we shall replace them with the generous spirit of a people who feel at home with one another.

Our rich texture of racial, religious and political diversity will be a Godsend in the 21st century. Great rewards will come to those who can live together, learn together, work together, forge new ties that bind together.

As this new era approaches we can already see its broad outlines. Ten years ago, the Internet was the mystical province of physicists; today, it is a commonplace encyclopedia for millions of schoolchildren. Scientists now are decoding the blueprint of human life. Cures for our most feared illnesses seem close at hand.

The world is no longer divided into two hostile camps. Instead, now we are building bonds with nations that once were our adversaries. Growing connections of commerce and culture give us a chance to lift the fortunes and spirits of people the world over. And for the very first time in all of history, more people on this planet live under democracy than dictatorship.

My fellow Americans, as we look back at this remarkable century, we may ask, can we hope not just to follow, but even to surpass the achievements of the 20th century in America and to avoid the awful bloodshed that stained its legacy? To that question, every American here and every American in our land today must answer a resounding "Yes."

This is the heart of our task. With a new vision of government, a new sense of responsibility, a new spirit of community, we will sustain America's journey. The promise we sought in a new land we will find again in a land of new promise.

In this new land, education will be every citizen's most prized possession. Our schools will have the highest standards in the world, igniting the spark of possibility in the eyes of every girl and every boy. And the doors of higher education will be open to all. The knowledge and power of the Information Age will be within reach not just of the few, but of every classroom, every library, every child. Parents and children will have time not only to work, but to read and play together. And the plans they make at their kitchen table will be those of a better home, a better job, the certain chance to go to college.

Our streets will echo again with the laughter of our children, because no one will try to shoot them or sell them drugs anymore. Everyone who can work, will work, with today's permanent under class part of tomorrow's growing middle class. New miracles of medicine at last will reach not only those who can claim care now, but the children and hardworking families too long denied.

We will stand mighty for peace and freedom, and maintain a strong defense against terror and destruction. Our children will sleep free from the threat of nuclear, chemical or biological weapons. Ports and airports, farms and factories will thrive with trade and innovation and ideas. And the world's greatest democracy will lead a whole world of democracies.

Our land of new promise will be a nation that meets its obligations—a nation that balances its budget, but never loses the balance of its values. A nation where our grandparents have secure retirement and health care, and their grandchildren know we have made the reforms necessary to sustain those benefits for their time. A nation that fortifies the world's most productive economy even as it protects the great natural bounty of our water, air, and majestic land.

And in this land of new promise, we will have reformed our politics so that the voice of the people will always speak louder than the din of narrow interests—regaining the participation and deserving the trust of all Americans.

Fellow citizens, let us build that America, a nation ever moving forward toward realizing the full potential of all its citizens. Prosperity and power—yes, they are important, and we must maintain them. But let us never forget: The greatest progress we have made, and the greatest progress we have yet to make, is in the human heart. In the end, all the world's wealth and a thousand armies are no match for the strength and decency of the human spirit. (Applause.) Thirty-four years ago, the man whose life we celebrate today spoke to us down there, at the other end of this Mall, in words that moved the conscience of a nation. Like a prophet of old, he told of his dream that one day America would rise up and treat all its citizens as equals before the law and in the heart. Martin Luther King's dream was the American Dream. His quest is our quest: the ceaseless striving to live out our true creed. Our history has been built on such dreams and labors. And by our dreams and labors we will redeem the promise of America in the 21st century.

To that effort I pledge all my strength and every power of my office. I ask the members of Congress here to join in that pledge. The American people returned to office a President of one party and a Congress of another. Surely, they did not do this to advance the politics of petty bickering and extreme partisanship they plainly deplore. No, they call on us instead to be repairers of the breach, and to move on with America's mission.

America demands and deserves big things from us—and nothing big ever came from being small. Let us remember the timeless wisdom of Cardinal Bernardin, when facing the end of his own life. He said: "It is wrong to waste the precious gift of time, on acrimony and division." Fellow citizens, we must not waste the precious gift of this time. For all of us are on that same journey of our lives, and our journey, too, will come to an end. But the journey of our America must go on.

And so, my fellow Americans, we must be strong, for there is much to dare. The demands of our time are great and they are different. Let us meet them with faith and courage, with patience and a grateful and happy heart. Let us shape the hope of this day into the noblest chapter in our history. Yes, let us build our bridge. A bridge wide enough and strong enough for every American to cross over to a blessed land of new promise.

May those generations whose faces we cannot yet see, whose names we may never know, say of us here that we led our beloved land into a new century with the American Dream alive for all her children; with the American promise of a more perfect union a reality for all her people; with America's bright flame of freedom spreading throughout all the world.

From the height of this place and the summit of this century, let us go forth. May God strengthen our hands for the good work ahead—and always, always bless our America.

Articles of Impeachment for President William Jefferson Clinton (1998)

105th Congress, 2d Session, H. RES. 611 in the Senate of the United States, December 19, 1998

Resolved, that William Jefferson Clinton, President of the United States, is impeached for high crimes and misdemeanors, and that the following articles of impeachment be exhibited to the United States Senate:

Articles of impeachment exhibited by the House of Representatives of the United States of America in the name of itself and of the people of the United States of America, against William Jefferson Clinton, President of the United States of America, in maintenance and support of its impeachment against him for high crimes and misdemeanors.

Article I

In his conduct while President of the United States, William Jefferson Clinton, in violation of his constitutional oath faithfully to execute the office of President of the United States and, to the best of his ability, preserve, protect, and defend the Constitution of the United States, and in violation of his constitutional duty to take care that the laws be faithfully executed, has willfully corrupted and manipulated the judicial process of the United States for his personal gain and exoneration, impeding the administration of justice, in that:

On August 17, 1998, William Jefferson Clinton swore to tell the truth, the whole truth, and nothing but the truth before a Federal grand jury of the United States. Contrary to that oath, William Jefferson Clinton willfully provided perjurious, false and misleading testimony to the grand jury concerning one or more of the following: (1) the nature and details of his relationship with a subordinate Government employee; (2) prior perjurious, false and misleading testimony he gave in a Federal civil rights action brought against him; (3) prior false and misleading statements he allowed his attorney to make to a Federal judge in that civil rights action; and (4) his corrupt efforts to influence the testimony of witnesses and to impede the discovery of evidence in that civil rights action.

In doing this, William Jefferson Clinton has undermined the integrity of his office, has brought disrepute on the Presidency, has betrayed his trust as President, and has acted in a manner subversive of the rule of law and justice, to the manifest injury of the people of the United States. Wherefore, William Jefferson Clinton, by such conduct, warrants impeachment and trial, and removal from office and disqualification to hold and enjoy any office of honor, trust or profit under the United States.

Article II

In his conduct while President of the United States, William Jefferson Clinton, in violation of his constitutional oath faithfully to execute the office of President of the United States and, to the best of his ability, preserve, protect, and defend the Constitution of the United States, and in violation of his constitutional duty to take care that the laws be faithfully executed, has willfully corrupted and manipulated the judicial process of the United States for his personal gain and exoneration, impeding the administration of justice, in that:

(1) On December 23, 1997, William Jefferson Clinton, in sworn answers to written questions asked as part of a Federal civil rights action brought against him, willfully provided perjurious, false and misleading testimony in response to questions deemed relevant by a Federal judge concerning conduct and proposed conduct with subordinate employees.

(2) On January 17, 1998, William Jefferson Clinton swore under oath to tell the truth, the whole truth, and nothing but the truth in a deposition given as part of a Federal civil rights action brought against him. Contrary to that oath, William Jefferson Clinton willfully provided perjurious, false and misleading testimony in response to questions deemed relevant by a Federal judge concerning the nature and details of his relationship with a subordinate Government employee, his knowledge of that employee's involvement and participation in the civil rights action brought against him, and his corrupt efforts to influence the testimony of that employee.

In all of this, William Jefferson Clinton has undermined the integrity of his office, has brought disrepute on the Presidency, has betrayed his trust as President, and has acted in a manner subversive of the rule of law and justice, to the manifest injury of the people of the United States.

Wherefore, William Jefferson Clinton, by such conduct, warrants impeachment and trial, and removal from office and disqualification to hold and enjoy any office of honor, trust or profit under the United States.

Article III

In his conduct while President of the United States, William Jefferson Clinton, in violation of his constitutional oath faithfully to execute the office of President of the United States and, to the best of his ability, preserve, protect, and defend the Constitution of the United States, and in violation of his constitutional duty to take care that the laws be faithfully executed, has prevented, obstructed, and impeded the administration of justice, and has to that end engaged personally, and through his subordinates and agents, in a course of conduct or scheme designed to delay, impede, cover up, and conceal the existence of evidence and testimony related to a Federal civil rights action brought against him in a duly instituted judicial proceeding. The means used to implement this course of conduct or scheme included one or more of the following acts:

(1) On or about December 17, 1997, William Jefferson Clinton corruptly encouraged a witness in a Federal civil rights action brought against him to execute a sworn affidavit in that proceeding that he knew to be perjurious, false and misleading.

(2) On or about December 17, 1997, William Jefferson Clinton corruptly encouraged a witness in a Federal civil rights action brought against him to give perjurious, false and misleading testimony if and when called to testify personally in that proceeding.

(3) On or about December 28, 1997, William Jefferson Clinton corruptly engaged in, encouraged, or supported a scheme to conceal evidence that had been subpoenaed in a Federal civil rights action brought against him.

(4) Beginning on or about December 7, 1997, and continuing through and including January 14, 1998, William Jefferson Clinton intensified and succeeded in an effort to secure job assistance to a witness in a Federal civil rights action brought against him in order to corruptly prevent the truthful testimony of that witness in that proceeding at a time when the truthful testimony of that witness would have been harmful to him.

(5) On January 17, 1998, at his deposition in a Federal civil rights action brought against him, William Jefferson Clinton corruptly allowed his attorney to make false and misleading statements to a Federal judge characterizing an affidavit, in order to prevent questioning deemed relevant by the judge. Such false and misleading statements were subsequently acknowledged by his attorney in a communication to that judge.

(6) On or about January 18 and January 20–21, 1998, William Jefferson Clinton related a false and misleading account of events relevant to a Federal civil rights action brought against him to a potential witness in that proceeding, in order to corruptly influence the testimony of that witness.

(7) On or about January 21, 23 and 26, 1998, William Jefferson Clinton made false and misleading statements to potential witnesses in a Federal grand jury proceeding in order to corruptly influence the testimony of those witnesses. The false and misleading statements made by William Jefferson Clinton were repeated by the witnesses to the grand jury, causing the grand jury to receive false and misleading information.

In all of this, William Jefferson Clinton has undermined the integrity of his office, has brought disrepute on the Presidency, has betrayed his trust as President, and has acted in a manner subversive of the rule of law and justice, to the manifest injury of the people of the United States.

Wherefore, William Jefferson Clinton, by such conduct, warrants impeachment and trial, and removal from office and disqualification to hold and enjoy any office of honor, trust or profit under the United States.

Article IV

Using the powers and influence of the office of President of the United States, William Jefferson Clinton, in violation of his constitutional oath faithfully to execute the office of President of the United States and, to the best of his ability, preserve, protect, and defend the Constitution of the United States, and in disregard of his constitutional duty to take care that the laws be faithfully executed, has engaged in conduct that resulted in misuse and abuse of his high office, impaired the due and proper administration of justice and the conduct of lawful inquiries, and contravened the authority of the legislative branch and the truth-seeking purpose of a coordinate investigative proceeding in that, as President, William Jefferson Clinton refused and failed to respond to certain written requests for admission and willfully made perjurious, false and misleading sworn statements in response to certain written requests for admission propounded to him as part of the impeachment inquiry authorized by the House of Representatives of the Congress of the United States.

William Jefferson Clinton, in refusing and failing to respond, and in making perjurious, false and misleading statements, assumed to himself functions and judgments necessary to the exercise of the sole power of impeachment vested by the Constitution in the House of Representatives and exhibited contempt for the inquiry.

In doing this, William Jefferson Clinton has undermined the integrity of his office, has brought disrepute on the Presidency, has betrayed his trust as President, and has acted in a manner subversive of the rule of law and justice, to the manifest injury of the people of the United States.

Wherefore, William Jefferson Clinton, by such conduct, warrants impeachment and trial, and removal from office and disqualification to hold and enjoy any office of honor, trust or profit under the United States

Presidential Address to a Joint Session of Congress and the American People (2001)
George W. Bush

The White House, Office of the Press Secretary
September 20, 2001

Mr. Speaker, Mr. President pro tempore, Members of Congress, and fellow Americans:

In the normal course of events, Presidents come to this chamber to report on the state of the Union. Tonight, no such report is needed. It has already been delivered by the American people. We have seen it in the courage of passengers, who rushed terrorists to save others on the ground—passengers like an exceptional man named Todd Beamer. Please help me to welcome his wife, Lisa Beamer, here tonight.

We have seen the state of our Union in the endurance of rescuers, working past exhaustion. We have seen the unfurling of flags, the lighting of candles, the giving of blood, the saying of prayers—in English, Hebrew, and Arabic. We have seen the decency of a loving and giving people, who have made the grief of strangers their own.

My fellow citizens, for the last nine days, the entire world has seen for itself the state of our Union—and it is strong.

Tonight we are a country awakened to danger and called to defend freedom. Our grief has turned to anger, and anger to resolution. Whether we bring our enemies to justice, or bring justice to our enemies, justice will be done.

I thank the Congress for its leadership at such an important time. All of America was touched on the evening of the tragedy to see Republicans and Democrats, joined together on the steps of this Capitol, singing "God Bless America." And you did more than sing, you acted, by delivering forty billion dollars to rebuild our communities and meet the needs of our military.

Speaker Hastert and Minority Leader Gephardt—Majority Leader Daschle and Senator Lott—I thank you for your friendship and your leadership and your service to our country. And on behalf of the American people, I thank the world for its outpouring of support. America will never forget the sounds of our National Anthem playing at Buckingham Palace, and on the streets of Paris, and at Berlin's Brandenburg Gate. We will not forget South Korean children gathering to pray outside our embassy in Seoul, or the prayers of sympathy offered at a mosque in Cairo. We will not forget moments of silence and days of mourning in Australia and Africa and Latin America.

Nor will we forget the citizens of eighty other nations who died with our own. Dozens of Pakistanis. More than 130 Israelis. More than 250 citizens of India. Men and women from El Salvador, Iran, Mexico, and Japan. And hundreds of British citizens. America has no truer friend than Great Britain. Once again, we are joined together in a great cause. The British Prime Minister has crossed an ocean to show his unity of purpose with America, and tonight we welcome Tony Blair.

On September the eleventh, enemies of freedom committed an act of war against our country. Americans have known wars—but for the past 136 years, they have been wars on foreign soil, except for one Sunday in 1941. Americans have known the casualties of war—but not at the center of a great city on a peaceful morning. Americans have known surprise attacks—but never before on thousands of civilians. All of this was brought upon us in a single day—and night fell on a different world, a world where freedom itself is under attack.

Americans have many questions tonight. Americans are asking: Who attacked our country? The evidence we have gathered all points to a collection of loosely affiliated terrorist organizations known as al-Qaida. They are the same murderers indicted for bombing American embassies in Tanzania and Kenya, and responsible for the bombing of the U.S.S. Cole. Al-Qaida is to terror what the mafia is to crime. But its goal is not making money; its goal is remaking the world—and imposing its radical beliefs on people everywhere.

The terrorists practice a fringe form of Islamic extremism that has been rejected by Muslim scholars and the vast majority of Muslim clerics—a fringe movement that perverts the peaceful teachings of Islam. The terrorists' directive commands them to kill Christians and Jews, to kill all Americans, and make no distinctions among military and civilians, including women and children.

This group and its leader—a person named Usama bin Ladin—are linked to many other organizations in different countries, including the Egyptian Islamic Jihad and the Islamic Movement of Uzbekistan.

There are thousands of these terrorists in more than sixty countries. They are recruited from their own nations and neighborhoods, and brought to camps in places like Afghanistan where they are trained in the tactics of terror. They are sent back to their homes or sent to hide in countries around the world to plot evil and destruction.

The leadership of al-Qaida has great influence in Afghanistan, and supports the Taliban regime in controlling most of that country. In Afghanistan, we see al-Qaida's vision for the world. Afghanistan's people have been brutalized—many are starving and many have fled. Women are not allowed to attend school. You can be jailed for owning a television. Religion can be practiced only as their leaders dictate. A man can be jailed in Afghanistan if his beard is not long enough. The United States respects the people of Afghanistan—after all, we are currently its largest source of humanitarian aid—but we condemn the Taliban regime. It is not only repressing its own people, it is threatening people everywhere by sponsoring and sheltering and supplying terrorists. By aiding and abetting murder, the Taliban regime is committing murder. And tonight, the United States of America makes the following demands on the Taliban:

> Deliver to United States authorities all the leaders of al-Qaida who hide in your land.
> Release all foreign nationals—including American citizens—you have unjustly imprisoned, and protect foreign journalists, diplomats, and aid workers in your country.
> Close immediately and permanently every terrorist training camp in Afghanistan and hand over every terrorist, and every person in their support structure, to appropriate authorities.
> Give the United States full access to terrorist training camps, so we can make sure they are no longer operating.

These demands are not open to negotiation or discussion. The Taliban must act and act immediately. They will hand over the terrorists, or they will share in their fate.

I also want to speak tonight directly to Muslims throughout the world: We respect your faith. It is practiced freely by many millions of Americans, and by millions more in countries that America counts as friends. Its teachings are good and peaceful, and those who commit evil in the name of Allah blaspheme the name of Allah. The terrorists are traitors to their own faith, trying, in effect, to hijack Islam itself. The enemy of America is not our many Muslim friends; it is not our many Arab friends. Our enemy is a radical network of terrorists, and every government that supports them.

Our war on terror begins with al-Qaida, but it does not end there. It will not end until every terrorist group of global reach has been found, stopped, and defeated. Americans are asking: Why do they hate us?

They hate what we see right here in this chamber—a democratically elected government. Their leaders are self-appointed. They hate our freedoms—our freedom of religion, our freedom of speech, our freedom to vote and assemble and disagree with each other.

They want to overthrow existing governments in many Muslim countries, such as Egypt, Saudi Arabia, and Jordan. They want to drive Israel out of the Middle East. They want to drive Christians and Jews out of vast regions of Asia and Africa.

These terrorists kill not merely to end lives, but to disrupt and end a way of life. With every atrocity, they hope that America grows fearful, retreating from the world and forsaking our friends. They stand against us, because we stand in their way.

We are not deceived by their pretenses to piety. We have seen their kind before. They are the heirs of all the murderous ideologies of the twentieth century. By sacrificing human life to serve their radical visions—by abandoning every value except the will to power—they follow in the path of fascism, and Nazism, and totalitarianism. And they will follow that path all the way, to where it ends: in history's unmarked grave of discarded lies.

Americans are asking: How will we fight and win this war?

We will direct every resource at our command—every means of diplomacy, every tool of intelligence, every instrument of law enforcement, every financial influence, and every necessary weapon of war—to the disruption and defeat of the global terror network.

This war will not be like the war against Iraq a decade ago, with its decisive liberation of territory and its swift conclusion. It will not look like the air war above Kosovo two years ago, where no ground troops were used and not a single American was lost in combat.

Our response involves far more than instant retaliation and isolated strikes. Americans should not expect one battle, but a lengthy campaign, unlike any other we have seen. It may include dramatic strikes, visible on television, and covert operations, secret even in success. We will starve terrorists of funding, turn them one against another, drive them from place to place, until there is no refuge or rest. And we will pursue nations that provide aid or safe haven to terrorism. Every nation, in every region, now has a decision to make. Either you are with us, or you are with the terrorists. From this day forward, any nation that continues to harbor or support terrorism will be regarded by the United States as a hostile regime.

Our Nation has been put on notice: We are not immune from attack. We will take defensive measures against terrorism to protect Americans.

Today, dozens of federal departments and agencies, as well as state and local governments, have responsibilities affecting homeland security. These efforts must be coordinated at the highest level. So tonight I announce the creation of a Cabinet-level position reporting directly to me—the Office of Homeland Security.

These measures are essential. But the only way to defeat terrorism as a threat to our way of life is to stop it, eliminate it, and destroy it where it grows.

Many will be involved in this effort, from FBI agents to intelligence operatives to the reservists we have called to active duty. All deserve our thanks, and all have our prayers. And tonight, a few miles from the damaged Pentagon, I have a message for our military: Be ready. I have called the armed forces to alert, and there is a reason. The hour is coming when America will act, and you will make us proud.

This is not, however, just America's fight. And what is at stake is not just America's freedom. This is the world's fight. This is civilization's fight. This is the fight of all who believe in progress and pluralism, tolerance and freedom.

We ask every nation to join us. We will ask, and we will need, the help of police forces, intelligence services, and banking systems around the world. The United States is grateful that many nations and many international organizations have already responded—with sympathy and with support. Nations from Latin America, to Asia, to Africa, to Europe, to the Islamic world. Perhaps the NATO Charter reflects best the attitude of the world: an attack on one is an attack on all.

The civilized world is rallying to America's side. They understand that if this terror goes unpunished, their own cities, their own citizens may be next. Terror, unanswered, can not only bring down buildings, it can threaten the stability of legitimate governments. And we will not allow it.

Americans are asking: What is expected of us?

I ask you to live your lives and hug your children. I know many citizens have fears tonight, and I ask you to be calm and resolute, even in the face of a continuing threat.

I ask you to uphold the values of America, and remember why so many have come here. We are in a fight for our principles, and our first responsibility is to live by them. No one should be singled out for unfair treatment or unkind words because of their ethnic background or religious faith.

I ask you to continue to support the victims of this tragedy with your contributions. Those who want to give can go to a central source of information, libertyunites.org, to find the names of groups providing direct help in New York, Pennsylvania, and Virginia.

The thousands of FBI agents who are now at work in this investigation may need your cooperation, and I ask you to give it.

I ask for your patience, with the delays and inconveniences that may accompany tighter security—and for your patience in what will be a long struggle.

I ask your continued participation and confidence in the American economy. Terrorists attacked a symbol of American prosperity. They did not touch its source. America is successful because of the hard work, and creativity, and enterprise of our people. These were the true strengths of our economy before September eleventh, and they are our strengths today.

Finally, please continue praying for the victims of terror and their families, for those in uniform, and for our great country. Prayer has comforted us in sorrow, and will help strengthen us for the journey ahead.

Tonight I thank my fellow Americans for what you have already done and for what you will do. And ladies and gentlemen of the Congress, I thank you, their representatives, for what you have already done, and for what we will do together.

Tonight, we face new and sudden national challenges. We will come together to improve air safety, to dramatically expand the number of air marshals on domestic flights, and take new measures to prevent hijacking. We will come together to promote stability and keep our airlines flying with direct assistance during this emergency.

We will come together to give law enforcement the additional tools it needs to track down terror here at home. We will come together to strengthen our intelligence capabilities to know the plans of terrorists before they act, and find them before they strike.

We will come together to take active steps that strengthen America's economy, and put our people back to work. Tonight we welcome here two leaders who embody the extraordinary spirit of all New Yorkers: Governor George Pataki, and Mayor Rudy Giuliani. As a symbol of America's resolve, my Administration will work with the Congress, and these two leaders, to show the world that we will rebuild New York City.

After all that has just passed, all the lives taken, and all the possibilities and hopes that died with them, it is natural to wonder if America's future is one of fear. Some speak of an age of terror. I know there are struggles ahead, and dangers to face. But this country will define our times, not be defined by them. As long as the United States of America is determined and strong, this will not be an age of terror; this will be an age of liberty, here and across the world.

Great harm has been done to us. We have suffered great loss. And in our grief and anger we have found our mission and our moment. Freedom and fear are at war. The advance of human freedom—the great achievement of our time, and the great hope of every time—now depends on us. Our Nation—this generation—will lift a dark threat of violence from our people and our future. We will rally the world to this cause, by our efforts and by our courage. We will not tire, we will not falter, and we will not fail.

It is my hope that in the months and years ahead, life will return almost to normal. We'll go back to our lives and routines, and that is good. Even grief recedes with time and grace. But our resolve must not pass. Each of us will remember what happened that day, and to whom it happened. We will remember the moment the news came—where we were and what we were doing. Some will remember an image of fire, or a story of rescue. Some will carry memories of a face and a voice gone forever.

And I will carry this. It is the police shield of a man named George Howard, who died at the World Trade Center trying to save others. It was given to me by his mom, Arlene, as a proud memorial to her son. This is my reminder of lives that ended, and a task that does not end. I will not forget this wound to our country, or those who inflicted it. I will not yield. I will not rest. I will not relent in waging this struggle for the freedom and security of the American people.

The course of this conflict is not known, yet its outcome is certain. Freedom and fear, justice and cruelty, have always been at war, and we know that God is not neutral between them. Fellow citizens, we will meet violence with patient justice—assured of the rightness of our cause, and confident of the victories to come. In all that lies before us, may God grant us wisdom, and may He watch over the United States of America.

Thank you.

Bibliography

Abbott, Carl. *The New Urban America.* Chapel Hill: University of North Carolina Press, 1987.

Allen, Walter, and Reynolds Farley. *The Color Line and the Quality of Life in America.* New York: Russel Sage Foundation, 1987.

Ambrose, Stephen. *Nixon: Ruin and Recovery, 1973–1990.* New York: Simon & Schuster, 1991.

Anderson, Paul. *Janet Reno: Doing the Right Thing.* New York: Wiley, 1994.

Arblaster, A. *The Rise and Decline of Western Liberalism.* New York: Oxford University Press, 1986.

Archer, Michael. *Art since 1960.* New York: Thames & Hudson, 1997.

Balmer, Randall. *Mine Eyes Have Seen the Glory: A Journey into the Evangelical Subculture of America.* New York: Oxford University Press, 2000.

Barnouw, Erik. *The Tube of Plenty: The Evolution of American Television.* New York: Oxford University Press: 1990.

Barone, Michael. *Our Country: America from Roosevelt to Reagan.* New York: Free Press, 1990.

Barrett, David. *World Christian Encyclopedia.* New York: Oxford University Press, 2001.

Baughman, James L. *The Republic of Mass Culture: Journalism, Filmmaking, and Broadcasting in America since 1941.* Baltimore: Johns Hopkins University Press, 1992.

Berkowitz, Edward. *America's Welfare State: From Roosevelt to Reagan.* Baltimore, Md.: Johns Hopkins University Press, 1991.

Berman, Harold. *Faith and Order: The Reconciliation of Law and Religion.* Atlanta, Ga.: Scholars Press, 1993.

Bernstein, Carl, and Bob Woodward. *All the President's Men.* New York: Simon & Schuster, 1974.

Bibby, John F. *Two Parties—Or More?: The American Party System.* Boulder, Colo.: Westview Press, 1998.

Brisbin, Richard. *Justice Antonin Scalia and the Conservative Revival.* Baltimore, Md.: Johns Hopkins University Press, 1997.

Broder, David, and Bob Woodward. *The Man Who Would Be President: Dan Quayle.* New York: Simon & Schuster, 1992.

Brooks, Tim, and Earle Marsh. *The Complete Directory to Prime Time Network TV Shows: 1946-Present,* 3rd ed. New York: Ballantine Books, 1985.

Cairncross, Frances. *Costing the Earth: The Challenge for Governments, The Opportunities for Business.* Cambridge, Mass.: Harvard Business School Press, 1991.

Cameron, Charles M. *Veto Bargaining: Presidents and the Politics of Negative Power.* New York: Cambridge University Press, 2000.

Carter, Dan. *The Politics of Rage: George Wallace, the Origins of New Conservatism, and the Transformation of American Politics.* New York: Simon & Schuster, 1995.

Clancy, Paul, and Shirley Elder. *Tip: A Biography of Thomas P. O'Neill, Speaker of the House.* New York: Macmillan, 1980.

Cockcroft, James. *Latin America—History, Politics, and U.S. Policy,* 2d ed. Chicago: Nelson Hall, 1996.

Cohodas, Nadine. *Strom Thurmond and the Politics of Southern Change.* New York: Simon & Schuster, 1991.

Congressional Quarterly. *Guide to the U.S. Supreme Court.* Washington, D.C.: U.S. Government Printing Office, 1990.

Critchlow, Donald T. *Intended Consequences: Birth Control, Abortion, and the Federal Government in Modern America.* New York: Oxford University Press, 1999.

———. *The Politics of Abortion and Birth Control in Historical Perspective.* University Park, Pa.: Pennsylvania State Press, 1996.

Daniels, Roger. *Asian Americans: Chinese and Japanese in the United States since 1850.* Seattle: University of Washington Press, 1988.

D'Emilio, John, and Estelle B. Freedman. *Intimate Matters: A History of Sexuality in America,* 2d ed. Chicago: University of Chicago Press, 1997.

Derr, Mary Krane, ed. *Pro-Life Feminism.* New York: Sulzburger & Graham, 1995.

Derrida, Jacques. *Speech and Phenomena, and Other Essays on Husserl's Theory of Signs.* Translated by David B. Allison. Evanston, Ill.: Northwestern University Press, 1973.

Duffy, John. *From Humors to Medical Sciences: A History of American Medicine.* Urbana: University of Illinois Press, 1993.

Dunkley, Graham. *The Free Trade Adventure: The WTO, the Uruguay Round and Globalism—a Critique.* New York: St. Martin's Press, 2000.

Echols, Alice. *Daring to Be Bad: Radical Feminism in America, 1967–1975.* Minneapolis: University of Minnesota Press, 1989.

Edwards, Lee. *The Power of Idea: The Heritage Foundation at 25 Years.* Ottawa, Ill.: Jameson Books, 1997.

Elving, Ronald D., ed. *Congress and the Great Issues, 1945–1995.* Washington, D.C.: Congressional Quarterly Inc., 1996.

Felsenthal, Carol. *The Sweetheart of the Silent Majority: The Biography of Phyllis Schlafly.* New York: Doubleday, 1981.

Flowers, Charles. *A Science Odyssey: 100 Years of Discovery.* New York: Morrow, 1998.

Follett, Ken. *On Wings of Eagles.* New York: Morrow, 1983.

Freeman, Jo. *Women: A Feminist Perspective.* Mountain View, Calif.: Mayfield Publishing Company, 1995.

Gaddis, John Lewis. *Strategies of Containment: A Critical Appraisal of Postwar American National Security Policy.* Oxford, U.K.: Oxford University Press, 1982.

Garrow, David. *Liberty and Sexuality: The Right to Privacy and the Making of "Roe v. Wade."* New York: Macmillan, 1994.

Gates, Henry Louis, Jr., and Cornel West. *The African American Century: How Black Americans Have Shaped Our Country.* New York: Free Press, 2000.

Genovese, Michael A. *The Watergate Crisis.* Westport, Conn.: Greenwood Press, 1999.

Gerber, Scott Douglas. *First Principles: The Jurisprudence of Clarence Thomas.* New York: New York University Press, 1999.

Goldberg, Bernard. *Bias: A CBS Insider Exposes How the Media Distort the News.* Washington, D.C.: Regnery Publisher, 2002.

Goodrum, C., and H. Dalrymple. *Advertising in America: The First 200 Years.* New York: Harry N. Abrams, 1990.

Gorn, Elliot J., and Warren Goldstein. *A Brief History of American Sports.* New York: Hill & Wang, 1993.

Guttman, Allen. *From Ritual to Record: The Nature of Modern Sports.* New York: Columbia University Press, 1978.

Hadden, J. K., and A. D. Shupe. *Televangelism.* New York: H. Holt, 1988.

Hall, Kermit, ed. *The Oxford Companion to the Supreme Court.* New York: Oxford University Press, 1992.

Hammond, Paul Y. *Cold War and Detente: The American Foreign Policy Process since 1945.* New York: Harcourt Brace Jovanovich, 1975.

Hawkins, Gordon. *Pornography in a Free Society.* New York: Cambridge University Press, 1988.

Hayward, Steven. *The Age of Reagan: The Fall of the Old Liberal Order, 1964–1980.* Roseville, Calif.: Forum/Prima, 2001.

Hitchcock, H. Wiley. *Music in the United States: A Historical Introduction,* 4th ed. Upper Saddle River, N.J.: Prentice Hall, 2000.

Hunter, James D. *Culture Wars: The Struggle to Define America.* New York: Basic Books, 1991.

Hutchinson, Dennis J. *The Man Who Once Was Whizzer White.* New York: Free Press, 1998.

Irogbe, Kema. *The Roots of United States Foreign Policy toward Apartheid South Africa, 1969–1985.* Lewiston, N.Y.: E. Mellen Press, 1997.

Jackson, Kenneth. *Crabgrass Frontier: The Suburbanization of the United States.* New York: Oxford University.

Jacobs, Ron. *The Way the Wind Blew: A History of the Weather Underground.* New York: Verso, 1997.

Jennings, Francis. *The Founders of America.* New York: W. W. Norton, 1993.

Jewell, Malcolm E., and Sarah M. Morehouse. *Political Parties and Elections in American States.* Washington, D.C.: Congressional Quarterly Press, 2000.

Kammen, Michael. *American Culture American Tastes: Social Change and the 20th Century.* New York: Alfred A. Knopf, 1999.

Kessler, David A. *A Question of Intent: A Great American Battle with a Deadly Industry.* New York: Public Affairs, 2001.

Kinder, Donald. *Divided by Color: Racial Politics and Democratic Ideals.* Chicago: University of Chicago Press, 1996.

Kohn, Richard H. *Military Laws of the United States from the Civil War through the War Powers Act of 1973.* New York: Arno Press, 1979.

Kutler, Stanley I. *The Wars of Watergate: The Last Crisis of Richard Nixon.* New York: Alfred Knopf, 1990.

Kyvig, David E. *Explicit and Authentic Acts: Amending the Constitution, 1776–1995.* Lawrence: University Press of Kansas, 1996.

Laumanny, Edward O. et. al. *The Social Organization of Sexuality.* Chicago: University of Chicago Press, 1994.

Lawson, Steven. *Running for Freedom: Civil Rights and Black Politics in America since 1941.* New York: McGraw-Hill, 1997.

Levin, Doron P. *Irreconcilable Differences: Ross Perot vs. General Motors.* Boston: Little Brown, 1989.

Long, Robert Emmet, ed. *Religious Cults in America.* New York: H. W. Wilson, 1994.

Luck, Edward C. *Mixed Messages: American Politics and International Organization, 1919–1999.* Washington, D.C.: Brookings Institution Press, 1999.

MacIntyre, Alasdair. *Three Rival Versions of Moral Enquiry.* Notre Dame, Ind.: University of Notre Dame Press, 1990.

Maisel, Sandy L. *Parties and Elections in America: The Electoral Process.* Lanham, Md.: Rowman & Littlefield, 1999.

Marty, Martin. *Modern American Religion.* Chicago: University of Chicago Press, 1986.

McCloskey, Robert G. *The American Supreme Court.* Chicago: University of Chicago Press, 2000.

Meltz, Robert. *The Takings Issue: Constitutional Limits on Land-Use, Control and Environmental Regulation.* Washington, D.C.: Island Press, 1999.

Meyer, M. A. *Response to Modernity: A History of the Reform Movement.* New York: Oxford University Press, 1988.

Mielke, Arthur J. *Christians, Feminists, and the Culture of Pornography.* Lanham, Md.: University Press of America, 1995.

Mintz, Steven, and Susan Kellogg. *Domestic Revolutions: A Social History of American Family Life.* New York: Free Press, 1988.

Muller, Thomas. *Immigrants and the American City.* New York: New York University Press, 1993.

Nash, George H. *The Conservative Intellectual Movement in America since 1945.* New York: Basic Books, 1976.

Newhouse, John. *Cold Dawn: The Story of SALT.* Washington, D.C.: Pergamon/Brassey, 1989.

Novas, Himilce. *Everything You Need to Know about Latino History.* New York: Plume, 1994.

Olasky, Marvin. *Abortion Rites: A History of Abortion in America.* Wheaton, Ill.: Crossway Books, 1992.

O'Neill, Thomas P., with William Novak. *Man of the House; The Life and Political Memoirs of Speaker Tip O'Neill.* New York: Random House, 1987.

Posner, Gerald. *Citizen Perot: His Life and Times.* New York: Random House, 1996.

Posner, Richard. *An Affair of State: The Investigation, Impeachment, and Trial of President Clinton.* Cambridge, Mass.: Harvard University Press, 1999.

Powaski, Ronald E. *Return to Armageddon: The United States and the Nuclear Arms Race, 1981–1999.* New York: Oxford University Press, 2000.

Quayle, Dan. *Standing Firm: A Vice-Presidential Memoir.* New York: HarperCollins Publishers, 1994.

Ravitch, Diane. *The Troubled Crusade: American Education, 1945–1980.* New York: Basic Books, 1983.

Rehnquist, William H. *The Supreme Court.* New York: Alfred Knopf, 2001.

Reiss, Edward. *The Strategic Defense Initiative.* New York: Cambridge University Press, 1992.

Ricci, David. *The Transformation of American Politics: The New Washington and the Rise of Think Tanks.* New Haven: Yale University Press, 1993.

Robbins, William G., and James C. Foster, eds. *Land in the American West.* Seattle: University of Washington Press, 2000.

Rodman, Peter. *More Precious Than Peace: The Cold War and the Struggle for the Third World.* New York: Scribners, 1994.

Rosenberg, Roslind. *Divided Lives: American Women in the Twentieth Century.* New York: Hill & Wang, 1992.

Rudenstine, David. *The Day the Presses Stopped: A History of the Pentagon Papers Case.* Berkeley: University of California Press, 1996.

Rusk, Dean. *As I Saw It.* New York: W.W. Norton, 1990.

Savage, David. *Turning Right: The Making of the Rehnquist Supreme Court.* New York: Wiley & Sons, 1992.

Schippers, David, with Alan Henry. *Sellout.* Washington, D.C.: Regnery, 2000.

Singer, Edward Nathan. *20th Century Revolutions in Technology.* Boston, Mass.: D.C. Heath, 1998.

Skidmore, Thomas, and H. Wayne Smith. *Modern Latin America.* New York: Oxford University Press, 1997.

Sklar, Robert. *Movie-Made America: A Cultural History of American Movies.* New York: Vintage Books, 1994.

Smith, James Allen. *The Idea Brokers: Think Tanks and the New Policy Elite.* New York: Free Press, 1991.

Sniderman, Paul, and Edward Carmines. *Reaching beyond Race.* Cambridge, Mass.: Harvard University Press, 1997.

Sobel, Robert. *Dangerous Dreamers: The Financial Innovators from Charles Merrill to Michael Milken.* New York: John Wiley & Sons, Inc., 1993.

Sullivan, Shannon "New Philosophical Directions," *In Encyclopedia of American Cultural and Intellectual History.* Volume 3. Edited by Mary Kupiec Cayton and Peter W. Williams. New York: Houghton Mifflin, 2001.

Strobe, Talbott. *Endgame: The Inside Story of SALT II.* New York: Harper & Row, 1980.

Thomas, A.M. *The American Predicament: Apartheid and United States Foreign Policy.* Brookfield, Vt.: Ashgate, 1997.

Thomas, Andrew Peyton. *Clarence Thomas: A Biography.* San Francisco, Calif.: Encounter Books, 2001.

Ullman, Sharon. *Sex Seen: The Emergence of Modern Sexuality in America.* Berkeley: University of California Press, 1997.

Urofsky, Melvin, ed. *The Supreme Court Justices.* New York: Garland, 1994.

Wallis, Rodney. *Lockerbie: The Story and the Lessons.* Westport, Conn.: 2001.

Ware, Alan. *Citizens, Parties and the State: A Reappraisal.* Princeton, N.J.: Princeton University Press, 1987.

Watson, Mary Ann. *Defining Visions: Television and the American Experience since 1945.* Fort Worth, Tex.: Harcourt Brace, 1998.

Weinstein, B. L., and R. E. Firestine. *Regional Growth and Decline in the United States: The Rise of the Sunbelt and the Decline of the Northeast.* Westport, Conn.: Praeger, 1978.

Woloch, Nancy. *Women and the American Experience: A Concise History.* New York, McGraw, 2002.

Wright, Jim. *Balance of Power.* Atlanta, Ga.: Turner Publishing, 1996.

Wright, Russell O. *A Twentieth Century History of the United States Population.* Lanham, Md.: Scarecrow Press, 1996.

Wuthnow, Robert. *Christianity in the Twenty-first Century.* New York: Oxford University Press, 1993.

Yarnold, Barbara. *Abortion Politics in the Federal Courts.* Westport, Conn.: Praeger, 1995.

Zeiler, Thomas W. *Dean Rusk: Defending the American Mission Abroad.* Wilmington, Del.: Scholarly Resources Inc., 2000.

Index

Boldface page numbers denote extensive treatment of a topic. *Italic* page numbers refer to illustrations; *c* refers to the Chronology; and *m* indicates a map.